The Turn of the Ermine

An Anthology of Breton Literature

Merged

(um o oveuen y Both)

[signature]

The Turn of the Ermine

An Anthology of Breton Literature

Selected and translated by

Jacqueline Gibson and Gwyn Griffiths

With a Preface by Bernard Le Nail

Francis
Boutle
Publishers

First published by Francis Boutle Publishers
272 Alexandra Park Road
London N22 7BG
Tel/Fax: (020) 8889 7744
Email: info@francisboutle.co.uk
www.francisboutle.co.uk

ISBN 1 903427 28 2

Printed by Biddles Ltd

Acknowledgments

While every effort was made to trace the authors included in this anthology, it has not always been possible to do so. We apologise for any oversight, which will be rectified in further editions. We would like to thank those authors who gave their permission to reproduce their work and to Éditions Plon for permission to reproduce the extract from the Breton version of *Le Cheval D'Orgueil* by Per-Jakez Helias. We would like to thank Mrs Lowri Williams for permission to translate and publish extracts from the works of her father, W. Ambrose Bebb, and Madame Anne-Marie Stockmans-Malmanche for permission to publish and translate extracts from *Ar Baganiz* by her father Tangi Malmanche. While the vast majority of texts in Breton and Welsh have been translated by the editors, we would like to thank Penguin Books for their permission to reprint extracts from *The Description of Wales* by Gerald of Wales and *The History of the Kings of Britain* by Geoffrey of Monmouth; we would also like to thank the estate of H.G. Wells for permission to reprint the extract from *Apropos of Dolores*. We would also like to thank the following Breton publishers who have given their permission to reproduce works or parts of works previously published by them: Brud Nevez, Al Lanv, Al Liamm and Skol Vreizh. Further, we would like to thank Kuzul ar Brezhoneg for their help in tracing some of the contemporary authors included in this anthology. Finally, we would like to thank Bernard Le Nail for agreeing to write the preface.

Contents

Preface

There are as yet very few books presenting Brittany, its own cultural identity and language to the outside world. Confined to the French and French-speaking world, the Bretons have often been locked in a sterile dialogue with the French central power which has always tried to deny the existence of a 'Breton problem' to international authorities, while at the same time hiding from the rest of the world its policy which amounts to the annihilation of Brittany's language and identity. Since the creation of regions in France, between 1971 and 1982, the French central government has done its utmost to limit Brittany's direct links with other regions and other countries. For many Bretons Paris is still 'the centre of the world' as they fail to realise that this city, formally the capital of a great European power and even, for a while, that of a colonial Empire spanning the planet, is now no more than the capital of an average power whose real influence in the world is in decline. If Paris was in the past one of the main creative centres in the world of fashion, arts and letters, it now lives in the memory of a splendour which belongs to the past. For many decades, the Breton people, who are the most Europe orientated of the inhabitants of France, have been aware of the fact that the stakes of the future were continent-wide and even worldwide. As Roparz Hemon himself recommended in 1930, it is vital for the Bretons to 'open windows on the world'. They must cease to see Paris as the obligatory stop, as the measure of all things, as the arbiter of elegance and good taste. Brittany has mostly prospered and been able to make a significant contribution to humanity when it looked outwards.

This book should usefully contribute to this wider vision by revealing for the very first time the richness and variety of Brittany's cultural identity. It offers numerous texts in the Breton language, introduced and translated into English, a language which is undoubtedly today and presumably will be for a long time, the worldwide language of communication.

The authors of this book have produced a thoroughly original work and succeeded in their task of gathering into a harmonious whole, texts of very different origins covering a period of over 2,000 years, from an extract of *The Conquest of Gaul* by Julius Caesar to the most recent writings of a young Russian university lecturer who learned Breton with striking facility and thus brought her contribution to the enrichment of the Breton literary inheritance. They managed to bring together with disconcerting audacity extracts from theatre plays, folksongs, poems from the Middle Ages and very contemporary poems, newspaper articles, extracts from letters, pages from history books, testimonies from travellers and other surprising and often unexpected writings. This anthology, which resolutely moves away from the beaten track resembles a treasure chest. It testifies both to the great cultural knowledge of its authors as well as to their lack of bias and conformity. Their choice will surely displease some, but will definitely appeal to many other readers who will feel the wind of freedom blowing through the pages, a wind carrying the smell of sea and sea-spray; in short, the spirit of Brittany. This book is not one-sided and does not attempt to indoctrinate its readers in any way. It simply gives them a wide choice of materials, some of which are very little known. This allows them to discover for themselves the secrets of the Breton soul, to understand and love this small country no bigger than Belgium or the Netherlands, which is situated at the extremity of Europe and at the end of the Old World.

Brittany as a unique human community has been many times on the brink of disappearing. Her identity is constantly under threat, her language is at the present time in a dire situation because of the inflexible and uncompromising stance of French politicians who fail to realise that the old centralist Napoleonic model is thoroughly out of date, that the world has changed and that Brittany, with her creative, open and friendly identity could be a major centre of new ideas and become a model for all other French regions. Far from being a threat to the unity of the country, the strong identity of Brittany looks, in the eyes of perceptive observers, a most precious asset.

This book contains many tragic and painful pages, such as those which recall the terrible civil war which took place in Brittany during the French Revolution, the butchery which marked the first world war or even the heart-rending events which took place during and immediately after the second world war. It must be said once again that the Bretons carry no blame and fought bravely for freedom and democracy, that the errors of a very small number of extremists, driven to desperate choices by the deafness of central government, cannot be used until the end of times to stigmatise the defenders of the Breton language and identity. At a time when the vast majority of the French abandoned their fate into the hands of Marshal Petain, many Bretons chose, and that as early as 1940, to go to England to continue the fight. At the end of 1940 the Bretons made up 70% of the Resistance while Brittany only comprises 7% of the French population. The Resistance went on to attract more and more men and women, yet at the end of 1943, only six months before the Normandy landings, the Bretons still represented 40% of the Free French. This is not to forget the Resistance in Brittany itself, a vast uprising of the whole people, which retained many German troops in the peninsula, for these, had they been allowed to reach the Normandy front, would have pushed the Allies back to sea. It is also thanks to the Bretons that France, whose authorities had massively collaborated with Nazi Germany from 1940 to 1944, could recover her honour. The brutal repression which was triggered after D-Day against all forms of Bretonness, seems all the more disgraceful.

It is sad to have to note that France still continues to this very day to discriminate against a European language which is the only remaining Celtic language still spoken on the continent, the last remains of a civilisation which used to stretch over the greater part of Europe and which contributed together with the Greco-Roman civilisation to create her original identity. Yet one constantly hears French political leaders state in a perfectly serious voice that France is 'the birthplace of human rights'. From a historical point of view this is not totally accurate since the Declaration of the Rights of Man was only adopted in France on 26 August 1789, i.e. more than thirteen years after the Declaration of Independence of the United States (4 July 1776) from which it borrowed many points. It is particularly inaccurate from the point of view of its actual application since, less than 4 years on, this beautiful declaration was violated by the establishment of a system of government which reigned through terror, much worse than any other system of government which preceded the Revolution. Human rights were trampled underfoot on many other occasions, particularly during the 1940–1944 period and during the dirty colonial wars in Indochina and even more so in Algeria. The policy of French leaders towards the Breton language is unworthy of a true democracy and one is obliged to recognise that it hardly basically differs from the policy of enforced germanisation carried out by the Third Reich in Lusace, from that of Mussolini towards the French-speaking population in the Val d'Aoste and that of the Franco regime towards the Basques, Catalans and Galicians.

The Breton language is today in dire straights. Yet this European language was still, in the 1930s, the most widely spoken Celtic language in the world with over 1, 200,000 speakers. The determination to drive it away from public life and from schools has finally reached its goal. Its use has collapsed dramatically in the last 50 years, but all hope is not yet lost. The people of Brittany have shown many times that they are able to forge by themselves the instruments and tools which are denied them, whether it be Breton-medium schools or ferry-crossings from their ports. In crucial moments, they retain this formidable aptitude to join forces for the good of their country. They look for examples and models which have been successful in other parts of the world, and make use of new technologies to forge their way forward. Not all hope is lost as long as there is a will. Being keener on the construction of Europe and more open to the rest of the world than other inhabitants of France, the Bretons have not said their last word.

Bernard le Nail

Foreword

There has never been linguistic unity in Brittany: in the Eastern part of the country known as Upper Brittany and in its two main towns of Nantes and Rennes where the ducal courts were held French, or the romance language from which it evolved, has always been in use; in Lower Brittany, i.e. in the Western part of the country, the mass of the people remained Breton speakers – or speakers of Gallo in a small area of North-East Brittany – until the beginning of the twentieth century, while the aristocracy, the social and administrative elite was either bilingual or French speaking. The French Revolution of 1789 marked the beginning of a number of repeated attacks against the various 'jargons', 'patois' and 'idioms' spoken on the French territory, a policy of linguistic repression which was carried out systematically until the middle of the twentieth century. Breton still survives in the heartland of Brittany, even though it is now spoken by a minority of people. But bizarrely, as the language loses its hold in Brittany, so literary production seems to increase.

Other languages point to the evidence of the existence of a rich body of literature referred to as the 'matter of Brittany' but there only remains a few words and glosses of Old Breton (8th to 11th century) which can be found in lists, charters and other documents. In the Middle Breton period (11th to 15th century) compositions were mainly oral and of unknown authorship until Yann Lagadeg (Jehan Lagadeuc) published his *Catholicon*, a Breton-Latin-French dictionary in 1499. In the nineteenth century efforts were made to standardise the language. Yann Frañsez ar Gonideg (Jean-Francois Le Gonidec) published his dictionary of modern Breton in 1821 and this had a profound effect on the written works which were published subsequently. The romantic period also put the spotlight on Brittany and, as elsewhere in Europe, serious collecting of folk literature began. Ballads, songs and folktales formed the core of the anthologies published by such famous collectors as Kervarker (Théodore Hersart de la Villemarqué) and Fañch an Uhel (Francois-Marie Luzel).

However until the late nineteenth century the bulk of published works originated from the clergy and was aimed at the religious and moral edification of the masses. Yet the second half of that century also saw the birth of a cultivated literature – mostly poems and stories – which was often heavily influenced by the French fashion of the time, but which also included a few works of note. Lexicographers and grammarians also continued the expansion, modification and standardisation of the language across the various dialects of Brittany, a task which carried on until the middle of the twentieth century.

The history of twentieth century Breton literature is dominated by the Gwalarn movement, founded by Roparz Hemon, who set to create and publish a large body of works in Breton which could be considered of international standing. He gathered around him a few gifted writers and published novels, short stories, poems, essays, dictionaries, grammars, translations and studies on the language. The influence of his work can be felt up to this day.

Although one of the aims of this book is to give an overall picture of the literary texts published in Breton, this is in no way intended to be a definitive anthology of Breton literature, for the writings are too rich, too plentiful, too varied and too wide-ranging to fit in the very few themes which have been selected. It is hoped that many contemporary writers who have not been included in this anthology will not be offended by their omission. Whenever possible the original Breton text has been used. In a few cases we have reproduced the standardised version published in a re-edition. Both poetry and prose are widely represented in this anthology. Very few pages however are devoted to the Breton theatre.

The decision to exclude authors writing in modern French was a difficult one to take and was sometimes arrived at with regret, as in the case of Albert Legrand, Anatole Le Braz, Emile Souvestre, Max Jacob, Pierre Loti, Alain Robbe-Grillet, Saint-Pol Roux, Tristan Corbière and Morvan Lebesque, and at times with fewer pangs of conscience when it came to the writings of Chateaubriand, Alphonse Daudet, Madame de Sévigné, Honoré de Balzac, O-L Aubert, Victor Hugo and others, these having been widely published in French and often translated into English.

Many nineteenth century authors who wrote in Breton but concentrated on painting hackneyed sentimental pictures of a Brittany that never was are not, as a rule, included in this collection. On the other hand, the views expressed by foreign writers have been taken into account. They cast an interesting look, free from national politics, on Brittany. The Lives of saints, Caesar's writings, Welsh and English authors who wrote about their travels all provide valuable testimonies of outsiders' opinions on Brittany.

Until the literary movement promoted by Gwalarn at the beginning of the twentieth century, the vast majority of writings in Breton were of a religious nature. The versification and content of Middle-Breton texts are of interest but because the literary value of modern religious writings is minimal they too have been excluded from this anthology. The emphasis is thus firmly placed on contemporary texts in an attempt to show how lively, modern and open to the outside world are today's Breton writers. This does not mean ignoring the religious past of the country, and many religious references – whether pagan or Roman Catholic – will be found in the chosen texts.

Some of the texts chosen may be found to be controversial, such as the letters published in *Baner ac Amserau Cymru* which have no literary value but bear testimony to the lasting links between Celtic lands. Other more literary texts written in Breton after the second world war also bear witness to the fight against the French State which imprisoned and condemned many Breton activists who refused political or language assimilation. In France, the native language of Brittany is still seen as a threat to the unity of the country, yet the Welsh example shows how a minority language can be promoted and turned into an asset for the nation as a whole.

The main aim of this anthology is to give a voice to those who are not normally heard because of the language in which they write. It is in no way complete, and yet it gives a picture of the liveliness of contemporary Breton creative writing which continues to thrive against all the odds.

This anthology is too scanty, too short, too subjective – as are all works of this type – and yet it is hoped that it represents a view of Brittany which is common to the vast majority of Breton men and women who are struggling, to this very day, to keep the language alive in its historical patch by using it daily and having their children educated through it.

Traces of a Lost Literature

Virtually nothing survives of medieval Breton literature, yet among the literatures of other languages, there is evidence of considerable respect, reverence even, for Breton tales and story-telling, be they spoken or sung to the accompaniment of musical instruments. The bilingual Breton entertainers, popular in the courts of Europe, and aided through later cultural cross-fertilisation by the *trouvères* of northern France would have taken these tales further afield. This would explain a Breton influence – mainly through oral transmissions in the European courts – from way back in time, helping to create a literary form that acquired widespread popularity in the Middle Ages, in Norman French, Middle English, Old Norse (or Icelandic) and Medieval German. These were the *Lais* or *Lays* (*Strengleikar* in Old Norse), fairly short tales in verse, which came to sudden popularity in the twelfth century. They describe a moment of crisis in a love relationship, intense and usually complicated. The *Lais* of the mysterious Marie de France, composed in the latter part of the twelfth century, are the best known works in this genre. Whether Marie considered herself to be writing *lais* or whether she was acknowledging the sources of her stories, is not clear. Whatever, the narrative verses now associated with her name became known as *lais*. She says in her Prologue to the *Guigemar lai*.

Les contes ke jo sai verrais
Dunt li Bretun unt fait les lais
Vos conterai assez briefment

The tales which I know to be true
Of which the Bretons composed lais
I shall relate to you concisely.

She ends the *Eliduc lai*:

De l'aventure de ces treis
Li auntien Bretun curteis
Firent le lai pur remembrer,
Que hum nel deust pas oblier.

Of the adventures of these three
The ancient courtly Bretons
Made a lai to remember them
Lest men should forget.

And this is how she begins the *Laustic lai*:

Une aventure vus dirai
Dunt li Bretun firent un lai.

A story I shall tell
Of which the Bretons made a *lai*.

All of Marie de France's *lais* contain similar acknowledgements either at the beginning or the end – or both – of each one. The same was true of her contemporaries, such as the composer or re-writer of the *Graelent Lai*, a *lai* mentioned in the tale of *Trystan and Esyllt*, that Trystan played to the accompaniment of the harp when he first arrives in Mark's court. It has been suggested that the composer of *Gralent* had lifted it with embellishments and name changing from Marie de France's *Lanval*, apparently to her intense disapproval. Another, *Lay le Freine*, is a straight translation of Marie's *Le Fresne*. There exist in Middle English a total of eight tales described as Breton Lays among which should be included Geoffrey Chaucer's *Franklin's Tale*. Chaucer pointedly refers to the *Lai* form in order to create an impression of antiquity, of a pre-Christian, twilight era of magic and fantasy. Antiquity, but not an obsolete literary form.

In his Prologue to the Franklin's Tale Chaucer wrote:

Thise olde gentil Britons in hir dayes
Of diverse aventures maden lays,
Rymeyed in hir firste Briton Tonge;
Which layes with hir instruments they songe,
Or elles redden hem for hir plesaunce ...

And then he begins the Tale:

In Armorik, that called is Britayne ,
Ther was a knight that loved and dide his payne
To serve a lady in his beste wyse;

English translators have shown little interest in Breton or Celtic influences on Marie de France. "Marie's romances derive farther back than any Breton or Celtic dream ... such stories are common property," wrote Eugene Mason dismissively in his Introduction to *Mediaeval French Romances*. Glyn S Burgess and Keith Busby in their Introduction to *The Lais of Marie de France* note that she would have been familiar with the *Trystan* romances and had used Geoffrey of Monmouth's *Historia Regum Britanniae* for the purpose of getting some useful geographical place names. She also shows that she can speak English. But there is not much more.

So what of the *lais* of Marie de France? Of the twelve, eight are set wholly or partly in Brittany. Three are set in Celtic-Brythonic or former Celtic-Brythonic lands; *Lanval* is set in Carlisle, *Yonec* in Caerwent and Caerleon in South-east Wales, and *Chevrefoil*, the shortest, is a cameo from the Trystan and Esyllt story set in Wales and Cornwall. Of the twelve only one is set outside the Celtic-Brythonic lands, *Les Deus Amanz,* which is set in Normandy. The eight Breton Lays in mediaeval English – of a later period, extant manuscripts dating from the fourteenth and fifteenth centuries – acknowledge Breton origins and influences but geographically the tales are spread across Germany, Rome, Sicily, Greece, Austria and include references to the Saracens. Three present tales from the Celtic-Brythonic lands: Chaucer's *Franklin's Tale* is set firmly in Brittany. Thomas Chestre's *Sir Launfal*, another embellished re-working of *Lanval* is set in Arthur's court in Carlisle and the tale takes us to Caerleon, Lombardy and Brittany. The English *Lay le Freine*, as already mentioned, is a translation of Marie de France's *Le Fresne* and is set totally in Brittany.

It would appear that the *lais* of Marie de France were not intended to be sung but rather to be read by an emerging literate society. Yet there are numerous references suggesting that the form was traditionally associated with a musical performance. Chaucer in his Prologue to the *Franklin's Tale* suggests as much. Trystan when he first appears in King March's court is described performing the *Graelent Lay* (Gottfried von Strassburg version): "He sang the notes of his *lay* so beautifully in Breton, Welsh, Latin and French that you could not tell which was sweeter or deserving of more praise, his harping or his singing." And in the Thomas of Brittany version we find Esyllt singing "Her hands are fair, her *lay* is good, her voice sweet, and her tone low."

A subtle atmosphere of the supernatural is a particularly Celtic element surrounding the *lais*. *Lanval* goes to Avalon with his fairy love. *Guigemar, Milun, Yonec* and *Deuz Amanz* all have supernatural elements, not an ingredient vital to any of the stories but a suggestion of Celtic influences, comparable to the *Mabinogi*. Death, a particular preoccupation of the Celts, is present in the *lais*.

As for the feminine aspect of the *lais*, it has been argued, that the women have forceful personalities. They are involved in an exploration of love, not platonic love but a love that was often adulterous, the ultimate aim being physical union. Marie does not show disapproval for the extra-marital affairs of her characters. She asserts the value of love for women as well as for men. For the (male) troubadours – there were women poets in the Languedoc courts of love – women were an inspiration for heroic deeds to enhance the moral traits of the men. Marie went a few steps further than the songs of the southern troubadours.

Have some Celtic influences filtered through in her attitudes to women? Hints, perhaps, of the Welsh Laws of Hywel Dda (c. 930), which even by present day standards, showed progressive attitudes towards women and children. It is now being suggested that the Tales of the *Mabinogi* were the work of a woman. The great Breton writer and theologian, Ernest Renan, wrote in his *Essai sur la poésie des races Celtiques* in 1859 that if we were to assign sex to nations we would have to say without hesitation that the Cymric/Breton branch of the Celtic race is an essentially feminine race. "No human family... has carried so much mystery into love," he wrote. "No other has conceived with more delicacy the ideal of woman, or been more fully dominated by it."

As to the form of the original Breton *lai* we have a few pointers. The term *laid* or *loid* was used to describe verses inserted in ancient prose Irish sagas. Rachel Bromwich noted that in the twelfth century the *laoidh* corresponded to the ballad part of the saga of Finn Mac Cumhaill and his warriors, the *laithe fiannaidheachta* (Fenian *lais*). Sir Ifor Williams in his introduction to *Canu Llywarch Hen* raised the point that primitive *englynion* in the *Red Book of Hergest* and the *Black Book of Carmarthen* appear to be lyrical interludes within a prose saga. He also mentioned that the most complete Welsh versions of the tale of *Trystan and Esyllt* is in the form of these *englynion* interspersed with explanatory prose to help move the story forward. So are we thinking of something similar to the allegedly unique work, *Aucassin et Nicolette*, a *conte-fable* set in Beaucaire in Languedoc but recorded in the French dialect of Champagne? It is said to be unique, at least in France, a complete story told alternately in verse and prose. The oldest extant manuscript also includes the music. Could this be the one written record of the presentation of a *lai*?

We have suggested that no Breton *lai* has survived. However, there is in Kervarker's/Hersart de la Villemarqué's *Barzaz Breiz* a ballad which he claims to be an example of a *lai*. We include it in this anthology in spite of some doubts, along with Marie de France's version of the same story. While the reputation of Kervarker has generally been redeemed it would appear that it is not so in relation to this ballad.

We would merely note that it is much shorter than Marie de France's version. Would it require some spoken prose explanation as part of its presentation if not of the extent of *Aucassin et Nicolette* but of the kind mentioned by Sir Ifor Williams vis-à-vis *Trystan and Esyllt*? Marie's title, *Laustic*, is an obvious Frenchified version of the Breton 'eostig' for nightingale – '*Ann Eostik*' is the title of the version in *Barzaz Breiz*, a fact often ignored by translators.

Kervarker

Ann Eostik, *from the 1839 edition of Barzaz Breiz*

Greg iaouang a Zant-Malo, deac'h,
D'he frenestr a oele, d'ann neac'h:

"Sioaz! sioaz! me zo tizet!
Va eostik paour a zo lazet!"

"Livirit d'in, va greg nevez,
Perak 'ta savit kelliez,

Kelliez diouz va c'hostez-me,
E kreiz ann noz, diouz ho kwele,

Diskabel-kaer, ha diarc'henn,
Perak 'ta savit evelhenn?"

"Mar zavann, den ker, evel-se,
Ekreiz ann noz, diouz va gwele,

Da eo ganin, setu, gwelet
Al listri braz mont ha donet."

"Ne d'eo ket, vad, evid eul lestr,
Az it kelliez d'ar prenestr;

Ne d'eo ked evid al listri,
Nag evid daou nag evid tri;

Ne d'eo ked evid ho gwelet,
Ken neubed al loar, ar stered.

Va itron, d'i me livirit,
Da berak bep noz e savit!"

"Sevel a rann da vont da zell
Ouz va bugel enn he gavel."

"Ne d'eo ket ken evit sellet,
Sellet ouz eur bugel kousket;

Ne d'eo ket gevier a fell d'e,
Da berak savit evel-se?

"Va denik koz, ma na derez,
Me lavaro ar wirionez:

Eunn eostig a glevann bep noz,
Er jardin war eur bodik-roz;

Eunn eostik bep noz a glevann;
Ken ge e kan, ken dous e kan!

Ken dous e kan, ker kaer, ken flor,
Bep noz, bep noz, pa zioul' ar mor!"

Ann aotrou koz dal m' he c'hlevaz,
Enn he galoun a brederiaz;

Ann aotrou koz dal'm he chlevaz,
Enn he galoun a levaraz:

"Pe mar 'ma gwir, pe ma ne ket,
Ann eostig a vezo paket!"

Antronoz-beure, pa zavaz,
Da gaout ar jardinour ez eaz.

"Jardinour mad, sentit ouz-in;
Eunn dra zo a ra glac'har d'in:

E'r c'harz a zo eunn eostik-noz
Ne ra nemet kana enn noz;

Hed ann noz ne ra met kana,
Ken e ma ounn dihunet gant-ha.

Mar 'ma paket fenoz ganid,
Eur gwenneg aour a roinn-me d'id."

Ar jardinour pa'n deuz klevet;
Eunn ulmenig en deuz stegnet,

Hag ann eostig en deuz paket,
Ha d'he aotrou neuz hen kaset,

Hag ann aotrou, pa hen dalc'haz,
Awalc'h he galoun a c'hoarzaz,

Hag he vougaz, hag he daolaz,
War barlenn wenn ann itron geaz.

"Dalit, dalit, va greg iaouank;
Setu aman hoc'h eostik koant;

Me 'm euz hen paket evid hoc'h;
Me chans, va dous, e plizo d'e-hoc'h."

He den iaouank d'al ma klevaz,
Gand glac'har vraz a lavaraz:

"Setu ma dous ha me tizet;
Ne hallfomp mui en em welet,

Da sklerder loar, d'ar prenester,
'Vel ma oamp boazet da ober."

Translation

The Nightingale

A young wife from Saint-Malo, yesterday,
At her window, cried:

"Alas! Alas! I am lost!
My poor nightingale has been killed!"

"Tell me, my newly-wed wife,
Why do you get up so often,

So often, lying next to me,
In the middle of night, you leave your bed,

Your head is bare, and also your feet,
Why do you get up thus?"

"I rise, dear man, like this,
In the middle of night, from my bed,

Because I like to see
The tall ships come and go."

"It is not, surely, for a ship,
You go so often to the window,

It is not for the ships,
Neither for two nor for three.

It is not to see them,
Or the moon, or the stars.

My lady, tell me,
Why each night, you rise!"

"I rise to go and look
At my baby in his cradle."

"Neither is it to go and see,
See a sleeping baby;

I do not want to hear lies,
Why do you get up like this?"

"My little old man, to calm you down,
I shall speak the truth:

There is a nightingale I hear every night
In the garden on a rose-bush;

A nightingale which I hear each night;
Her song is so joyful, her song is so sweet!

Her song is so sweet, so beautiful, so harmonious,
Each night, each night, when the sea calms down!"

The old man, when he heard this,
Thought it over in his mind;

The old man when he heard this,
Spoke to himself thus:

"Whether she speaks true or false,
That nightingale shall be caught!"

The following morning when he rose,
He went and sought the gardener.

"Good gardener, listen well,
There is something that pains me:

In the hedge there is a nightingale
Which does nothing but sing at night:

All night it does nothing but sing,
So much that it keeps me awake.

If you catch her tonight,
I'll give to you a golden coin."

The gardener when he heard this;
Went to set a trap,

He caught the nightingale,
And to the master took it,

The master, when he received it,
Laughed heartily.

He strangled it, and threw it,
On the white lap of his poor lady.

"Here, here, my young wife;
Here is your fine nightingale;

I went and caught it for you;
I hope, my sweet, it pleases you."

Her young lover, when he heard of this,
With great sadness did he speak:

"My love, I have been found out,
No more can we see each other,

Under a clear moon, at the window,
As we used to do."

Marie de France

Laüstic

Une aventure vus dirai
Dunt li Bretun firent un lai.
Laüstic ad nun, ceo m'est vis,
Si l'apelent en lur païs;
Ceo est russignol en franceis
E nihtegale en dreit engleis.
En Seint Mallo en la cuntree
Ot une vile renumee.
Deus chevalers ilec manëent
E deus forz maisuns i aveient.
Pur la bunté des deus baruns
Fu de la vile bons li nuns.
Li uns aveit femme espusee,
Sage, curteise e acemee;
A merveille se teneit chiere
Sulunc l'usage e la manere.
Li autres fu un bachelers
Bien coneü entre ses pers
De prüesce, de grant valur,
E volenters feseit honur.
Mut turnëot e despendeit
E bien donot ceo qu'il aveit.
La femme sun veisin ama.
Tant la requist, tant la preia
E tant par ot en lui grant bien
Que ele l'ama sur tute rien,
Tant pur le bien quë ele oï
Tant pur ceo qu'il iert pres de li.
Sagement e bien s'entr'amerent.
Mut se covrirent e garderent
Qu'il ne feussent aparceüz
Ne desturbez ne mescreüz;
E eus poeient bien fere,
Kar pres esteient lur repere;

Preceines furent lur maisuns
E lur sales e lur dunguns.
N'i aveit bare ne devise
Fors un haut mur de piere bise.
Des chambres u la dame jut,
Quant a la fenestre s'estut,
Poeit parler a sun ami
De l'autre part e il a li,
E lur aveirs entrechangier
E par geter e par lancier.
N'unt gueres rien que lur despleise;
Mut esteient amdui a iese,
Fors tant k'il ne poent venir
Del tut ensemble a lur pleisir;
Kar la dame ert estreit gardee,
Quant cil esteit en la cuntree.
Mes de tant aveient retur,
U fust par nuit u fust par jur,
Que ensemble poeient parler.
Nul nes poeit de ceo garder
Que a la fenestre n'i venissent
E iloec ne s'entreveïssent.
Lungement se sunt entr'amé,
Tant que ceo vient a un esté,
Que bruil e pré sunt reverdi
E li vergier ierent fluri.
Cil oiselet par grant duçur
Mainent lur joie en sum la flur.
Ki amur ad a sun talent
N'est merveille s'il i entent.
Del chevaler vus dirai veir:
Il i entent a sun poeir
E la dame de l'autre part,
E de parler e de regart.
Les nuiz, quant la lune luseit
E ses sires cuché esteit,
Dejuste lui sovent levot
E de sun mantel se afublot.
A la fenestre ester veneit,
Pur sun ami qu'el i saveit
Que autreteu vie demenot
E le plus de la nuit veillot.
Delit aveient al veer,

Quant plus ne poeient aver.
Tant i estut, tant i leva
Que ses sires s'en curuça
E meintefeiz li demanda
Pur quei levot e u ala.
"Sire", la dame li respunt,
"Il nen ad joië en cest mund
Ki n'ot le laüstic chanter.
Pur ceo me vois ici ester;
Tant ducement l'i oi la nuit
Que mut me semble grant deduit.
Tant me delit e tant le voil
Que jeo ne puis dormir de l'oil."
Quant li sires ot que ele dist,
De ire e de maltalent en rist.
De une chose se purpensa:
Le laüstic enginnera.
Il n'ot vallet en sa meisun
Ne face engin, reis u laçun,
Puis les mettent par le vergier;
N'i ot codre ne chastainier
U il ne mettent laz u glu,
Tant que pris l'unt e retenu.
Quant le laüstic eurent pris,
Al seignur fu rendu tut vis.
Mut en fu liez quant il le tient;
As chambres a la dame vient.
"Dame", fet il, "u estes vus?
Venez avant, parlez a nus!
J'ai le laüstic englué,
Pur quei vus avez tant veillé.
Desor poëz gisir en peis:
Il ne vus esveillerat meis."
Quant la dame l'ad entendu,
Dolente e cureçuse fu.
A sun seignur l'ad demandé
Et il l'ocist par engresté.
Le col li rumpt a ses deus meins;
De ceo fist il que trop vileins;
Sur la dame le cors geta,
Se que sun chainse ensanglanta
Un poi desur le piz devant.
De la chambre s'en ist atant.

La dame prent le cors petit;
Durement plure e si maudit
Ceus ki le laüstic traïrent
E les engins e laçuns firent,
Kar mut li unt toleit grant hait.
"Lasse", fet ele, "mal m'estait!
Ne purrai mes la nuit lever
Ne aler a la fenestre ester,
U jeo suil mun ami veer.
Une chose sai jeo de veir:
Il quidera ke jeo me feigne;
De ceo m'estuet que cunseil preigne.
Le laüstic li trametrai,
L'aventure li manderai."
En une piece de samit,
A or brusdé e tut escrit,
Ad l'oiselet envolupé.
Un sun vatlet ad apelé;
Sun message li ad chargié,
A sun ami l'ad enveié.
Cil est la chevalier venuz;
De part sa dame dist saluz,
Tut sun message li cunta,
Le laüstic li presenta.
Quant tut li ad dit e mustré
E il l'aveit bien escuté,
De l'aventure esteit dolenz,
Mes ne fu pas vileins ne lenz.
Un vaselet ad fet forgeer;
Unques n'i ot fer ne acer,
Tut fu de or fin od bones pieres,
Mut precïuses e mut cheres;
Covercle i ot tresbien asis.
Le laüstic ad dedenz mis
Puis fist la chasse enseeler.
Tuz jurs l'ad fet od lui porter.
    Cele aventure fu cuntee,
Ne pot estre lunges celee.
Un lai en firent li Dictun.
Le Laüstic l'apelë hum.

Translation

The Nightingale

An adventure I shall tell
Of which the Bretons made a lai.
Laüstic the name, I believe,
They call it in their land;
That is 'rossignol' in French
And 'nightingale' in correct English.
Saint-Malo, in that country,
Stands as a city of renown.
Two gentlemen dwelt there
Each one in a fine house.
Through the generosity of these two men
The city acquired respectability.
One had married a woman,
Wise, courteous and gracious
She conducted herself marvellously
In the fashion of the time.
The other knight was a bachelor
Well known among his peers
For his strength and great valour,
And performing deeds of honour.
Many tournaments he attended
And gave freely of what he had.
He loved his neighbour's wife.
By his persistence, by his entreaties
And through his generosity
She loved him more than anything,
By the good things she heard of him
And because he lived close by.
Wisely and well they loved each other,
Yet they took care and avoided
Being seen together,
Disturbed or suspected;
This they were able to do,
Because their dwellings were so close
And their rooms and their keeps.
There was nothing to separate them
But a high wall of grey stone.
From the bedroom where the lady stood,
By the open window,
She could talk to her beloved

And also he to her,
And exchange gifts
Which they threw to each other.
There was little to displease them;
Both were contented, at their ease
Except that they could not come
Together for their pleasure;
For the lady was well guarded,
When her husband was about.
But not so that they could not
During the night or day,
Speak a word together.
None could prevent them
From coming to the window
And seeing each other there.
For long they loved each other
Until a summer came.
In its heat, the fields
Grew green and the orchards bloomed.
Birds with great sweetness
Sang their joy from the flower-heads.
If love is in the heart
No wonder it now grows stronger.
Of the knight the truth I'll tell:
He did his utmost
And the lady too,
To speak and see each other.
At night, when the moon shone
And her lord slept soundly,
From his side she often rose
And donned her mantle.
At the window she would stand,
For her love she waited
Knowing he would come
And most of the night kept vigil.
They took delight in what they saw
As they could not have more.
So often did she rise, so often did she get up,
That her husband impatiently
And repeatedly asked her
Why she got up and where she went.
"My lord," the lady did reply,
"There is no greater joy in the world

Than hearing a nightingale sing.
That is why I come here to stand;
So sweet the song I hear at night
Which gives me the greatest pleasure.
Such is my delight and desire for it
That I cannot sleep at all."
When her husband did hear this,
He gave a malicious laugh.
And then he plotted something:
To catch the nightingale.
Every servant in the mansion
Made a trap or a snare
To set within the garden;
There was no hazel nor a chestnut tree
That did not have a snare or glue,
Until the bird was caught.
When the nightingale was captured,
The knight was given it, still alive.
He was delighted to hold it in his hands
And went to the chamber of his lady.
"Madame," he said, "where are you?
Come forth and speak to me!
I have now caught the nightingale
Which has been keeping you awake.
Now you shall sleep in peace:
It will never wake you again."
When the lady heard this,
She was pained and sorrowful.
To her husband she then asked
To have the bird for herself.
Its neck he broke with his two hands;
Killing it in sheer spite.
At the lady he threw the body,
So that her dress was bloodied
And spots cast on her breast.
Then he left her chamber.
The lady took the tiny body;
Bitterly she wept and cursed
Those who caught the nightingale
And made the snares and glue,
And she was full of hate.
"Alas," said she, "woe betide me!
I can no more get up at night

To go and stand at the window
Where once I saw my love.
One thing I know too well:
He will think my love is spent;
So I must take action now.
The nightingale I'll send to him
And tell him what has happened."
And in a piece of satin,
Embroidered in gold and designed,
She wrapped the little bird.
Then she called a servant;
She charged him with a message,
And sent him to her lover.
To the knight he went,
From his lady he brought a greeting,
The message he repeated,
And presented him with the nightingale.
When the message had been given
And all had been well listened to,
At the news he was much distressed,
But he was not discourteous nor impolite.
A little vessel he had made;
Not of iron nor of steel,
But of pure gold and fine stones;
Most precious and expensive;
With a lid tightly covering it.
The nightingale then he put inside
And sealed the casket firmly.
Every day henceforth he carried it with him.
      This adventure was told
And could not for long be hidden.
A lai was composed by the Bretons:
They called it Le Laüstic.

The Pagan Past

Druids and druidism are mysteries of the Breton and Celtic world. The waters have been somewhat muddied by the neo-druidism of the stonemason, antiquarian and occasional literary forger Edward Williams (Iolo Morganwg). Through his creation, the Gorsedd of Bards in Wales, later copied in Brittany and Cornwall, he gave new prominence to druidism. He was by no means the first to try and resurrect the cult. References by Julius Caesar, Tacitus, Loukianes and others provide proof of their existence and much of the available information about them.

Julius Caesar

The Conquest of Gaul (Extract)

(Written circa 52 B.C. Translation by S. A. Handford, Penguin Classics, 1951)

Everywhere in Gaul there are only two classes of men of any account or consideration. […] The two privileged classes are the Druids and the Knights. The Druids officiate at the worship of the gods, regulate public and private sacrifices, and give rulings on all religious questions. Large numbers of young men flock to them for instruction, and they are held in great honour by the people. They act as judges in practically all disputes, whether between tribes or between individuals; when any crime is committed, or a murder takes place, or a dispute arises about an inheritance or a boundary, it is they who adjudicate the matter and appoint the compensation to be paid and received by the parties concerned. […] All the Druids are under one head, whom they hold in the highest respect. On his death, if any one of the rest is of outstanding merit he succeeds to the vacant position; if several have equal claims, the Druids usually decide the election by voting, though sometimes they decide by combat. On a fixed date in each year they hold a session in a consecrated place in the country of the Carnutes, which is the centre of Gaul. Those who are involved in disputes assemble from all parts, and accept the Druids' judgement and awards. The Druidic doctrine is believed to have been founded in Britain and thence imported into Gaul. Even today those who want to make a profound study of it generally go to Britain for the purpose.

The Druids are exempt from military service and do not pay taxes like other citizens. These important privileges are naturally attractive: many present themselves of their own accord to become students of Druidism, and others are sent by their parents or relatives. It is said that these pupils have to memorize a great number of verses – so many, that some of them spend twenty years at their studies. The Druids believe that their religion forbids them to commit their teachings to writing, although for most other purposes, such as public and private accounts, the Gauls use the Greek alphabet. But I imagine that this rule was originally established for other reasons – because they did not want their doctrine to become public property, and in order to prevent their pupils from relying on the written word and neglecting to train their memories; for it is usually found that when people have the help of texts, they are less diligent in learning by heart, and let their memories rust. A lesson which they take particular pains to inculcate is that the soul does not perish, but after death passes from one body to another; they think that this is the best incentive to bravery, because it teaches men to disregard the terrors of death. They also hold long discussions about the heavenly bodies and their movements, the size of the universe and of the earth, the physical constitution of the world, and the power and properties of the gods; and they instruct the young men in all these subjects.

It is true that the Empire persecuted the Druids. They were attacked (partly doubtless, for political reasons) under the laws regarding human sacrifice, murder and magic (Lex Cornelia de Sicariis) *by Tiberius and Claudius. At that time if we are to take a passage in Pomponius Mela literally, they continued to teach the young in secret.*

Sabine Baring-Gould and John Fisher

Lives of the British Saints (Extract)

With the acceptance of Christianity, the saints simply occupied the shells left vacant by the Druids. […]

The institution of schools for the young was certainly much older than Christianity in Britain and Ireland. We know from classical authorities, as well as from Irish writers, that the Druids formed communities, and these were presided over by an Arch-Druid, that in them were educated the sons of the kings and nobles, and that the heads of these schools had lands for their support. By no way can we explain the marvellous expansion of the educational establishment which took place after Ireland became Christian, than on the supposition that the saints entered in upon an institution already existing, and brought into it a new life.

The office of cursing originally formed part of the duties of the Druid. He was a functionary called in likewise at the conclusion of contracts. When two individuals entered into a compact, the Druid was present to utter imprecations on him who should break the agreement. Beside the Druid there was the poet who would guarantee to compose a lampoon against one who should break the contract. This was part and parcel of the legal process. In Ireland, when Saints Patrick, Carentoc, and the rest of the Commission revised the laws, the least possible interference was made with existing social and legal systems.

As the Druid ceased to be esteemed, the saint gradually took over the functions. He had thrust on him, the duties formerly discharged by the Druid. From being professional curser of the tribal foes, it was but natural that the saint should take on him to curse those who interfered with the privileges of the monastery, even gave him personal offence. […] A man who thought he had been wronged, and could not forcibly put things right according to the law, went to a Druid in Pagan times, to a saint in Christian days, and asked him to "ill-wish" the wrong-doer, just as now he goes to a lawyer and solicits a summons.

Anonymous

The Life of Saint Samson of Dol (Extract)

This was written in the early seventh century, not long after the saint's death. Most of the other Lives were written several centuries after their time. The following paragraph about Illtyd, who was born in Armorica, suggests that he was both a Druid and Christian.

[…] with a common purpose, they rose up together and […] set about conducting their son [Samson] to the school of the famous master of the Britons, Eltut by name. Now this Eltut was a disciple of St. Germanus and St. Germanus himself had ordained him priest in his youth. And in truth Eltut was of all the Britons the most accomplished in all the scriptures, namely of the Old and New Testaments, and in those of philosophy [science] of every kind, of geometry namely, and of rhetoric, grammar and arithmetic, and of all the theories of philosophy. And by birth he was a most wise magician, having knowledge of the future.

Kervarker

Ar Rannou

In the 1867 edition of Barzaz Breiz, Kervarker suggests that the following is one of the oldest poems in the Breton language. He believed it to be a catechism in which the Druid teaches the child the secrets of the Druidic world. He heard it for the first time sung by a young man in the parish of Nizon, near Pontaven. He also said that Brizeux had told him that he had heard a version of it in Scaër. Luzel found many versions of the poem in all parts of Breton-speaking Brittany, but principally in Cornouaille and Tréguier, in which the identity of the speakers or singers are not identified. He said it was known as 'Gosperou ar Râned' (The Frogs' Vespers). Jean-Marie de Penguern believed it to be an encoded "history of the coming of the island

Britons". François-Marie Luzel saw it simply as a song to train the memory and the speech of young children. He also said that he never came across the word 'drouiz' for 'druid' – only the term 'Eskop derv' (Bishop of the oaks). Luzel also made the point that none of the people who sang it to him were able to explain what it meant. We need not place much significance on that last point. How many know that the popular English nursery rhyme 'Ring-a-ring o' roses' dates from the Great Plague of 1665? Donatien Laurent says that the song is evidently very old and suggests that the ludicrous title, 'Gosperou ar Râned', came about through a confusion between the words 'rann' (game, couplet) and 'ran' (frog).

In his lengthy notes attempting to give meaning to this poem Kervarker makes extensive use of the Myvyrian Archaiology of Wales. *It may be that he is equally indebted to Edward Davies's* Mythology and Rites of the British Druids *(London, 1809), a work that also draws on the* Myvyrian Archaiology.

Stanza I. *Reflects the importance the cult of the dead and fear of the supernatural to the Druids. Anatole Le Braz described the Catholicism of the Bretons as a kind of mystical paganism. Suicide – the ultimate sin according to the Catholic Church – was an accepted part of its culture up to the present time.*

Stanza II. *A reference to the Welsh tales of the oxen of Hu Gadarn dragging the monstrous 'avanc' from the lake and saving the world from the flood. One died from his exertions, the other from grief at the loss of its partner.*

Stanza III. *Might be derived from an ancient and obscure Welsh poem 'Gwarchan Maelderw,' which quotes Hu Gadarn as saying he wants men to be born again (Edward Davies). Taliesin says "Thrice was I born. I know how to meditate. It is woeful that men will not come to seek all the sciences of the world, which are treasured in my bosom; for I know all that has been, and all that will be hereafter."*

Stanza V. *In the* Life of Illtyd *(Vita Sancti Iltuti) there is statement that the saint was blameless in the five stages of life.*

Stanza VI. *Wax models of children were an important part of sorcery in the middle ages. The cauldron has an important place in Celtic mythology.*

Stanza VII. *Seven suns, possibly seven days; seven moons, seven nights?*

Stanza VIII. *The Irish lit bonfires on hilltops in May. White heifers might be an allusion to a sacrifice to a Celtic goddess worshipped on the Isle of Anglesey.*

Stanza IX. *According to Pierre Le Baud, children were sacrificed on an altar in Aber-Wrac'h, at a place called Porz Keinvan, the Port of Lamentations – where the mothers would grieve over the loss of their children. The dancing elves might refer to moon worship, sometimes symbolising Ceres. Kervarker cites references to a cult of Koré or Kori on an island near Armorica (Île de Sein?). Ceridwen, or Keridwenn, was the Celtic equivalent of Ceres. Citing 'Monde Primitif, Volume IV,' Edward Davies said that the priests of the Cabiri were called 'Sues', i.e. 'swine'. Greece and Rome consecrated the sow to Ceres, and named it the mystical animal. She is prolific and ploughs the land with her snout. The Welsh, according to Davies, went further in that Ceres (or Ceridwen) herself assumed the form of a sow. She addressed her children as 'porchellan' ('piglets.')*

Stanzas X and XI. Could they be the Romans coming to attack the Veneti? Or a reference to the slaughter of the Anglesey Druids by the Romans? A rare reference to Christians massacring Druids occurs in the seventeenth century work of Toussaint de Saint-Luc.
Stanza XII. Are the signs of the Zodiac an omen? Is the killing of the sacred cow of the Bretons followed by the end of the World? Your guess is as good as ours!

Ann Drouiz
Daik, mab gwenn Drouiz; ore;
Daik, petra fel d'id-de?
Petra ganinn-me d'id-de.

Ar Bugel
Kan d'in euz a eur rann,
Ken a oufenn breman.

Ann Drouiz
Heb rann ar Red heb-ken:
Ankou, tad ann Anken;
Netra kent, netra ken.
Daik, mab gwenn Drouiz; ore;
Daik, petra fel d'id-de?
Petra ganinn-me d'id-de.

Ar Bugel
Kan d'in euz a zaou rann,
Ken a oufenn breman.

Ann Drouiz
Daou ejenn dioc'h eur gibi;
O sachat, o souheti;
Edrec'hit ann estoni!
Heb rann ar Red heb-ken:
Ankou, tad ann Anken;
Netra kent, netra ken.
Daik, mab gwenn Drouiz; ore;
Daik, petra fel d'id-de?
Petra ganinn-me d'id-de.

Ar Bugel
Kan d'in euz a dri rann, &c.

Ann Drouiz
Tri rann er bed-man a vez:

Tri derou, ha tri divez,
D'ann den ha d'ann derv ivez.
Teir rouantelez Varzin:
Frouez melen ha bleun lirzin;
Bugaligou o c'hoarzin.
Daou ejenn dioc'h eur gibi; &c.
Heb rann ar Red heb-ken: &c
Daik, mab gwenn Drouiz, ore; &c.

Ar Bugel
Kan d'in a bevar rann, &c.

Ann Drouiz
Pevar mean higolin,
Mean higolin da Varzin
Higolin klezeier blin.
Tri rann er bed-man a vez, &c
Daou ejenn dioc'h eur gibi; &c
Heb rann ar Red heb-ken: &c
Daik, mab gwenn Drouiz, ore; &c.

Ar Bugel
Kan d'in euz a bemp rann, &c.

Ann Drouiz
Pemp gouriz ann douar;
Pemp darn enn hoar;
Pemp mean war hor c'hoar.
Pevar mean higolin, &c
Tri rann er bed-man a vez, &c
Daou ejenn dioc'h eur gibi; &c
Heb rann ar Red heb-ken: &c
Daik, mab gwenn Drouiz, ore; &c.

Ar Bugel
Kan d'in euz a c'houec'h rann, &c.

Ann Drouiz
C'houec'h mabik great e koar,
Poellet gand galloud loar;
Ma n'ouzez-te, me oar.

C'houec'h louzaouen er perik

Meska'r goter ra'r c'horrik;
Enn he c'henou he vezik.
Pemp gouriz ann douar, &c
Pevar mean higolin, &c
Tri rann er bed-man a vez, &c
Daou ejenn dioc'h eur gibi; &c
Heb rann ar Red heb-ken: &c
Daik, mab gwenn Drouiz, ore; &c.

Ar Bugel
Kan d'in euz a zeiz rann, &c.

Ar Drouiz
Seiz heol ha seiz loar,
Seiz planeden gand ar Iar,
Seiz elfen gand bleud ann ear.
C'houec'h mabik great e koar, &c
Pemp gouriz ann douar, &c
Pevar mean higolin, &c
Tri rann er bed-man a vez, &c
Daou ejenn dioc'h eur gibi; &c
Heb rann ar Red heb-ken: &c
Daik, mab gwenn Drouiz, ore; &c.

Ar Bugel
Kan d'in euz a eiz rann, &c.

Ar Drouiz
Eiz avel o c'houibannat;
Eiz tan gand an Tantad,
E miz mae e menez kad.

Eiz onner wenn-kann-eon,
O puri enn enez don;
Eiz onner wenn d'an Itron.
Seiz heol ha eiz loar, &c
C'houec'h mabik great e koar, &c
Pemp gouriz ann douar, &c
Pevar mean higolin, &c
Tri rann er bed-man a vez, &c
Daou ejenn dioc'h eur gibi; &c
Heb rann ar Red heb-ken: &c
Daik, mab gwenn Drouiz, ore; &c.

Ar Bugel

Kan d'in euz a nao rann, &c.

Ar Drouiz

Nao dornik gwenn war dol leur,
E kichen tour Lezarmeur;
Ha nao mamm o keina meur.

E koroll, nao c'horrigan,
Bleunvek ho bleo, gwisket gloan,
Kelc'h ar feunteun, d'al loar-gann.
Gouiz hag e nao forc'hell all,
E toullik dor ann houc'hzal,
O soroc'hal, o turc'hial,
O turc'hial, o soroc'hal:
Torc'h! torc'h! torc'h! d'ar wezen aval!
Ann houc'h koz d'ho tiorreal.
Eiz avel o c'houibannat, &c
Seiz heol ha eiz loar, &c
C'houec'h mabik great e koar, &c
Pemp gouriz ann douar, &c
Pevar mean higolin, &c
Tri rann er bed-man a vez, &c
Daou ejenn dioc'h eur gibi; &c
Heb rann ar Red heb-ken: &c
Daik, mab gwenn Drouiz, ore; &c.

Ar Bugel

Kan d'in euz a zek rann, &c.

Ar Drouiz

Deg lestr tud gin a welet
O tonet euz a Naoned:
Goa! c'hui; goa! c'hui, tud Gwenned!
Nao dornik gwenn war dol leur, &c
Eiz avel o c'houibannat, &c
Seiz heol ha eiz loar, &c
C'houec'h mabik great e koar, &c
Pemp gouriz ann douar, &c
Pevar mean higolin, &c
Tri rann er bed-man a vez, &c
Daou ejenn dioc'h eur gibi; &c
Heb rann ar Red heb-ken: &c

Daik, mab gwenn Drouiz, ore; &c.

Ar Bugel
Kan di'n euz a unnek rann, &c.

Ar Drouiz
Unnek Belek houarneset,
O tonet euz a Wened,
Gand ho c'hlezeier torret;
Hag ho rochedou goadek;
Prenn-kolvez da vaz-loaek;
Euz a dri c'hant ho unnek.
Dek lestr tud gin a welet, &c
Nao dornik gwenn war dol leur, &c
Eiz avel o c'houibannat, &c
Seiz heol ha eiz loar, &c
C'houec'h mabik great e koar, &c
Pemp gouriz ann douar, &c
Pevar mean higolin, &c
Tri rann er bed-man a vez, &c
Daou ejenn dioc'h eur gibi &c
Heb rann ar Red heb-ken: &c
Daik, mab gwenn Drouiz, ore; &c.

Ar Bugel
Kan d'in euz a zaouzek rann, &c.

Ar Drouiz
Daouzek miz, daouzeg arouez,
Ann diveza-an-divez,
Saezer, 'hellink flimm he zaez.

Daouzeg arouez en em zraill,
Ar Vuc'h gen, ar Vuc'h Zu-baill,
O tonet o'ch Koad-ispail;
Flemm ar zaez enn he c'herc'hen,
He goad o redeg o'chpenn;
O vlejal hi, sonn he fenn.

Korn o son boud: tan ha taran;
Glao hag avel, taran ha tan!
Tra ken mui-ken; tra na rann!
Unnek belek houarneset, &c

Dek lestr tud gin a welet, &c
Nao dornik gwenn war dol leur, &c
Eiz avel o c'houibannat, &c
Seiz heol ha eiz loar, &c
C'houec'h mabik great e koar, &c
Pemp gouriz ann douar, &c
Pevar mean higolin, &c
Tri rann er bed-man a vez, &c
Daou ejenn dioc'h eur gibi; &c
Heb rann ar Red heb-ken: &c
Daik, mab gwenn Drouiz, ore; &c.

Translation

The Series

The Druid
Tell me, fair son of the Druids; loveliest one;
Tell me, what do you want?
What would you have me sing to you?

The Child
Sing to me the parts of one,
So that I may know it now.

The Druid
There is no part of one, it is alone by right:
Death, the father of sadness,
Nothing before, nothing after.
Tell me, fair son of the Druids; loveliest one;
Tell me, what do you want?
What would you have me sing to you?

The Child
Sing to me the parts of two,
So that I may know it now.

The Druid
Two oxen tied to a cart;
They pull, they are going to die;
See the wonder of it.
There is no part of one, it is alone by right:
Death, the father of sadness,

Nothing before, nothing after,
Tell me, fair son of the Druids; loveliest one;
Tell me, what do you want?
What would you have me sing to you?

The Child
Sing to me the parts of three, &c.

The Druid
There are three parts to this world:
Three beginnings and three endings,
For man, and for the oak, too.

Merlin's three kingdoms:
Golden fruit and bright flowers,
Children laughing.
Two oxen tied to a cart; &c.

The Child
Sing to me the parts of four, &c.

The Druid
Four honing stones,
Honing stones of Merlin
To sharpen blunt swords.
There are three parts to this world: &c
Two oxen tied to a cart: &c
There is no part of one, it is alone by right: &c
Tell me, fair one of the Druids; loveliest one; &c.

The Child
Sing to me the parts of five, &c.

The Druid
Five circles of the earth;
Five stages of time;
Five rocks on our sister.
Four honing stones, &c
There are three parts to this world: &c
Two oxen tied to a cart: &c
There is no part of one, it is alone by right: &c
Tell me, fair son of the Druids; loveliest one; &c.

The Child
Sing to me the parts of six, &c.

The Druid
Six sons made of wax,
Given life by the moon's light,
If you do not understand, I do.

Six herbs in a cauldron
Stirring the mix the dwarf
His thumb in his mouth.
Five circles of the earth; &c
Four honing stones, &c
There are three parts to this world: &c
Two oxen tied to a cart: &c
There is no part of one, it is alone by right: &c
Tell me, fair son of the Druids; loveliest one; &c.

The Child
Sing to me the parts of seven, &c.

The Druid
Seven suns and seven moons,
Seven planets including the Pleiades,
Seven elements of the air's flour.
Six sons made of wax, &c
Five circles of the earth; &c
Four honing stones, &c
There are three parts to this world: &c
Two oxen tied to a cart: &c
There is no part of one, it is alone by right: &c
Tell me, fair son of the Druids; loveliest one; &c.

The Child
Sing to me the parts of eight, &c.

The Druid
Eight winds whistling;
Eight fires and the Bonfire,
In May on battle mountain.

Eight heifers, white as foam,
Grazing on a deep island;

Eight white heifers of the Dame.
Seven suns and seven moons, &c
Six sons made of wax, &c
Five circles of the earth; &c
Four honing stones, &c
There are three parts to this world: &c
Two oxen tied to a cart: &c
There is no part of one, it is alone by right: &c
Tell me, fair son of the Druids; loveliest one; &c.

The Child
Sing to me the parts of nine, &c.

The Druid
Nine white hands on a threshing table,
Near the tower of Lezarmeur;
And nine mothers lamenting much.

Nine dancing elves,
Flowers in their hair, dressed in wool,
Around the fountain in the full moon.
A wild sow with her nine young boars
At the entrance of her lair,
Grunting and digging,
Digging and grunting:
Come! Come! Come! To the apple tree!
The old boar teaches them.
Eight winds whistling, &c
Seven suns and seven moons, &c
Six sons made of wax, &c
Five circles of the earth; &c
Four honing stones, &c
There are three parts to this world: &c
Two oxen tied to a cart: &c
There is no part of one, it is alone by right: &c
Tell me, fair son of the Druids; loveliest one; &c.

The Child
Sing to me the parts of ten &c.

The Druid
Ten enemy ships you see
Coming from Nantes;

Woe! You! Woe! You, people of Vannes!
Nine white hands on a threshing table, &c
Eight winds whistling, &c
Seven suns and seven moons, &c
Six sons made of wax, &c
Five circles of the earth; &c
Four honing stones, &c
There are three parts to this world: &c
Two oxen tied to a cart: &c
There is no part of one, it is alone by right: &c
Tell me, fair son of the Druids; loveliest one; &c.

The Child
Sing to the parts of eleven, &c.

The Druid
Eleven priests clad in iron,
Coming from Vannes,
With their swords broken;
And bloodied robes;
And hazel branches for crutches;
From more than three hundred down to eleven.
Ten enemy ships you see, &c
Nine white hands on a threshing table, &c
Eight winds whistling, &c
Seven suns and seven moons, &c
Six sons made of wax, &c
Five circles of the earth, &c
Four honing stones, &c
There are three parts to this world: &c
Two oxen tied to a cart: &c
There is no part of one, it is alone by right: &c
Tell me, fair son of the Druids; loveliest one; &c.

The Child
Sing to me the parts of twelve, &c.

The Druid
Twelve months, and twelve signs,
The last but one,
The Archer, firing his arrow with its dart.

Twelve signs in conflict.

The beautiful Cow, the black cow with the white star,
Coming from the Wood of Spoils;
The dart of the arrow in her flank,
The blood flowing freely;
She bellows, ear-splitting.

The horn sounds: fire and thunder;
Rain and wind, thunder and fire;
No more; no more divisions!
Eleven armed priests, &c
Ten enemy ships you see, &c
Nine white hands on a threshing table, &c
Eight winds whistling, &c
Seven suns and seven moons, &c
Six sons made of wax, &c
Five circles of the earth, &c
Four honing stones, &c
There are three parts to this world: &c
Two oxen tied to a cart: &c
There is no part of one, it is alone by right: &c
Tell me, fair son of the Druids; loveliest one; &c.

Urvan Perennes

Kan an drouiz

In Pe Is ... Pe Ahes? *published in 1943, Urvan Perennes traces the transformation of Brittany into a Christian land. He first describes the pagan religion with its druids, its cult of nature, its cruel gods who require human sacrifices carried out on dolmens. He then moves on to the progress brought to man and to the land of Brittany by christianisation as forests were cleared under the direction of the early Celtic Saints, and ends with the victory of the Lady of Rumengol, (i.e. the Virgin Mary), over Ahès, pagan daughter of King Gralon in the legend of Kêr-Is. The opening poem mentions druidism.*

"Kanomp an Eienenn
A ro kresk d'ar vezenn,
D'ar yeotenn teneredigez
Ha diskan d'al labouz
En traoniennou didrouz:
Skuilha' ra yec'hed... levenez.

Kanomp an Avel o yudal
A dreuz ar c'hoadou doñ,
Pe c'hoaz ar Gurun o strakal:

Tarann 'ro nerz-kaloñ!
Kanomp ar Bann-heol, ar Barr-Glao
A ro d'an douar frouez aho!"
Hag an Drouiz koz a gane
En e sav war lein an Are.

★★★

"Kanomp, kanomp an Tan!
Kuzet er prenn, er mean
'Man o para a-us d'hor penn
Gwir elfenn, a vuhez;
Ha drezan Teutates
A ro ha nerz ha sklerijenn.

Kanomp ar C'hleze hag an Dir,
Ar Gâd, ar gwad o ruilh!
Kleze lemm da zifenn hor gwir
Ha d'e vinji gwad puilh,
Hesus eo a ra'r boblou krenv
Ha digabestr, dindan an eñv."

★★★

"Kanomp hor Tîr karet
A vag tud ha loened
Druz ha ken kaer en heol skedus!
Tirienn hor C'hentadou
Goloet a goadou
War e ribl, ar mor peskedus.

Kanomp ivez ar C'hentadou
O c'halloud, o lealded.
Hon tîr eo poultrenn o c'horfou,
O ene 'chom bepred.
Keit ha ma vevo eun Drouiz
E vezo meur-veulet Galliz."

★★★

"Kanomp an Uhel-varr
Lakeet war an douar
'Vit pellaat pep droug, pep terzienn.

Beleien an Dero
Hep dale hen falc'ho
Gant ar Fals aour war an Dervenn.
Kanomp erfin ar Wir Furnez!
Eman skrivet er bed:
Da bep steredenn Teutates
En deus merket e sked,
Roudennet e hent da heuilha;
Ha da bep den, hevelep tra."

Hag an Drouiz koz a gane
En e sav war gern ar Menez.

Translation

The Druid's Song

Let's sing the Source
Which makes the tree grow
The grass tender
And the bird sing
In the silent valleys:
It brings forth health and joy.

Let's sing the Wind howling
In the depths of the woods;
Also the Thunder roaring:
Taranis[1] gives courage!
Let's sing the ray of Sunshine, the Shower of Rain
Which give fruit to the earth!"

Thus the old Druid sang
Standing on the top of Monts d'Arrée.

★★★

"Let's sing, let's sing the Fire!
Hidden in the wood, in the stone.
It shines above our heads
A true component of life;
Through it Teutates[2]
Gives strength and light.

Let's sing the Sword and the Steel,

The Battle, the blood which flows!
The sharp sword which defends our right
And avenges it in blood.
Hesus[3] makes the nations strong
And free, under the heavens."

★★★

"Let's sing our beloved Land
Which feeds men and animals
How fertile and magnificent it is in the shining sun!
The land of our Ancestors
Is covered in woods
And on its fringe, the sea is full of fish.

Let's us also sing our Ancestors,
Their power, their faithfulness.
Our land is their bodies' dust,
Their souls remain.
As long as a single Druid lives
The Gauls will be much praised."

★★★

"Let's sing the Mistletoe
Which grows on earth
To banish all evils, all fevers.
The priests of the Oak grove
Will soon cut it
With the golden Sickle, from the oak-tree.

Let's finally sing the True Wisdom!
It is written in the world:
To each star Teutates
Has given its radiance,
Has traced its given path;
And to each man, he did the same."

Thus the old Druid sang
Standing on the top of the Mount.

[[1]*Taranis was the pagan God of Thunder,* [2]*Teutates the main god of the Gauls,* [3]*Hesus the god of war.*]

G B Kerverziou

Matezh al loar, *1950*

> – War an hentig, 'dan goulou loar
> piv a goroll, piv a goroll?
> deus da welout enta, va c'hoar:
> elf eo pe zuz, pe deuz, pe droll?
>
> – Matezh al loar eo, o wiañ
> ar bannou skañv, an aour lijer,
> hep dont a-benn da ziviañ
> danvez ar meurdouell euver.

Translation

The Moon's Maidservant, *1950*

> – On the narrow path, in the moonshine,
> Who is dancing, who is dancing?
> Do come and see, sister;
> Is it an elf, an imp, a ghost or a troll?
>
> – It is the moon's maid spinning
> The pale light beams and delicate gold,
> But she cannot use up the yarn
> Of this hazy hallucination.

The Invasion from Britain

According to the following extracts, the first settlements in Brittany – or Armorica – by the Brythonic Celts took place between 383 and 388 AD. French – and Breton – historians tend to dismiss the Maximus (or Maximianus or Macsen Wledig) tradition that Brythonic Celts under Conan Meriadec had settled in Brittany at such an early date. Arthur de la Borderie traces the growth of the legend through Nennius, Geoffrey of Monmouth, Le Baud, Albert de Morlaix, Toussaint de Saint-Luc to de Roujoux's *Histoire des Roi et des Ducs de Bretagne* (1828) – each, suggests la Borderie, adding his own embellishments. Also, there is a tendency to ignore Breton kings before Nominoe. But it is accepted that troops from Britain were used in defence of the Roman Empire on the continent and were reputed to be fierce warriors. The most detailed account is in Geoffrey of Monmouth's *History of the Kings of Britain* – see below. Geoffrey's work is not reliable history, but there are references in other sources supporting this tradition – Nennius, *The Dream of Macsen Wledig*, *The Welsh Triads*. William of Malmesbury suggests an even earlier settlement under Constantine and we have included extracts from historians who support this claim.

Gerald of Wales

The Journey Through Wales (Extract)

c.1190. Translation by Lewis Thorpe, Penguin Classics, 1978

There is a third group of Britons left unconquered, and these occupied Brittany, in Southern Gaul. They were moved there by the tyrant Maximus, long before the fall of Britain. Their young soldiers supported Maximus in many hard battles, and in gratitude the imperial authorities gave them these lands, which protrude from Gaul.

Geoffrey of Monmouth, *c.1136*

History of the Kings of Britain (Extract)

Translation by Lewis Thorpe, Penguin Classics, 1966.

[Caradocus] gave the kingship of Britain to Maximianus, and his daughter with it. When Conanus Meridiadocus saw this, he was angrier than anyone could think possible. He went to Albany and busied himself raising an army, in order to trouble Maximianus. Once he had gathered together a force, he crossed the Humber and ravaged the lands on both sides of the river. As soon as Maximianus was informed of this, he assembled his entire army and hurried to meet Conanus. He fought with him and left the field having won the day. But Conanus was not so reduced that he could not begin destroying the countryside again, as soon as he had re-organised his army. Maximianus returned to the fray, they fought again, and the King withdrew only after he had been defeated. Finally, after each had done as much harm as he could to the other, they made their peace, with the blessing of their friends.

Five years passed, Maximianus developed an obsession with power, because of the vast amounts of gold and silver that flowed in to him daily. He prepared a fleet and conscripted every armed soldier in Britain. The kingship of Britain was not enough for him; he wanted to conquer the Gauls too. He crossed the Channel and went first to the kingdom of the Armorici, which is now called Brittany. He began to attack the Frankish race, which lived there. The Franks came to meet him, under their leader Himbaldus. They fought against him, but finding themselves in dire straits, the Franks turned in flight. Duke Himbaldus himself had fallen, together with 15,000 men gathered from the entire kingdom. Maximianus was delighted that he had slaughtered so many men, for he knew that after such immense casualties the country could easily be taken. He summoned Conanus to him, some way from the soldiers, and said to him with a quiet smile:

"We have seized one of the fairest kingdoms of Gaul. We have every reason to hope that we shall capture the rest. We must occupy their towns and strongholds as quickly as we can, before the news of their danger penetrates into the Gallic hinterland and the entire nation is called to arms. If only we can hold this kingdom, then I have no doubt that we can subjugate the whole of Gaul. You must not let it depress you that you have permitted the kingship of the island of Britain to pass into my hands, when you had hopes of possessing it yourself. Whatever you have lost in Britain I will make good to you in this country. I will raise you to the kingship of this realm. This will be a second Britain, and once we have killed off all the natives we will people it with our own race. The land produces heavy crops of corn and the rivers are full of fish. The forests are attractive and the pastures most pleasant. In my opinion no country is more agreeable."

Conanus bowed his head and thanked Maximianus, promising that, as long as he lived, he would be faithful in doing homage.

Without more ado they drew up their lines of battle and marched to Rennes, taking it that same day. The savagery of the Britons was already well known, as was the number of men they killed. The townsfolk fled, leaving behind their wives and children. Everyone else in the cities and castles followed their example, so the Britons marched in, meeting no resistance. Wherever they came they massacred the men, sparing only the women. Finally, when they had killed every single male in the land, they garrisoned the cities and castles with British soldiers and fortified the high hills. The inhumanity of Maximianus became known throughout the other territories of Gaul. [...] When he realized what a source of terror he was, Maximianus became even bolder. He quickly increased the size of his army by offering lavish bribes. [...] Maximianus assembled what he considered to be a force large enough to conquer the whole of Gaul.

At the same time he put off acting in his own savage way until the kingdom, which he had captured, could settle down and he would re-stock it with people from Britain. He issued an edict that 100,000 ordinary men and women be gathered together in the island of Britain and come out to him; and with them 30,000 soldiers, to protect them from enemy attack. As soon as he achieved all this, he distributed these people among all the tribes of the Armorican kingdom. In this way he created a second Britain, which he gave to Conanus Meridiadocus. Maximianus, with his soldiers, went off to the remoter parts of Gaul. [...]

Meanwhile the Gauls and Aquitanians were causing great trouble to Conanus and his Armorican Britons. They harassed the newcomers by attacking them time and time again. Conanus resisted these attacks, returning bloodshed for bloodshed and defending with great manliness the country committed to his charge.

Once he was victorious, he decided to find wives for his troops, so that heirs might be born from them who should hold the land forever. To prevent any mixture of blood with the Gauls, he ordered women to come from the island of Britain and to be married to his men. [...] The fleet was made ready, the women went on board the ships, and they put to sea down the river Thames. On the last part of the journey, just as they were turning their sails towards the men of Armorica, contrary winds sprang up against the fleet, and this scattered the whole company in a very short time. The ships ran the hazard of the seas and most foundered. Those who escaped this terrible danger were driven ashore on islands inhabited by barbarians. The women were either slaughtered by the uncivilized islanders or sold into slavery.

Nennius

Selected Documents of Early British History, *c.800* (Extract)

Translated by John Morris, Phillimore, Chichester, 1980.

The seventh emperor to reign in Britain was Maximus. He went forth from Britain with all the troops of the British and killed Gratian, the king of the Normans, and held the empire of all Europe. He refused to send the soldiers who had gone forth with him back to Britain, to their wives and children and lands, but gave them many districts from the lake on top of Mount Jove to the city called Quentovic, as far as the Western Mass, that is the Western Ridge. *[For the Armorican British, who are overseas, went forth there with the tyrant Maximus on his campaign, and, since they were unwilling to return, they destroyed the western parts of Gaul to the ground, and did not leave alive those who piss against the wall. They married their wives and daughters and cut out their tongues, lest their descendants should learn their mothers' tongue. That is why we call them in our language 'Letewicion,' that is, half-dumb, because their speech is muddled.] They are the Armorican British, and they never came back, even to the present day.

*The sentences between the brackets are not included in the text of L. Faral (La Légende Arthurienne, Vol 3, Paris 1929, but they appear in Mommsens' edition (Chronica Minora, Berlin, 1892).]

Anonymous
The Dream of Macsen Wledig (From *The Mabinogion*)

Translation by Gwyn Jones and Thomas Jones, Everyman Library, 1948.

And then the emperor [Macsen, Maximus or Maximianus] said to Cynan [Conanus] and Gadeon, "Good sirs," said he, "I have gained possession of all my empire. And this host I give you to conquer what region of the world you will." And then they set out and conquered lands and castles and cities, and they slew all their men, but the women they left alive. And in this wise they continued until the youths who had come with them were hoary-headed men with the length of time they had been about that conquest. And then Cynan said to Gadeon his brother, "What wilt thou," said he, "remain in this land or go to the land whence you were sprung?" So he determined to go to his land, and many along with him; but Cynan and another company stayed on to live there. And they determined to cut out the tongues of the women, lest their language be corrupted. And because the women were silenced of their speech, and the men spoke on, the men of Llydaw were called Brytanieid. And thence there often came, and still come from the Island of Britain, men of that tongue.

Hugh Williams
Footnote to *The Life of Gildas*

From a footnote by Hugh Williams in his translation of Vita Gildae *(Life of Gildas) written by a monk of the Monastery of Ruys in Brittany (London 1889).*

Letavia. The writer expressly informs us that this was a name employed by the **Britanni**, i.e., the Bretons themselves. Generally speaking, the only name we find in Latin writers, from Gregory of Tours down to the Middle Ages, is **Britannia**, sometimes with the adjective **minor** added, to imply the smaller Britain as distinguished from the island Britannia. Gregory has both the singular **Britannia** and the plural **Britanniae**, while the people in his pages are everywhere called **Britanni**, though once, seemingly, we read of a **quidam Britto**. Other writers employ the form **Brittones**, as for instance, Samson is made to say to King Hilbertus: "I have come into the country of the **Brittones**" – **in Brittonum patriam deveni**. These names, whatever date be given to the emigration or emigrations to Armorica, must have been carried out by the people themselves, and many other old names found new places to designate, such as Dumnonia (Devon), Cornubia (Cornwall), Léon, etc. Of such names of places or peoples conveyed to Armorica, **Letavia** is an instance.

In the **Vita S. Iltuti** the form is also **Letavia**; but the **Vita Cadoci** twice gives us the name as **Lettau**. Nennius (**Historia Brittonum**) is probably the earliest writer to mention Brittany under this name; or, to speak more correctly, two MSS of his work, which insert an interpolation of considerable length. After the record that the Britons who had left Britain with Maximianus (Maximus, more correctly) for the continent, never returned, but became the "Britons of Armorica" (**Brittones Armorici**), the interpolation proceeds to say that having married Gallic wives, they cut the tongues of all, lest the children should learn their mother's language. "For which reason those are called in our tongue **Letewicion**, that is, half mutes, because they speak confusedly (**id est, semi-tacentes quoniam confuse loquuntur**)." The derivation so given to **Letewicion** is from **let** (= modern Welsh **lled**) in the sense of "partly"; and **tewicion** (**tewi**, **tewigion**, **tawel**), "silent ones": **Letewic**, however, is **Letevicus**, meaning an inhabitant of **Letau** or *Letaw*, which in modern Welsh is **Llydaw**. Henry of Huntigdon repeats the assertion of Nennius as to the settlement of Britons in Armorica in the time of Maximus: "**Brittones vero quos Maximus secum adduxerat in Gallia Armorica usque hodie remanserunt.**"

Edward Stillingfleet

The Antiquities of the British Church, *1685* (Extract)

The author makes the following point about the name Brittany:

The first time we find the name of Brittania given to the country is in the subscription of Mansuetus to the Council of Tours, where he is named Episcopus Britannorum, after which it was frequently called Britannia Cismarina, Minor, Celtica &c.

William of Malmesbury

The Kings Before the Norman Conquest, *Early 12th century*

Severus and Constantius, two of their [the Romans'] greatest princes died upon the island, and were interred with the highest pomp. [Severus died A.D. 211 and Constantius A.D. 306.] The former, to defend this province from the incursion of the barbarians, built his celebrated and well-known wall from sea to sea. The latter, a man, as they report, of courteous manners, left Constantine, his son by Helena [...] a youth of great promise, his heir. Constantine, greeted emperor by the army, led away, in an expedition destined to the continent, a numerous force of British soldiers, by whose exertions, the war succeeding to his wishes, he gained in a short time, the summit of power. For these deserving veterans, when their toil was over, he founded a colony on the western coast of Gaul, where to this day their descendents, somewhat differing in language and manners from their parent stock, remain with wonderful increase.

In succeeding times, in this island, Maximus, a man well fitted for command, had he not aspired to power in defiance of his oath, assumed the purple, as though compelled by the army, and preparing immediately for his passage over into Gaul, he despoiled the province of almost all its military force. Not long after, also, one Constantine, who had been elected emperor here on account of his name, drained its whole remaining warlike strength; but both being slain, the one by Theodosius, the other by Honorius, they became examples of the instability of human greatness. Of the forces which followed them, part shared the fate of their leaders; the rest fled to the continental Britons.

Anonymous

The Welsh Triads (Extract)

Translation by Rachel Bromwich, University of Wales Press, 1961.

The Welsh Triads – 11th century bullet points to aid the memory of the storyteller – allude to the tale of the Breton settlement as it appears in The Dream of Macsen Wledig. *Llychllyn – meaning Scandinavia – is an obvious copying error for* Llydaw.

Porth a aeth y gan Yrp Luydavc hyt yn Llychllyn [...] A'r eil a aeth gan Elen Luydavc a Maxen Wledig hyt yn Llychllyn. Ac ny daethant byth y'r Ynys honn.

An army (of assistance) went with Yrp of the Hosts to Llychllyn [...] And the second [army] went with Elen of the Hosts and Maxen Wledig to Llychllyn. And they never returned to this island.

David Powel

History of Cambria, London, *1584* (Extract)

Little Brytaine is a countrie in France, called in Caesars time, Armorica, and after inhabited by Brytaines, who about the yeare of Christ 384, under the conduct of Conan, Lord of Meriadoc, now Denbighland, went out of the Isle with Maximus the tyrant, to his aid against the Emperour Gratianus, and winning the said countrie of Armorica, (which Maximus gave Conan and his people) slew and drove out all the old inhabitants thereof, planting themselves in the same, where they to this daie speake the Brytish toong, being the third remnants of the ancient Brytaines.

Names of the subsequent Kings of little Brytaine
(as given by Powel)

1. Conan
2. Gradlonus
3. Salomon 1
4. Auldranus
5. Budicus 1
6. Howelus Magnus [This Howel was with King Arthure in his warres]
7. Howelus 2
8. Alanus 1
9. Howelus 3
10. Gilquellus
11. Salomon 2
12. Alanus 2 [who descended of a daughter of Rune, son of Mailgon Gwyneth, King of Great Brytaine, which was married to the forenamed Howel the Second, King of little Brytaine]
13. Conobertus
14. Budicus 2
15. Theodoicus
16. Rualhonus
17. Daniel Dremrost
18. Aregstanus
19. Maconus
20. Neomenius
21. Haruspogius
22. Salomon 3 [who was slaine by his owne men, and then was that Kingdome turned to an Earldom, whereof Alan was the first Earle, who valiantlie resisted the Normans, and vanquished them oftentimes].

Edward Stillingfleet

The Antiquities of the British Church, *1685* (Extract)

It seems hard to determine when the first colony of Britons was settled in the parts of Armorica. For in the declining times of the Roman Empire, there was so frequent occasion of the British soldiers removing into the continent, and so little encouragement to return hither, that it is not improbable, that after the troubles of Maximus and Constantine a colony of Britons might settle themselves upon the sea coasts near to Britain where they might be ready to receive or to go over to their countrymen, as the condition of affairs should happen. This I am very much induced to believe, not from the authority of Nennius, or Geoffrey, or William of Malmesbury, or Radulphus Niger &c but from these arguments:

First from Sidonius Apollinaris, and there are two pages in him which tend to the clearing of this matter. The first is concerning Aruandus, accused at Rome of treason, in the time of Anthemius, for persuading the king of the Goths to make war upon the Greek emperor i.e. Anthemius, who came out of Geece, and upon the Britons on the Loire, as Sidonius Apollinaris expertly affirms, who lived at that time, and pitied his case. This happened about A.D. 467 before Anthemius was the second Consul. From whence it appears, not only that there were Britons then settled on the Loire, but that their strength and forces were considerable, which cannot be supposed to consist of such miserable people as fled for fear of the Saxons. And it is observable, that about this time Ambrosius had success against the Saxons, and by Vortimer's means, or his, the Britons were in great likelihood of driving them out of Britain. So that there is no probability that the warlike Britons should at that time leave their native country.

A second passage is concerning Riothamus, a king of Britons in the time of Sidonius Apollinaris, and to whom he wrote, who went with 12,000 Britons to assist the Romans against Euricus, king of the Goths, but were intercepted by him, as Jornandes relates the story, and Sigebert places it A.D. 470. Now what clearer evidence can be desired than this to prove that a considerable number of Britons were there settled, and in a condition not only to defend themselves but to assist the Romans; which cannot be imagined of such as merely fled thither after the Saxons coming into Britain. Besides, we find in Sirmondus's Gallican Councils, Mansuetus, a Bishop of the Britons, subscribing to the first Council at Tours, which was held A.D. 461. By which we see the Britons had a full settlement then, as not only to have habitations but a king and bishops of their own; which was the great encouragement for other Britons to go over, when they found themselves so hard pressed by the Saxons at home. For a people frightened from hence, would hardly have ventured into a foreign country, unless they had been secure before hand of a kind reception there. If they must have fought for a dwelling there, had they not far better have done it in their own country? From whence I conclude, that there was a large colony of Britons in Armorica before those numbers went over upon the Saxon cruelties; of which Eginhardus and other foreign historians speak. Archbishop Usher seems to think this Riothamus himself to have been the first leader of them. But it is hard to think a person of his valour and experience would leave his country in that distressed condition it was brought into by the Saxons.

But Florentius, the author of the Life of Judocus says, that his name was Rivoal, a prince here in Britain, who gathered a good army and fleet together, and with that subdued the people who lived on the Armorican coasts, being then left destitute and unable to defend themselves. For that was the effect of the Roman government, which was kept up by the force of the Roman legions in all parts of it, and so when these were broken, the nations were so unaccustomed to war that they lay open to all invaders. So that the aggressors did generally succeed in their attempts where the Roman legions were withdrawn, and next to the wise providence of God which ordereth all things, there was no one cause which contributed so much to the miseries of those time, and the strange revolutions which happened in them, as the natives being not trained up to martial discipline, but depending wholly on the Roman legions for their defence and security; thence whatever people had the courage to invade, did usually take possession of the country where the Roman legions were at a distance, or otherwise engaged against each other. […] But to return to the Armorican Britons, whether they came over under Rivoal in the beginning of the distractions here, when the people were so rebellious against their princes, as Gildas relates, or whether they went over to assist Constantine and his son, and so remained there, I shall not determine. But that the Britons were well settled there before Sampson, Archbishop of York and his company passed the seas, appears by what Mat. Paris (A.D. 1199) says, that they went to their fellow citizens and countrymen, hoping to live more quietly there. And after the death of the Bishop of Dol, he was by the consent of the Britons put in his place, and from thence forwards exercised his Archiepiscopal power there; the kings of that province, not suffering his successor there to pay any obedience to the Archbishop of Tours. Which begot a suit which held 300 years in the Court of Rome, and was this year manfully decided by Innocent III as Mat. Paris there relates: who states the case very unskilfully, laying the weight of it upon the Archbishop's bringing over his Pall from York, which the Pope had given him there. Suppose this were true (although the Popes gave no Palls then, nor a great while after) yet this were no reason to contest it in the Court of Rome [for] so long together. But the difficulty of the case lay upon another point, viz. according to the Old Canon of the Church, if a Province were divided into two, each Province was to have a Metropolitan. Now this reason held much stronger when new kingdoms were erected out of the Roman Provinces. For what reason was there why the Bishop of Dol in the Kingdom of Brittany should yield subjection to the Bishop of Tours in a distinct kingdom, as appears by the account given of this Cause by Innocent III in his Epistles lately published by Baluzius. On the other side it was pleaded, that all Brittany was under the jurisdiction of the Archbishop of Tours, but that the Britons conspiring against the King of France, and setting up a kingdom of their own, they made use of Sampson, Archbishop of York, coming to establish a Metropolitan power within that kingdom: and upon complaint being made to Rome, the Popes had put it upon this issue, whether any of their predecessors had granted the Pall to the Bishop of Dol, which not being proved, the Pope, as it is easy to imagine, gave sentence against the Bishop of Dol. But it is certain that they went upon a false suggestion, viz. that the Kingdom of Bretagne was set up in rebellion to the Kingdom of France. For Childeric had not extended his dominions in France as far as the Loire: and before his time, the Britons were in quiet possession of those parts of Armorica; and the best French historians (Mezeray) now grant that the Britons came thither in the time of Merovée, who obtained but little in Gaul as Hadrianus Valesius confesses. And the author of *The Life of Gildas* observes, that the power of the kings of France was very inconsiderable in the time of Childeric, son of Merovée, at what time Gildas went over to Armorica, as his school fellows under Iltutus, Sampson and Paulus had done before him: whereof one succeeded the other Sampson at Dol, and the other was made Bishop of Oxismii, the most northern people of Bretagne; which diocese is since divided into three, Tréguier, St. Pol de Léon and St. Brieuc.

Algernon Herbert

Britannia After the Romans, *1836* (Extract)

The armies which Maximus led over to Gaul were chiefly composed of the natives of Britannia whom he enrolled into his service in numbers so great, that the island was never afterwards secure against the irruptions of the Scots, Picts, Saxons, and other marauding or piratical neighbours. Gildas, Tysilio and The Triadists are all agreed on deploring the drain of British manhood in this revolution of the declining empire, as one of the main sources of ruin to the island. [...]

The British – though nominally Roman – reign of Carausius, followed by the mildness of re-conqueror Constantius and perhaps a somewhat incomplete reconquest, brought back upon the stage some of those un-Romanised and Celtic-tongued chiefs of clans, when the civilization and discipline of the Quinque Provinciae had previously kept in obscure subjection in the remoter districts. Cynedda, the founder of the North-Welsh dynasty, established himself in Anglesea and the neighbourhood about A.D. 371; and at the same time with Maximus the emperor or tyrant, one Conan of Meriadawg (now Denbighshire or a part thereof) made his appearance as a British chieftain. Maximus removed him into Gaul with a considerable power of native Britons and settled him in the maritime district called Armorica, the same which in consequence of that memorable settlement has since been termed Lesser Britain or Brittany. It was a military colony of some strength in the first instance, soon after reinforced by the remains of the unfortunate armies of Maximus, and, a century later, by refugees from this invaded and desolated island. Their establishment stood firm, and the fall of Maximus did not compel the emigrants to evacuate their new possessions. But they were not made independent of the Roman system of administration and the authority of the Roman magistrates was still maintained in the municipalities of that part of Gaul. The naval power of Maximus and the British, in the channel, could never have been shaken with such a formidable outwork as Armorica on its eastern shores. Excellent harbours, both deep and shallow, broad lagunes and the impregnable promontories – some of them even insulated at high water, rendered the Armorican Britain an inexpugnable barrier to Britain and British waters. But he was not wise unto the end.

The *Bruts* relate that Maximus established Conan in the Gauls by virtue of a pacification between them, and after a war in which Conan had been worsted. It is indeed probable that Maximus acted with a double policy. The same Celtic clans, whom it was most useful both for example and immediate tranquillity to transport, were those whose language and manners would keep them most distinct from the Romanising Gauls, and therefore make them the most efficient outwork to Britannia on that side. To bind them more effectually to the mother island, a multitude of British women were sent over to marry all amongst those colonies who had not wives; and the mischance of some of these adventurous damsels gave rise to the legend of the 11,000 virgins.

Armorica was no barrier to Britannia as against the Picts or Saxons, whilst, by affording an obvious and natural asylum to those who wished to fly, it may have weakened her defence against them. But the passionate Cumbrian Gildas, and the Welsh, are unreasonable in their condemnation of Maximus, who did not contemplate his own ruin, and still less that of the Roman empire itself, and actually employed the most vigorous means in his power to secure and civilize the island.

This whole passage in the history of Maximus has been denied by the modern French writers, and that denial has been taken up by the historian of the Anglo-Saxons. It is said that the Little Britain was not established in Armorica by him and Conan under him, and by surviving adventures in the unfortunate expedition, that no such man as Conan Meriadawg lived in the fourth century, and that Little Britain was constituted no earlier than the middle of the fifth or beginning of the sixth century, under the auspices of Rhiwallon a princely Briton who fled from the anarchy and Saxon and devastation of his island, in 513 according to most opinions, or in 453 according to Father Lobineau.

The doubts raised upon this subject by Vignier, Vertot and others of the French, did not arise in fair unbiased argument. Their desire was to establish that no distinct sovereignty had existed in the Armorican Gaul previously to the establishment of the Merovingian Franks in that country. By such means they sought to justify the degradation of the British kings into counts, the claim of liege homage into lieu of simple homage, and all the series of usurpations which have made Brittany a part of France. There are many occasions for condemning the spirit of falsehood in the British chroniclers, but in this instance we need not mistrust the

substance of their statement, though a want of accuracy is discernible in several of its particulars.

Gregory of Tours, by his observation that "ever since the death of king Clovis (i.e. for about 80 years) the Britons have been under the power of the Franks, and have been called counts not 'kings' implies that Breton kings used to reign anterior to Clovis".

John Hughes
Studies in Ancient British History, *1819* (Extract)

The dismissing of the tradition that Armorica had been settled by Conan Meriadec prior to the invasion of Britain by the Saxons by eighteenth century French and Breton historians appears to have incensed English and Welsh historians as indicated above. The Abbé Vertot's Histoire des Bretons *is also censured by John Hughes.*

Maximus had a son named Victor, born of a British lady, and to whom he expected the Britons would be ardently attached. This youth headed an army who engaged in defending the cause of the usurper and his son, in Gaul; but the son shared the misfortunes of the father, for the British troops were defeated, and Victor fell at the head of them. In this most pitiable condition they had been left exposed to the insults of a triumphant enemy, forlorn and destitute, until that in their wanderings, they found an asylum in Armorica. This account has been contradicted, most strenuously, by the French historians, who deny that our insular Britons formed any settlement on the continent, until after the Saxon invasion. But whether it was from this circumstance, or rather from subsequent events, that the British race obtained a decided predominance in the territory of Armorica, we shall not take upon us to decide. [*In a footnote re. Vertot he adds: "That author being determined to espouse the hypothesis of the dependence of Brittany on the French crown from the time of Clovis, seems too partial to be altogether depended upon, even by those who are rather sceptical as to the affirmations of Geoffrey of Monmouth".*]

We shall not, therefore, detain the reader here, in either controverting or defending what has been commonly asserted, as to the establishment of a dynasty among the French Bretons, under Conan Meriadoc, and the princes who are said to have succeeded him from the year 384. The statements of the British chronicle on that subject are of considerable antiquity; although the Abbé Vertot, and other writers, will not admit of the coming over of the insular colony before the invasion of the Franks, nor allow that the Bretons were ever independent of that people. Of this, however, we are assured, from our most ancient documents, that, of the large host that followed Maximus, none returned home; we must therefore, from the nature of the case infer, that they obtained settlements somewhere; and tradition states that it was Armorica. The connection between the Cambro-Britons and the people of Armorica was of very ancient standing, as appears by the languages of both people, which are so nearly allied even in this remote age.

Conan, Lord of Meriadoc, of the region of Denbigh, was nephew to Eudaf, or Octavius, Lord of Ewias, whose daughter Elen was married to Maximus. This Conan is said to have obtained a territory in Armorica for himself and his countrymen, and to be succeeded by princes of the same race. These were probably chieftains that had power over a small territory, comprising a part of Brittany, and the whole of that extensive province, which it is probable, was never strictly independent of the Romans, nor afterwards of the Franks.

Edward Davies

Celtic Researches on the Origin, Traditions & Language of the Ancient Britons, *1804* (Extract)

The romantic tales which describe the extermination of the inhabitants, by those Britons, who accompanied the tyrant Maximus – the fifty thousand virgins, who were drowned or butchered, – the Armorican women, whose tongues were cut out, &c &c are not the materials of history. […]

Armorica, is a *relative* term, describing the region as a part of Gaul; but the inhabitants were Britanni in the time of Pliny, and perhaps before the name was known in this island. When they became detached, as well as independent, they dropped the *relative*, and used the *absolute* name.

All that seems to be historical, in the account of settlement from this country, is, that a race either descended from *British* nobility, or connected with it, sat upon the throne of Brittany, and that an asylum was there given to noble families of Britain during the Saxon conquest, though not so many of them, as to affect the language of the people.

But the "Armorican tongue," we are told, "is related nearly, to the Welsh, and Cornish." It must be so, if it be Celtic.

The Gauls, and Britons, were originally one people.

The sons of Gaulish families came to Britain for education (Caesar, *De bello Gallico*). In both countries, the disciples of Druidism learnt the same ancient poems, and studied the same oral maxims. The Druids of Britain, and Gaul, could therefore, have differed but little in their language.

But in so large a country, as the jurisdiction of Druidism, there must have been shades of peculiarity, amongst the vernacular idioms of the populace: and the Armorican, or Celtogalatian language, in the days of Caesar, appears to have differed from the Welsh, much in the same degree as at present.

In order to prove this, I must have recourse to Etymology, who though a rash leader, is a most valuable subaltern. Caesar calls the district, *civitates Armoricae*. *Armorica* was, undoubtedly, a Gaulish term, describing the locality of these states. In Welsh, *ar*, is *upon* – *môr*, the *sea*, – whence *morig*, *maritime*: the name, in that case, would import, *supermaritime*, a very awkward phrase. In Bas-Breton, *ar – the*, *mor– sea*, whence *moric* or *morec*, *maritime* – the *maritime* (*states*).

The Welsh call that country *Llydaw*, from *Lled* (*Let*) a side, and *aw*, *water*. But for the Welsh *T*, the Armoricans, at the end of their words, uniformly substitute *S* – hard, which the Romans frequently mark by the letter X. The *Lexovii* are mentioned by Caesar, as a people by the waterside.

This word is *Armorican – Les*, a *side*, and Govea, *in composition*, ovea, water; literally *the water side*.

The people of Le Perche, in the western extremity of the country are called *Diablintes. Diabell*, in Bas-Breton, is *longinquus*, plural, *diabellint – the remote ones*. In Welsh they would have been called *Pellenigion*.

From *Belen*, mentioned by *Ausonius*, [...] comes the Amorican *Bel-ec, priest*, pl. *Beleien. Patera*, a minister of Apollo, is nothing more than the Armorican *paotr*, a *boy*, *servant* or *attendant*.

Divona must come, according to the interpretation of the *Gallic Board*, from the Armorican *Doue, God* and *fonn, abundant, overflowing*.

The Arrival and Worship of Breton Saints

A characteristic of Breton religion is the worship of saints. The parish churches do not differ much from those of other countries. But in the countryside it is not uncommon to find as many as ten or fifteen chapels in a single parish, solitary buildings on desolate moors or sheltered by barren rocks on stormy coasts. Most are one-room buildings with a single door and window, dedicated to a local saint unknown to the rest of Christendom. These saints, of whom there are hundreds, date from the fifth and sixth century emigration. Most of them existed, but time and tradition has woven around them a rich tapestry of tales, tales absorbed into Brittany's glorious oral tradition, but the seeds of many of them are found in the *Lives* of the saints.

"The strange and terrible physiognomy of these saints, more Druidic than Christian, savage and vindictive, pursued me like a nightmare," wrote Ernest Renan in his *Souvenirs d'enfance et de jeunesse*, describing the wooden statues of the saints, the only adornment in these buildings. On another occasion, Renan wrote of Saint Ronan: "He was more a spirit of the earth than a saint, and his power over the elements were endless."

There are other suggestions in the following extracts of Druidic influence on the Christianity of the early Celtic church. It has been argued, convincingly, that the Celtic saints were following, literally, in the footsteps of the Druids, on the network of roads and centres throughout Gaul and Britain.

The *Life of Samson* is one of the earliest, probably written in the eighth century, while it is estimated that the *Life of Gildas* –by the Monk of Rhuys – was a product of the ninth century.

Anna Vezmeur

Amzeriou kenta hon bro, *1855* (Lodenn)

Neket dre ar brezel hepken oa douget e peb lec'h hano ar Vretoned, be oant ivez ar c'henta skolaerien euz ar bed. En amzer-se ne oa ket eur skol brudet evel hini sant Iltud, en eul loden euz a Vreiz-Veur galvet ar Glamorgan; hag en holl gouenchou euz an diou Vreiz e vije desket an oll skianchou, ken re sakr, ken re ar bed. Piou a hello lavarout mad avoalc'h pegen desket a oa an dud iaouank eno? Pedavare a vo kavet eur seminer evel hini sant Iltud? Euz ar skol-se eo deuet er vro-man sant Samson, sant Weltaz, sant Pol a Leon. Eno oa bet desket daou vab ar roue Rivoal, sant Pabu pe Tugdual, ha sant Lenor. Hag a hellin-me, paour-kez dall, gant ken neubeut a skiant, komz deoc'h euz a eskibien ker gouiziek, bet evel steret ar vro-man? Ouspen meuleudiou Doue, a vije klevet e peb lec'h euz an diou Vreiz hag a ree estlam ar broiou all, e oa ive brudet mad e peb lec'h Arthur, Rivoalen, ar marc'heien pe soudardet kalounek, ha dreist pep tra Merlin an divinour ha Taliessin, mab Onys. Rag an daou-man o deuz great guerziou kaer oa meulet gant an oll.

Deveziou a voalheur a gouezaz var an enez a Vreiz. Ar Saozon zo erruet gant eun niver spountuz a listri. An iliziou, ar c'houenchou zo diskaret; e skol sant Iltud ne veler mui an niver braz euz he ziskibien. E lec'h ma oa guelet araok Samson, Magloar ha Pol o pourmen var an aod, hag o komz eno euz a Zoue, ne veler mui nemet al lapousset mor en em welc'hi pe o c'hlebia beg o diouaskel en eon euz an toennou. E lec'h moueziou dudiuz ar venec'h, ne glever mui nemet iud ar morvini hag ar gueleni; rag deuet oa an amzer ker poaniuz evit an enez a Vreiz ha ken euruz evit ar vro-man. An oll dud pinvidik ha gouiziek a bignaz var listri evit dont e Breiz-Izel. Neuze a erruaz aman, Seva hag eun nombr braz a venec'h; douari a rejont en enezen Kermorvan, e parrez Ploumoguer. Sant Pabu a zeuaz er ger a Osismor, galvet breman Kastel-Paol, evit goull grad ar c'hont a Leon da sevel ur gouent e lec'h hanvet breman Trebabu, var dro 520.

Pa oe klevet a oa deuet mab Rivoal-ar-Braz en he vro, he zaou vreur a zeuaz gant joa d'he zigemer. Deroc'h, kont Guenet, hanvet ive Gueroc'h pe Erec'h, he gonduaz en he balez e pelec'h ar roue Rivoal II a zeuaz d'he velet. Neuze c'hoaz, en eun devez kaer meurbet evit bro Leon, oe digemeret e Osismor sant Pol, eskop Guikastel. Hen, goude beza tremenet tri bloaz en enez Eussaff, a zouaraz e Kernik, e parrez Plounevez. Sant Jaoua a oe taolet gant eur bar-avel dreist mor Brest e steir ar Faou.

Sant Philibert, eur maread goudeze, a zouaraz e beg Rostudel. Renta a reas kristenien mad an dud a jome eno, hag a oa neuze paganet; el lec'h ma zeo breman parrez mad Krozon pe Kraon, kichen Brest. Douar Krozon, ken dizolo breman, a oa neuze kasi goloët a wez dero, eno a oa ive eun iliz an Drouized. Guelet a reer c'hoas mein hir ha dolmen aleiz e Krozon hag e Kamelet. Sant Philibert en doa c'hoant da vont larkoc'h da brezeg an Aviel; hag araok guitaat ar Grozonis e roaz ar velegiach da Hernot, den iaouank euz ar vro, oajet a eur bloaz varn-ugent, hag hen c'hargaz

da labourat da silvidigez he genvroiz. Kement a breder a gemeraz d'ho renta kristenien vad, ma savjont dezan eur japel evit he henori hag he bedi goude he varo.
Pedennou kristenien vad Krozon a zo atao selaouet gant sant Hernot. Sant Philibert
ne ket dizonjet kenneubeut gant Krozoniz; savet zo ive dezan eur japelic elec'h ma
zireder evit beza pareet euz certen klenvejou. Lenn a reer ive an aviel sant Iann eno
da eur maread bugale vihan.

Breiz Huel a zigemeraz ive sant Samson hag he niz sant Meen. Sant Weltaz ha
Taliessin, mab Onys, en em dennaz en eneziou euz ar Morbihan, ha sant Malo a
zeuas er ger a Aleth. Sant Luner, mab Rivoal-ar-Braz, a zeuaz e Pontual gant he
vreudeur a oa neuze mignonet. Ho c'harantez an eil evit egile ne badaz ket pell.
Konomor, unan anezo, en doa bet Kerne evit he lod, ha c'hoantaat a ree ouspen
kaout lod ar re all; hag evit-ze e reaz laza Rivoal, hanvet ive Ian Reith, he vreur hag
he roue, gant Budik, eur breur all dezan. Klaskout a reaz ive laza he nis Alan pe
Judual; mæs an diaoul, en doa kemeret evit he vestr, neket galloudek dirag Doue.
Sant Luner, o klevout oa maro he vreur Rivoal II, a zeuaz d'he balez hag a gemeraz
he nis evit he gundui da balez ar roue a Frans. Konomor, leun a fulor, a ieaz da dy
he vreur hag a c'houleunas digantan he nis, ma ne felle he unan beza lakeet d'ar
maro. Sant Luner na roaz dezan respount ebed, en em gontanti a reaz da ziskuez al
lestr, gant he lien guen en avel, a gasse da lez ar roue a Frans ar guir roue a Vreiz.

En amzer-se, evel ma leverer, sant Pol a drec'haz eun dragon euzuz, a ree distruj
er vro en dro da Osismor. Den na grede mont gant sant Pol beteg toull an dragon,
nemet eun den iaouank euz a barrez Kleder, hanvet Kergournadec'h; euz ar famil-
ze eo bet lavaret: "Araok ne oa aotrou a nep lec'h oa eur marc'hek e
Kergournadec'h." Ha c'hoaz: "Mar ezoc'h euz Kergournadec'h, savit ho pen d'an
ec'h." Sant Pol oa gret eskob a Leon, hag o velout ne oa ket ar roue er vro, mont a
reaz d'he glask beteg lez ar roue a Frans e pelec'h Judual he zigemeraz gant kalz a
garantez. Sant Pabu, eskob Landreger, a oa deuet eno ive evit guelout e nis ker. Evel
ma na ouie ket ar gallek na elle ket komz gant ar Fransizien nemet e latin. Judual a
gomze gant he yountr e brezonek; rag eun den euz ar Vreiz na glaske ket neuze dis-
onjal he vrezonek.

Pa zeuaz sant Pol en dro en he eskopti, e reaz sevel kouenchou: unan en enez
Vaz, eun all e parrez Kerlouan, unan e Plougar hag eun all c'hoaz e Lampol.

Translation

Our Country's Early Times, *1855* (Extract)

The Bretons did not build their fame on war feats only. They were also the world's
earliest teachers. In those times there was no school more famous than that of Saint
Illtud in a part of Great Britain known as Glamorgan. It seems that all the sciences,
the holy ones as well as those of the world, were taught in all the monasteries of the
two Britains. Who cannot but speak well of what was taught to the young people
there? When will one find another school like that of Saint Illtud? It was from that
school that Saint Samson, Saint Gildas, Saint Pol de Léon came to this land. Here

two sons of king Rivoal, Saint Pabu (also known as Tugdual) and Saint Lunaire were educated. How could I, poor thing who knows so little, tell you about such learned bishops who have shone like stars in this land. As well as God's praises, which were heard everywhere throughout the two Britains and which other countries exclaimed about, there was the great fame attached to Arthur, to Rivoalen, to the brave knights and soldiers and above all to Merlin the Magician and to Taliesin, son of Onis, for these last two have composed beautiful songs which were admired by all.

Then days of calamity swept over the island of Britain. The Saxons arrived in a frightening number of ships. The churches and abbeys were destroyed. The number of pupils in Saint Illtud's school fell dramatically. On the beaches where Samson, Magloire and Pol had been seen walking and talking of God, there were only sea birds preening and wetting the tips of their wings in the foam of the rough waves. Instead of the gentle voices of the monks, one heard only the wailing of cormorants and seagulls. The time, so painful for the island of Britain and so fortunate for our own land, had indeed come. All the wealthy people and scholars boarded ships to come to Lower Brittany. This is how Seva and numerous monks arrived here; they landed on the island of Kermorvan, in the parish of Ploumoguer. Saint Pabu went to the town of Osismor, now known as Saint-Pol-de-Léon, to ask the Count of Léon for permission to build a convent in a place now called Trebabu. This was around AD 520.

When news came that the son of Rivoal the Great had arrived in the country, his two brothers came joyfully to welcome him. Deroc'h, Count of Vannes, also named Gweroc or Erec, led him to his palace where king Rivoal II came to see him. On another occasion, on a day when the sun shone over Leon, Saint Pol, bishop of Guikastel, was welcomed in Osismor. He had spent three years on Ushant island before landing in Kernik, in the parish of Plounévez. Saint Jaoua had been blown by a strong storm to the other side of the narrows of Brest and into the Faou river.

Some time later, Saint Philibert landed on Rostudel Point. He converted the former pagans who lived there into good Christians, in the place which is now the good parish of Crozon, not far from Brest. The land of Crozon which is now so open was at that time nearly entirely covered in oak trees. Here too was a Druidic temple. Many standing stones and dolmens can still be seen in Crozon and Camaret. Saint Philibert wanted to go further to preach the Gospel. Before leaving the peninsula he chose to ordain as a priest Hernot, a young man of the district aged twenty-one, and asked him to work for the salvation of his countrymen. He took such care to make good Christians of these people that a chapel was built to honour him and pray to him after his death. Prayers of the good Christians of Crozon are still listened to by Saint Hernot. However Saint Philibert has not been forgotten by the people of Crozon. A little chapel was built for him where people come to be cured of certain illnesses. The Gospel of Saint John is also read there to groups of young children.

Upper Brittany also welcomed Saint Samson and his nephew, Saint Meen. Saint

Gildas and Taliesin, son of Onys, withdrew to the isles of the Morbihan and Saint Malo went to the town of Aleth. Saint Lunaire, son of Rivoal the Great, came to Pontual with his brothers who were also his friends at the time. Their mutual love did not last long. One of them, Conomor had inherited Cornouaille but also wanted the others' share. In order to achieve this, he arranged for Budik, one of his brothers to assassinate Rivoal, also named Ian Reith, who was also his brother as well as his king. He also tried to kill his nephew Alan or Judual; but the devil he had taken as his master has little power when facing God. Saint Lunaire, after hearing of the death of his brother Rivoal II, came to the palace and took his nephew to the safety of the palace of the king of the Franks. Conomor, enraged, went to his brother's house, and threatening to kill him, asked him to hand over his nephew. Saint Lunaire made no reply. He simply pointed to the ship with her white sail swollen by the wind who was bringing the true king of Brittany to the court of the king of the Franks.

In those days, so one tells, Saint Pol defeated a fearsome dragon which was destroying the countryside around Osismor. No one would go with Saint Pol to the lair of this dragon except one young man from the parish of Cleder, name of Kergournadec'h. Of that family it is said: "Before noble men existed, there was a knight in Kergournadec'h." Also: "If you are of Kergournadec'h, hold your head high in the air." Saint Pol was ordained bishop of Léon, and realising that there was no king in the land, he went to the court of the king of the Franks to get him, and Judual welcomed him lovingly. Saint Pabu, bishop of Tréguier, had also travelled there to see his dear nephew. As he could not speak French, he only conversed with the Franks in Latin. Judual talked to his uncle in Breton as, at that time, the sons of Brittany were not trying to forget their own language.

When Saint Pol returned to his bishop's palace, he established monasteries: one on Ile de Batz, others in the parish of Kerlouan and in Plougar and yet another in Lampaul.

Gildas

De Excidio Britonum/On the Destruction of Britain (Extract)

This was written some time before the Battle of Badon Hill – AD516. Translation by Michael Winterbottom, Phillimore, Chichester, 1978.

So a number of the wretched survivors were caught in the mountains and butchered wholesale. Others, their spirit broken by hunger, went to surrender to the enemy; they were fated to be slaves for ever, if indeed they were not killed immediately. Others made for lands beyond the sea; beneath the swelling sails they loudly wailed, singing a psalm that took the place of a sea shanty: "You have given us like sheep for eating and scattered us among the heathen".

Anonymous
The Life of Teilo (Extract)

From Liber Landavensis – The Book of Llandâv *or* Llandaff Chronicles.

The Book of Llandâv *was compiled and edited between 1108 and 1132 by Galfrid, brother of Bishop Urban, Bishop of Llandaff at the time. A similar, shorter, version of this description of the emigration to Brittany also appears in* The Life of Oudoceus – *also included in* The Book of Llandâv. *Oudoceus was Bishop of Llandaff, c. AD 562 –610. The suggestion here is that a plague instigated the migrations of the fifth and sixth centuries from Britain to Brittany. Various sources suggest the plague ended between AD 550 and 560. Gerennius [Geraint] of Cornwall is believed to have died around AD562.*

St. Teilo received the pastoral care of the Church of Llandaff, to which he had been consecrated, with all the adjacent diocese, that had belonged to Dubrucius (Dyfrig); in which, however, he could not long remain, on account of the pestilence which nearly destroyed the whole nation. It was called the Yellow Pestilence because it occasioned all persons who were seized of it, to be yellow and very pallid, and it appeared to men as a column of a watery cloud, having one end trailing along the ground, and the other above, proceeding in the air, and passing through the whole country like a shower going along the bottom of the valleys. Whatever living creatures it touched with its pestiferous blast, either immediately died, or sickened to death. If any one endeavoured to apply a remedy to the sick person, not only did the medicine have no effect, but the dreadful disorder brought the physician, together with the sick person, to death. For it seized Maelgwn Gwynedd, King of North Wales, and destroyed his country; and so greatly did the aforesaid destruction rage throughout the nation, that it caused the country to be nearly deserted.

In the meantime, while this disorder raged not only against men, but also against beasts and reptiles, St. Teilo cried to the Lord in fasting and lamentation, saying, "Spare, O Lord, spare thy people, who willest not the death of a sinner, but his life, and thou shouldst not give thy inheritance to perdition." Then the anger of the Lord, through means of his prayers, and those of other holy persons, being appeased for a time, he was admonished from heaven, and with those who were the residue of the nation, departed into distant countries; some of whom went into Ireland, but many, he leading them, removed into France, until God should intimate to them to return to their country. And an angel thus spoke, and ordered St. Teilo, saying: "Arise, and go beyond the sea, and gather the remains of thy nation, that they may follow thee, until God, full of mercy, seeing the misery of thy nation, and thee, a servant of God labouring for the nation in prayers and fasting, will grant, on the removal of the persecution from them and you, that you should return from banishment, and be free from danger of this kind for ever." And again the angel said: "Go without hesitation, for an angel of the Lord will accompany thee back with thy followers, to thy country with prosperity."

Therefore St. Teilo arose, and took with him some of his suffragan bishops, and men of other orders, with sons of both sexes, men and women, and came first of all, to the country of Cornwall, where he was well received by Gerennius (Geraint), King of that land, who treated him and his pupils with great honour. And in an interval of his hospitality, King Gerennius addressed Teilo, the Bishop, familiarly, saying unto him, "I request and desire that thou wilt receive my confession, and be my confessor in the Lord." And the Bishop consenting, received his confession, and promised him, saying with confidence, that he should not see death before he received the body of the Lord, which he should consecrate. These things being done, the holy man with his companions went to the Armorican nations, and was well received by them. Samson, Archbishop of the Church of Dol, hearing of the arrival of his co-brother in the country, met him with joy, for they were born in the same district, and had the same language, and were taught at the same time by St. Dubrucius, the Archbishop, by the laying on of whose hands St. Samson was consecrated Bishop, as is related in his life. And he requested St. Teilo to live with him, and he assented, and resided with him a long time, and there left some beneficent proofs of his sanctity, that is, the salutiferous fountain, called Cai, which he obtained from the Lord to flow. And besides the recoveries, which the sick obtained from it in the name of God, and Teilo, a remarkable miracle remains to this day. For the sailors of that nation of Armorica, in order to their obtaining the accustomed wind for their ships, to enable them to sail direct in whatever course they intended, had a custom of cleansing that salutiferous fountain, and often, through the intercession of the Holy Bishop, the Lord granted their request, that is the wind for the sails of their ship, whereby they sailed pleasantly on the smooth sea where they would.

Also, he left there another testimony of his patronage, for he and the aforesaid St. Samson planted a great grove of fruit-bearing trees, to the extent of three miles, that is from Dol as far as Cai and those woods are honoured with their names until the present day for they are called the groves of Teilo and Samson. And from that time forth the Bishopric of Dol is honoured, and celebrated by the testimony of all the Armorican Britons, on account of the conversion and reverence of St. Teilo.

In the meantime, whilst these things were taking place and performed, it happened that Christ, through his mercy, ordered that the aforesaid pestilence, which was called the Yellow Pestilence, should depart and vanish from the whole island of Britain. Which the faithful leader Teilo having heard, greatly rejoiced, and being summoned by the Holy Spirit, he sent messengers both into France, and beyond the Alps into Italy, wherever it was known to him that his countrymen had fled, and he collected them together, that as the pestilence was extinguished, and peace affected in every respect, all might return to their own country. Therefore he prepared three great ships for the numerous people to pass over. The holy man came to the sea port, as they were weeping and mourning on account of the departure of so great a father; and while they waited for a prosperous wind for their voyage, lo! The King of the district, Budic by name, came to meet him with a large army of Armoricans. And immediately the King, and his whole army knelt down before him; and on his asking what this meant, the King answered him, "We bend our knees for this purpose, that thou mayest beseech God, for me and my country, on account of the calamity which we at present sustain; for a huge serpent has lately appeared which has nearly destroyed the third part of my kingdom."

And the holy Bishop for some time hesitated, and dreaded to go with him, for terrible things were related of the serpent; and suddenly an angel of the Lord appeared to him, and comforting him, said, "Fear not to go with them, for the power of Christ will be present with thee, which will destroy the serpent under thy hands; and on thy account the Redeemer and Saviour will save and deliver all the country." The holy Prelate following the advice of the angel, dared to approach the flying and winged dragon; and being inspired by heaven, he immediately took off one of his vestments, and tied it round his neck, and ordered him by the Lord's commandment, to follow him as far as the sea, and cease to emit his poisonous and pernicious breath. And lastly, the pestiferous beast, according to the commandment of the Bishop, having become mild and gentle, did not lift up his wings to terrify, nor show its teeth to gnash with them, nor put out his tongue to emit his fiery breath. And immediately the pious Prelate went towards the sea, leading after him the enormous monster by the portion of his vestments, wherewith he had tied him, and immediately, in the name of the Lord, fixed him to a great rock in the midst of the sea. And the Armoricans seeing this, entered into counsel with St. Samson, and said to him, "Holy father, take care of us, for if the man of God leaves us, the serpent will come again and destroy us and our country; be pleased therefore to keep him with us, and earnestly entreat him to consent to remain, so that we may not die from that calamity."

And the pious father hearing that St. Samson, and King Budic, with the people, had consulted that they might retain him by their entreaty for some time, was displeased, and resolved in himself not to do what they agreed on and proposed. And, lo! An angel of the Lord appeared to him that night, and said, "Do not hesitate to remain with them, for through means of thee, the country shall receive protection and assistance, and this will be proof to thee, that I am sent from the Lord; tomorrow the King and the aforesaid Prelate, with a numerous attendance of people will come to thee, and suppliantly entreating, will strongly offer to thee the Episcopal care and privilege of all Armorica; and consenting to them according to my advice, accept what they offer to thee for some time; in the mean while shall be collected thy countrymen, who are still dispersed on all sides, and say unto them I will remain with you as long as may please God whilst waiting for the assembling of all my exiled countrymen."

And again the angel said: "Lo! Another proof will be shown to thee from God through me. Tomorrow the Prelate and King with a large company of people will meet thee, that they may lead thee honourably, and gloriously, to the Episcopal seat;

and when they will zealously offer to thee the best of their horses for thee to ride thereon, do not thou consent to receive it all from them; for thou shalt immediately have, as a testimony of the divine permission, a most excellent steed sent to thee from God through me; and mounting him cheerfully and triumphantly, thou shall go with them to the bishopric of Dol, which has been prepared and pre-destined by God for thee."

All these things, therefore, took place the following day, as the angel had promised; for the King, and Prelate, with a multitude of people met him, that they might conduct him with due honour to the Episcopacy of Dol, and exalt him into the Episcopal seat. And, lo! Suddenly, as the heavenly messenger had predicted, when they offered to him one of their best horses, and he refusing to receive it from them, there appeared near him a most beautiful steed, sent by God to him. And mounting him, he went with them to Dol; and there, as he had been commanded by God, he consented to remain, until the time afore-appointed by God the Father. And at that instant of time, he called to him King Budic, and with the bestowing of much blessing on him, gave him the aforesaid horse. Before all the people, the Bishop St. Teilo requested of God, and suppliantly prayed, that the soldiers of Armorica might excel in horsemanship all other nations, and thereby defend their country, and avenge themselves victoriously on their enemies. And that privilege which St. Teilo obtained from the Lord to be conferred by him, remains until this day, according to the testimonies and historical accounts of all the old men of that country. For the Armoricans are seven times more valiant as horsemen than as foot soldiers.

In the meantime, whilst these things were performed, the Bishop St. Teilo, called to him his family, that is, the common people of his country, and conversing with them familiarly, at last said to them: "Know ye, my little children, that our king Gerennius is afflicted with a serious disorder, and I believe, as an angel has informed me, that he will die of this illness. When I came to that country, passing through his territories, I visited him, and he honourably received me and my companions, treating us hospitably for some days. And I engaged to him, promising in the Lord, that he should not see death, nor his last day, until he received from me the body of the Lord, and that then he should depart from this world. Prepare, therefore, for us our ship, that through means of knowledge divinely communicated, we may return to our native country, which has been a long time desired, and divinely promised us." A large ship being therefore prepared, and seven years and seven months expired, during which St. Teilo had resided in the country of the Armoricans, he entered into it with many doctors, and some other bishops, by whose sanctity the British nation should be refreshed after the pestilence. And then he enjoined his companions, saying, "Take with you this stone coffin, that the body of Gerennius may be buried there in." And they, wondering, declared they could not obey the command, on account of its great size. "For," they said, "ten yoke of oxen can scarcely move it from this place." But he, trusting in the Lord, and the prayers of the bishops and people, directed that it should be cast into the sea before the prow of the ship, and that through the power of God it would be brought to the bank without using an oar, which was accordingly done. And as they sailed in the middle of the sea, another ship met them, and the sailors coming together, conversed with each other, and a bishop sent by King Gerennius mentioned that the King was dying, but expected the arrival and coming of St. Teilo. Sailing together from thence, they got to a harbour called Dingerein. And lo! Immediately the aforesaid stone, that had been thrown into the sea, having arrived, appeared between the two ships and according to the faith of the holy pastor of Christ, manifested the glory of his majesty. St. Teilo, coming to the King, found him still living, and having received the body of the Lord from his hand, joyfully migrated to the Lord; and his body was carefully buried in the aforesaid stone coffin, and by his holy confessor committed to God.

After these things, the holy man went to his own Episcopal see, with a great number of the clergy and people who accompanied him, and there he remained to the end of his life, holding supremacy over all the churches of the whole of southern Britain, according to the appointment of the fathers who consecrated him at Jerusalem, as before mentioned.

Anonymous *(written by Monk of the Monastery of Ruys, Brittany, about the 9th century. Translated by Hugh Williams, Cymmrodorion, London, 1889.)*

The Life of Gildas (Extract)

The end of this passage suggests that Gildas wrote his De Excido Britonum *in Brittany. It seems almost certain from his own testimony that he wrote it in South Wales around AD 540 when he was 43. It would appear that he went to Brittany in his later years – later than the thirtieth year suggested in this extract. But the quotation is proof, at least, that copies of this work existed and were read in Brittany in the early ninth century.*

When he [Gildas] was afterwards making arrangements to return to his own country, God, who willed to magnify His mercy unto us would not permit him to do so. For when, at God's command, he had come to Armorica – formerly a territory in Gaul, but it was at that time called Letavia by the Bretons, in whose possession it was – he was received by the inhabitants with honour and great joy. But he himself, while shunning worldly and vanishing honours, was longing more and more to lead a life of contemplation. At that time, however, the resources of the kings and kingdom of the Franks were small. For in those days, as any wise reader can learn from the histories of the ancients, it was Childericus, the son of Meroveus, a man devoted to the error of the heathen, who was ruling over the Franks. St Gildas, therefore, in the thirtieth year of his age, came to some island which lay in sight of the district of Reuvisium, and there, for a considerable time, spent a solitary life. But, after no long time, as the lamp that had been lit could no longer remain under a bushel, but upon a stand, that all his neighbours and acquaintances, both near and far away, might enjoy the light of its brightness, the people began to flock to him

from all directions, and to entrust their sons for their instruction to his superinten-
dence and teaching. He gladly took them under his charge, and began instructing
them in spiritual knowledge. Coming, therefore, to some fort on a mountain in
Reuvisium, situated in sight of the sea, he built there a monastery of more skilful
workmanship, and in it he constructed defences after the fashion of cloisters.
There his life shone forth so brilliantly that a large number of sick and maimed
persons and lepers, who were in the country round about, came to him, and were
restored to health by his actions and merits – a wonder which, even up to the present time, by the merits of the saint, Almighty God has not ceased to work in that
place.

He then, finally, built a small oratory on the bank of the river Blavetum under a
certain overhanging rock: he hollowed out the rock itself from west to east, raised a
wall on its right side, and thus made a suitable oratory, underneath which he caused
a fountain of clear water to issue forth from the rock; and from that very rock, by
the bountifulness of the Lord, he brought excellent glass. He also made a mill
there, to which he put the wheat, and which he turned with the hand. This mill is
preserved in the same place up to the present day; and into it, as the merits of the
saint avail with Christ, sick Christians banish all their ailments. […]

He also was the meekest of all the men of that time. He was, moreover, wise
both in his teaching and in action, truthful in conversation, diligent in prayers, continuing though the nights in vigils, torturing his body with fastings, long-suffering
in wrongs, affable in conference, bountiful in alms, distinguished in all goodness.
And, further, he was wont to teach that heretics, after the first and second reproof,
should be avoided; and in his sermons, he exhorted men to atone for sins by alms,
to feed the hungry, to give drink to the thirsty, to clothe the naked, to visit the sick
and those cast into prison, to bury the dead, to return evil for evil to no man, to love
fasting, to be always assiduous in vigils and prayers. It was thus that the illustrious
teacher instructed the clergy, thus the monks, and thus too the laics; and he
enjoined upon others nothing save what he himself was wont to do. […] Those
who quarrelled he would call back to peace, but reproved murderers, adulterers,
sacrilegious persons, robbers, and plunderers, of whatsoever condition they might
be, being no respecter of persons […]

Once more: the holy man, at the request of brother monks who had come to
him from Britain, ten years after he had departed from that country, wrote a short
epistolary book, in which he reproved five of the kings of that island who had been
ensnared by various crimes and sins. I have, therefore, thought it proper to add on
this page a few words to show how elegantly and how concisely he has related their
worthlessness, and censured each of them by name for his iniquities.

"For, of a truth," says he, "will the citizens conceal not only what belongs to our
(kings), but what the nations round about are now casting in our teeth? For Britain
has kings, but they are despots. It has judges, but they are impious men. They are
often engaged in plunder and rapines, but always preying on the innocent; exerting
themselves to avenge or protect, but in favour of criminals and robbers; having an

abundance of wives, whores and adulteresses; they constantly swear false oaths; they make vows, but almost immediately act falsely; make wars, civil and unjust, rigorously prosecuting thieves throughout the country, but not only loving but even remunerating those thieves who sit at table with them; giving alms plentifully, but, in contrast to this, piling up a huge mountain of crimes; sitting in the seat of judgement, but rarely seeking for the rule of right judgement; despising the innocent and the lowly, but seizing upon every chance to exalt to the stars the bloodyminded, the proud, murderers, adulterers, the enemies of God, who with their very name ought to be utterly destroyed; having many prisoners in the gaols, loading them with chains, whom they maltreat more in treachery than as a deserved punishment; entering among the altars and abiding there, and yet despising these altars shortly after, as if it were a heap of dirty stones."

Anonymous

The Book of Llandâv (Extract)

St. Oudoceus was Bishop of Landaff from AD 562 to around 610. According to his 'Life' he was born in Brittany, his father being Budic and his mother Anauued – sister to St. Teilo.

Be it known to you, dearly beloved, that in the time of Bishop Oudoceus, Gwaednerth, by diabolical instigation, killed his brother Meirchion, through contention for the kingdom, and having committed murder, the fratricide was excommunicated by St. Oudoceus, at a synod assembled together at Llandaff from the mouth of the Wye to the mouth of the Towy; and he remained, with crosses laid on the ground, and inverted bells, for three years, under the same excommunication, and without the communion of Christians. The three years being expired, he sought pardon from St. Oudoceus, which being granted to him, he was sent on a pilgrimage to Dol, in Armorica, on account of the ancient acquaintance and friendship which the holy fathers, his predecessors, that is St. Teilo, and St. Samson, the first bishop of the city of Dol, had between each other, and also because the said Gwaednerth, and the Bretons, and the Archbishop of that country, had the same language, and were of the same nation, although separated by a large portion of the earth, and he could consequently the better renounce his crime, and request indulgence, as his language was understood.

Anonymous

The Life of Gildas (Extract)

The story of Conomor and Triphine – Conomor is spelt variously as Conomerus, Commotus and Conomore – could be the true source of the Bluebeard legend, the inspiration for Bartok's opera. South of the estuary of the Loire – still in Brittany – in Pornic lived a baron, Gilles de Rais (1404–1440). There is a tradition that he murdered his wives and abused and killed many young boys. The French novelist, J. K. Huysmans, who was fascinated by the Gilles de

Rais story and used it in his novel (Là-bas) stated that "Gilles de Rais was not the true 'Barbe-Bleue' but the Breton king, Conomor, the ruins of whose sixth century castle lies on the edges of Carnoet."

A classical version of the tale is of a husband going away and giving his wife the keys of the castle telling her she can go to any room, bar one. Her curiosity gets the better of her, she goes to that room and finds the murdered bodies of her husband's previous wives. In terror she drops the keys into a pool of blood on the floor and is spite of every effort she cannot clean the blood from the keys. Her husband discovers that she has disobeyed him and she is murdered, too.

It is a very modern tale dealing with some of the worst aspects of the relationships between men and women – men who insist on proving that their wives are faithful, men who abuse their wives, women who insist on knowing all their husband's secrets and are punished for doing so. In one Breton version there is a suggestion that Conomor, when he discovers Triphine is pregnant, suspects her of being unfaithful. It also suggests the terror of pregnancy which women had in the Middle Ages when they often died in childbirth.

There lived in those days, in the upper parts of that country, a certain tyrant whose name was Conomerus, a man allured by a perverse credulity and a diabolical crime, who made it a practice, as soon as he learnt that his wife had conceived, to put her to death at once. After he had already done away with many women sprung from noble families, parents began to feel much saddened on this account, and to move further away from him. Seeing that he was despised by everyone, he sent for Saint Gildas asking him to observe the petition of his words. But the saint, perceiving the cunning of his wickedness, refused his request, but removed far away from him lest in any way, through intercourse with him, the nobles and princes of that part of the country might be deceived. Unable to achieve his objection, Conomerus sent to Werocus, Count of Vannes, demanding his daughter in marriage. When Werocus heard this, he answered the messenger, saying: "How can I give my daughter to be slain by your master's accursed sword? Have I not heard of the massacre he has made of the ladies who were married to him? I certainly will not do so: for my daughter shall not risk death as long as I can help it."

The messengers returned to Conomerus with Werocus's reply. But Conomerus desisted not from the course he had begun, and again and again charged Werocus, saying: "Whatever hostages or sureties thou desirest, I will give thee; do thou but grant me my request." Werocus replied: "Thy suit is in vain; to no purpose dost thou labour in thy request. For unless thou givest me Saint Gildas as surety, thou wilt in no way succeed in thy petition; for to no one, except through his hands, will I deliver my daughter." The king at once sent messengers to Saint Gildas, desiring him to come with all speed, and receive, on the promise of his protection, a daughter from her father's hand, and give her to him in legitimate wedlock as his wife. But the saint, in disapproval of their words, said in answer to them: "You know that your master is a very cunning man, and ruined by a tyrannical savageness. If I assent, and if he pledge me as a surety and then kill the maiden, I shall have fallen into a grievous sin before the Lord, and have separated her parents from me by the violent bereavement of their child, and caused them to sigh deeply with intolerable grief. But, nevertheless, I will come with you, and discuss the wishes of both parties, even of the parents and of him who has directed you to me." Then he goes along with them, and finds the princes themselves had assembled to discuss this matter. And while they were deliberating about this matter, the maiden's father said to Gildas: "If thou wilt receive my daughter under thy charge, I will trust thee, I will deliver her to thee. But if thou refuse to take her, this man shall never have her." Saint Gildas said to him: "Deliver her to me, and I, protected by the power of God, shall restore her to thee safely." The aforesaid tyrant, therefore, received her to be joined in marriage to him. Gildas, mighty in glorious virtues, returned to his monastery.

When the marriage had been celebrated, the tyrant began to caress his beloved bride: and, as soon as he learnt that she had conceived, he meditated killing her as had been his custom. But dreading the oath which he had sworn to Saint Gildas, he said to himself that he could not deceive a holy man. For he feared to incur God's anger if he attempted to murder, with his accursed sword, a lady whom he had received from the hands of Saint Gildas. But the devil supplied him with pretexts, declaring that he ought not to fear the holiness of Saint Gildas to such a degree as, like a coward, to give up, for the sake of a mere monk, what he had set his heart on. As the woman, in the meantime, perceived, by many indications, that his heart was enraged against her because she had conceived, she was struck with fear and secretly escaped. When her wicked husband learnt this, he was now incensed with greater anger, and pursued her. Having found her on the road-side, hiding under some leaves – for she was wearied by her journey – he drew out his sword, cut off her head, and then returned home.

When her father had heard what had befallen his daughter, he was stricken with deep grief, and sent at once, with great haste, to Saint Gildas, saying: "Give me back my daughter; for it is owing to thy intercession that I have lost her. For know that he who received her in marriage from thy hand, has murdered her with his own sword."

Thereupon the saint, deeply moved, hurried to a small fortification where the aforesaid tyrant used to dwell, desiring to hear from him whether, as the rumour was, he had slain his wife with his own hands. But when the tyrant saw Saint Gildas approaching, he charged the porter of the house not on any account to let the saint enter in to him; for he knew that, through the murder of his wife, he had sinned against God and against the holy man. But although he was not ignorant of this, he nevertheless disdained to request that the saint should prevail with God in prayer to grant him a contrite and humble heart to do penance for the evil he had done. When, therefore, Saint Gildas had knocked long at the door and no one opened to him, but rather he was mocked by those within, he prayed unto God that unless it was His will that that man should be changed for the better, it might seem good to Him to put an end to his wickedness. Having ended his prayer, he went round the whole fortification in which the tyrant dwelt, took a handful of earth, and cast it upon that dwelling; and immediately, by the will of God, it all fell to the ground.

He then left for the place where lay the lifeless corpse of the murdered woman with her offspring in her womb, and prayed in this way: "Lord God, who didst form man of the dust of the earth, and who, in order to deliver him from the power of Satan, under whose dominion, when he transgressed Thy commandment, he cast himself of his own free will, didst will that thy Son, whom Thou hadst begotten, from eternity before the generations, should die, I invoke Thee to hearken unto me. Hear me, I say, Oh Lord, for I beseech Thee in the name of Thine Only Begotten, our Lord Jesus Christ, it seemed good to promise unto them that believed on Him that, if they should ask Thee aught in His Name, Thou Wouldst not turn away the ear of Thy mercy from their supplication." When he had prayed, he took the head and fastened it on the trunk of the body, and said: "In the name of our Lord Jesus Christ, Trifina, I say unto thee, Arise, and stand on thy feet, and declare unto me what thou hast seen." And forthwith she arose whole and safe from all corruption, and in answer to the saint she said: "As soon as I was slain, I was borne in an angelic chariot, as if to be carried away, and joined to the band of martyrs; but at thy call I returned to thee." Then Gildas brought her to her father and, taking her right hand, restored her to him, saying: "Behold the trust which thou didst commit to me. Guard her as thy daughter, and the progeny too, which she bears in her womb. See that he be diligently nurtured when he is born, until he reaches the age of understanding." But she protested with an oath: "Father, I will never leave thee." Saint Gildas answered her: "It becomes a woman in no wise to follow a monk; but meanwhile abide thou in thy father's house until thou givest birth; and when thou hast done so, we shall lead thee into a nunnery where, in company with other virgins, thou mayest be able to lead a life of chastity." Then did the words of the man of God seem good to her, and she tarried a few days in her father's house.

Not long after, when her time was come, and the woman gave birth to a son, the news was told to Saint Gildas. He ordered the child to be baptised, and to be called after his own name; and when weaned, he had him taught in the liberal pursuits of literature, and caused his mother to abide in a nunnery along with other maid-servants of God. Afterwards, while serving God in chastity, and leading a life of vigils and prayers, she was at length called by the Lord and laid to a blessed rest. Her son also was distinguished for his virtues and miracles, and completed with a blessed end the saintly life he had led. Now the Bretons, in order to distinguish him from the other Saint Gildas, do not call him Gildas, but Trechmeur.

Anonymous

The Life of Samson, (Version found in the *Liber Landavensis*) (Extract)

In those days Count Commotus [Conomor or Conomerus – *see above*], a foreigner, and a cruel and tyrannical person, governed all Brittany, having slain Jonas, the native Count of the Bretons, and delivered up his son to King Hildebert and his Queen, to be kept in captivity. Which Saint Samson hearing, he was grieved at their misery, and quickly went to king Hildebert, desiring to redeem Judual from confinement, and to deliver the people from a foreign ruler. When Samson entered into the king's palace, he found a certain Count, who was a demoniac, whom he anointed on the face and breast with consecrated oil, and thereby liberated him from the devil. The King hearing this, and that he came to supplicate for Judual, and having consulted his nobles, received Saint Samson with suitable honour, and invited him to dine with him. The Queen, however, as she held Judual bound in captivity, would not release him; and by rejecting the entreaties of Saint Samson, and abusing him with a reproachful expression, irritated him; and that she might destroy him, she prepared a deadly drink for him.

And when the King, and the holy Archbishop, sat down to dinner, and all who were present, congratulated him on his arrival, the Queen at the instigation of the devil, mixed poison with wine in a glass, and through her servant offered it to Saint Samson to drink. Then he, being divinely inspired, made the sign of the Cross upon the glass, which thereby broke in four parts, and the poison being shed on the hand of him who held it, the flesh and skin, in the sight of all present, were burnt to the very bone. Then Saint Samson said, "This drink is not fit to be drunk," and the King being disturbed, and all the people wondering, Saint Samson marked the hand of him who had been hurt, and completely restored it.

After they had dined, Saint Samson, with the permission of the King, hastened to the place where Judual was kept, to meet whom, the Queen sent a wild horse to destroy him, but the chosen of God marked him with the Cross, and his saddle being placed on him, he mounted, and the animal became as mild as if he had been tamed by the King of Heaven. Having her heart still hardened, the Queen ordered that a fierce lion, with its keepers, should meet him, that it might seize him, but the hand of God protected his elect, and as if struck with a stake, it betook itself to flight; but Saint Samson looking after it, said, "I command thee, in the name of Jesus Christ, that thou hurt no one any more, and that thou speedily die." When it immediately leaped headlong, and expired. And the King beholding so many miracles performed by the holy man, bought forward Judual, released him from his chains, and gave him up to him. The Queen likewise, with her favourites, prostrate at his feet, asked pardon of the holy man.

Which being done, and all being pardoned by the grace of God, and greatly rejoicing, the King said to Saint Samson, "There is a serpent in this province, which afflicts all who dwell around; and because we see thee to shine with miracles, we request that thou wouldst vouchsafe to deliver us from it." To whom Saint Samson said, "Find me a guide for the way, and in the power of God, I will expel it from your parts." A guide therefore being found, he took with him two brethren, and leaving the others with Judual in the place, being confident and always exulting in the Lord, he quickly set out upon his journey; and when he came to the cave in which the serpent was, he entered there, with bended knees, and commanded it to swim beyond the river called Sigona, and there remain under a certain stone; which soon after, by his word alone he drowned in the sea. And in the same place he built a monastery, and place therein brethren who should serve Christ. Lastly King Hildebert greatly loved Saint Samson for having performed such great miracles, and freely gave him valuable gifts, namely in gold, and silver, in precious vessels, in farms, and various possessions, and commended himself to his prayers.

Taking with him Judual, he went to Lesia [Lisieux in Normandy] and Angia [Anjou or possibly Angers], and there collected an army, and returned with it to Brittany; Saint Samson praying and fasting, and Judual fighting with the army against Commotus. Judual, by the prayers of the holy man, at one blow overcame his enemy, and from that time, he and the successors of his family, held the Government of Brittany. Soon after, Judual was triumphantly received by his countrymen, and elected Governor over all Brittany; and he rendered himself, and all who belonged to him, subject to Saint Samson, and devoutly commended himself to his prayers. "Let the Governor return thanks to the Redeemer, and the people rejoice, being committed to the care of such a pastor." Whence the government of all Brittany is observed to belong justly to Dol until this day. For what great miracles the Lord, on this side of the sea, and beyond it, has by him performed, how much his learning shone, the eloquence of no writer, or doctor doth relate.

Being perfect in life, and in age, and adorned with all virtues, he was attacked by severe illness in the monastery of Dol, and the clergy flocking around, he gave his body to the earth, and his soul to heaven. The clergy buried his body with unguents, and in their hearing, the heavenly host with hymns and praises conveyed his soul to Christ.

The Monk of Rhuys
The Life of Gildas (Extract)

The author of this Breton Vitae Gildae *(Life of Gildas), describes Gildas's education at the feet of Saint Hildutus (the Breton-born Iltud) who also educated Samson of Dol and Paul Aurélien (of Saint-Pol-de-Léon).*

The blessed Gildas, destined to become the honour and glory of his nation, is entrusted by his parents to Saint Hildutus to be instructed by him. He took the holy child to himself, and began to teach him in sacred literature; and seeing he excelled in outward beauty, and was most eagerly bent upon the liberal studies, he loved him with tender love, and strove to teach him with attentive zeal. The blessed Gildas was, therefore established, under a master's training, in the school of divine scripture and of the liberal arts. Observing, however, the knowledge imparted in both kinds of teaching, he was anxious to be taught rather in the divine doctrines, desiring to imitate a kind of contemplation, and altogether deserting the reputation of man's opinion.

Kervarker

Buhez Sant Ronan

Kervarker in the 'Notes' at the end of the ballad 'Buhez Sant Ronan' in Barzaz Breiz, 1867 *edition, suggests that Kéban, or Keben, was a Druidess, a fierce Queen of the Sacred Wood. The ballad then becomes a symbol of the conflict between the old pagan religion and the new Christianity. Anatole Le Braz, on the basis of the folktale sees it merely as a case of an angry, hard-working wife furious at her husband for wasting his time talking to the saint instead of working his land.*

> Ann otrou Ronan benniget
> Enez Iverni a oa ganet,
> Bro-zaoz, enn tu-all d'ar mor glaz,
> Demeuz a bentieien vraz.
>
> Eur wech ma oa enn he beden,
> En doa gwelet eur sklerijen
> Hag eunn el kaer gwisket e gwenn,
> A gomzaz out-han evelhenn:
>
> "Ronan, Ronan, kerz alese;
> Gourc'hemennet eo gand Doue,
> Evit savetei da ene,
> Mont da chom e douar Kerne."
>
> Ronan ouz ann el a zentaz,
> Ha da chom e Breiz e teuaz,
> Kent e traon Leon, ha goude,
> E Koat Nevet, e bro Kerne.
>
> Daou pe dri bloa oa pe ouspenn,
> M'oa eno ober pinijen,
> Pa oa eur pardae toull he zor,
> War he zaoulin, dirag ar mor;
>
> Ken a lammaz eur bleiz er c'hoad,
> Adreuz enn he veg eunn danvad;
> Ha war he lerc'h eunn den, timad,
> Hag a oele, gant kalonad;
>
> Ha Ronan gant true out-han,
> A bedaz Doue evit-han:

"Otrou Doue, ha me ho ped;
Grit na vo ann danvad taget!"

Ne oa ked he beden laret,
Pa oa ann danvad digaset,
Heb droug e-bed, war dreuz ann nour,
Dirag Ronan hag ann o'ac'h paour.

Ac'hano da zont ann den kez,
Deue d'he welet aliez;
Gant plijadur vraz e teue
Evit klevet komzou Doue.

Hogen eur c'hreg a oa gant-han,
Hag hi gwall-bez, hanvet Keban,
Hag hi a zeuaz d'argarzi
Ronan enn abeg d'he hini.

Eunn deiz a oa bet d'he gaouet
Ha trouz d'ean hi devoa gret:
"Chalmet hoc'h euz tud ma zi-me,
Ma goaz kouls ha ma bugale:

Ne reont met ho tarempred holl,
Ha ma danvez a ia da goll.
Ma na zentet ouz-in muioc'h,
Kaer po chilpat, me rei gen-hoc'h!"

Enn he fenn e lakaz neuze,
Da c'hoana den santel Doue.
Hag hi mont da gaout ar Roue,
Gradlon, enn-tu-all d'ar mene:

"Otrou Roue, ha me ho ped;
Ma flac'hik-me zo bet taget:
Ronan Koad Neved deuz her gret;
O vont da vleiz meuz hen gwelet."

Evel ma oa bet tamallet
Ronan da Gemper oa kaset,
Ha tolet ebarz eur c'hao don,
Aberz otrou roue Gradlon.

Mez ac'hane pa oa tennet,
Dioc'h eur wezen e oa staget,
Ha daou gi gwez ha diboellet
Warn-ezhan timad oa losket.

Hag hen heb man na kaout aon,
A reaz eur groaz war he galon;
Ken a dec'haz ar chas raktal
Evel dioc'h ann tan, oc'h harzal.

Gradlon pa welaz kement-se,
A lavaraz d'ann den Doue:
"Na petra vad a rinn-me d'hoc'h
P'e ma Doue enn tu gen-hoc'h?"

"Netra vad me na c'houlennan,
Nemed true d'ar c'hreg Keban;
He bugelik ne ket maro,
Gant-hi enn arc'h oe klozet beo."

Ann arc'h a oa bet digaset,
Ar bugel enn hi oe kavet,
Hag hen war he goste, maro;
Ha sant Ronan he lakaz beo.

Ann otrou Gradlon hag he dud,
Souezet-braz gand ar burzud,
'N em strinkaz dirak sant Ronan,
O c'houlenn trugarez out-han.

Hag hen e mez, d'ar c'hoad endro,
Da chom di beteg he varo;
Eno oc'h ober pinijen
Eur men kaled dindan he benn;

Gant-han krogen eunn ounnar vriz,
Eur skoultrik gweet da c'houriz,
Ha da eva dour ar poull du,
Ha bara poazet el ludu.

Pa zeuaz he dremen divea,
Pa eaz kuit deuz ar bed-ma,

Daou ejen gwez kaen dioc'h ar-charr,
Tri eskob d'he gas d'ann douar.

Hag i digouezet gand ar ster,
Ha kaout Keban diskabel-kaer,
Oc'h ober liziou d'ar gwener,
Daoust da wad Jezuz, hor Salver;

Hag hi sevel he golvaz prenn,
Ha darc'ha gant korn eunn ejenn,
Ken a zilammaz gwall-spontet,
He gorn gand ann tol diframmet.

"Ke, map-gaign, ke d'az toull endro!
Ke da vreina gant chas maro!
Ne vei ket kavet brema mui
Oc'h ober goab ac'hanomp-ni."

N'oa ked he genou peur-sarret,
Pa oa gand ann douar lonket
Etouez moged ha flammou-tan,
E lec'h ma c'helver Bez-Keban.

Mont a eure ato ar c'harr,
O kas Sant Ronan d'ann douar;
Pa chomaz sonn ann daou ejen,
Heb kerzet mui na rog na dren.

Eno e oe laket ar sant,
Evel ma kreder oa he c'hoant;
E penn-ann-nec'h euz ar c'hoad glaz,
Eeunn-hag-eeunn dirag ar mor-braz.

Translation

The Life of Saint Ronan

The blessed Saint Ronan
Was born on the isle of Hibernia,
England, beyond the blue sea,
Descendant of noble race.

One day while he was praying
He saw a bright light

And an angel dressed in white
Spoke to him thus:

"Ronan, Ronan, leave this place;
It is God's command,
To save your soul,
Go and stay in the land of Cornouaille."

Ronan obeyed the angel,
And went to Brittany,
First in Lower Leon, and then,
In the Sacred Forest, in Cornouaille.

There he was for two, three years or more
Doing his penance,
When, one afternoon, on his doorstep,
On his knees, facing the sea,

A wolf sprang from the wood,
With a sheep in its mouth;
And after it, a man, in haste,
Crying, in despair;

And Ronan, with pity for him,
Prayed to God on his behalf:
"Lord God, I pray Thee;
Let not the sheep be strangled!"

Hardly had the prayer been said,
That the sheep was laid down,
Unharmed, on the doorstep,
In front of Ronan and the wretched farmer.

From that day on, the dear man
Came to see him often;
Coming with great pleasure
To hear about the Word of God.

But he had a wife,
A wicked woman, named Kében,
And she came to chase away
Ronan because of her husband's visits.

One day she went to seek Ronan
And hurled abuse at him:
"You have bewitched the people of my house,
My husband as well as my children.

"They do nothing but visit you, I am being ruined.
If you do not start obeying me,
No matter how much you yap,
You'll have to deal with me."

Then she hatched a scheme
To play a dirty trick on God's saint.
She went to seek the King,
Gradlon, beyond the mountain:

"Lord King, I pray you;
My little girl has been strangled:
Ronan of the Sacred Forest has done it;
I saw him change into a wolf.

As Ronan had been accused,
He was taken to Quimper,
And thrown into a dark dungeon
In the name of King Gradlon.

On being taken from there,
He was tied to a tree,
And two wild and fierce dogs
Were set upon him.

Without the slightest worry or fear
He made the sign of the Cross on his heart;
The dogs ran off immediately
As if from a fire, barking.

Gradlon, on seeing this,
Said to the man of God:
"What reward shall I give you
Since God is with you?"

"I ask for no reward,
Except for the pardon of the woman Kében;

Her child is not dead,
She put her alive in the chest."

The chest was brought
And the child found inside,
Lying dead on her side;
But Saint Ronan brought her back to life.

Lord Gradlon and his people
Amazed by the miracle,
Threw themselves at Saint Ronan's feet
Asking for forgiveness.

He went out, returned to the forest,
Where he stayed until his death;
Doing his penance,
A hard stone for a pillow;

For his cloak, a heifer skin with dark markings,
A plaited twig around his waist,
And to drink, water from a black pool,
And bread baked in the ashes.

When he passed away,
And left this world,
Two big wild oxen were yoked to a cart,
Three bishops came to bury him.

They came by a river,
They found Kében bare-headed,
Washing clothes on a Friday,
Regardless of the blood of Jesus, our Saviour;

She raised her wooden battledore,
And struck the horn of an ox,
So that it leapt back in great fear,
Its horn broken off by the blow.

"Go, carrion, go back to your hole!
Go and rot with dead dogs!
You will no longer
Make mockery of us."

No sooner had she opened her mouth,
That she was dragged inside the earth,
Surrounded by smoke and flames,
In a place now known as Kében's Grave.

The cart continued its journey
To bring Saint Ronan to his burial place;
Until the two oxen stopped suddenly
Without another step, neither forward nor backward.

There the saint was buried,
As such was his wish, it was thought,
On the hill top, in a green wood,
Right in front of the ocean.

Anonymous

Gwerz Sant Kado

[*This ballad was heard sung by Guillaume Quellien of La Roche, Tréguier, and published in* Chansons et danses des Bretons, *Paris, 1889. They were collected and edited by Narsis Kelien (Narcisse Quellien)*]

A bell a zo me 'm a dezir
Da diskleria ar pez zo gwir,
Trei ar galleg en brezonek
Eur c'hantik ker am euz kavet.

Klewet ac'h eus komz dre ar vro
Demeuz ann otro sant Kado?
He viraklo nag he vue
N'ac'h euz klewet biskoaz an-he.

E Ragoustand e oa ganet
Ha Raourach e oa hanvet;
He vamm a oa Lorans Konstans,
Merc'h d'eur roué braz a Irland.

Eunn ermid e oa tost d'ar vro,
Lec'h m'a oa ganet sant Kado,
Deuaz d'hen goul da vadein,
Hag he dad prest da gonsantin,

Enostant ma oant paianed,
Med Doue en euz permetet.

Ann ermid a gas an-ehan
Eunn dewez da wit tan d'ehan
Da lochen ar bastored
Elec'h oant o vesa ann denved;

Ar pastor kri o laret d'ehan
Na roje ket a dan d'ehan,
Nemed hen lakat a raje
De vonet gant-han n' he jave;

Sant Kado dre umilite
A lakaz glaou en he jave
Ewit kas d'he vestr ann ermit,
Hep poan d'he gorf na d'he abit;

Neuze oe hanvet eur zorser,
Eur majisian, eunn tromper;
Ar mestr-pastor a fell d'ehan
Mond 'n he ermitach d'hen lazan;

En ermitach p'int ariet,
Dal war ar plas int bet rentet,
Ha mantret ho oll izili,
Na ellent mui bo remuin;

Sant Kado dre gompasion
Ouz ho c'hlewet o c'houl pardon,
O c'heaz en orezon fervent
Hag ho greaz iac'h en eunn instant.

P'oa ari sant Kado en oad,
A fellaz d'he vamm ha d'he dad
Hen lakaet da gomandin
War ann armeo ha d'ho reglin;

Mes sant Kado na c'houle ket
Kombatin ewit treo ar bed;
'Barz ann desert en em rentaz
Ha sant Gouard hen saludaz,

En plas de welet sant Andre
Oa eur mignon braz da Doue.

Sant Kado laka batisan
War ar mor eur pond ar c'heran,
War eur vrec'h-vor deus ann Indrez,
Pini oe hanvet revier Estez;

Unan deuz ann artizaned
Gant re all a oe lazet,
Ha ma hen toljont en eur stank:
Pebez maleur d'ann dud mechant!

Sant Kado emez hen tennaz,
Sant Kado hen resusitaz.
Daouzek bla e oa bet eno
O resusitan tud varo,

Ouz ho c'honvertisan d'ar fe
Hag o lenn ann awiel d'he.

War-dro 'n anter-noz eo kemeret
Ker gant arme ar baianed
O vasakrin ar gristenien;
Dre ma o c'hevent, na vane den.

Oa sant Kado en he oviz,
Ec'h antrejont 'barz an iliz;
Eur barbar kri ha digonsianz
O treuzin dre he gorf eul lans.

Eunn neubeut goude-se oe interet
Gant eunn toullad relijiuzed.
Ha m'a re miraklo 'n he vue,
A re c'hoaz kalz mui goude-ze.

Translation

The Ballad of Saint Cadoc

For a long time I have wanted
To tell that true tale,
To translate from French into Breton
A fine hymn that I have come across.

Have you heard in this land
Of holy Saint Cadoc?
His miracles and his life
You never heard anything of them.

He was born in Ragoustant
And Raourach it was called;
His mother was Laurence Constance,
Daughter of a great Irish king.

A hermit near the place,
Where Cadoc was born,
Came and asked to baptise him,
And his father readily agreed,

Although they were pagans,
But God gave his permission.

The hermit sent him
One day to fetch fire
To the hut of the shepherds
Where they grazed their sheep;

The cruel shepherd said to him
That he would not give him fire,
Unless he would carry it
Against his chest;

Saint Cadoc very humbly
Placed the glowing coals in his shirt
To take them to his master the hermit,
Without damaging his body or his clothes;

He was then called a sorcerer,
A magician, a cheat;
The head shepherd wanted
To go to his hermitage and kill him;

At the hermitage when they arrived,
They were suddenly struck blind,
Their limbs were stunned,
They could no longer move;

Saint Cadoc taking pity on them
On hearing them begging his pardon,
Led them into fervent prayers
And healed them instantly.

When Saint Cadoc came of age,
His mother and father wished to
Put him in command
Of an army and be their leader;

But Saint Cadoc did not want
To fight for the things of this world:
He went to the desert
And Saint Gouard saluted him,

There he saw Saint Andrew
Who was a great friend of God.

Saint Cadoc then had a fine bridge
Built over the sea,
Across a stretch of water near Lorient
Which is called the river Etel;

One of the workers
Was killed by the others,
And they threw him into a pond:
Worst luck for the wicked men!

Saint Cadoc pulled him out,
Saint Cadoc revived him,
For twelve years he was there
Reviving the dead,

Converting them to the faith
And reading to them the Gospels.

At about midnight he was captured
By the army of pagans
Who massacred the Christians;
Of those they caught, none survived.

As Saint Cadoc was at his prayers,
They entered into the church;

A cruel barbarian with no conscience
Pierced his body with a lance.

Soon after he was buried
By a number of monks.
And if he made miracles during his life,
He made many more after his death.

Brittany and the Revolution

Brittany was heavily involved in the French Revolution. Louis-René de Caradeuc de la Chalotais had led a revolt in Rennes against the French Crown in 1788. It was a revolt of the nobility in protest against the erosion of the (very limited) powers of the ancient Breton Parliament. It was a revolt that for a short period united nobility and peasants, bourgeois and scholars. As the Revolution spread, the main towns in Brittany – Rennes, Nantes, Saint-Brieuc, Tréguier, Lannion, Quimper amongst them – gave their support. Then divisions began to appear. The nobility and the bishops sided with the Royalists. In 1791, the Assembly in Paris voted to subject bishops and parish priests to the same regime as the secular authorities and ordered them to take the oath to observe the Civil Constitution of the Clergy. This was too much for the parish priests, who initially had welcomed the Revolution, and they too changed sides. Those who refused to take the oath went into hiding, into exile or were executed. When the Abbé Sieyes abolished the traditional bishoprics of Saint-Malo, Dol, Léon and Tréguier Breton support for the church plunged the country into civil war. It has been said that the Abbé Sieyes, whose career in the church began in Tréguier, should have known better! It has been argued that, without the exhortation of the clergy, the counter-revolution would not have succeeded for so long. It is usually seen as a conflict of the Right and the Left, the Church and the State. Emmanuel Le Roy Ladurie in *Le Territoire de l'historien* interprets it as a revolt of the peasantry against the bourgeoisie, of country folks against townsfolk, as the urban bourgeoisie – in the wake of the Revolution – snapped up the lands formerly owned by the Church, out-bidding even the richest of the tenant farmers. The 'Chouan' counter-revolution began near Landean, north-east of Fougères, in March 1793, and there was another major revolt in the Vendée, the area to the south of Brittany's ancient border, south of the Loire. In November 1793 the counter-revolutionaries of the Vendée and Brittany came together in Fougères, intent on de-stabilising the new order.

Yann-Vari al Lae

Reflexionou Christen war Revolution Franç, *1836* (Lodenn)

P'eur eta, ô ma Doue, e teuyo an termen
Ma welin c'hoas ma c'hontre, douar ar Francisien!
Ma c'horf zo pell diouté, mæs noz-de ma speret
Gant quement o deus gret din, a sonch enne bepret.

Pell amzer a so deja ma'z on deut da Vro-Saoz;
Pa zezir cals ar galon, e scuiser o c'hortoz;
Ha n'em euz nep esperanç da dremen c'hoas ar mor!
Allas! en Franç ne souffrer na belec na pastor.

Azezet voar eur garrec en tal bordic an od,
Lies a vech an daerou a red var ma diou jod,
Pa velan reus ar pec'het hac hini ar muntro
Hep na fin na chenchamant o ravaji ma bro.

Truezus eo ma doare ha pitoyabl ma stad,
Chaseet deus ma c'hontre ha collet ma oll vad;
Mæs ar chagrin am zevor eo clevet a bep tu
Ar feiz, ar religion en Franç a so achu.

Ah! ma maleur ma-unan a ve neubeut a dra;
Mæs hini ar gristenies! hennes eo a laqa
Da redeq voar ma diou jod eur feunteun a zaerou,
Pa sonjan en abandon eus va denvedigou.

Ne allan quet en compren, eur bopl quen gracius,
Quen poli, quen amiabl, guechall quen vertuzus,
En quen neubeut a amzer en defe collet cren
Bep santimant a enor, gwirione he greden.

Da zizamman ma c'halon em eus sonjet canan,
N'em eus gret nemet essa, bep notenn e fazian.
Rac en eur vro estranjour, ma zeod stag ouz ma staon,
Ma oll rimou so chanchet en canticou a gaon.

Dre agremant ar rimou, eur vouez melodius
E deus calmet aliez sperejou furius,
Ha tennet huanadou deus calon eur mechant
A vije bet goal diæz da c'honid autramant.

Mar fel d'ac'h-hu soulaji eur buguel a so clan,
Invantet eur rimastel, canet eur son dezan:
Laket gant legerete mel ous bordou an tas
Hac ec'h evo ar remed hep ma santo ar blas.

En dezir-se, ma broïs, em eus gret ar vers-man,
Evit essa ho conid: mæs na ouffen canan;
Avoalc'h eo d'in rapportin, clasquet doc'h un all an ton,
Abominationou ar revolution.

Translation

Christian Thoughts on the French Revolution, *1836* (Extract)

Tell me, dear God, when will come the time
When I shall see again my country, the land of the French?
My body is far from them, but day and night my thoughts
Dwell on it, because of what they did to me.

I arrived in England a long time ago;
When the heart is filled with longing, one tires of waiting;
I have no hope of journeying back by sea!
Alas! In France, neither the priest nor the pastor are welcome.

Sitting on a rock by the edge of the sea,
Tears often run down my cheeks
As I think of the harm done by the sins and murders
Which are steadily and relentlessly tearing my country apart.

My state is pitiful. My condition is lamentable.
I was driven out of my country and lost all my possessions.
But the grief which gnaws at me comes from hearing around me
That France has done away with faith and religion.

My own misery would be of no consequence;
But what of the Christians! This is what makes
A stream of tears run down my cheeks,
When I think how neglected my flock is.

I cannot understand it. A nation so gracious,
So well behaved, so pleasant, so virtuous in the past,
How could it, in such a short time, totally discard
Any feeling of honour and the truths of its creed?

To get some comfort, I thought of singing,
I made a single attempt, but the notes fail me.
Because, in a strange land, my tongue sticks to my palate,
And my verses turn into hymns of lamentations.

Due to the appeal of rhymes, a melodious voice
Has often soothed angry minds,
And drawn sighs from wicked hearts
Which would have been very hard to obtain in any other way.

Should you wish to relieve a sick child,
Make up a rhyme, sing him a song:
Put a few drops of honey on the rim of the cup
And he will drink the medicine without feeling its taste.

This is why, dear compatriots, I have composed these verses,
To try and win you over; but I cannot sing them myself.
I just report the facts; find another to put to music
The abominations of the Revolution.

Lan Inizan

Emgann Kergidu, *1877* (Lodenn)

Gant an Aotrou de la Marche, eskob Kastell, ec'h en em gavas gwashoc'h c'hoazh, rak ouzhpenn ma ranke, evel an eskibien all, touiñ sentiñ ouzh al lezennoù nevez, e voe c'hoazh lamet digantañ e eskopti. An dra-se a yoa un dra graet e Pariz gant ar re a yoa e penn ar c'houarnamant, hep kas keloù ebet d'hon Tad Santel ar Pab. Diskleriet e voe dezhañ gant ar re a yoa e karg e Montroulez, n'oa ken eskob, rak n'oa hiziviken eskopti ebet ken e Kastell, al lezenn her lavare.

An Aotrou de la Marche ne soublas ket evit-se. Skrivañ a reas da baotred Montroulez en ul lizher hir ha kalonek-meurbet oa bet anvet eskob e Kastell, a-berzh Doue, gant hon Tad Santel ar Pab, hag, evel eskob, n'en doa da sentiñ nemet ouzh ar pab; war e garg a eskob, tud ar bed-mañ n'o doa pe wel: d'hon Tad Santel ar Pab hepken oa terriñ e eskopti, ha tamm da dud hag a rank sentiñ o-unan ouzh an Iliz hag ouzh an eskibien; rak un eskob eo pastor e eskopti, ha n'eo ket d'ur pastor sentiñ ouzh e zeñved, mes d'an deñved sentiñ ouzh o fastor. Hag ouzhpenn, pa c'hourc'hemenn Doue un dra hag an dud un dra all a-enep, e tleer sentiñ ouzh Doue ha dilezer lezennoù an dud. Hon Tad Santel ar Pab, emezañ en ur echuiñ, en deus staget ac'hanon ouzh eskopti Leon, ha n'eo ket ho lezennoù-c'hwi eo a viro.

Ar feiz n'oa ket c'hoazh mouget e kalonoù an holl: barnerien Montroulez a chomas sebezet o lenn ul lizher ker kalonek hag a lezas, evit ur pennad, an Aotrou de la Marche e peoc'h. Chom a reas didrabas war-dro ur bloaz. Neuze e teuas, eus a Bariz, urzh d'an dud-a-lezenn a Vontroulez da gas an Aotrou de la Marche er-

maez eus e eskopti, pe d'hen dastum er prizon. An Aotrou de la Fruglaye, eus a
vaner Keranrous, e Plouiann, e-lec'h m'emañ bremañ o chom e vab-bihan, an
Aotrou de Champagny, a ra kement a vad dre ar vro, a gasas ur mevel kalonek en
doa en e di da lavaret dezhañ bezañ war evezh, rak deuet oa da Vontroulez urzh da
gregiñ ennañ. An Aotrou de la Marche a voe glac'haret, mes ne dec'has ket: re a
ziegi en doa o tilezer e vugale. Antronoz ec'h en em gavas e Kastell un archer, ha
gantañ, en e sac'h ler, urzh a-berzh ar c'houarnamant d'an Aotrou de la Marche,
eskob kozh Leon, da vont er-maez eus e eskopti.

P'oe klevet ar c'heleier-se e Kastell, e voe glac'har e pep ti. An dud diwar ar maez
a deuas e kêr hag a yeas war-eeun d'an eskopti da gaout an eskob, o zad; tud kêr a
yae ivez war o lerc'h: holl e lavarent:

"Aotrou 'n Eskob, chomit ganeomp! N'ho pet ket aon rak archerien
Montroulez; ne daio hini da gregiñ ennoc'h nemet lammat a rafe dreist hor c'horf-
ni, rak ni a skuilho betek ar berad diwezhañ eus hor gwad kentoc'h eget ho tilezel."
An Aotrou de la Marche a rede an dour eus e zaoulagad o klevet komzoù ker
kalonek. Lavaret a reas d'ar bobl a yoa e toull-dor an eskopti:

– "It pep hini d'e gêr, va bugale vat, mont a ran da c'houlenn kuzul digant va
vikeled-vras, ha digant tud vat all a zo amañ en eskopti. Bennozh Doue deoc'h evit
ar garantez a ziskouezit din: me, n'hoc'h ankounac'hain biken, n'ho tilezin ket, mar
gellan."

Distro d'e gambr, an Aotrou de la Marche a c'houlennas digant ar veleien hag an
dud a renk uhel eus a Gastell a yoa en em zastumet en eskopti, petra en doa da ober.
An holl, o welet penaos ez ae an traoù, hen alias da gemeret an tec'h. Ma n'her raje
ket e vije emgann etre Kastelliz hag an archerien, n'oa ket war zivin, ha neuze, an
Aotou 'n Eskob a vije pennkaoz e varv meur a hini. An Aotrou de la Marche a voe
glac'haret-bras o klevet an ali-se, evelato e sentas dre garantez ouzh e bobl: ne
falveze ket dezhañ e vije skuilhet evitañ berad gwad hini anezho.

Penaos e tec'has kuit? Ne oufen ket, evit her lavaret deoc'h gant gwirionez. Lod
a lavar oa degouezhet warnezhañ, en e balez, e-pad m'edo en e gambr o skrivañ e
alioù diwezhañ hag e gimiad da dud e eskopti, pevar archer warn-ugent degaset eus
a Vontroulez evit e gerc'hat d'ar prizon.

An Aotrou de la Marche a c'houlennas diganto petra glaskent.

– "Deuet omp, eme vestr an archerien, d'ho kerc'hat da vont d'ar prizon da
Vontroulez.

– D'am c'herc'hat da vont d'ar prizon! Ha perak?

– Her lavaret a zo bet graet deoc'h a-raok bremañ; abalamour ne fell ket deoc'h
sentiñ ouzh lezennoù ar c'houarnamant. Alo! savit diwar ho kador, ha deuit
ganeomp.

– Evelato e root amzer din da lakaat dilhad all ha da zastum ur c'hrez bennak da
vont ganen. Ha gedal a rafec'h aze ur pennadig, war ar palier, e-pad ma vezin oc'h
ober kement-se?"

Mestr an archerien, gant taol-lagad efedus an archer, a sellas pizh ouzh ar gambr
a-dro-war-dro. Evel ne wele nemet levrioù, bern-war-vern, renket an eil e-kichen

egile, e lavaras d'an Aotrou 'n Eskob e chomje d'her gedal. Ur gwall bennad a kave dezhañ e ranke gedal hag e tigoras ar gambr. Siwazh! n'oa eskob ebet ken enni, aet e ranke bezañ kuit diwar nij...

Neuze e savas kabal e-touez an archerien: dont a rejont holl er gambr; furchañ a rejont kement kogn a yoa... Unan anezho, o sellet pishoc'h, a welas ur renkad levrioù ha n'edo ket a-renk gant ar re-all: sachañ a reas war ar planken edo al levrioù warnezhañ, hag e laoskas ur griadenn. Eno oa un nor, hag, e-tal an nor-se, oa ur skalier evit diskenn d'ar jardin... Ker buan, an archerien, an eil war-lerc'h egile, evel chas chase o vont dre un ode vaen hanter distank, a ziskennas dre ar skalier-se er jardin hag a c'haloupas a-dreuz hag a-hed evit klask o eskob kollet. Kaer o devoe klask ne gavjont den.

Lod all a lavar oa aet anezhañ e-unan eus e eskopti, a-raok m'oa en em gavet an archerien, an Aotrou de la Marche, goude m'oa bet kuzuliet war gement-se gant e veleien ha gant an dud all a Gastell a yoa en-dro dezhañ.

Pehini eus an div istor-se eo an hini wir? Ne ouzon ket: Kastelliz a gont anezho o-div. N'eus forzh penaos, an Aotrou de la Marche a dec'has da vihanañ, rak n'en doa ket a c'hoant e vije skuilhet evitañ ur berad zoken eus a wad e vugale, hag e yeas da guzhat da di an Itron Jegou du Laz.

Translation

The Battle of Kergidu, *1877* (Extract)

The state of affairs was even worse for His Lordship de la Marche, bishop of Saint-Pol-de-Léon. Not only did he have, like all other bishops, to swear he would obey the new laws, but his diocese was taken away from him. The decision had been taken in Paris by top government men without referring to our Holy Father, the Pope. The men in charge in Morlaix explained to him that he was no longer bishop, as the diocese of Saint-Pol-de-Léon had been abolished, so said the law.

Bishop de la Marche did not give in. He wrote a long and very courageous letter to the authorities in Morlaix, stating that he had been named bishop of Saint-Pol-de-Léon by the Pope, our Holy Father, by the will of God, and that his only allegiance as a bishop was to the pope. Lay people had nothing to say about the duties of his office; only the Pope, our Holy Father, could get rid of the bishopric and not the people who must themselves obey the Church and the bishops, as a bishop is the shepherd of the diocese. It is not up to a shepherd to obey his sheep, but up to the sheep to obey their shepherd. In addition, when God orders one thing and laymen an opposing one, one must obey God and contravene human laws. In his conclusion he wrote: "The Pope, our Holy Father, has linked my name to the diocese of Saint-Pol-de-Léon, and your own laws will not prevent this."

The faith was not yet stifled in everyone's heart: the judges in Morlaix were astounded on reading such a courageous letter and left Bishop de la Marche in peace for a while. He was not troubled for about a year. But then, the Paris authorities ordered those in Morlaix to remove Bishop de la Marche from his diocese and send him to prison. Monsieur de la Fruglaye, from Keranrous manor in Plouiann – Monsieur de Champagny, his grandson who does so much good in the countryside is now living there – sent one of his brave servants to tell him to be on his guard, as the order to arrest him had arrived in Morlaix. Monsieur de la Marche was grieved but he did not flee: he did not wish to abandon his flock. The following day, a gendarme arrived in Saint-Pol-de-Léon. In his leather bag was the order from government to Monsieur de la Marche, former bishop of Leon, to leave his diocese.

When the news was heard in Saint-Pol-de-Léon, everyone was distressed. The country folk came to town and went straight to the bishop's palace to see the bishop, their father; town people followed them. They all said: "Your Lordship, stay with us! Don't be afraid of the Morlaix gendarmes. None of them will be able to arrest you unless they walk over our dead bodies, because we shall give the last drop of our blood rather than abandon you."

Tears were running from Bishop de la Marche's eyes as he heard such brave words. From the threshold of his palace he said to the people:

"Return home, my good children, I shall seek advice from my vicars-general and from other good men who are here, in the palace. God bless you for the love you show me. I will never forget you. I will not abandon you if I can."

After returning to his office, Bishop de la Marche asked the priests and the high ranking people of Saint-Pol who had by now gathered in the palace what he should do. All of them, seeing how things were going, advised him to flee. If he did not do so, it was obvious that the people of Saint-Pol and the gendarmes would fight one another, and then the Bishop would be responsible for many deaths. This piece of advice distressed Bishop de la Marche, and yet he complied with it for the love of his flock. He did not wish that a single drop of blood should be shed because of him.

How did he flee? I would not know, to tell you the truth. Some say that twenty-four gendarmes, sent from Morlaix, came upon him in his palace in order to send him to prison at the time when he was in his office writing his last recommendations and his farewell to the people of the diocese. Bishop de la Marche asked them what they wanted:

"We have come to fetch you and bring you to prison in Morlaix," said the chief gendarme.

"Fetch me and send me to prison? Whatever for?"

"You have already been told; it is because you do not want to obey the laws of the government. Come on! Get off your chair and come with us."

"Surely you will give me a few minutes to change my clothes and gather a shirt or two before I accompany you. Would you wait here for a little while, on the landing, while I go and do this?"

The head gendarme, with the efficient glance of his profession, examined the room closely. As he could only see books, lots of books, side by side, he said to the Bishop that he would wait for him. Then, thinking that he had been waiting for a long time, he opened the door. Unfortunately, there was no bishop to be seen; he must have flown away...

This caused a commotion among the gendarmes; they all came into the room; they searched through all the nooks and crannies. One of them, looking closer, saw a row of books which was not aligned with the others. He pulled on the bookshelf and let out a scream. He found a door and, behind it, a staircase which led down to the garden. In single file, the gendarmes, like hunting dogs making their way through a gap partially blocked by stones, rushed down the staircase to the garden and ran hither and thither searching for their lost bishop. Although they looked everywhere, they found no one.

Other people say that Bishop de la Marche left his palace of his own accord, before the arrival of the gendarmes, thus following the advice of the priests and of the people of Saint-Pol who were with him.

Which of these two stories is the true one? I don't know. The inhabitants of Saint-Pol tell them both. All that is known is that Bishop de la Marche did manage to flee, as he did not want to shed a single drop of the blood of his flock, and that he went to hide in Madame Jegou du Laz's house.

Yann-Vari Branelleg

Testamant an Aotrou Branellec, *c.1794* (Lodenn)

Douguet eo an arret,
Nen deus mui a dermen,
Da choas d'in eo roet
A-zaou gant al lezen
Pe renonç dam fei,
Pe bea dibennet;
O divis cruel ha calet!

Mes me choas ar maro
Eus a greiz ma c'halon
Ha sur ha brefero
Ar guir Riligion
Da ul lezen impi,
Deun doctrin ampoeson
Sourcen eus ar berdition.

Ma c'hrim ha ma zorfed
Dirac an nation
Eo ma meus preseguet
An aviel guirion
Ha tretet he lezen

Demeus a schismatiq
Hac ouspen eus a heritiq.

Na breseguen netra
Nen deo guir christinen
Gat ma goat er sinan
Me er graï laouen;
Ya, eur poeson eo,
Hag eur poeson marvel
Pa ro ar maro eternel.

Pobl dign eus ar drues
Ur weich choas quen mervel
Quitta da zallente
Distro dan aviel
Malheur mil guech malheur
Dan nep ne heuillio quet
Rac assur evezo daonet.

[...]

Adieu pobl a Gastel
Ma finitantet ques,
Bezit ato fidel,
Ha dalc'hit mad do feis,
Nep a gol ar vues
Evit lezen Doue
Tra certen enem savete.

Adieu, ma breur Guillou
Adieu breur Gabriel,
Arretet ho tailou;
Er Religion santel
E cafot motivou
A gonsolation
Heuliet hy agreis ho kalon.

Ya sur, madoue
Me arra volontier
Eus ma c'horf, ma bue
Ur sacrifis antier,
Bizit doch agreabl;
Pardonet, me oped

Tud coupabl ha tud revolted.

Ma breudeur beleyen
Neve merseriet
Poc'h eus ho curunen
Sur en eon recevet,
Pedet evageste
Da roi din ho courach
M'am bezo ar memes partag.

Translation

Testament of Jean-Marie Branellec, *c.1794* (Extract)

The sentence has been passed,
There is no more time left.
I am given the choice
According to the law
Either to renounce my faith
Or to be beheaded;
Oh, cruel and hard choice!

But I choose death
From the bottom of my heart
And I, surely will prefer
The true Religion
To an impious law,
To a poisoned doctrine,
The source of perdition.

My crime and my offence
In front of the nation
Is that I have preached
The true Gospel
And that I have called the law
Schismatic
And even heretic.

I do not preach anything;
Which is not truly Christian.
I sign this with my blood
I shall do it joyfully;
Yes, it is a poison,
And a mortal poison

For it gives eternal death.

People worthy of pity,
Once again before dying,
Abandon your blindness,
Return to the Gospel.
Woe, yes, woe betide
Those who will not follow it,
For they certainly will be damned.

[...]

Adieu, people of St-Pol,
My dear penitents.
Always be faithful,
And keep well to your faith.
Whoever loses his life
In the name of God's law
Certainly saves himself.

Adieu, my brother Guillaume;
Adieu, my brother Gabriel,
Stop crying;
In the Holy Religion
You will find grounds
For solace.
Follow it with all your heart.

Yes, certainly, my Lord,
I willingly agree
To the full sacrifice
Of my body, of my life;
Take them in your trust;
Forgive, I pray you,
The culprits and the revolted.

My brother priests
Recently martyred
You have certainly received
Your crowns in heaven.
Pray for me
To give me your courage
So that I meet the same destiny.

Erwan ar Moal

Kloareg Kersaozon, *1927* (Lodenn)

Ar 27 a viz meurs, ar bla 1793, e oa tud a vil-vern wardro lezvarn Lanuon. An hevelep trouz a oa gante evel gant ar mor war an tornod, pep-hini o lavaret e c'hir, uheloc'h pe izeloc'h.

– Gwashoc'h 'vit paouez a rêr, eme unan, o stourm ouz ar gouarnamant. Ouz hennez ne c'honeer nep gwech.

– Goneer! eme eun all o tremen, ha c'hoaz e vo gret hirie!

– Gwell eo d'ac'h serri ho keno, pôtr yaouank; 'n hon mesk aman 'zo polis hep gouzout d'imp.

– Ar polis? Me rey ar polis, me, aman hirie! 'me ar pôtr yaouank, ken rok ha tra.

– Marvad, heman 'zo meo, 'me eun ozac'h, goustadik, rak n'houlle bean klevet na gant ar polis na gant ar pôtr yaouank.

– Penôs? 'me eur Yan bennak, n'anveez ket te hennez? Hennez zo Kevarek, breur mager Kloareg Kersaozon, an hini a vo barnet aman breman-zouden-Doue. Marvad, p'an eus klevet lavaret e oa paket ar c'hloareg, eo deut da welet penôs e vo e gont.

– Arsa, kont d'in 'ta reiz, mar gouies, perak eo bet tapet ar c'hloareg-ze?

– Dilun diwezan e oa an invantor en e barouz. Kannaded ar gouarnamant a zo êt di evel el lec'hiou-all, da gemer roll madou an iliz, evit gwerzan anê diwezatoc'h. Ar c'hloareg an eus difennet toull-dor an iliz, hen e-unan, rak e gamaradou 'oa tec'het rak ar jendarmed. Kroget zo bet warnan, ha hirie 'vo barnet aman. Darn a lavar e vo dibennet.

– Dibennet o deus eur roue, perak ne dibennfent ket eur c'hloareg?

– Peuc'h! eme unan eus ar gompagnunez; aman 'z eus eur gwaz o tont hag a zo da zizfiout anean.

Setu pep-hini a viras e deod hag en em lakas da zellet endro d'ean. Mes war an taol e savas mesk war-zu penn ar blasen: jendarmed war varc'h a vije gwelet o tont, eun daouzek anê. Dre ma tostajont, e weljod re-all war droad e-kreiz tre ar re war varc'h; gant ar re-ze e oa ar c'hloareg.

Bean 'oa heman eun den bihan dister, tres eur bugel warnean, hag hen pevar bla warn-ugent, eur stum d'ean dizrouk ha dizeblant, nemet pa zave e zaoulagad war an dud dre ma tremene; neuze e kemere eun êr poaniet ha nec'het, hag e seblante furchal e-touez ar bobl da glask unan bennak.

Den na ranne eur gir war hent ar jendarmed: an trouz a oa tavet, sioul an holl evel ar maro.

Pan eas ar c'hloareg el lezvarn, ar bobl, avat, a reas evel divatan: a gement korn a oa d'ar blasen e sachjont war dresek toull an nor, en eur voutan, evel pa vije bet eno eur men arc'hant da c'honit. An trouz a hadkomansas, mes e tavas adarre mik pa gomzas prezidant al lezvarn. Ar re 'oa chomet er-meaz, (hag e oa manet an darn-vuian), a zavas o skouarn da êsat klevet a-dreuz d'ar prenechou digor.

Ar prezidant a c'houllas digant ar c'hloareg e hano; disklerian a reas petra 'oa tamallet d'ean; ar c'hloareg na dizanzavas netra.

– Perak, eme ar prezidant, ho peus-hu êsaet stourm ouz ar polis? C'hoant ho poa da dennan warnoc'h sellou ho konsorted ha da voutan anê war ar jendarmed?

Kersaozon a respontas:

– Ma c'honsorted a oa tec'het endro. 'Vidon-me, ne glaskan ket bean sellet mat gant den, mes c'houllan ket ive bean sellet fall, dre ma vijen chomet a-dre. N'am eus ket a geun, o vean kloareg, da vean stourmet evit difenn ma iliz. Ma 'm ije bet eur fuzuilh, am ije grêt impli anezi.

– Eur fuzuilh? Ha te ne vijes ket 'vit he dougen!

Ar vouez a oa deut eus a vesk an dud.

Ar c'hloareg a respontas dak:

– Gwir eo, 'vit ar ganfarded a oa eno ne oa ezom nemet euz ar vaz!

– Bôn! kloareg!

Ar wech-man adarre, unan eus an dud an evoa komzet.

Ar c'hloareg a daolas e zellou warnean hag a reas d'ean eur minc'hoarz; e vreur-mager a oa eno, hed ter gammad dioutan. Raktal e laouenas.

– Jendarmed, eme ar prezidant; piou bennak a gomzo, kroget warnean!

Ar varn na badas ket pell; an advokad a gomzas kaer, mes ne oe ket chilaouet. Ar c'hloareg a oe barnet da chom er prizon, da c'hortoz mont da Zant-Brieg; eno 'oa arru ar c'hilhotin.

O vont er-maez, triwec'h jendarm oa adarre war e dro. Koulskoude, pa bôzas e dreid er ru, unan a gavas an tu da darc'ha eun tôl gantan. Kersaozon a zizroas; mes kerkent-all, Kevarek a digoueas a-dreuz d'an engrouez ha d'ar jendarmed; kregi reas dre e ziouskoa en den an evoa skoet, hag e reas gantan eun dro evel eur c'haz-meo:

– Gôut a rez, emean, oun-me breur hennez?..

Ha kerkent hag ar gomz, an taol; hag ar c'hanfard d'an traou, evel eur pen-ejen dindan an horz.

– Kroget war ar re-ze! eme mestr an archerien.

– Adrê, jendarmed! eme Kevarek, a-bouez e benn. – Hola, pôtred!

Dek pe daouzek gwaz, tud a nerz ha tud iskwit, a'n em gavas souden e-kichen an archerien. Seiz a oe stlapet diwar o c'hezeg ken lip ha tra. Kevarek an evoa tennet digant unan e zabren hag a c'hoarie anei ken ne vije gwelet nemet eul luc'heden endro d'ean, evel ma ra eur skod tân en dorn eur bugel.

Kevarek, gant e zaou zorn hag e zaou droad, an ije darbaret c'houec'h den difall; mes pa vije eur c'hleze 'n e zorn, an diaoul hen e-unan na vije ket deut warnean. En eur skei, e souze dirak an tri archer a oa war e dro, hag e lavare d'ar c'hloareg, manet eno evel eun den notet:

– Tap eur marc'h ha touch d'ar gêr!

Hen e-unan a zouze war-zu ar c'hezeg. An dud a'n em voute evel ma ra an toliou-mor gant an avel grenv. Kompagnunez Kevarek a skoe start gant o fennou-baz; tri ane 'oa mestr da gezeg; mes archerien-all a dostae.

– War lein! war lein! eme Kevarek. Dao! dao! hag hen o tigori e benn d'eur jendarm hag e gof d'eun all, ha war varc'h! Ar c'hloareg a dap 'vel eur bugel a-dreuz war e jo:

– Plas! Plas!

Tri varc'h-all, e dud war o c'hein, 'oa war e lerc'h hag a dripe war ar pave hag a vounte gant o bruched. Ar penbaz hag ar sabren a yee endro evel freilhou. Mes ar bobl a roe toull da Gevarek ha d'e bôtred; d'ar jendarmed, avat, ne rent ket.

Ekreiz an dourni hag ar safar, e luient 'ne, e rent d'ê kouean, hag i o-unan a gouee gante. Malloziou ha toliou a valee stank evel ar grizilh etre ar jendarmed hag an dud. Pôtred Kevarek, ar re ane n'o devoa ket tapet a gezeg, a dapas eur roud-all da'n em jach: kollet e oent en engroez.

Neuze, etre Lanuon ha Ploubêr, e oe kas war an henchou: pevar a gezeg arôk ha nao warlerc'h, gant archerien. Ar re-man, souchet war o c'hezeg; ar re-ze, o tornan gant o zreid hag o daouarn, ken ma leze o loened, war o lerc'h, eun eonen ru war boultren an hent. Tostaat a rent d'eur c'hoad. Kevarek a huchas war e dud:

– Da Doull-an-Ouc'h breman zouden!... Lezet ar c'hezeg war wrimen ar c'hoad...

Eï do! Eï do!...

Pa oent arru en doare eus ze, o pozjont 'n eun tôl krenn. An anevaled a vennas torri o divesker. Lampat e traou na oe ket hirr, ha d'ar red d'ar c'hoad. Klevet e oe ar jendarmed o youc'hal; ar re-man all a rede dindan ar brankou, pleget o choug, o fri rez d'an douar.

– Lez int da zont! eme Kevarek.

A-boan o devoa gret eur c'hart leo, hep ne oa meneg a netra, an hini kentan a oe kollet ar gwel warnean; ar re-all na spontjont ket, ha pep hini d'e dro a voutas e ziouhar etre diou wrien eun derven vras, en eun toull konifl, hag a dremenas evel eul lizer er vouest. Kevarek, an diwezan, a daolas plê mat ma ne oa chomet roud ebet war o lerc'h; boutan reas e zabren 'n e rôk; goude e hadtennas e benn ermeaz an toull da chileo hag-en e klevje ar jendarmed. Seblant ebet! Red eo lavaret penda-ben ar wirione, e tennas ive e deod warzu d'ê 'rôk disken en e guz.

Hogen, a-boan e oa d'ean 'n em glenket, eur pôtr yaouank, 'n e c'hourvez war hed tôl, 'drek eun torkad drez, a zavas da zellet gant eur pikol daoulagad dilontet.

– Ken gwir 'vel eo ma hano Al Louarn, emean, 'man Kevarek 'barz ar pech.

Translation

Cleric Kersaozon, *1927* (Extract)

On the 23rd March 1793, a huge crowd had gathered in front of the Courts of Justice in Lannion. The noise was like that of the sea breaking on the cliffs as everyone had something to whisper, say or shout out loud.

"One could do worse than stop fighting the government," said someone. "You can never win against them."

"Not true, and we shall prove it again today," replied a passerby.

"You'd better keep quiet, young man. There are policemen hiding among us."

"Policemen? I shall police this place today!" replied the young man arrogantly.

"He must be drunk," said another in a low voice, in case he was overheard either by the police or by the young man in question..

"What!" said someone else, "You don't know him? This is Kevarek, the foster-brother of Cleric Kersaozon, the one who is going to be sentenced here, right now. When he heard that the cleric had been arrested, he must have decided to come and see what was going to happen to him."

"Well then! Tell me straight, if you can, why has this cleric been caught?"

"Last Monday, the inventory of the parish goods was to be carried out. The government's envoys went there, as everywhere else, to make a list of the church belongings, in order to sell them later. But the cleric prevented them from entering. He was on his own, as his companions had scampered off before the arrival of the police. He was arrested and today he is going to be sentenced. Some say that he will be guillotined."

"They have guillotined a king. Why wouldn't they guillotine a cleric?"

"Quiet!" said a voice in the crowd. "The man who is coming is not reliable."

They all stopped talking and were looking around, when, suddenly, chaos broke out at the top of the square: it seemed that a dozen or so mounted gendarmes had arrived. As they drew nearer, the onlookers saw, between the two rows of horses, other gendarmes on foot. The cleric was with them.

The cleric was an insignificant little man who looked like a child although he was twenty-four years old. He appeared innocuous and indifferent, except that, when he looked at the people as he walked past them, there was a pained and worried look on his face. He seemed to be searching amongst the crowd for a particular person.

No one spoke as the gendarmes went past. All noise stopped. There was deadly silence.

However, when the cleric entered the court, the onlookers seemed to recover consciousness. From all corners of the square, they pushed and shoved their way towards the door, as though it led to a mountain of coins they could get their hands on. The noise picked up again but stopped again suddenly when the President of the Court started talking. Those who had stayed outside – and that was true for most of them – craned their necks to be within earshot by the open windows.

The President asked the cleric for his name and read out the charges. The cleric did not object to anything.

"Why did you try to interfere with the work of the gendarmes?" asked the President. "Did you want to attract the attention of your colleagues and make them attack the gendarmes?"

"My colleagues had already fled," replied Kersaozon. "As for myself, I do not look for anyone's good opinion, but neither did I want to be badly thought of, should I have stepped back. As a cleric, I do not regret having fought to defend my church. If I had had a gun, I would have used it."

"A gun? You're not strong enough to carry one!" said someone in the crowd.

"That is true," replied the cleric, quick as a flash, "but considering the rogues who were there, a stick would have been enough!"

"Well said, Cleric!" said another voice in the crowd.

The cleric turned his eyes towards the man and gave him a smile. His foster brother was there, no more than three steps away from him. He immediately felt better.

"Gendarmes!" said the President; "If anyone else interrupts, arrest them!"

The trial did not last long. The lawyer for the defence spoke well but was not listened to. The cleric was sentenced to prison before being transferred to Saint-Brieuc where the guillotine had arrived.

When he left the court, eighteen policemen were again surrounding him. However, when he stepped onto the street, someone found a way to give him a blow. Kersaozon deflected it. Immediately, Kevarek made his way through the crowd and the gendarmes. He took hold of the shoulders of the man who had struck the blow, and made him spin round like a top:

"Don't you know that I am this man's brother?" he said.

A blow accompanied the words; the attacker fell down like an ox under the weight of a burden.

"Arrest them!" said the chief gendarme.

"Step back, gendarmes!" screamed Kevarek. "Come now, boys!"

Ten to twelve strong and fast men suddenly appeared at the policemen's sides. Seven of these were dragged down from their horses without further ado. Kevarek had taken one of the gendarmes' sabre, and was twirling it so furiously that, like a child waving a piece of charcoal, one could only see glinting flashes around him.

With his bare hands and feet Kevarek could overcome six strong men; but put a sword in his hand, and the devil himself could not get the better of him.

As he continued to strike, he was drawing back from the three gendarmes fighting against him. He then said to the cleric who was rooted to the spot:

"Get yourself a horse and get home!"

He was himself stepping back towards the horses. The crowd was heaving like high waves in a strong wind. Kevarek's men were striking hard with their cudgels; three of them had taken hold of the horses; but other gendarmes were approaching.

"On horseback! On horseback!" said Kevarek. Swish! Swish! He hit a gendarme in the head and disemboweled another before jumping on a horse. He picked up the cleric as though he were a child and laid him across his horse.

"Make room! Make room!"

Three of his men, now on horseback, followed him. The horses were stamping their hooves on the cobble-stones and pushing forward. Cudgels and sabres were twirling in the air like threshing tools. The crowd was making way for Kevarek and his men, but not for the gendarmes.

As the racket and din were going on, the people poked fun at the gendarmes, made them fall from their horses and tumbled down with them. Curses and blows fell like hailstones on both sides. Kevarek's men, those who had not managed to get a horse, found another way to vanish: they lost themselves in the crowd.

And then, between Lannion and Ploubezre, the chase took to the roads: four horse in front and nine, with gendarmes on their backs, going after them. These were crouching on their horses while Kevarek's men were spurring their horses so hard with their feet and hands that they left behind them, on the dust of the road, a trail of red foam. On approaching a wood, Kevarek shouted to his men:

"To Toull-an-Ouc'h! Right now! Leave your horses at the edge of the wood!" Gee up! Gee up!

Once there, they came to such an abrupt halt that the animals nearly broke their legs. The men immediately jumped off and ran into the wood. The gendarmes could be heard yelling as the others dashed underneath the branches, bent in half, their noses to the ground.

"Let them come and get us!" said Kevarek.

Hardly had they covered a quarter of a league, without exchanging a single word, when the first man disappeared from sight. Not that it frightened the others as, one by one, they pushed their legs between two roots of a big oak tree, in a kind of rabbit hole, slipping down it like a letter in the letter-box. Kevarek, holding the rear, checked carefully for traces of their passage and pushed his sabre in front of him; his head then poked up again from the hole as he pricked up his ears to find out if he could hear the gendarmes. No sign of them! But to tell the full truth, he also pulled out his tongue in their direction before vanishing into the hiding-hole.

However, hardly had he been lost from sight that a young man, who had been lying low behind a thorn bush during this commotion, stood up, his eyes nearly popping out of his head.

"As true as my name is Al Louarn," he said, "Kevarek is trapped."

Kervarker

Ar Chouanted, *1839*

> Er re goh hag er merc'hed hag er botred vihan
> Ha re pere n'int ket goest de vonet d'en emgann,
> A laro enn ho zier, abarh mont de gousket,
> Ur *Pater* hag eunn *Ave* eùit er Chouanted.
>
> Er Chouanted zou tud vad, hi zou gwir grechenion,
> Saùet de zifenn hon Bro klouz el hun beleion;
> Mar skoont ar tal hou tour, m'hou ped, digouret d'e!
> Doue else, me zud vad, digorai d'hoc'h, eunn de.
>
> Julian bleù-ru a lare d'he vamm goh, ur mitin:
> – "Me ia me ged Tinteniak, pe monet a blij d'ein

– De deu vreur dez me losket, ha te me losk eùe!
Mes, mar plij d'id de vonet, ra de renai Doue"!

Pe zeie er Chouanted ez a bob korn a Vreih,
A Dreger hag a Gerne hag a Wenned ileih,
Er re C'hlaz digoueh get-he, e maner Koatlogen,
Ez a gosteeu Bro-C'hall, tri mil enn ur vanden.

– "Chetu enn heur e sonein, chetu enn heur sonet,
Me emgafemp, eur wech c'hoah, ged er c'hoh soudarded.
Bec'h ar-n-hoc'h, potred a Vreih, bec'h ar-n-hoc'h, ha gwelemp!
Mar m'ann Diol enn-tu get-he, ma Doue enn tu gen-emp"!

Ha pe oant deit de grogein, hen darc'he el-unn oac'h:
Get he bop a vuzul vad, get hen meit he benn-bah,
He benn-bah hag he chaplet ez a Zantez-Anna,
Ha kemed e dosteie, a oa pilet get ha.

Ha touellet ker oa he dok, ha toullet e chupen,
Ha loud hag he vleù troc'het ged eunn tol a sabren,
Hag er goed a zivere demeuz toull he goste,
Ha n'arzaoue e tarc'hout, hag oc'hpenn e kane.

Ken n'hen gwelez ket mui tamm, hag hen gwelez endro,
Hag hen tennet a goste didan ur ween dero,
E ouilein leih he galon, chouket get hon he benn,
Enn Eutreu Tinteniak por a-drez ar he varlen.

Ha p'achiue enn emgann ar dro enn nozeoh,
Chouanted a zidoste, re ieuang ha re goh,
Hag a denne hou zokeu, hag a lare else:
– "Chetu ma goneit gen-emp, ha hon, siouah! marue!"

Translation

The Chouans, *1839*

Old people, women and young boys,
All those who are not able to go and fight,
Will say in their homes, before going to sleep,
A *Pater* and an *Ave* for the Chouans.

The Chouans are good people. They are true Christians
Who have risen to defend our Country as well as our priests;

Should they knock on your door, I beg you, open it!
God, my dear people, will also open the door for you, one day.

Red-haired Julien[1] said to his old mother, one morning:
– "I am going with Tinténiac, for I want to go!"
– "Your two brothers have left me, and you leave me too!
But, if you want to go, may God be with you!"

As the Chouans were arriving from all corners of Brittany,
From Tregor, from Cornouaille, and many from the Vannes region,
The Republicans met with them, at the Manor of Coëtlogon.
These were coming from France, three thousand of them.

– "The hour is coming, the hour has come,
When we shall fight, once more, these miserable soldiers.
Be brave, children of Brittany, be brave, and let us see!
If the Devil is on their side, then God is with us!"

When they started fighting, Julien fought like a man:
Everyone had a good gun, but he only had his cudgel,
His cudgel and his rosary from Saint Anne,
Yet anyone who came near him was defeated by him.

His hat was pierced many times, his jacket too,
A sabre blow had cut some of his hair.
He was shedding blood from a wound in his side,
But he never ceased to strike; what is more, he was singing.

I no longer saw him, and then saw him again,
He had retired under an oak tree,
And was shedding many tears, his head bowed;
Poor Monsieur de Tinténiac[2] resting across his lap.

When the battle finished, at nightfall,
The Chouans approached, young and old.
They took off their hats, saying these words:
– "We have won the battle, but, alas, he is dead!"

[[1]*Red-haired Julien was one of the brothers of Georges Cadoudal, the famous Chouan leader executed in 1804.* [2]*De Tinténiac was also a leading Chouan.*]

The Two World Wars

During the first world war a million Bretons fought for France. A quarter of them did not return. As Breton troops were often used on the front line they were decimated at twice the rate of the national average. On the other hand, contact with France and French people of other regions did more than compulsory schooling to integrate Brittany into the French State and accelerate the decline of the Breton language which parents saw as a handicap they had no wish to transmit to their children. The Breton clergy also encouraged patriotism and set the example: many priests worked as stretcher-bearers on the front line while many nuns worked as nurses in field hospitals.

Yann-Ber Kalloc'h, a poet from the Vannes region who died on the battlefield in 1917, thought that, at the end of the war, the sacrifice and faithfulness of Bretons would be recognised by the French State. He drew up a petition which he intended to send to the Paris government asking for Breton and the History of Brittany to be taught in schools. Subsequent requests made in 1919 by the Marquis de L'Estourbeillon to Members of the Peace Conference and to Wilson, President of the USA, fell on deaf ears.

The PNB (Parti Nationaliste Breton) was founded in 1919 and their journal, *Breiz Atao* (Brittany forever) also includes many calls for the cultural renewal of Brittany. The party's true agenda however was the creation of an independent fascist State. Its rulers adopted the old IRA philosophy: "the enemy of my enemy is my friend", and openly supported German policy decisions before and during the second world war.

The 1940 armistice was generally welcomed in Brittany. However, as months and years went by and the demands of the German occupying troops increased, many Breton men took refuge in the 'maquis' and joined the Resistance. After the assassination of a prominent nationalist priest, Perrot, by a communist resistant, the 'Bezen Perrot,' a small auxiliary police force of the Waffen SS – which according to Yann Fouéré had been originally founded to defend cultural nationalists who were being assassinated in the name of the Resistance – waged an open war on resistants and the warring factions within Brittany began to settle old scores. After the liberation of France, the French Authorities arrested over a thousand Bretons and began purging Brittany of so-called 'collaborators' who were ruthlessly hunted down, interned in camps and sent to court to face either the death penalty or civil degradation and banishment from the region. In fact, many of those arrested had done no more than attend a Breton language evening class or subscribe to a Breton magazine.

Abeozen

Dremm an Ankou, *1942* (Lodenn)

The action in the following extract from his war novel, Dremm an Ankou, *takes place in 1916 near Verdun.*

Dirazo "Esnes" a zispak he dismantrou a-liou gant an uloc'h hag ar c'heuneud los-ket. Izelaat a ra an deiz, ma kemer pep tra eun doare truezus. Kleier an iliz a zo diskaret war lez ar straed veur. C'houez ar rost a glever gant an tiez, evel pa vefe o paouez laza an tan gwall.

– "Rakkambr an Ifern," eme Erwan etre e zent. "Piou a soñj d'ezañ emaomp e miz Mae, miz ar bleuniou!"

Tost d'ar vered ar serjant-fourrer a zo aet tre en eur c'heo da c'houlenn diskle-riaduriou. Setu heñ er-maez.

– "Amañ tostik, war an dorgenn, emañ ar rann foziou a dleomp derc'hel."

Hag e savont a-dreuz al liorzou gwastet, gant o gwez mogn, strobet a orjal dreinek. Erruet int. War lez ar foz, kouezet a-c'houen e gein, eur pikol morian – lazet abaoe peur? – a zigor war an oabl goullo, gwenn e zaoulagad divuhez. Nozi a ra. War an araok, n'ouzer dare pelec'h, eur soudard gloazet a c'halv e gamaladed war e sikour. Skuisoc'h-skuiz e sav e glemm er serr-noz kridiennus. Soñjou pennfollet a ziroll e penn Erwan. Diskennet eo an daou serjant en eur c'heo bennak, hag heñ, skuiz-maro, ken gwiridik e dreid dindanañ ma n'hell mui chom en e sav, a c'hourvez war lez ar foz, e benn war e sac'h evel ar morian-hont. Distrempet eo an douar gant ar glao a ra bep noz. Daoust ha santout a ra Erwan an anoued o tont d'e gorf diouz ar pri, a-dreuz e zilhad, gleb gant ar c'houezenn? Marteze. Met petra 'vern! en em rei a ra da gousket.

★★★

Dihunet trumm eo bet gant ar safar. Sevel a ra, dispourbellet e zaoulagad en e benn. Sklerijennet eo an noz teñval gant eur skleur euzus. Aze en traoñ, dismantrou "Esnes" a zo an tan gwall enno. Obuziou a bep seurt, a bep nerz, e-leiz a re loskus en o zouez, a darz dibaouez.

– "Rakkambr an Ifern?" eme Erwan. "An Ifern end-eeun, ya!"

Hag ez en em sant dister ha dinerz dirak an arvest braouac'hus ma n'eus den d'hen emskeudenni nemet ar re, siouaz! o deus paret o daoulagad warnañ.

– "An dennadeg-harz war ar vourc'h," eme eur vouez e-kichen Erwan. "Deiz ha noz e krog evelse, bep eur, aliesoc'h a-wechou. Daou zervez 'zo, hon eil batailhon a zo bet paket gantañ. Eun den war dri a zo chomet e-barz, gloazet pe lazet."

Eur soudard eo, deut er-maez eus ar c'heo gant ar serjeant Rivet, a gomz evel-se. Emañ o prienta e sac'h da vont kuit.

– "Hag ar paour kaez a zo aze en tu bennak o c'hervel, ne daio den d'e gerc'hat?" a c'houlenn Erwan.

– "Eo, m'en deus unan bennak c'hoant da chom da vervel gantañ!" eme ar soudard en eur samma e sac'h hag e fuzuilh, hag ez a kuit.

★★★

Deut eo Rivet e-kichen Erwan ha, skoaz-ouz-skoaz, e sellont ouz an tantad boemus, leun a darziou kurun. Dre aze eo e tle dont ar gompagnunez dizale. Dre aze eo d'ezo mont war hec'h ambroug.

– "Ar c'houlz eo," eme ar serjant-fourrer, tost d'ezo. "Ret mat eo ez afe unan ac'hanoc'h diouztu."

– "Piou a gav deoc'h a c'hello mont a-dreuz eur seurt dislonkerez tan hag houarnaj?" eme Erwan c'houero, o soñjal en e gamalad Livier, lazet e Posen-Champagn. "Fur e ve gortoz ma loskaio eun tamm an dennadeg-harz."

Munutennou a dremen, e-leiz pe nebeut? Hini anezo ne soñj sellout ouz e vontr, nemet ar fourrer, marteze, rak e vouez a glever adarre, startoc'h.

– "Ret eo! Ret mat eo!" emezañ, o soñjal e gourdrouzou ar c'habiten ma ne ve ket aet eeun an traou.

– "Aesoc'h eo gourc'hemenn eget ober!" eme Erwan outañ e-unan.

Sellout a ra ouz Rivet. Rivet a sell outañ. O daoulagad a dle beza evel re an dud kondaonet d'ar maro, ha Rivet, bet e Maroko, bet gloazet e "Montmirail", e penn kenta ar brezel, a lavar sioula ma c'hall:

– "Mont a ran da welout." Hag heñ kuit.

★★★

Kouezet eo Erwan adarre war an douar yen. Ne chom ket gantañ nerz a-walc'h zoken evit sellout.

. . . .

– "Erwan," eme mouez wenn ar serjant Rivet harp outañ, "n'em eus ket gallet kaout va hent!"

– "Ret eo mont! Ret eo," eme raktal mouez hegasus ar fourrer.

– "Deomp!" eme Erwan imoret, hag e sav war an dachenn, diwisket gantañ e harnez soudard nemet e dokarn hag e voestl-vaskl. Diskenn a ra d'ar red etrezek an tangwall. Eul lamm. Ger Kambron a darz etre e vuzellou. Eun eil. Eun trede. Luziet brao e-kreiz eur rouedad orjal dreinek hanter guzet er geot hir. Torret krenn eo an tiz a oa warnañ.

– "Ar serjant en deus bet aon," emezañ e-unan, "Perak n'em bije ket?"

Hag en-dro. An dennadeg-harz, avat, a baouez tamm ha tamm, pa ziskenn Erwan er foz-difenn, eo evit lavarout d'ar serjant Rivet:

– "Ne gavan ket va hent kennebeut, serjant. Ha mar dafemp hon-daou a-gevret?"

– "Deomp!" eme ar serjant sederaet. Hag e tiskennont en dro-mañ, dorn ouz dorn, evel daou vugelig o vont d'ar skol. Trouz ebet ken. Mervel a ra an tan er vourc'h. Ne dle mui beza kalz a dra da zevi er paour kaez dismantrou-se; hag e kerz an daou zen, digor eveziek o diouskouarn war-du an adreñv, ma teu ar maro ken trumm ha ken puilh, pa grog da skei. Emaint deut en tu all da "Esnes," war an hent bras a gas da "Monzéville." Azeza a reont war eur bern postou prenn a zo aze, yac'hoc'h d'ar c'horf eget an douar gleb. Hag e c'hortozont...

★★★

Ouz skleur disliv al loar o sevel a-us d'ar Run 304, e welont o tont gant an hent eur renkennad skeudou spisoc'h-spis.

– "Piou a zeu aze?" eme ar serjant.

– "Unnekvet kompagnunez," eme mouez start ar c'habiten Renaud.

Hag e savont.

– "Mat eo aet an traou ganimp betek-hen," eme ar c'habiten, en eur sellout ouz an dismantrou, c'houez ar suilh ganto. "N'eus bet den gloazet."

Hag e teuont war raok. Moueziou faez a glever er renkadou:

– "An ehan! An ehan!"

– "Skuizh an dud," eme ar c'habiten en eur drei ouz Erwan. "Daoust ha gallout a rafemp ober eun tamm ehan amañ?"– "Amañ?" eme Erwan, o skrija betek bleñ-chou e vleo. "O nann, kabiten! Mar krogfe adarre da skei an dennadeg-harz a zo bet bremaik, n'ouzon dare hag unan ac'hanomp a yafe kuit dibistig!"

Hag e kendalc'h da vale.

– "Reder an diaoul, te 'zo skañv da dreid!" a glever o c'hourgomz, gwech amañ, gwech ahont. "Amzer a-walc'h ac'h eus bet da ziskuiza e-keit ha m'edomp o poania dindan hor samm. Te, n'eo ket pounner da hini, reder an diaoul, landreant!"

Klevout a ra Erwan, moarvat; hogen ne soñj nemet fraesoc'h a se en tan-gwall leun a darziou kurun, hag e kerz, hag e kerz, ar c'habiten, hep ur ger, war e roudou, hag, adreñv, ar c'hlemmou o vont war devel. Sed amañ an iliz. Eur pennadig c'hoaz hag emaomp e-tal ar vered.

Petra c'hoarvez? Evel pa vije aet, en eun taol kont, an oabl a-bez e tammou, eo.

– "An dennadeg-harz!" eme Erwan d'an ofiser, hep trei e sell diouz e hent el liorzou.

Sell 'ta! Diskuizet krenn eo ar glemmerien. N'emañ ket ken Erwan hag ar c'habiten e penn ar gompagnunez. A-gleiz, a-zehou, en despet d'o samm, e krap ar soudarded d'ar piltrotig gant an dorgenn.

– "Paotrig! Paotrig!" eme unan en eur vont e-biou," saveteet brao ec'h eus d'imp hor c'hroc'hen, genaoueien ma'z oa ac'hanomp!"

Erruet er foz-difenn an holl a chom mantret, troet war du an ifern bouzarus, ma c'hallfent beza bet ennañ o youc'hal o garmadenn diweza, paneve...

Hag e sell ar c'habiten Renaud, hir-hir, hep ranna grik, ouz e reder yaouank m'en deus talvezet e spont, fenoz, o buhez, evit eur pennadig c'hoaz da vihana, da gement a dud.

Translation

In The Face of Death, *1942* (Extract)

In front of them, the town of Esnes displayed its dust and burnt wood coloured ruins. Daylight was fading and everything looked miserable. The church bells had been blown to the edge of the main street. A smell of burning hovered over the houses, as though a fire had just been put out.

"It is the gateway to Hell," said Erwan between his teeth. "Who could possibly think we are in May, the month of flowers!"

The quartermaster sergeant had gone into an underground shelter near the churchyard to get his orders. He was now emerging from it.

"The section of trenches that we have to hold are close by, on the hill."

They set off across the ravaged fields lined with tree stumps wrapped in barbed wire. They reached their goal. On the edge of a trench, a huge black soldier laid on his back. When had he been killed? The whites of his lifeless eyes were open on the empty sky. Night was falling. Towards the frontline, nobody knew exactly where, a wounded soldier was calling his comrades for help. His cries were getting fainter and fainter in the chilly dusk. Frightening thoughts rushed through Erwan's mind. The two sergeants had gone down in some shelter or other. Exhausted, his feet so painful that he could no longer stand up, Erwan laid down by the edge of the trench, his head resting on his haversack, like the black man over there. The ground was waterlogged as it had been raining every single night. Did Erwan feel the cold creeping up his body through the clay, through his clothes wet with perspiration? Maybe he did. But it did not matter. He fell asleep.

★★★

He was suddenly woken up by the din. He stood up, his eyes nearly coming out of his head. The dark night was lit by a ghastly light. Down there, the ruins of Esnes were on fire. Shells of every kind, of every strength, including numerous incendiary ones, were bursting constantly.

"The gateway to Hell?" said Erwan. "No. This is Hell, pure and simple."

He felt small and powerless in front of this terrifying scene which no one can conjure up except those who have had the bad fortune to witness it.

"It is the defensive artillery fire on the village," said a voice next to Erwan. "It is like this day and night, once every hour, sometimes more often. Two days ago, our second battalion got trapped in it. One man in three caught up in it was either wounded or killed."

These were the words of a soldier who had come out of the shelter with Sergeant Rivet. He was busy packing his haversack before leaving.

"What about the poor man who is calling somewhere over there? Will no one go and get him?" asked Erwan.

"It depends if someone wants to go and die with him!" said the soldier, picking up his kit and his gun before setting on his way.

★★★

Rivet was now standing next to Erwan and, shoulder to shoulder, they watched, spellbound, the thundering inferno. The company was meant to come through there at any moment. And their orders were to go and meet them.

"The time has come," said the quartermaster sergeant next to them. "One of you must go immediately."

"And who do you think can cross such a torrent of fire and scrap iron?" said Erwan bitterly, thinking about his friend Livier killed in Pose-Champagne. "It would be wiser to wait until the barrage of artillery has eased off a little."

Minutes passed by. Were there many of them or just a few? No one thought of looking at their watches, except maybe the quartermaster who was heard to say in a very firm voice:

"I order you to go! I order you to go!" He was thinking of his captain's reprimands if things did not go according to plan.

"It's easier to give orders than to follow them!" thought Erwan.

He looked at Rivet. Rivet looked at him. Their eyes must have been like those of people condemned to death. Rivet, who had done the Moroccan campaign and been wounded in Montmirail at the beginning of the war, said in a very low voice:

"I'll go and take a look." And off he went.

Erwan fell again on the cold earth. He did not have enough strength left to look.

. . . .

"Erwan," said the cold voice of Sergeant Rivet close to him, "I haven't been able to find a way through."

"I order you to go! I order you to go!" said the quartermaster in an irritated voice.

"I'll go!" snapped Erwan. He stood up, shed off his kit, keeping his helmet and gas mask for protection. He ran towards the fire. A jump. He swore. A second jump. A third. He got entangled in a network of barbed wire half hidden in the high grass and came to a sudden halt.

"The sergeant was frightened," he said to himself, "Why shouldn't I be too?"

He turned back. The artillery fire slowly came to a standstill. As Erwan jumped into the trench he said to Sergeant Rivet:

"I haven't been able to find a way through either. What about both of us going?"

"Let's go!" said the sergeant in a calm voice.

This time, they went down hand in hand like two children going to school. The noise had stopped. The fire was dying over the village. There could not have been many things left to set fire to in those miserable ruins. So the two men walked on, listening intently for noises coming from the rear, from the direction where death comes so quickly and so often, should the artillery fire start again. They reached the other side of Esnes and were now on the main road leading to Monzéville. They then sat on a pile of wooden poles, more welcoming to the body than the wet earth. And they waited.

***

By the shine of the pale moon rising over Hill 304 they saw a row of shadows becoming more and more distinct as they got closer to them on the road.

"Who goes there?" asked the sergeant.

"Eleventh company," said Captain Renaud's strong voice.

They stood up.

"Things have gone well for us, up to now," said the Captain looking at the ruins which smelt of burning. "No one has been wounded."

They marched on. Tired voices rose in the ranks: "Let's have a rest! Let's have a rest!"

"They are tired," said the captain turning towards Erwan. "Could we not take a rest here?"

"Here?" said Erwan, shuddering with horror. "Absolutely not, Captain! If the artillery fire we have just heard was to start again, I don't know if one of us would escape unscathed!"

He carried on walking. Mutterings rose behind his back:

"Hell runner! Light-footed bastard ! All you did was rest while we were walking with our full kit. You're carrying nothing, hell runner, loafer!"

Erwan certainly heard these remarks; but they made him concentrate even more on the possibility of a renewed thundering inferno and he carried on walking relentlessly. The captain followed him without a word and the protests coming from the rear died off. They reached the church and, a little while later, they drew level with the churchyard.

But what was happening now? It was as if the sky had suddenly been blown apart.

"The artillery fire!" said Erwan to the officer, keeping his eyes on the path among the fields.

Would you believe it! The moaners suddenly felt refreshed. Erwan and the captain were no longer leading the company. On both sides of them and in spite of their kit, the soldiers were scampering up the hill.

"Young man! Young man!" said one of them as he was overtaking him. "Well done! You have saved our skins. It was stupid of us to complain!"

Once in the trench, they all looked dismayed, their heads turned towards the deafening inferno in which they could have been screaming their last scream, if it had not been for...

Captain Renaud looked without a word and for a long, long time at his young envoy, whose fear, on this very night, had saved, at least for a little while longer, the lives of so many men.

Loeiz Herrieu

Kammdro an Ankoù, *1916* (Lodenn)

6-09-1915 – An enderv-mañ e sav penn-komz genomp ag hor stad dañjerus. Oc'hpenn 6000 soudard omp, tolpet amañ, hep tachad erbet d'en em guzhet a pa vehe tennet àrnomp. Ha nend omp nemet seizh kardlev ag an eneberion. E-pad ma komzomp, setu ur potarn é kouezh e-kreiz ar vourc'h. Lâret a zo deomp em dolpiñ a gompagnunezhoù ha monet, àr-un-dro, er-maez ag ar vourc'h, met ankouaet eo ar c'hemenn. Pep unan n'en deus soñj nemet anezhoñ e-unan. Monet a raomp daou pe dri, krommet doc'h kostez an hent-bras, ur 400 metr bennak àr hent Hans, lec'h mah eus tolpet soudarded arall. A gement tu a zo e welan tud ec'h achap, èl logod a vehe fondet o neizh, e-pad ma talc'h ar potarnoù da darzhal. Donet a ra tammoù betagomp. Setu kenseurted é tonet, ar gwad é redek doc'hte. Ha ni d'o lieniñ get hor pakadoù gronn-gouli. Reiñ a ran-me ma hani d'ur c'haezh a zo daet da gouezh e-talon, toullet e c'hoûg, e vrec'h hag e zivhar get tammoù potin. E-kreiz ar vourc'h, e klevomp re a c'harm get an droug. Ur brav a zevezh!

Da bemp eur neoazh ema ret din kas ar paperioù da sin d'ar c'hapiten. En ur zegouezh er vourc'h, e welan, e-kreiz an hent, dilhad roget, tammoù kig gwadek tud ha roñseed, neudennoù telefon a-skourr, karrezioù gwer brezhilhet. 38 a re gouliet a zo ha 8 a re lazhet.

7-09-1915. Daet eo kaer-bras. Hag eh aomp en heol d'en em laoua; rak kompagnunezh a zo genomp!

A-tro an noz e vehomp é kann doc'hte; met 'gozik emaint ken diaes da herzel èl ar Jermaned.

An enderv-mañ e kaser d'an douar an eizh den lazhet dec'h.

Translation

The Twists and Turns of Death, *1916* (Extract)

6.09.1915: This afternoon we talked of the dangers we were facing. There are over 6,000 soldiers gathered here, without the slightest spot in which to hide if we were fired at. And we are only two miles away from the enemies. During the conversation, a shell fell in the middle of the village. We were told to regroup into companies and then quit the village, but the order fell on deaf ears: everyone was only thinking of himself. With bent backs, we ran in groups of two or three along the main road in order to reach the Hans road, about 400 metres further up, where other soldiers had gathered. From all sides, I could see men fleeing, like mice whose nests have been wrecked, while shells continued to explode. Shrapnel flew around us. Fellow soldiers then started arriving, blood streaming from them. We dressed up their wounds with our rolls of bandages. I gave mine to an unfortunate man who had just fallen next to me, his neck, one of his arms and both his legs cut open by shrapnel. We could hear men screaming in pain in the village centre. What a day!

Despite everything, at 5 pm, I had to bring some papers for the Captain's signature. Arriving in the village, I saw, in the middle of the road, torn clothes, bloody bits of human and horses' flesh, telephone wires hanging where they had fallen, and smashed window panes. There were 38 wounded and 8 dead.

7.09.1915: A gorgeous day. We went in the sunshine to delouse ourselves, as we are far from being on our own!

The fight against the lice lasted until evening, but they are nearly as difficult to get rid of as the Germans.

This afternoon we buried the eight men killed yesterday.

Loeiz Herrieu

O Huidérig euruz! *c.1916*

Er mitin-ma, é doustér hag é splanndér yaouank tarh en dé, é hwélan un huidér é seùel én êr ag en amzér, én ur ganal tér-tér, étré orsal merglet en diù linenn. Hag é sonjan:

"Huidérig, me mignon, hoantâd e hran te eurusted! E te galon vihan, léh n'en des ket d'er Hâs e lan on hani-ni. …pad mah om stummet de zistruj a zifeh, saùet e tes un néh, eid er vuhé karantéuz ha disoursi, émesk laseu treisuz stennet d'or hasoni.

Med goap é hrez ag en houarnaj govellet de vabdén én é araj. Adreist é botarneu hag é orsal, te saù diflaù, é glazdér en èbr glan, én ur ganal, heb déhan, te bozieu bresk, te sonenn skañù.

Te bousined bihan, én o néh nifl, o selleu d'er lué, tréhiet d'az ihuélded, bamet d'az leùéné, e hoanta en dé, ma helleint eùé parein, ged o eskell, dumed flour er hogus ha flourikâd o 'flu doh flamm en héol loskuz; seùel ihuél, pell doh en douar, pell doh mabdén hag é safar, doh é randon ha fallanté.

O huidérig euruz!

Perag n'em es ket mé eveldout diùaskell?

Ma hellehen neijal, èl ma hra me spered, de vro klet el lanneu, hañù ha gouiañù é bleu, em es lézet abarh, setu pell-zo, siouah! ar dreuzeu er mor braz, un néh èl te hani, karantéuz eùé, e hirvoudan dehoñ, a zonded me halon, noz-dé, ged melkoni..."

Translation

O Happy Skylark, *c.1916*

This morning, in the mildness and bright glory of dawn, I saw a lark flying up freely in the sky, singing insistently between the rusty barbed wire of the two lines and I thought:

"Lark, my friend, I envy your happiness. In your little heart, there is no place for the Hatred which fills ours. Whilst we are trained to destroy and mutilate, you have built a nest in order to lead a loving and carefree life among the treacherous traps set by our hatred.

But you make light of the weapons forged by a human race seething with rage. You rise with ease above the shells and barbed wire, up into the pure blue sky, singing continuously the delicate phrases of your gentle song.

Your little ones, in their graceful nest, look up, amazed at how high you fly. They delight in your jubilation and long for the day when they too will be able to brush the soft down of the clouds with their wings, stroke their feathers at the flame of the burning sun and fly high, far from earth, far from man and his cries of rage, far from his arrogance and spitefulness.

O happy lark!

Why don't I have wings like you?

If only I could fly, as does my mind, to that cosy place in the ever-flowering heath, on the edge of the ocean. This is where, a long time ago, alas, I left a nest like yours, and just as loving too, a nest that I miss sorely, in the depth of my heart, night and day."

Reun Menez Keldreg

Lili, *1969* (Lodenn)

En amzer-se ne oa mui joaüsted dre ar bed. Ur gorventenn c'hlac'har a c'hwezhe war dremm an douar o lezel anezhi sonnet, gant roufennoù a boan, evel gorre ul lenn skornet a-daol-trumm e-kreiz ar spontusañ barr-avel. Ie bai da zremm ur c'hozhiad falc'het d'ar marv, e-pad ar skrijusañ spont.

Pep hini a blege e choug dindan beli an alouberien. Rannet oa ar Bed. Ha rannet pep Bro. An aer a anale ar skevent a oa pounneroc'h d'ar spered, eget samm ar gozhni; eget ar vizer; eget an dienez.

Aer ar Gwalleur. Aer ar Brezel.

Nijet oa ar sioulder; teuzet an habaskter, evel fronnd ur rozenn disec'het war bav na ginnig mui d'al lagad nemet delioù gweñvet ha brein.

Trouz ar reuz hag ar freuz, o ruilhal e pep empenn, gant dasson taolioù seulioù pounner bagadoù soudarded dre ar straedoù. Ar gasoni o sevel a-ziwar an dienez, a-ziwar ar morc'hed ouzh an amzer dremenet, o lakaat an dud d'en em zrailhañ.

Met piv, pe betra, a viro ouzh ur rozenn da vleuniañ er fank? Piv pe betra a viro ouzh ar garantez da greskiñ e kalon ur goantenn?

Paotred o blev melen a gerzhe dre gêr; re a bep ment, a bep neuz. Disoursi. O klask magañ c'hoantegezh o yaouankiz gant o brud a vrezelourien.

Unan anezho eo a gutuilhas e c'hopr, war muzelloù Lili!

★ ★ ★

Dilezet he doa re he Gouenn.

Va dilezet.

En un taol-trumm; hep ur ger; evel ma faout ur vouc'hal ur geuneudenn e daou, en em gavis rannet diouti. Goullo va fenn; heug em c'halon, leun barr.

Diskredik e chomis pell amzer. Betek an devezh ma welis anezho, o daou, kazel-a-kazel, e lanneier en Enez.

Ar vrec'h he starde ne oa ket mui va hini. Davet un estren e save e selloù; hag un estren a gutuilhe war he diweuz ar pokoù orgedus am boa tañvaet ar c'hentañ.

– Kollet em boa Lili!

M'he doa lakaet hec'h evezh, da gentañ, da guzhat en deñvalijenn pe war ar maezioù he darempredadur, goude un nebeut sizhunvezhioù en em ziskouezhas, hep mezh na keuz, dindan lagad an holl.

Na skandal, da gentañ, na flac'hadoù goude, digant he re, nag alc'houez, d'ar fin war he dor, ne zeuas a-benn d'he herzel war an hent dibabet ganti.

Santout a rae re vat, e oa tonket dezhi mervel, hep dale. Ha dreist pep skoilh ez ae, ur wir leskidigezh en he c'hreiz.

Barnet eo bet. Gant ar re yac'h.

He brud? Hec'h enor? Komzoù goullou pa geñverier anezho gant ar pal ma oa bountet davetañ a-enep dezhi.

Gourc'hemennoù al lezenn? Alioù an nesañ? Ar furnezh? Ar resped, ha me oar? Kaelioù houarn an dud sentus; ar re a zo o buhez eeun ha plaen da vevañ betek kreiz ar gozhni; ar re a sav dirazo bloavezhioù hir ha didro; hep ar paz; hep an droug-skevent.

Eviti, evel un dorn he degemere, he dedenne. Na harz, na kil, na rae d'an dorn-se dispegañ. Ha ma loske he buhez, ne rae nemet sentiñ ouzh ar c'hleñved a loske he c'hreiz.

Fellout a rae dezhi pegañ, leizh he genou, er mizioù a chome ganti. O gwaskañ evit ober dezho diverañ eviti, betek an disterañ takenn a blijadur.

Hep lezel na keuz na truez war he lerc'h.

Daoust hag e verze kement-se an estren he daremprede?

Miz Eost a dremene, o tizhout d'e fin, pa oa gwelet, a-nevez, bagadoù soudarded o treuziñ kêr; diouzh renk. En ur ganañ e kemerent hent an disparti. Tamm ebet aer ur c'himiad gant o c'han. Yaouankiz o vont, dic'hoanag ma n'eo ket digeuz, d'an emgann.

Kollet en o zouez, ar Frank pe an Ernst a garas Lili. O tilec'hiañ, ur wech muioc'h; en ur lezel a-dreñv, ur plac'h, unan muioc'h, ha netra ken. Boued d'e sorc'hennoù evit an amzerioù kriz a zeue davetañ.

Adalek an devezh-se, den, pe koulz lavaret, ne welas mui Lili.

An teodoù a vrudas e oa klañv. Lavaret oa ez ae ar medisin d'ober war he zro. Gwir pe c'haou, ne selle ket ouzhin. Ne glaskis ket he gwelout. Torret oa, da vat, al liammoù am stage outi. Ne guitaen mui an ti am implije.

'N em daoned 'doa en he c'hlorenn hep ober van ouzh tra. Nag an dud, nag o barnedigezh.

Ur yaouvezh koulskoude, hec'h adwelis.

Da zevezh ar foar. War he fouez e valee, harpet war brec'h he mamm. E derou miz Gouere edomp. Fellout a rae d'am mestr prenañ ur c'houblad moc'h, hag e heuliet em boa, rak devezh ar foar a verk, evidomp, kouerion, kement hag ar sul; hag ouzhpenn, kaer e plije d'an den va alioù war al loened.

E-touez an engroez e vanis, harpet ouzh ur c'hased, va selloù kollet war ar boblad a dud o voudal o safar en-dro din, pa verzis anezho.

Tost da dizhout va bagad e tremenjont. Dianavez oant o div d'ar baotred a'n em gave em c'hichen. Gallout a ris eta hec'h arvestiñ, leun va daoulagad. He liv, gwennet dija pevar pe bemp miz a-raok pa he darempreden, oa deut da vezañ par da liv ar plastr gleb. Ar ruz, re ruz, a verke he muzelloù a falc'he he bizaj d'an hanter. Krommet oa hec'h izili evel dedennet davet an douar gant pouez, pe samm ar c'hleñved. Meur a sell a baras warni, estonet. Va re hec'h heulias, pell amzer, betek ar mare ma troas, pouezus, war brec'h he mamm, korn ar straed.

Digalonekaet-naet, e tistrois d'ar gêr.

Gant an hañv, hervez a glevis, e teuas ur welladenn en he yec'hed. Ken e teuas da vezañ gwelet a-wechoù, da serr-noz o pourmen er vanell a dremene dirak he zi.

Daoust ha brudet 'oa bet kement-se? Ha fellet 'oa d'ar boatred yaouank hec'h adwelout? Pe dre zegouezh, marteze, e teuent, da dremen dirak he zi? N'ouzon ket.

Un abardaevezh sul e c'hoarvezas an dra. Ur bagad paotred yaouank, re dommet gant ar gwin, a dremenas er vanell. Harpet ouzh he zi Lili a rambree an douster an devezh oc'h echuiñ. Ur vouskanenn oc'h heuliañ trouz o fazioù o tont daveti a glevas, a-raok o gwelout. P'az hec'h anavezas, ne fellas ket dezhi 'n em dennañ en he zi. En ur welout anezhi e tavjont gant o c'han, ha kuzulig a zeuas etrezo. Daoulagad an holl a bare warni dre ma tostaent. Herzel a rejont en he c'hichen. War emglev. Unan anezho a dostaas outi. Hep ur ger he c'hemeras war e vruched ouzh he briatañ. (Kinniget 'doa muioc'h, kea! d'an amprevaned a enebourien.)

Ne reas ket ar plac'h ur jestr. Ne rannas grik. Met pa dostaas egile e vuzelloù,

leizh nerzh he dent a begas. Gwadañ a reas at paotr; en ur youc'hal. Kilañ a reas ur paz pe zaou, hag a-dro-brec'h he flac'hatas, a-gleiz, a-zehou. Dilavar, ar re all a selle. Ne reas ket muioc'h an den fuloret, ha kemeret aon emichañs gant an holl e troas ar vandenn kein hag e tilec'hjont. Ar plac'h a yeas d'he zi.

Brudet oa bet an taol.

Goude-se, ma oa enebiezh en a-raok en he c'heñver, e teuas da vezañ kasoni, ha kounnar hag enebouriezh.

An dismegañs gouzañvet gant ar baotred a fouetas o lorc'h, heskinus evel un draen. Ha touiñ a rejont ober dezhi paeañ.

Translation

Lili, *1969* (Extract)

This short story is set at the end of the second world war.

At that time, there was no joy left in the world. A wind of misery was blowing on the face of the earth, leaving it set in wrinkles of pain, like the surface of a lake suddenly iced over during a very strong gale, like the face of an old man hacked by death in the middle of a nightmare.

Everyone bowed their heads under the weight of the invader's power. The World was split. Every country was split. The air which the lungs inhaled was heavier to the mind than the burden of old age, poverty or destitution.

The air of Calamity, the air of the War.

Serenity had vanished. Tolerance had melted away like the scent of a dead rose only able to proffer the world the withered and rotten leaves on its stem.

The noise of destruction and devastation was rumbling in every brain, echoing that of the heavy boots of squads of soldiers marching through the streets. Hate, fuelled by hardship and by the grieving for the recent past, made the people tear one another apart.

But who or what can prevent a rose from blooming in a mire? Who or what can prevent love from growing in the heart of a pretty girl?

Confident blond-haired boys, of all sizes and shapes, were walking through the town, trying to feed their youthful desires with their reputation as warriors.

One of them picked his reward on Lili's lips!

★ ★ ★

She had abandoned her own people.

She had abandoned me.

Suddenly, without a word, like an axe chopping a branch in half, I found myself cut away from her. My head was empty, my heart full to the brim with loathing.

I could not believe it for a long time. Then one day I saw them, the two of them, arm in arm, on the moors of Enez.

The arm which held her tight was no longer my own. She was raising her eyes to an outsider, and the outsider was picking on her lips the voluptuous kisses I had been the first one to taste.

I had lost Lili!

At first she took care to hide her relationship in the shadows of the night or in the countryside, but after a few weeks she met him openly, without shame or regret, for everyone to see.

Her parents first reprimanded her, then beat her up and finally locked her indoors, but nothing could make her diverge from the path she had chosen.

She knew well that she was destined to die soon. The fire burning inside her made her overcome every difficulty.

She was sentenced. By the healthy.

Her reputation? Her honour? These were empty words compared to the target towards which she was unwillingly propelled.

The constraints of the law, neighbourly advice, common sense, respect and the like? These are iron gates for obedient people, for those who lead a simple and uneventful life until old age sets in, for those who have long and uncomplicated years in front of them, without the cough, without tuberculosis.

For she was gripped by a hand which beckoned her and held her captive. No obstacle, no remission made this hand lose its hold. It could be said that she was burning her life out, but she was only obeying the illness which was burning inside her.

She wanted to bite, as deeply as possible, into the few months which were left to her, to squeeze them dry and make them give up to their very last drop of pleasure.

Leaving neither regret nor pity behind her.

Was the foreign boy she went out with aware of this?

The month of August was reaching its end when squads of soldiers were seen again marching though the town. They were singing as they took to the road which led them away, but their song did not bid the slightest note of farewell. They were young people going to battle, without hope and though possibly with regret.

Somewhere in their midst was the Frank or the Ernst who had loved Lili. On the move once again, and leaving behind a girl, yet another girl, and nothing more. She would feed his daydreams in the cruel times ahead of him.

From that day on, virtually no one saw Lili any more.

Rumour had it that she was ill. Apparently, the doctor had been called. Whether that was true or false had nothing to do with me. I did not try to see her. The links that bound me to her were well and truly cut. I no longer went out of my employer's farm.

She had condemned herself to loneliness without any regard to anything or anyone, without any care for other people's bad opinion of her.

I saw her again however. It was on a Thursday, the day of the fair. She was walking slowly, leaning on her mother's arm. It was at the beginning of July. My employer wanted to buy a couple of pigs, and I had accompanied him, as the day of the fair, for us farmers, means as much as a Sunday. Furthermore, this man valued my advice on animals.

I was standing amongst other men, leaning on a crate, my eyes lost on the noisy crowd around me, when I noticed them.

They passed close the group of people I was with. Neither of them was known to the men standing by my side. I could therefore observe her at ease. Her complexion, which was already white four or five months earlier when I was going out with her, had become sallow, like the colour of wet plaster. The far too intense red which defined her lips cut her face in half. She had bow legs, as if the burden of her illness made them bend towards the ground. Many astonished heads turned to watch her. I followed her with my eyes, for a long time, until she turned the corner of the street, leaning heavily on her mother's arm.

Thoroughly depressed, I returned home.

I heard that she made a recovery at the beginning of summer, so much so that she was sometimes seen at twilight taking a walk in the alleyway running alongside her house.

Did many people hear about this? Did the young men decide to see her again? Or did they just happen to pass by her house? I don't know.

The incident happened on a Sunday afternoon. A group of young men, who had drunk too much wine, took the alleyway. Leaning against the house, Lili was daydreaming in the mildness of the falling day. She heard a faint song punctuating their footsteps before she saw them. When she could make out the words, she decided not to retreat inside the house. As soon as they saw her, the singing stopped, and they started deliberating among themselves. All eyes were watching her as they drew closer. They stopped next to her, of a common accord. One of them approached her. Without a word, he put his arms around her and pushed her on to his chest. She had offered the foreign louts a lot more, hadn't she? The girl did not make a move, did not say a word. But when the boy attempted to kiss her, she bit him as hard as she could, drawing blood. He screamed, took a couple of steps backward and smacked her on both left and right cheeks, again and again. The others watched silently. The irate man did nothing more, and the young men, probably afraid, turned round and went away. The girl entered her house.

The story got around.

Thereafter, the bad feelings that were felt towards her before turned into hatred, indignation and hostility.

The insult endured by the boys spurred their pride, as prickly as a thorn. They swore they would make her pay.

Per Denez

Aelig Va Buhez, *1995* (Lodenn)

Mari-Vadalen a gomz da gentañ:

"Gwelet em eus merc'hed en noazh, touzet o fennad-blev... pourmenet e vezent war ar straed gant paotred... karet em bije gouzout petra o doa graet ar baotred-se da gas an Alamaned kuit... marteze... met ne vern."

Paouez a reas adarre.

"Ni, ne vezemp ket er c'hoari-se... Adsevel ar vro a felle deomp ober... hag e labouremp... Ha setu un deiz ar varc'hadourez-bleunioù-se o tont en hon ti... Bali Waldeck e oa... Un ti brav... gant ul liorzh... Kemeret e oa bet gant ur strollad kenlabourerien... marteze digant Yuzevien kaset da vervel er c'hampoù... ha ni hor boa hen kemeret digant ar genlabourerien tec'het kuit... Ur brav a di, ya... ul liorzh a-dreñv... tri estaj... hor sekretourezed a laboure en eil estaj... Hag un deiz e oa deut honnezh, ar varc'hadourez-bleunioù, dichadennet, o youc'hal, spontus penaos e c'helle ar vaouez-se youc'hal: "Deuit da begiñ ennañ!... Er Gestapo eo bet!... Pet den n'int ket bet kaset d'ar marv gantañ, an Italian laou-se!"

"A, Italian e oa?"

"Soñj am eus eus an anv: Umberto Prampolini. Mont a reas daou pe dri eus hor bagad da gerc'hat anezhañ... Ar varc'hadourez-bleunioù bepred war-lerc'h, o choual, o vallozhiñ, o tegas d'he heul div pe deir all dedennet gant an talabao. "Tregont da nebeutañ en deus lakaet fuzuilhañ." Degaset e voe an Italian bihan en ti, er burevioù a-rez an douar.

"Ha neuze?"

"Pennfollet e oa. Gant ar geben all, ur gwir vleizez, ne oa gouest da lavarout netra nemet "N'eo ket gwir! N'on ket kablus! N'eo ket gwir! Morse n'em eus graet droug da zen!" Hag eben o tont gant rimadelloù anvioù na ouie den ha gwir pe faos e oant... Nerzh a oa gant honnezh avat... Ha kasoni... hag an Italian bihan atav warnes leñvañ..."

"Kablus e oa?"

Ur c'hruz a reas Mari-Vadalen d'he skoaz.

"Piv oar? Piv a ouio morse?"

"Ha neuze?"

"E gorf a voe kavet da vintin dirak an ospital gant ur medisin o tont d'e labour."

Fromet e oan bet. Diwar re. Hi ivez. Dav e mont da vale e fru ar mor.

Gwelloc'h c'hoazh eget kustum e oa ar boued da greisteiz.

"Ne zebrez ket?" eme C'hustav, a-zevri oc'h ober e stal d'ur c'hrank saoz.

"N'em eus ket naon. Poan-benn a zo ganin."

"Ur banne gwin memes tra a yelo ganit... Ar gwin a blij dit am eus goulennet... Bourgogn gwenn..."

"N'em eus na naon, na sec'hed... Mar plij! Mar plij!" Dec'hervel ar mevel. "Ur banne dour gant un Aspirin, mar plij!"

Em c'hambr e chomis goude lein.

"Nann, nann, n'en em chalit ket... Un enderverzh em gwele a raio vad din..."
Ha gant aon e teufe menozioù droch en e spered: "C'hwi oar, ar merc'hed, a-
wechoù, n'emaint ket war o zu mat... N'eo ket o fazi... It da bourmen, muiañ-karet.
Hag arabat en em chalañ. Fenozh e vo mat pep tra."

Da noz e ris va c'hoan gant ur volennad vouilhoñs – eus ar gwellañ! – hag un
tamm turbodenn dre an dour – pezh na oa ket fall ivez! Ur frouezhenn war-lerc'h.
Hag ar valeadenn gant Mari-Vadalen.

"Neuze eo bet lakaet d'ar marv en ho ti?"

"El liorzh... Unan a yeas da lavarout d'ar sekretourezed chom hep sellout dre ar
prenestr en enderverzh, chom hep sellout el liorzh... Ne selljont ket. Met klevout a
rejont. Me ivez a glevas. Aspediñ a rae, an Italian bihan. Prampolini. "Kredit
ac'hanon! N'em eus graet netra... N'em eus graet droug ebet... Da zen ebet... It da
c'houlenn gant va gwreg... Va gwreg, ne lavar morse gaou... It da c'houlenn gant va
amezeien... va amezeien all..." Ne ouie ket mui petra lavarout, an Italian bihan
paour, ne ouie ket penaos lakaat an hini a oa dirazañ da gemer truez... an hini a oa
dirazañ gant ur bistolenn en e zorn... Skiltrañ a rae e vouezh... Aspediñ ar Madonna
da zont d'e sikour... Marteze e oa ar Madonna ouzh e zegemer en he divrec'h pa
darzhas an tenn..."

Kazel-ha-kazel e tistrojomp d'an ostaleri. Hep ur ger. Eno e oant en-dro gant o
reuz, evel an noz a-raok.

"Memestra e oa tu da c'hortoz... d'e gas dirak ul lezvarn..." a lavare Fulub.

"Ne oamp sur eus netra." Tro Remont e oa bet.

Gustav: "Hag an tregont den kaset d'ar marv?"

"Piv a lavare kement-se? Ar varc'hadourez-bleunioù pennsodet! Evit peseurt
abeg e oa war e lerc'h evel-se, te a oar? Ma oa gwir, e oa abred a-walc'h d'ul lezvarn
e gastizañ."

Gustav: "N'em eus ket keuz da vezañ lazhet an amprevan. Da vezañ lazhet
anezhañ gant va dorn. Ha ma vefe da ober en-dro e rafen c'hoazh."

Dav e voe din azezañ. Stardañ a ris dorn Mari-Vadalen.

"Gustav," emezi, "gouzout a ran e c'hoarvez ur bern traoù divalav e mareadoù
trubuilhet evel-se... Met un dra 'zo n'on ket gouest da zisoñjal... Ar paotrig ken
brav, ken bihan, seizh vloaz, eizh d'ar muiañ, rodellet kaer e vlev du ha ken glan e
zaoulagad c'hlas... "Itron, emezañ din, va zadig a zo amañ... Va zadig Umberto...
Prampolini eo e anv..." Petra em bije lavaret?... E oa marv e dadig Umberto?
Flourañ a ris e bennad-blev. "Ya, mabig... amañ 'mañ..." Levenez en e zaoulagad.
"Degaset em eus ur pallenn dezhañ... gant aon en defe riv en noz-mañ... Me n'em
bo ket riv... me a gousko gant va mammig en he gwele..." Kemer a ris ar pallenn.
"Prometiñ a rit din, Itron, reiñ ar pallenn dezhañ? Va zadig a zo un tadig ken mat...
'Fell ket din e vefe yen dezhañ... ha gouzout a ray evel-se ivez en deus soñjet e vab
ennañ." Ne ouien ket petra lavarout. Ober a ris ya gant va fenn. "Trugarez, Itron...
Va anv eo Angelo..." Hag e gwir e oa un aelig.

Diaes e oa da Vari-Vadalen derc'hel gant he c'homz.

"Gustav... Me an hini eo am eus rediet ac'hanout da lezel e baperioù gantañ en e chupenn ha da bakañ ar c'horf er pallenn a-raok hen teurel dirak an ospital. Evel-se da nebeutañ en deus soñjet ar paotrig e oa bet tomm d'e dad pa oa o vervel."

Gwelout a raen ibilien-lagad Gustav o strizhañ evel ma raent pa oa ar gounnar o vont da begiñ ennañ.

"Klasket em eus disoñjal Umberto Prampolini, hag a-wechoù e kav din, Gustav, on deut a-benn. Disoñjal ar paotrig-se, avat, ne c'hellin biken."

Ne yeas ket Gustav e fulor. Gwelloc'h em bije karet e vije bet peget unan eus e varradoù ennañ.

"Ar brezel eo ar brezel! Dav e oa dilastezañ. Hag em eus graet..."

Gervel a reas ar mevel.

"Champagn d'an holl!"

Yen e voe din. Sevel a ris.

Translation

My Life's Little Angel, *1995* (Extract)

A young Sicilian girl, whose mature lover, Gustav, has been a member of the PNB (Parti Nationaliste Breton) during the second world war, talks to one of her lover's friends. Mari-Vadalen speaks first:

"I have seen women, their hair shaved off, being forced by men to walk naked through the streets. I would have liked to know what they themselves had done to get rid of the Germans. Who knows? But never mind."

She stopped talking again for a while.

"We ourselves were not playing that game. What we wanted to do was rebuild our country. And we worked at it. Then, one day, that flower-seller came to our house on Waldeck-Rousseau Street. It was a lovely house. With a garden. It had been taken from a group of collaborators. Maybe it used to belong to Jews sent to die in the camps. We had taken it over from collaborators who had fled. It was a lovely house, with a back garden and three floors. Our secretaries worked on the second floor. Then, one day, that flower-seller came in, ranting and raving. You wouldn't believe how strongly this woman screamed: "Arrest him! He was in the Gestapo! Goodness knows how many people this bloody Italian sent to their deaths."

"Oh! He was Italian, was he?"

"I remember his name: Umberto Prampolini. Two or three men from our organisation went to get him. The flower-seller was still following us, shouting, swearing. She had brought with her two or three others attracted by the hullabaloo. "At least thirty people have been shot because of him." The small Italian was brought to the house, in the ground-floor office.

"And then?"

"He lost his head. What with that woman being there, and a real shrew she was too, all he could say was: "It's not true! I am not guilty! It's not true! I have never hurt anyone!" But the other was carrying on with her litany of names which no one knew if they were true or false. She was forceful however, and vented her hate, while the small Italian could hardly repress his tears."

"Was he guilty?"

Mari-Vadalen shrugged her shoulders.

"Who knows? Who will ever know?"

"So?"

"His body was found in the morning in front of the hospital by a doctor coming on duty."

All this had upset me. A lot. She too was distraught. We had to go and take a walk in the sea spray.

The food at lunch-time was even better than usual.

"Are you not eating?" said Gustav busily eating a crab.

"I am not hungry. I have a headache."

"Surely you will have a glass of wine. I ordered the wine you like. A white Burgundy."

"I am neither hungry nor thirsty. Please leave me alone!" The waiter was called. "A glass of water and an aspirin, please."

I stayed in my room after lunch.

"Don't you worry! An afternoon in bed will do me good." And in case this should give him sinful thoughts I added: "You know, women, at times... They don't feel right. It's not their fault. Go and take a walk, darling. And don't worry. I'll be fine by tonight."

At dinner time I ate a bowlful of excellent clear soup, a piece of boiled turbot, which was not bad at all either, and a fruit for dessert. Then I went for a walk with Mari-Vadalen.

"So he was put to death in your house?"

"In the garden. Someone went to tell the secretaries not to look out of the window during the afternoon, not to look in the garden. They did not look. But they heard. I heard too. The little Italian, Prampolini, was begging: "Believe me! I have done nothing. I have done no harm... to no one. Go and ask my wife! My wife never lies. Go and ask my neighbours, my other neighbours!" The poor small Italian no longer knew what to say. He no longer knew how to make the man facing him take pity on him, the man facing him who was holding a gun in his hand. His voice was shrill. He begged the Virgin to come to his help. Maybe the Virgin took him into her arms when the gun went off."

We returned to the hotel arm in arm. Without a word. There they were again, turning over the past, as on the previous night.

"However, we could have waited. We could have sent him to court," said Fulup.

"We were not sure of anything," replied Remont.

Gustav: "And what about the thirty people he had sent to their death?"

"Who said that? The enraged flower-seller! Why did she hate him so much? Do you know? Even if what she said was true, we could have waited for a court to sentence him."

Gustav: "I don't regret killing the bastard. Killing him with my own hand. If it was to be done again, I would do it again."

I had to sit down. I squeezed Mari-Vadalen's hand.

"Gustav," she said, "I know that lots of ugly things happen in such troubled times. But there is one thing I cannot forget. It is that little boy, so handsome, so small, seven, maybe eight years old at the most, with black curly hair and pure blue eyes. "Madame", he said to me, "My daddy is in there. My daddy Umberto. Umberto Prampolini." What could I say? That his daddy was dead? I stroke his hair. "Yes, son, he is here." His eyes shone with happiness. "I brought him a blanket, in case he got cold during the night. I won't be cold. I'll sleep with my mummy in her bed." I took the blanket. "Promise me, Madame, that you will give him the blanket. My daddy is such a good daddy. I don't want him to feel the cold. And he'll also know that his son was thinking about him." I did not know what to say. I nodded. "Thank you, Madame. My name is Angelo." And, to tell the truth, he was a real angel."

Mari-Vadalen was finding it hard to carry on talking.

"Gustav... I am the one who forced you to leave his papers in his jacket and to wrap the body in the blanket before throwing it in front of the hospital. That way, at least, the little boy could think that his father was warm when he was dying."

I could see the pupils of Gustav's eyes narrowing as they always did when he was about to throw a fit of anger.

"I have tried to forget Umberto Prampolini, and sometimes, Gustav, I think I managed to. However, I will never be able to forget that little boy."

Gustav did not get angry. I would have preferred it if he had gone into a rage.

"War is war. It was necessary to muck out. That's what I did."

He called the waiter.

"Champagne for everyone!"

I felt cold and got up.

Herve Bihan

Remi, *2000* (Lodenn)

En devezh-se a Vae, ma oa kaer-eston an amzer, en devoa kuitaet ar skol a-gevret gant Jañ. Ildud en devoa ranket mont war-eeun d'ar gêr da sikour gant e dad grignoliañ sac'hadoù greun da gas diwezhatoc'h da valañ d'ar vilin. Anat e oa diaesoc'h dezho, da Jañ ha da Remi, derc'hel d'o c'hoari boas. En taol-se ne voe mui na Hitler, na de Gaulle na Churchill. Ne voe mui nemet daou soudard eus un armead kuzh deuet da zieubiñ ar vro, evel ma klevent diouzh komzoù radio tad Remi. Gant tammoù koad hanter stummet anezho e raent pep a fuzuilh. Kuzhet e vezent ganto en argaeenn ar park en tu all d'an ti-skol. Ret e oa dezho tremen dre ar Groaz-Ruz hag ac'hano pep hini da vont gant e hent war-du ti o zud, Jañ war-du ar Manati ha Remi war-du Keriliz.

Remi a guitaas Jañ hag e-lec'h heuliañ an hent e krapas war ar c'hleuz a oa dic'harzhet eno ha mont war-du Keriliz a-dreuz ar parkeier. Kaer e oa an amzer ha plijout a rae dezhañ splujañ trumm er geot uhel pan spurmante an enebour ijinet gantañ prest da lakaat an arigrap warnañ pe da dennañ ar boled a lakfe an termen d'e vuhez soudard kuzh! Ur wezh ar mare e ankouae e c'hoari da selaou kan an evned, pe c'hoazh da eñvoriñ anvioù ar plant e bleuñv anavezet gantañ bremañ. Hag a-greiz-holl e adkroge gant e argadoù, ha paoñ! paoñ! Reizhet meur a enebour, ha tostoc'h a se eur dieubidigezh ar vro!

Tost da Geriliz e oa bremañ, hag eus krec'h ar c'hleuz ma kerzhe warnañ e wele yer an amezeien e-kreiz ar porzh sko ouzh ti e dud. Pladañ a reas a-greiz-holl ha tennañ div c'heunadenn, a oa daou bezh maen kavet gantañ e-harz ar c'hleuz. Ne darzhjont ket, anat, met ar yer a darnijas pennfollet en ur gammigellat evel tud mezvet, ha pebezh cholori! Remi a zic'hargadennas hag a zistagas meur a denn fuzuilh. Ur wezh echu e gefridi e ruzas, war e galabosoù, betek penn ar c'hleuz, souezhet ne vije ket deuet gwreg an amezeg da grial anezhañ evit e dorfed. Diskenn a reas prim ha heuliañ mur ar porzh da dizhout dor a-dreñv ti e dud. Sur e oa an enebour o c'hedal en un tu bennak, ha paoñ! emezañ en ur vukañ war ur paourkaezh yar, dizurzh en he fluñv goude ar redadenn foll.

Tizhout a reas an nor ha digeriñ goustad. Ne oa ket echu ar c'hoari, soudard un arme guzh a dle bezañ gouest da vont tre hep reiñ da c'houzout da zen. Em gavout a reas en trepas teñval. Ne oa trouz ebet, nemet skoadennoù balañsinenn an horo-laj bras, du-hont, er gegin. Diouzhtu e klevas evel ur c'hwezh iskis, hakr ha kreñv, evel pan veze fardet gwadegennoù goude bezañ lazhet ar pemoc'h lart e menaj tud Jañ. Difennet groñs outañ o devoa e dud debriñ eus ar seurt bevañs, soñj mat en devoa, iskisoc'h a-se e kave klevet ar seurt c'hwezh er gêr. Mont a reas pelloc'h, goustad, diaezet, ne oa mui e c'hoari o ren e gammedoù. Stekiñ a reas ouzh un dra bennak war al leur. Hag eñ sellet. Tata! Tata eo! Beuzet en e wad o poulladiñ, e zaoulagad dispourbellet paret warnañ gant ur mousc'hoarzh yen o tiskuliañ e zent gwenn. Tata! Lazhet o deus Tata! E galon a bennfolle, a lamme, a c'hourlamme. C'hoant en devoa da ziskargañ e vouzelloù. Redek a reas war-du e gambr, hag eno eus ar prenestr e welas e vamm hag e c'hoar, morlivet ha ruz o daoulagad, dindan gward en unan eus an div wetur sach-diaraok a-steud en tu all d'an hent. N'en devoa ket Remi dilezet e fuzuilh koad ha stardet-mat e oa gant e zaouarn, ar pezh a vire outañ a vezevelliñ, moarvat. Mont a reas betek ar gegin hag eno e klevas ur c'hwezh kreñv all a anaveze: hini lêr lifre an Alamaned a dremene dre an hent bras ur wezh an amzer. Em gaout a reas fri-ouzh-fri gant un ofiser bras en e goazez war gador e dad, pevar soudard gantañ. An ofiser bras a lavaras dezhañ, en ur yezh n'en devoa ket klevet abaoe m'en devoa kuitaet ar gêr vras all, meur a vloavezh a oa: "Sellit 'ta, mab gagn ar Yuzev terrorist! Penaos emañ ar bed ganit, loustoñ?" Eñvor ar bloavezhioù kent a zeuas dezhañ d'un tizh ne c'hell ket meizañ spered mab-den: Jeremi e anv evit gwir, yuzev bihan deuet da repuiñ eno gant e dad, e vamm hag e c'hoar Rachel, divadezet Izabel...

Ur paotr eürus eizh vloaz e oa Remi. Nag eñ na Jeremi ne voent mui gwelet.

Translation

Remi, *2000* (Extract)

On this exceedingly lovely day in the month of May, he walked out of the school together with Jañ. Ildud had had to go straight home to help his father put in the attic the bags of grains which, in due course, would be sent to the mill for grinding. It was obviously harder for the remaining two, Jañ and Remi, to carry on with their usual game. On that occasion, there were no Hitler, de Gaulle or Churchill. There were only two soldiers of a secret army come to free the country, as they had heard on Remi's father's radio. They had each made a gun from two wooden sticks of roughly the right shape. They usually hid them in the high hedge of the field on the other side of the schoolhouse. They then had to go past Kroaz Ruz and, from there, took the road leading to their respective homes, Jañ towards Ar Manati and Remi towards Keriliz.

Remi left Jañ but, instead of taking to the road, he climbed on the embankment at a point where it had been cleared of brushwood and went, across the fields, towards Keriliz. The weather was lovely and he enjoyed diving suddenly in the high grass when he caught sight of an imaginary enemy ready to arrest him or to shoot a bullet which would put an end to his life as an underground soldier! Once in a while he would forget his game to listen to the song of the birds or to recall the names of the flowering plants which he now knew. But all of a sudden, he would launch another offensive. Bang! Bang! A few more enemies were thrashed, bringing the time of the liberation of the country that little bit closer!

He was now approaching Keriliz. From the top of the dike on which he walked, he could see his neighbours' hens in the courtyard next to his parents' house. He dived down suddenly and threw two grenades, two stones he had picked up at the foot of the hedge. They obviously did not explode, but the terrified hens scampered away in all directions as if they were drunk. What an uproar! Remi burst out laughing and pulled the trigger several times. His attack over, he crawled on all fours to the end of the hedge, amazed that the neighbour's wife had not come out and screamed at him for his misdeed. He ran down, keeping close to the yard's wall, in order to reach the back door of his parents' house. He was sure the enemy was lying in wait somewhere. "Bang!" he said, aiming at a poor hen whose feathers where still in disarray after her frenzied flight.

He reached the door and opened it slowly. The game was not over. A soldier in a secret army must be able to enter without anyone being aware of it. He was now in the dark corridor. The only noise was that of the pendulum of the grandfather's clock, ticking over there, in the kitchen. Right away, he smelt a strange, pungent, strong smell which reminded him of the black puddings prepared in Jañ's parents' farm when a fat pig had been slaughtered. His parents had strictly forbidden him to eat such food, he remembered that well. He found it all the more strange to find this kind of smell at home. He walked on, slowly, unnerved, his game well and truly forgotten. He bumped into something on the floor and looked down. Daddy! It was Daddy! Drowning in his own congealing blood, his wide-opened eyes, staring at him, a cold smile revealing his white teeth! Daddy! They killed Daddy! His heart jumped, flinched, lurched. He wanted to go to the toilet. He ran towards his bedroom. Out of the window, he saw his mother and sister, white as sheets, their eyes red, under surveillance, in one of the two front-steering cars parked, one behind the other, on the other side of the road. Remi had not put down his wooden gun. He was gripping it tightly with both hands and this probably prevented him from blacking out. He went to the kitchen where he smelt another strong and well-known smell, that of the leather uniform of the Germans who were, at times, seen on the main road. He found himself face to face with a high-ranking officer sitting in his father's armchair and four soldiers. The senior officer said to him in a language he had not heard since he had left the city where he used to live a few years ago: "Here you are then, bastard son of that Jewish terrorist! How are you, you little turd?" The memories of earlier years came flooding back, at a speed no one can imagine. Jeremi was his real name; he was a young Jew who had come to take refuge here with his father, mother and sister Rachel, renamed Izabel...

Remi was a happy seven year old boy. Neither he nor Jeremi were ever seen again.

Youenn Olier

Barnedigezh laouen, *1951* (Lodenn)

Dres d'ar mare-se avat e savas e penn all ar sal un hiboud difraezh, mouezhioù tud ha trouz boteier war ar plañchod. Saeoù du a fiñvas du-se. Edo ar varnerien o tont evit embann ar varnedigezh. Un den a grogas da lenn un tamm paper a vouezh izel; ne oa ket tu da gompren mann. Buan e voe torret evezh an Treut, ne glaskas ket mui selaou: e vignon a larfe dezhañ. Heuget e voe a-greiz-holl. Adarre ne oa mui nemet ar c'hoadachoù gwerniset, teñval, an dremmoù lintrus lu gant an dour-c'hwez endro dezhañ, ar warded polis du dirazañ, ha pell, dreistdiraez, penn disliv ha stouet an tamaliad, hag e-skoaz da hennezh ar prenestr bras ha gouloù an heol en tu dehoù, e-tal saeoù du ar varnerion hanter gousket, ha flaer an holl dud-se o c'hweziñ ouzhpenn-se ha mesket gant aer vac'h ar sal anken, skuizhnez, levenez ha konnar.

Ar boubou a savas endro dezhañ damc'houde a roas dezhañ da c'houzout e oa echu lenn ar varnedigezh. Fin a oa d'an arvest. Mont a rae kuit ar c'hoarierion o saeoù du, faezh meurbet, met laouen holl gant ar soñj e oa echu o devezh labour hag e c'hellfent bezañ er gêr a-benn ur c'hardeur. Ha neuze e oa sach ha bont gant an arvesterion da dapout an nor, laouen ivez evel tud o deus kannet ul loen drouk; An Treut a yeas ganto kaset gant ar froud.

Er-maez, er garid, e kavas e vignon ar Beulz. Ruz un tamm e oa hennezh, hanter serret e zaoulagad a-dreñv e lunedoù tev, rouestlet un disterañ e vlev du evel ma c'hoarveze gantañ pa veze nec'het. Treiñ a reas e selloù outañ, alvaonet ha dilavar, ha tremen ur wech ouzhpenn e vizied en e vlev. Mont a rejont a-gevret dre ar sal vras hag an diri-maen, ha diboufañ el leurgêr hep rannañ grik: arabat e oa degas an evezh gant o brezhoneg. Eno e voent trellet gant ar gouloù: ar blasenn hag he ziez uhel hag ar straedoù a gase davet tachenn Veurzh en tu all d'ar pont a baras trumm e kannder grizias an heol-sklêrijenn. Tostoc'h dezho e oa freskadurezh c'hlas leto-nennoù al liorzhig-kêr. Ur pennadig e chomjont a-sav e-tal ar bolomoù-maen bras a-raok adkregiñ gant o hent. An dud en em zispartie buan, hep lavarout nemeur a dra e-keñver ar prosez. Daou bolis a chome c'hoazh e-tal dor ti ar Breujoù, o sevel gward. Safar kirri-tan o loc'hañ, dorikelloù o strapañ, storlok an tram o tostaat war-du kreiz kêr, garmoù an avreloded o c'hoari el liorzh. Aze e oant, war a riblenn-straed. Stagañ a rejont da ziskenn gant ar blasenn, dilavar atav.

"Ha neuze petra 'zo bet a-benn ar fin," a c'houlennas an Treut o chom a-sav dindan garidoù ar c'hoariva, e leurgêr an ti-kêr, kant metrad pelloc'h, pa ne oa mui den en-dro dezho. Egile a zibrederias a-greiz-holl. Un hir a huanad a zeuas gantañ. "E varnet o deus d'ar marv," emezañ, ha diouzhtu goude e ouzhpennas o treiñ outañ: "Gouzout a rez, e vourreviet o deus spontus: gwelet ec'h eus pebezh penn en doa." Ha neuze, war-lerc'h ur pennad dilavar: "Pebezh bruderezh mat a c'hel-limp ober."

Tevel a reas en ur vousc'hoarzhin. Laouen e oa. War an toal ne respontas netra an Treut dezhañ: treiñ a reas kein outañ, strafuilhet, kerseet, glac'haret holl, ha sellout ouzh al leurgêr kann. Dremmoù laouen a zañsas tro-dro dezhañ, arvesterion, c'hoarierion; soñj en devoe pegen tomm e oa er sal du-se. C'hoant en devoe ivez da skrignal, da leñvañ ha da gonnariñ. "An hini all ne vo ket re domm dezhañ da vihanañ," a soñjas. Adarre e wele dirazañ ur bern tud laouen o fichal dindan an heol, – hag un dra da sabatuiñ, – en o mesk un den disliv, e-unan-penn, skeud an Ankoù en e gerc'henn.

Translation

A Good Sentence, *1951* (Extract)

At that very time, a blurry noise rose from the front of the room, that of people's voices and of shoes treading on the wooden floor. Over there, black robes were moving. The judges were coming back to pass sentence. Someone started to read a piece of paper in a low voice. In no way could one understand what he said. An Treut soon stopped paying attention and trying to listen. His friend would tell him. He suddenly felt nauseous. Once again, he was surrounded with darkly-varnished woodwork, ludicrous faces gleaming with sweat. Black-clothed policemen were standing guard in front of him. Further on, he could see, over other people's heads, the black robes of the drowsy judges, the pale and bowed face of the accused, and next to him, on the right, the big window which let in the sunlight. But add to that the stench rising from of all these sweating people, mixed with the sultry atmos-

phere of the narrow room, the weariness, the exhilaration and the feelings of anger.

A little while later, he realised, from the mutterings around him, that the sentence had been read. The show was over. The black-robed players were leaving, exhausted but happy to think that their day's work was over and that they could all be home within a quarter of an hour. The spectators then pushed and shoved their way to the door, feeling as happy as people who have got the better of an unruly animal. An Treut went with them, carried by the current.

He met his friend outside, in the corridor. Ar Beulz's face was red, his eyes were half-closed behind his thick glasses, his black hair slightly tangled, as happened when he was upset. He looked at his companion, silent and dazed and passed, once again, his hand in his hair. They crossed the main hall and walked together down the stone staircase which leads to the forecourt without saying a word: they did not want to attract attention to them by speaking Breton. As soon as they were outside, they were dazzled by sunlight: the torrid glare of the sun was beating down on the square with its high houses, and on the streets which lead, over the bridge, to the Champ de Mars. Closer to them was the green freshness of the public park lawns. They stopped for a while near the big statues before setting off again. The others were scattering off quickly without saying much about the trial. Two policemen were still standing guard at the courts' doors. Noise of the departing cars, clanking of the automatic barriers, clatter of the tram on its way to the town centre, shouts of the boys playing in the park. There they were, on the pavement. They started to walk down the square, still not talking to each other.

When there was no longer anyone near them, they stopped under the theatre arcades, on Town Hall Square, a hundred yards further on, and An Treut asked: "So, what was the final verdict?" His companion suddenly came back to earth. He heaved a long sigh. "They condemned him to death," he said, and turning towards him, he immediately added,: "You know, they tortured him a lot; you saw his face, didn't you?" Then, after a short silence: "Just think of the publicity we can get out of that."

He stopped talking and smiled, pleased. An Treut did not reply: he turned round, upset, disappointed, distressed and looked at the sunbathed square. Happy faces danced around him, the audience, the players. He recalled how hot it had been in the courtroom back there. He wanted to snigger, to cry, to have a fit of anger. "At least he won't feel the heat," he thought. Once again he saw, in front of him, a crowd of happy people moving in the sunlight, and – amazing sight – in their midst, a pale man, on his own, wearing the mark of death.

The Breton Movement

The Romantic movement of the nineteeth century put the spotlight on Brittany and was thus partly instrumental in the creation of the first Breton Movement – 'Emsav' in Breton – which lasted until the first world war. The movement reflects a quest for identity from Bretons caught between their own culture and that of France. It has its roots in the defence and promotion of the language, the values and way of life of Brittany, and reacts against the central government's endeavours to eradicate regional differences and totally assimilate a formally independent nation into the French State. While on the cultural side it can claim several victories such as the creation of many magazines in the Breton language, the intransigence of Paris politicians towards the teaching of Breton in schools and towards some measure of self-determination gave rise in the 1930s to calls for autonomy and even independence from a determined minority of people for whom the end justified the means. During the second Emsav, which spans the period between the two world wars, a handful of Bretons nursed the dream of creating an independent Breton State with the help of the Third Reich. This was at odds with the desires of the vast majority of Bretons who stayed faithful to the French Republic.

The first four texts chosen relate to the first Emsav and have a strong romantic flavour. The next six concern the second Emsav and describe the clampdown of the French authorities at the end of the war. The last five texts give a partial illustration of the aspirations of the third Emsav which still fights on the cultural, literary, economic and political scenes to secure a future for Brittany and for her language.

Anna-Vari Roparzh

Dihun Breiz, *1913*

Dihun 'ta, Breiz-Izel, hon Mam muia karet;
N'eo ket mad e chomfez re hir ken da gousket;
Glac'haret a vemp holl mar dalc'hez, morgousket,
Da hunvreal pelloc'h en amzer dremenet.

Fin 'zo breman d'an noz, arru eo ar beure;
Me wel ar sklerijen 'para war ar mene;
An heol tom ha skedus a lugerno prestik:
Sao eta, Breiz-Izel, chilaou mouez ar Barzik.

Deuz peb brank e tiskenn eur c'han melodius,
Dousder ar mintiniou rent ar galon joaüs,
Hag ar gliz-noz, kouezet war ar ieoten wenvet,
A ra d'ezhi sevel kaëroc'h en he c'hened.

Iouc'hadennou skiltrus a glevan dre an aer
O laret: "Breiz-Izel, arru eo an amzer!"
Ma vemp holl unanet da sikour hon Mam-Bro
Da derri al liam he chadenne pell zo.

Kerne, Treger, Leon ha potred vad Gwened
A zo war-zao breman, p'ho deuz an drouz klevet
'Vo prestik goueliou braz var Vre hag en Pontreo
Da enori hon Breiz, diston rei an ekleo.

Deut eta, ma Broïz, deut holl, deut da glevet
Mouez ken drant ar Varzed a zo ho mignoned:
Komz a refont ouzhoc'h var galz demeuz a draou
'Vit m'o laket ar Gwir en pep lec'h trec'h d'ar Gaou.

Dihun 'ta, Breiz-Izel; lez da gousk hirvoudus,
Kemer peurz 'vit biken en da renk enorus,
Difenn gant lealded da iez, da gustumou,
Goull frankiz d'az mibien gwasket gant ar mestrou.

Goull da iez, er skoliou, en kenver ar gallek,
Ha te vo, dreist ar Gall, 'n eur c'hout ar brezonek;
Da spered zo digor, da benn a zo kaled:
Na blegi ket dindan ar bec'h warnout tolet.

Translation

The Awakening of Brittany, *1913*

Wake-up, Brittany, our beloved Mother;
You must not sleep any longer;
We would all worry if you kept on dozing and
Dreaming about past times.

The night is at an end. Morning has come;
I see the morning light on the mountain top;
The hot and sparkling sun will soon shine:
Get up, Brittany, listen to the voice of the Bard.

From every branch comes a melodious song,
The morning mildness makes our hearts rejoice.
The night dew which fell on the wilted grass
Makes it spring back up again, sweeter than ever.

I hear vibrant cries in the air:
"Brittany, your time has now come!"
Let us unite to help our country
Throw off the shackles she has worn for so long.

Cornouaille, Trégor, Léon, and the good men of Vannes
Are now standing up, for they have heard
Of the forthcoming celebrations on Menez-Bré and in Pontrieux
In honour of Brittany, and the news is spreading.

Come, fellow countrymen, come without fail and hear
The joyful voices of the Bards, your friends:
They will talk to you about many things
And will make Truth prevail upon Lies everywhere.

Wake up, Brittany; shake off your doleful sleep,
Regain your honoured rank for ever more;
Fight loyally for your language, your traditions,
Request freedom for your sons oppressed by the rulers.

Request that your language be given the same status as French in schools,
You will be better than France, if you keep your language;
You have an open mind, you keep to your decisions:
Do not bow under the burden you were made to carry.

Narsis Kelien

Gouspero ann Anaon, *1880* (Lodenn)

– "Aboe ann ele milliget
Euz ann env m'int bet diskaret,

Doue 'n euz tolet ho zelen
D'ann douar, 'vit hon c'hanerien.

Hag hon zado koz evelse,
Pa oe dalc'het ho Bro out-he,

Dindan ar gwelio war ar mor,
Treuz ar mor o tont enn Arvor,

Ken klemmuz hag ann tonn ganent,
Ia, ha meulent Doue velkent.

Emgann aliez ho doe bet
Ha mervel peb gwech m' vize ret:

Arog mervel 'iouc'h ar bleizi,
Evel ann er hon Barzed-ni.

En hon c'hozni ma omp gwasket,
Estiged Breiz na dawfont ket.

Euz ann dud vad na vo evor
Pa vo torret Telen Arvor.

Ha piou 'veulo Doue aman
Pa vo eet Breiz-Izel ac'han?" –

'Pad *in Exitu* ar Vreiziz,
A dinse ar c'hloc'h e Ker-Is.

– "Nan, ma breudeur, eme eunn dall,
N'eo ket Arvor eet d'ar bed all;

Ha mad ve laret ar *Credo*
Hor boe disket gant hon zado:

Doue da genta, Breiz goude,
Gant fe, fizianz ha karante.

Ken gwir hag ann heol lugernuz,
Doue ha Breiz a zo paduz;

Keit vo war ann aod eunn dolmen,
Hag a divoano eunn dervenn,

Ann dero 'barz ar c'hoajo braz,
Ar bruk e lannek, hag ar Groaz,

Keit vo eur Groaz-hent enn he zao
Hag huel war c'hleun er parko,

Keit draillo war mor ann awel,
Biken na varvo Breiz-Izel!"

Translation

Evensong for the Dead, *1880* (Extract)

"When the fallen angels
Were thrown out of heaven,

God threw their harp
On earth, for our bards to use.

This is why our forefathers,
When their country was taken from them,

Taking to sailing boats and
Crossing the sea to come to Arvor,

Sang melodies as plaintive as the waves,
And yet they were praising God.

They fought many battles,
And died when they had to;

Before dying the wolves howl.
Our bards' eagle screeches too.

In our old age, although we are oppressed,
The nightingales of Brittany will sing on.

The memory of our good people will disappear
When the Harp of Arvor is broken.

And who will praise God on this earth
When Lower Brittany is no more?" –

As the Bretons were ceasing to be
The bells of Ker-Is were ringing.

"No, brothers", said a blind man,
"Arvor has not passed away;

Let us say the *Credo*
That we learnt from our fathers:

God first, Brittany next,
In faith, trust and love.

As true as the sun shines,
God and Brittany will last;

As long as there are dolmens on the shore
And the acorns grow,

As long as there are oak trees in the forests,
Heather on the moor, and the Cross,

As long as a Cross marks the meeting of two roads
And the fields are surrounded with high hedges,

As long as the wind rages over the sea,
Brittany will not die!"

Ronan de Kermene

Pa vin maro, *1913*

Pa vin maro, c'houi a deuio, ma mignoned,
D'ar sul, d'an abardaez, goude ar gousperou,
Tost d'an iliz vihan, e kornig ar vered,
War ma bez ken dister e-touez an holl veziou.

C'houi a zigaso d'in bleuniou koant ar mene:
Lann melen, brugou glas hag ar balan dispar,
Ha, da skeudenn buhe peurbadus ma ene,
E lakfet en o zouez eur bodig uhel-var.

C'houi a lavaro d'in ha Barzed 'zo dalc'h-mat
O kanan ar Frankiz, an tan sakr en o c'hreiz,
C'houi a lavaro d'in (o pebez kelou mat!)
Ha trec'het eo d'ar fin ar Gall, enebour Breiz.

Neuze, mignoned ker, e trido ma c'halon
E goueled ar bez du, dreist planken an arched,
Ha, keit ma vo douget a-dreuz d'an nenvou don,
Gant eur barr-levenez e trido ma spered.

Translation

When I Am Dead, *1913*

When I am dead, you will come, my friends,
On a Sunday evening after Evensong,
By the small church, to a corner of the churchyard,
And find my modest grave among many others.

You will bring me pretty mountain flowers:
Golden broom, green heather, and splendid gorse,
And, to symbolise the eternal life of my soul
You will place among them a sprig of mistletoe.

You will tell me if there are still Bards
Singing Freedom whole-heartedly.
You will tell me – O such good news!–
If at last the French, Brittany's enemies, have been vanquished.

Then, dear friends, my heart will flutter
At the bottom of the black grave, and over the coffin lid,
Then, as my soul is carried through the deep heaven,
It will radiate a glow of happiness

Pêr Mokaer

Er Glaù, *1913*

En amzér gouh a huéharal,
Pa goéhé glaù ar hur bro-ni,
E té de vout fréhus en doar,
'Vleué er park, eùe er bar,
E oé milén éd en érùi!

Rak én amzér 'm es ké déhi,
En amzér gouh a huéharal,
Hon tud e oé mestr en ou zi,
Tud digabestr ha tud léal!

Hiniù en dé, en treu ia fal:
Spontet, ni gleu safar ar glaù,
Glaù miliget er modeu gal,
Deit a véz-bro er modeu fall,
D'hon diskarein, hag hemb arsaù

Rak en amzér bremen zo kri;
Hiniu en dé, en treu ia fal;
Ur Breihad mat 'n 'es melkoni,
Pe huel é vro soublet hé zal.

Ur Bobl el Breih n'hel ket bout gal!
E me halon ur voéh e lar:
"Goarnet berpet en espérans!
D'emb é vo hoah un dé hon doar!
Né veimp ket feahet get ré Frans!

"Rak én amzér e zei un dé
Er Vretoned ne veint ket gal,
Diliam e vo hor Bro arré
Ha treh hor gouen èl guéharal!"

Translation

The Rain, *1913*

In the old days of yesteryear,
When rain fell on our country,
The earth became fertile,

Flowers grew in the fields, the branches were in bloom;
The golden wheat was ripening in the furrows!

I long for these past times,
For the old days of yesteryear,
When our ancestors were their own masters,
When they were free and loyal men!

Today, things are going badly:
The noise of the falling rain frightens us,
That accursed rain of French ways,
Those bad ways coming from abroad
To annihilate us, without respite!

Present days are cruel;
Today, things are going badly;
A good Breton's heart is filled with sadness
When he sees his country bow her head.

And yet Bretons cannot be French!
In my heart I hear a voice say:
"Keep hope alive!
One day, our land will be ours again!
We shall not be wiped out by the French!

Because the day will come
When the Bretons will not be French;
Our Country will lose her chains
And, as in the old days, our people will triumph!"

Fañch Elies-Abeozen

Hervelina Geraouell, *1943* (Lodenn)

Fromet e oa Hervelina, pa save, da-heul an daou baotr, gant an diri, betek burev
Breizh da Viken. Ur skritellig oa war an nor. Skeiñ a rejont hag e voe diouzhtu
digoret dezho. An den yaouank, o doa gwelet e sal ar c'heltieg, oa dirazo. Un dra
bennak a laouen oa en e zaoulagad bev hag un doare mousc'hoarzh a c'hournije war
e c'henoù start.

"Moarvat eo laouen o welout unan bennak, n'en deus ket gwelet betek-henn, o
tont war e dro," a soñje Hervelina oc'h azezañ war ar gador kinniget dezhi. "Ne dle
gwelout atav nemet an hevelep pennoù."

Job a anaveze dija Denouel, merour ar gelaouenn. Goude ur gerig diwar-benn
piv oant ha war be studi e labourent e troas an diviz war dachenn ar brezhoneg.

"Ur chañs vras hoc'h eus," eme Zenouel da Anton hag Hervelina, "da vezañ brezhonegerien. Ni, amañ, Breizhuheliz, a glask addeskiñ yezh hor bro. Ne deo ket aes avat, n'eus kreizenn vrezhonek ebet e Roazhon ha ne deo ar skol-veur nemet un ti gall da zeskiñ kelennerien evit ar skolioù gall. Ha n'en deus ket ar brezhoneg e-barzh kement a dalvoudegezh zoken hag ar portugaleg a vez kelennet en hevelep sal. Perak e kav deoc'h ne deu ket ar studierien muioc'h war-dro kentelioù Per ar Gall?"

"Labour a-walc'h o deus gant o studioù a-hend-all," eme Job an Dred. "Ar brezhoneg ne gas da neblec'h. Pa vez echu o labour, an darn vuiañ eus ar studierien a glask en em ziduiñ ha ret eo karout ar brezhoneg evit mont war-dro sal ar c'heltieg."

"Ma ne vije nemet ar re a gar al latin, ar gresianeg, ar saozneg pe ar galleg zoken," a droc'has neuze Hervelina, "o vont war-dro ar skol-veur, ne vefe ket re sammet ar gelennerien gant o labour."

"Koulskoude," eme Zenouel, "an notered, ar vedisined hag all, mar deuont da Vreizh Izel, o devo ezhomm da vont e brezhoneg ouzh an dud."

"Ne deo ket er skol-veur e teskint ar brezhoneg-se, mar o deus da zeskiñ," eme Anton d'e dro. "Eno e vez disklêriet ur bajenn eus *Pipi Gonto* evel ur pennad eus Kikero pe Milton, ne vez ket desket penaos toullañ kaoz gant tud Koadout pe Garaez."

"Ya, ret eo magañ karantez-vro evit karout ar brezhoneg ha kemer plijadur en e studi. Seblantout a ra din," eme Zenouel, "ez a war an dachenn-se ar maout gant Breizhuheliz. Ar vrezhonegerien a chom morgousketoc'h. Ne gomprenomp ket perak."

"Me 'gav din," eme Hervelina, "e kredont ez eo a-walc'h komz brezhoneg evit bezañ Bretoned, ha pa ne ve en o fenn nemet mennozhioù a vro estren. Pa ra an aotrou Turkantin ur brezegenn e brezhoneg, da goulz ar votadegoù, e vez kavet tud da grediñ ez eo dre m'eo ur Breton mat. An aotrou Turkantin ne soñj nemet e mouezhioù e genvroiz hag e politikerezh Pariz. Ne ra forzh eus Nevenoe na Pontkalleg, ne deu war e vuzelloù nemet anvioù Janed Ark, ar marichal Foch, Dixmude, Verdun hag all. An aotrou Turkantin hag all ne dint ket enebourien da Vreizh ha d'ar brezhoneg, nann, nemet e servijo kement tra er vro-mañ da vrasañ gloar ar Frañs. An aotrou Turkantin zo skouer tud ar blasenn e kement kêrig a Vreizh Izel. Anaout a reont c'hoazh ar brezhoneg, e gomz a reont ouzh an dud vunut. Ar galleg, avat, zo, pell zo, yezh o empenn hag o c'halon. Ar vrezhonegerien rik n'o deus nag an amzer vak nag an deskadurezh ret da garout ur yezh. Mont a reont da heul tud ar blasenn hag o brasañ c'hoant eo e teufe o bugale da vezañ par da re tud ar blasenn."

Denouel a selle gant un tamm eston ouzh ar plac'h yaouank. Hervelina, eus he zu, ur wech chomet a-sav, a soñje: "Petra 'c'hoari ganen? Setu me oc'h ober politikerezh a-greiz-holl, diwar-benn ar brezhoneg. Biskoazh kemend-all!"

"War a welan," eme Zenouel a-benn ur pennadig, "ne welit ket gwall vat stad ar brezhoneg en ho pro."

"O!" eme Hervelina. "Ne varvo ket c'hoazh diouzhtu. Un dra a c'hellomp gwelout, avat. Eus an tri studier omp amañ, n'eus nemet Anton Benneg a ve bet moarvat dija ar galleg yezh e gavell, daoust m'en deus desket brezhoneg a-vihanig gant mitizhien e vamm ha moused ar skol. Mat, Job an Dred ha me ne domp ket hon-daou ken beuzet e-barzh ar brezhoneg ha m'eo bet hor c'herent en hor raok. Ar brezhoneg en deus kollet tachenn ennomp hag a gollo c'hoazh mar rankomp mont da vevañ er-maez eus Breizh Izel. Ma ne gemm ket stad an traoù e teuio un deiz bennak ar brezhoneg e penn e hent."

"Ret eo dihuniñ ar garantez-vro e kalon ar Vretoned," eme Job an Dred, "ha ne deo ket aes; ar skolioù, an Iliz ne reont nemet ar c'hontrol, zoken en iliz ha zoken e brezhoneg. Daoust ha Breizh a c'hell bezañ evit an darn vuiañ eus ar veleien estreget bugel devotañ merc'h henañ an iliz?"

"Da c'houzout eo ha niverus e teuy da vezañ, deiz pe zeiz, ar Vretoned dihunet," a glozas Denouel. "Grit abostelerezh en-dro deoc'h. Studiit ar brezhoneg ha savit pennadoù evidomp mar doc'h dornet evit ober se. Studiit hon istor peogwir eno eo emañ diazez ar garantez-vro."

Savet eo Hervelina hag he daou geneil da vont kuit. Ur sell a daolas war ar gambrig. Kartennoù-post peget ouzh ar mogerioù. Un engravadur war goad: ur Breizhad o sevel ur maen-bez ma lenned warnañ *Amañ eo beziet Breizh*. Stardañ e zorn da verour *Breizh da Viken* a reas Hervelina hag e soñje, tra ma tiskenne gant an diri. "Daoust ha dibenn un amzer zo bet eo a zo o kenderc'hel da vevañ-bevaik er gambrig-se, er gelaouennig a vez savet enni evit kant lenner bennak, skignet e-touez tri milion a dud, pe deroù un huñvre gaer a deuio, deiz pe zeiz, da wir? Piv 'oar!"

"Petra 'soñjit eus Denouel?" eme Job an Dred ouzh Hervelina.

"Un den a feiz moarvat," emezi. "N'on dare ha dont a raint, eñ hag e gamalad-ed, a-benn da zihuniñ o bro. Ar pezh a vije bet trist, avat, eo ne vije ket bet kavet unan bennak er vro-mañ da vagañ ur seurt huñvre."

Translation

Hervelina Geraouell, *1943* (Extract)

Hervelina felt nervous as she followed the two lads up the stairs leading to the office of *Brittany for Ever*. There was a small sign on the door. They knocked. The door was opened at once. The young man she had seen in the Celtic Room was standing in front of them. His bright eyes were shining with pleasure and there was a shadow of a smile on his closed lips.

"He is presumably pleased to see someone he has not spoken to before come to see him," thought Hervelina as she sat on the chair she was offered. "He must always see the same faces."

Job already knew Denouel, the magazine's editor. After giving their names and stating the subjects they were studying, the conversation turned to the question of the Breton language.

"You are very lucky to be native speakers," said Denouel to Anton and Hervelina. "Here, in Higher Brittany, we have to relearn our country's language. It is not easy however. There is no Breton Centre in Rennes, and the University is no more than a French institution training teachers for French schools. The Breton taught there is not as highly valued as, let's say, Portuguese, which is taught in the same room. But why do you think students do not attend Per ar Gall's lessons more often?"

"They have enough to do studying their own subjects," said Job an Dred. "Breton leads nowhere. When the students have done their homework, most of them want to relax and they would need to love Breton to attend the Celtic Room."

"If only those who loved Latin, Greek, English or even French attended University, the lecturers would not be overworked," interrupted Hervelina,

"Yet" said Denouel, "lawyers, doctors etc... who go and work in Lower Brittany will need to be able to speak Breton."

"It's not at University they will learn that kind of Breton, if they need to learn it," said Anton in turn. "There, a page of *Pipi Gonto* is analysed like a passage from Cicero or Milton. They are not taught how to converse with the people of Koadout or Carhaix."

"Yes, one must love the country in order to love the Breton language and enjoy studying it," said Denouel. "It seems to me that, on this account, the Higher Bretons have the upper hand. Native-speakers are more indifferent. We don't understand why."

"I think," said Hervelina, "that they find it is enough to speak Breton in order to be Breton, even though their minds may only be invaded by foreign thoughts. When Monsieur Turkantin makes a speech a Breton, at elections time, some people think that he does so because he is a good Breton. Yet Monsieur Turkantin only thinks of his compatriots' votes and of Paris politics. He does not care about Nominoe or about Pontcallec. The only names who ever pass his lips are those of Joan of Arc, Marshal Foch, Dixmude, Verdun and the like. Monsieur Turkantin and his colleagues are not enemies of Brittany or of Breton, not at all, as long as all things Breton help to increase the glory of France. Monsieur Turkantin is the very example of public figures found in every village in Lower Brittany. They still know Breton and use it to speak to ordinary people. French however has been for a long time the language of their brains and of their hearts. Those who only speak Breton have neither the time nor the necessary education to love the language. They take their cue from public figures and their greatest wish is that their children would be like those of public men."

Denouel gazed at the young girl with surprise. Having stopped talking, Hervelina suddenly thought: "What's happening? Here I am taking a political view on the Breton language. This is amazing!"

"From what I can see," said Denouel after a while, "you don't think much of the state of Breton in your part of the country."

"Oh!" said Hervelina "It is not going to die straightaway. However, one thing is obvious: among the three students gathered here, only Anton Benneg has had French as his mother tongue, although he soon learnt Breton from his mother's servants and from his schoolmates. Fine. As for Job an Dred and myself, we are not as immersed in Breton as were our own parents. Breton has lost some ground in us, and will continue to do so if we have to go and live outside Lower Brittany. If things don't change, there will come a day when Breton will no longer be spoken."

"The love of our country must be instilled in the hearts of the Bretons," said Job an Dred, "and that is far from easy: the schools and the Church work in exactly the opposite direction, even in church when mass is celebrated in Breton. Do you really think that, for the majority of priests, Brittany can be anything other than the most devout elder daughter of the church?"

"We don't yet know whether, in days to come, many more Bretons will become active," concluded Denouel. "Preach around you. Study Breton, write articles for us if you can do so. Study our history because that is the very basis of patriotism."

Hervelina and her two comrades stood up to go. She glanced at the small room: postcards stuck to the walls; a wood engraving showing a Breton putting up a gravestone on which was written: *Here lies Brittany*. Hervelina shook the hand of the editor of *Brittany for Ever*, and walked down the stairs thinking: "Is this the end of a civilisation struggling to stay alive, in this little room where they publish a small-size magazine which is sent to roughly a hundred readers living among three million people, or is it the beginning of a beautiful dream which will, one day, come to life? Who knows?"

"What do you think of Denouel?" said Job an Dred to Hervelina.

"He is a true believer," she replied. "But I have no idea if he and his comrades will manage to arouse other people's interest. It would have been far worse, however, if no one in Brittany had ever been found to entertain such a dream."

Fañch Elies Abeozen

Kell 5, *1948*

At the end of the second world war, Abeozen was imprisoned for his activities during the war.

Tavet 'oa blejadennoù an dud vazhatet. Noziñ a rae ha ne wele mui daoulagad Yann Kere pikoù ar c'haoc'h kelien war vurioù gwenn-razet e gell. Erru 'oa warnañ, ur wech muioc'h an noz lugudus gant he frederiadennoù luziet ha dispi. Bec'h en doa tommañ d'e dreid. N'oa ket yen miz Du koulskoude ha ne zeue ket a-benn da enebiñ ouzh ar riv, ken dinerzh e rede ar gwad en e wazhied. Gwir eo neket gant soubenn ar c'haol da nav eur veure, gant soubenn ar patatez diouzh ar pardaez ha tri c'hant hanter kant gramm bara sec'h ez eus peadra da herzel ouzh an anoued.

Padal gwelloc'hik ez en em sante abaoe miz. Ur bakadenn c'hwec'h lur bitailh a reseve bremañ pep sizhun da Wener digant e wreg hag e fetisae e bredoù goular gant ur begad amann, un tammig kilhevardon hag un aval. Ne sante mui e benn o vezevelliñ pa stoue d'an douar na pa'z ae en e c'hourvez war e c'holc'hedad plouz.

Un doare anken a samme e galon da bep tro er sizhunioù kentañ. Krediñ a rae dezhañ e kendalc'he da vont war draoñ zoken goude ma oa deut e benn da harpañ war e wele. An diouer a voued magus eo moarvat a rae kement-se.

Abaoe an derc'hent n'oa mui e unan-penn en e gell. Daou gamalad a oa deut dezhañ. Edont bremañ o zri gourvezet pep hini war e c'holc'hed plouz, tamolodet en o daou ballenn, o c'hortoz ar c'housk da droc'hañ evit un nebeut eurvezhioù war ar soñjoù kasaüs ha doanius a grigne dibaouez o empenn. Paol Riwall a oa e-kichen an nor ha Per ar Gwenn keñver-ha-keñver da wele Yann Kere, o daou war ar planchod.

Bremañ e kleve adarre mouezh mabden. Rak mouezh ar warded daoust hag ober a c'heller anezhi mouezh tud bet dezho ur vamm hag un tad? N'oant e gwir nemet doareoù ardivinkoù, bouetet o c'heflusker gant kasoni ha krizder. N'oa ket puilh ar gerioù-skorn a zistagent. Da eizh eur veure e tigore ar gell: "Kafe..." hag e veze diskennet dezhañ ur c'hartad tizan goular hag e damm bara pemdeziek. Ur pennad da c'houde e wigoure adarre ar potailh: "Soubenn!..." Etre div eur ha peder eur abardaez gwigour adarre: "Bale!" hag ez ae d'ar red war-du ar porzh, e vogerioù pemp metr uhelder gant e brenestr kaelet gant barrennoù houarn war an diaraok. Dre eno, dreist ar vur mein ruz a rae tro liorzh digempenn ar prizon, e wele bleñchoù ur wezenn bennak, melenet o delioù, ha toennoù tiez ma veve enno – pebezh burzhud! – kerent ha bugale etrezo tan un tammig karantez an eil evit ar re all. E-unan en e borzh evel en ur gell, al loen gouez a oa anezhañ, e sante n'oa mui e gwirionez nemet un niverenn, an niverenn 82. Amañ er-maez avat, e c'helle chom en e sav, harpet ouzh ar voger troet war-du heol gwan an diskar-amzer. Santout a rae, war e valvennoù kloz, pokoù klouar lagad an deiz hag e soñje, un dioanag skrijus o vroudañ e galon, ez oa, en un tu bennak er-maez, ur galon dener o hiraezhiñ dezhañ hag ur bugelig bloaz hanter n'e anavezfe mui evit e dad pa vefe divac'het. ...Met ha divac'het e vefe un deiz?... Daoust hag ar vuhez dieub ken eürus, zoken pa veze tenn, n'oa ket bet anezhi un huñvre?... N'ouie dare ha dont a rafe en-dro an tremened-se c'hwek d'e galon gour. Ar bremañ put ha garv a oa marteze da badout da viken evel Ifern Yen kantikoù e vro... E vro?... C'hoarzhiñ trenk a rae, pa zeue ar ger-se war veg e deod. C'hoazh un huñvre c'houllo m'oa bet touellet ganti abaoe bloavezhioù ha bloavezhioù ma klaske he degas da wir. Ha bremañ e oa kouezhet warnañ ar c'hastiz, ur c'hastiz didruez a-berzh tud a lavare bezañ e genvroiz pa ziskouezent bezañ e wir enebourien hag enebourien aheurtet kement tra a gare. Ne vije ket bet re bounner ar samm d'e ziskoaz, lakaomp ne vije bet chomet er bed-se, ma oa harluet dioutañ, krouadurien Doue, ezhomm dezho eus e labour hag eus e skoazell evit bevañ. Petra ober?... Gortoz en ur uzañ unan hag unan munutennoù diniver ur bremañ rannet e daou gant an deiz hag an noz ken ha ken disaour.

Gwigour adarre. Echu ar bourmenadenn. Ha d'ar red en-dro betek e gell, pri-zonidi all o redek en e raok, o daouarn a-dreñv o c'hein, herr warno evel chas gour-drouzet o skampañ d'o loch. Alc'houezet an nor. Bremañ peoc'h betek ma klevo evit an eil gwech: "Soubenn"... Ha da c'houde ar mare arvarus. An deiz o louediñ hag an holl dasmantoù karet pe gasaet o tont da c'hournijal er gell. Anken ha c'hwervoni o tispakañ evel bleunioù sklas ur goañvezh hep dibenn. Sed amañ o seniñ ar c'hloc'h digristen. Poent eo diwiskañ, lakaat an dilhad war ar gador bostek, reut d'e beñsoù treutaet, hag o dougen er-maez gant e votoù-ler hag e skudell houarn gwenn. Ha d'ar gwele da grenañ un nozvezh-pad muioc'h, tamolodet en e ballennoù rust evel ur sae reun, da c'hortoz tarzhig an deiz disliv da skleuriñ war vurioù gwenn-lous ar gell. Tost e oa dezhañ koulskoude bezañ laouen daoust d'an anhun, pa ne gleve ket, ur wech aet war e wele, kunujennoù ha keinvan a-us d'e benn. Rak re ingal e tibabe ar warded ar mare-se da vont da vazhata hemañ pe henhont, hervez froudenn chatalek o c'hasoni sec'hedik. Ken goullonderet e oa bet e empenn gant an darvoudoù m'en deus bet mil boan o tegas d'e eñvor un drailhenn bedenn bennak. N'eus nemet unan o reiñ dezhañ un tamm frealz gwirion, ar *Salve Regina* eo. Hag e tibun, meur a wech lerc'h-ouzh-lerc'h, ar gerioù latin, kanet ken alies gwechall er skolaj.

★★★

Setu ma n'oa mui e-unan-penn. Souezhet e oa bet o welout daou all en hevelep kell gantañ. Diaes e kavas zoken da gentañ, abaoe un devezh hag hanter kant ma oa e-unan gant e soñjoù, daoust pegen pounner e oant, degemer tud en e vuhez digenvez. Ha peseurt tud e oa anezho?.. Frealzet e oa bet dizale. Harzet e oa bet Paol Riwall, d'e veno, en abeg d'e venozioù breizhek ha d'e zarempredoù re start gant an Alamaned. Per ar Gwenn a oa anezhañ ur c'henwerzhour, tamallet dezhañ gant kenseurted warizius da vezañ gonezet re a vil lurioù e-pad aloubidigezh ar vro ha da vezañ degemeret ar soudarded wer-louet en un doare re seven en e gafeti.

Marvailhoù hir a oa bet ganto en nozvezh kentañ, pep hini o tisplegañ e afer en doare direbechañ evel-just, hogen tostoc'h ouzh ar wirionez rik eget an drevezadenn disneuziet ma vefent barnet diwarni.

Per ar Gwenn a vage ar spi da vezañ divac'het dizale, dinoaz-krenn evel m'oa bet war dachenn pep politikerezh, emezañ. Un dell-gastiz a vefe sammet warnañ, sur a-walc'h. Ur wech paeet gantañ, e tivrofe pell diouzh kasoni diboell ur gêr deut par d'un ospital ar re sot.

Paol Riwall ha Yann Kere, avat, ne grede ket dezho e vefent kwitez ken buan-se. Enebourien douet o menozioù a oa deut adarre war lein ha n'o doa truez ebet da c'hortoz eus o ferzh. Harp ebet da gaout digant ar re, eus an Emsav, a oa chomet dilabour evit Breizh, war zigarez e oa an Alamaned war he douar. Mat e oa graet dezho, da veno ar re-mañ, sur a-walc'h. N'o doa nemet chom fur evelto, tremen hep alanat e brezhoneg ha gortoz un amzer habaskoc'h da ober gant doujañs ouzh pennoù ar Stad goulennoù bet nac'het keit amzer ha tonket da vezañ dismegañset en dazont, nemet dont a rafe ar gomunistiezh war c'horre. C'hoariet o doa o flanedenn war daol an darvoudoù kemmus ha kollet ar barti. Setu.

A eur da eur, pa glevent an enaouerien dredan o strakal ha trouz kammedoù pounner pe skañvoc'h o tostaat, e tavent trumm. Dizale e teue war elum al lamp a-us d'o fennoù ha lagad ar gward a selle, dre an toullig-spiañ en nor, hag aze edont c'hoazh o zri. Hag e tivere gorrek ha diseblant munutennoù an eurioù teñval betek ma teue ar c'housked da glozañ o daoulagad, e korf an noz.

***

Aet e oa gouelioù Nedeleg e-bioù. "Peoc'h war an douar d'an dud a youl vat," a gane e gwechall an aelez a-us da grec'hienn Bezleem Judea. N'en doa ket kresket kalz niver an dud-se moarvat, rak bremañ evel gwechall ne rene etre ar pobloù hag ar rummoù-tud e pep bro nemet brezel ha kasoni. "An den a zo ur bleiz d'an den" a zo ul lavarenn zereatoc'h da ziskleriañ istor un denelezh o nac'h bemdez he Dasprener.

Mont a raent o zri bep pemzektez d'an oferenn. N'oa mui troet nikun anezho da vont kalz war-dro an iliz kent bezañ bountet er prizon evel torfedourien. Amañ, avat, peñseidi anezho, e klaskent tapout krog e feiz o bugaleaj evit chom war c'horre mor an dioanag. Met arabat da brizonidi disoñjal, zoken e-pad un hanter-eurvezh ez int tud kablus. Setu perak o deus ijinet ar saverien brizonioù doareoù archedoù prenn en o sav, digor hepken war an araok betek bruched an den. Pep unan a vez kraouiet en e logellig e doare ma klev an oferenn hep gwelout nikun nemet ar beleg ouzh an aoter, ar c'hurust o respont hag ar gward war ur chafod dirazo, gant e selloù bepred o parañ warno. Buan e oa deut Yann Kere da anaout ar re eus e genseurted a oa boas bezañ bazhatet. Pa dremene unan anezho dirak ar gward, en e sav e toull dor an trepas a gase d'an archedoù, e rae ur c'hildro trumm evel da dec'hout rak un taol-troad en e revr.

Kozh e oa aluzenner ar prizon. Lenn a rae dezho aviel ar Sul, met dibaot e sermone. Ha moarvat ez oa gwell e-giz-se. Ken sachet eo bet ar veleien e tabutoù gwadek hon amzer ma n'ouzont ket chom bepred hep distagañ, war zigarez prezeg ger Doue, komzoù na drid ket enno nemeur a vadelezh e keñver an dud faezhet, pa n'o deus ket ar re-mañ menozioù a-liv gant o re. E-lec'h kenderc'hel da vezañ neptu, e-harz an aoter da nebeutañ, etre kostezennoù a-zevri gant un emgann dibardon, e savont a-du gant homañ pe honhont. Un doare iskis da gompren spered ar gatoligiezh, liamm etre holl bobloù ar bed ha nann relijion vroadel ar stad-mañ-stad. Setu perak eo frealzusoc'h da drec'hidi klevout hepken komzoù an Aotrou Krist eget diskleriadennoù re zenel.

***

Nebeut amzer goude storlok boas bailhoù ha chotoronoù ar gegin o kemenn dezhañ e oa war-dro pemp eur, en deus klevet Yann Kere trouz kammedoù pounner ur strolladig tud o tont tre er prizon. Meur a wech endeo eo bet divorfilet gant an hevelep trouz. Potailh ur gell o stirlinkat bremañ. Kuzuligoù.

"Petra eo an dra-se ken abred-mañ?" eme Baol Riwall.

"Ur paour kaezh den o vont d'e dro-vale ziwezhañ," eme Yann. "A-benn un eur amañ e vo graet e stal dezhañ ha ne vo mui nemet ur c'horf marv toull-didoullet dirak daou renkad fuzuilhoù o tivogediñ."

"Añ?" eme Baol Riwall o sevel trumm en e goazez. "Sur oc'h?"

"Ya, sur on," eme Yann.

Hag e chomont o daou dilavar da selaou trouz ar c'hammedoù o pellaat.

Per ar Gwenn a vorede bepred.

★★★

Galvet eo bet Paol Riwall er beure-mañ da vont da vurev ar barner enklasker. An daou all a zo gant o marvailhoù boas evel kezeg ouzh an dornerez.

Soñjal a reont, avat, en hini a zo o strivañ da zifenn e frankiz ha marteze e vuhez rak skilfoù an tamalloù gwir pe faos. Santet o deus ez oa c'hoazh prederietoc'h egeto o-daou. Marteze dre m'oa dimezet abaoe bloaz hepken. N'en doa ket gwelet ar verc'hig ganet abaoe ma oa en toull. Marteze ivez dre ma touje riskloù kuzh n'en doa ket meneget dezho. Traoù a zo m'eo furoc'h d'un den o mirout evitañ e-unan. N'eus nemetañ da c'hellout barn e gwirionez diwar be abeg en deus graet an dra-mañ-dra d'ar poent-mañ-poent. Neket ar varnerien, en un amzer bennfollet gant ar gasoni, a zo gouest da gompren peragoù un den. Barn a reont hervez reolennoù dizamant ur Reizh, sujet da venozioù o c'hostezenn.

"Ni a zo ar Wirionez Peurbadus," emezo. "Labouret ec'h eus en hon eneb. Kastizet e vezi."

"Gwa an drec'hidi," a lavare Brennos kozh da senedour Roma. Taolet eo bet an hevelep ger ouzh fas e ziskennidi, meur a wech abaoe. Emaomp adarre ouzh tu ar re faezhet.

★★★

Da serr-noz, liv an erc'h war an oabl a welent dre brenest uhel ar gell, eo deut Paol Riwall en dro. Teñvaloc'h c'hoazh e benn eget diouzh ar beure, ha skuizh-divi eo, war a seblant. Gant doñjer e kas d'an traoñ e skudellad soubenn disall, dalc'het klouar dezhañ dindan e ballennoù. Dizale e son ar c'hloc'h hag emaint bremañ o zri tamolodet war o flouz. Peur e vo tomm d'o zreid yen-sklas? Bremaik, avat, e santo Yann an aouidoù o flemmañ e dreid hag e zaouarn. Ar boued re dreut hag ar vuhez difiñv a zo bet kiriek d'e vizied da goeñviñ adal miz Here.

Paol Riwall n'en deus respontet nemet gerioù dispis a-walc'h d'ar goulennoù o deus graet outañ war e zistro. Hag abaoe ez int chomet dilavar. Teñval eo an noz bremañ hag e vanont pep unan sebeliet en e ezeved, o santout pegen dister ar c'honfort a c'hellont reiñ an eil d'egile.

Ur skeudenn garet, mistr ha gwevn a c'hournij en dro da benn Yann Kere, ken buhezek a-frapadoù m'eo darbet dezhañ klemm dindan flemmadenn ul laonenn o vroudañ e gig. Diaes meizañ pegen treantus eo tourmant un den beziet ez vev en ur gell vorailhet ha kaelet mat, pa soñj er garantez virvidik m'eo bet diframmet diouti. Hag e teu d'e eñvor ur bomm fromus eus ur ganaouenn eus an Inizi Gall. Ur

peñsead a gan d'e garantez o leñvañ dezhañ war an aod:

Na leñv ket e giz-se va ene,
Rak diskenn a ra da zaeloù
Em betek e strad ar mor
Ha leskiñ a reont va c'halon...

Hag hep gouzout dezhañ e tistag a vouezh dam-uhel:
"Un den, dezhañ gwreg ha bugale n'en deus ket ar gwir da vont en un Emsav ha pa ne ve da hemañ nemet ur pal speredel."
"Re wir a larez, Kere," eme Baol Riwall evel pa gomzfe dre e huñvre. "N'en deus ket ar gwir-se pe e sach e dud gantañ e gouelec'h e reuz."
"Daou vloaz war-nugent oan p'eo deut an Alamaned da vistri war ar vro-mañ. Unan oan eus soudarded an arme-se a zo bet skignet evel pell en avel e Mezheven 1940. Ruilh-diruilhet a-hed an hentoù betek e Kreisteiz Bro-C'hall, ne vagen ken c'hoant nemet da zistreiñ d'ar gêr. A-wechoù war droad, a-wechoù e lost kirri-dre-dan, d'an diwezh war ur marc'h houarn dilezet gant unan bennak e foz an hent, on deut en-dro da Vreizh, ur wech disoudardet. Kavet em eus dre amañ va mignoned, birvilh en o speredoù gant ar spi en un amzer welloc'h o vont da hinoniñ war Vreizh. Tuet mat a-walc'h e oa, a lavared, an Alamaned da Emrenerien hor bro. N'oa keloù er mare-se nag evit ar Soviedoù da freuzañ o emglev gant an Alamaned nag evit Amerika, ken pell, da zont da aberziñ he feoc'h war aoter an dismantr. Un Europa nevez a zeue war wel hag hor gerig hor boa da rannañ en dael, hol lod da ober el labour adsevel ur C'hornog peoc'hus hag oberiant war holl dachennoù buhez mab-den. En em roet on me ivez d'ar striv-se ha n'en deus ket fellet din gwelout pegen bras kemm a zeue er gudenn dre m'en em skigne ar brezel dre ar bed holl.
"Dre ma teue pounneroc'h-pounner samm ar brezel war o diskoaz, an Alamaned n'o deus mui pledet gant kudennoù ar C'hornog Pellañ. Gonit ar brezel er Reter a rankent da gentañ. Abostelerezh grignous skingomz London en deus aloubet ar speredoù, doñvaet un tammig gant stok an drouziwezh. Gant ar str-ishaduriou, ar gernez, ar brizonidi dalc'het pell diouzh o bro, ar yaouankizoù gal-vet da labourat e labouradegoù an estren, an enebiezh he deus kresket a-zeiz-da-zeiz betek dont d'ur chouanerezh a-enep an alouberien hag ar re a save a-du ganto. Ur c'hastiz didruez a gase an dorzh d'ar gêr d'ar re, sponterien pe vroga-rourien, a skoe gwall-daolioù a bep seurt ouzh an Alamaned, en desped d'an arsav-brezel.
"Kendalc'het o deus, avat, an Alamaned d'ober ganeomp, gant lod ac'hanomp kentoc'h, da skoazellerien en o stourm a-enep o holl enebourien diabarzh ha diavaez ha n'hon eus ket merzet e poent n'oa mui ar stourm-se hini hor bro. N'hon eus ket bet a renerien da reiñ deomp e kentel an alioù fur a oa o dever kemenn d'o zud. Marteze ivez e oa re ziwezhat deomp da ziskregiñ diouzh an erv boulc'het. Ur wech deut da vat an dilestradeg, omp bet plaouiet e drouziwezh ar re a oa dec'h

mistri ha ne dint bremañ nemet emgannerien galonek o ren betek dibenn o nerzh diwezhañ emgann o bro evit he buhez.

"Graet e vo deomp evel da drubarded. N'eus netra da herzel ouzh kazoni mistri nevez ar Stad. Mat; me n'asantin da ansav on bet un treitour nemet gwelout a rafen, mar bezan lezet da vevañ, aotreet d'ar Vretoned ar frankizioù goulennet hag azgoulennet dibaouez gant ar re anezho n'eo ket dallet o daoulagad. Keit ha ma vo laret nann d'ar goulennoù-se e vo ar gwir diouzh hon tu, daoust d'hon fazioù. Nemet faezhet omp hag hor gwellañ strivadennoù a seblant bezañ bet graet en aner. Noz ar spont a zo bremañ war an Emsav. Ne gredan ket, avat, e teufe a-benn d'ober, nann gwelloc'h, met kenkoulz ha ni, ar re a damalle deomp bezañ staget gant an hent fall. Gwir eo e kavint an tu da lavarout, ar re n'o deus ket fiñvet ur biz e-pad pevar bloaz evit an Emsav, eo ni a vo kiriek ma vez nac'het ar goulennoù a raint gant azaouez ouzh ar re n'o deus morse gouezet nemet rannañ gerioù mel ouzh kenvroiz Yann-Ber Kalloc'h. Morse, ne zeu d'o soñj e c'houlenne ar barzh, meulet ganto dre m'eo marvet war vaez ar stourm, an hevelep frankizoù ha ni, e save an hevelep klemmoù a vo kavet adarre war ziweuz ar re yaouank a zeuio deiz pe zeiz da adstagañ gant an Emsav.

"Met ni a zo graet hor stal deomp... Keuz a c'hellomp da gaout 'd'hon eurvad douarel aet da goll'... rak ne welimp ket o parañ war hor bro-Vreizh ar frankiz bevañ brezhon... Marteze zoken eo toc'hor da vat spered Breizh... Gwazh a se!... Krediñ a ran ez eo planedenn ar Vretoned an hini end-eeun m'int dellezek anezhi... Doaniet on hepken evit ar re a zo stag o buhez ouzh va hini hag evit an hiniennoù a gemer perzh en hor c'hañv d'un huñvre gaer aet da get."

Per ar Gwenn a zo moredet ur pennad 'zo. Dilavar e chom Yann Kere. Ar vouezh er gell aloubet gant an noz a seblant dezhañ dont eus ur vered: melen fresk ar pri berniet e-kichen ar bezioù nevez toullet, hag, e-tal pep toull, un arched koad sapr gant un niverenn livet e du warnañ... Trouz ebet nemet klemm an avel er gwez pin...

★★★

En noz yen deut adarre war ar gell, Yann Pere ha Per ar Gwenn o deus klevet ar brizonidi o tont en dro eus ar varn. N'o deus mui gwelet Paol Riwall. Ur gward a zo deut da gemer e ballennoù hag an traoùigoù a oa dezhañ er gell. Aner e oa goulenn keloù digant ur seurt penn beuz. An nebeutañ a c'houlennoù a reer amañ a zo bepred ar gwellañ. Un dra, avat, a zo diarvar: unan bennak a zo bet barnet d'ar marv. Klevout a reont chadennoù o stirlinkat. Lakaat a reer un den da redek gant e hualoù. Ul lamm a bak hag e skoont warnañ moarvat d'e lakaat da sevel buanoc'h.... hag ur vouezh a zistag gant ul levenez kriz: "En em voazañ a raio!"

Ya, en em voazañ a raio hag ivez ouzh pri yen ar bez pa vo deut e zeiz.

Deiz ar vourevien, avat, a zeuio ivez.

Translation

Cell No 5, *1948*

The beaten men had stopped howling. Night had fallen and Yann Kere could no longer see the black spots left by the flies on the white-washed walls of his cell. Once again, the tedious night had come upon him with its retinue of complex and hopeless thoughts. He was finding it hard to keep his feet warm. The month of November was mild, but he could not manage to keep the chill at bay, so slowly was the blood running in his veins. To tell the truth, neither the cabbage soup served at 9 am, nor the potato soup of the early evening, nor the daily ration of 350 grams of dry bread could help him fight the cold.

This past month however he had felt a little better. Every Friday he was now getting a six pound food parcel from his wife, and was able to supplement his tepid meals with a pat of butter, a slice of dried sausage and an apple. He no longer felt dizzy when he bent down nor when he laid on his straw mattress. In the first few weeks, a feeling of anxiety had oppressed him. He felt as though he was falling further and further down, even after his head had come to rest on his bed. This sensation probably came from lack of nourishing food.

Since the previous day he was no longer on his own in his cell. Two companions had come to join him. The three of them were now lying down on their straw mattresses, curled up in their two blankets, waiting for sleep to interrupt for a few hours the dreadful and painful thoughts which constantly gnawed at their minds. Paol Riwall's bed was near the door. Per ar Gwenn's mattress was opposite Yann Kere's on the bare floor.

Once again he heard what was meant to be a human voice. Wardens' voices, can one call them voices of men who have had a mother and a father? They were in truth nothing more than some machine or other, whose engine ran on hate and cruelty. They only uttered a few icy words. At 8 am, the door of the cell would open: "Coffee!" They then poured a mug of tepid brew and handed him his daily piece of bread. Some time afterwards, the lock would squeak again: "Slopping out!" At 9 am he would hear another word: "Soup!" Between 2 pm and 4 pm, another squeak: "Stroll!" and he would run towards the yard surrounded by fifteen foot walls. The only window on the front wall was barred with iron. Through it, above the brick wall which surrounded the unkempt prison garden, he saw the branches of a yellowing tree, and the roofs of houses in which lived – how astounding! – parents and children who were fond of one another. As alone in the yard as he was in his cell, he felt like a wild beast, he knew he had become a number, number 82. Once outside however, he could stand up, his back against the wall which faced the weak autumn sun. He felt the warm caress of the sunshine on his closed eyelids, but, as an overwhelming hopelessness invaded his heart, he thought that there was, somewhere on the other side, a young woman who longed for him, and an eighteen months child who would no longer recognise his father when he came to be released. But would he be released one day? His life as a free man, which had been happy, even when times were hard, had it only been a dream? He had no idea whether the recent past he cherished so much would ever come again. Perhaps the harsh and bitter present was to last for ever, like the Cold Hell of his country's hymns. His country? He would laugh bitterly whenever that word came upon his lips. That was another empty dream which had deceived him during the many years when he was trying to turn it into reality. The punishment had now fallen upon him, a merciless punishment from people who claimed to be his fellow countrymen, but who, in fact, had turned out to be his true enemies and the persistent enemies of everything he loved. The burden on his shoulders would not have been too heavy if there had not been in this world – the world from which he was exiled – a few of God's creatures who needed his help and support to live. What could he do but waste away, one by one, the countless minutes of a present cut in half by the humdrum of day and night.

Another squeak. The stroll was over. He ran back to his cell. Other prisoners were running in front of him, their hands behind their backs, hastily, like dejected dogs scampering off to their kennels. The door was locked. Now there would be peace until the second cry of "Soup!" would be heard. Then would come the treacherous moment when daylight started failing, when all his loved or hated ghosts would flutter about in his cell, when depression and bitterness would open up like the icy flowers of an endless winter. The bell rang raucously. It was time to undress, put his clothes on the heavy chair that was so hard to his wasted backside, and put them out with his leather shoes and his tin bowl. Then go to bed and shiver for another night, curled up in his blankets, as rough as a hair-shirt, waiting for a colourless dawn to light dimly the cell's dirty white walls. Although he could not sleep, he felt rather good, lying there on his bed, as he could not hear, above his head, the insults and groans of pain so usual at that time of day, when the guards, fuelled by the bestial and brutal fads of their intemperate hatred, went to beat up one prisoner or other. His mind had been so emptied by the recent events that he had to strive to remember a few words from a prayer. In fact, only one of them, the *Salve Regina*, gave him some real consolation. And he recited, several times in a row, the Latin words he had sung so often at school, years ago.

★★★

He was now no longer on his own. He had been surprised to see two other men join him in his cell. At the beginning, after fifty-one days spent alone with his thoughts, however painful they were, he had found it difficult to make room for others in his lonely life. What sort of people were they? His mind was soon put at rest. Paol Riwall claimed that he had been arrested because of his sympathy for the Breton cause and his easy relations with the Germans. Per ar Gwenn was a shopkeeper, accused by jealous fellow traders of having earned far too much money during the country's occupation and of having welcomed the green-clad soldiers in too polite a fashion in his café.

On the first night, they had chatted for a long time, each one explaining his case in the most irreproachable way, of course, but in a way which was closer to the real truth than the deformed version which would be used to judge them.

Per ar Gwenn hoped to be released soon, as he claimed he had taken no part in the political wrangle. He expected a fine. Once paid, he would leave and go far away from the senseless hatred of a town which had turned into a madhouse.

Paol Riwall and Yann Kere however, did not believe that they would be let off the hook so easily. The sworn enemies of their ideas were again in power and they could not expect any pity from them. There was no help to be got from members of the Emsav who had refused to work for Brittany, on the pretext that the Germans were on her soil. They would simply think that they deserved what they were getting. What they should have done was keep quiet, as they themselves had done, stop breathing in Breton and wait for the coming of more moderate times when they would respectfully ask politicians for requests which had always been turned down in the past and which were bound to be held in contempt in future, unless the communists were to win. They had played their fate by putting it on the table of changing events and they had lost the game. That was all.

Once every hour they heard the light switches being turned on and the noise of heavy footsteps approaching. They would suddenly stop talking. Soon afterwards, the light above their heads would shine and the guard's eye would peer through the peep-hole in the door, to check that the three of them were still there. The minutes of the dark hours would go by slowly and indifferently until sleep came to close their eyes, in the middle of the night.

★★★

The Christmas festivities were over. "Peace on earth to men of good will," as the angels used to sing a long time ago above the crib of Bethlehem in Judea. It would seem that their numbers had not grown much, because now, as in the old days, there was nothing but war and hatred between nations or between groups of people in every country. "Man is a wolf to man" is a fitter phrase to explain the history of humanity which denies its Redeemer every day.

Once every other week, the three of them would go to mass. They had all stopped going regularly to church long before being incarcerated as criminals. Here, however, like castaways, they tried to rekindle the faith of their youth in order to stay afloat on the sea of despair. But prisoners must not forget, even for half an hour, that they are guilty. That was why the prison architects had come up with a kind of upright wooden coffin, only open towards the front, up to a man's chest height. They were all ensconced in their boxes, which allowed them to hear mass without seeing anyone except for the priest at the altar, the altar boy who gave the responses and the warden on a platform in front of them, watching them constantly. Yann Kere had quickly come to recognise those of his fellow prisoners who were frequently beaten up. When one of them approached the warden standing by the door of the corridor which led to the coffins, he would turn away suddenly, as if to avoid a kick in his backside.

The prison chaplain was an old man. He did the day's reading from the Gospel, but did not usually give a sermon. That was probably better. The priests had been so drawn into the bloody fight of the time that they did not always know how to stop saying words – on the pretext of spreading God's message – words which could be unkind to the ears of the disheartened men, if their own views happened to be different. Instead of showing neutrality, at least at the foot of the altar, they sided with one or the other of the determined factions engaged in a bitter fight. It was a strange way to interpret the spirit of Catholicism which is a link between the nations of the world and not the national religion of one State or other. That is why defeated men found it more consoling to hear only the words of Christ rather than explanations given by men.

★★★

Soon after the usual banging of pans and cauldrons in the kitchen, which told him that it was about 5am, Yann Kere heard the heavy footsteps of a small group of people entering the prison. This was not the first time he had been roused by such a noise. The jangle of a cell lock. Mutterings.

"What's happening so early?" asked Paol Riwall.

"It's a wretched man going on his last stroll," said Yann. "In an hour's time, it will be over for him and there will only be a dead body riddled with bullets in front of two lines of smoking rifles."

"What?" said Paol Riwall sitting up suddenly. "Are you sure?"

"Yes, I'm sure," said Yann.

Both of them fell silent, listening to the decreasing noise of the footsteps. Per ar Gwenn was still dozing.

★★★

In the morning Paol Riwall was led to the investigating magistrate's office. The lives of the other two carried on in the usual way, like horses at the threshing machine. However, their thoughts were with the one who was striving to defend his freedom and maybe his life from a clutch of charges which could be true as well as false. They felt that his worries were bigger than their own, possibly because he had only been married for a year and had not yet seen his baby daughter born after his incarceration, possibly also for secret reasons he had not mentioned to them. Certain things were better kept to oneself. He was the only one who could really judge why he had done what he did at a particular time. In these times so full of hatred, professional judges were unable to understand a man's motives. They passed sentence according to the relentless rules of a Justice which was subject to their own political ideas.

"We are the Eternal Truth. You have worked against us. You will be punished."

"Woe betide the vanquished," said old Brennos to Rome's senator. The same phrase has been said, more than once, to his descendants, and we, once again, are in their ranks.

★★★

At twilight – the sky seen through the cell's high-set window told them that snow would soon fall – Paol Riwall returned. He looked even gloomier than he had done in the morning and seemed to be exhausted. He gulped down with disgust the bowl of insipid soup they had kept warm for him under his blankets. Immediately afterwards the bell rang and the three of them curled up on their mattresses. When would their icy feet warm up? Soon after, Yann would feel the pain creeping up in his feet and hands. The insufficient food and sedentary life had made them swell since October.

Paol Riwall had replied with short and vague answers to the questions they had asked him on his return. Then they had fallen silent. The night was dark now and they were all lost in their thoughts, aware that they could not give one another much solace.

A loved, thin and supple shadow flew around Yann Kere's head. At times it was so life-like that he felt on the verge of shouting out, so sharp was the blade which cut into his flesh. It is hard to realise how deep is the torment of a man buried alive in a locked and barred cell, when he thinks of the intense love which has been taken away from him. A few lines of a French West Indian song came to his mind, the story of a shipwrecked man singing to his beloved crying on the beach:

Do not cry so much, my lovely.
Your tears reach down
To me, at the bottom of the sea,
And they burn my heart...

And without realising it, he said in a quiet voice: "A man with a wife and children has no right to belong to the Emsav, even if his aims are purely intellectual."

"That's right," said Paol Riwall, as if talking in his dreams. "He has not got this right because he drags his family to the desert of his misfortune."

"I was twenty-two when the Germans became the rulers of this country. In June 1940, I was one of the soldiers in this army which was deployed like snow flakes in the wind. Always on the road, carted about right down to the south of France, my only wish was to return home. When I was demobilised, I returned to Brittany, on foot, in the trailer of a motorcar, and finally on a bike found in a ditch by the road-side. Once back home, I met up with my friends whose minds were set ablaze by the anticipated bright future which was shining on Brittany. It was said that the Germans were rather sympathetic to the autonomists' cause. At that time, there was no sign that the Soviets would break their agreement with the Germans, nor that the distant United States would come to sacrifice their peace on the altar of ruin. A new Europe was appearing and we had our word to say in the debate, our work to do in all fields of man's life, in order to rebuild a peaceful and dynamic West. I devoted myself to this effort and I did not want to acknowledge the major changes brought to the problem when the war became worldwide.

"As the weight of war was getting heavier and heavier on their shoulders, the Germans disengaged themselves from the problems of the extreme West. They first had to win the war in the East. The grating words of the London radio invaded minds which the impact of the rout had calmed. Because of the restrictions, of the famine, of the prisoners kept a long way from home, of the young men called to work in foreign factories, the hostility against the invaders was growing day by day, until it turned into a kind of guerrilla warfare against them and those who agreed with them. A ruthless punishment awaited those, be they called terrorists or patriots, who were setting up all sorts of attacks against the Germans, in spite of the armistice.

"However, the Germans continued to use us, some of us at least, to help them in their fight against all their enemies – whether in Brittany or abroad – and we did not notice in time that this fight was no longer the fight for our country. We did not have leaders to give us in time the wise advice that they should have given to their men. Maybe it was also too late for us to get away from what we had started. When the Normandy landings happened, we were caught in the debacle of those who had been yesterday's rulers and who were now nothing more than brave fighters, fighting to the last for the life of their country.

"We shall be treated as traitors. There is nothing to stop the hatred of the new rulers of the State. Well, I am not ready to confess to being a traitor, until I see – if I am left to live – that Brittany is given those rights which have been requested, on so many occasions, by those Bretons who never lost sight of her. As long as these requests are not met, we have the right on our side, whatever mistakes we made. But we have lost and our best efforts seem to have been made in vain. A dark time of terror is now gripping the Emsav. Yet I do not think that those who accuse us of having gone astray would achieve more, or even as much as we did. Those who have not lifted a finger in the past four years for the Emsav will certainly find a way to say that we are the guilty ones, should their polite requests to those who have done nothing but give a few words of praise to Yann-Ber Calloc'h fellow country-men be turned down. The thought never enters their heads that this poet, who wins their praises because he died on the battlefield, was in fact asking for the same rights as we are. He made the same complaints as those which will be heard from the young people who, in days to come, will rejoin the Emsav.

"As for us, we shall be punished. We can regret 'the disappearance of our earthly happiness', for we shall never know in our country, Brittany, what it is like to live as free Bretons. Maybe the spirit of Brittany is truly dying. Too bad! I believe that the Bretons are getting whatever destiny they truly deserve… I only feel pain for those whose lives are linked to mine and for the few who take a share in our loss of a beautiful dream which came to nothing."

Per ar Gwenn had been half-asleep for a while. Yann Kere did not reply. The voice in the darkened cell seemed to him to have risen from a churchyard: the heap of clay on the side of the recently dug graves is bright yellow; beside each hole, there is a pine coffin bearing a number painted in black. The only sound is that of the wind lamenting in the yew trees.

★★★

As the cold night invaded their cell, Yann Kere and Per ar Gwenn heard the prisoners returning from court. They never saw Paol Riwall again. A warden came into the cell to take his blankets and the few objects which belonged to him. There was no point in asking such a beast what had happened. In this place, the fewer the questions raised, the better. One thing however was certain. Someone had been condemned to death. They heard the clinking of chains. A fettered man was made to run. He fell down and they beat him to make him stand up faster. A cruel voice said cheerfully: "He'll get used to it!"

Yes, he will get used to it and also to the cold clay of the grave when his time comes.

The day of the torturers, however, will also come.

Roperzh ar Mason

Evit ket ha netra, *1951* (Lodenn)

In this novel, Fant, a Breton woman from the Vannes region, recalls how she was converted to the Breton cause by her sister-in-law, learnt Breton and joined the Emsav when she was in her twenties. During the second world war she became a member of the PNB (parti nationaliste breton). Her elder brother Jili also supports the cause though he stayed clear of any involvement with the party, while her younger brother Alan joined the ranks of the Free French in England. When retribution starts at the end of the war, Fant goes into hiding in a presbytery. On hearing of the death of her childhood friend Herri, murdered by the men of the maquis on suspicion of having been in the 'Bezen Perrot', (a pro-Reich militia) she rushes to his home to pay her last respects. Brec'hed, Herri's widow welcomes her and hides her. Jili now comes to visit his sister Fant and tell her and Brec'hed the latest news.

– "Diaesoc'h diaes e oa bevañ war ar maez e-pad mizioù diwezhañ an dal-c'hadur. Monedonet an Alamaned ha gwazed ar maki n'arsavent ket hag ar beizant-ed paour, preizhet gant an eil hag egile, a veze e riskl bras seul gwezh ma roent boued d'unan bennak.

Soñj ac'h eus Fant em boa bet c'hoant da chom sourzien an holl. Dañjerus e oa ar c'hoari ha koulskoude, dever rik hor micher, e-keñver pep seurt tud klañv.

Un noz e tegouezhas e Kerandro ur paotr gloazet gant an Alamaned. Nen doa mui ofiserion er c'hastell a-c'houde daou viz. Degemer a ris an den hag e wellais dezhañ e korf pemzek deiz. Her c'huzhet em boa barzh an dachenn en un ti-plouz bihan, ne servije mui nemet da zastum benveger-liorzh hag un dumporell a reas ur gwele evitañ. Daoust da dri enklask e Kerandro n'hen dizoloas ket an Alamaned. Pa voe yac'h e tistroas ar paotr hep droug d'e vagad. A Benc'hesten e oa.

Pa zegouezhas an Amerikaned da lakaat ar seziz war an Oriant, daoust da bennoù fall Bubri, o devehe sur klasket trouz ouzhimp abalamour d'hor menoioù, ec'h embannas an hini gloazet em boa graet un taol kaer a-du gant ar maki. Setu me bremañ e-touesk gouroned ar politikerezh nevez!

Alan a zo deuet d'am gwelout, ur groaz Loren war e vruched. Komzet en deus din diwar-benn Fant evit lavarout gant droug he devoa heuliet Herri en e dreisoni hag e oa bet ret dezhañ tabutal evit ne vize ket serret. Dre gomzoù arall didouell a-zivout kailhed a zo, diaes da zoñvaat, e komprenis mat e voe spontet eñ ivez gant drouglazh Herri ha ne grede ket lavarout petra 'soñje diwar an torfed. Hañval ganin e teuy dimp arre, un deiz bennak, ene diboellet hor breur...

Betek gouzout emañ dav chom war evezh. Leun eo ar vro a spierion diharak, hon enebourion a barrez Vubri da gentañ. Ar gouarnamant nevez ne glask nemet distrujañ an Emsav, sevenadurel evel politik, dre vougañ mouezh e renourion. Dija, a larer, ez eus bet war-dro kant den drouklazhet ha tri mil toullbac'het. A-c'houde 1793 n'hor boa anavet en hor bro un hande seurt gant henhen!

D'holl ar Vretoned o deus harpet an Emsav e-pad ar brezel e tamall ar gouarnamant dezhe o devout kenlabouret gant an Alamaned, hep klask abegoù arall. Ur sigur en deus allas! Farioù amoet ar re daer o deus emgannet edan sae ar re nazi."

– "Nen dint ket stank," emezon. Unan evit Gwened a-bezh. Mar behe onest ar gouarnamant n'en devehe tamallet nemet ar re-se, daoust m'emañ muntrer an abad Perrot an hini klablusañ.

– "Onest? Paour-kaezh Fant! Pell eo siwazh an onestiz diouzh prederioù hor politikerion. Nen deo ket ur brezel hepken hon eus bet, un dispac'h ne lavaran ket. Ar re ruz, deut amañ dre sotoni ar Saozon, ne vint ket skarzhet an tazoù. Gwirioù Breizh ne zifennont ket, rak katolik omp, evel Kroatiz ha Slovakiz. Setu ar pezh n'o deus ket komprenet kristenion Vreizh a vlej bremañ gant ar bleizi hag a baeo ker tuchant o dalledigezh. Spi am eus e vo graet neuze unaniezh ar re a volontez vat enep ar gailhed..."

– "Ha goulennoù an Emsav e vo selaouet oute koulz pe ziwezhat," eme Vrec'hed gant feiz. "Gant merzherion ar vro e vimp harpet sur."

Displegañ a ra neuze da Jili devezh kriz ar muntr, donedigezh c'harv an dorfedourien, o fardañ e-barzh an ti evel gouezidi, chupennoù kousiet ha frondennoù ruz gante, mindrailherezed en o daouarn. Edo Herri o skrivañ en e vurev. Zoe, he devoa heuliet ar gailhed, leun a spont, en em daolas diraze en ur grial:

– "Na lazhit ket ma mestr!"

Ur reklom boledoù a ziskaras war un dro Herri ha Zoe. Brec'hed hag he bugale, a oa neuze el liorzh, ne zegouezhas nemet evit klevout o huanad diwezhañ, e-pad mac'h ae kuit dija an drouklazherion dre ar rabin, en ur c'hoarzhin gouez.

– "Paour-kaezh Herri," eme Jili fromet. "Ur wezh arall ec'h in da bediñ war e vez. Ret eo ma kuitain Gwened kent gouloù-deiz."

Hag o treiñ trema Brec'hed:

– "Ober a rin Itron holl ar pezh a c'hellin evit ho harpañ en arnod-se ken skrijus."

Jili a ambrougan d'an nor-dal e-pad ma heuilh Anna gozh Brec'hed betek he c'hambr nevez.

★★★

E ti Bernuz, daoust d'hon tristidigezh, e teue en-dro ar vuhezegezh voas. Lies en he sal-c'hegin e kroge Anna da ganal a bouez-penn arre:

Joli, joli bébé rose...

hag an tonioù kozh-se a zreboule evel galvadennoù ar bed arall.

Jili a zeuas arre d'hor gwelout daou viz diwezhatoc'h, war-greiz an deiz ar wezh-mañ, rak habaskaet e oa un tammig spered an dud, d'e soñj.

E breder a veze ma frosez a ranke degouezhout er gambr-sivik e miz Meurzh hag hini Gweltaz, toullbac'het atav e prizon Gwened, a zeuhe kentizh war e lerc'h.

N'en devoa gellet netra evidomp nemet goulenn ma vize digabestret Gweltaz goude e varn. "Da fin ar brezel," a respontas ar Prefed. Skraperezh ar madoù a risklemp hon daou met, paour evel ma oamp, ne vehe nemet ur fent.

War an tu-se, dre eurvad, ne zoujed mui netra evit Brec'hed. Direizhted euzhus muntr Herri a oa ken splann ne voe boulc'het prosez erbet enep dezhañ. Pinvidigezh re ar Fur ha gwirioù-oberour Herri a warante bevañs Brec'hed ha desav he bugale. Herve, an hini koshañ a seblante dija bout hañval pakret ouzh e dad. C'hwec'h Breizhad a galon a savo un deiz da gemer lec'h Herri. Nann! Nen deo ket achu preder gwaskerion Bariz!

Ne badas ma frosez nemet div euriad. Troet en devoa dija spered an dud, skuizh ma oant gant rogoni ha gouezoni ar vistri nevez, dreist-holl e-touez ar gatoliked, nec'hañset a-fed o skolioù, harpet gant Vichy hag en arvar bremañ gant al likelezh o kregiñ arre. Met ne grede ket ar varnerion lakaat o brud e riskl.

E-pad ar breudoù e laris didro dezhe o fegement, ar pezh a vamas seul vui ma talc'hen, daoust d'an dek vloaz tremenet, d'am zrolinenn ha d'am dremm blac'h-yaouank.

Ma gopr a voe an dizenor broadel ha skraperezh ma danvez. Imor fall an dud e karg en em ziskouezas en ur pennad ag ar gazetenn o tistalmiñ e gounnar ma c'helled ober c'hoazh "Meuleudi entanet ar dreisoni, evel pa vizemp atav edan gwask an Alamaned."

D'an enderv-noz pa zistroen da Vernuz, disammet ma c'halon gant holl ar pezh am boa laosket, en em gavis gant an abad Maogwenn:

– "Kevelloù mat a zo, Fant! Kembreiz ha Kelted arall tramor a sav o mouezh enep an hande gall e Breizh. Un degouezh a bouez eo, hon digollo ag hon diouer kriz. Sur on, gant harp hor breudeur geltiek mac'h ay an Emsav war-raok arre, gant ar bobl marse war hol lerc'h ar wezh-mañ!"

Translation

For Practically Nothing, *1951* (Extract)

"In the last months of Occupation, life in the countryside was getting harder and harder. The comings and goings of the Germans and of the men of the maquis went on relentlessly and the wretched farmers, plundered by both sides, were running a big risk every time they gave anyone some food.

You remember, Fant, that I wanted to carry on looking after all patients, whoever they were. It was a dangerous choice but it is the strict duty of our job to do so.

One evening, a man wounded by the Germans arrived in Kerandro. All the officers had left the castle two months previously. I welcomed the man whose health recovered within a couple of weeks. I hid him on the farm, in a tiny thatched cottage which was by now only used to store garden tools. His bed was a farm cart . Although Kerandro was searched three times, the Germans did not find him. Once recovered the man went back to rejoin his group. He was from Pénestin.

When the Americans came to put the siege on Lorient, a few malicious inhabitants of Bulbry would certainly have tried to denounce us because of our ideas, but the injured man said loud and clear that I had done a great deed for the maquis. That's how I come to be one of the heroes of the new political scene!

Alan came to see me, a Lorraine cross on his chest. He talked to me about Fant, and there was anger in his voice as he said that she had followed Herri in his treachery, and that he had had to fight for her not to be thrown into prison. Other disillusioned words about certain wild and brutish men made me understand that he too had been frightened by Herri's murder and that he was not saying what he really thought about the murder. I do think that, one day, the strayed soul of our brother will come back to the fold.

However we need to stay on our guard. This place is full of dangerous spies, our enemies from Bulbry to start with. The new government are doing their best to destroy the Emsav, whether cultural or political, by stifling the voice of its leaders. I have already heard that a hundred people have been executed and that three thousand have been put into jail. There has not been such persecution in our land since 1793.

The government are accusing all the Bretons who helped the Emsav during the war of having collaborated with the Germans, without taking any other fact into consideration. Unfortunately, they have the upper hand because of the stupidity of violent men who fought under the uniform of the Nazis."

"There weren't many of them," I replied. "Only one for the whole town of Vannes. If the government were honest, they would have accused specific individuals and no one else. The murderer of the parish priest, Jean-Marie Perrot, is the most guilty of all."

"Really? Poor Fant! Honesty is unfortunately far from the minds of our politicians. We have lived not only through a war but through a revolution too. The communists, who arrived here because of the foolishness of the English, will not be ousted for a long time. They do not fight for the rights of Brittany because we are Catholic, like the Croatians and the Slovaks. This is what Christians in Brittany have not understood. They now cry with the wolves but will soon pay dearly for their blindness. And when this happens, I hope that the people of goodwill unite against the rogues..."

"... and that the questions raised by the Emsav will be listened to one day or other," said Brec'hed vehemently. "We shall surely get the support of our country's martyrs."

She then explained to Jili the fateful day of the murder, the brutal arrival of the murderers dressed in dirty jackets and red scarves who had rushed into the house like savages, machine guns in hand. Herri had been at his desk, writing. Zoe, on their heels, ignoring her fear, had thrown herself in front of them screaming:

"Don't kill my master!"

A burst of machine-gun had slaughtered both Herri and Zoe. Brec'hed and her children, who were in the garden at the time, only came into the house to witness their last breaths, while the murderers were already leaving through the tree-lined front path, laughing wildly.

"Poor Herri," said Jili in a voice trembling with emotion. "Another time, I'll go and pray on his grave, but I must leave Vannes before dawn."

And turning towards Brec'hed, she added:

"I shall do everything I can to support you in this very tragic time."

I accompanied Jili to the front door and old Anna followed Brec'hed to her new bedroom.

★★★

Despite our sadness, daily routine returned to our lives in the Berné house. As in the past, Anna could often be heard in the kitchen, singing, at the top of her voice:

Joli, joli bébé rose...

and other old tunes which, like calls from the other world, were deeply moving.

Jili came back to see us two months later, in bright daylight this time, as he thought that people's ideas were now more moderate.

He talked about my court-case which was to take place in the Civic Chamber in March, and about that of Gweltaz, who was still incarcerated in Vannes, and which was due a few days after mine.

He had not been able to do anything for us, except ask that Gweltaz might be set free after the trial. "At the end of the war," the Prefet had replied. We were both likely to lose all our possessions, but we were so poor that it would feel like a joke.

On this point, thank goodness, we no longer feared for Brec'hed. The wickedness of Herri's murder was so evident that the charges against him had been dropped. The wealth of the Le Fur family and the royalties from Herri's publications would provide for Brec'hed and for the education of her children. Herve, the eldest, was already the spitting image of his father. Soon, six brave Bretons would rise to take Herri's place. No! The oppressors in Paris will not be able to rest!

My own court-case lasted only two hours. People's minds had changed. They were tired of the arrogance and brutality of the new leaders. This was especially true of the Catholics who were worried about their schools which had had the support of the Vichy government but were now threatened by the return to secularism. The judges however did not want to risk their reputations.

In my defence speech, I resolutely spoke my mind, to everyone's surprise, as, ten years on, I still had the body and the face of a young girl.

I was condemned to national dishonour and to the loss of all my property. The anger of the authorities was revealed in a fiery newspaper article which stated that one could still "praise treachery, as though we were still under the yoke of the Germans."

Later that afternoon I was feeling light-hearted from having spoken so frankly. On the way back to Berné, I met a priest, Maogwenn:

"I have good news, Fant! The Welsh and other overseas Celts are raising their voices against the French persecutions in Brittany. This is an important event, which will make up for our cruel losses. I am sure that, with the help of our Celtic brothers, the Emsav will be reborn, and maybe this time, the majority of people will be with us."

Letters from *Baner Ac Amserau Cymru*

Towards the end of 1945 and throughout the following months of 1946 a series of letters, mostly anonymous, appeared in the Welsh weekly journal Baner Ac Amserau Cymru. *These letters contained allegations that the French authorities had persecuted Breton nationalists and those who supported the Breton language and culture after the liberation of Brittany in 1944. It has been estimated that fewer than eighty Breton nationalists collaborated openly with the Germans in the war years, a tiny figure in comparison with other parts of France and other German occupied countries. The biggest collaborators of all, suggested Helmut Kochen, the head of the Gestapo in France, at his trial in 1954, were the Police Nationale Française, the Gendarmerie Française and the French justice system. The French Gendarmerie administered the prison camp in Drancy, on the outskirts of Paris. Every week, from August 1940 until the liberation, three thousand French Jews were transported from this holding camp to Auschwitz. One who died in Drancy was the Jewish writer and artist from Quimper, Max Jacob.*

But this was of little importance. This was a great opportunity to blacken the name of Breton nationalism, cultural and political, and above all, to destroy the Breton language. Articles written by the Rev John Dyfnallt Owen, a Welsh Congregational Minister, who before the war had close connections with leaders of the Breton cultural movement, sparked off the interest. The series of letters then appeared during which Dewi Watkin Powell (later Judge Watkin Powell), as a journalist for Baner Ac Amserau Cymru, *went to the trial of the leader of the Breton literary renaissance, Roparz Hemon. The presence of a foreign journalist caused panic and con-*

fusion in the court with frantic telephone calls being made to Paris. It had been anticipated that Hemon would have been sentenced to death. In the event he was sentenced to civil degradation, i.e. lost his citizenship for life. He moved to Ireland where he lived as a highly respected academic for the rest of his life. The following are brief extracts from some of the Breton letters – one of which defends the French authorities.

From Breton I, Baner Ac Amserau Cymru, *December 26, 1945*

It has for a long time been the intention of the French Government to exterminate the Breton language. This was made clear by M. Doumergue, former President of the Republic, and by M. de Monzie, a former Minister of Education. The latter said publicly in 1926, "for the linguistic unity of France, Breton should be exterminated".

In 1939, in spite of frequent protests by town councils, and societies of all kind, Breton was still not studied in the schools of Brittany. We were allowed just two hours of Breton at Rennes University. Every opportunity was taken to destroy our language. We suffered under the French Republic the same oppression as that suffered by the people of Bolsen under Mussolini, the Catalans under France and the Koreans under Japan.

In 1941, during the German occupation, our language was allowed on radio for the first time. It was never used for political purposes. Breton private schools were opened and, through the Breton Celtic association, Breton studies were promoted at the highest level.

When the French government returned in 1944, the persecution of all things Breton resumed.

I can testify that

(1) around 3,000 Bretons have been arrested for being nationalists since 1944. It should be noted that many other nationalists – not included in that figure – are in hiding. The arrests were made at the end of November 1944, at the command of General Allard.

(2) The majority of these alleged nationalists were not involved in politics. M. R. Tanguy of Rennes was taken to the local prison camp accused of "stating that France should be re-Celticized". It is true that Breton dancing has not been prohibited, but some of those who belong to these clubs have been arrested. Members of Breton pipe-bands have also been arrested. Many priests in Léon (North Finistère) and Cornouaille have been arrested.

(3) Those arrested (among them young girls and women) have been forbidden from speaking Breton or writing letters in their own language. Many have been treated roughly and some have been beaten. M. Charles was beaten so badly in the prison camp in Rennes that he had to be taken for a time to a mental hospital.

(4) Many have been killed – people who took no part in politics. Among them were Father Lec'hvien of Quimper-Gwezenneg and the Countess du Guerny. The

latter, a well known Breton writer, was arrested in her house in Côtes-du-Nord by soldiers from Toulouse and killed in front of her children.

(5) A few local (news?) bulletins have been permitted recently. But even as early as August 1944 all Breton papers have been banned, even the children's magazine *Olole*. That was also the fate of such periodicals as *Feiz ha Breiz, Galv, Nemeton, Sav, Breiz Atao, Gwalarn, Dihunamb, Galerne*, etc.

(6) The *Brezoneg er Skol* movement, which provides books for teachers and pupils, was deemed illegal in December 1944. As the name suggests (Breton in the Schools) the only purpose of *Brezoneg er Skol* was to promote the language. Its chairman, Yann Foueré, was thrown into a prison camp in October 1944.

(7) The teaching of Breton history in primary schools has been prohibited by the Commissaire de la République. It has never been allowed in secondary schools.

(8) Anyone in Britain can listen to Radio-Rennes on 288 metres and discover that our native language has also been prohibited here. Because he used the Breton language in talks to farmers about our literature, Roparz Hemon, founder of the Breton cultural renaissance, is now in a prison camp under the incredible charge of "cultural relations".

[There follows a list of Bretons condemned to death, some of whom had been executed.]

This is not all. There has been torture – as in Dachau – of members of the Parti Nationaliste Breton. Le Ruyet, one of its young members, had his leg broken in Rennes prison camp while being interrogated by policemen.

How can this be called democratic freedom? How is it possible to reconcile this with the United Nations Charter (chapter 1, paragraph 1), "The right of everyone to live in peace, regardless of language or sex".

★★★★

From Breton II, January 23, 1946

I have myself opposed the Germans and deeply desired to see them defeated. I managed to avoid all contact with them and I was sorry to see some who believed they would be victorious and would do something for our language. Such stupidity! The agents of the enemy have tried to take advantage of us in this and other ways. But the majority of my countrymen have not fallen into the trap; they have done nothing but continue to work for our language and culture.

Alas, the idea has been fostered that working for Brittany was the same as working for the Germans. This is totally false and the Bretons cannot be held responsible for the evil of the paid employees of the enemy nor for the errors of half a dozen of our compatriots who were tricked and led astray.

I knew the Abbé [Yann-Vari Perrot] very well, and can assure you he never worked for the Germans. Many malicious stories have been spread about him and there is no truth in any of them. People have said he welcomed enemy soldiers into his home and offered them champagne. He never drank anything but water! Others claimed he bought pigs for their army. I know he once bought a pig, for himself, and had to borrow money from his curate to do so. He had very little money. Yet, as everyone knew, his house, his table and his purse were at the disposal of all.

I heard, too, that people said he saw a great deal of the Germans. It is not surprising! His house had been taken over – or a large part of it – by them and they moved around in it day and night. I remember he fed a dog belonging to them that received nothing from them but kicks. I know that the Abbé was severely critical of Hitler and that he had to pay a fine to the Germans for breaking a curfew. Others have claimed that he did not support the young men who went into hiding to avoid being sent to work in Germany. All I know is that he gave every assistance to my son who was in exactly such a situation.

Roparz Hemon is about to appear before the Court of Justice in Rennes – next month from what I understand. During the war he has done nothing but write books and tried to get more Breton on Radio-Rennes. […] If he is found guilty it will be a terrible blow for the Breton language. Many feel that it is the language itself that is on trial.

[Abbé Perrot, a parish priest in Scrignac, was assassinated on the instructions of the Resistance and the communists on Sunday, December 12, 1943.]

★★★★

From Dr Yann Ezel, rue des Réservoirs, Douarnenez, March 13, 1946. This is the only letter by a Breton for which the name of the writer is published. Dr Ezel was born in Ploare in 1908 and died in Douarnenez in 1967. He was a writer of short stories in the Breton language.

I shall only write of what I saw or that which I have personal knowledge. I think I have every right to do so, for I was arrested in my own home in rue des Réservoirs Douarnenez, where I am a practising doctor. The only reason given for my arrest, which happened on November 20, 1944, was that I was a local leader of the Parti Nationaliste Breton in the Douarnenez area. I stress that I was not accused of having any contact with the Germans during the occupation, and that there had been no contact between them and myself. Nevertheless I was interned in the Saint-Charles prison camp in Kerfeunteun, near Quimper, and I was kept there until May 17, 1945. I was accused by the *Chambre Civique* in Quimper on May 16, 1945, of being a member of the Breton Nationalist Party, and I was sentenced to civil degradation for the rest of my life. I have lost all my rights as a citizen.

The rules of Saint-Charles were not those of a political camp but of a prison. We were kept there for many months, confined to a tiny cell and only permitted 20 minutes for exercise each day and two hours towards the end of our internment.

Mid-day we had potato soup, potatoes boiled in half a litre of water; in the evening we had three-quarters of a litre of watery vegetable potage. Once a week we were given a little meat. The cells were damp and dirty, with no heating and health conditions were very bad. I will not dwell on cases such as that of our compatriot Joseph Le Poinse, a barber in Carhaix, who was treated so badly that he could not stand for a week.

This was the treatment meted for months to Breton patriots whose only crime was their love of Brittany and the Breton language. I saw in Saint-Charles many members of the Parti Nationaliste Breton thrown into prison because they were patriots and not for any crime of contact with the Germans. I cannot give you detailed figures, nor the names of all my compatriots imprisoned in Saint-Charles. I enclose the names of about sixty with this letter. [*These were published separately in the same issue of the paper.*]

During the summer of 1945 the prison camps were emptied as the prisoners were brought to trial. The majority on my list were sentenced to loss of citizenship for life; many were deprived of all their property and were no longer permitted to reside in Brittany. This last measure, preventing the more prominent nationalists from remaining in Brittany is proof that their crime was not collaboration with the Germans but that it was their Breton activities which worried the authorities, and they wanted to stifle them.

The detail I have just given is about the Saint-Charles prison camp. There were many similar camps in Brittany, filled with Breton nationalists, e.g. the camp in Langueux in Côtes-du-Nord; Saint-Pabu and Pont-de-Buis in Finistère; Chateaubriant in Loire-Inférieure. I should mention in particular the Marguerite Barracks in Rennes because I know thousands of Breton nationalists have been imprisoned there. [...] I do not wish to accuse anyone in particular, but I feel it is my duty, for the sake of truth, to state that Breton nationalists, by the hundreds since 1944, have been thrown into prison or prison camps and sentenced to further imprisonment or loss of national citizenship, also that their property has been taken from them, and they cannot live in the country of their birth; and this has happened to us simply because we loved Brittany. We therefore believe that these sentences do us credit, rather than being a disgrace.

Whoever claims that Breton patriots now live under a free government that allows Breton culture to develop, is either mistaken, or deliberately misleading.

★★★★

From Breton III, writing from Morlaix, in the edition dated March 13, 1946 – the same edition as the letter from Dr Yann Ezel. The author was almost certainly the journalist and author Francis Gourvil, a fluent Welsh speaker. It is believed that he also translated into French, extracts at least, of Ambrose Bebb's Dyddiadur Pythefnos, *a diary of a journey around Brittany undertaken by Bebb on the very eve of war. Bebb was actually in the company of Loeiz Herrieu when the siren sounded announcing that war had been declared. The book includes interviews with leading Breton nationalists and these were subsequently used against them as evidence in their trials.*

No French Government has ever tried to prohibit the speaking or writing of Breton. It has to be said, however, that there has never been in Brittany any popular movement to appeal to the government on behalf of the Breton language. This has only ever been done by a small group of academics.

There is no truth whatsoever in the claim that 3,000 Bretons have been imprisoned since 1944 because of their patriotism. Those who are in prison are there because they collaborated with the Germans, or because of suspicion that they had been traitors to their country.

Leaders of the *Parti Nationaliste Breton* with the aid of the Germans, published *L'Heure Bretonne* to spread Nazi ideas and oppose the Allies.

Based on my own experience of imprisonment by the Germans, I can say that the treatment given to prisoners by the French government cannot be compared to what we suffered at the hands of the Germans.

The Bretons condemned to death or hard labour have been found guilty by all-Breton juries. Madame du Guerny was a woman who did all in her power to assist the Germans. She was condemned to death because she gave the Germans details of a place near her home where a number of Breton *maquisards* were hiding.

Breton publications produced with the assistance of the Germans have not been prohibited, they died naturally after the liberation because no publisher would stock them.

The reason why Radio-Rennes has not broadcast anything in Breton after liberation is that the transmitter has not returned to full power after the Germans had destroyed it before leaving. Because of its geographical situation, it cannot broadcast to the Breton-speaking parts of Brittany.

Roparz Hemon was imprisoned because he broadcast during the war as an officer in the service of the Germans.

I can assure the people of Wales that there is no persecution in Brittany and we do not believe that sympathy should be shown to those who collaborated for five years with the enemy who oppressed us so heavily and cruelly. Those who deserve our sympathy are the families of the hundreds who were tortured and killed by the Germans and their bodies thrown into the long and deep trenches discovered after the enemy was driven from our country.

★★★★

From Breton IV, mainly in response to Breton III. This letter was published on April 24, 1946:

The attitude of France has always been one of opposition to the Breton language. The language is not taught in the schools and in many schools it is forbidden to

speak it in the playground. Combes, the Culture Minister, has declared that the language shall not be used in the churches [...] Last month (February) it was announced that prisoners would not be permitted to speak Breton in Fontrevault prison.

It is incorrect to say that there has never been a popular movement in support of the Breton language. In 1934 hundreds of town councils called – in vain – for the teaching of Breton in the schools. In 1945, hundreds of students in Brittany called for the same right in a letter to the Education Minister.

If the Germans were cruel towards their prisoners, so too were the French. In Vannes, in particular, there was deliberate malnutrition; prisoners were tortured with cigarette burns on their bodies when they were interrogated. In Chateaubriant, sadistic practices were common; old men were forced to run on all fours and even made to eat their own faeces.

Madame du Guerny was not tried, she was tortured and shot.

No one can believe, after a year and a half, that there has not been a Breton language broadcast on Radio-Rennes because the transmitter was destroyed.

I wonder who, in Brittany, are the Nazis. The Bretons who want their freedom, inside or outside the French State, or those who continue to abuse those they perceive as their enemies, seeking excuses to commit the most vile murders, and preventing patriots from publishing any journal?

[The letter also points out that many journals received assistance from the Germans, in one instance a paper that was very pro-Nazi was allowed to continue after liberation as its editor had taken an anti-Breton stance before the war – and did so again at the end of hostilities.]

Valère Depauw

Breiz Atao, *1968* (Extract)

This novel was originally written in Flemish and published in Belgium. It has been translated and published in Welsh and German but not, as far as we can tell, French. Maiwenn Kloareg's husband, Erwann, a Breton nationalist, was shot by the French authorities – unjustly it turns out – for collaborating with the Germans. Maiwenn, unable to face her neighbours, goes to live in Paris. This passage describes her return to Brittany.

The train arrived in Nantes, and Maiwenn felt the joy of an exile returning after many years in a foreign land. She was once more in Nantes, the old Naoned that France through the centuries had eyed with a view to plunder. Today, as before, it was necessary to fight to keep Nantes Breton, but with weapons other than those used by the celebrated Duke Alain Barbe-Torte. She saw for herself in the station how the battle was being fought today, because painted on the wall of one of the buildings were the words 'Brittany without Nantes is not Brittany. Breizh Hor Bro!'

The train stopped, the door opened suddenly, so suddenly that the man sleep-

ing in the opposite corner of the carriage woke, startled. Maiwenn studied the confused look on his face, but the next moment her attention was drawn elsewhere.
Three, four, five young men came into the carriage, each with a yellow card and the
letters *Kemper, Gouel Kernev* in the lapel of his coat. They sat noisily, one of them
opposite Maiwenn. She smiled at him. He smiled back, a youthful smile, friendly
as if they knew each other. Why did she think of Yolo and Patrick Ar Braz?

The train resumed its journey. The young men settled down and the man in the
corner closed his eyes and tried to sleep again. But in the next carriage there were
other lads who had got on the train in Nantes, and it was not long before they disturbed the silence. One of them started singing a song that Maiwenn knew perfectly well: '*Ma Frañsez er velin avel* – In the misery of his windmill, Frañsez thinks
of his beloved Mari-Joseb.

Maiwenn smiled to herself. She remembered dancing to the song with Erwann
in the Kernascléden festival soon after they were married. Erwann was Frañsez and
she was Mari-Joseb. It is a happy song, the words at least, but like all Breton songs
the music retains the rhythm of the ballads and the *cantiques*. And she heard it again,
like an echo of happy days from the past, hearing it on her way home …

A youngster sang a line, with the others responding, repeating the line; he sang
another line which was again repeated. By the time they got to the first line of the
second verse the young men in Maiwenn's carriage were joining in, uncertainly,
humming quietly … And not only the men; Maiwenn could not resist, because she
felt again the spirit of the days when singing was as natural to her as speaking. And
she started singing. The others took this as a sign to stop humming and to sing
loudly so that their fellow-travellers in the next carriage could hear them. The man
in the corner sat up in his seat, there was no hope of sleep.

At the end of the song, the young man sitting by her side turned to Maiwenn:
"Are you going to the Cornouaille festival, Madame?"

He asked the question in French, and hearing French spoken after the Breton
song surprised Maiwenn. But, she thought, the young men should not be blamed.
In Nantes, at the borders of the old country, far from Breton-speaking Brittany, not
many would know the language.

"Yes," she answered, also in French. "And you too, I see … Will there be many
from Nantes in Quimper?"

"Oh, yes, many, the majority are already there. The Nantes *Kevrenn* [section]
were there yesterday in the concert of Breton music, and four of the *sonerien*
[pipers] were also taking part. And our choir was also there singing Breton songs."

"So you are not a member of the *kevrenn* or the choir?" asked Maiwenn with a
smile.

But there was no smile on his face when he replied:

"The battle cannot be won only through singing, playing instruments and dancing. Other things have to be done."

It was what Paol Hulen had told her in the past.

It was broad daylight by now – a brilliant morning, the country fresh in the sunlight, at the same time green and gold, a sight not to be seen anywhere except in Brittany. It was the sight she had never been able to forget, a sight that constantly came to her mind in her hours of grief and longing. For so many years she had renounced it, of her own will, and accepted the greyness of Paris, its illusions and disenchantments. If she had ever been aware of that voluntary sacrifice, this was it. But she could think of it without sorrow or bitterness, because it had not been in vain. Bitterness and sorrow? No, to the contrary, it was pure joy to have suffered the disgrace for so long, as if the accusations of villainy had been brought against her. Because of that she could not be as one with Erwann, able to return, proud and strong, to settle her account with those who had disgraced both of them, Erwann and herself.

In the next carriage they were singing again: love songs, battle songs, a ballad. And the young men who were with Maiwenn started singing too, but they soon stopped, perhaps because she was not singing with them. She was staring through the window, and the names of the villages and the small towns that the train sped through sounded familiar, even in their French forms: Chantenay, La Basse Indre, Saint Herblain-Couéran, Saint-Etienne de Montluc … On the wall of a building in Saint-Etienne de Montluc Maiwenn saw – stirring her to the depths of her soul – painted in huge letters the war cry of former days and of all time: *Breiz Atao!* – Brittany for ever!

"And we must ensure that those words come true," said a voice.

It was the young man at her side who had spoken. She looked at him. There was no need to explain, she had understood.

Afterwards she asked him:

"Do you speak Breton?"

"No," he answered, with more than a little regret. "But we understand it pretty well, thanks to the Breton songs we are learning. And the young people are becoming keener than ever to learn it."

"Well, there is a way of learning it. Lessons by post, for instance."

"Yes, we know. And if we have to, that's how we'll learn it. But there is a lot of talk of organising evening classes next winter, and a good number are keen to join them. We're all very keen," he said pointing to his four friends.

The four moved closer, so that all five men and Maiwenn were a private little group apart from the man in the corner. He had listened to them singing, but now he picked up his newspaper, but perhaps he only pretended to read, listening to them talking behind the paper.

"Where are you from, Madame?" asked one of the young men.

"From Cornouaille. To be more precise from the Bigouden area … But I lived in Paris for seven years …"

She realised that she had spoken of the past: had she not said that she had lived in Paris? This was how she definitely announced her decision, in the presence of these lads from a part of the country that was under the greatest threat, five Bretons who didn't know her, but perhaps even that had its significance.

"And now I'm returning to Brittany," she said.

The man in the corner went off the train in Savenay, without saying a word, and it was a relief to see him leave. Two girls came in. They, too, were going to Quimper, and the lads honoured them by singing a lovely lament from the hills of Cornouaille, *Ar Gwennilied*.

The girls smiled, shyly, then they sang, a song that was one of Maiwenn's favourites: *An hini a garan* – The one I love. A song inspiring such memories! Things had changed very little, she thought, and young people today were no different from her and Erwann and their friends.

When her compartment became silent once more, Maiwenn could hear the joyful singing in the next compartment and other compartments – a train swelling in song on the way towards Quimper. Could she have ever hoped for such a joyful return ..? The countryside became increasingly familiar, villages and towns awakening myriads of memories. Here, she and Erwann had given a day to propaganda; there she and others had arranged to defend Frañsez Debauvais when he came to speak in spite of being banned by the authorities ...

Then Saint-Gildas-des-Bois, Redon, Questembert, Vannes – town of Nominoë, who inspired the Bretons to unity. Then Auray, and nearby, Kerleano, where Georges Cadoudal was born and where his bones were buried, but just his bones, because after he had been executed by the French his body was given to medical students of the University of Paris. Thus, against his will, was the anti-revolutionary put to the services of France.

Lorient, then Gestel. A little beyond Gestel they saw a man standing on a heath, alone in the great expanse, waving the Breton flag – a magnificent picture of a rapturous vision from a distant past. [...]

Then came Quimperlé, faithful Quimperlé. Then Rosporden, Saint-Ivy. At last Quimper.

Maiwenn let herself be carried by the powerful flow of the crowd. Here, inside the station, everything was in French, the name 'Quimper,' every sign, every noticeboard. But the young army that walked onwards was Breton, the echoing songs were Breton, then everyone joined in one song: *Gwir Vretoned!* – True Bretons.

Maiwenn came out of the station and there before her was Quimper. And a massive baner proclaiming the words of welcome:

Eus Brest betek Naoned, holl Vretoned breudeur. From Brest to Nantes, all Bretons are brothers.

She was home at last, home.

Per Denez

Milliget ra vezin ma tisoñjan ac'hanout Jerusalem, *1981* (Lodenn)

N'em boa ket da glemm evit ar sizhunvezh-se. A-benn ar fin, ha da vat, e teue frankoc'h an traoù ganin: e oa echu, emichañs, gant an trubuilhoù arc'hant. Ken kustum e oan da vezañ sammet ganto ma ne oan ket evit disouezhiñ. Daoust ha krog e oa evidon maread ar saout lard? Marteze ne oa ket c'hoazh... da nebeutañ 'oan gouest da zigeinañ... Na brav e oa ober un ehan ha tennañ goustadik an anal!... Start oa bet an traoù. Den n'oufe krediñ pegen start oant bet. Da vloaz warn-ugent oa bet lamet diganin ma diplomoù Skol-Veur peogwir oan bet e-barzh ar Strollad Broadel, keit hag ober oa bet difennet ouzhin, gant kastiz an 'dizenor broadel' – 'felle ket dezho kompren pehini oa ma bro – bezañ skolaer, kelenner, kazetenner, medisin, alvokad, ha me 'oar! Diaes e oa krediñ, e 1945, e talveze Diskleriadur Gwirioù Mab-den evit Breizhiz ivez. Trubuilhoù, dibaouez. Mont a ra unan skuizh. Un hent avat a oa kinniget deoc'h da dec'hout diouzh an holl drubuilhoù. Un hent digor-frank d'ar C'hallaoued fall, koulz ha d'ar C'hallaoued vat aet war an tu fall, da enebourien dec'h savet keuz enno a-greiz-holl da vezañ bet enebourien: ne oa ket an hent-se unan strewet gant roz and jesamin, met war-eeun e kase d'an digastizañ. Ret e oa, evit daspren pec'hedoù un emgann, mont d'ober un emgann all, ar wech-se evit ar frankiz anat eo, ar gwir, ar sevenadur, tout an traoù petra, an emgann e menezioù hag e rizegi Bro-Vietnam, a veze anvet c'hoazh Indochina gant ar re a gase ar re all da vervel di. Ha neuze 'ta oan aet. Pa oan deut en-dro, pevar bloaz war-lerc'h, oan ket mui dizenoret. Ur vedalenn bennak a zegasen ganin zoken, hag ivez skeudennoù em eñvor na oa ket re vat prederiañ hir warno. Adenoret e oan, hag e c'hellen bezañ skolaer, kelenner, kazetenner, medisin, pe alvokad. Ya. Gant m'am bije bet arc'hant, hag amzer, da studiañ en-dro. Gant ma n'em bije ket bet gwreg ha bugel da vagañ... Hag e soñjen: daoust ha n'int ket bet pell a-walc'h, o-daou, o fritañ mizer? Petra 'm bije graet neuze nemet mont da veajour koñvers? En em lakaat a ris da werzhañ gwin. Mont a di da di, a zor da zor, ha lakaat an den-mañ-den, n'en doa bet morse ar seurt soñj en a-raok, da gaout c'hoant bras, a-greiz-holl, da brenañ ur c'hesad boutailhadoù Bourgogn gant etiketennoù brav hag un anv brudet, brudet mui pe vui. Ar c'hesad-se a oa, evidon hag evit ma familh, boued evit an devezh: boued treutik, met boued memestra. Ne oan ket, anat eo, ma-unan-penn war an hent gant ar vicher-se hag alies e soñje din e vije bet aesoc'h gwerzhañ ur skornerez d'un Eskimo eget un dousennad bout-aihadoù gwin d'ur mondian. Koulskoude eo 'kartennoù mat', e-giz ma vez lavaret, a oa ganin. Koulskoude e oan deut ken helavar war berzhioù dispar ma mar-c'hadourezh ha tad misioner ar retred-katekiz war levenez ar baradoz prometet d'ar vugale fur. Hag e labouren start, e valeen a-hed straedoù na baouezent ket da ziger-iñ war straedoù all c'hoazh, e pignen gant dirioù a seblante ken diziwezh ha skeul Jakob, ha n'eo ket alies e paken ma lein en ur restaoldi: daoust da se n'hellan ket lavarout eo bevañ a raemp, chom hep mervel gant an naon hepken. Ha ret-mat e oa din bezañ mousc'hoarzhus, ha lavarout trugarez evit ar pakadoù dilhad kozh, evit an nebeud bilhiji-bank – "c'hwi 'oar, trapenn d'ar bugel an hini a reomp kement-se, Itron Poulpiked" – a veze astennet din gant va zud, dismegañsus a-walc'h an tamm anezho, din-me, an hini er familh hag a oa troet-fall. Aze 'm boa lonket anezhi avat! Ha bloavezhioù 'oa padet! Tenn oa bet derc'hel penn. Sevel tammig ha tammig ar penn. Tenn! Ma Chezuz, un ifern! Ur gwir ifern! Pa teue neuze kamaraded kozh, bet ganto ar chañs da dremen a-dreuz melloù ar roued, pe da zivellañ abred a-walc'h, dezho ur vicher vat e Pariz hag un ti-hañv bihan e Breizh – un ti mod kozh anat eo –; pa c'hoarveze da gamaraded eus an amzer gozh, hag eus an emsav kozh, kavet ganin war hentoù put va foanioù pemdeziek, dont d'ober ouzhin tamalloù: "penaos, ur stourmer eveldout, bezañ lezet pep tra da gouezhañ... bezañ troet kein... penaos biskoazh e c'hellfe ar vro bezañ saveteet...", pa teuent din evel-se gant o c'hof tev hag o sac'had reprochadoù, e raen outo ur risign ken divalav, e tiguzhen en ur mousc'hoarzh ken drouk ma dent faos (ma dent-me a oa aet gant ar skorbud), ken e tennen a-grenn diouto ar c'hoant da genderc'hel. Kerkoulz all e tennen diouto ar c'hoant da brenañ gwin diganin. Met eus an dra-se e raen foutre-kaer, foutre-kaer... Ha p'o dije goulennet, 'm bije ket gwerzhet dezho. Trawalc'h am boa graet, nann?, memestra..

Translation

May I Be Cursed if I Forget You Jerusalem, *1981* (Extract)

I had no complaints to make about that particular week. At long last, my life was getting easier. With a bit of luck, my money problems were over. I was so used to worrying about them that I could not get used to the idea. Were more affluent days upon me? Maybe not yet, but at least I could relax. How nice it was to be able to stop and take a long breath! Things had been hard. No one will ever believe how hard they had been. At twenty-one, my university degree was taken away from me because I had been a member of the PNB. What is more, I had been condemned to 'national dishonour' by people who did not want to understand which was my true country. This meant that I could no longer become a schoolmaster, a teacher, a journalist, a doctor, a solicitor, and goodness knows how many other things. In 1945, it was hard to believe that the Declaration of Human Rights also applied to the Bretons. Nothing but problems, incessantly. One gets tired. However, there was a way to redeem oneself and forget all these worries. It was a way open to bad Frenchmen, as well as to good Frenchmen who had made the wrong choices, to the former enemies who suddenly regretted having been enemies. That way was not paved with rose and jasmine, but it led straight to forgiveness. To atone for the sins of one battle, one had to take part in another battle, a battle for freedom this time round, of course, but also for the law of the land, for culture, and for everything else you can think of. That battle was taking place in the mountains and rice fields of Vietnam, which, at the time, was still called Indochina by those who sent other people to die there. So, I went there. When I came back, four years later, I was no longer dishonoured. I also brought back some military medal or other, as well as livid memories which I had rather not dwell on. I had recovered my honour, and could now become a schoolmaster, a teacher, a journalist, a doctor or a solicitor. That would have been all well and good if I had had the money and the time to return to studying, if I had not had a wife and a child to feed. What I thought was:

"Haven't the two of them had enough misery to cope with during all this time?" There was no real choice for me but to become a commercial representative. So I started selling wine. I went from house to house, from door to door, to convince people who had never thought of it before that they suddenly craved for a crate of Burgundy bottles carrying beautiful labels and a famous name – famous or not quite so famous. That crate was, for me and my family, food for a day: not a lot of food, but food all the same. Obviously I was not the only one on the roads doing this particular job, and I often thought that it would be easier to sell fridges to Eskimos than a dozen bottles of wine to the wealthy. Yet, I worked for so-called prestigious winegrowers. I had become as eloquent about the excellent quality of my merchandise as a missionary priest talking, during a confirmation retreat, about the joys of paradise promised to all good children. I worked hard. I walked along streets that never stopped leading on to other streets. I climbed stairs which seemed as endless as Jacob's ladder. I did not often stop to have lunch in a restaurant. In spite of all this, I can't say that we really lived. We just managed to keep hunger at bay. What's more, I had to keep a smile on my face, say thank you for the parcels of second-hand clothes, for a few banknotes – "You know, we're only doing this for the child, Mrs Poulpiked" – given by members of my family who looked contemptuously down on me, the one in the family who had turned out badly. Didn't I have to swallow my pride! This went on for years! It had been hard to keep afloat, to learn little by little to keep my head high. Hard? Dear God, it was hellish! Truly hellish! When I received the visit of old comrades who had been lucky enough to slip through the net or to find a way out early enough, and they now had a good job in Paris and a holiday cottage in Brittany – one of those old cottages, obviously – when companions of the old days, of the old Emsav, encountered on the rocky roads of my daily toil, came to admonish me: "What! a fighter like you! You dropped everything. You turned your back. How do you ever think our country could be saved?" When they came thus, with their big bellies and their sacks of rebukes, I sniggered so nastily, I smiled so maliciously to uncover my false teeth – scurvy had made my real teeth fall out – that I suddenly removed from them the wish to carry on talking. Obviously they no longer fancied buying any wine from me. But I didn't give a damn about it. Had they asked me, I wouldn't have sold it to them. I had done my fair share, hadn't I? Don't you think so?

Roparz Hemon

Pirc'hirin ar mor, *1933* (Lodenn)

       Da-unan-penn!
               Ya, sav ha kerzh. Atav,
      Etrezout ha da vreur, ul latar yen
             A vougo flammig lent ar gengarantez,
      Kerkent ha ganet.
             Douster, hegarated,

Madelezh kuñv hag habask, haelded leun!
Te 'oar, ne dint netra, mar chom da zremm
Difiñv 'vel dremm un delwenn, war he gweuz
Ur mousc'hoarzh hir ha skornet, 'vit an holl
Heñvel.
      Ma!
          Tonket ez eo dit!
             Pirc'hirin,
Ne deus er bed evidout den na lec'h
Da'z kervel pe da'z mirout.
              Neuze, kerzh!
Da-unan-penn en doan hag el levenez!

Skañv eo da samm, an hent 'zo frank ha ledan,
Start eo da dreid!
        Pa weli dremm pe vleunienn,
Arabat sellout hir!
           Ne'z karont ket,

Da-unan-penn out deut. Ha mont a ri,
E skilf ar Maro kriz, da-unan-penn!

Ha neuze, pa vo sec'h da eskern, mik,
E kornig klouar ur vered, hag ar bed
O tec'hout mil ha mil lev diouzh da amzer,
Piv 'oar?
      Un denig seven, sioul eveldout,
A zeuio kuñv d'azezañ 'dan ar gleuzeur;
Gant e vizied onest e tigoro
Al levrig kozh deut melen gant an oad.

Ha 'vel pa rog ur barrad gwent ar c'hoabr,
E vezi trumm dirazañ, kig hag ene.

Hag eñ, aketus-bras, ha fur, a welo
An Den 'zo bet ac'hanout.
          Eñ, an estren,
A-dreuz d'ar gerioù iskis ha diampart,
D'ar c'hoantoù aner, d'al lorc'hentez vugel,
A gavo hent e galon hag a chomo
Sebezet.

Translation

Pilgrim of the Sea, *1933* (Extract)

On your own!
            Yes, get up and walk. From now on,
Between you and your brother, a cold fog
Will smother the faint flame of mutual affection
As soon as it is kindled.
            Sweetness, affability,
Pure and patient gentleness, true magnanimity
Don't you know? They are nothing if your face remains
As lifeless as that of a statue with
Its everlasting frozen smile. The rule
Applies to all.
            And so
                This is your fate!
                    Pilgrim,
There is no man and no place in the world
To beckon you or make you stay.
                    So, walk!
On your own, through sorrow and through joy.

Your burden is light; the road is open and wide,
Your feet are firm on the ground.
            When you catch sight of a face or a flower,
Don't look too closely.
                    They don't love you.

You got here on your own and, when you fall into
The clutches of death, you will be on your own.

But then, when your bones are fleshless and dry
In a cosy corner of a churchyard; when the world
Will have raced far, far away from your own time,
Who knows?
            Maybe a gentle man, as quiet as yourself,
Will calmly come to sit beneath the light;
With his candid hands he will open
The old book yellowed by time.

And like a gust of wind ripping the clouds apart,
You will appear in front of him, in flesh as in spirit.

And he, so attentive and wise, will see
The Man you used to be.
                        And this stranger,
Will find, through strange and inadequate words,
Through unfulfilled desires and childish arrogance,
The way to his own heart and he will be
Astonished.

Roparz Hemon

Ar Marc'heg bale-bro, *1960*

Va jav ha me o vont a-hed an hent,
Hag a-dreuz park pa n'eus mui hent ebet,
A-hed, a-dreuz, ne vern, ez eomp bepred.
Hor pal bemdez 'zo keit hag en derc'hent.

D'an noz e kouskan, gwech en ur c'hastell,
Gwech en ur peniti, gwech war vein.
Din-me, ne vern, evit astenn va c'hein,
Roc'h noazh, plouz gleb, pe wele dimezell.

Traonienn pe run, douar ed pe ouelec'h,
N'o gwelan ken. Din-me int holl heñvel.
Goañv pe hañv, glav pe heol, kalm pe avel,
N'eus din na warc'hoazh, nag hiziv, na dec'h.

Translation

The Wandering Knight, *1960*

My horse and I go along the road,
And across fields when the road leads nowhere.
Walking on, cutting across; what matters? We go on.
Every day our goal is as far as ever.

At night I sleep, sometimes in a castle,
Sometimes in a refuge, sometimes on the ground.
It does not matter to me where I lie,
On bare rocks, on wet straw, or in a girl's bed.

Valley or hill, fertile land or desert,
I no longer see them. To me they all look the same.

Winter or summer, rain or sunshine, fair wind or gale,
I have no future, no present, no past.

Youenn Gwernig

Ni hon-unan, *c.2000*

Ha klevet hoc'h eus paotred
O tarzañ en noz yen,
Youc'hadennoù entanet
Ha c'hoarzh ha kanaouenn?
Klevit kan ar broadoù
O sevel diouzh o bez,
Klevit trouz ar chadennoù
O kouezañ el lastez.

'Mañ heol ar frankiz o sevel
Du-hont 'us d'an dremmwell,
Ni hon-unan, ni hon-unan,
Ni a gerzho dispont,
Ni hon-unan, ni hon-unan,
War hentoù hon dazont.

Hed-a-hed ar c'hantvedoù,
Dre o nerzh hag o feiz,
Poaniet o deus hon tadoù
'Vit sevel hor bro Vreizh.
Keit a chomo hon bro-ni,
E galloud an estren,
'N vodomp kenvroidi
D'an emgann deomp laouen.

A-vern dre gant miliadoù
A-hed harzoù Bro-C'hall
Gwazed hor ouenn 'n o bezioù
A c'hourvez en noz dall.
Ma'z eo ret mat bout falc'het,
Bleunienn hor yaouankiz,
Ni a varvo a-gevret,
'Vit difenn hor frankiz.

Translation

By Ourselves *c.2000*

Young men, have you heard
Bursting in the cold night,
The fierce howls
The laughing, the singing?
Hear the song of the nations
Rising from their graves.
Hear the noise of the chains
Falling into the gutter.

The sun of freedom is rising
Over there above the horizon.
By ourselves, by ourselves
We shall walk fearlessly,
By ourselves, by ourselves,
On the roads of our future.

All along the centuries,
With their strength and their faith,
Our fathers have struggled
To create our Brittany.
As long as our country stays
In the power of foreigners,
Let us get together, fellow countrymen,
Let us go happily to combat.

Piled up by the thousands
Along the borders of France
Our countrymen in their graves
Lie in the dark night.
Since we have no choice but to die,
Righteous young men,
We shall die together
To defend our freedom.

Reun ar C'halan

Emsav, *1985*

Meur a wech e oamp bet trec'het er brezelioù
A-benn emberr e vefe cheñchet penn d'ar vazh
Tremen poent e oa treiñ ar bed penn evit penn

Ar gounnar a save er c'halonoù hesent
An dud aonik a zeue da vezañ kadarn
Krignet e oa ar re zic'hrad gant ar morc'hed
Aet e oa da netra ar spont, al laoskentez
An dispac'h a skede e sell ar vugale
Den ebet ne gouezhfe ken e roued an estren
Ha petra a rae deomp ma tremenfe an hent
Dre an tangwall, ar vombezenn hag ar marv?
Edo ar geder o c'hortoz en e wardlec'h
Ne oa an dazont nemet ur sparfell dall

Translation

The Breton Movement, *1985*

We have been vanquished many a time in wars
This state of affairs would change soon
It was high time to turn the world upside down
The anger was rising in compliant people
Fearful people were becoming brave
And perfidious ones were filled with remorse
Fear had disappeared, cowardice too
Rebellion was shining in the eyes of children
No one would ever fall again in the foreigners' net
And what did we care if the road ahead was paved
With fire, bombs or death?
The watchman was waiting in his sentry box
The future was but a blind hawk

Paol ar Meur

Kontadennoù an Emsav, *1992* (Lodenn)

Deuet e oamp tre. Goude lakaat an tan en ur bern skirioù war an oaled ledan, ez is em c'hoazez ouzh an daol derv, en he c'hichen war ar bank pounner a oa stok ouzh ar voger.

"Ne vefemp ket evit tremen an eil diouzh egile war a seblant," emezon en ur zistoufañ ur voutailhad sistr. "Me ne vezen ket evit an enkrez a save ennon en engroeziadoù tud dizanv ar gêr vras. Amañ ez anavezan an holl re a gejañ ganto. Klok en em gavan e-kreiz ur seurt endro."

"N'emañ ket dazont hon hêrez vroadel er maezioù diboblet. Arabat deomp ersaviñ evel difennerien sevenadur Yann Gouer, ur sevenadur war an diskar, peotramant e vo tonket yezh hon tadoù-kozh da vont da get."

"Tonket eo an holl sevenadurioù da vervel mod pe vod e dirolloù ar c'hêrioù bras. Seul diventoc'h ar c'heodedoù seul vreinoc'h an emglev etre o annezidi. Ne

zasorc'ho ket hor pobl enno. Ne vo biken tizhet palioù pennañ an Emsav keid-all diouzh e wrizioù."

"Ne ouien ket e kellide c'hoazh seurt mennozhioù kilebenus en Emsav. Emaout o klask distreiñ d'ar grennamzer endra m'emañ da genvroidi o pukañ o selloù leun a spi war gemmoù burzhudus an dazont."

"Pebezh dipit pa zeuio anat dezho n'eus pare ebet d'ar c'hleñvedoù a zo o krignat o bed eus an diabarzh."

"Nag a gasoni maget ez kalon a-enep an araokaat."

"Arabat krediñ e nac'han kement aezamant eus an teknikoù nevez. Tamall a ran mistri ar govelioù bras da gas o gopridi da ostilhoù diene. Ar c'hêrioù bras n'int ken laboù ar strobadoù uzinoù. Renket e vez enno ar binviji kig hag eskern a zo eus ar vicherourien. Laourerien douar, artizaned eus an amzer paseet a gaver en o zouesk barzhed, arzourien ampart evit magañ o sevenadur gwerinel. Bez' ez eo bili-raz ar bed ijinerezhel maen-bez awen ar beorien."

"Kavell un eil ijin poblek kentoc'h. Diwanet eo ar muzik rock da skouer e-skeud al labouradegoù ramzel."

"Ar yaouankizoù a c'hoari ur seurt muzik entanet ne reont ken diavaeziñ ar feulster hadet en o c'halon gant an dizenelaat."

"Ar gwir zo ganit pa lavarez n'omp ket evit tremen an eil diouzh egile. Hervezon e saouromp dre zañsal, dre c'hoari ar rock, an trivli fardet en hor c'hreizon gant lusk strobinellus an endro nevez emaomp o frammañ."

"Emañ an endro nevez o'n em frammañ e-unan. Re wan eo skiant-varn mabden evit efediñ war donkad ar bed, evit mirout outañ da stummañ ar spered. Panevet koun fromus kantreadennoù ma amzer gentañ war ar maez, e kemerjen perzh ivez e kerzhadeg kollus ma c'hempredidi trema'n islonk. N'eus diskoulm ebet da enkadennoù ar c'henelioù dihengoun. Aner dezho klask mirout ouzh an emlazh. Hep sklêrijenn an hêrezh ne c'hell ket ar youl-bevañ kenderc'hel da virviñ ennomp."

Tavet e oa ar glav. Ne dabouline mui war gwer ar prenestr a-drek hor c'hein. Edo an tan o strakal ferv er siminal, ar flammoù o korolliñ laouen. Dont a reas betek ennomp begeliadenn glemmus un dañvad diouzh al lochenn follennoù houarn a oa stok ouzh talbenn an ti. En derc'hent e oa deuet ma amezeien dostañ da zougen dorn din da ziskoultriñ ar gwez a vevenne an hent-karr a gase da'm foenneg. O c'houviet am boa da bakañ o c'hoan du-mañ evit o zrugarekaat. O vezañ ma ne oan ket kustum da skaotañ al listri kentizh ha loc'het kuit ma degemeridi, dreist-holl pa ne c'hortozen den en deizioù war-ierc'h, ne oa ket an disterañ gwerenn brop war an daol.

"N'eus ket da vezañ ken tonkeour memes tra," emezi pa skois trema an dar. "Gouest omp da eilpennañ planedenn hor pobl dre gemer penn an traoù e kement skourr a zo er velestradurezh."

"Ur c'hwitadenn e vefe ur seurt strategiezh a dra sur, ha pa vefe dilennet Jezuz-Krist evel pennrener ar vro. N'eo ket neptuek frammoù ar stad. Aze emañ an dalc'h. Goveliet eo bet ar mekanik bras a zo eus al levierezh gant beleien an ideologiezh. Kaer c'hoari gant an dornelloù e kendalc'ho da seveniñ al labourioù a oa bet fiziet ennañ gant e saverien," a respontis dezhi en ur strinkañ dour tomm er gwerennoù.

"Sed ar pezh a lakaan bec'h da ober evelato dre blediñ gant studioù eus ar re startañ. Seul uheloc'h kargoù an emsaverien er velestradurezh, seul efedusoc'h ar stourm evit dihun broadel ar Vretoned."

"N'eus ket tu da implij ar stad C'hall hep mougañ hor breizhadelezh. Strivañ a ran da vevañ hepti, da zisoñjal ez eus anezhi."

"Ra lavaro an dazont gant piv emañ ar gwir," emezi kent pakañ krog er werennad sistr edon oc'h astenn dezhi.

Lenn a ris en he sell karget a skuizhnez he doa c'hoant klozañ ganti. Deuet e oa anat dezhi ne zeufe ket a-benn da'm darboellañ, e chomfe berr hec'h arguzennoù da ziswrizienniñ ma mennozhioù. Mechal hag aon he doa ivez na vefe horjellet ma c'hredennoù e-kerz ur seurt breud?

"Ha laouen e vefes da gargañ da vouzelloù gant un alumenn vioù, ar vioù dozvet gant ma yer hiziv vintin?" a c'houlennis outi en ur zigeriñ an armel yen.

"Al lichouzenn a zo ac'hanon ne vo ket evit nac'hañ seurt kinnig," emezi, ur mousc'hoarzh o lugerniñ trumm en he daoulagad.

"Ne vin ket pell o poazhañ ar meuz lipous az po da bred," a lavaris en ur dennañ kement a zo ret evit keusteurenniñ diouzh ar ganastell, ar pezh arrebeuri kozhdouar am boa bet da hêrezh digant ma zad-you.

"Distreiñ a ri da Vrest warc'hoazh?" a atersas, o fardañ ur vutunenn.

"Evel bemdez-doue evit seveniñ ma endervezhiad labour er porzh-kenwerzh," a respontis en ur derriñ ar vioù a-us d'ur volenn grag.

"N'eo ket skuizhus d'ar c'horf plediñ gant div vicher?"

"N'on ket eus ar sammetañ gant al labour. Maer ar barrez, anezhañ ul labourerdouar diouzh ar c'hiz nevez, ne blij ket dezhañ e klaskfe gopridi zo sevel loened eveltañ. Ne vimp biken ali an eil gant egile keit ha ma vo hennezh o tifenn ur vicher ha me ur sevenadur."

Gant ur seblant prederiek e taolas bemmen moged glas war-du al lein. Kent steuziañ etre an treustennoù du e stummjont troellennoù espar, par d'an tresadennoù kelt.

"Ne gavan penn ebet dezhi," emezi, blaz ar souezh en he mouezh. "Disheñvelbras omp an eil diouzh egile. Anat eo. Koulskoude e tifoup un elfenn a from diouzh donañ ma c'halon seul wech ma sankañ ma selloù ez re."

Ne gredis ket anzav outi e save hevelep trivliadenn em boud pa veze luc'hennoù a levenez o skediñ en he mammenn-lagad. Ha peadra oa da sebeziñ? Evidomp da gaout mennozhioù kontrol e oamp ganet war ar memes douar, e oamp a-unan gant ar memes broad. N'eo ket bet dlazezet spered Breizh war ul levr.

Translation

Tales From the Breton Movement, *1992* (Extract)

We went inside. After lighting the kindling in the large fireplace, I went to sit at the oak table, next to her, on the heavy bench against the wall.

"It looks as if we can't agree," I said as I opened a bottle of cider. "I could no longer stand the torment I felt amongst crowds of unknown people in the city. Here I know everyone I meet. I feel at ease in such surroundings."

"The future of our national heritage does not lie in the deserted countryside. We must not react as though we were defending a peasant culture; it's a disappearing culture. Otherwise the language of our ancestors is bound to disappear."

"In the frenzy of big cities, all civilisations are bound to die one way or the other. The more gigantic the town, the more disharmony between its inhabitants. Our people will not be reborn in cities. The main objectives of the Emsav will never be reached so far from its roots."

"I was unaware that such retrograde ideas still existed in the Emsav. You are trying to return to the Middle Ages when your fellow countrymen are putting all their hopes in the miraculous changes the future will bring."

"How disappointed they will be when they realise that there is no cure to the illnesses which are attacking their world from the inside."

"Why do you hate progress so much?"

"Don't think that I turn my back on all the comforts brought by new techniques. I only accuse the masters of big industry of turning their workers into soulless machines. Big cities are like a multi-factory warehouse in which the tools of flesh and blood, I mean workers such as farmers, craftsmen of the old days, including poets and gifted artists, are stored in order to feed popular culture. The whitewashing of the industrial world is the gravestone of the ordinary man's inspiration."

"Or rather the cradle of a renewed popular imagination. Rock music, for instance, was born in the shadow of the giant factories."

"The young who play such lively music are only expressing their anger at so much dehumanisation."

"You are right to say that we cannot be of the same mind. I personally think that when we dance, when we play rock music, we enjoy the inner sensation brought by the magical rhythm of the new environment we are building."

"The new environment is building itself all on its own. Man's judgement is too weak to have any effect on the fate of the world and to prevent the world from shaping our minds. If it were not for the tender memories of the first rambles I took in the countryside, I would also take part in the tragic walk of my contemporaries towards the precipice. There is no solution to the crises of peoples without traditions. It is useless for them to try and prevent suicide. Without the light of inheritance, the will to live cannot survive in us."

The rain had stopped. It was no longer beating against the windowpanes behind us. The fire was raging in the fireplace, its flames dancing happily. We heard the bleating of a forlorn sheep in the corrugated iron shed which adjoined the side of the house. On the previous day, my closest neighbours had come to give me a hand to cut the branches of the trees which bordered the path leading to my meadow. To thank them, I had invited them back home for supper. Since I was not in the habit of washing the dishes as soon as my guests left, particularly when I was not expecting anyone to come and visit me on the following days, there was not a single clean glass on the table.

"There is no need to be so pessimistic," she said, as I walked towards the sink. "We are quite capable of reversing the destiny of our people by leading every branch of administration."

"Such a strategy is sure to fail, even if Jesus Christ were elected as leader of the country. The framework of the State is not neutral, that is the problem. The big machine which rules us has been forged by the priests of this ideology. No matter how much one fiddles with the knobs, it will continue to do the job it was programmed to do by its inventors," I answered, while filling the dirty glasses with hot water.

"Yet this is what I am aiming for, and that is why I have chosen to enrol on a particularly difficult course. The higher the positions held by Breton activists in administration, the more efficient the fight for the national awakening in Brittany."

"We cannot use the French State without stifling in us what make us Bretons. I do my best to live without it, to forget it exists."

"Let the future tell who is right," she said, before taking the glass of cider I was offering her.

I saw in her tired eyes that she wanted to drop the subject. She was well aware that she could not persuade me, that her arguments were not strong enough to make me change my mind. She was also possibly afraid that such a discussion might shake her own beliefs.

"Would you like to eat an omelette made with the eggs laid by my hens this very morning?" I asked her as I opened the fridge door.

"I like my food and cannot refuse such an offer," she replied, her eyes suddenly brightening up.

"It won't take me long to cook the delicious fare you will be given to eat," I said, taking out of the ancient dresser left to me by my great-grandfather all the kitchen utensils I needed.

"Are you going back to Brest tomorrow?" she asked as she rolled a cigarette.

"Tomorrow as every other day, I'll do an afternoon's work in the commercial port," I replied, while breaking the eggs into a stoneware bowl.

"Don't you find it tiring to have two jobs?"

"I am far from being overworked. The mayor of the village, one of these modern farmers, does not like to see wage-earners competing with him in animal farming. We shall never see eye to eye as long as he tries to defend a job and I a culture."

She seemed to be deep in her thoughts as whiffs of blue smoke curled up towards the ceiling. Before disappearing between the black beams, they made beautiful arabesques, like those in Celtic drawings.

"I can't make sense of it," she said in a surprised voice. "It is obvious that the two of us are very different. Yet I feel this stirring in my heart every time I look into your eyes."

I did not dare admit to her that I felt the same when gleams of happiness were shining in her eyes. But what was there to be surprised about? Although we held opposite views, we were born on the same land, we fought for the same nation. The love of Brittany does not come from a book.

Tales and Legends from Brittany

In the evening, the household used to gather around the hearth to hear those tales and rhymes which form part of the oral literature of Brittany and which have been gathered and set in print by collectors in the nineteenth century. Yeun ar Gow recalls the deep impression these tales made on his mind when he was but a child. A few of these legends and ballads are reproduced here to give but a flavour of this very rich tradition. This chapter concludes with a contemporary short story which casts a humorous look on the theme of witchcraft.

Yeun ar Gow

E Skeud tour bras Sant Jermen, *1955* (Lodenn)

Diouzh an noz, e korn an oaled, e lennen ar *"C'hourrier"* ha *"Feiz ha Breiz"* da dud an ti, sikouret a-wechoù gant ma maeronez pa ne vezen ket gouest da zistagañ mat ar gerioù diaes. Ar pezh a blije ar muiañ d'an holl a oa ar romantoù hag ar c'hontadennoù hir embannet tamm-ha-tamm bep sizhun. Plijadur ha dudi a gavent o selaou an istorioù sebezus-se, hag an evezh a daolent em c'homzoù a ziskoueze sklaer pegement a vall o deveze da c'houzout penaos ec'h echujent. Hogen dav e vefe gortoz ac'hann d'ar sizhun war-lerc'h evit kaout ar c'hendalc'h pe ar fin eus an danevelloù kaer-se a oa o anv *Lena, An Divroet, Lapous an Eürusted* ha... me 'oar.

War-lerc'h ma lennadenn, e troe ar gaoz peurvuiañ war draoù ar vuhez pemdeziek hag ar c'heleier a rede dre ar barrez: dimezioù, euredoù hag interaman-choù. Pa veze anv eus ar marv hag ar bed-all, e kave pep hini e bezh da gontañ. Ar c'hoñchennoù glac'harus-se a strafuilhe ma c'halon gizidik hag a sile nec'h em spered. Dont a ris da c'houzout petra e oa ar sinadoù, ar spesoù, al lutined, an hoperig-noz, an drougsperedoù hag an Ankoù hag e garrigell. Bep un tamm e kle-vis komz eus ar c'horriged ha paotred ar sabad, eus an tier sorset, eus an dud a ouie lenn ar Vif hag ober sorserezh, eus ar re a rae marc'had gant an Diaoul hag eus ar re o devoa ur c'hazh du da zegas aour dezho bep mintin, evel an den-se anavezet

gwechall e Pleiben, a rae an holl Filip ar C'hazh Du outañ.

Aonik e oan deuet da vezañ ha ne felle ket din mont d'am gwele ma-unan. War an deiz zoken, pa vezen kaset d'ar c'halatrez da gerc'hat ur panerad chalotez pe ognon, a-boan ma kreden mont d'an nec'h. Met, gant ar vezh, e klasken trec'hiñ war ar spont diskiant-se, hag e pignen gant an diri en ur ganañ da gas an nec'h diwar va zro.

Hogen ne veze ket enkrezus atav hon nozvezhioù e korn an oaled. Alies, e-lec'h an traoù skrijus am eus komzet anezho, e tisplege hiniennoù eus hor mevelien, rak mistri-konterien a oa en o zouesk, kontadennoù kaer hag am sabatur. Rimodelloù a oa an anv a raemp outo, o vezañ, moarvat, ma oant bet savet gwechall-gozh e gwerzennoù pe e rimoù. Ne oa ket bet ankouaet ar re-mañ tre gant hor c'honte-rien, hag e teue ganto bommoù anezho, gwech a-barzh krogiñ da gontañ ha gwech e-kreiz o c'hoñchennoù, evit lakaat ar selaouerien da c'hoarzhin. Ran e oan gant ar c'hontadennoù hag an neb a ouie unan bennak n'en deveze peoc'h ebet diganin ken en divije asantet he dibunañ. Neuze, goude bezañ bet pedet hag aspedet n'ouzon ket pet gwech ha graet ur skarzh d'e c'houzoug da sklaeraat e vouezh, e kroge ar c'honter evel-hen:

Gwechall ha gwechall
An neb 'n devoa daoulagad ne oa ket dall
Ha, brema, an neb an neus
A wel eün pe a-dreuz...

"Gwechall, eta..." Hag e selaouen, gant dudi, displegañ taolioù-kaer *Yann e Vazh Houarn* hag e genseurted, tost da vat ken souezhus hag eñ, aet da redek ar bed da glask o chañs.

Translation

In the Shadow of Saint Germen's Tower, *1955* (Extract)

In the evening, by the hearth, I used to read "*Courrier du Finistère*" and "*Feiz ha Breiz*" to the household, with a little help from my godmother when I came up against difficult words. The novels and the long tales serialised on a weekly basis were everyone's favourites. They all enjoyed listening to these marvellous stories, and the attention with which they listened to me showed only too clearly how keen they were to know how these tales would end. But they had to wait for a whole week for the follow-up or for the end of these beautiful tales entitled '*Lena*', '*The Expatriate*', '*The Bird of Happiness*' etc.

My reading over, the conversation usually turned to events of daily life and local news such as engagements, weddings and funerals. When the subject of death and the other world came up, they all had their word to say. These distressing anecdotes used to upset my sensitive nature and fill me with anxiety. I came to learn about premonitions, ghosts, imps, goblins of the night, evil spirits and about the Ankou and his cart. Once in a while, they would talk about korrigans, malicious elves, bewitched houses, people who could read the 'Vif' and do witchcraft, about those who made a bargain with the Devil and those who had a black cat who brought them gold every morning, just like that man known many years ago in Pleiben who was nicknamed 'Filip of the Black Cat' by all.

I became fretful and I did not want to go to bed by myself. Even during the day, when I was sent to the attic to get a basketful of shallots or onions, I was reluctant to go up. Ashamed of myself, I tried to get the better of this silly apprehension and, in an attempt to dispel my uneasiness, I would sing as I walked up the stairs.

But our evenings by the hearth were not always so upsetting. Often, instead of the wondrous things I have already mentioned, some of our servants who were master storytellers told beautiful tales which enthralled me. 'Rimings' was the name we gave them, because, I suppose, they had been composed, many years ago, in verses or in rhymes. Our storytellers still vaguely remembered the rhymes, judging by the extracts which came to their lips either at the very beginning or in the middle of the tales, to make the audience laugh. I loved these folk-tales and I did not leave those who knew them in peace until they agreed to tell them. But I had to beg and plea I don't know how many times before the storyteller cleared his throat and uttered the introductory words:

In the old days, this is what I find:
If you had eyes, you were not blind.
In the present time, I shall just hint
That, if you can't see straight, you might have a squint...

"Once upon a time, therefore..." And I listened spellbound to the feats of Yann and his iron stick and other similar strange tales whose heroes travelled the world in search of fame and fortune.

Tristan and Iseult

Tristan and Iseult are the best known European great tragic lovers. It's a tale deeply embedded in the European psyche with a lasting influence on European literature and other branches of the arts reaching its pinnacle with Wagner. "Thus Chateaubriand, the Breton, rediscovered the Celtic idea, expressed once and for all in 'Tristan', of the fatal suddenness of love," wrote André Maurois in his biography of the great writer. Two people falling in love after drinking the magic love potion, two people with no particular reason to like each other, with more reason to be hostile to each other, bound together in eternal love. A tragic tale of love that has captured the imagination for a thousand years, inspiring story-tellers, poets, artists and composers.

It is commonly acknowledged that the original Tristan was Drust, son of Talorc, a Pict who ruled in the Hebrides around 780 (R. M. Loomis, Introduction to The Romance of Tristram and Ysolt, *Columbia University Press, 1931). What fragments survive of a Pictish*

language – names of kings and place-names – would suggest the Picts were also (Brythonic) Celts. (Jackson, K. cited by Peter Berresford Ellis in The Celtic Empire*). A substantial part of the Tristan story – from where he decides to do battle against Morhaut, the Irish warrior who comes to exact tribute from Mark of Cornwall up to when Ysolt in Ireland discovers that it was Tristan who killed Morhaut, her uncle – resembles the Irish saga 'Wooing of Emer'.*

The story moved south and Drust, son of Talorc, became in Welsh, Trystan ap Tallwch. Ystoria Trystan, recorded in a sixteenth century manuscript but obviously based on a much older poem comes in the form of 28 early three-line englynion with some explanatory prose to move the story along, introduces Cai Hir (alias Sir Kay, Kaherdin, Kaerdin) and Arthur into the story as well as Brengain (Golwg Hafddydd in the Welsh version). The amusing Welsh tale has Mark, son of Meirchion, husband of Esyllt demanding that Arthur should intervene because of Trystan's adultery with Esyllt. Neither is prepared to give way and Arthur judges they should each spend six months with Esyllt. Mark chooses the six months when there are no leaves on the trees – and the nights are longer! Esyllt responds that the holly, ivy and the yew have leaves every month of the year so she will gladly spend all her time with Trystan. This tale appears to be uniquely Welsh.

*The basic Pictish story was developed by Cornish story-tellers – bringing Tintagel into the story. It crossed the channel and by AD 1000, at the latest, had gained great popularity in Brittany. R. S. Loomis says that a famous Welsh "fabulator", Bledhericus or Bleheris (or Bledri ap Cadifor), told stories of Arthurian themes in the court of the Count of Poitiers possibly in the time of the "first" troubadour, Guilhem VII, Duke of Aquitaine (1071 – 1127). Andrew Sinclair (*Dylan the Bard, Robinson 2003, *citing Robert Graves,* The White Goddess, *London, 1961) writes: "He was the 'fabulous translator' of Arthurian legend into Norman French, and he was commemorated by two rivals as someone who knew the history of all the counts and all the kings of Britain, and 'all the stories of the Grail'."*

Brittany, now, figures prominently in the tale. It begins and ends in Brittany and some of the surviving versions of the tale include fine examples of descriptive writing, notably of the siege of Carhaix and the hall of statues. (It has been suggested that the huge caves under the Pointe de Dinan on the Crozon peninsula inspired Wagner in his adaptation of the tale.) Tristan's father becomes a Breton lord from Leon, Rivalon, Tristan now becoming the son of Rivalon.

Early surviving European versions of the tale were written by Thomas of Brittany around 1160, by Eilhard von Oberge around 1170 and Béroul around 1200. It has been argued that the German Eilhart and Norman-French Béroul versions are the closest to the basic original tale. Gottfried von Strassburg, whose source was Thomas, proceeded to produce a masterpiece in Middle High German, in the form of one of the finest narrative poems of the middle ages, and the inspiration for Wagner. It is as well to remember, too, that Marie de France's 'Chevrefoil' (Honeysuckle) – c. 1180 – is a tiny fragment of the Tristan and Iseult story.

Thomas of Brittany
Rivalon, Tristan's father

Rivalon, Tristan's father, is described in 'Tristrams saga ok Isondar', translated from the French of Thomas of Brittany by Friar Robert into Old Norse (or Icelandic) in 1226 at the request of the King Hakon Hakonarson of Norway. It is the only complete version of the Thomas's tale.

There lived in Brittany a young man, handsome, the wisest in council, strong, wealthy with many castles and forts. He was learned in all branches of the arts, brave and skilled in deeds of knighthood, trustworthy and high-minded, of great foresight, surpassing all other men in the land of that time in all accomplishments. His name was Rivalon. To the fierce he was the fiercest, to those with no mercy, he was merciless. He had with him a large number of trusted knights and he would happily have kept more had he the means of sustaining them. He was generous with gifts, considerate towards others and such was his prowess and bravery in battle that he acquired lands and booty from his enemies and his fame and fortune was considerable. In his third year of bearing the arms and armour of knighthood he gathered a large army and attacked many a king and duke, inflicting on them severe losses of men and property. He burnt down royal castles and strongholds, defeated and captured many of the king's knights for which he demanded high ransoms in the form of gold, silver, jewels as well as horses and armour. Sometimes, he also lost men as can happen in the course of battle. Rivalon's attacks on the king were so fierce, devastating his kingdom and capturing his men, that the king with the assent of his wisest men finally sought a truce and they met to agree a peace treaty.

Langleiz
Tristan hag Izold, *1950* (Lodenn)

This is a modern Breton version of the siege of Carhaix, in the centre of Brittany, in which Tristan defeats and captures Riol, the count of Nantes. Duke Howel, in gratitude offers him the hand of Izold of the Fair Smile in marriage and the two are married. Langleiz's work is based in the main on Joseph Bédier's retelling of the story [Roman de Tristan, Paris: Société des Anciens Textes Français, 1902].

E-pad daou zevezh, e treuzas Tristan ha Gorwenal meur a vourc'h ha meur a gêriadenn hep gwelout nag un den nag ur c'hi, nag ur c'hilhog zoken. D'an trivet deiz, koulskoude, da vare an navet eur, e tegouezhjont gant ur run koadek, m'edo kluchet war e lein ur chapel gozh hag, e-kichen ar chapel-se, ul logellig. Gwisket en ur c'hroc'hen-gavr a ziwalle e gorf diouzh ar fall-amzer, ur manac'h a oa etalti.

Daoulinet war an douar, edo dres o pediñ Mari Magdalena da reiñ dezhañ muioc'h a geuz c'hoazh eus e bec'hedou. Saludiñ a reas Tristan hag e floc'h hag, endra ma stage Gorwenal ar c'hezeg ouzh moger ar c'hraou, e sikouras ar marc'heg yaouank da lemel e dokarn hag e roched stamm-orjal, hag ec'h aozas ar pred.

Ne voe ket gwall fonnus hemañ: dour ar stivell dostañ ha bara heiz, pobet dindan al ludu, ha setu holl!

Echu ar goan, ec'h azezjont e-tal an tan. Diskenn a rae an noz. Tristan a c'houlennas ouzh ar manac'h anv ar vro rivinet-se ma veve enni.

"Aotrou ker," eme ar manac'h, "douar Breizh-Izel an hini eo. E dalc'h an dug Howel emañ. Ur rouantelezh pinvidik a oa anezhi gwechall, gant pradoù glas aret kaer, ma kreske war o bevennoù gwez-avaloù e-leizh. Ac'houdevezh, siwazh! ez eo bet drastet ha freuzet penn-da-benn ar vro-mañ dre an tan hag ar skraperezh, gant soudarded an aotrou Riol, kont an Naoned, ken ne chom mui enni ur voudennig douar na vefe ket gwastet. Evel-se emañ kont gant ar brezel ..."

"Breur," eme Dristan, "daoust hag e ouiec'h perak en deus graet ar c'hont kement-se a noaz d'an dug Howel hoc'h aotrou."

"Bez e c'hellan, aes tre, aotrou ker, displegañ deoc'h sigur ar brezel. Riol a oa dindan beli an dug Howel. Ur verc'h en doa hemañ, koant e-touezh ar re goantañ. Riol en dije karet he c'hemer da bried, hogen e ouie mat n'en dije ket fellet d'an dug Howel reiñ e verc'h a galon vat da unan eus e zalc'hidi ... Setu perak en deus klasket he skrapañ dre heg ha gwidre."

Tristan a c'houlennas, ouzhpenn:

"Ha ne c'hell mui an dug Howel derc'hel penn d'e enebourion?"

"Nemet gant kalz a boan. Ha, koulskoude, kreñv eo mogerioù Karaez, ar c'hastell n'eus nemetañ a chom c'hoazh e dalc'h an dug, ha ken kreñv all kalon e vab Kaerdin, ar marc'heg dispont. Emañ e enebourion o pouezañ muioc'h mui warnañ, evelato! Daoust hag e vo gouest da stourm outo hir-amzer ?..."

Tristan a c'houlennas, neuze, ha pell edo c'hoazh diouzh Karaez. "War hed ul lev bennak, hepken," a respontas ar manac'h.

An tronoz vintin, e kimiade Tristan diouzh e ostiz, e pigne war e varc'h hag e skoe, a-herr, trema Karaez, heuliet bepred gant Gorwenal. A-benn un hanter-eur bennak, e tegouezhe e-tal mogerioù ar c'hastell. Soudarded a oa en o sav war an hent-ged. Goulenn a reas komz ouzh an dug. Edo dres Howel e-touez e wazed, ha Kaerdin war-un-dro gantañ.

"Tristan, roue Bro Leon on, un niz da Varc'h roue Bro Gerne. Klevet em eus lavarout en deus en em savet unan bennak eus ho talc'hidi a-enep d'ho peli hag ez on deut da ginnig deoc'h va c'hleze."

"Siwazh! aotrou Tristan, Doue d'ho pinnigo evit ho madelezh! Kerzhit hoc'h hent koulskoude. Na penaos e c'hellfemp ho tegemer amañ pa n'hon eus mui na gwinizh na kerc'h na segal, na boued all ebet, koulz lavarout, paneve piz-fao ha dour?"

"Ne vern," eme Dristan, "bevet em eus en ur c'hoad gouez, e-pad daou vloavezh, diwar wriziennoù ha greunennoù sec'h, ha ne gaven ket fall, tamm ebet, ar vuhez-se. Gourc'hemennit, eta, ma vo digoret din an nor vras!"

"Roit dezhañ an aotre a c'houlenn, va zad," eme neuze Kaerdin, "peogwir eo ken uhel-se e galon; ha ra vo liammet e blanedenn ouzh hon hini, el levenez evel er glac'har."

Ha, neuze, e voe degemeret Tristan gant lid hag enor. E ambroug a reas Kaerdin dre an hentoù-ged da weladenniñ ar mogerioù. Na kreñv e tiskoueze bezañ an tour-kreiz, harpet evel ma oa, a-bep tu, gant difennoù koad, ma c'helle ar waregourion en em guzhat a-dreñv dezho... Eus e lein, koulskoude e weled, er pelloù, an teltoù savet gant Riol e-kreiz ar gompezenn.

Distroet er porzh enor, e kinnigas Kaerdin da Dristan:

"Arsa! Keneil ker, pignomp bremañ betek ar sal e-lec'h m'emañ va mamm ha va c'hoar."

Hag int da vont tre e kambr ar gwragez, dorn an eil krog e dorn egile.

Azezet war ur pallenn ruz moug, kinklet gant broderezhioù prizius, edo, dres, ar vamm hag ar verc'h a-greiz kanañ ur sonnenn-nezañ savet en enor da Janedig ar goantenn, skuizh o c'hortoz dindan ar spern-nevez Yann, he muiañ karet, en deus he dilezet. Tristan o saludas hag, aotreet ganto d'hen ober, a azezas etalto, endra ma kroge Kaerdin er stol a vroude e vamm:

"Tostait da welout, keneil ker! Pebezh micherourez eo va mamm! Met – emezañ kerkent goude, gant karantez – bez e c'hellfen lavarout kenkoulz-all diwar-benn va c'hoar, neketa! Sellit gant pegement a ampartiz he deus kinklet ivez an danvez prizius-mañ ..!"

Ar plac'h yaouank, plijet gant ar c'homzoù-se, a savas neuze he fenn davet he breur, en ur vinc'hoarzhin gant kement a goantiz hag a levenez didroidell ma lavaras Kaerdin da Dristan:

"Evel ma welit, keneil ker, n'eo ket hep abeg mat hon eus he lesañvet Izold Gwenn-He-Minc'hoarzh ..!"

O klevout digant e geneil e veze graet Izold anezhi, e vinc'hoarzhas Tristan, diouzh e du hag, adal neuze, e sellas outi gant muioc'h a zouster.

E gamp brezel en doa savet Riol a-hed un hanter-lev bennak diouzh Karaez hag, abaoe un nebeut sizhunvezhioù, ne grede mui gwazed an dug Howel treuziñ dorioù kêr evit e argadiñ. Kerkent ha deut an tronoz, avat, Tristan ha daouzek marc'heg yaouank a guitaas kêr, d'ar ruzell veure, armet holl penn-kil-ha-troad, hag a varc'hekaas e gwaskedenn ar c'hoadoù pin betek teltoù kentañ ar c'hamp enebour ha, deut eno, a zifoupas eus o c'huzhiadell en ul lamm hag a skrapas unan eus ar c'hirri a gase gwinizh da gamp ar c'hont.

Abaoe an deiz-se, ne voe mui da badout ganto: a-wechoù e eilpennent teltoù Riol, gwardoniet fall, a-wechoù all e kouezhent, a-greiz-holl war un nebeut kirri, o c'hloazañ loened ha soudarded; ha bepred ec'h ijinent gwidreoù-brezel nevez hardisoc'h hardisañ, ken ne zistroent mui da Garaez hep kas ganto ur preizh bennak.

Ne oa ket en aner e c'houzañve Tristan ha Kaerdin kement-se a riskloù a-gevret. Deiz goude deiz, e tomme o c'halonoù an eil evit an hini all hag en em skoulme etrezo liammoù a vignoniezh ken start ha ken niverus ma touas an daou varc'heg ne c'hellfe den na tra o disrannañ nepred.

Hag, evel ma welot goude, e vint feal d'o ger.

Pa zeuent endro eus ar c'hrogadoù risklus-se, en ur varc'hekaat glin ouzh glin, e varvailhe a-wechoù Kaerdin diwarbenn he c'hoar, Izold Gwenn-He-Minc'hoarzh, ar plac'h koant ha didro, ha bepred e oa evit he meuliñ gant teneredigezh.

Tristan, diouzh e du, hag eñ feal memestra e don e galon da Izold ar Veleganez, ne c'helle ket en em virout a vezañ gounezet, tamm ha tamm, gant dremm leun a goantiz an eil Izold.

Nann! n'en doa ket ankounac'haet e geneilez! Nemet e oa bremañ gant nebeutoc'h a hiraezh, hag a vall d'he gwelout en-dro, e soñje enni, distanet ma oa bet e boan gant douster ar Vreizhadez yaouank.

Ur wech m'edo a-greiz kanañ ur sonenn en doa savet gwechall en enor d'e vuiañ karet, e voe klevet gant Kaerdin ... Anv Izold a zistage dres, d'an ampoent. O verzout anv e c'hoar war ziweuz an telennour, e soñjas Kaerdin gant dudi ne c'hellfe ket ar plac'h yaouank bezañ karet gant ur marc'heg gwelloc'h eget Tristan. Ne lavaras netra d'e geneil, hogen, adal an deiz-se, e kavas alies an dro d'o lezel o-unan-penn da guzulikat an eil gant egile.

Hirbadout a rae ar seiziz ...

Un deiz bennak, avat, d'ar ruzell-veure, e tiskennas ur gedour, a-herr bras, a-ziwar an tour-kreiz en ur huchal:

"Kousket hoc'h eus re bell, aotrounez! Savit a-herr, setu ma tered soudarded Riol d'hon arsailhañ."

Marc'heion ha bourc'hizion a dapas krog, buan ha buan, en o armoù hag a zeredas d'ar mogerioù. Tokarnoù, klezeier ha goafioù soudarded ar c'hont a lintre dija war ar gompezenn. Edo e lu-brezel o tostaat ouzh Karaez; ur burzhud e welout, ken kempenn ha ken reizh!

An dug Howel ha Kaerdin a lakaas o marc'herion war deir linenn dirak an norioù ha, pa voe tost a-walc'h lu Riol ez ejont d'e ziambroug, o c'hentroù sanket e kof o roñseed, endra ma kouezhe ar birioù warno, evel grizilh e miz ebrel.

Dihunet e oa bet Tristan gant ar gedour e-touez ar re ziwezhañ. En em wiskañ a ra a-herr. E roched stamm-orjal hag e weltroù houarn strizh a laka, e gentroù aour a stag. Kregiñ a ra en e dokarn hag en e gleze hag, en ul lamm, e sailh war e varc'h hag e tered, d'an daou-lamm ruz, trema ar gompezenn.

Ha setu ma tifoup en ur youc'hal "Karaez, Karaez!" Mall bras e oa!

Kilañ a rae, dija, gwazed Howel trema difennoù kêr, daoust da leoù-touet ha da c'halvadennoù o fennoù-brezel. Nag ur safar, nag ur firbouch, nag ul levenez kriz hag ur c'hañv war un dro!... Kaerdin, gant e varc'heion yaouank, a zalc'h mat koulskoude. Kerkent ha ma klev youc'hadenn Tristan, e tastum adarre an dec'hidi: ar wech-mañ ne vrallo mui den! Setu ma kil, bremañ, tud Riol.

Eus ar pelloù, e tered ur marc'heg, ur breur d'ar c'hont Riol e-unan. Taer ha dispont eo. Kaerdin a chom d'e c'hortoz. En em argadiñ a reont an eil egile, hogen ne bado ket pell an emgann. Dibradet diwar e loen gant goaf Kaerdin, an estren a laosk ur c'harm skiltr hag e kouezh war ar prad, marv mik.

Pa glev Riol galvadenn e vreur o vervel, e tilamm d'e dro, arflevet holl evit talvezout d'an trec'hour ur seurt kañv. Tristan en deus spurmantet riskl e geneil hag e klask distreiñ Riol diouzh e hent. En em stekiñ a ra an daou varc'heg gant kement a nerzh ma tarzh o goafioù a dammoù. Tizhet en e gerc'henn, e vransell hag e kouezh marc'h Tristan.

"Mallozh-ruz war an neb a zilez ar mestr evit gloazañ al loen. Salv da vuhez bremañ, mar gellez!"

"Fougeour!" a skrign Riol, en ur vroudañ e jav evit flastrañ e enebour di-arbenet.

E gleze en deus savet Tristan. Na spontus an taol a zarc'haou war benn ar c'hont! Al laonenn a riskl, avat, eus skoaz an den da skoaz al loen a horjell war e dreid hag a gouez ivez. Burzhud n'eo ket bet flastret Riol war un dro gant e varc'h!

Dispennet eo bremañ o skouedoù, roget o rochedoù houarn ha distagellet o hel-moù. N'eus forzh! A-walc'h a nerzh a gavint c'hoazh en o c'hasoni evit en em gan-nañ war droad.

Ur pezh klezeadenn a zistag neuze Tristan war dokarn e enebour ha ken rust eo ar stok ma kouezh Riol war e grabanoù, badaouet holl.

"Sav 'ta, mevel!" a youc'h Tristan; "deut out war ar prad-mañ evit da wall; ret e vo dit mervel!"

Riol a glask sevel endro. Diskaret eo, koulskoude, gant un taol a faout e dokarn, a droc'h e gabell hag a gign kroc'hen e benn noazh betek an askorn. Ar wech-mañ e c'houlenn truez hag e asped Tristan da lezel e vuhez gantañ. Ar marc'heg a gemer e gleze. Poent bras e oa rak, a-bep-tu, e terede Naonediz da skoazellañ o mestr.

Re ziwezhat ... E c'her en doa roet hemañ d'e drec'hour.

Kaset dirak an dug Howel, Riol a douas adarre bezañ feal hiviziken a keñver e aotrou. Grataat a reas, ouzhpenn, adsevel en o stad a-gent ar c'hêriadennoù hag ar bourc'hioù losket gant e soudarded.

Trec'het e oa bet ...! War e urzh e pellaas neuze al lu enebour.

Ur wech distro e Karaez, Kaerdin a lavaras d'e dad:

"Aotrou ker, n'eus marc'heg yaouank all ebet ken kalonek ha Tristan, e Breizh-Vihan a-bezh. Talvoudous bras e vefe deoc'h e skoazell. Goulennit outañ chom en ho kichen."

An dug Howel, aliet gant e varoned, a c'halvas, eta, ar marc'heg yaouank.

"Difennet hoc'h eus gwir va lignez war an douar-mañ diwar-gaoust ho kwad, emezañ. Biken ne c'hellin ho trugarekaat en un doare brokus a-walc'h ... Anavout a rit va merc'h, Izold Gwenn-He-Minc'hoarzh; emañ a ouenn uhel hag e tiskenn eus duged ha roueed. A galon vat en he rofen deoc'h. Kemerit-hi da bried, mar karit."

"Hag e ran gant dudi, aotrou," eme Dristan.

A! Perak e lavaras ar c'homzoù difur-se? En abeg d'ar c'homzoù-se, avat, e varvo ...

Dibabet e voe an deiziad. Dont a reas an dug gant e geneiled ha Tristan gant e re. Goude an oferenn, a oa bet kanet e-tal an abati kozh, e voe unanet Tristan hag Izold Gwenn-He-Minc'hoarzh, an eil ouzh egile, gant liammoù santel ar briedelezh. Hir ha kaer e oa bet al lidoù; bras e oa bet niver ar gouvidi deut war c'houlenn an dug; laouen e seblante bezañ an holl.

Translation

Tristan and Iseult, *1950* (Extract)

For two days, Tristan and Gorwenal travelled through many towns and villages without seeing a single man, not a dog, not even a cockerel. On the third day, however, around the ninth hour, they arrived at the top of a wooded hill which sheltered an old chapel and, close by the old chapel, a hermit's cell. Nearby, dressed in goat-skin to shield his body against bad weather, was a monk. Kneeling on the ground, he was praying to Mary Magdalene to make him regret all his sins. He welcomed Tristan and his servant and, while Gorwenal tied the horses at the stable wall, he helped the young knight out of his helmet and armour, and prepared a meal.

This was not a fine feast: water from the nearby spring and rye bread, baked in the ashes, and that was all!

After supper, they sat by the fire. Night was falling. Tristan asked the monk the name of the wasted land in which he lived.

"Dear lord," said the monk, "it is the land of Lower Brittany. It is owned by Duke Howel. It was once a rich kingdom, with beautiful meadows bordered by many orchards. Then, alas! The whole country was plundered and destroyed by fire and thieving, by the soldiers of Lord Riol, the count of Nantes. There is not a strip of turf which has not been laid to waste. That's how it is in times of war ..."

"Brother," said Tristan, "do you know why this count has done such harm to Duke Howel, your lord?"

"I can, very easily, dear lord, explain to you the reason for the war. Riol was the vassal of Duke Howel. The duke has a daughter, the most beautiful of all. Riol would have liked to take her for his wife, but he knew for sure that Duke Howel would not give his daughter to one of his vassals... This is why he has tried to kidnap her by foul means."

Tristan then asked:

"And so Duke Howel cannot continue to withstand his attacker?"

"Not without much pain. And, yet, the walls of Carhaix are strong. It is the only castle still held by the duke. His son Kaerdin is of good heart, a fearless knight. The enemies, nevertheless, have the upper hand! I doubt whether he can fight them off for long ..."

Tristan then asked whether he was far from Carhaix. "About a league, that's all," replied the monk.

The following morning, Tristan said farewell to his host, mounted his horse and rode hurriedly, towards Carhaix, followed by Gorwenal. He arrived at the walls of the castle within half an hour. There were soldiers on the rampart walk. Tristan asked to speak to the duke. Howel was standing there among his men, as was Kaerdin.

"I am Tristan, king of Bro Leon, nephew of Mark, king of Cornwall. I have heard it said that one of your vassals has risen up against you and I come to offer you my sword."

"Alas! Lord Tristan, God bless you for your kindness! Nevertheless, continue on your journey. How can we welcome you when we have practically no more wheat nor oats nor rye nor any other food, but only beans and water?"

"No matter," said Tristan, "I lived in the woods for two years, eating roots and dried seeds. This kind of life does not displease me. Please give the order to open the main gate!"

"Give permission to his request, my father," spoke Kaerdin, "since he is so brave; be it to tie his fate with ours, in joy or grief."

Tristan was thus welcomed with due ceremony and honour. Accompanied by Kaerdin, he walked along the parapet to inspect the walls. How powerful the central tower seemed to be with its wooden defences behind which the archers could shelter! From the top, however, they could see, in the distance, the tents raised by Riol in the middle of the plain.

After returning to the courtyard, Kaerdin invited Tristan:

"So! Dear friend, let us go up now to the room where my mother and sister are."

And they went, each holding the other's hand, to the women's room.

Seated on a richly embroidered rug, the mother and daughter were singing a weaving-song composed in honour of Janedig the beautiful, weary from waiting under the hawthorn for Yann, her beloved, who has gone away. Tristan greeted them and was invited to sit with them while Kaerdin took in his hand the stole his mother was embroidering:

"Come close and take a look, dear friend! How skilful is my mother! But," said he in a loving voice immediately after, "the same could be said about my sister, wouldn't you agree? See with how much skill she has adorned this precious cloth ...!"

The young girl, pleased with those words, raised her eyes towards her brother, with a smile of such beauty and sincere pleasure that Kaerdin said to Tristan:

"As you see, dear friend, it is not without good reason that she is called Izold of the Fair Smile ...!" [*In other versions she is referred to as Iseult of the White Hands.*]

After hearing from his friend that she was called Izold, Tristan smiled secretly and, from then on, he looked at her more gently.

Riol had established his camp about half a league from Carhaix and, over the past few weeks, Howel's men had not dared cross the gates of the town to attack him. On the following day, however, Tristan and twelve young knights left the town, at the crack of dawn, all armed from head to toe, and rode under cover of a pine wood to the first tents of their enemy's camp and, having arrived there, quick as lightning, they leapt from their hideout and took a cart which carried wheat to the count's camp.

From that day on, they gave the enemy no respite: sometimes they would cut down Riol's badly guarded tents; at other times they would suddenly attack some carts, wounding animals and soldiers. They were constantly thinking up ever bolder new tricks and never returned to Carhaix without some booty or other.

Tristan and Kaerdin did not face so many dangers together in vain. Day after day, their hearts warmed one towards each other and the knots of friendship which linked them were so strong and many that the two knights swore that no man could ever separate them.

And, as we shall see later, they were true to their words.

When they returned from these dangerous skirmishes, riding together knee to knee, Kaerdin sometimes talked about his sister, Izold of the Fair Smile, the beautiful and sincere girl, always praising her with tenderness.

Tristan, however, although he had given his heart to Izold of the Fair Hair could not prevent himself from being overcome, little by little, by the wholly beautiful face of the second Izold.

No! He had not forgotten his first love! But he pined less for her, he did not long so much to see her again, for his pain was tempered by the sweetness of the young Breton lady.

One day, as he was singing a song he had composed a while ago to his beloved, he was overheard by Kaerdin just as he was mentioning the name Izold. Hearing the name of his sister on the harpist's lips, Kaerdin thought with pleasure that the young girl could not be loved by a better knight than Tristan. He said nothing to his friend, but, from that day on, he often found an opportunity to leave them together to speak quietly to each other.

The town was still besieged...

One day, as dawn broke, a guard descended in a great hurry from the central tower shouting:

"You have slept too late, my Lords! Rise quickly, Riol's soldiers are coming to attack us."

The knights and burgesses hurriedly grabbed their arms and rushed to the ramparts. The helmets, swords and lances of the count's soldiers were already glinting on the plain. The army was approaching Carhaix; it was a wondrous sight, so orderly and so close they were!

Duke Howel and Kaerdin deployed their knights in three rows in front of the gates, and when Riol's troops came near enough, they went to meet them, spurs pressed into the flanks of the horses, while arrows showered on them like April hailstones.

Tristan was one of the last to be awakened by the guard. He dressed himself in a hurry. He put on his coat of mail and his steel gaiters, then fixed his golden spurs. He took his helmet and his sword and quickly leapt on his horse and galloped wildly towards the plain.

He arrived there shouting "Carhaix, Carhaix!" It was high time! Howel's men were already retreating towards the town defences, in spite of the oaths they had sworn and the calls of their army chiefs. Such noise, such confusion, such cruel joy and such lamenting at the same time ...! Kaerdin, with his young knights, stood firm in spite of everything. As soon as the runaways heard Tristan's shout, they gathered around him again; and this time not one of them took a backward step! Soon Riol's men started retreating.

In the distance, a knight was galloping towards them. He was a brother of Count Riol himself, a determined and brave man. Kaerdin waited for him. They both attacked, but the battle did not last long. The stranger was lifted from his horse by Kaerdin's lance, gave a sharp cry and fell dead to the ground.

When Riol heard the death cry of his brother he turned, furious for revenge, on the victor who was causing him grief. Tristan saw the terrible danger his friend was in and tried to divert Riol from his path. The two knights struck with such ferocity that their lances shattered into pieces. Tristan's steed, struck in the flank, lost its balance and fell to the ground.

"A curse on anyone who avoids the rider to wound his animal. Save your own life, now, if you can!"

"Braggart!" snarled Riol, spurring his horse towards his foe to annihilate him.

Tristan raised his sword and struck a terrible blow on the head of the count! The blade glanced, however, from the shoulder of the count to that of the horse, which staggered on its feet and also fell. It was a miracle that Riol was not squashed there and then by the horse!

Their shields were in pieces, their iron mail torn and their helmets undone. No matter! They still found enough strength in their mutual hate to continue battling on foot.

Then Tristan, with one massive blow with his sword, struck the helmet of his enemy so mightily that Riol fell on all fours, totally dazed.

"Get up, vassal!" screamed Tristan, "You unwisely came to this field; now you must die!"

Riol tried to stand again. However he was felled by a blow which split his helmet, went through his head-piece and cut the skin of his skull to the bone. This time he pleaded for mercy and begged Tristan that his life be spared. The knight took his sword. He did so just in time as, from all directions, the men from Nantes were rushing to their master's help.

They were too late ... their leader had surrendered to his victor.

Taken before Duke Howel, Riol swore to pay homage from then on to his lord. He agreed, also, to restore to their former condition the villages and towns which had been burnt by his soldiers.

He was defeated ...! He gave orders for his army to break camp.

When they had returned to Carhaix, Kaerdin said to his father:

"Dear Lord, there is nowhere in the whole of Brittany a young knight so brave as Tristan. His support would be very valuable. Ask him to stay with you."

Duke Howel, after seeking the advice of his barons, called for the young knight and said:

"You have defended my lineage on this earth with your blood. Never will I be able to thank you with sufficient generosity ... You know my daughter, Izold of the Fair Smile; she is of noble birth, descended from dukes and kings. I would give her to you with all my heart. Take her for your wife, should you wish to."

"I shall take her gladly, Sire," said Tristan.

Ah! Why did he speak those unwise words? Because of those words he would meet his death ...

The day was chosen. The duke came with his friends and Tristan with his. After the mass, which was sung in front of the ancient abbey, Tristan and Izold of the Fair Smile were joined together in holy matrimony. The celebrations were long and beautiful; many were the guests invited by the duke; they all appeared to be very joyful.

Kêr-Iz

There is a strong probability that the legend of Kêr-Iz ('The low town' in Breton) records a fifth century historical event, when a coastal town was submerged after a particularly strong storm. The sinking of the coastline into the sea has given birth to many related legends to be found in Ireland, Wales and Scandinavia. Although the exact location of Iz has never been ascertained and continues to be debated, the strongest contender seems to be the Bay of Douarnenez.

In the ninth century, the germs of the legend were put in writing by the chronicler Gurdisten who mentioned the name of the town of Iz and that of King Gralon (also spelt Gradlon, or even Graalent, as in Marie de France's 'lays'). The first accounts, inspired by the pagan harp players of Brittany, make no mention of either Saint Gwenole, or of the king's daughter, Dahud (also called Ahès in some versions of the legend). As the centuries went by, new episodes came to enrich the story of the sunken city.

The christianised version – used for the edification of the masses – was first recorded by Canon Pierre Le Baud in the sixteenth century. It tells how Kêr-Iz was submerged in punishment of the sins of its inhabitants, and how Gralon was saved by to the intervention of Saint Gwenole. A century later, Albert le Grand, in 'Les Vies des saincts de la Bretagne Armorique' introduced the character of the debauched king's daughter, Dahud, who stole the key – still no more than a symbol of royalty – from her father. In a further edition of this book, Kernadet added the dike, the sluice gates, and the stolen key given by Ahès to one of her lovers. She became the legend's main character in the writings of Cambry, Pitre-Chevalier and Hersart de la Villemarqué and, in the twentieth century, her story was recalled by Ernest Renan, Per-Jakez Helias, Jean Markale, Yves Brekelien and many others. The legend has also been transposed into operas, theatre and radio plays, children's stories, comic strips and has inspired several painters and ceramists.

The first ballad by Olier Souetr (Olivier Souvestre) is based on a nineteenth century ballad and on Kernadet's retelling of the legend.

Olier Souetr

Ar Roue Gralon ha Kear Is, *1853*

Petra 'zo 'neve e kear Is,
Mar d-e ken drant ar yaouankis,
Mar klevan-me ar biniou,
Ar vombard hag ann telennou?

N'eus e kear Is netra neve,
Rak ar festou-ma 've bemde,
N'eus e kear Is nemet traou koz,
Rak ar festou-ma 've bemnoz.

Bojennou drez zo divoannet
E dor an ilizou serret,
Ha, var ar beorien o voëla,
E losker ar chas d'ho drailla.

D'ho c'hoezek vla, an holl verc'hed
N'ho deus Doue, met ar peched;
Ha, da ober he gurunen,
E roont ho c'haëra rozen.

Ahès, merc'h ar Roue Gralon,
Tân an ifern en he c'halon,
Er penn kenta deus an diroll,
A drein d'he c'heul ar gear da goll.

Sant Guenole, gant kalonad,
Zo bet meur vech o kaoût he zad,
Ha, gant daëlou, an den Doue
En deuz lavaret d'ar Roue:

"Gralon, Gralon, laka eves
D'an dizurzou a rên Ahès:
Rak tremenet vo an amzer,
Pa skuillo Doue he goler.

El lec'h ma voa c'hoarzadek kent,
E vo neuze skrignadek dent,
El lec'h ma voa kanaouennou,
E vo klevet skrijadennou!..."

Hag ar Roue fur, spouronet,
He verc'h en deus bet kelennet:
Mes, diskaret dre ar gosni,
N'eus mui an ners da stourm out-hi.

Ha, skuiz gant rebechou he zad,
Evit mont d'eus he zaoulagad,
Hi 'deus gret, gant droug sperejou,
Eur palès kaër tost d'ar sklujou.

Eno, gant he amourouchen,
Ema fenos an abaden,
Eno, en aour hag er perles,
Evel an heol, e par Ahès…

"Plijadur d'ec'h er palès-man,
Merc'hed chentil ha potred skan,
Plijadur d'ec'h ha nozvez c'hrën,"
Eme eur Prinç, en eur antren.

Ar Prinç, a zoughe dillat ru,
He varo a voa hir ha du,
He oll izili a verve,
Hag e zaoulagad a zeve.

"Ra viot deut mad, estranjour,
Eme Ahès, gant eur bek flour,
Ia, ra viot deut ar gwëlla,
Mar annaveït an traou falla."

– "Neuze em bo dighemer mad,
A respontas an divroad:
Rak me er fall zo ken disket
Hag an hini 'neus her c'hrouet."

Ha kerkent Ahès d'her pedi
Da ober eun dro zanz gant-hi,
Hag an oll, a eneb Doue,
Goassa ma c'hallent a doue.

Pa voa fin d'ar sacrilejou,
Messager an droug sperejou,

Chomet he-eunan er palès,
A dostaas da gaoût Ahès:

"Va douçik koant, merc'h da C'hralon,
Ha muia karet va c'halon,
Ha n'alfen me ket e neb ghis
Gwelet alc'houe sklujou kear Is."

– "Va zad a zoug en he gerc'hen,
An alc'houe aoûr deus eur chaden,
Ha va zad brema zo kousket,
Ha kaout an alc'houe n'allan ket."

Mes hen d'he zreid en em strinkas,
Ha d'he dornik flour a bokas,
Hag he chalmas dre he zellou
Karghet a dân hag a zaëlou.

Heb gout ar pez a dremene
Neuze, eur pennad ac'hane,
En he balès, ar Roue koz
A voa kousket e kreiz ann noz.

Kampr paour Gralon ne voa enn-hi,
Netra nemet eur grucifi
Deuet a zorn eur mignon ker,
Sant Caourantin, Eskop Kemper.

Netra nemet eun Aviel,
Roët c'hoas gant eün den santel,
Roët d'ezhan gant Gwenole,
Evel eur merk a garante

Kaër en he gosni, 'vel eun Ael,
E kouske Roue Breiz-Izel,
Hag en dro d'he dall, he vleo gwenn
A ree, dispak, eur gurunen.

Neuze, Ahès, ar Brinces fall,
Evel pa vije skoët dall,
En he gampr, heb aon rag Doue,
Ha deu da laëres an alc'houe.

En eur vale, var bek he zroad,
Ar verc'h a dosta skanv d'he zad,
Ha goustadik, deus he gerc'hen,
E tenn, 'neur c'hoarzin, ar chaden.

Piou a deu du-hont gant ar ru,
Pignet va eun hinkane du,
Hag en d'an daou lamm var he ghein,
Ken a strink an tân deus ar vein?

Hennes eo messager Doue,
Digasset en Is d'ar Roue,
Hennes eo abostol ar Feiz,
Sant Gwenole, karet e Breiz.

Tostât a ra 'neur c'haloupat,
En he zorn deou he vaz Abad,
Hag eur stôl aour var he zaë venn,
Hag eur c'helc'h tan en drô d'he benn.

'Nem gavet e dôr ar palès
He pini e kousk tad Ahès,
Divar he varc'h, an den santel
A c'halv, en nos, a voëz huel:

"Gralon, Gralon, sao heb dale,
Sao evit heuilla Gwenole,
Sao evit tec'het deus ar mor:
Sklujou Kear Is a zo digor!"

Hag ar Roue koz, trubuillet,
Er meaz he velo zo zaillet:
"Din-me, din-me, va marc'h prima!…
Siouas! Peurgollet ar gear-ma!…"

Ha gant glac'har, e ber amzer,
E kerz da heul he vignon ker,
Ha var ho lerc'h, en eur iudal,
E klevont ar môr o ruillal.

Neuze ar Brincès dirollet,
He amourous gant-hi kollet,

Dre gear Is, a glei hag a zeo,
A rede, dispaket he bleo.

Mes pa gleo daou lamp ar c'hezek
Araog ar môr o tiredek,
Dre al luc'hed, gant nec'hamant,
E c'hanve he zad hag ar zant.

"Va zad, va zad, ma em c'harit,
Var ho marc'h skanv va c'hemerit:
Hag heb respont, an tad tener
A zav he verc'h var ann tailler.

Kerkent ar môr a vuanna,
Ha Gwenole, en eur grena,
A gri: "Gralon, tôl an diaoul-ze,
"Diwar dailler da hinkane!…"

Kouskoude c'hoas, leun a enkres,
An tad a zalc'h ar bec'heres:
Mes ar sant a ra sin ar groaz,
A deu hag a sko gant he vaz.

Kerkent mestres an droug speret
A ruill er môr bras fuloret,
Hag e kleo tost ar Roue koz
Eur c'hoarzin skiltr e kreiz an noz.

Mes, rentet skanvoc'h, heb dale,
E sail prim da c'heul Gwenole,
Hag he varc'h, gleb he beder c'har,
A lamp deus ar môr d'an douar.

Da zao-heol, ar Sant ha Gralon
A bigne var lein Mene-Hôm,
Pini, he dreid ebarz en trez,
A zao a uz Douarnenez.

Ac'hane, Roue Breiz-Izel,
Var he lerc'h a dolas eur zel:
Mes, e lec'h Is, gant he dek dor,
Ne velas mui nemet ar môr.

"Eur ghear em boa deus ar gaëra,
ha chetu hi et da netra!…"
Hag he galon oll a fraillas,
Hag he zaoulagad a voelas.

"D'an daoulin, eme Gwenole,
Gralon, d'an daoulin ganen-me."
Ha Gralon, dindan he c'hlac'har,
A goë d'an daoulin d'an douar.

Hag eno, dispak he vleo gwenn,
Hag he dall pleghet er boultren,
E lavare c'hoas ar Roue:
"Ra vo gret bolonte Doue!…"

Pa zavas divar he zaoulin,
Dindan tân flam heol ar mintin,
E velas, a dreuz he zaëlou,
O lugherni *Ru-Men-Goulou*.

Var ar men-ze, hon tadou koz
A skuille goad d'eun Doue fos,
Hag ar Roue, e ber amzer,
A lavaras d'he vignon ker:

"Du-hont, e memor a ghear Is,
Me a raï sevel eun Ilis,
Hag evit testeni d'an oll
M'he galvo Ilis Remengol.

Pa vo an doueou maro,
Ha koëzet meur a goat dero,
Eun de, deus ar peval avel,
E teuio d'y pobl Breiz-Izel."

Translation

King Gralon and Kêr-Iz, *1853*

What is new in Kêr-Iz
For the young to be so cheerful,
For me to hear the bagpipes,
The bombard and the harps?

There is nothing new in Kêr-Iz,
As parties are thrown there everyday,
There are only old goings-on in Kêr-Iz,
As parties are thrown there every night.

Thorn bushes have grown
In the doorway of the closed churches.
Dogs are unleashed on the wailing poor
So that they tear them to pieces.

By the age of sixteen, all the girls
Have only one God, that of sin.
And, to celebrate his crowning,
They give their most beautiful rose.

Ahès, daughter of King Gralon,
The fire of hell burning in her heart,
Is at the head of this depravity
And leads the town to its loss.

Saint Guénolé, with a heavy heart,
Went several times to see her father.
With tears in his eyes, the saintly man
Said to the king:

"Gralon, Gralon, do take notice
Of the dissolute life which Ahès runs;
As it will be too late,
When God decides to shed his wrath.

Where there used to be laughter,
There will be gnashing of teeth,
Where there used to be songs,
Screams will be heard!…"

And the wise king, terrified,
Admonished his daughter:
But overwhelmed by old age,
He no longer had the strength to fight her.

Weary of her father's reproaches,
And to remove herself from his sight,

She built, with the help of demons,
A superb palace near the sluice gates.

There, with her lovers,
A ball is to take place tonight,
There, covered in gold and pearls,
Ahès shines like the sun.

"Enjoy yourselves in this palace,
Noble young ladies and light-footed men,
Enjoy yourselves and happy night,"
Said a prince as he came in.

The prince wore scarlet clothes;
His beard was long and black;
His limbs seethed with eagerness
And his eyes were fiery.

"Welcome to you, stranger,"
Said Ahès in a flattering voice,
"Yes, a very warm welcome to you,
If you are acquainted with the worst depravities."

"Then, I shall be more than welcome,"
Replied the unknown man;
"For I am as well versed in evil
As the one who created it."

Upon this, Ahès invited him
To have a dance with her,
And all of them, repeatedly,
Took the Lord's name in vain.

After more sacrilegious acts,
The messenger of the demons,
Now the only guest left in the palace,
Came up to Ahès:

"Pretty sweetheart, Gralon's daughter,
Beloved of my heart,
Could I not, in some way,
See the key to the sluice gates of Iz?"

– "My father wears around his neck,
The golden key on a chain.
My father is now asleep,
Therefore I cannot get the key."

But he threw himself at her feet,
And kissed her dainty hand.
He charmed her with his gaze
Full of fire and of tears.

Not knowing what was happening,
A little way from there,
In his palace, the old king was asleep.
It was the middle of the night.

In Gralon's bare room
There was only a crucifix
Given to him by his dear friend,
Saint Corentin, Bishop of Quimper.

There was a Gospel too,
Also given by the holy man,
Given to him by Guénolé,
As a token of their friendship.

Handsome in his old age, angel-like,
The king of Lower-Brittany slept.
Around his forehead, his white flowing hair
Formed a crown.

Ahès, the malicious princess,
As if struck by insanity,
In his bedroom, without fearing God,
Comes to steal the key.

Walking on tiptoe,
The girl gently comes up to her father,
And slowly, from his neck,
She removes the chain, laughing.

But who now comes up the street
Riding a black horse,

At such a full gallop
That sparks shoot up from the cobbles?

This man is God's messenger,
Sent to Iz to see the king.
He is the apostle of Faith,
Saint Guénolé, much loved in Brittany.

He approaches at a gallop,
His abbot's staff is in his right hand,
A golden stole over his white dress,
And a flaming halo around his head.

On arrival at the door of the palace
Where Ahès father sleeps,
Still on horseback, the holy man
Calls in the night, out loud:

"Gralon, Gralon, get up at once,
Get up to follow Guénolé,
Get up to escape from the sea:
The sluice gates of Iz are open!"

The old man, confused,
Has now risen from his bed:
"My fast horse, come to me! come to me!
Alas! The town is lost for good!"

Distressed but losing no time,
He follows his dear friend,
And behind them,
They hear the roaring sea rushing in.

The debauched princess,
Who has now lost her lover,
Runs through Iz, hither and thither,
Her hair undone.

But as she hears the gallop of the horses
Fleeing in front of the sea,
In the glimmer of lightning, terror-stricken,
She recognises her father and the saint.

"Father, Father, if you love me,
Take me on your nimble horse."
Without a word, the loving father
Helps his daughter to ride pillion.

At once, the sea gathers speed,
And Guénolé, in a quivering voice,
Exclaims: "Gralon, throw that devil
From the back of your horse!…"

And yet, in his distress,
The father lets the sinner ride on;
But the saint makes the sign of the cross,
Gallops back to him and strikes with his staff.

Directly, the mistress of evil
Rolls in the raging ocean,
And close to the old king,
A shrill laughter rises in the middle of the night.

Having less weight to carry,
Gralon dashes at once after Guénolé.
The waves were already licking his horse's hooves,
As it leapt from the sea to the shore.

At sunrise, the saint and Gralon
Climbed to the top of Ménez-Hom,
Which, rising from the sands,
Stands above Douarnenez.

From there, the king of Lower-Brittany
Glanced back;
But, instead of Iz and its ten gates,
He could only see the sea.

"I had a most beautiful town,
And now it has disappeared!…"
He was heart-broken,
And his eyes filled with tears.

"Get on your knees, said Guénolé,
Gralon, on your knees, next to me."

Gralon, overwhelmed with grief,
Fell to his knees on the ground.

There, his white hair loose,
And his forehead in the dust,
The king added:
"Thy will be done!"

When he stood up,
In the fiery glow of the rising sun,
He saw shining across his tears,
The stone of *Ru-Men-Goulou*.

On this stone, our ancestors
Used to spill blood to honour a pagan god.
The king then
Said to his dear friend:

"Over there, in memory of Kêr-Iz,
I shall have a church built,
And, as a testimony to all men,
I shall call it Rumengol's church.

After the death of pagan gods
And that of many oak groves,
One day, from all points of the compass,
The Breton people will come here."

Roparz Hemon

Santez Dahud, *1935* (Lodenn)

In the accounts describing events of the fifth or sixth centuries, women are often seen as conservative, resistant to change, and therefore tend to be associated with paganism. This is true of Dahud, as well as of Keben, the female character who opposes Saint Ronan. They are vilified and chastised for their non-adherence to the Christian faith. In his reconstruction of the story, Roparz Hemon rehabilitates the king's daughter and explains how she saved the souls of the inhabitants of Kêr-Yz. Souvestre's Red Prince is here called Abred.

VI

Un abardaevezh edo Gwenole o tremen war ar voger e-tal ar mor. Gwener ar Groaz e oa, hogen den ne soñje mui en traoù-se e Kêr-Iz. Er Sul a-raok, Sul ar Bleunioù, pa oa deut ar manac'h en iliz-veur da brezegenniñ, en doa kavet al lec'h-se goullo, ha korfoù marv daou veleg astennet, troc'het o gouzoug dirak an aoter.

Gwir eo, ne zeue ken nemeur a dud bremañ da selaou komz an Aotrou. Distroet e oa ar Sant d'ar c'hastell, pounner e galon evel ur maen en e greiz.

A-daol-trumm, dre ma kerzhe, e kavas dirazañ ur frailh er voger, ken ledan ma rankas lammat en tu all. Nevez digoret e oa, ha ken don ma ne weled ket ar strad anezhañ. Sellout a reas ar manac'h un tammig pishoc'h, ha setu ma tizoloas frailhoù all, bihanoc'h, o redek evel naered du a-dreuz d'an dinaou betek ar mor a darzhe dibaouez en ur eonenniñ e-touez peulioù prenn ha mein plat ar wrimenn. Pell 'zo ne veze mui dalc'het ar voger veur a-ratre. Ar rev, ar gwall amzer o doa graet o reuz a-hed ar goañv, hep nikun da soursial. Eno, e-unan dirak an noz o tont, war ar riblennad-se o hiraat a-gleiz hag a-zehou ken kompez ha dizudi dindan an oabl izel, e krede d'ar Sant klevout an dour o toullañ sioulik ha didruez pell-bras a-is d'ar geot ha d'ar bleunioùigoù glas a greske etre daroù greunvaen.

Hag e gwir e teue davetañ evel un hiboud, ken na chomas a-sav, o selaou. Heñvel oa ouzh aroun an tonnoù, hag e teue koulskoude diouzh kêr, a-boan ma weled an toennoù anezhi, damveuzet er vrumenn-noz. Gwech e tave an trouz, gwech e save uheloc'h. Gwech e pellae dioutañ, gwech e hañvale tostaat. Gwech e teue diouzh un tu hepken, ha gwech a bep tu. Lavaret e vije edo kêr a-bezh o virviñ. Dre ma selaoue gwelloc'h, e kleve sarac'h kammedoù ha safar mouezhioù engroezioù tud o vont-dont dre ar straedoù. "Ur gouel bennak adarre," a soñjas. Hag evelato, ne oa ket garmoù a levenez a dizhe e skouarn. Hag i damvouget gant an avel, merzout a c'helled enno kounnar ha strafuilh. En un taol e kreskas an dourni, ha huchadennoù a savas sklaeroc'h:

"D'ar marv, Gralon gozh! D'ar marv ar manac'h! Bevet Abred, hor Roue!"

Un darn eus ar voger veur a skoe tost ouzh ar c'hastell, hag el lec'h-se e oa un tour, a dalveze war un dro da dour-tan ha da greñvlec'h. Di e redas Gwenole, ur menoz hepken en e spered: saveteiñ Gralon, saveteiñ Dahud.

Ur goulou a lintre e beg an tour, peoc'hus-meurbet, o tegas eñvor an deizioù gwechall. Dre vurzhud e oa chomet war enaou, rak eno ne oa den ebet. Dor an tour diouzh tu ar voger a oa digor. Hogen teñval e oa an diabarzh, netra o lugerniñ ennañ nemet hirgarrezennoù strizh ar prenester. Ar manac'h a dostaas ouzh unan. Parañ a rae al loar. Skalier bras ar c'hastell a oa sklerijennet-holl, ha distro. En traoñ avat, troad ar menez a oa leun a dud o youc'hal hag o fiñval, ha muioc'h a oa c'hoazh o tont diouzh ar voubouadeg a gleved o c'hournijal e straedoù a dro-war-dro.

A-vec'h m'en doa bet ar manac'h amzer da deurel ur sell ma strakas ur youc'hadeg vras, ha setu an holl vrec'hioù savet er vann. Krediñ a reas e oa bet gwelet hag edod o tont d'e gerc'hat betek lein an tour. Kuzhet e oa er skeud koulskoude, hag ouzhpenn, ne oa ket davetañ e oa troet ar pennoù, hogen etrezek dor ar c'hastell. Sellout a reas d'an nec'h d'e dro. Dindan ar volz e oa ur plac'h, hec'h-unan-penn, en he sav, gwisket e gwenn-kann. Edo o tont war-raok. Goustad e tiskenne an diri, ken sonn ha ken uhel he fenn ma vije bet lavaret un delwenn o vale. Un talgen aour a oa war he blev, hag e luc'he ouzh bannoù al loar ar bravigoù a c'holoe he brennid hag he divrec'h. Evel-se e veze fichet e Kêr-Iz ar plac'hed

yaouank o vont da vezañ euredet, hag ivez ar re o vont da vezañ kaset d'ar vered. Strakal a rae ar youc'hadennoù muioc'h-mui. Edo ar bobl o c'hoapaat: "Bevet muiañ-karet Abred! Bevet hor rouanez! Bevet Dahud!"

VII

Ur rouedad hentoù dindan-douar a oa bet kleuzet gwechall e menez ar c'hastell. Anavezet e oant gant un nebeud tud hepken. Unan a gase d'ar voger veur. Re all a gase war ar maez. Gwenole ne voe ket pell oc'h en em gavout e-tal ar roue, hag a oa morgousket en ur gador. Eno e oa bet dilezet gant e servijerien, a oa kroget aon enno, hag a oa tec'het o kas ganto kement tra a briz a c'hellent sammañ.

Tenn e voe d'ar Sant dihunañ an den kozh, ha tennoc'h c'hoazh e sachañ d'e heul dre ar riboulioù kailharek ha leizh, ma riskle an troad war ar pazennoù lenkr ha ma venne ar goulou bezañ mouget gant an dour o tiverañ diouzh al lein.

Diboukañ a rejont en diwezh e porzh ur maner bihan en diavaez da vogerioù kêr. Didud e oa ar maner-se. Hogen en ur park e-kichen e oa daou varc'h kozh, blevek o favioù. Er marchosi e kavas Gwenole dibroù ha rañjennoù louedet ha merglet en ur c'horn. Harnezet al loened, e stagas ar roue war gein unan, hag o pignat war gein egile, ez eas en hent, pell diouzh ar gêr villiget.

Klouar e oa an noz, luc'hed o treuziñ an oabl alies, hag ar gurun o strakal a-dreñv ar c'houmoul ledet a-hed an dremmwel. Ar c'hezeg, hag a oa bet diegus da gentañ, a drote bremañ buanoc'h, o hejañ o fenn a bep eil hag o c'hwesha dibouez. Ur strakadenn drumm, ha da heul un hiboud souezhus, o lakaas da vont d'an daoulamm. Damc'houde e stroñsas an douar, tra ma voe entanet an oabl ha pep tra gronnet a flammoù. Al loened pennfollet a grape gant tor ur menez. Pa dizhjont al lein hepken e chomjont a-sav, gleb-holl, o c'hwirinat gant ar spont.

War-zu ar c'hornog, ouzh troad ar menez, tonnoù ramzel a ruilhe hag a spoume, gwenn ha limestra ouzh skleur al loar. Ahont, en un tu bennak, e oa bet Kêr-Iz.

A-boan ma lintras an heol en deiz war-lerc'h. Gwenole ha Gralon a dremenas an devezh-se hag an nozvezh goude en ul lochenn savet da reiñ goudor d'ar vesaerien.

VIII

Antronoz ez eas ar Sant, beure-mat, da bediñ e-tal ar mor. Brav e oa an amzer, un dudi. Pleg-mor Douarnanez (rak siwazh, pleg-mor Kêr-Iz ne oa ken) a oa ledet kompez, o skediñ ken sioul ha tra dindan an heol. En un taol e oa deut an nevez-amzer. Ar geot, ar gwez hag ar girzhier a c'hlaze hag a wenne, hag an takennoùigoù a lugerne war beg pep briñsenn ha pep bleñchenn ne ouie den petra oant, pe rev teuzet, pe c'hlizh. C'hwek e oa an aezhenn. An oabl a oa glas-lirzhin a-us da Venez-Hom, glas-teñval a-us da vro ar C'hab, glas-tener a-us d'an donvor.

Tra ma pede, ez ehane ar Sant ur wech an amzer da selaou. Un trouz marzhus a hañvale dont a-bell eus strad ar mor, ur sarac'h hag ur safronerezh, izeloc'h ha kreñvoc'h tro-ha-tro. Ne oa ket gwigour ar bili charreet gant an tonnoù don. Ne oa ket boud an tarzhoù o skubañ an islonkoù dindan-vor. Ne oa ket yud an hou-lennoù o kribañ ferv ar c'herreg ganas kuzhet e-tal ar gorre. Ne oa ket fraoñv gwagennoù hir diniver ar Mor-Bras. Bez' e oa evel an holl drouzioù-se mesk-ha-mesk, ha muioc'h c'hoazh: ur sonerezh anavezet hag iskis koulskoude, glac'harus-meurbet, ennañ avat, a vare da vare, evel tonioù laouen.

Seul vui e selaoue ar Sant, veul vui e kreske an hiboud. Ha seul vui e kreske, seul vui e laouenae, mouezhioù seder o sevel trumm, ha neuze mouezhioù drant, o tridal hag o tridal, tra ma tave a-nebeudoù ar mouezhioù a anken hag a enkrez, ar sonioù sklintin o tont sklaer hag oc'h ober cholori mil evn o richanañ.

Hag a-greiz-holl e tarzhas sklêrijenn e spered ar Sant evel ur luc'hedenn: an trouz-se a oa trouz kleier Kêr-Iz o vrallañ. Bremañ o anaveze mat: kleier pep chapel, pep iliz, pep kouent ha pep manati, hag uheloc'h eget ar re all, kleier tour bras an iliz-veur, adal Arc'hantael, ar gwidorig, skiltr e c'harm evel diskan ur c'hurust bihan, betek Klodleun, ar c'hloc'h-boud, kleuz e c'halv evel kan ur c'hiniad en e vrud.

Ha setu: (penaos en doa ankounac'haet, ne ouie ket, — youl Doue marteze e oa) ar mintin kaer-se a oa mintin Pask, ha brallañ a rae ar c'hleier evel gwechall, pa veze an holl e Kêr-Iz mat ha sentus hag oberiant, pep hini o seveniñ laouen e zlead, o wareziñ ar re yaouank, o toujañ ar re gozh, leal e-keñver e nesañ, feal da Zoue ha d'ar roue, pa veze o ren dre gêr an aked hag an onestiz, pa veze kalonek pep gwaz ha fur pep maouez, pa veze an devezhioù labour gwir zevezhioù gouel.

"Ha salvet int bet daoust da bep tra?" a soñjas ar Sant. Ha ne vern pegen bras e ouie e oa madelezh an Aotrou, goude kement a ziroll, kement a renavierezh, ne oa ket evit kompren.

Dizaoulinañ a reas ha mont ur pennad a-hed an aod. Tavet e oa an trouz. Ne gleved mui nemet ar c'hoummoùigoù o sourral en ur vervel war an douar, hag an aezhenn o c'hwibanañ lizidour en ur ober tro an torgennoù.

E selloù, ha na oant e gwir troet ouzh netra, ken beuzet edo en e soñjezonoù, a baras trumm war un dra hag a lakaas e galon da ober ul lamm en e vruched. Nepell dioutañ, astennet war ur bern bezhin bras, e oa korf ur plac'h. Ar gwagennoù a zirolle war an aod, a ruilhe goustad tro-dro d'ar bezhin, hag a gile neuze, lentik ha sioulik, o sunañ an douar dindan ar meinigoù. Hag evel-se bep tro. Lavaret e vije e oa aon gant ar mor da vont pelloc'h.

Ar Sant a dostaas buan, hag oc'h anavezout merc'h ar roue, e vanas, den kozh santel ma oa, en doa gwelet meur a souezh ha meur a vurzhud, saouzanet-holl dirak an dremm-se, ken glan en he c'hened.

IX

Diwezhatoc'h en devezh, e teuas ur c'houer d'ar red da gaout ar Sant, o stardañ ur goulmig wenn-kann war e vruched. An evnig, skuizh-marv, a oa kouezhet dirak e dì. Dougen a rae ul lizher. Ne oa ket hir: "Abred en deus touet mont kuit diouzh Kêr-Iz da viken mar dan davetañ. Mont a ran". Da heul e oa siell Dahud.

Doue en doa miret ouzh Abred da ober e dorfed diwezhañ, ha distrujet Kêr-Iz. Hogen en ur reiñ he buhez, he doa ar plac'h dinamm gounezet grasoù d'he c'henvroiz da gaout keuz d'o fec'hedoù kent mervel.

X

D'al lec'h ma oa kouezhet ar goulm e voe douget korf Dahud. Hag eno e voe beziet, ha savet ur chapel warni. Ha goude kement a vurzhudoù, e voe enoret evel ur
Santez, hervez giz hon tadoù-kozh.

Translation

Saint Dahud, *1935* (Extract)

VI

One afternoon, Gwenole was walking on the dike which ran along the sea. It was
Good Friday, but everyone in Kêr-Iz had forgotten about it. The Sunday before,
Palm Sunday, when the monk had entered the cathedral to preach, he had found it
empty, except for the body of two priests lying on the floor in front of the altar.
Their throats had been cut. It is true to say that not many people now came to listen
to the word of God. The saint returned to the castle, his heart as heavy as a stone.

As he walked on, he suddenly saw in front of him a crack in the dike which was
so wide that he had to jump to reach the other side. It had appeared recently but
was so deep that he could not see where it started. The monk examined it and discovered other smaller cracks running like black snakes all the way down to the sea
which was constantly breaking and foaming among the wooden poles and the flat
stones of the sea defences. The wall had not been repaired for a long time. The
frost and bad weather had damaged it during the winter, but no one seemed concerned. There, alone in the falling night, in the middle of the narrow path, flat and
characterless under the high sky, the saint thought that he could hear, much below
the grass and the small blue flowers which were growing between the granite slabs,
the water digging consistently and relentlessly.

He could definitely hear a soft sound. He stopped to listen. It was like the clam-
our of the waves, and yet it came from the town, the roofs of which he could just
about see, half-hidden in the night mist. The noise was sporadic. It came and went.
At times he heard it from one side only and at other times from everywhere. It was
as though the whole town was vibrating. As he listened more carefully, he heard the
sound of footsteps and the wild cries of a mob pacing up and down the streets. "Yet
another feast'" he thought. However these were not cries of joy. Although they
were muffled by the wind, he noted irritation and anger in them. Suddenly the roar
increased, and the shouts became clearer:

"Death to Old Gralon! Death to the monk! Long live Abred, our king!"

The dike was connected to the castle, and at the junction, there was a tower
which served both as a lighthouse and as a fortress. Gwenole ran to it, a single
thought in his mind: he had to save Gralon, to save Dahud.

A light was calmly shimmering at the top of the tower, and this reminded him
of the old days. That it should still be burning was a miracle, as the place was
deserted. On the dike side, the door to the tower was open. It was dark inside as the
only glimmer came from the narrow rectangles of the windows. The monk walked

up to one of them. The moon was shining. The main staircase of the castle was fully lit but deserted. Down below however, at the foot of the mountain, the crowd was screaming and jostling as yet more people arrived, as the murmur floating above the surrounding streets seemed to imply.

The monk had hardly had time to take in the scene that a loud roar was heard. All arms were pointing upwards. He thought that he had been seen and that they were coming for him on the top of the tower. He was however hidden in the shadow, and in fact the heads were not turned towards him but towards the castle. He too looked up. Under the archway stood a girl, alone, dressed in pure white. She took a few steps forward, then slowly walked down the staircase, her head held so high and still that she looked like a walking statue. She wore a golden headband in her hair. The jewels around her neck and arms were glinting in the moonlight. This is how the girls of Kêr-Iz used to be dressed on the day of their wedding but also on that of their funeral.

The noise was getting louder as the people shouted defiantly: "Long live Abred's fiancée! Long live our queen! Long live Dahud!"

VII

A network of tunnels had once been dug in the mountain under the castle. Few people knew about them. One of them led to the big dike, others led outside. Gwenole lost no time to reach the king who was dozing in a chair. He had been abandoned there by his frightened servants who had run away, taking with them all the precious objects they could carry.

Waking the old man was not an easy task. The saint found it even harder to make the king follow him through the damp and dirty tunnels where their feet slipped on the slimy steps and where the torch was all but extinguished by the water dripping from the vault.

They finally arrived in the courtyard of a small manor, on the other side of the town walls. The manor was deserted, but in a nearby field they found two old horses with tufts over their hooves. In a heap, in a corner of the stables, Gwenole found mouldy and rusty saddles and reins. When the horses had been saddled, he helped the king to mount one, and riding the other, they set off, far from the cursed town.

The night was warm. Lightning crisscrossed the sky and the thunder was rumbling behind the clouds which lined the horizon. The horses, which had started at a slow pace, were now trotting faster, shaking their heads from side to side and constantly snorting. A sudden clap of thunder, followed by an unusual buzz, made them gallop. Immediately afterwards, the earth shook as the sky was set ablaze and everything was engulfed in flames. The panic-stricken horses rushed up the side of a mountain. They only stopped when they reached the top, sweating and neighing from fright.

On the western side, at the foot of the mountain, giant waves, white and purple in the moonlight, were rolling and foaming. The town of Kêr-Iz used to stand over there, somewhere in that direction.

The following day the sun hardly shone at all. Gwenole and Gralon spent the day and the following night in a hut built for shepherds.

VIII

The next day, at dawn, the saint went to the seashore to pray. It was a particularly nice day. The bay of Douarnenez – it can no longer be called the bay of Kêr-Iz – was calm, its glassy sea sparkling in the sunshine. Spring had suddenly sprung. The grass, the trees, the hedges were turning green and white. There was no way of knowing whether the small drops, which glimmered on every twig and every branch, were melted frost or dew. The air was pleasant. The sky shone bright blue above Ménez-Hom, dark blue above the Crozon peninsula, and a light-blue above the high sea.

From time to time, the saint interrupted his prayers to listen. A secret and distant sound seemed to rise from the bottom of the sea. It was a kind of rustle, a kind of buzz, which grew and declined; nothing like the whine of pebbles swept under by the waves, nor like the droning of the waves sweeping the sea floor. Nor was it the groaning of the surf violently hitting the treacherous rocks hidden just under the surface. It was not the loud purring of the usual ocean breakers. It was all these noises together and yet more: it was a well-known yet strange music, very sad except for what seemed to be a few happy notes.

The more the saint listened the more the buzzing gathered strength. And the more it increased the more joyful it became. Serene voices suddenly rose, then cheerful ones, exhilarating and thrilling. Gradually, the sorrowful and mournful voices ceased, making way for crystal-clear joyful sounds, like those made by a thousand twittering birds.

Suddenly, in a flash, the saint realised that the noises he was hearing were those of the ringing of Kêr-Iz bells. He could recognise them all now: the small bells of every chapel, of every church, of every convent and of every monastery were ringing in unison with the louder bells of the cathedral: here was Arc'hantael, the small bell with its pitch as high as the voice of a young altar-boy, and now Klodleun, with its grave tone as deep as a cantor's voice.

How could he have forgotten? He did not know. Was it God's will? This beautiful morning was, of course, that of Easter Sunday. The church bells were ringing, as they used to in the old days when the inhabitants of Kêr-Iz were obedient and hard-working, when all were happily doing their duty, protecting the young, respecting the old, when all were loyal to their neighbours, faithful to God and to the king, when, throughout the town, there was industry and integrity, when every man was brave and every woman wise, when working days were truly days of work and holidays truly holy days.

"Could they have been saved in spite of everything?" thought the saint. Although he knew that the Lord's goodness was infinite, how could it be? There had been so much debauchery, so much vilification.

He stood up and started to walk along the shore. The bells had stopped ringing and he could only hear the murmur of the tiny waves licking the sand, and that of the breeze whistling softly as it rounded the cliffs.

He was lost in his thoughts and not looking at anything in particular, when suddenly he saw something which made his heart jump in his chest. Not far from him, lying on a large pile of seaweeds, was the body of a girl. The waves, which broke angrily on the shore, spread themselves gently around the seaweeds, withdrawing warily and quietly as they sucked the sand from under the pebbles. And this happened again and again. It was as if the sea was frightened to go any further.

The saint quickly approached, and recognising the king's daughter. He, the old virtuous man who had seen many strange things and many miracles, stood there, mesmerised by the girl's pure and beautiful face.

IX

Later that day, a farmer came running up to the saint, holding a white dove to his chest. The little bird, exhausted, had fallen from the sky in front of his house. It was carrying a letter. It was a short note: "Abred has sworn he would leave Kêr-Iz for good if I gave myself to him. I shall do so." It ended with Dahud's seal.

God had prevented Abred from committing his last crime and had destroyed Kêr-Iz. By sacrificing her life, the unsullied girl had won God's grace for her fellow citizens who came to repent their sins before dying.

X

Dahud's body was carried to the place where the dove had fallen. She was buried there, and a chapel was built on her grave. After many miracles, she came to be revered as a saint, as was the way amongst our ancestors.

Marianna Abgrall

Ar Roue Grallon hag an Doktor Laenneg, *1920*

Bremañ ez eus un nebeut amzer e oa e Kemper un devezhour kozh a raed Jozek anezhañ. Daoust dezhañ da chom e kêr e touge atav dilhad diwar ar maez, un tog ledan voulouzet hag ur chupenn glazik. Jozek a gare un tammig e vannig met morse ne veze mezv: tommedik-tommedig, netra ken, ha neuze e parlante outañ e-unan dre maz ae gant e hent. An dra-se ne rae droug da zen ebet. Bemdez, goude e zervezh, e oa boas da lakaat ur c'horniad ha da evañ ur bannig da di ur mignon dezhañ a oa o chom er penn all da ru Kereon. Da vont ha da zont e ranke tremen dre vlasenn an iliz-veur. D'an taol a nav eur e teue atav d'ar gêr. En hañv e veze d'an eur-se kalz tud war ar blasenn o kemerout an aer-noz met er goañv, avat, Jozek ne wele den ebet, ral e veze. Ha setu un nozvezh goañv hag eñ ha klevout, pa oa tost d'ar blasenn, unan bennak o pasaat, mantrus klevout pegen kreñv e oa e baz. Hor paotr kozh ne reas ket a van met div, teir nozvezh diouzhtu e klevas ar memes taolioù paz hag o devoa doare da zont eus a uhel ha Jozek da sellout ouzh ar prenestr, da nec'h an tiez. Ne wele den. Erruet war ar blasenn, dirak an iliz, e klev un taol paz e-giz pa zeuje eus unan eus an tourioù pe diwar doen an iliz. "Sell 'ta, sell 'ta", eme Jozek, "piv an tanfoeltr a zo aze o pasaat d'ar mare-mañ? Serret eo dor an iliz, mil bell zo, hag ar sakrist, me zo sur, a zo en e wele!" Ha va den da sevel e benn, da sell-out ouzh en aer. Al loar a bare hag e welas mat daou dour hag ar roue Grallon war e varc'h maen e-kreiz. Hag e klevas adarre un taol paz a lakae da dregerniñ ar blasenn a-bezh. "Sell, sell, tanfoeltr" emezañ en ur chom krenn en e sav, "daoust ha n'eo ket ar roue kozh eo a vefe o pasaat. Setu aze un dra zrol, avat, ha, koulskoude, n'on ket souezhet tamm ebet hag en defe tapet ur gaouad abaoe an amzer m'emañ aze din-dan an avel, ar glav, ar frim hag an erc'h! nann, nann, n'on ket souezhet tamm ebet avat!" Ha Jozek dre ma 'z ae d'ar gêr, a zalc'he da goazeal outañ e unan. "Nann, avat, n'on ket souezhet: en hañv, emañ brav a-walc'h aze: netra da ober e-doug an deiz nemet sellout ouzh an dud o tremen ha selaou ar marc'hadourezed d'en em rezoniñ war ar blasenn, met er goañv, avat, gwelloc'h eo ganin bezañ o faoutiñ koad er goudor!"

En noz war-lerc'h, d'an taol a nav eur, Jozek a oa adarre o tizreiñ d'ar gêr, ur ban-nac'hig brav gantañ dindan e fri. Degouezhet e-kreiz ar ru Kereon, e klev evel en nozvezhioù araok un taol paz kreñv, mantrus.

– "Alo!" emezañ, "daoust hag an tourioù a zo o vont da gouezhañ. Hag e sav e benn da sellout: ur goumoulenn a c'holoe al loar a oa dres aet e-biou hag ar paotr kozh a welas mat an daou dour sonn en o sav, hag, e-kreiz, marc'h ar roue Grallon met roue ebet ne wele.

– "Tanfoeltr!" emezañ, "biskoazh kemend-all! Daoust ha me a vefe berrwelet bremañ?" Hag e frote e zaoulagad gant e zaou zorn. Kaer en devoa sellout ne wele atav nemet ar marc'h. En tour, avat, e kleve trouz egiz pa vijed bet o reiñ taolioù horzh war an derezioù. Jozek a grogas un tamm aon ennañ. "Petra an tanfoeltr a zo aze? Mat! Me 'rank gwelout, ya 'vat, hag e rakfen chom amañ betek warc'hoazh vintin, me 'welo, me 'welo, pe n'eo ket Jozek va anv!"

Mont a ra da azezañ war derezioù ar porched. Atav an trouz: Poum-poum! Tostaat a ra; bremañ e vefe lavaret unan gant ur botoù pounner o vale en iliz. En un taol, div zor vras an iliz a zigor hag ar roue Grallon, ya, ar roue Grallon maen, o tont eus an iliz war e bouez en ur lakaat da dregerniñ gant e votoù maen pavez ar porched hag eñ war ar blasenn ha, war-eeun, war-du patrom Laenneg. Jozek a oa chomet sioul, sebezet o welout ar roue met pa voe aet e-biou dezhañ, e oa savet en e sav hag o krenañ c'hoazh gant ar spont e lavare: "Biskoazh kemend-all! Me 'zo bet martolod, em eus graet brezelekadenn Sina ha n'em eus biskoazh klevet na gwelet kemend-all! Met, sell 'ta, da belec'h ez a ar roue kozh!" Hag eñ d'e heul sioulañ ma c'helle. N'en devoa ket a ezhomm da gaout aon da vezañ klevet o vale daoust ma oa laosk ha faout e votoù: RE AR ROUE A RAE KEMENT A DROUZ ma oa souezhet Jozek ne zeue ket an dud da sellout en o frenester. Prenestr ebet ne zigo-ras, hag, e feiz, e oa un tamm lorc'h ennañ o soñjal e vije-eñ, Jozek kozh, e-unan test eus un dra ken estlammus. Lavarout a rae goustadik: "Sell 'ta, sell 'ta, o vont da welout e amezeg emañ evit doare. D'ober petra an tanfoeltr ez a da vihanañ?" Ar roue a yae atav war e bouez. Bep an amzer en deveze taolioù paz hag e ranke chom a-sav, evel evit kaout e alan. Pa voe degouezhet pemp pe c'hwec'h paz diouzh patrom Laenneg, hemañ a ziskennas diwar e gador. Soublañ a reas e benn izel evit saludiñ ar roue. Hemañ a reas eveltañ pa voe degouezhet e-kichen ar gael a ra an dro da batrom Laenneg. Jozek a glevas anezho o koazeal met re bell e oa evit klevout mat petra lavarent. Sur e oa, avat, e komzent e brezhoneg rak klevout a rae Laenneg o lavarout: "Mat, mat-tre!" Neuze, hemañ a grogras gant e zaou zorn en divkoaz ar roue; treiñ a reas e gein war-du ennañ hag e lakaas e skouarn da selaou e-giz ma ra ar medisin pa vez war-dro an dud klañv; selaou a rae a-gleiz a-zehoù ha, gant kil e vizied e skoe war gein maen ar roue kozh. E c'hellit krediñ ne reas ket a drouz kleuz: temperamant mat en devoa c'hoazh. Goude e lakaas e skouarn war e beultrin, e gostezioù. Ar roue en deveze taolioù paz bep an amzer ha Laenneg a lavare: "Mat, n'eus netra, netra!" Pa voe echu gant Laenneg e lavarjont adarre ur ger bennak an eil ouzh egile. Neuze, Laenneg a saludas ar roue en ur lavarout: "Kenavo, aotroù roue!" Hag ez eas da azezañ adarre war e gador. Ar roue a respontas: "Bennozh Doue deoc'h, va mignon!" Ha, war e bouez, ez eas war-du an iliz. Jozek her gwelas o vont ebarzh. An div zor a serras diouzhtu ha klevout a rae trouz botoù maen ar roue o sevel e derezioù an tour. Neuze, Jozek a zeuas ur soñj dezhañ hag a lakaas un enkrez vras en e spered. "Daoust," emezañ, "hag ar roue kozh a ouezo mont e-unan war e varc'h. Me 'rank gwelout, avat!" Hag ez eas da harpañ e gein ouzh moger an ti-korn a sko war ar ru ha war ar blasenn. Ac'hano e welo mat rak al loar a zo o parañ eeun war an iliz-veur. Prest e wel ar roue Grallon o tegouezhout war an doenn blat a zo etre an daou dour. Mont a ra eeun war-du e varc'h. Lakaat a ra e droad er stleug, e zorn war gein e varc'h ha flip! en ul lamm, evel ur paotr yaouank emañ gwintet warnezhañ.

Jozek a denn un huanadenn hir e-giz pa vije bet disammet diouzh ur bec'h pounner hag o sevel e dog ledan en aer e lavaras: "A han! Ni, avat, a zo daou baotr kozh start war o divesker. Kenavo, va roue!" Hag ez eas d'e wele. Abaoe Jozek a ya, evel kent, bemnoz da lakaat ur c'horniad ha da evañ ur banne da di e vignon. "Mat! Biskoazh abaoe," emezañ, " n'em eus klevet ar roue Grallon o kaout un taol paz: pare klok eo."

Ha setu aze va c'hontadenn. Mar he c'havit brav kontit anezhi d'ho pugale e-kichen an tan pa vezot o veilhañ evit m'o devezo soñj eus ar roue Grallon meur hag eus o c'henvroad brudet Laenneg.

Translation

King Grallon and Doctor Laennec, *1920*

Born in Quimper in 1781, Laenneg (Laennec) was the inventor of the stethocope.

A little while ago, there lived in Quimper an old day labourer called Jozek. Although he lived in town, he always used to wear country clothes, a wide rimmed hat with a velvet ribbon and the traditional blue jacket. Jozek liked his drink but was never drunk, just a little inebriated. On such occasions, he used to speak to himself as he went about his business. That did not hurt anyone. Every day, after work, he used to light his pipe and go for a drink to one of his friends' house who lived at the other end of Kereon Street. To get there and back, he had to cross the cathedral square. He always came home at the stroke of nine. On summer evenings there were plenty of people out on the square, but in winter Jozek hardly ever saw anyone, if at all. One winter evening, he heard someone coughing as he was approaching the square. The coughing was so bad that it was painful to hear. The old man did not at first take much notice of it, but, three nights in a row, he heard the same fits of coughing which seemed to come from high above. Jozek looked up towards the windows and the tops of the houses. He saw no one. As he arrived on the square and walked in front of the cathedral, he heard a burst of coughing which seemed to come from the church towers or from the roof of the cathedral. "Well, fancy that!" said Jozek, "Who the devil is up there at this time coughing his lungs out! The door of the church was shut hours ago and I bet that the sexton is in his bed!" He looked up, right up. The moon was shining and he clearly saw the twin towers and, right between them, King Grallon on his stone horse. "Well, well, fancy that!" he said straightening himself right up, "It sounds as if the old king is coughing. How weird! yet it is no surprise that he should have caught a bad cold. He has been out there in the wind, rain, frost and snow for such a long time! No, I'm not a bit surprised." On his way back home, Jozek went on talking to himself. "No, I'm not surprised. In summer things aren't too bad for him. He has nothing to do during the day but look at the passers-by and listen to the stallholders arguing on the market square, but in winter, I much prefer chopping up wood under shelter!"

The following evening, as the clock struck nine, Jozek was again on his way home, having drunk a little more than usual. As he got half-way down Kereon Street, he heard again, like on the previous nights, an appallingly loud cough.

"Well then!" he said, "are the towers going to tumble down. He looked up: the cloud which had been concealing the moon had just moved away and the old man clearly saw the two towers in their full height. Half-way between them, he saw King Grallon's horse, but there was no sign of the king himself.

"Fancy that!" he said, "I can't believe my eyes! Am I getting short-sighted?" He rubbed his eyes with his hands. He looked and looked but could only see the horse. However, in the tower itself, he could hear a noise resembling that of a sledgehammer hitting the stairs. Jozek was getting scared. "What the devil is happening? Well! I must know for sure, even if I have to stay here until tomorrow morning. I'll find out for sure, or my name is not Jozek!"

He went up to the church porch and sat down on the steps. The noise was still there: Bang! Bang! It was getting closer and now sounded like boots pounding the nave. Suddenly, the two main doors of the church opened and King Grallon, yes, the stone-carved King Grallon left the church unhurriedly, his stone boots ringing out on the cobble-stones of the porch. He reached the square and walked on towards Laennec's statue. Jozek had been rooted to the spot, amazed at the sight, but after the king had passed by him, he stood up, and still trembling with fright, said: "Fancy that! I have sailed the seven seas and fought the war in Indochina but I have never heard or seen anything like this! I wonder where the old king is going!" He then followed him as quietly as he could. He needed have no fear that his badly-fitting, loose old shoes would be heard. THOSE OF THE KING MADE SO MUCH NOISE that Jozek was surprised that no one came up to their windows to see what was going on. Not a single window opened, and to tell the truth, he was quite proud of the fact that he, old Jozek, was the one and only witness to such an amazing event. He mumbled on: "Well, well, he seems to want to pay his neighbour a visit. Whatever for? I ask you." The king was walking on unhurriedly. Every so often he coughed and had to stop to get his breath back, or so it seemed. Five or six steps before the king reached the statue, Laennec stood up from his chair and bent down to salute the king who returned the honour as he reached the iron enclosure surrounding Laennec's statue. Jozek heard them talking but he was too far behind to hear clearly what they were saying. However, he was sure they were speaking Breton as he could hear Laennec saying: "Mat, mat-tre!" [Very well, very well then!] Then Laennec put his hands on the king's shoulders, turned him round and put his ear against his back, just as a doctor does with his patients. He listened to the right side, to the left side. He tapped with his knuckles the stone back of the old king. I can assure you it did not make a hollow sound: the king was still in good shape. He then listened carefully to his chest. Every so often, when the king had coughing fits, Laennec would say: "Don't worry! This is nothing!" When Laennec straightened up, they exchanged a few words. Finally, Laennec saluted the king, said: "Goodbye, Sire!" and went back to sit on his chair. The king replied: "Thank you very much, dear friend!" before returning unhurriedly to the cathedral. Jozek saw him enter the church. The two doors closed immediately behind him and he heard the noise of the king's boots going up the tower. Jozek then thought: "I wonder if the old king can climb on his horse without help. I need to see that, for sure!" He walked away and leant against the wall of the corner house which gives both on to the main street and on to the square. This was a good vantage point as the moon was now illuminating the cathedral. Soon afterwards he saw King Grallon stepping on the flat roof which links the two towers. The king walked straight to his horse. He put a foot in the stirrup, a hand on the back of the horse, and Hop! He jumped on the saddle like a young man.

Jozek heaved a long sigh. What a relief! He lifted up his wide cap and said: "Well done! Both of us are old but we are still sprightly old men. Goodbye, Sire!" He then went back home to sleep. After that day, Jozek carried on smoking his pipe and having a drink in his friend's house. "Would you believe it! I have never heard another cough from King Grallon;" he said, "he is fully cured."

My tale is at an end. If you liked it, tell it by the fire-place to your children in the evening, so that they remember great King Grallon and his famous compatriot, Laennec.

Kervarker

Bosen Elliant, *1839*

The theme of plagues is found in many ballads and songs in Brittany. Bozen Elliant – The Plague of Elliant – is one of the ballads in Hersart de la Villemarqué's Barzaz Breiz, the 1867 edition. Villemarqué suggests that this was the plague that ravaged much of sixth century Europe. Ratian, the bard-saint, was a contemporary of Saint Guénolé. Donatien Laurent points out that the ballad could be referring to a fourteenth century plague or one even later than that. He points out that there may have been confusion between "Rasian" and "Basian" (i.e. Sebastien) another saint invoked against plagues. The description of the woman pulling the cart loaded with her nine dead sons, her mad husband walking behind whistling, inspired a painting by Louis Duveau which can be seen in the Musée des Beaux Arts in Quimper.

Tre Langolen hag Ar Faouet
Eur Barz santel a vez kavet;
Hag hen Tad Rasian hanvet.

Laret en deuz d'ar Faouediz:
Laket eunn oferen beb miz,
Eunn oferenn enn hoc'h iliz.

Eet eo ar vosen a Elliant,
Hogen ne ket eet heb forniant,
Eet zo gat-hi seiz-mil ha kant!

E bro Elliant, heb laret gaou,
E ma diskennet ann Ankou,
Maro ann holl dud nemed daou;

Eur c'hroegik kouz tri-ugent vloa
Hag eur mab ken e devoa.

"Edi ar vosen 'penn ma zi;
Pa garo Doue 'teui enn ti;
Ni iei 'mez pa deui," emez-hi.

E kreiz Elliant, er marc'hallec'h,
Geot da falc'hat e kafec'h,

Nemed enn hentig euz ar c'harr
A gas re varo d'ann douar.

Kriz vije 'r gallon na welje,
E bro Elliant, neb a vije:

Gwelit triouec'h charr tal ar vered
Ha triouec'h all eno tonet.

Lec'h oa nao mab enn eunn tiad,
Eent d'ann douar enn eur c'harrad,
Hag ho mamm baour oc'h ho charrat.

Ho zad adren o c'houibannat:
Kollet gat-han he skiand-vad.

Hi a iude, galve Doue:
Reustlet e oa korf hag ene:

"Laket ma nao mab enn douar,
Ha me roi d'hoc'h eur gouriz koar,

A rei teir zro endro d'ho ti,
Ha teir endro d'ho minic'hi,

Nao mab em boa em boa ganet,
Setu gad ann Ankou int eet;

Gad ann Ankou e toull ma dour;
Den da houl d'in eul lommik dour!"

Leun e'r vered rez ar c'hleuziou,
Leun ann iliz rez ann treuzou;

Red eo benniget ar parkou,
Da lakat enn ho ar c'horvou.

Me wel er vered eunn derven,
Hag enn he beg eul liser wenn:
Eet ann holl dud gad ar vosen.

Translation

The Plague of Elliant, *1839*

Between Langolen and Le Faouët
A holy bard lives;
Father Rasian is his name.

He said to the people of Le Faouët:
"Celebrate a mass every month,
A mass in your church."

The plague has gone from Elliant,
But not without its load,
Seven thousand and a hundred have gone with it.

Around Elliant, in truth,
The Ankou has descended,
All the people are dead, save two;

An old woman of sixty years
And her only son survive.

"The plague is on the threshold of my home;.
When God wills it, it will enter;
We shall leave when it comes," she said.

In the centre of Elliant, on the market place,
You will find grass to scythe down,

Except on the cart lane
Which carries the dead to their graves.

Those not crying would be hard-hearted;
Around Elliant, there would not be any:

See the eighteen carts, at the cemetery gate,
And another eighteen arriving there.

There were nine sons in one household,
Who were brought to their graves in a single cartload.
Their poor mother was pulling it.

Their father followed whistling:
He had lost his reason.

She was howling, imploring God,
Broken in body and soul.

"Bury my nine sons in the earth
And I shall give you a waxed cord,

Which will go thrice around your home,
And thrice around your sanctuary.

I had nine sons who were born to me,
Now they have gone with the Ankou.

With the Ankou on my doorstep,
No one will ask me for a sip of water!"

The cemetery is full, right up to its walls
The church is full, right up to its porch;

They have to bless the fields,
To bury the corpses in them.

I see an oak-tree in the cemetery,
And at its top a white sheet:
Everyone has been taken by the plague.

Anonymous

Iannik Kokard

This 'gwerz' or ballad, of which there are many examples, first appears in nineteenth-century manuscripts, but undoubtedly refers to fifteenth century events when leprosy was common in Brittany.

Iannik Kokard a Blouilliau,
Braoa mab kouer 'zo er vro,
Ar pabor euz ann holl baotred,
Kalonik ann demezelled.

Pa 'z ee Iann Kokard d'all Lewdreaz,
Ar merc'hed koant 'lamme e-meaz,

Ann eill d'eben a lavare:
"Iannik Kokard 'zo vont aze!"

Iannik Kokard 'n euz lavaret
Er ger, 'he dut, p'eo arruet:
"Ma zad, ma mamm, mar veoc'h kontant,
Me eureuife ur plac'hik koant,

Me eureuife Mari Tili,
Ur madou-braz 'roer gant-hi;
Reï 'reur d'ez-hi seiz komanant,
Ha leiz ar bouezell a arc'hant;

Leiz ar veol-vraz a neud-gwenn,
Ur c'harr houarnet hag un denn!"
Ar C'hokard a lavare
D'he vab Iannik, eno neuze:

"Mari Tili n'ho pezo ket,
Rag dac'h ha dimp 've rebechet,
Dac'h-c'hui ha dimp 've rebechet,
Rag ur gakouses ho pe bet!"

"Ma zad, ma mamm, da vihana,
Ma lest da vont da bardona;
Ma lest da vont da bardona
D'ar Folgoat, pe d' Zantes-Anna."

"Mar et d'ar pardon d'ar Folgoat,
Doue ra reï dac'h beaj-vad!
Doue ra reï dac'h beaj-vad,
D'ho tud er ger kezelo mad!"

Pa oa o tremenn Montroulez,
Hag hen o kaout he Gakousez:
"Iannik Kokard, ma c'harante,
Na pelec'h et-c'hui er giz-ze?"

"Me 'ia da bardon ar Folgoat,
Diloer, diarc'henn, war ma zroad."
"Iannik Kokard, ma c'harante,
Ma lest da vont ganec'h iwe,

Da c'houlenn 'r c'hraz digant Doue
Ma kouskfomp er memeuz gwele;
Kousket 'n ur memeuz gwelead,
Debri er memeuz skudellad."

Euz a Vontoulez da Blouvorn,
Ez int et ho daou dorn-euz-dorn.
Mari Tili a lavare,
Toul porz hi zad pa dremene:

"Iannik keiz, gortoït un tamm,
Ma 'z inn en ti da gaout ma mamm,
Da c'houlenn ha 'zo peadra
Da rei d'imb hon daou da goania."

"Ma merc'hik, me am euz klewet
Iannik Kokard 'zo dimezet;
Pa vezo ouz taol o koanian,
Ma merc'h, goulennit digant-han;

Euz ma laro, mar eo kristenn,
Roït d'ezhan he groaz-nouenn:
Roït d'ezhan he groaz-nouenn,
Un arched a bewar flankenn!"

"Iannik Kokard, ma c'harante,
Anzaovit d'inn ar wirione;
Anzaovit d'inn ar wirione,
Ha c'hui 'd'h euz groeg ha bugale?"

"Ia, me 'meus groeg ha bugale,
me garrie beza 'r ger gant-he."
"Iannik Kokard, ma c'harante,
Evit 'r banne diganin-me;

Na roinn ket d'ac'h a winn-gwenn,
Gant aouenn na zavfe d'ho penn;
Me diskenno dac'h gwin-kleret,
Wlt ma roï dac'h nerz da gerzet."

P'iee Iannik Kokard da vouit dour,
Na ouie ket ez oa klanvour;

Na ouie ket ez oa klanvour,
Ken a zellas ebars ann dour.

Bars ar feuntenn dre ma selle,
Gant al louarnes e tispenne!
Iannik Kokard a lavare
D'he dad, d'he vamm, pa arrue:

"Ma Zad, ma mamm, mar am c'haret,
Un ti-newez d'inn a zavfet;
Zavet-han d'inn en lez al lann,
Tost d'ann hent a ia da Zant-Iann;

Grit ur prenestr en he bignon,
Ma welinn ar prosession,
Ar baniel braz a Blouilliau,
O vont etrezeg Sant Kado.

Ar baniel braz tro ar vered,
Hag a wes am euz-han douget!
Mar 'm euz-han douget lies-braz,
N'hen doginn ken brema siouas!"

He dad he vamm a lavare
D'Iannik Kokard eno neuze:
"Iannik Kokard, d'in lavaret,
Gant petra ez oc'h bet laouret?"

"O eva gwinn, leiz ar werenn
Digant ur plac'hik a garienn;
O eva gwinn ampouezonet
Gant ur gakouses milliget!"

Mari Tili a lavare
En Montroulez pa arrue:
"Tric'houec'h kloarek am euz karet,
Hag ho zric'houec'h am euz laouret;

Iannik Kokard, ann diwesa,
Laka ma c'halon da ranna!
Ur strill-goad euz ma biz-bihan,
A laourfe kant, koulz hag unan!

Translation

Iannik Kokard

Iannik Kokard from Ploumilliau,
The finest farmer's son in the land,
Leader of the lads,
Heart-throb of the girls.

When Iann Kokard went to Lewdreaz,
The pretty girls rushed out
Saying to each other:
"There goes Iannik Kokard!"

Iannik Kokard said
When he got home, to his parents:
"Father, Mother, if you agree,
I shall marry a pretty girl,

I shall marry Mari Tili,
She will be given a fine dowry;
She will be given seven smallholdings,
And a full measure of silver;

A barrel full of white yarn,
A cart with iron fittings and a harness."
Old Kokard then said
To his son Iannik, there and then:

"You cannot have Mari Tili,
Because you and we get the blame
You and we would get the blame,
For you will marry a leper.

"Father, Mother, at least
Let me go to the pardon;
Let me go to the pardon
Of Le Folgoat, or of Sainte-Anne."

"If you go to the pardon of Le Folgoat,
God grant you a pleasant journey!
God grant you a pleasant journey,
And good wishes to your parents at home!"

As he was passing through Morlaix,
He chanced upon his leper girl
"Iannik Kokard, my beloved,
Where are you going thus?"

"I'm going to the Folgoat pardon,
Sockless, shoeless, on foot."
"Iannik Kokard, my love,
"Let me come with you too,

To seek the grace of God,
That we may sleep in the same bed;
Sleep in the same bed,
And eat from the same bowl."

From Morlaix to Plouvorn,
They both went hand in hand.
Mari Tili said
As they passed the door of her father's house:

"Iannik, dear, wait a little
While I go inside to see my mother,
To ask if she has anything
To give us both for supper."

"My daughter, I have heard
That Iannik Kokard is married;
When he is at the table eating supper,
My daughter, ask him then;

Depending on what he says, if he's a Christian,
Give him his last rites:
Give him his last rites,
And a coffin made of four planks!"

"Iannik Kokard, my love,
Admit the truth to me;
Admit the truth to me,
Have you a wife and children?"

"Yes, I have a wife and children,
I wish I was home with them."

"Iannik Kokard, my love,
Drink a glass of wine with me.

I shall not give you white wine,
In case it should go to your head;
I shall pour you some red wine,
To give you strength to walk."

When Iannik Kokard went for water,
He did not know he was sick;
He did not know he was sick,
Until he looked at the water.

As he looked into the fountain,
He was rotting with leprosy!
Iannik Kokard then said
To his father and his mother, when he returned:

"Father, Mother, if you love me,
Build me a new house;
Build it on the edge of the moor,
By the road which leads to Saint-Jean.

Make a window in the gable-end,
So that I can see the procession,
With the great banner of Ploumilliau,
Going to Saint-Cadoc.

The great banner round the churchyard,
That I have carried at times!
Though I have carried it many times,
I shall no longer carry it, alas!"

His father and mother then spoke to
Iannik Kokard thus:
"Iannik Kokard, tell us,
What gave you leprosy?"

"Drinking wine, a full glass
From a girl I loved;
Drinking wine poisoned
By a cursed leper girl!"

Mari Tili said
In Morlaix when she returned:
"I have loved eighteen clerics,
And given leprosy to the eighteen.

Iannik Kokard, the last,
Has broken my heart!
One drop of blood from my little finger,
Would kill a hundred as easily as one."

Kervarker

Ar C'hakous, *1839*

Ann den iaouank

Krouer ann neñv hag ann douar!
Mantret va c'halon gant glac'har.
O kounan eun noz hag enn de
D'am dousik koant, d'am c'harante.

Me zo war va gwele chomet,
Dalc'het, sioaz! Gand ar c'hlenved;
Ma ve va dousik a deufe,
E berr-amzer am frealzfe.

Evel gand ar werelaouen,
Goude eun nozvez a anken;
Mar deufe ma dous d'am gwelet,
E venn gant hi dizoaniet.

Ma lakafe beg he geno
War bordik skudul va louzo,
Da evan goude pa iefeun
Gwelleet raktal e vizenn.

Ar gallon az poa d'in roet,
Va muian karet, da viret,
N'em euz kollet na distroet,
Na laket da uz fall e-bed;

Ar gallon az poa d'in roet,
O va dousik koant, da viret,

Em euz mesket gand va hini;
Pini da hini va hini?

Ar Plac'h
Piou a gomz ouz-in evel-se,
Ha me ken du hag eur vran ve?

Ann den iaouank
Pa vec'h ken du hag ar mouar,
Gwenn-kann oc'h d'ann hini ho kar!

Ar plac'h
Den iaouank, eur gaou a leret!
Va c'halon d'hac'h, n'em euz roet;
N'em euz ker mui ac'hanoc'h,
Fur c'hakous a ouzonn-me oc'h!

Ann den iaouank
'Vel eunn aval e beg ar ween
E ma kalon ar femelen;
Kaer ve ann aval da welet,
Hag eur prenv e kreiz zo kuet.

Evel eunn delien war ar brank,
E ma gened ar plac'h iaouank;
Ann delien gouez war ann douar,
Ar c'hened ive a ziskar.

'Vel ar bleun glaz diouz lez ar stank,
Ma karante ar plac'h iaouank;
Ar bleunig a dro wechigo,
Ar bleunig a dro, a zistro;

Ar bleunig a dro wechigo,
Karante ar plac'h tro ato.
Ar bleun a ielo gand ann dour
Ha gand ann ankoun ann traitour.

Me a zo eur c'hloaregik paour,
Me a zo mab da Iann Kaour;
Beann onn bet tri bloa o studi,
Hogen breman na inn ket mui.

Benn eur pennad me iei endro,
Me iei endro kouit deuz ar vro;
Benn eur pennadik vinn maro,
Ha d'ar purkator me ielo.

Translation

The Leper, *1839*

The Young Man
Creator of Heaven and Earth!
My heart is heavy with pain.
As I remember day and night
My sweet love, my sweetheart.

I have to stay on my bed,
Confined, alas, by sickness;
If only my love would come,
Swiftly she would console me.

Like the morning star,
After a night of anguish;
If my love would come and see me
She would comfort me.

If only with her lips she'd touch
The rim of my medicine cup;
When I later drank from it,
Cured in an instant I would be.

The heart you gave me,
Sweetest love, to keep,
I have neither lost nor given back,
Nor ill-used in any way;

The heart that you gave to me,
My sweet love, to keep,
I have mingled it with mine;
What part is mine, what is yours?

The Girl
Who talks to me like this,
Who is as black as any crow?

The Young Man
Were you as black as blackberries
White you'd be to the one who loves you!

The Girl
Young man, falsely you speak!
My heart to you I did not give;
I no longer am attracted by you,
I know that you are a leper.

The Young Man
Like an apple on the tip of a bough
Is the heart of women;
The apple you see is beautiful
But a worm hides in its centre.

Like a leaf upon a branch
Is the beauty of a young girl;
The leaf falls upon the ground,
Beauty disappears.

Like the blue flower on the surface of the pond
Is the love of a young girl;
The little flower turns sometimes,
The little flower turns, this way, that way.

The little flower sometimes turns,
The love of a girl always turns;
The flowers will go with the water
And the treacherous with their anguish.

I am a poor clerk,
I am the son of Iann Kaour;
Three years I spent studying
But I shall no longer do so.

In a while, I shall no longer be,
And from this land I will be gone;
Shortly, I shall be dead,
And I shall go to Purgatory.

Fañch an Uhel

Ar Plac'h hag an naer, ganet war an hevelep tro gant ur wreg, *First published in 1939*

Ur wezh e oa un aotrou pinvik hag e bried, euredet pell amzer a oa, ha n'o devoa bugel ebet; hag e oant glac'haret a gement-se. Bet e oant en kalz a lec'hioù santel, o pediñ Doue hag e vamm benniget da reiñ dezhe ur bugel, paotr pe blac'h, ha ne ouient ken petra da ober.

Un deiz, e-pad an nevez amzer, pa oant o tont eus ar Folgoad, e welent a bep tu, en hentoù hag er parkoù, laboused-nij, ha naered, ha touseged, hag holl o devoa klodadoù re vihan, hag e tiskouezent bezañ eürus. Ma teuas neuze ar wreg da lâret, o welet kement-se:

– Mar rofe an Aotrou Doue ur bugel din, ha pa rankfen genel gantañ un naer, pe un touseg, ne raen forzh!

Kement-se na oa ket ur gomz vat. Setu ma teuas da vezañ brasez hepdale, hag e oa stad enni, hag en he fried ivez. Pa voe deut an amzer, e c'hanas ur plac'h vihan, ur bugel kaer a-walc'h, met un naer a oa rodellet en-dro d'he goûg. An naer a em dirodellas eus en-dro a c'hoûg ar bugel, hag ac'h eas er-maez an ti da em guzhañ indan ar geot, el liorzh a oa drek an ti.

Badezet e voe ar bugel ha anvet Levenez, abalamour da levenez he mamm hag he zad, hag e teue da greskiñ bemdez en yec'hed hag en koantiri, met roud an naer a oa chomet en-dro d'he goûg, evel ur c'harkan ruz, ha netra n'halle hen kas kuit, kaer a oa frotañ gant bep seurt louzoù.

Pa voe deut Levenez da vezañ ur grenardenn war-dro daouzek vloaz, un deiz pa oa he-unan o vale 'barzh al liorzh, drek an ti, e voe souezhet-bras o klevet ur vouezh o lâret:

– Demat, ma c'hoarig! Demat dit, ma c'hoarig Levenez!...

Kaer he devoa sellet, ne wele den, hag ar vouezh a oa koulskoude tost dezhi. Ma em lakaas da glask e-touez ar bodennoù, hag e kavas un naer. Ma leuskas ur griadenn gant an aon. Met an naer a gomzas neuze evel un den hag a lâras dezhi:

– N'ho pet ket aon, n'am eus droug ebet da ober deoc'h, ma c'hoarig!...

– Jezuz! C'hwi ma c'hoar, un naer!

– Ya, an hini he deus ho kanet he deus ma ganet ivez war an hevelep tro.

– Ha penaos e c'hallfe kement-se bezañ?

– Setu penaos: ho tad hag ho mamm a oa euredet pell amzer a oa, ha n'o devoa bugel ebet. Un deiz ma oant aet d'ar Folgoad da bediñ Doue da reiñ dezhe ur bugel, evel ma oa koulz an nevez-amzer, pa oant o tistreiñ d'ar gêr, e welent a bep tu, en henchoù hag er parkoù, a bep seurt loened hag amprevaned ha ganto-holl klodadoù re vihan, betek an naered hag an tougesed. Ma teuas hon mamm da lâret neuze:

– Mar kar Doue reiñ din ur bugel, ha pa rankfen genel gantañ un naer, ne ran ket a forzh!

Ma voe graet evel ma lâras, hag e c'hanas ur plac'h vihan hag un naer; ar plac'h eo c'hwi, an naer eo me, hag evel-se ez oc'h va c'hoar. En-dro d'ho koûg ez oan rodellet, ha ma roud a zo eno c'hoazh, ha n'eus nemedon hag a c'hallfe hen kas kuit. N'hoc'h eus ket ezhomm da gaout aon, na mezh ivez ouzhin-me, rak ne c'hoantaan deoc'h nemet pep vad, evel ma welfet diwezhatoc'h. Hepdale e teufet da zimeziñ....

– O! Nann avat, a lâras Levenez, me na youlan ket dimeziñ.

– Eo, dimeziñ a refet, ha koulskoude e ve welloc'h deoc'h ne zimezfec'h ket.

– Met penaos kas kuit ar c'harkan ruz a zo en-dro d'am goûg?

– It d'ar gêr, ha degaset din amañ un hanaf leun a laezh livrizh, hag ul lien gwenn, hag e welfet neuze.

Mont a ra Levenez d'an ti, ha distreiñ kerkent d'al liorzh, ha ganti un hanaf leun a laezh livrizh, hag ul lien gwenn. N'he devoa ken aon eus an naer. Lakaat a eure an hanaf war an douar, hag an naer a lammas kerkent e-barzh. Goude chom el laezh ur pennadig, e teuas arre er-maez, hag e lâras da Levenez gourvez war ar c'hlazenn. Pa voe gourvezet ar plac'hig, e em rodellas en-dro d'he goûg, e chomas evel-se ur pennadig, hag e em dirodellas neuze, hag e lâras dezhi:

– Frotet bremañ ho koûg gant al lien gwenn, el-lec'h emañ ar c'harkan ruz.

Ar plac'hig a reas evel-se, ha kerkent setu aet kuit ar c'harkan.

– Na lâret ket d'ho mamm, na d'ho tad ivez, eme an naer, penaos hoc'h eus graet evit kas kuit ar c'harkan.

An naer a em guzhas arre indan ar geot, ha Levenez a deuas d'ar gêr, ha stad enni.

– Sellet, a lâras kerkent d'he mamm, sellout ma goûg; ar c'harkan ruz a zo aet kuit!...

– Ha penaos eo c'hoarvezet kement-se; petra a' teus graet?

– Netra, mamm; anezhañ e-unan eo aet kuit, dre youl Doue.

– Lâret din, ma merc'h, eme an tad, piv en deus graet kement-se, ha me a roio kalz a arc'hant dezhañ.

– N'eo den ebet, ma zad; youl Doue, ha netra ken.

Dre ma teue Levenez en oad, ez oa koantoc'h bemdez, hag ar baotred yaouank ar muiañ pinvik eus ar vro a deue da ober al lez dezhi; met lâret a rae dezhe-holl ne dimezje ket. Dont a eure ivez un aotrou yaouank, a vro bell, emezañ, ha ne anaveze den anezhañ. Hemañ a blijas dezhi. Setu ma voent dimezet hag euredet. Pa voe fin d'ar gouelioù ha d'ar festoù, ar pried nevez a gasas e wreg gantañ d'e gastell, ur c'hastell ar c'haerañ. Eno n'he devoa netra da ober bemdez nemet bale er jardinoù ar c'hastell, ha gwiskañ bep seurt dilhad kaeroc'h-ouzh-kaeroc'h, hag em sellet er melezouroù. Holl kement a c'hoantae a vije kavet dezhi.

He fried ac'h ae alies eus ar gêr, da vale, e-pad daou, tri devezh, hag ouzhpenn, hag e leze ganti holl alc'hwezoù ar c'hastell, nemet unan hepken, hini ur gambr vihan. Bale a rae dre holl gambroù ar c'hastell, hag e wele a bep seurt traoù, holl kaeroc'h pe gaeroc'h. Pa dremene e-biou d'ar gambr difennet, e lâre bep tro: "Daoust petra a zo aze ivez?" Hag he devoa c'hoant bras d'he digeriñ, rak an alc'hwez a oa ganti ivez, evel ar re all; met ne grede ket. Dougerez e oa. He fried, o welet anezhi un tammig trist, un deiz, dre ma oa he spered troet bepred gant ar gambr difennet, a c'houlennas diganti:

– Petra a c'hoantaet, ma c'halonig? Lâret din, ha n'eus forzh petra a c'houlennfet, ho pezo.

– Ne c'hoantaan netra evit bremañ, emezi, nemet ur c'hrank-mor.

Mont a ra kerkent d'an aod, da glask dezhi ur c'hrank-mor. Met kerkent ha ma voe troet e seulioù, Levenez, na bade ken gant ar c'hoant da c'hoût petra a oa er gambr difennet, a digoras an nor... Met kerkent e kouezhas d'an douar, gant ar spont hag an euzh, o welet nav gwreg yaouank, hag holl dougerezed, en istribilh eus un treust, hag ur c'hrog houarn indan groñch pep hini anezhe!... Pa difallaas, e tastumas an alc'hwez, a oa kouezhet er gwad, hag e serras an nor, hag ec'h eas buan da skrivañ ul lizher da lâret d'he zad ha d'he mamm dont d'he c'herc'hat hep koll amzer, dre ma oa o vont da goll he buhez, mar ne deujent prim-ha-prim. Pa voe skrivet he lizher, e stagas anezhañ en kerc'henn ur c'hi bihan a oa deut ganti eus ar gêr, hag e lâras dezhañ:

– Kas al lizher-se d'am zad ha d'am mamm ha na goll ket a amzer, ma c'hiig kaezh, rak emañ ar marv war ma seulioù!

Mont a ra ar c'hi, buanañ ma c'hall; lennet eo al lizher gant an tad hag ar vamm, ha setu-int kerkent da ouelañ, ha da estlammiñ. An naer a degouezhas neuze en ti, hag a lâras dezhe:

– Hastet pignat war varc'h, ho-taou, ha na gollet ket a amzer, pe e vo marv ho merc'h pa errufet!

Hag ec'h eas er-maez kerkent neuze. Pa errujont en kastell o mab-kaer, ez oa hemañ o stlejañ o merc'h dre ar porzh, diwar-bouez he blev. Un naer fuloret a erruas ivez er porzh kerkent hag i, hag ec'h eas war-eeun d'an den fall, hag e flemmas anezhañ en e droad. Ma kouezhas kerkent d'an douar. An naer a lammas warnañ hag a dennas dezhañ e daoulagad er-maez e benn, hag e varvas kerkent, gant un eonenn en e c'henoù.

Levenez a c'hanas neuze war al lec'h ur bugel bihan, hag he zad hag he mamm, pa weljont se, a lâre e oa mat lazhañ ar bugel, gant aon e vije heñvel eus e dad. Ar pezh a voe graet. Neuze e c'hoantajont ober badeziñ an naer: met ar veleien na youlent ket he badeziñ, ha ne voe ket graet.

Ma en divije gallet mestr ar c'hastell lazhañ Levenez, evel e wragez all, e vije bet e dekvet, hag en divije lazhet ugent o lazhañ dek, hag e vije aet neuze da sorser. Ez oa o vont da vezañ, met Doue na youlas ket.

Translation

The Girl and the Snake Who Were Both Born to a Woman, 1939

Once upon a time there was a rich man and his wife who had been married for many years but did not have any children, and this saddened them greatly. They had been on pilgrimages to many holy places to pray to God and to his blessed Mother to give them a child, a boy or a girl, and they no longer knew what to do. One day, during spring, as they were on their way back from Le Folgoat, they could see everywhere – on the roads and in the fields – birds, snakes and toads who all had clutches of little ones and looked happy. On seeing them all, the wife said:

"If God were to give me a child, I wouldn't mind if I had to give birth to a snake or a toad at the same time!"

This was not a wise thing to say. Soon afterwards, she became pregnant and was very happy, and so was her husband. When the time came, a little girl was born, a rather beautiful child, except that a snake was twisted around her neck. The snake untwisted itself from the neck of the child and went out to hide in the grass of the back garden.

The child was christened Levenez [Joy], because of the joy she had brought her mother and father. She grew everyday in health and beauty, but the birthmark left by the snake looked like a red necklace around her throat. Nothing could make it go away, no matter how hard she rubbed it with all sorts of herbs.

One day, when Levenez was a young girl of about twelve, she went for a stroll by herself in the back garden, and got quite a surprise on hearing a voice saying:

"Good morning, my little sister; good morning to you, my little sister Levenez!"

She looked around but she could see no one, and yet the voice was close to her. She started searching amongst the bushes and found a snake. She cried out with fright. But the snake spoke to her like a human and said:

"Do not be frightened; I won't harm you, little sister!"

"Jesus! You are my sister, you, a snake!"

"Indeed I am; the one who gave birth to you gave birth to me at the same time."

"How can this be?"

"This is how: your mother and father had been married for a long time and did not have any children. One day during spring-time, on their way back from Le Folgoat where they had been to pray to God that He might give them a child, they saw everywhere, on the roads and in the fields, all sorts of animals, like snakes and toads and even insects, with their little ones. In the end, our mother said:

"Should God wish to give me a child, even if I had to give birth to a snake at the same time, I do not mind!" And it was done as she said. She gave birth to a child and to a snake. The girl is you, the snake is me, and that is how you are my sister. I was rolled around your neck, have left a mark there and I am the only one who can make it disappear. You do not need to be frightened or ashamed of me, because I only wish you the very best, as you will see later. Soon you will get married."

"Oh, no," said Levenez, "I do not want to get married."

"Yes, you will get married, and yet it would be better for you if you didn't."

"And how can I remove the red circle which is around my neck?"

"Go inside the house, bring back a bowl of fresh milk and a white cloth, and then you'll see."

Levenez went inside the house and returned at once to the garden with a bowlful of fresh milk and a white cloth. She no longer feared the snake. She put the bowl on the ground, and immediately the snake jumped in it. It stayed in the milk for a while, then came out and told Levenez to lie on the grass. When the girl was lying down, it twisted itself round her neck, stayed there for a while before unrolling itself and saying:

"Now, rub your neck with the white cloth, where the red circle is."

The girl did so and the circle disappeared.

"Do not tell your mother or father what you did to remove the red circle," said the snake.

The snake hid again among the grass and Levenez, delighted, went inside the house.

"Look!" she immediately said to her mother; "look at my neck; the red circle has disappeared!"

"And how did this happen? What have you done?"

"Nothing, Mother. It went away all by itself. It was the will of God."

"Tell me, Daughter, who has done this and I shall make him rich," said the father.

"It was nobody, Father. God's will and nothing else."

As Levenez went on in years, she became prettier every day, and the wealthiest young men of the region came to court her, but she turned them all down. A young noble man, claiming to come from afar, also came. Nobody knew him and she was fond of him. And so they were engaged and married. At the end of the celebrations, the groom brought his bride to his castle, a most beautiful castle. All she had to do there was walk in the castle garden, wear all kinds of beautiful clothes and look at herself in the mirror. Everything that she wished for would be brought to her.

Her husband would often leave home, for two, three or more days at a time, and left her all the castle keys except for one, the key to a small room. She used to visit all the rooms and saw all kinds of exceedingly beautiful things. Every time she walked past the forbidden room she would say: "Whatever can be in there?" She longed to open it, as she had been given its key together with the other ones, but she did not dare. She was pregnant. One day, seeing her a little sad – her thoughts were focusing on the forbidden room – her husband said to her:

"What do you wish for, my dear? Tell me and you will have whatever you ask for."

"I don't want anything at the moment," she said, "except crab meat."

He immediately went to the shore to get a crab for her. But as soon as his back was turned, Levenez, who could no longer repress her desire to know what was in the forbidden room, opened the door... But she immediately fainted from fright and disgust on seeing nine young wives, all of them pregnant, hanging from a beam, their necks split by an iron hook! When she came back to her senses, she gathered the key which had fallen into a pool of blood, closed the door and quickly went to write a letter to her parents to tell them to come and get her without delay, as she was going to die if they did not come right away. She then tied the letter around the neck of the small dog who had been her childhood companion at home, and she said to him:

"Bring this letter to my parents. Don't waste any time, my dear little dog, because death is on my heels!"

The dog ran as quickly as he could. Her parents cried and screamed on reading the letter. The snake then came into the room and told them:

"Hurry, you two! Get on a horse now. Do not waste any time, or your daughter will be dead before you arrive!"

The snake went out immediately. When they arrived at their son-in-law's castle, he was dragging their daughter by her hair through the forecourt. An angry snake also appeared in the forecourt at that very time. It went straight to the wicked man and bit him in the foot, making him fall at once to the ground. The snake then jumped on him and poked his eyes out. The man died at once, his mouth foaming.

Levenez gave birth there and then. Seeing what was happening, her parents said it was better to kill the child in case he took after his father. And this was done. They also wanted to have the snake baptized, but the priests refused to baptise it and so it was not done.

If the master of the castle had been able to kill Levenez, as he had killed his other wives, she would have been the tenth. He would have killed twenty by killing ten and would have turned into a wizard. This nearly happened, but God did not want it so.

Yann Gerven

Walpurgisnacht, *1992*

Splannat a rae al loar en oabl boull ha lintrañ a rae ar stered ur wech pellaet diouzh ar c'helc'h. Kousket e oa Burtuled Vras a-gleiz, hag a-zehoù; en traoñ e oa c'hoazh ul lutig war elum e Mi'n ar Foll. Rag-eeun dirak Marijan Morvan e oa skeud teñval ar chapel hag ar gwez pin en-dro dezhi; lakaat a ra troad ar skubellenn da sonnañ un tammig muioc'h, ha diskenn a ra goustadik betek santout ar briñsoù bezv o skubañ ar brug hag al lann brezhoneg a c'holo Menez Burtuled hañv-goañv. Chom a ra a-sav dirak ur c'hleuz izel, ma lak he skubellenn harp outañ.

Evel boas e oa an hini gentañ, ha ne oa ket diaes dezhi: etre Kernaered ha Menez Burtuled n'eus ket ouzhpenn ur c'hard lev. Bremazon e teufe ar re all: Roz Prijant eus Krec'heur, Ameli Roperzh eus ar Gollod, Katrin Chato eus Toull Gordenn, evit ar re dostañ, hag ar re all eus Purid, Kerien, ha betek harzoù ar Vro C'hallo, hag a oa en hent dija evit dont. N'eus trouz kristen ebet en noz: klevet a reer ul louarn o c'h-lipat deus tu Gwern ar C'hogoù, ha meur a gaouenn a ziskouez bezañ bev. Peogwir n'eus nemet gortoz d'ober, e tenn Marijan ur c'horn-boud eus he godell hag e tosta anezhañ ouzh he skouarn: mouezh hoalus Katrin Gwern a grog neuze da ganañ Son ar C'hwenn.

Ur skeud all er Su dindan bannoù al loar: Katrin Chato, moarvat, o tont eus tu Sant-Nigouden. Douarañ a ra chik ha brav nepell diouzh al lec'h ma oa Marijan o selaou muzik, hag e teu da renkañ he balaenn e-kichen hini Marijan. A-zoug ar wech eo bet gwelet Katrin war ur skubellenn valan, tra ma 'c'h ae ingal Marijan war unan vezv. Pep hini hervez he goud: bezv pe valan, se zo ingal; re kostez Jañjili ha Sant-Konan a gav gwelloc'h zoken ar skubellennoù plouz riz. N'eus forzh penaos, n'eo ket an danvez a ya d'ober ar valaenn a cheñch kalz an doare da nijal, met an implij a vez graet diouti pa skuber an ti a-hend-all: ar gwellañ skubellenn da nijal eo an hini a zo bet implijet an aliesañ da skubañ, gant un dorn ampart da heñchañ anezhi. Ha graet zo bet taolioù esae evel-se: ur valaenn kelenn evit skubañ ar skiber a gustum nijal propik, ha betek ur fagodenn spern du, gant ma vo bet implijet div pe deir gwech da skarzhañ ar skiminalioù e c'heller ober un dra bennak ganti: ret eo lâret ne nij ket gwall vuan, ouzhpenn ma eo tenn a-walc'h chom azezet warni gant an drein, hep kontañ meur a froc'h el lostenn da c'houde. Met nijal a ra memes-tra, evel kement balaenn a zo, etre douarn ur vaouez kozh a-walc'h evit kaout akuitez hardi war ar skubañ.

Dont a ra an holl re all an eil war-lerc'h eben: re Rostren, Gwareg, Sant-Nikolaz, re kostez Plourac'h ha Poullaouen. E-pad ur frapadig e tenn Menez Burtuled da Roissy-Charles de Gaulle, met ne bad ket. Trawalc'h a dud zo bremañ evit gelver an drougsperedoù: e-kreiz ar breoù e teu tro-ha-tro Lusifer, Asmode, Belzebut, Astarot hag un nebeud re all izeloc'h o renk da bourchas o vertuz hag o fouvoar d'ar re a zo ouzh o aspediñ. Kreskiñ a ra ar cholori ha chaok ar sorserezed en-dro d'ar moged soufr fetis a c'holo an dorgenn bremañ.

– Sell, n'eo ket deuet Marielle Goubil? a c'houlenn ur vouezh, hini Ameli Roperzh marteze.

C'hoarzhin a ra peder pe bemp dre ma teu soñj dezhe eus ar mod ma oa erruet Marielle ar wech diwezhañ, gant ur skubell nevez-flimm-flamm: da gomañs e oa bet darbet dezhi mont a-benn d'ur post telefon, da c'houde he doa klasket spazañ ar c'hure war ar peuri, moarvat, rak pemp pe c'hwec'h lamm he doa graet a-raok kouezhañ e-kreiz ur vodenn lann galleg evit echuiñ. Petra 'faot deoc'h, kaer he deus bezañ gouest da lakaat an hanter eus archedi Kallag da vont war an aouryeotenn (dimezet eo gant ar brigadier Moreau eno), ur plac'h ha ne grog gwech ebet en ur skubellenn er gêr ne c'hell ket ober kalz a dra a-c'haoliad warni goude-se.

– Re yaouank, paour-kaezh Ameli. Ne c'heller ket laoskel mekanikoù evel-se etre daouarn merc'hedigoù! a respont Marijan Morvan.

A ya. War vourzh un F 16 pe ur Mig 23 eo gwelloc'h bezañ dindan daou-ugent vloaz. War un troad balaenn eo gwelloc'h kaout daou-ugent vloaz pe zoken tri-ugent, hag ar Marielle-se, hag a labour e ti an Tailhoù hag a bae tud da zelc'her he zi, eo ral dezhi kregiñ en ur skubellenn, ar chostrom yaouank-se!

Klevet a reer neuze un dra bennak o voudal en aer, evel ur mell taol gwenan, ha setu Marielle o touarañ plaen ha kaer e-kreiz al lanneg.

– Eskuzit ac'hanon, c'hoarezed, emezi, met ur film a oa war Canal+ gant Brigitte Lahaye o tiskouez he nunu hag he chaflutenn, setu ne'm boa ket kavet an tu da gas an hini kozh du-mañ d'e wele a-raok ma vije bet fin an abadenn. O, ur film laou, sellit, met chomet on memes tra betek ar fin da sellet outañ, pa oa an hini Lahaye o...

N'eo ket nec'het ar c'hoarezed gant nunu ha chaflutenn Brigitte Lahaye, nann da! Emaint oc'h ober ur c'helc'h en-dro da jao Marielle, rak deuet eo war... O, Sant Tomaz na gredas ken na welas!

– A, ya, emezi, ma sunerez-poultrenn. Ur Zanuzzi C125, efedusoc'h un tamm mat evit n'eus forzh peseurt skubellenn. Prenet ganin pemzektez 'zo ti Derrien, e traoñ ar blasenn du-mañ. Tizhañ a ra, un drugar, hag aesoc'h eo azezal warni evit war n'eus forzh petra 'mod all.

Chom a reont holl da sellet gant disfiz ouzh ar mekanik.

– Pegeit 'peus lakaet evit dont? a c'houlenn a-benn ar fin Jermen Gurudeg, hag a zo deuet eus Groñvel.

– 'M eus ket lakaet dek munud.

Dek munud! Lod anezhe o deus lakaet un eur hanter evit dont eus Kaorel pe Sant-Hern. Tostaat a ra darn ouzh an ardivink. Gwelet a reer zoken Roz Prijant oc'h azezal warnañ da c'houzout hag-eñ eo brav, ha flourañ anezhañ ha tout. Gast, ken antilin eo Roz gantañ ha ma oa Robert Heinlein gant merc'h ar pastor an deiz m'he doa pedet anezhañ da bignat ganti e tour an iliz da ziskouez dezhañ he spered santel!

– Ti biv a lâret 'peus prenet anezhañ? a c'houlen Ameli Roperzh.

– Ti'n If Derrien, du-mañ. Ha n'eo ket seurt ker-se.

– Ma, eme Katrin Chato, hag a zo brudet evit bezañ an hini akuitañ da leviañ troadoù skubellinier, me ne gredan nemet ar pezh a welan. Greomp ur pennad tizh: mont kuit eus amañ da gaout ar chapel, souhañ en-dro d'an tour, dont en-dro. Gwelet e vo piv a c'hounezo.

– Mat eo. Me zo mut dit pa gari.

Emañ c'hoazh Katrin o kemer lañs evit distokañ diouzh an douar m'he deus graet Marielle an hanter eus an hent sa'r chapel dija, ha gwelet a reer anezhi dizale o tremen timat a-zioc'h o fennoù, o vont d'ober un dro ouzhpenn a-us da Wazh Skavenn hag o tont en-dro ha douarañ brav e-kreiz ar menez. Daoust ha troet he deus Katrin en-dro d'an tour, seulamant?

– Geo, gwelet a ran bremañ he daoulagad o lugerniñ evel div c'hlaouenn dan. Emañ o tont davedomp, eme Terez Tenneg.

Rak gant ar skubellennoù ez eo ar c'hontrol eus ar c'hirri-tan. Pa weler div c'houlaouenn ruz, neuze e vez o tont e-fas deoc'h.

Douarañ a ra Katrin Chato, kemeret ganti penn Sinead O' Connor rak kollet he deus he ferukenn, ha klemm a ra abalamour d'an drêz ha d'al lann ha d'an avel, met n'eus den ebet evit taoler pled outi. Emañ an holl c'hoarezed en-dro d'ar sunerez-poultrenn.

Ha 'n If Derrien ne gomprenas morse perak e oa deuet er memes sizhun seitek plac'h ha tri-ugent eus kement korn a oa e Kernev-Uhel da brenañ gantañ pep a sunerez-poultrenn Zanuzzi C125.

Translation

Walpurgisnacht, *1992*

The clear night sky was getting brighter. The stars further away from the moon circle were twinkling. On the left, Burtuled Vras was asleep, and on the right, down below, there was still a tiny light shining in Mi'n ar Foll. Straight ahead, there were the dark shadows cast by the chapel and by the pine-trees which surround it. Marijan Morvan slightly straightened the foot of the broomstick and gradually started on her downward path until she felt the birch twigs brush against the heather and high broom which cover Mount Burtuled throughout the year. She stopped by a low embankment and rested her broomstick against it.

As usual, she was the first to arrive, but this achievement held no merit as there cannot be more than half a mile between Kernaered and Mount Burtuled. The others would arrive soon: Roz Prijant from Krec'heur, Ameli Roperzh from Ar Gollod, Katrin Chato from Toull Gordenn; they all lived close-by. The others, coming from Puried, Kerien and even from the borders of the Pays Gallo, were already on their way. There was not a Christian sound to be heard in the night, though she heard the yelping of a fox somewhere towards Gwern ar C'hogou and the hooting of a few owls keen to prove that they were alive. As she had nothing to do but wait, Marijan took a conch from her pocket and brought it up to her ear: the seductive voice of Katrin Gwenn started singing the Song of the Fleas.

Another shadow appeared in the moonshine from the South. It could only be Katrin Chato from Sant-Nigouden. She landed expertly not far from the place where Marijan was listening to music and parked her broom next to Marijan's. Katrin had been known to use a broomstick made of broom, but Marijan always used one made of birch. Each to her own: birch or broom, it does not matter. Those living around Jañjili and Sant-Konan even seem to prefer straw brooms. In any case, it is not the material used to make the broom which makes a lot of difference in the flying technique, but how often it has been used to sweep the house: the best flying brooms are those which have often been held by expert hands for housecleaning tasks. Many tests have been carried out to prove the point: a holly broom made for the shed floor usually flies nicely. One can even use a bundle of sloe branches, as long as it has been used two or three times to sweep the hearth. Not that it flies quickly or that it is comfortable to sit on, on account of the thorns, not to mention the resulting rips in the skirt. But it does fly, like any other broom, if it is put in the hands of a woman old enough to be experienced in the art of sweeping.

One after the other, the others arrived, from Rostrenen, Gwareg, Saint-Nicolas, Plourac'h ha Poullaouen. For a short while, Mount Burtuled looked like Charles de Gaulle airport, but it did not last. The assembly was now big enough to start calling in the demons: during the incantations, Lucifer, Asmode, Belzebut, Astarot and a few lower ranking evil spirits took it in turn to shed virtues and favours on their worshippers. The din of the witches' twaddle reached a peak as a thick cloud of sulphur shrouded the hill.

"Tell me! Where is Marielle Goubil?" asked a voice which could well have been that of Ameli Roperzh.

Four or five of them laughed as they recalled how Marielle had arrived at the previous gathering on a brand-new broom: she had first nearly crashed into a telephone pole, then probably tried to skim pebbles on the hillside because she had done five or six rebounds before ending up her flight by falling in the middle of a low gorse bush. Let me tell you that, although she is capable of making half of Callac policemen lose their heads – she is married to Sergeant Moreau who works there – a woman who never uses a broom at home cannot ride one easily.

"She is too young, poor Ameli. You can't put such machines into the hands of little girls!" answered Marijan Morvan.

How true! If you are on board a F16 or a Mig 23, it is better for the pilot to be under forty. But if you are flying a broomstick, it is better to be forty or even sixty, and this Marielle, who works for the Income Tax Office and who pays for others to do her housework, well, it is not often that you see her with a broom in her hands, and what is more, she does not even give a decent wage to her cleaning lady!

Then they heard something of a buzz in the air, like a huge swarm of bees, and there was Marielle landing skilfully in the middle of the moor.

"Please excuse me, dear sisters," she said, "but on Canal+ there was a film starring Brigitte Lahaye showing her tits and her pussy, so I just could not get my old man to go to bed before the end of the programme. I know it was a bad film but I still watched it right to the end because that Lahaye was..."

Her dear sisters were not interested to hear about Brigitte Lalaye's tits and pussy, not a bit! They were all standing around Marielle's means of transport, because she had come on a.... Oh, dear Saint Thomas who did not believe until he had seen!

"Well, yes," she said, "it is my vacuum cleaner. A Zanuzzi C125. It is a lot more efficient than any old broomstick. I bought it a couple of weeks ago in Derrien's, the shop on the town square, back home. It's amazingly fast and a lot easier to sit on than any other contraption.

They were all looking suspiciously at the appliance.

"How long did it take you to get here?" finally asked Jermen Gurudeg who had made the journey from Gronvel.

"It took me ten minutes."

Ten minutes! Some of them had travelled for half an hour to get from Kaorel or Saint-Hern. A few women got closer to the machine. Roz Prijant even sat on it to know if it felt right. She was running her hand on it and goodness knows what. Goddammit! Roz was as taken by it as Robert Heinlein with the vicar's daughter on the day she asked him to climb with her to the top of the church steeple in order to show him her holy spirit!

"Where did you say you bought it from?" asked Ameli Roperzh.

"From Yves Derrien's shop, in my village. And it isn't all that expensive."

"Well," said Katrin Chato who is known as the champion of all broomstick pilots. I only believe what I see. Let's give it a go: we'll go from here to the chapel, turn left around the steeple, and come back, and we'll see who wins."

"Fine. You're on!"

Katrin was still running to gather enough speed to take off from the ground when Marielle was already half-way to the chapel. They then saw her above their heads making a detour via Gwazh Skavenn, returning and making a perfect landing on the mount. And you know what? Katrin had not even reached the steeple!

"Yes, she has. I can see her eyes glowing like two ambers. She is coming towards us," said Terez Tenneg. Broomsticks are the opposite of cars: when you see two red lights, you know they are coming towards you.

Katrin Chato landed. She looked like Sinead O'Connor as she had lost her wig. She was complaining of the brambles, of the moor, of the wind, but no one was taking the slightest notice of her. All the sisters were gathered around the vacuum-cleaner.

Yves Derrien never understood why, that very week, seventy-seven women came from all corners of Haute-Cornouaille to his shop to buy a Zanuzzi C125.

Love

Youenn Drezen

An Dour en-dro d'an inizi, *1932* (Lodenn)

Edon, digomz, o prederiañ gant ar gudenn vilvedel, pa dostaas va c'heneilez ouzhin. Skrijañ 'rae evel diwar anoued. He divrec'h a oa noazh, skoaz hag all, ha gwenn-kann en amc'houloù. He brennid, evel an houlenn war ar c'hal, a bigne hag a ziskenne. Sevel a reas davet va re daou lagad, ul lufr enno ha n'am boa gwelet biskoazh. He diweuz a grene un disterañ. Lakeat a reas un dorn war va brec'h, un dornig gwenn ha mistr.

Me, skrignet va dent, tenn va anal.

– "Enaouerez!"

Hi, duet he sell raktal, a grogas gant un nerzh souezhus em divrec'h.

– "Enaouerez? Ma sankfen dit va dent en da fas, e komprenfes..., marteze."

Me eo an hini a sankas va dent en he skoaz, ken na wadas. Lammet e oa an derzhienn warnon. Tennañ 'reas un dic'hwezhadenn verr, hag unan hir kerkent goude. Plegañ 'reas evel ur gorzenn weüs-meurbet, ma rankis kregiñ enni dre an dargreiz da virout outi da gouezhañ. Ar wech kentañ, abaoe m'hec'h anavezen, e tistagas va lesanv:

– "Herri!"

A! Iribe, santout, goude bloavezhioù, en-dro d'am gouzoug, gwask an divrec'h-se, gwenn, ha sin, ha kuñv! A! Iribe, an daou-lagad-se, re splann kent, ha re vliv ha bev, aet en un taol da ziv regezenn o tangwallañ da wad! Marteze, n'em eus ket meizet, pa oa poent c'hoazh, o fedenn c'hrizias: "Lavar din ar gomz a c'hortozan!" Marteze 'oa er pennig-se ur goanag a oa din da seveniñ.

Bezañ dalc'het ar c'horf-se etre va divrec'h, bezañ chouret an izili-se, flour ha start, fresk ha klouar war un dro, ha bezañ o lezet da vont... pebezh drouk-huñvre!

He bizied a c'hoarie lentik gant va blev, hag a spine va divjod, ha va chink, ha va malvennoù, goustad. Hag e lavare din gerioù-mamm ha kariadez.

Ne ouien mui petra 'raen, hag e c'holoen he zal, he diweuz, he c'herc'henn gant pokoù gouez, hag e sanken va dent en he c'higennoù, ken na hirvoude.

A! bevañ hiziviken – da viken! – a-gevret gant Anna Bodrig, ober anezhi pried muiañ karet va buhez, kenloderez va strivoù davet an uhelvennadoù a lufre dirak va daoulagad! N'he dije ket bet lavaret nann. He daoulagad a gomze eviti. Huanadet he doa adarre, gant ur vouezh o krenañ, div notennig heson.

– "Herri!"

Peget e oa he furmoù ouzh va izili, ha me stigned va izili ken na ginnigent tarzhañ. Tripal a rae hec'h askre sko em c'halon. Ma tassone mein ar grugell gozh gant hon div anal denn. Aet e oan mezv ha kroget ar c'hrenerezh em divesker. Ha va dorn gourel ha karget a allazigoù, a ziskenne davet teñzor prizius an divronn gwenngen, frouezh miret ez-elevezel ar gwerc'hezed yaouank.

– "Herri Maheo, nann!"

Ur bedenn! Hag he biziad a waskas va arzorn. Kerderc'hel a ris, ha va mouezh, hec'h-unan, a ouezas pediñ ha kemenn, hag e santen, daoust d'hec'h eneberezh, an dra klouar ha bev, flour evel seiz, o tridal dindan va biziad. Hogen ur wech all:

– "Nann!"

Krenn e oa bet distaget ar c'hemenn. Ha me:

– "O, Naig, perak?"

Teurel a reas he fenn, ur pennig evel ma ne garin hini ebet biken mui, war va bruched, hag e chomas harpet warnon ur reuziad hir, o tic'hwezhañ. Marteze e ouele. Ne greden ket fiñval. Kerse am boa, ha dudi ivez.

Ra'm bije bet laosket, neuze, ar gerioù 'oa boureviet va zeod ganto. Ra'm bije bet lavaret dezhi e oan trelatet ganti, e oan aet diskiant, ya! diskiant gant he spered, hec'h ene, gant he c'horf, ha n'em bije gallet bevañ gant parez all ebet nemeti. Setu ar gerioù a c'hortoze.

... Siwazh!

Aet er-maez eus krugell Gavr-Iniz, torret ar gazell-ge! Graet he doa Anna Bodri eus he zu kement a zo aotreet d'ur plac'h yaouank e Breizh. Krediñ a c'hellas n'am boa nemet ar c'hoant a vroud an den davet pep maouez korfet ouzh e zoare.

Me – petra an diaoul a viras ouzhin da gomz? – a oa chomet mut evel ar peul ma oan. Hag Anna Bodri he doa adkemeret he stumm a-ziagent.

Redek a reas trumm davet ar maez, hag e chomas en he sav war dreuzoù dor ar grugell. C'hoarzhin a rae gant he c'hoarzh lirzhin ha gwerc'h.

Evel ma ne vije bet c'hoarvezet netra.

– "Che! Emezi, ni 'zo droch hon-daou!"

Me avat, drouklaouen ha genaouek, a gave din, pa droen an alc'houez en nor houarn, edon o sebeliañ un huñvre, mouget kerkent ha ganet.

Translation

The Water Around the Islands, *1932* (Extract)

I was silent, thinking about the mystery of the ancient cairn, when my companion came up to me. She was shivering from the cold. Her bare arms and shoulders were standing out in the purest white in the faint light. Her chest, like a wave on the slipway, was rising and falling. She raised her eyes to mine. There was a shine in them that I had never seen before. Her lips were trembling slightly. She put her hand on my arm, a dainty, white, slim hand.

I held my breath and clenched my teeth:

"You're teasing me!"

Her eyes darkened immediately and she suddenly gripped my arms.

"I'm teasing you? If I sunk my teeth into your face, maybe then you would understand..."

But I was the one who sunk my teeth into her shoulders till I tasted blood. A fever gripped me. She heaved a short sigh, then a long one. She bent backwards like a supple reed, so far back that I had to put my arm around her waist to prevent her from falling. For the first time since I knew her, she uttered my first name:

" Herri!"

Ah! Iribe. Many years later, I can still feel around my neck these two lithe arms, so white, so fresh, so soft! Yes, Iribe! I still see these eyes which had been so radiant, so lively, so sparkling, turn suddenly into two glowing embers which set my blood on fire! Maybe, I did not notice in time their fervent request: "Tell me the words I want to hear!" Maybe there was, in her lovely head, a wish I had to fulfil.

I have held this body in my arms, I have caressed these arms, so soft and yet so firm, fresh and yet warm, and I have let them go... What a nightmare!

Her fingers were gently playing with my hair and lightly caressing my cheeks, my chin and my eyelids as she uttered tender and loving words.

I no longer knew what I was doing. I covered her forehead, her lips, her throat with wild kisses, and I bit so hard into her flesh that she moaned.

Ah! To live for ever, for ever more, with Anna Bodri; to make her my beloved spouse in life, that she might share my endeavours to reach my cherished aims! She would not have refused. I am sure she would not have refused. I saw it in her eyes. In a trembling voice, she slowly repeated the two melodious notes: "Herri!"

Her body was tight against my body, and all my muscles were so taut that I thought they would burst. Her heart was beating hard next to mine and the stones of the ancient cairn were echoing the sound of our two panting breaths. My manly hand full of caresses was descending towards the precious treasure of her white breasts, towards the fruit which young virgins guard modestly.

"No! Herri Maheo."

A plea! Her fingers tightened on my wrist. I carried on, and my voice which felt detached from me, begged and implored and I felt, in spite of her opposition, a warm and lively thing, as soft as silk, coming to life under my fingers. But she repeated: "No!"

The command had been curt, and I said: "Oh, Naig, Why?"

She threw her head, a dainty head such as I will never love again, upon my chest, and leant on me for a long time to get her breath back. Maybe she was crying. I did

not dare move. I felt disappointment, but also delight.

If only I had then pronounced the words which were on the tip of my tongue. If only I had told her that she sent me into raptures, that her mind, her soul, her body made me go wild, yes, wild, and that I could never live with anyone else but her. Those were the words she wanted to hear.

...Alas!

Outside Gavrinis cairn, the spell was broken. Anna Bodri had done as much as a young Breton girl could do. She could well have thought that I only felt for her the desire which stings a man who courts all the women whose body pleases him.

Whatever had prevented me from talking? – Why had I stayed silent like the stupid man I was?

Anna Bodri had recovered her composure. She ran out quickly, stopping on the threshold of the cairn. She laughed in a cheerful and innocent way.

As if nothing had happened.

"Well!" she said, "That was naughty of us."

As for myself, feeling discontented and stupid, I thought, on turning the key in the iron door, that I was burying a stillborn dream.

Ronan Huon

Ar Gwennili-mor, *1959*

– "Alan, savit ho prec'h pa zebrit!" eme e vamm d'ar paotr yaouank.

Ruziañ a reas Alan ha sellout, hep sevel e benn, ouzh an daoliad a-dal. Nann. Tekla n'he doa ket klevet evezhiadenn e vamm. Edo re brederiet war-dro he c'hoar vihan ha ne zeue ket a-benn da dennañ ar boued diouzh meudoù ar c'hrank kousker o doa pesketaet o daou diouzh ar beure.

Prenestroù bras sal-debriñ an ostaleri a skoe diouzh un tu war ar c'hoad, diouzh an tu all e skede ar mor etre brankoù gwez pin al liorzh.

– "Re Dorval a ya kuit hiziv," eme tad Alan, "gwelet am eus o fakadoù er hall."

– "Erru eo miz Gwengolo," a respontas ar vamm.

Daoust da se e chome glas ar mor ha digoumoul an oabl. Ur stlakadenn a dregernas er pellder.

– "Ar vag-dre-dan o tont er-maez eus ar porzh," eme dad Tekla en ur zerc'hel da glukañ e dasad kafe du. Dre an nor digor e welent mogerioù ar porzh en tu all d'an aber hag ar vagig o haketal en ur leuskel bouilhadoù moged en aer, evel un deskard butuner.

Sellout a rae Tekla ouzh relegenn ar vag pesketa dizolo bremañ en ouf an *Dourig*. Ar besketarien granked, a soñjas, a c'hellfe treuziñ ar pleg-mor war droad.

– "Morad zo hiziv," a lavare un denig moal ha kromm e-tal an nor.

– " 'Mañ ar paotr kozh oc'h ober e lez," a farsas tad Tekla.

– "Mont a rit da chevreta?" a gendalc'he an den, oc'h ober e arsav pemdeziek e-kichen ur plac'h yaouank kozh kramennek a zebre ouzh un daol hec'h unan bemdez, eveltañ.

Echu gantañ e bred e troas tad Alan war du e amezeg:

– "Neuze, graet eo an darbaroù evit loc'hañ, Aotrou Kerlaban?"

– "Ar mintinvezh hon eus tremenet o pakañ an traoù," a respontas mamm Dekla, an hanter muioc'h zo bremañ eget pa oamp deut.

Alan a savas ha kemer diwar gein e gador aozilh e stammenn.

– "Dont a rez, Tekla?" a c'houlennas

– "Na vez ket re ziwezhat, te oar emañ ar c'harr da bemp eur," eme an Aotrou Kerlaban.

Sellout a raent ouzh an daou zen yaouank o tiskenn gant ar wenodenn dindan ar pin.

– "Setu daou a gavo poanius mont an eil diouzh egile," a lavaras unan bennak.

A-dal dezho en em astenne an aber. Ur wern gant funioù a-istribilh a save, kosteziet, a-us d'ar mor.

– "N'int ket deut a-benn da saveteiñ o bag c'hoazh," eme Alan, "moarvat e vo izel a-walc'h ar mor fenoz evit he sevel."

Kemer a rejont o hent boas a-dreuz ar c'hoad, gant o binvioù pesketa war o skoaz. Sioul e voent ur pennadig. Alan a soñje en disparti. Dibenn miz Eost a oa bet ur wir dec'hadeg.

– "Un dra am eus da laret dit araok ma'z i kuit," a vesteodas Alan.

– "Lavar 'ta," eme Dekla o treiñ davetañ.

– "Pa vimp war an aod."

Tremen a rejont tiez hañv damguzhet o zalbennoù gwenn e-mesk at gwez. Serret e oa o stalafioù ha dreist d'ar c'hlouedoù raoskl e welent ur porched livet e ruz, distaget dioutañ ar vrañsigell hag an holl funioù.

– "Ar familh Gwiader a zo aet kuit er beure-mañ ivez."

– "Ya, o gwelet am eus o sammañ ar c'harr. Ne chomo ket mui kalz a dud pa vimp aet."

– "N'eus forzh penaos, ar skol a grog 'benn teir sizhun. Echu eo ar vakañsoù."

Ne oa takenn avel ebet ha traezh an hent ma sanke o zreid ennañ a save, poul-trennek, dindan o c'hammedoù. War lezenn an hent delioù an drez hag ar raden a oa goloet gant un troc'had poultr gwenn. Mizioù 'oa ne oant ket bet gwalc'het gant ar glaveier.

Lavaret e vije bet kreiz an hañv pa ziboukjont dirak ar mor o skediñ.

Kerzhout a raent diarc'hen war ar reier. Alan a sellas dirazañ ouzh Tekla o c'hao-liata ar poulloù dour gant he divesker kilhog-raden. En noz diwezhañ e oa savet eus e wele. Stouet war varlenn ar prenestr, er beuznoz e spurmante ar pin hag ar wenodenn. A-boan ma veze klevet ar gwagennoù o lipat an traezh. Sevel a rae ur c'hwezh douar, sev ha bezhin kemmesket betek ennañ. An ti a oa sioul. Soñjet en doa e Tekla. He gwelout a rae, he fenn war ar blueg gant he c'huchenn-vlev a-dreuz d'he jod. Sioul ha peoc'hus evel bremañ, ar pezh a damalle dezhi pa oa-eñ ken prederiet. He muzelloù a oa treset spis. Stouiñ a rae a-us dezho, lavarout a rae dezhi he c'hare hag e poke d'he diweuz.

Un tu bennak en ti en doa stirlinket ur plad pe ur voutailh bennak. 'Ar beure eo', en doa soñjet. Stouet en doa un tammig muioc'h war ar barlenn evit sellout dre brenestr ar sal-debriñ dindanañ. Ne wele netra. A-nevez e oa deut trouz eus an dia-barzh. Sonerezh arabek e oa, o tont eus ar gegin moarvat.

O soñjal en he disparti e venne e galon frailhañ en e greiz. Echu e oa an 'hanv' e gwirionez daoust ma ne seblante ket, pep tra nemet an amzer a ziskoueze e oa war e dalaroù. En ostaleri e oa goullo an drederenn eus an taolioù. Dec'h da noz pa dremenent e-kichen 'La Belle Etoile' o doa merzet e oa c'hoazh nebeutoc'h a dud er sal-debriñ sklerijennet. Amañ war an draezhennig en tu all d'ar reier ne wele nemet ur bugel o c'hoari war vevenn an dour hag o kilañ dirak pep ourlig mor.

Ur flapadeg a-us dezho o lakaas da sevel o fennoù. Ur bagad evned heñvel ouzh skreved a dremene:

– "Gwennili-mor," a zisplegas Alan hag a oa barrek war al laboused.

An nijad gwennili a dremenas he skeud evel ur goumoulenn drumm war ar mor.

– "'Maint o vont kuit," emezañ.

– "Perak ez eont kuit ken abred. Tomm eo c'hoazh an amzer," a lavaras Tekla he selloù o heuliañ an evned war an oabl boull.

– "Pep hini a ya kuit, e-touez ar re ziwezhañ emaomp, Tekla."

Treiñ a reas Alan ur maen hag un armead kranked bihan a dec'has da glask repu dindan ar bezhin.

– "Te ouie ez eo pa sav ar mor ez eo ret pesketa chifretez?" a c'houlennas ouzh Tekla.

Homañ ne respontas ket hag a reas sin dezhañ da devel. Edo kluchet a-us d'ur poull du o furchal, habask evel pa ne vefe bet netra, evel pa vefe bet an deiz-mañ un deiz evel ar re all.

– "N'eus nemet bugale anezho," emezi a-benn ar fin.

Alan a azezas war ar bezhin mouest, e sell kollet war ar mor.

– "Sell ouzh ar vag o tont er-maez eus ar porzh en tu all. N'he deus ket a linen-noù honnezh? Daoust petra eo? Marteze ez eo an hini hon eus gwelet dec'h e Konk o kargañ kement a gasedadoù gwin ruz."

– "Perak e vefe honnezh?" emezi o tigeinañ diwar he labour.

Chom a rae selloù Allan kollet war ar mor hag e komze outañ e unan:

– "Mont a reont pell. D'ar Maoritani," emezañ, ha, goude un ehan, "pelec'h emañ ar Maoritani?"

Mistr, en he sav, Tekla a zic'hourde he c'hein skuizh o vezañ bet pleget re bell. Ne oa tamm lusenn ebet en aer, an tiez en tu all d'ar pleg-mor ha mogerioù kreñv ar gêr-gozh a oa fraezh hag a seblante tost-tre. Tremen a reas he dorn war he zal evit sevel he blev a gouezhe war he daoulagad.

– "Skuizh out, peskataer huñvreoù?"

Evel ma ne responte ket e c'houlennas:

– "Petra peus Alan?"

– "Netra."

– "Geo."

– "Fin ar vakañsoù," emezañ kintus.

Ar mor a oa sioul evel ul lenn. E-kreiz an aber ur ouel vras a stlake dousik, distignet. Tekla a azezas war ur roc'h da c'hortoz ar paotr chomet war he lerc'h.

Edo o tont gant ur sailh bihan en e zorn. En em santout a rae e unan ha bihan e oa e galon evel d'ar sul da noz er gêr pa echue an devezh koñje. Gwelout a rae Tekla azezet en heol hag ar c'hoant d'he stardañ en e zivrec'h a greskas ennañ.

– "Me gred, Tekla..." emezañ o tostaat.

Risklañ a reas war un tamm bezhin ha tra ma tastume e gregin ha chifretez munut er bezhin glep e tirolle c'hoarzh sklaer ha didro ar plac'h yaouank.

A-drek dezhi ur vag glas a astenne he lien, ar mor a skede atav dindan heol gor un dibenn hañv trugarezus.

– "Petra edos o vont da laret?" emezi neuze.

Alan a oa fuloret a-enep dezhañ e-unan hag a-enep d'he c'hoarzh-hi.

– "N'am eus ket soñj."

Bremañ ma tiskenne ar mor e save c'hwezh ar bezhin hag e kleve trouz ar c'hregin o fiñval dizehan er reier. Daoulagad glas-lin ar verc'h a glaske lenn en e re.

– "Petra peus laret?" a c'houlennas adarre.

Ar paotr a gilas ur wech c'hoazh.

– "Mann ebet, emezañ hag e talc'has: oan o vont da laret e kavfen hir va amzer."

– "Ne vo ket pell araok ma'z afec'h kuit ivez."

Risklañ a rae ar vag glas a-drek ar choaser en tu all d'ar bae. Dizale ne voe mui gwelet nemet tric'horn ar ouel rouz o vont war-raok a-us d'ar chaoser.

Sevel a reas Tekla en ur zigrosañ he sae skañv gant bizied o ivinoù torret hag e kemeras dorn Alan evit lammat dreist ar reier.

Distreiñ a rejont dorn ha dorn a-hed an draezhenn. Ne gomzent ket nemeur. Tremen a rejont dirak ostaleri 'La Belle Etoile'. El liorzh ne chome nemet ur gwaz hag ur vaouez war an oad azezet dirak un daolig houarn livet e gwenn.

Sellout a raent ouzh ar mor en o c'heñver ha pa dremenas an daou zen yaouank e paras o daoulagad warno evit o heuliañ betek ar penn all eus an aod.

Ur c'heginer gant e dog gwenn, en e goazez war vardell ur prenestr izel, a selle ivez ouzh ar mor. Pa dremenas ur vatezh o tastum un disheolier e tistagas ar paotr ur farsadenn. C'hoarzh skiltr ar plac'h a dregernas hag e voe sioul pep tra adarre.

Alan a roas un taol troad en ur bern kokouz dilizet war an traezh gant ur pesketaer re sammet.

– "Distreiñ a rez d'al lise?"

– "Eveljust," emezi.

– "Dont a ri amañ er bloaz a zeu?"

– "O ya, me soñj. Pet eur eo Alan?"

– "An hanter."

– "Poent eo din tostaat," emezi en ur bellaat diouzh ar ribl, ur pakad bennak am eus d'echuiñ.

Hag e hastjont etrezek an ostaleri a-dreuz askol berr an erin.

War an hent gwenn a-hed an aod e tifrete an dud en-dro d'ar c'harr-boutin ruz.

Bugale en o dilhad-neuial ha diarc'hen o doa dilezet o c'hoarioù war an traezh evit arvestiñ a-dost ouzh an disparti. Sammet e oa bet war lein ar c'harr binvioù pesketa, avanelloù a bep ment, seier kein ha daou zen a oa o klask eren ur wetur bugel.

Alan ha Tekla a c'hortoze kichen-ha-kichen.

An dichal a oa deut da vat hag an aber a oa dizoloet betek al lec'hid.

– "Emaint o lakaat ar yacht en e blomm," eme Alan.

Teñval e oa e benn. Bemañ e oa re ziwezhat evit komz pe pokat dezhi. Sellout a reas tro dro. Pep hini a oa prederiet gant e labour. Kemer a reas bizied hir Tekla en e zorn hag o stardañ.

Tekla a voe an hini diwezhañ o pignat er c'harr a loc'has e-kreiz hopadennoù ar grennarded. Dre ar prenestr e heje ar plac'h yaouank ar mouchouer en devoa gwelet war he blev an deiz kentañ, daou viz a-raok. Troet en doa pell a oa ar c'harr er c'horn-pleg gant ar wetur bugel o vrañsellat war lein hag e chome difiñv Alan. Evel en ur huñvre e kendalc'he da welout ur mouchouer a liv o flapañ en avel.

– "Sellit ouzh ar gwennili o vont kuit," eme unan bennak en e gichen.

Distreiñ a reas Alan. Ar paotr kozh eo a oa o komz outañ. Ruziañ a reas, mezhek, hag e-lec'h mont endro gantañ d'an ostaleri e skoas adarre etrezek ar mor ha gant e sac'h mezher stlepet war e gein, e vragoù-neuial glep oc'h ober ur merk teñval er foñs, e pellaas a-hed an aod.

Translation

The Terns, *1959*

"Alan, lift up your elbow when you eat!" said the boy's mother.

Alan blushed. Without lifting his head, he looked at the people on the opposite table. Good! Tekla had not heard his mother's remark. She was too busy helping her younger sister who was struggling to take the flesh out of the claws of the sleeper crab which they had caught that very morning.

The large windows of the hotel dining-room looked out on to the wood on one side; on the other side the sea was sparkling between the branches of the garden pine trees.

"The Dorvals are leaving today," said Alan's father. "I saw their luggage in the hall."

"It's the beginning of September," replied the mother.

And yet, the sea was still blue and the sky cloudless. In the distance they heard a bang.

"That's the motor boat leaving the harbour", said Tekla's father between two gulps of black coffee. Through the open windows, they could see the harbour walls on the other side of the estuary and a small boat sputtering puffs of smoke in the air, like someone smoking his first cigarette.

Tekla was looking at the hull of the old fishing boat now exposed in Dourig creek. People looking for crabs can now walk across the bay, she thought.

"It is a spring tide today," said a small, bald and slightly hunch-backed pensioner as he came in.

"That's the old man's chat up line," joked Tekla's father.

"Will you try and catch prawns today?" said the man as he stopped by the side of the scruffy spinster who, just like him, was always eating alone.

His meal over, Alan's father turned to his neighbour:

"So, you're ready to go, Mr Kerlaban?"

"We spent the morning packing," replied Tekla's mother, "and we have twice as many things now as when we arrived."

Alan got up and picked up his jumper from the back of the wicker chair.

"Are you coming, Tekla?" he asked.

"Don't be too late. You know the coach leaves at five," said Mr Kerlaban.

They watched the two youngsters walk down the path under the pine trees.

"These two will find it hard to be torn apart," said someone.

The estuary stretched in front of them. A mast with its loose rigging was lying at an angle above sea level.

"They haven't yet managed to rescue the yacht," said Alan. "The sea will be low enough tonight to raise it."

They took their usual path across the wood, their fishing gear on their shoulders. They stopped talking for a while. Alan was thinking of the separation. The end of August had simply flown by.

"I must tell you something before you go," stammered Alan.

"What is it, then?" said Tekla as she turned toward him.

"I'll tell you when we get to the water's edge."

They walked past summer houses half-hidden among the trees. All the shutters were closed. Over the reed fences, they saw a red frame from which the swing and all the ropes had been removed.

"The Gwiaders left this morning too."

"Yes, I saw them pack their car. There won't be many people left once we are gone."

"Anyway, it's back to school in three weeks. The holidays are over."

There was not a breath of air. The sand of the path, in which their feet sank, turned to dust under their feet. On the edge of the path, the brambles and bracken leaves were covered with a layer of white dust. They had not been washed by rain for months.

One would have thought it was the middle of the summer. Suddenly the glimmering sea appeared in front of them.

They walked on the rocks barefooted. Alan looked at Tekla's long thin legs as she stepped over the ponds, a little way in front of him. During the previous night, he had risen from his bed and had seen, leaning out of the window, the contours of the pine trees and of the path in the clear night. He could hardly hear the soft sound of the waves licking the sand but smelled the mixture of earth, sap and sea-weeds. The house was silent. He had thought of Tekla. He had visualised her with her head on the pillow and a strand of hair across her cheek. She had looked as calm and serene as she was now. How could she be so unconcerned when he himself felt so upset? Her lips were full. He had bent down over her, told her he loved her and kissed her lips.

Somewhere in the house he had heard the jingle of a dish or of a bottle. "It's morning," he had thought. He had leant further down over the ledge to look through the dining-room window underneath him, but had not been able to see anything. He had heard another noise from the inside of the house, some Arabic music probably coming from the kitchen.

When he thought of her leaving, he felt he was being torn apart. The summer was truly over although it did not feel like it. Everything except the weather told him that it was reaching its end. In the hotel, a third of the tables were now empty. Yesterday evening, as they were walking past 'La Belle Etoile,' they had noticed how few people were sitting in the lit dining-room. Here, on the little beach beyond the rocks, he could only see one child playing at the edge of the water, step-ping back in front of each wavelet.

A flapping of wings above their heads made them look up. A flock of birds which vaguely looked like terns flew past:

"Common terns," explained Alan who knew about birds.

The flock of birds went past, casting a shadow, like that of a cloud over the sea.

"They are off," he said.

"Why are they leaving so soon? The weather is still hot," said Tekla as her eyes followed the birds in the clear sky.

"Everyone is leaving. We are amongst the very last, Tekla."

Alan turned over a stone. A horde of tiny crabs scampered off to find refuge under the seaweeds.

"Did you know that shrimps are caught when the tide comes in?" he asked Tekla.

She did not answer and made a sign for him to be quiet. She was squatting by a dark pond, searching through it, thoroughly unflustered, as though nothing special was happening, as though this was a day like any other day.

"They are so tiny," she said in the end.

Alan sat on the wet seaweeds and looked pensively at the sea.

"Look at that boat over there getting out of the harbour. There's no fishing gear on board. What can it be? It could well be the boat we saw yesterday in Concarneau loading all those wine crates."

"Why should it be that one?" she replied, straightening her back.

Alan kept looking at the sea and said to himself:

"They travel far. To Mauritania." After a while he added: "Where is Mauritania?"

Tekla stood up. She looked thin as she stretched her back bent for so long. There was no hint of mist in the air. The houses on the other side of the bay and the walls of the old town were clearly visible and seemed very close. She put her hand to her forehead to brush aside the strand of hair which had fallen in front of her eyes.

"Are you tired, dream-catcher?"

As he did not reply, she asked:

"What's the matter, Alan?"

"Nothing."

"I know there is something."

"It's the end of the holidays," he mumbled.

The sea was as smooth as a lake. In the middle of the estuary, a loose sail was gently flapping. Tekla sat down on a rock to wait for her companion who was somewhere behind her.

He came towards her holding a small bucket in his hand. He felt as lonely and miserable as on Sunday nights, at the end of his day off at home. He saw Tekla sitting in the sunshine and longed, more than ever, to hold her in his arms.

"Tekla, I think ...." he said, walking up to her.

But he slipped on the seaweeds. As he started collecting the shells and small shrimps fallen among the wet wrack, the young girl was merrily laughing her heart out.

Behind her a blue boat unfurled its sails. The sea was still shimmering in the warm sun of this lovely Indian Summer.

"What were you going to say?" she finally asked.

Alan felt angry at himself, and at her for having laughed.

"Can't remember."

The receding sea filled the air with the smell of seaweeds. He could hear the shellfish moving ceaselessly under the rocks. The girl's lavender-blue gaze settled upon him, as she tried to read his thoughts.

"What were you saying?" she asked again.

The boy recoiled once more.

"It was nothing," he said. Then he added: "I was going to say that I'll be bored."

"It won't be long before you leave too."

On the other side of the bay, the blue boat was gliding behind the pier. Then there was only the triangle of its red sail sliding along above the pier.

Tekla got up and smoothed out her summer dress. Her fingers nails were broken. She took Alan's hand to jump over the rocks.

They came back hand in hand along the beach. They hardly spoke. They walked past 'La Belle Etoile'. The only people in the garden were a middle-aged couple sitting at a small iron table painted white.

They looked at the sea stretching in front of them, then at two young people who were passing by, and their eyes followed them to the end of the creek.

A cook, wearing his white hat, was sitting on a low window ledge. He too was looking at the sea. When a waitress went past him to collect a parasol, the man

cracked a joke. She laughed out loud, and then all was quiet again.

Alan kicked a pile of cockles left on the sand by a cockle-digger who had been too burdened.

"Will you be going back to school?"

"Of course."

"Will you come back here next year?"

"I suppose so. What time is it, Alan?"

"Half-past."

"It's time I got back," she said, as she left the water's edge. "I have a few things to pack yet."

They hurried back to the hotel, over the sand dune covered with dwarf thistle.

There was a flurry of activity around a red coach parked on the sandy road which ran along the beach.

Barefooted children in their swimsuits had left their beach games to come and watch it go. Fishing tackle, small and large fishing nets and rucksacks had been heaped on the roof-rack to which two men were now trying to strap a pram.

Alan and Tekla were waiting side by side.

The tide was very low, exposing the mud banks of the estuary.

"They are raising the yacht," said Alan.

He looked sad. It was now too late to talk to her or to kiss her. He looked around him. Everyone was busy. He took Tekla's long fingers in his hand and squeezed them.

Tekla was the last passenger to get on the coach. The children cheered as it left. Through the window, the girl waved the scarf she had worn two months ago, when he had first met her. The coach, with the pram swaying on the roof rack, had turned the corner. Alan stood there for a long time. As in a dream, he kept seeing a bright scarf fluttering in the wind.

"Look! The terns are leaving," said a voice next to him.

Alan looked round. The old man was talking to him. He felt ashamed and blushed. Instead of going back to the hotel with him, he turned to face the sea. He threw his linen bag over his shoulder. On the rear of his bathing trunks, there was a dark wet spot. He walked away along the shore.

Filip Oillo

Blaz an holen, *1996* (Lodenn)

Douget e oa e huñvreoù gant hiboud ar mor. Ar mor divarvel, pasianted ennañ ken ha ken, abaoe ur viken o krignañ pennek an tornaodoù galloudus.

Hag aze en e gichenik edo Anna, ken kaer, war e aod-traezh kuzh, ken kaer all. Devezh benniget! Ha ne oa ken nemet kaerded en-dro dezhañ. Hini ar mor, hini ar reier, hini an tornaodoù, hini Anna. Met ur pec'hed e oa he dilhad-kourankañ. Ur pec'hed marvel.

Un devezh brav e oa bet. Romantel and romantok. Dorn ha dorn, o pourmen a-hed an aod. Ne oa ket gwall hent d'ober, ken bihan ma oa an aodig kuzh. Met meur a dra a oa da zizoleiñ warni. Ur bedig. Abaoe kanvedoù edo ar reier en o flas. Pet koublad amourouzien o doa klevet o vale warno hag en o c'hichen?

Diskouez a reas dezhi mougev gevrinus e vugaleaj a oa dindan an tornaod. Bet tud ar vro, gwechall gozh, o verniañ peñse enni, diwar-wel d'ar valtouterien, hervez e dad-kozh. Fresk e oa en diabarzh. Ha tomm-grizias er-maez.

Dorn ha dorn e teujont en-dro eus kouronkañ. Yen e oa an dour. "Dre belec'h an diaoul e vez ar Gulf Stream o tremen?" a soñjas pa oa e vizied o klask un hent e-touesk he blev fuilh, e-keit ma oa kemmesket don o selloù, hag int o-daou en o sav, o zreid en dour c'hoazh.

Stardañ a reas anezhi etre e zivrec'h, ha pokañ d'he genoù. Blev gleb Anna a-fuilh war he fas a strinkas ennañ fulennoù a follentez. Bountañ a reas goustadik brikoloù dilhad-kouronkañ Anna diwar he divskoaz. Ha. souezhusañ tra, hi hec'h-unan a sikouras anezhañ d'ober, en ur dennañ ar brikoloù diouzh he divrec'h. Ha setu penaos e zaoulagad a reas anaoudegezh gant begoù teñval he divronn bihan ha sklaer, ront ha stegn, difluket a-greiz pep kreiz eus dilhad-kouronkañ rust ha teñval al Légion d'Honneur, koantig ha tres ar brasañ eston warno. Anton, e galon o kalkenniñ ken ha ken en e vruched, e gasas e c'henoù da dañva blaz kroc'hen Anna. Gwall sebezet, rak hi a laoske anezhañ d'ober, en ur flourat goustadik e vlev, tra ma sente-eñ begoù he divronn o reutaat dindan e pokoù.O virvi gant ar c'hoant, ha deuet kalon dezhañ, e stagas da gas goustadik he dilhad-kouronkañ d'an traoñ. Redek a rae e deod ouzh he c'hroc'hen, o tastum an holen laosket gant ar mor, ha dousik e talc'he an danvez glas da riklañ diwar digroazlez Anna. E-pad un hanter eilenn bennak, e c'hellas deskiñ Anton penaos e oa ur gwir veleganez eus Anna, pa voe diboulzet a-greiz-holl war e giz ganti.

"Arabat, Anton, arabat!" emezi, en ur sachañ buan an danvez war he c'horf hag e wiskañ en-dro. "C'hwi paotred n'eus ken nemet ar soñj-se en ho penn" a zichekas.

Treiñ a reas Anton e benn ha bale toutek ha mont un tammig larkoc'h da deurel e bouez war ur roc'h ront. Dilavar, e zivrec'h kroazet gantañ war e zaoulin, hag e elgezh gantañ war e arzorn, e selloù kollet en tu-hont d'ar c'heinvor.

Aet e oa Anna diouzh he zu da azezañ war he serviedenn. Dilavar e chomjont e-pad ur reuziad mat. Ar mor hepken a gleved e huanadennoù pa zeue e zeodoù da lipat an traezh.

"Naon ha sec'hed am eus ac'hanout, Anna," a lavaras Anton a-greiz-holl, hep krediñ sellet outi, blaz holen an daeroù war e vouezh daskrenus.

Ur vatimant bras-divent a oa o tremen dirazo, e kanol ar Forn. Eus pelec'h e oa o tont? Eus Iwerzhon?

"Gouzout a rez," emezi. "Fall-kenañ e oa tremenet an traoù bewech gant ar baotred all. Ar re am eus anavezet araozout." Mantret e oa Anton. Biskoazh n'en dije soñjet he dije anavezet paotr all ebet.

Mil binijenn en doa o chom mestr war ar c'hoant a oa o virviñ ennañ c'hoazh.

Tennet gantañ e selloù diouzh an tu all d'an dremmwel, e paras anezho war re Anna.

"Sot on ganez, Anna. Keit ha ma vo dour er mor, em boa joa ouzhit."

Dilavar e chomas Anna, a-raok sevel en he sav: "Kenkoulz deomp loc'hañ, 'gav ket dit? Pelloc'h e vimp diwezhat er glinikenn."

Deuet e oa ar poent da zistreiñ d'ar gêr vras. Da seizh eur e kroge en-dro Anna gant he labour. Anton ne oa ket da labourat en noz-se. Met ur gouel a oa da gaout er glinikenn. Helmut Schneider, ar surjian eus Bro-Alamagn, hag a oa o labourat ganto abaoe pemp bloaz, en doa kavet ur post-labour e-giz isrener en ur glinikenn e Glotertal, er Schwarzwald, nepell eus Freiburg. Evit lidañ a-zoare e zistro d'e vro, e oa bet divizet gant tud ar glinikenn en em zic'hizañ.

"Na pegen dinamm an aer tro-dro amañ! Pakomp ur fronellad vat a-raok mont d'ar gêr vras en-dro" emezi.

Anton, avat, ne oa ket troet d'ar poent-se da gargañ e skevent. Rak ur gwall vec'h a oa war e spered. Anna ne gomprene ket anezhañ. Met daoust ha gouest e vefe da gompren anezhañ deiz pe zeiz?

"Anton," emezi. "Re vuan ez ez ganin. Me 'zo e-giz louarnig ar Priñs Bihan. Ret e vo dit doñvaat ac'hanon. Tamm-ha-tamm."

Doñvaat... Soñjal a reas Anton e *Keben Doñvaet*, gant Shakespeare. Ar ger doñvaat ne zeree ket ouzh Anna. Erfin... Betek gouzout....

Translation

The Taste of Salt, *1996* (Extract)

The whispering sea was carrying his dreams. Everlasting, ever patient, it had been nibbling stubbornly at the majestic cliffs since time immemorial.

Anna, pretty Anna, was there, by his side, on his secret creek which matched her prettiness. What a blessed day! There was nothing but beauty all around him: the sea, the rocks, the cliffs, and of course, Anna. But that swimsuit of hers! What a shame! What a frightful shame!

It had been a romantic and idyllic summer's day as, hand in hand, they had walked along the shore. Not that there was far to walk on his tiny secret creek, but there was plenty to discover. It was a little world of its own. The rocks had been standing there for centuries. How many loving couples had they ever heard walking on them or past them?

He showed her the secret cave of his youth, right under the cliff. According to his grandfather, the local people used it in the old days to store the booty gathered from shipwrecks, far from the inquisitive eyes of the customs officers. Inside, it was cool, outside it was burning hot.

They returned from their swim hand in hand. The sea was cold. "Where on earth is that Gulf Stream supposed to be?" he thought, his fingers trying to find a way out of her tangled hair as they stood, feet still in the water, looking deeply into each other's eyes.

He took her in his arms and kissed her lips. The strands of Anna's tangled hair on her face lit sparks of passion in him. He gently slid the straps of her swimsuit off her shoulders. By the strangest of happenings, she helped him and freed her arms from the straps. This is how his eyes made acquaintance with the dark nipples of her pale, round, firm little breasts, now freed from the cups of the rough dark swimsuit which bore a resemblance to that worn by girls in the Legion of Honour school. Her nipples looked lovely but were seemingly very surprised. His heart beating wildly in his chest Anton brought his lips closer in order to get a taste of Anna's skin. He was most amazed that she let him carry on whilst she gently caressed his hair. He felt her nipples harden under his kisses.

Burning with desire and now feeling very brave, he started to slide her swimsuit further down. He was running his tongue on her skin, gathering the salt left on it by the sea while the dark blue swimsuit was slowly slipping from Anna's hips. For half a second or so, in a glimpse, Anton saw that Anna was a real blonde, but suddenly she pushed him away.

"Don't! Anton, don't!" she said pulling her swimsuit up quickly and sliding the straps on again. "You, men, that's the only thing you ever think about," she added in a voice full of defiance.

Anton turned round and sheepishly went to sit on a rounded rock, a little way further on. Silent, with his arms crossed around his knees and his chin resting on his wrist he looked far away towards the other side of the ocean.

Anna had gone back to sit on her towel. Neither of them talked for a long while. The only heaving sound was that of the sea as its tongue came to lick the sand.

"I hunger and thirst for you, Anna," said Anton suddenly, not daring to look at her. His tear salted voice was shaking.

A huge ship glided in front of their eyes in the Chenal du Four. Where did it come from? From Ireland?

"Just let me tell you," she said. "In the past, things have always turned out badly with men, others, those I have known before you." Anton was dismayed. Never would he have thought she had known other men.

He was fighting hard to control the desire which was still burning in him.

He looked away from the horizon, and his eyes met Anna's.

"I am mad about you, Anna. I shall love you for as long as there is water in the sea."

Anna stood up and replied: "We'd better go, don't you think. Or else we'll be late at the hospital."

It was time to go back to town. Anna's shift started at seven o clock. Anton was not on duty that evening, but there was a party at the hospital. Helmut Schneider, the German surgeon who had been working with them for the past five years, was leaving to become assistant manager in a hospital in Glotertal, in the Black Forest, near Freiburg, and in order to celebrate his return to his homeland, the hospital staff had decided to throw a fancy dress party.

"The air around here is so pure! Let's breathe it in once more before returning to town," she said.

Anton did not feel like filling his lungs at that particular time. A heavy burden was on his mind. Anna did not understand him. Would she ever be able to understand him?"

"Anton," she said "you go too fast. I am like the fox in *The Little Prince*. You will have to tame me, little by little."

Tame her? Anton thought about Shakespeare's *Taming of the Shrew*. The word 'tame' did not quite fit Anna. "Well!" he thought, "Who knows?"

Alan Botrel

Ar Pok, *1995*

Edo-hi, difiñv, en he sav, e penn an trepasig, parfet he dremm, dic'hoarzh daoust ha gant ur seurt kuñvded, ha diskouez a rae dor ar sal gant he biz e penn he brec'h astennet. Heuliañ a eure an hent, hesent hag enkrezet war un dro, ha digeriñ an nor. Ur sal a vent etre e oa, goullo ha dizolo he mogerioù, o paouez bezañ diannezet pe o c'hortoz taolennoù, gloestroù pe draezoù nevez evit un diskouezadeg all.

Edo Giana en he sav dirak ar prenestr uhel met ne wele diouti nemet ur stumm du beuzet e gouloù gwenn ar goañv en he gronne diouzh an diavez. Tostaat a eure goustad ha dre ma nesae outi e tiveuze diouzh ar stumm-se livioù he dilhad, takad sklaer he dremm, he daoulagad glas-mor, betek d'ar stumm dispis dont da vezañ Gianna evit gwir, nes-holl outañ.

Nes ha n'eo ket kar ken. An daoulagad-se a oa bet dezhañ evel daou buñsad gouloù glas a spluje hag a veuze enne bep tro ma pare he sell warnañ a oa deuet da vezañ kloz outañ, berzet. Gouloù ne oa mui; ur gouloù, glas atav, traken: dall-disked e selle outañ, yen.

"Da lizher am eus bet," a lavaras dezhi. Ret e oa kregiñ gant ur gomz bennak met keuz en doe raktal da vezañ staget gant ur seurt bomm amoet. E zont amañ, d'an eur lakaet, a ziskoueze anat... P'en dije ouzhpennet "...er beure-mañ", pe un dra bennak e-giz-se, e vije bet muioc'h abeget e frazenn.

"Lavaret em boa dit paouez a bellgomz din er gêr. Met ne fell ket dit kompren, evit doare. Gouzout a ouzout ne vez ket eurioù labour reoliek gant ma gwaz. Ha ma gwaz a garan a-nevez. Muioc'h eget n'eus forzh piv. Kompren a rez. Piv bennak e ve ar "piv"-se..." War betra he doa lakaet ar pouez, war "piv" pe war ar "bennak"-se, faeüs, tagus, blaz an dismeg gantañ? Hag e mouezh ken tomm, ken flour ne oa ket keit-se, ken yen, ken dianav bremañ. Gwasket e voe e galon gant un dorn yen. Pe gant krabanoù tan, ne ouie ket. Skeiñ a rae ar gwad dizingal dindan e zaouividig, yen ivez gant ar c'hwezenn. "Paouez a bellgomz din, a skrivañ din, a gomz ouzhin... Paouez a sellout ouzhin!" a c'harmas Gianna, gant taeroni. Doueez ar gened o vont en egar. Kilañ a reas, pellaat diouti tamm-ha-tamm, aon ha doan e don-donañ e galon. Gouloù gwan ar goañv en diavez he gronnas adarre a-nebeudoù. Beuziñ a rae Gianna ennañ, didrouz, gorrek. Steuziañ a reas liv glas he daoulagad da gentañ, hag he dremm da c'houde, gwenn er gouloù gwenn. Merzhout a eure ur stumm da ziwezhañ, un drolinenn du pell-holl dirak ar prenestr uhel, er gambr noazh. An dourenn en e zaoulagad a lakae ur seurt gouel daskrenus war bep tra.

Dizreiñ a reas a-daol-trumm.

Daoust d'ar flav ma oa e zivc'har dindanañ en doa c'hoant redek, tec'hout a-dizh, pell alese, pell diouzh Gianna, da virout en e eñvor dremm e garantez, da ank-ouazh mouezh an doueez konnaret.

★★★

Edo-hi atav difiñv e penn an trepas, o tiskouez an hent d'ar sal edo o paouez kuitaat. Chom a eure a-sav. C'hoant en doa sentiñ ouzh ar vrec'h, ouzh kemenn ar biz-se. Mont war e giz, komz ganti. Fulor Gianna a dregernas neuze en e zivskouarn. Pignat a reas war ar sichenn hag, en ur zifronkal, ouzh he briata, tanet e galon gant ar garantez, e pokas da zivweuz maen yen an delwenn.

Translation

The Kiss, *1995*

There she was, motionless, at the end of the short corridor. The oval of her face was perfect. Although she did not smile, there was a kind of sweetness on her lips. The index finger of her extended arm pointed towards the door of the room. He obediently followed her injunction, and, feeling nervous, opened the door. It was a medium-sized room with bare walls. It had just been cleared out, or else it was being made ready to receive paintings, furniture or other objects for a new exhibition.

Gianna was standing in front of the high window but he could only just make her out as the black shape standing out against the bright background of white winter light coming from outside. He slowly approached her, and as he did so, the shape relinquished the colour of her clothes, her lightly-coloured face, her sea-blue eyes, until the blurry shape truly became the real Gianna who was so close to him.

She was close to him, but she was no longer with him. Her eyes, these two springs of blue light in which he had dived and drowned every time she had looked at him, were now closed to him, prohibited. The sparkling light had gone; there was a veil, and blue it was, but that was all; she was looking at him in a blind, lifeless, cold sort of way.

"I got your letter," he told her. He had to broach the conversation somehow, but he immediately regretted having started with such silly words. His coming here, at the said time, showed it too well... Had he added "this morning" or anything else of the kind, his sentence would have laid him open to more criticism.

"I told you to stop phoning me at home. But you apparently don't want to understand. You know very well that my husband does not have regular working

hours. I love my husband again, more than anyone else. Try to understand."

Whoever could this 'anyone' be? Where had she laid the emphasis? On the word 'anyone', or was it on 'else', which sounded scornful and acrimonious with its tinge of contempt? Her voice, which had been so warm, so tender, not so long ago, was now so cold, so unfamiliar. His heart was squeezed by a cold hand or by fiery talons, he did not know which. His blood was pulsating erratically in his temples which were now cold with perspiration.

"Stop phoning me! Stop writing to me! Stop talking to me. Stop seeing me!" screamed Gianna vehemently. The goddess of beauty was flying into a rage. He stepped back, moved away from her gradually, his heart brimming with fear and sorrow.

The faint winter light of the outside surrounded her again little by little. Gianna disappeared into it silently, slowly. First the blue of her eyes faded away, then her face, white in the white light. In the end, he could only see a shape, a black outline, far away, in front of the high window of the bare bedroom. The tears in his eyes left a kind of quivering veil on everything.

He turned away suddenly.

Although his legs were giving way under him, he wanted to run, to flee at speed, far from this spot, far from Gianna, in order to keep in his memory her loving face and to forget the voice of the raging goddess.

★★★

She was still motionless at the end of the corridor, pointing the way to the room he had just left. Still standing up. He wanted to obey the arm, the command of her finger. But also to come back, to talk to her. Gianna's fit of anger rang again in his ears. He climbed on the pedestal. In tears, his heart burning with love, he put his arms around her and kissed the cold stone lips of the statue.

Fañch Elies-Abeozen

Hervelina Geraouell, *1943* (Lodenn)

Hervelina a oa bet evitañ ar vleunienn zianav na gaved ket e liorzh ar juloded. Ur plac'h eus e vro koulskoude, kizidikoc'h avat eget ar re a zaremprede dre amañ, eeunoc'h ivez, chomet tost d'an dud vunut, o sellout outo nann diouzh ur bazenn uheloc'h, hogen he daoulagad a-rez o daoulagad.

Ha ne blegfe ket Anton en dro-mañ da volontez e vamm.

En derc'hent, diouzh an abardaez, goude koan, aet an tad d'ober un tro d'ar jardin hag ar c'hoarezed pignet en o c'hambroù, Anton oa bet galvet gant e vamm e-kichen ar prenestr. Edo oc'h ober stamm. Pa voe distaliet an daol gant ar vatezh, e lezas ar vamm al loer da gouezhañ war he daoulin gant an nadozioù metal lufrus.

"Anton," emezi en ur lakaat da barañ war he mab selloù yen un daoulagad sklaer, aroueziet enno ur volontez didrec'hus. "Resevet hon eus ul lizher digant da eontr ha kaoz zo ennañ ac'hanout. O! Ne glemm ket diwar da benn, er c'hontrol, nemet e kemenn deomp ez out bet gwelet, meur a wech, da-unan-penn, gant ur plac'h yaouank eus ar vro, ur studierez, war a lavarer, merc'h un den-a-vor."

"Gwir eo," eme Anton diouzhtu. "Ur gamaladez eus ar skol-veur a zo eus Keraouell, e-kichen Ploueskad. Hi eo am eus gwelet eno."

"Ur gamaladez a glasker bezañ an-unan ganti," eme ar vamm, "zo gwell reiñ dezhi marteze un anv all! O! Da dad ne ra nemeur a van. N'heller ket mirout, emezañ, ouzh studierien ha studierezed d'en em zaremprediñ pa vezont bemdez mesk-ha-mesk: ar pezh ne gomprenan ket kalz, me. Peurvuiañ, pa reont al lez an eil re d'ar re all, eme da dad, ne deo nemet evit c'hoari ha ne deo ket stank an dimezioù a vez skoulmet diwar an darempredoù-se. Lakaomp ez eo gwir. Evelato e fell din gouzout petra eo ar vignoniezh a zo etrezout hag ar plac'h yaouank-se. Gwell-a-se ma ne deo nemet ur c'hoariell."

"Ne deo tamm ebet ur c'hoariell," eme Anton feuket. "Hervelina zo ur plac'h vat ha speredek ha n'eo bet morse deuet em fenn e c'hellfen c'hoari gant he c'halon."

"Soñjal a raen ne wele ket da dad ken sklaer ha ma krede dezhañ. Ur garantez da vat eo e kred dit magañ evit ar baotrez-se. Setu ar pezh a ra aon din. Gouzout a rez koulskoude, Anton, n'heller ket fiziout en un den ken yaouank ha te, da zilenn ar vaouez a ranki bevañ ganti da holl vuhez-pad."

"War a gredan, mamm, eo me koulskoude a dle hec'h anavezout ar gwellañ. N'ouzoc'h ket piv eo, na petra 'dalv."

"Koantig eo, war a lavar da gendirvi. Ne deo ket hep danvez, hervez da eontr. Ar familh avat ne deo ket brudet da vezañ gwall droet gant ar relijion. Ha pa vefe, n'eus abeg ebet dit da vont da glask maouez ken pell, pa vo kavet kalz gwelloc'h, kalz suroc'h dit dre amañ."

Anton, hegaset, a chome dilavar. Santout a rae o pouezañ war e ziskoaz yev reut bolontez meuriad ar juloded. En o bro ez eus evito daou rummad-tud: i hag ar re all. Netra da c'hounit o klask breutaat ouzh e vamm.

"Komz a rit, mamm, evel pa vefen o c'houlenn fortuniañ er bloaz-mañ. Un nebeud bloavezhioù a rankin c'hoazh gortoz, gouzout a rit. Un tamm re abred eo kemer chati adal bremañ gant un dra n'hell ket c'hoarvezout a-raok ma'm bo graet va servij."

"A zo gwir, va mab. Nemet arabat dit stagañ da galon e-lec'h ma n'hello ket chom evit mat. Gwell eo ganeomp da welout o taremprediñ ur plac'h dereat eget ur penn-skañv. Me avat ne gomprenan ket peseurt ezhomm a zo d'ur studier bezañ e-giz-se war-dro ar merc'hed. Da dad a lavar n'eus ket da ober van, nemet e c'hellen tennañ da evezh war an dra koulskoude, mar karen. Ha setu perak em eus lavaret dit va soñj. Bez fur, Anton! Taol evezh d'ober diotach!"

Anton, goude poket d'e vamm gant c'hwervoni, a oa pignet d'e gambr. Trubuilhet oa e galon. Evel pa vije bet taolet Hervelina er-maez eus an ti e oa. N'eo ket en un doare rust ha diseven, hogen gant ur c'henavo reut ha yen-sklas:

"Ne lavaromp ket sotonioù deoc'h. Ni zo tud savet-mat. Met na deuit ket mui

da lakaat ho treid dre amañ. N'hoc'h ket eus hor renk."

Kousket fall en doa gant huñvreoù enkrezet ma wele enno ar penn karet, e zaoulagad bras don o sellout outañ hep skuizhañ, hep fiñval o malvennoù, war c'hortoz eus ur respont d'o goulenn dilavar. Hag eñ, evel seizet e deod, n'helle distagañ na ya na nann.

Bet oa e vamm o pediñ Doue ma chomfe he mab fur ha dieub, ma virfe e galon evit ur baotrezig, onest ha difaltazi ha dilevenez evelti.

Darbet e voe dezhañ serriñ ar prenestr diwar ur fourrad kounnar. Habaskaat a reas diouzhtu e galon pa glevas e vamm o sevel gant an diri hag e reas an neuz da lenn *Galv ar Gouelec'h* gant Jack London.

Translation

Hervelina Geraouell, *1943* (Extract)

Hervelina had been for him the unknown flower which is not found in the gardens of the Julods [*well-to-do people in the district of Leon*]. She was a local girl however, but more sensitive than the ones he was acquainted with, more outspoken too, as she had stayed close to unpretentious people, looking at them not from a higher plane but straight into their eyes.

This time, Anton would not submit to his mother's will.

The day before, in the evening, after dinner, when his father had gone for a walk in the garden and his sisters had retired to their bedrooms, Anton had been summoned by his mother near the window. She was knitting. When the maid had finished clearing the table, the mother rested the sock and the bright metal needles on her lap.

"Anton," she said, looking at her son with pale cold eyes which reflected her unbending will. "We received a letter from your uncle. He mentions you in it. Oh! He does not say anything bad about you, on the contrary, but he writes that you have been seen, more than once, alone with a young local girl, a student apparently, a sailor's daughter."

"That's true," replied Anton at once. "She is a university friend who comes from Keraouell, near Plouescat. I went there to see her."

"A friend one tries to be alone with is surely called something else!" said the mother. "Not that your father minds. He says that one cannot prevent male and female students to get to know each other as they meet one another everyday. I can't say I understand this point of view, but according to your father, when they go out with each other, it is only to show off, and they don't usually end up marrying each other. Even if that is the case, I'd like to know more about this friendship between you and that young girl, and all the better if it is only a fad .

"It is in no way a fad," said Anton in an irritated voice. "Hervelina is a good and clever girl, and I never thought for one minute that I could play around with her feelings."

"I did think that you father was not judging the situation as clearly as he thought. So, you believe that you really love this girl. That's what frightens me. However, Anton, you know that one cannot entrust a man as young as yourself with the choice of the woman he will have to live with for the rest of his life."

"In my opinion, Mother, I am the one who knows her best. You don't know who she is or what she is like."

"According to your cousins, she is pretty. And not without a fortune, according to your uncle. However her family are not known to be regular churchgoers. And even if they were, you have no reason to go and find a companion so far, when we can find a much better and much safer one for you in our circle."

Annoyed by the reply, Anton stayed silent. He was feeling on his shoulders the heavy weight of the will of the Julod clan. According to them, there were only two kinds of people: them and the others. But he had nothing to gain by confronting his mother.

"Mother, you speak as though I was asking to get married this year. You know that I need to wait a few more years. It is a little early to start finding fault in something that cannot happen until I have done my national service."

"That's true, son. But don't attach your heart in a place where it cannot stay for ever. We prefer to see you going out with a decent girl rather than with a carefree one, although, as far as I am concerned, I don't understand why students feel the need to concern themselves with girls. You father says to take no notice, but he allowed me to draw your attention to the matter, if I wanted to. That's why I have told you what I thought. Be good, Anton! Beware of doing something stupid!"

After giving his mother a bitter goodnight kiss, Anton went up to his room. His heart was not at peace. It was as if Hervelina had been thrown out of the house, not in a violent or impolite way, but with a curt and icy-cold goodbye: "We are not telling you tales. We are courteous people. But don't ever come back here again. You are not of our class."

He slept badly and had fretful dreams in which he saw the beloved face and its large enigmatic eyes looking at him incessantly, without blinking, expecting an answer to the silent question he read in them. And he, as if tongue-tied, could say neither yes nor no.

His mother was praying God that her son might stay good and unattached, and that he kept his heart for a girl like herself, honest, dull and unimaginative.

He nearly banged the window shut in a fit of anger. His heart quietened suddenly when he heard his mother climb the stairs, and he pretended to read *The Call of the Wild*, by Jack London.

Langleiz

Feunteun Varanton, *1975* (Lodenn)

Pa zipoufas Marzhin a-ziouzh gwasked ar c'hoadmeur, edo ar plac'h yaouank en he c'hoazez e-kichen ar feunteun, ur mell levr, digor bras, war he daoulin. Trouz donedigezh ar marc'h hag ar marc'heger o waskañ hag o terriñ skourroù munut ar wenodenn pe ouzh o disteurel en ur vont, n'he lakeas ket zoken, da sevel he fenn.

An neuz da lenn a rae hepken Viviana rak, e melezour sklaer ha boull ar feunteun, e spie, e-kuzh, an hini a zeue.

Minc'hoarzhin a reas hemañ rak ur gorvigell ken aes da zizoleiñ. Hogen koantoc'h ha plijusoc'h da welout e oa c'hoazh Viviana eget na grede. Ha, kentizh, ec'h ankounac'haas e ragenebiezh evit soñjal hepken e douster an herradig-amzer a veve.

"Plac'h koant, emezañ dezhi, en ur rediañ e varc'h da chom a-sav a-benn un nebeut kammedoù, piv oc'h ha petra 'rit amañ? Ur mailh war e vicher e tlee bezañ an hini en deus desket deoc'h lenn er pikol levr-mañ!"

Adserriñ a reas Viviana he levr hag en e lakeas etalti, war ar pondalez marmor a dalveze dezhi da gador. Ha graet d'an estrañjour ur minc'hoarzh ken hoalus all, e respontas dezhañ:

"Perak va goulennata, o va mestr, c'hwi hag a oar pep tra? Va anv eo Viviana. Emañ va zad o chom nepell ac'halemañ, er maner a welit du-hont. Desket en deus din an nebeut a dra a ouzon... Ha bremañ, e c'hortozan ho kentelioù."

Diskennet a-ziwar e varc'h, Marzhin a stagas al loen ouzh skod un avalenn ouez hag a dostaas d'ar plac'h evit azezañ etalti. Houmañ a bare bremañ he selloù outañ dizouj kaer, hep paouez a vinc'hoarzhin. Luskellat a rae he divesker a-us da zour ar feunteun. En o mone-done, e spine a-wechoù begoù he zreid gorre ar melezour berus, a skrije neuze gant o allazig skañv; ken e sinklas, en diwezh, ur flistradig dour betek dremm an estrañjour azezet e-kichen ar verc'h yaouank. Hep rannañ ger, e sec'has Marzhin, gant palv e zorn, an takennoù lintrus a ziruilhe war e zivjod, evel pa vefent bet daeroù.

Daeroù!... Nag a zaeroù a skuilho a-raok pell amzer, da heul ar c'hoari bugel-se! Nep sin kevrinus, nep arouez ne c'helle mui avat e lakaat da zistreiñ war e giz. Re bell e oa aet bremañ. Nac'het en doa klevout mouezh e askre, a guzulie dezhañ pellaat diouzh ur seurt degouezhadenn. Dall e chomfe dirak sinoù.

Ha Marzhin ha lavarout dezhi, d'e dro, a-greiz minc'hoarzhin, eñ ivez:

"Ur mestr fur hoc'h eus bet. Perak klask unan all?

– Ne c'hell ket un tad deskiñ pep tra d'e verc'h."

Daoust ha graet he doa ar respont amjestr-se a-zevri pe dre ziouiziegezh? Diaes e vefe bet gouzout. Diskouez a rae bezañ ker glan, a gorf hag a galon, ha dour treuzwelus ar feunteun a adskeude, dres d'an ampoent, he stummoù mistr.

– Plac'hig koant, eme Varzhin, n'hoc'h eus ket soñjet, moarvat, er ster a c'hellfen reiñ d'ar gerioù emaoc'h o paouez distagañ?"

Hi, avat, hep distreiñ he selloù dioutañ, a eilgerias d'an estrañjour:

"Sklaer eo o ster, evidon-me!"

Edont bremañ kichen-ha-kichen. Marzhin en dije gellet he briata hag he stardañ ouzh e vruched, netra nemet oc'h astenn e zivrec'h. Ar wrez loskus en em sile en e wazied a lakae e galon da dalmañ buanoc'h.

Fromet holl gant an esmae hag un deneridigezh n'en doa merzet, betek-hen, evit plac'h all ebet, e klaske en em virout a grenañ. A-benn un herradig, e c'houlennas outi:

"Gant petore kentel e c'hellfen kregiñ d'ho kenteliañ?"

Dremm Viviana ne ziskulie netra eus he soñjoù don. Bez e selle atav outañ gant kemend-all a goantiz hag a zouster hoalus:

"Dre ar gentel a blijo ar muiañ deoc'h, aotrou ker, gant n'hon devo ket da ruziañ – na c'hwi na me – eus ar blijadur a dennimp diouti."

Minc'hoarzhin a reas adarre Marzhin dirak he soutilded.

– Hag ar gentel-se lakaet e-maez hon divizoù, petra 'rofec'h din en eskemm d'ar boan a gemerfen?

– Va c'halon a rofen deoc'h e prof, mignon ker. Va c'halon ha netra ouzhpenn…

– Ra vezo graet hervez ho c'hoant, mignonez ker, a eilgerias Marzhin o waskañ kement ha ma c'hellas war e gerseenn.

– Met, da gentañ holl, petra 'ouzoc'h ober?

– Gouzout a ran kerzhout war c'horre an dour, gourc'hemenn ouzh ar flammennoù hag ouzh ar seizh avel, lakaat da redek ur ster e-lec'h ne voe nepred gwelet unan; ha mil ha mil c'hoari all skañvoc'h pe bounneroc'h. Me 'oar ivez reiñ d'ur stlejennad vrumenn bennak ne vern pe liv, ne vern pe stumm: stummoù tud pe anevaled, pe euzhviled zoken. Gouzout a ouzon c'hoazh dibradañ ur c'hastell gant ar votenn zouar e zouge, an armead a strive d'e arzailhat hag ar soudarded e zifenne.

"Ha, da brouiñ ne glaskan ket ho lorbañ gant sorc'hennoù, ez on prest da ziskouez deoc'h ur gouel aozet evidoc'h-c'hwi hepken ha ne vefe nemedoc'h a gement a c'hellfe e welout, hep pellaat zoken diouzh pondalez ar feunteun-mañ."

Ken plijet e voe Viviana gant kinnig Marzhin ma stlakas he daouarn. Ha, kerkent, ec'h adsavas hemañ, hag ez eas da gutuilh ur skourrig kraoñkelvez en ur vod gwezigoù a greske nepell ac'halese. Ur c'helc'h a dresas goude, en-dro d'ar feunteun, gant beg ar skourr, hag un nebeut gerioù kevrinus a hiboudas a vouezh izel. Hag echu e lid-hud, e teuas da azezañ adarre e-kichen e vuiañ-karet. A-benn un herradig amzer, e seblantas ar c'hoadmeur fiñval. Ha neuze, dirak Viviana sebezet, e tifoupas a-zindan ar gwez marc'heion hag itronezed, hag en em zalc'he dorn ouzh dorn, dre goubladoù, o kanañ en un doare dispar hep paouez a gerzhout war o goar.

Goude bezañ en em renket war wrimenn ar c'helc'h a oa bet treset gant Marzhin, e krogjont holl da gorolliñ gant kemend-all a ampartiz, endra ma sone biniawoù ha bombardoù dihewel, da eilañ o c'hammedoù mibin.

Nepell ac'halehont, e c'helled gwelout, el lijor, stumm ur c'hastell kelc'hiet gant ul liorzh marellet a vleunioù dispar a bep seurt livioù, glas lin, ruz flamm, melen aour, ha leun a wezennoù o tougen frouezhioù dedennus ken dispar all.

Sorbet evel m'edo gant nevezenti an arvest en em zisplege dirazi, ne grede ket mui Viviana seniñ ger.

Padout a reas ar gouel iskis-se betek mare ar gousperoù. Goude ar c'horolloù, e voe astennet liñselioù gwenn-erc'h war ar c'hlazenn ha degaset meuzioù ha diedoù e-leizh. Echu ar banvez ha lamet listri ha liñselioù, e chomas an dimezelled da varvailhat ha da fistilhañ etrezo, e-pad ur pennad mat c'hoazh, endra ma tiduelle an aotrounez, distroet d'o c'hoarioù kadarn ha d'o mirc'hi, oc'h arsailhat jakoù-plouz e rabinoù al liorzh.

Pa zeuas ar goubanner-noz, e krogas ar varc'heion, ar floc'hed, an itronezed hag an dimezelled-se d'en em dennañ, goustadik hag evel gant keuz, trema ar c'hoad-meur, en ur gorolliñ adarre. O skeudennoù fuilhet a welas Viviana o teuziñ a silik, koublad warlerc'h koublad, a-feur ma sankent e amc'houloù ar gwez bras. Dambrest goude, e teuze ivez ar c'hastell el lusenn, hag e tianade d'e dro. Hogen, war c'houlenn ar plac'h, e chomas al liorzh, a voe anvet ganti, e koun ar blijadur he doa bet el lec'h benniget-se: "Repu Pep Levenez". Ha setu penaos e vez graet anezhi, c'hoazh hiziv zoken.

"Koantenn, ret eo din ho tilezel, a lavaras, erfin, Marzhin da Viviana.

– Ha perak kement-se a vall, keneil ker? Daoust ha ne c'hellfec'h ket deskiñ din unan all eus ar c'hoarioù dispar a ouzoc'h?

– Muioc'h a amzer vak eget n'am eus fenoz a zlefen kaout. Dont en-dro a rin hepdale. Ha neuze e teskin deoc'h ar re vravañ eus ar burzhudoù a ouzon sevel, gant ma vin asur ne nac'hot mui bezañ din, da c'houde.

– Gouzout a rit kenkoulz ha me, aotrou ker, e kollfen war un dro va brud-vat hag ho karantez, mar asantfen d'en em werzhañ deoc'h er c'hiz vezhus-se. Daoust ha n'on ket dija ho mignonez dre ar galon? Deskit din ar pezh am eus kement a c'hoant da c'houzout hep goulenn netra en eskemm. Hag, un deiz bennak, marteze..."

Ha Marzhin, "an den fur", div wech dallet peogwir e rakwele en amzer-da-zont ken aes ha ma lenne en amzer-vremañ, Marzhin a voe diboell hag hegredik a-walc'h evit tremen gant divizoù ar goantenn: bez e teskfe dezhi, neket hepken an holl ardoù-hud a ouie hag ul lod kaer eus al lezennoù kuzh a ren ar bed, met ivez ur sekred gouest da eilpenniñ e blanedenn-eñ. C'hoant en doa da vezañ gopraet en eskemm. Gopraet e vefe.

Na kriz e tlee bezañ avat e gerseadenn!

Translation

Baranton Fountain, *1975* (Extract)

When Merlin suddenly rode out of the cover of the forest, the young girl was sitting by the fountain, a big book open on her lap. The noise from the approaching horse and rider who were breaking or tossing aside the twigs of the path they were following did not even make her lift her head.

Viviana was only pretending to read. She was in fact secretly spying on the newcomer in the clear and transparent mirror of the fountain.

He smiled at this unsubtle stratagem, but Viviana was prettier and more pleasing to the eye than he had expected. He immediately forgot his antagonism to think only of the sweetness of the instant he was living.

"Pretty girl!" he said to her, forcing his horse to a halt after a few steps. "Who are you and what are you doing here? The one who taught you to read this enormous book must be an authority in his field!"

Viviana closed her book and put it down by her side, on the marble step on which she was sitting. She gave the stranger a most seductive smile and replied:

"Why question me, oh Master who knows everything? My name is Viviana. My father lives not far from here, in the manor-house you can see over there. He taught me the few things I know... And now, I await your lessons."

Merlin got off his horse, tied it round the trunk of a wild apple-tree, came up to the girl and sat next to her. She was now looking at him in a most impertinent way, still smiling. She was swinging her legs above the fountain pool, and as she did so, her toes would sometimes lightly brush the surface of the watery mirror which quivered under the light caress; so much so that finally, a spray of water reached the face of the stranger sitting beside the young girl. Without a word, Merlin dried with the palm of his hand the shiny drops which were running along his cheeks, just like tears.

Tears! He will soon shed many tears as a consequence of this childish game! It was too late for any secret warning, any omen, to make him turn back. He had gone too far now. He had refused to listen to the inner voice advising him to avoid this encounter. He would refuse to take heed of omens.

With a smile on his lips, Merlin asked:

"You have had a wise master. Why look for another?"

"A father cannot teach his daughter everything," she replied.

Had she given this hazardous answer in full knowledge or because she did not know? It would have been hard to know. She seemed to be as pure of heart and body as the transparent water of the fountain which now reflected her slim figure.

"Pretty girl", said Merlin, "you have presumably not thought of the meaning I could put on the words you have just uttered?"

But without looking at him, she replied to the stranger:

"Their meaning is very clear to me!"

They were now sitting side-by-side. Merlin could have taken her in his arms and clasped her on his chest. He only had to extend his arms. The boiling heat which ran in his veins made his heart beat faster.

Stirred by a flutter and a feeling of tenderness that he had never yet experienced for any other girl, he tried to prevent himself from trembling. After a short while, he asked:

"Which lesson should I start my teaching with?"

Viviana's face did not reflect her inner thoughts. She carried on looking at him, just as pretty, gentle and loveable.

"With the lesson you prefer most, dear Sir, as long as neither you nor I will have to blush for the pleasure we shall take from it."

Merlin smiled again at her subtlety.

"Leaving aside the content of this lesson, what will you give me in exchange of the pain I would take?"

"I would give you my heart as a gift, dear friend. My heart, but nothing else..."

"Be it as you wish, dear friend," replied Merlin, hiding his disappointment as much as he could.

"But, before we start, tell me what you can do," said the girl.

"I can walk on the surface of the water, order the flames and the four winds, make a source flow where none was ever seen, and a multitude of other simple or harder tricks. I also can give a wisp of fog any colour, any shape: make them into mountains or houses, men, animals, and even dragons. I also know how to lift a castle and its surrounding land together with the army which tried to attack it and the soldiers who defended it. And to prove that I am not trying to deceive you with daydreams, I am prepared to show you a feast, thrown just for you, as you will be the only one capable of seeing it, without even moving from the edge of this very fountain."

Viviana was so pleased with Merlin's offer that she clapped her hands. Immediately Merlin got up and went to get a branch of hazelnut in a clump of small trees growing nearby. He then drew a circle around the fountain with the tip of the branch while whispering a few mysterious words. His magic over, he came back to sit again next to his beloved. A short while afterwards, the forest appeared to be coming to life. And in front of the astounded Viviana, there suddenly appeared, from under the trees, knights and ladies holding hands, two by two, singing in a most melodious way as they slowly approached.

After lining up around the circle drawn by Merlin, they all started to dance nimbly, as invisible binious and bombards accompanied their dainty steps.

Close by but hovering in space, they could see the shape of a castle surrounded by a garden full of beds of exquisite and colourful flowers, lavender-blue, bright red, or golden yellow. The many trees bearing gorgeous fruit were just as stunning.

Absorbed in the novelty of the vision displayed in front of her, Viviana did not dare say anything.

This strange feast lasted until late afternoon. After the dances, tablecloths as white as snow were laid on the grass to receive a multitude of dishes and beverages. Once the banquet was over and the dishes cleared, the young ladies stayed quite a while to chatter and gossip together, as the knights entertained with daring games, sometimes on horseback as when they attacked straw men in the alleys of the garden.

When dusk fell, the knights, page-boys, ladies and noble young girls started retiring slowly, as if with regret, into the forest, dancing once again. Viviana watched as their hazy images melted away, couple after couple, as they sank in the shadow of the big trees. Soon after, the castle also melted away and disappeared in the mist. But, on the girl's request, the garden remained. In memory of the pleasure she had had in this wondrous place, she named it 'Refuge of Every Joy'. This is how it is still called today.

"My pretty, I will have to leave you now," said finally Merlin to Viviana.

"Why such a hurry, my dear? Could you not teach me another one of the excellent tricks you know?"

"I would need more free time than I have tonight. I shall return soon to teach you the most beautiful tricks of magic I can do, but you must not refuse to be mine afterwards."

"Yet, dear Sir, you know as well as me that I would lose both my good reputation and your love if I agreed to sell myself to you in such a shameful way. Am I not already your bosom friend? Teach me what I so much wish to know, without asking for anything in return. And maybe, one day…"

And Merlin, the so-called 'wise man', but in truth a man who was blind twice over, for he could foretell the future as easily as he could read in the present, Merlin was foolish and naive enough to believe the words of the young beauty: he would teach her, not only all the magic he knew and many of the hidden laws which govern the world, but also a secret capable of overturning his own destiny. He wanted to be paid in return. He would be paid.

How cruelly disappointed he must be!

Brizeug

Mari, *1844*

> Pa zeûann ken trist dré hô ker,
> Na spountit két, tûd ar Vouster,
> Mé glask va c'hoant, n'ounn kéd eul laer.
>
> Dré-man mé heûliaz aliez
> Em iaouankiz eur plac'hik kéz,
> Evel eul labous hé farez.
>
> Péléc'h éma ar plac'hik kaer?
> Na spountit kéd, tûd ar Vouster,
> Mé glask va douz, n'ounn kéd eul laer.
>
> Gand hé c'hoef digor d'an avel,
> Hi oa é-ghiz eunn durzunel
> Pa 'nem zispleg hé diou askel.
>
> Kolled é ann durzunel gher!
> Na spountit kéd, tûd ar Vouster,
> Mé glask va c'hoant, n'ounn kéd eul laer.
>
> Er vourc'h, goudé ar gousperô,
> Ann holl a laré, trô-var-drô:
> "Houn-nez éo flouren ar vrô!"

O iaouankiz flour ha ré verr!-
Na spountit két, tûd ar Vouster,
Me oel va douz, n'ounn kéd eul laer.

Translation

Mari, *1844*

If I walk through your streets looking sad,
Don't be afraid, people of Mouster,
I am looking for my lady, I am not a thief.

In these parts, I often walked
In my youth, with a dear girl,
As a bird following his mate.

Where is this pretty girl?
Don't be afraid, people of Mouster,
I am looking for my beloved, I am not a thief.

With her headdress open to the wind,
She looked like a dove
Extending her wings.

I have lost the dove.
Don't be afraid, people of Mouster
I am looking for my lady, I am not a thief.

In the village, after vespers
They used to say all around:
"She is the beauty of the district!"

O, tender youth, which is so short!-
Don't be afraid, people of Mouster,
I cry for my beloved, I am not a thief.

Yann-Bêr Kalloc'h

Er Vernikenn, *c.1910*

Gwélet em-es un dra heb par:
Ur garreg sonn ar hé diùhar,
Ha tro-ha-tro mor é konnar;

Hag er garreg, – ihuél hé fenn,
E oé staget doh hé hrohenn,
Bihan-bihan ur vernikenn.

Digabestret ha didruhé
En tonneu divent e darhé...
Med er vernikenn e zalhé.

Ha chetu deit er mor d'arsaù,
Hag er gêh verniken tenaù
D'er roh e oé staget ataù.

Er vernikenn e oui krogein:
'Zoh er roh é ma ar é gein,
Tra ne hello hé distagein...

Hama, n'en-des nitra gwirroh:
Él er vernikenn ar er roh,
Me halon zo staget dohoh!

Translation

The Limpet, *c.1910*

I have seen a wondrous thing:
A rock well set on its base,
And all around the furious sea;

The rock was holding its head high
And on its surface was attached
A tiny limpet.

Freely and pitilessly
The huge waves battered the rock,
But the limpet held on.

When the sea finally calmed down
The dear tiny limpet
Was still attached to the rock.

The limpet knows how to hold on.
From the back of the rock,
Nothing will make it break loose.

And so, here is the full truth:
Like the limpet on the rock
My heart is attached to you!

Farnachanavan

Diavaez, *1953*

Azezet edomp war ar geot glas.
    Hi ne lare grik.
    Me 'selle outi.
Avel fesk ar mor, 'n ur flourañ he zal,
A lakae a-fuilh va bleo teñval.

Sellet pizh he deus war-du an neñv glas
    ha gwelet he deus
    ar freuz hag ar reuz,
e-mesk ar c'houmoul o c'hostezioù du,
a bevarlamme evel kezeg feuls.

Ha laret he deus hep sellet ouzhin:
    O! perak ez eus,
    kement-all a freuz
e don ho kalon? Perak e welan
hoc'h ene bet glan ken du hag ar vran?

N'em eus laret tra, n'he deus komzet ken,
    hag eo savet,
    hag ez eo aet
war ar geot glas, a-hed ar mor glas,
'n ur ober an neuz da chom didrabas.

Translation

In The Open, *1953*

We were sitting on the green grass.
    She was not talking.
    I was looking at her.
The fresh wind of the sea which caressed her forehead
Was tangling my dark hair.

She stared at the blue skies
    and saw

mayhem and commotion
amongst the dark-sided clouds
tearing along like wild horses.

And she said, without looking at me:
    Oh! Why is there
    so much turmoil
in the depth of your heart? Why do I see
Your soul, formerly so pure, now as black as the crow?

I did not respond; she did not say anything more.
    She stood up,
    and walked
on the green grass, along the blue sea,
pretending not to care.

Charlez ar Braz

Son nevez war un danvez kozh, *1930*

Me am eus ur vestrezig e Pennanroz
Hag e redin d'he gwelet hep mui gortoz.
Hag e redin d'he gwelet disul da noz.

Ha mar teuez d'am gwelet, va c'hloareg koant,
Me'n em droio 'n ur pesk er stêr arc'hant.
N'az pezo ket va c'halon hervez da c'hoant.

Mar 'n em droez en ur pesk 'vel ma larez,
Me 'vo pesketaer, o va mestrez,
Me 'besketo va dousig dre garantez.

Mar teuez d'am fesketa ha d'am spouron,
Me 'm en droio en heizez er c'hoajoù don,
N'az pezo tamm, kloaregig, eus va c'halon.

Mar 'n em droez en heizez, 'vel ma larez,
Me a vezo chaseour, o va mestrez!
Me 'chaseo va dousig dre garantez.

Mar teuez d'am chaseal 'riskl d'am muntriñ
Me 'n em raio leanez 'n un abati,
N'az pezo ket va c'halon, o kloareg kri!

Mar 'n em rez leanez 'vel ma larez
Me a yelo da vanac'h, o va mestrez,
Me 'goveso va dousig dre garantez.

Ha mar teuez d'am c'hoves 'oueli c'hwero,
Gwenn-kann marv em gwele te am c'havo.
Roin ket dit va c'halon, kaer az pezo.

Mar da gavan gwenn-marv 'n da wele kloz,
Plas Sant Per a gemerin er Baradoz
D'hen digeriñ d'am dousig eus Pennanroz.

Translation

New Song on an Old Theme, *1930*

I have a sweetheart in Pennanroz
And shall hurry to see her without further delay
I shall hurry to see her on Sunday night.

If you come to see me, handsome cleric,
I shall turn into a fish in the silvery stream.
You will not have my heart as is your wish.

If you turn into a fish, as you just mentioned,
I shall be a fisherman, o my sweet love,
I shall try and catch my sweetheart for the love of her.

If you come to catch me and frighten me,
I shall turn into a doe in the deep woods.
Cleric, you will not even have a corner of my heart.

If you turn into a doe, as you just mentioned,
I shall be a hunter, o my sweet love!
I shall hunt my sweetheart for the love of her.

If you come to hunt me and risk murdering me
I shall become a nun in a convent.
You will not have my heart, o cruel cleric!

If you become a nun, as you just mentioned,
I shall become a monk, o my sweet love,
I shall come and confess my sweetheart for the love of her.

If you come and confess me, you will cry bitterly.
You will find me in bed, wearing the white mask of death.
I shall not give you my heart, whatever you do.

If I find you in your box bed, wearing the white mask of death,
I shall take Saint Peter's place in Paradise
And open its doors to my sweetheart from Pennanroz.

Death

The beliefs and superstitions which surround death were collected by Anatole le Braz at the very end of the nineteenth century. Although his informants were Breton speakers, we only know of their testimonies and tales through a translation into French which Le Braz published as *La Légende de la mort chez les Bretons armoricains*. Death is personified by the Ankou, a skeleton-like figure wearing a cloak and a wide-brimmed hat, who comes in his squeaking cart to fetch the living and bring them to the other world. However, the distinction between this world and the next is not necessarily clear-cut as many signs and omens allow people to read into the future, some of which are mentioned in the extract from Per Denez's short story, *Kontadenn Bobl*. But death is not necessarily frightening. For some it holds no fear – up to a couple of years ago, the suicide rate in Brittany was the highest in France – for others it brings hope of an inheritance, as in *Tartez an ognon* by Roparz Hemon. This short story is based on a play of words, the Breton word 'sekret' meaning both 'recipe' and 'secret.' The theme of death has also given birth to one of the most hilarious stories ever written in Breton, *Lannevern e kañv* by Jakez Konan.

Anonymous
Buhez Mab den

This long poem comprising fifty-nine stanzas – to which two were added, although their structure makes it plain that they do not belong to it – is one of the best example of middle Breton poetry. According to Roparz Hemon, it was probably composed in the XVth century but its source remains unknown. It first appeared in print in 1530. Being a succession of reflections on death, it brings to mind François Villon's 'Le Grand Testament', composed in the fifteenth century, although there is no ground to suggest that it was inspired by it. This poem is particularly remarkable for the richness and refinement of its versification. It follows the rules of middle-

Breton prosody, making use of a sophisticated system of internal rhymes as well as the end of line rhymes.

There are eight feet in each stanza. The end of line rhymes follow the pattern 'aabccb'. Each line contains either an internal rhyme repeated three times or two internal rhymes, each repeated twice. The main or penultimate rhyme in line 3 is the same as the final rhyme of lines 1 and 2; that of line 6 echoes the final rhyme of lines 4 and 5. Furthermore, the final rhyme of line 1 of the following stanza is usually the same as the 6th line of the previous stanza.

The perfectly formed thirtieth stanza runs thus:

Maz soyche den certen en bet	$- - -d - d\,d\;a$
Bout en iffern en cernn bernet	$- - - e - e\,e\;a$
En tan manet, hep guelet Doe	$-f\!f\,a - - a\;b$
Ha bezaf ret bepret seder	$- - - g - g\,g\;c$
Dre e blam iffam pep amser	$- - h - h - h\;c$
Ober a Luciffer he roe	$- c - - - c\,c\;b$

Key:
a = et, b = oe, c = er, d = en, e = ern, f = an, g = red, h = am

[If man thought seriously [when] in the world
that he would be in hell's circle thrown
to stay in fire, without seeing God,
and that he would have for eternity
through his fault, infamous at all times,
to call his king Lucifer ...]

The rhymes being lost in translation, we only present here a short extract taken from the beginning of the poem, to give an idea of its content. In the Middle Ages and for some time afterwards corpses were buried in or around the church. After seven years they were dug up, the bones were gathered and put in the parish ossuary, an open-work stone building which stood within the church enclosure.

Goude da stat ha pompadou
Guyscamant ha paramantou
Ez duy an Anquou ez louen
Pan troy enhaf da lazaff mic
Maz duy da neuz da bout euzic
Ha tristidic da bizhuyquen

Pan vezo da quic maru myc yen
Ne deux car oar an douar certen

Me-dest nac estren nep heny
Na tud da ty na da priet
Na ve mar dyspar ez carset
En deurffe quet da guelet muy

Iuez dan pret maz decedy
Guenez oar da chouc ne douguy
Nemet hep muy un coz lyen
Penheny ez vezy griet
Tizmat a lum ha dastumet
Tra en bet nez vezo quet quen

Goude se en douar oar da huen
Ez laquaher pan duy an termen
Mar cazr na quen oas a quenet
Eno coff ha quenyn ez breiny
Treyt ha penn hac ez dispenny
Lagat ha fry ha goaziet

Dou pe try glyzen tremenet
Treyt ha penn ez vyzy tennet
Certen ne ves quet leset muy
Ha ne goffe styn az lynez
Euyt da sellet a het dez
Pa ez lamer an bez pyou vezy […]

Ne gueus a nep stil quen abil ve
Na quen ruset diouz an beure
Pan ve quement den so en bet
A aznaffe querent diouz hentez
Na breuzr diouz hoar dre nep oarez
Ha pan vez en bez gouruezet

Tranalation

The Life of Man (Extract)

After your pride and vanity,
Lovely clothes and finery,
Death will eagerly come
In its own time, to kill you dead.
Your look will become repulsive
And sad for evermore.

When your flesh is dead, cold, icy
No one on earth, be sure of it,
I say it loud, be they strangers or friends,
Servants or spouse,
Whatever love they felt for you,
Would wish to see you anymore.

Besides, at the hour of your death,
On your shoulders there will only be
A miserable piece of cloth
In which you will be sewn up
Quickly, crudely until wrapped up;
You will not have anything else.

After which, in the ground, on your back
You will be put when the time comes;
However great and radiant your former beauty,
There, your belly and your back will rot,
Your feet and head will decompose,
Your eyes, your nose and your veins too.

Two or three years later,
You will be dug up, feet to head;
You won't be given longer, certainly;
And your relatives will not know who you are,
Should they look at you during a whole day,
When you are taken out of the grave. [...]

There is no one, however skilled he may be,
However wise since his very first day,
There is no one in the whole world
Who would recognise his parents from his friends,
His brother from his sister, in any way,
When one is lying in the grave.

Per Denez

Kontadenn bobl, *1953*

"Ma kontan deoc'h kement-se dre ar munud, Aotrou Barner, n'eo ket peogwir am eus aon eus ho kastiz. Ne vern din petra vezo graet. Ne vern din e vefen kondaonet d'ar marv. En enep. C'hoant am eus mervel. Ha kalz aesoc'h eo bezañ kaset gant ar re all betek ar chafod eget mont c'hwi-hoc'h-un e penn ar chaoser pe skoul-

mañ c'hwi-hoc'h-un ul las en-dro d'ho koug. Nann. Ho kastiz ne vern din tamm ebet. Pezh a garfen hepken eo ober deoc'h kompren. Evit netra. Just evit ober deoc'h kompren.

Kaer am eus avat, ne gomprenit ket. Moarvat ne c'hellit ket kompren. N'oc'h ket eus hor bro, setu! N'oc'h ket eus hor gouenn. Zoken pa vevit en hon touez abaoe keit all, n'oc'h ket eus hon tud. C'hwi n' hoc'h eus morse klevet karrig an Ankou o vont e-biou d'ho ti, kia? Pe, kentoc'h ha gwashoc'h, c'hwi n'hoc'h eus morse klevet ho mamm o tisplegañ e oa tremenet karrig an Ankou un noz dirak toull he dor, hag e oa bet kollet he gwaz er mor an deiz war-lerc'h. Me 'm eus klevet, Aotrou Barner, ouzhpenn ur wech. Ha pa veze lavaret an istor e welen, ouzh flammadeg an tan, stumm treut an ankou o tispakañ er milouer er penn all eus ar gambr, hag e stagen da youc'hal. Ar re all a youc'he ivez pa ouient petra am boa gwelet, hag an amezeien a yae kuit buan eus an ti en ur ober sin ar groaz.

Mousc'hoarzhiñ a rit, Aotrou Barner. Koulskoude e lavaran deoc'h ur wech c'hoazh: ma'z on-me kablus evit an dra-se, neuze eo klablus va mamm ivez, ha va zud-kozh, ha tud-kozh va zud-kozh. Va gouenn a-bezh. Va mamm he doa-hi klevet ur c'havell o vont en-dro er c'hrignol. Ha taolit evezh-mat: ne oa kavell ebet eno da luskellat. Padal e kleve anezhañ ha me gleve evelti. Pa savemp gant an dirioù da welout, e tave an trouz diouzhtu. Evel-se e-pad teir nozvezh lerc'h-ouzh-lerc'h. An teirvet nozvezh e oa deut Matilig ar Burev Tabok da gousket ganeomp, kement e oamp spontet. Ha pa oamp-ni o selaou trouz ar c'havell o vont en-dro, ingal-ingal e lusk, setu ma teuas un dra bennak, pe unan bennak, da skeiñ ouzh ar prenestr. Teir gwech diouzh renk. Evel ma skoan amañ gant va biz war an daol, Aotrou Barner. Piv, pe betra, oa deut, n'hon eus gouezet morse. Pa voemp disouezhet e oa tavet trouz ar c'havell er c'hrignol, ha va breur bihan a oa marv en e wele. Evel-se oa.

Ni hon eus gouezet atav pa oa unan bennak eus hon ti o vont da vervel. C'hwi ivez, a lavaroc'h. Met ar medisin an hini eo a lavare deoc'h: "Ho tonton kozh ne bado ket pell", hag ar familh a vire un devezh dieub evit an obidoù. Ar marv a zeue deoc'h en un doare sioul, rakwelet, a-wechoù gortozet. Evel un dibenn d'ar vuhez. Ganeomp-ni n'eo morse ar marv un dibenn d'ar vuhez: met un troc'h er vuhez. Mamm va zad a oa bet tapet klañv o walc'hiñ el lenn ha n'he doa ket bet amzer zoken da zegas he lien d'ar gêr. He zri bugel brasañ o doa ranket sammañ anezhi diwar an hent. Ma, an dud a ouie c'hoazh. Ne ouient ket piv a oa o vont da vervel. Met gouzout a raent e oa unan bennak eus ar familh o vont da dremen en tu all. Eizhtez a-raok e oa bet ul liñser e-kreiz al leurenn dirak an ti. Chanig an Intañvez ha Maouez ar Stilhogenned o doa gwelet anezhi pa oant o tont en-dro d'ar gêr eus ar fritur. Loar-gann a oa: tu ebet da faziañ. Ha zoken e oa ur bernig mein e pep korn anezhi d'he derc'hel displeg-mat.

Ober a rit goap, Aotrou Barner. Neuze, lavarit din perak am eus graet an dra-se? Gouzout a rit mat n'am boa ket kasoni. Gouzout a rit mat n'am eus ket kasoni. Karout a raen anezhañ kalz, ar paotrig kaezh. Bemdez e teue d'ar gêr da c'hoari gant va mab. Pe neuze ez ae va mab da c'hoari gantañ. Evel daou vreur e oant. Evel daou vreur. Met setu, ne oant ket daou vreur. Hag ur vamm a chom atav ur vamm. Ha mouezh ar gwad, Aotrou Barner, a vez atav kreñvoc'h.

An tonkadur, petra 'reoc'h, a zo an tonkadur, a rank an holl plegañ d'e grizder. Ha kement-se a oa tonket adal an deiz kentañ. Adalek deiz ar vadeziant, da lavarout mat. Ne gomprenan ket penaos e c'hell an dud ober seurt sotonioù. Met diouzhtu p'am eus klevet kement-se am eus gouezet e oa un droug bennak da c'hoarvezout. Hag a-benn ar fin ez eo c'hoarvezet. Klañvidik e oa bet, ar paotrig kaezh all, abaoe an derou, e-skoaz va bugel-me hag a oa ur mell babig, tev ka kreñv; met pa c'hoarveze d'am mab kouezhañ klañv – c'hwi oar, Aotrou Barner, ar vugale vihan a vez atav un dra bennak o c'hoari ganto – neuze e seblante egile kemer nerzh ha liv. Evel pa vije bet ur yec'hed hepken da rannañ etrezo. Dres: evel pa vije bet ur yec'hed hepken evito o-daou, d'unan d'e ziaoueriñ pa oa gant egile.

Nann, ne gomprenan ket penaos e c'hell an dud ober seurt sotonioù. Rak e vamm an hini eo a zo kaoz eus pep tra. Lakaet he doa en he fenn bezañ maeronez em zi. Me a oa laouen evel just o kaout anezhi da gomer, peogwir e oa-hi an hini diwezhañ deut er familh. Met neuze, ranket he dije lavarout din. Ne vijen ket bet feuket. Klasket am bije un all. Kavet am bije un all. Forzh petra a vije bet gwelloc'h eget sammañ war hon daou vugel un tonkadur ken spontus. O, kannet am bije anezhi pa 'm eus klevet ar c'heloù. N'he doa digarez ebet. Hi a ouie mat. Hi a ouie mat e varv unan eus an daou vugel pa vez dougerez ar vaeronez.

Bremañ e vefe gwelloc'h din tevel. Rak ar pezh a lavarin a gomprenoc'h nebeutoc'h c'hoazh. Met peogwir on krog da gontañ n'eus nemet kenderc'hel. E-pad daou zevezh e oa bet va mab gant ar ronkell. Ne ouie ket ar vedisined petra en doa. Unan a lavare e oa an droug en e benn, un all en e skevent. Sotonioù. Me, ar vamm, a ouie avat petra oa. Ha koulskoude e chomen kalonek. Mougañ 'rae va bugelig: glas e teue va zremm da vezañ hag e zaoulagad a ziskoueze ar gwenn anezho en un doare spontus. Ha koulskoude e chomen kalonek. Gouzout a ouien petra oa d'ober evit saveteiñ anezhañ. Met kalonek e chomen. Gwelloc'h e oa din kaout poan eget ober poan d'ar re all. Gwelloc'h eo din lezel va bugel da vervel, gwelloc'h e lezel da vervel, a lavaren dibaouez, da gas ar soñjoù aloubus diwar va spered. C'hwi 'wel e oan kalonek, Aotrou Barner. Ha n'eo ket va fazi m'eo deut he mab dezhi, d'ar vaeronez, betek va zi pa oa va bihanig o vont da dremen. N'eo ket me a oa bet o klask anezhañ. Gouzout a ouien e vije aet va c'halonegezh diganin m'am bije e welet. Hag aet eo va c'halonegezh diganin p'am eus e welet o tont, ruz e zivjod gwechall divliv, o sankañ e zent en un aval trenk, eñ hag a veze atav hep c'hoant ebet da zebriñ tra. Ha c'hwi, Aotrou Barner, a vije chomet kalonek, ma vije bet ho mab gant ar ronkell abaoe daou zevezh? Ha c'hwi a c'hell lavarout e vijec'h chomet kalonek? Me a ouie petra 'm bije graet m'am bije gwelet anezhañ. Ha pezh a ouien am eus graet. E lazhet 'm eus, Aotrou Barner.

Ya, gouzout a ran petra lavaroc'h. "Ha padal, ho mab a zo marv." Gwir, va mab a zo marv. Met se zo un dra all. Pa oamp o tont en-dro eus e vadeziant hor boa kejet gant interamant Luiz Marot o vont d'an iliz: neuze e ouien e oa tonket va mab da vervel yaouank-flamm. Klasket am eus hepken e virout un nebeut bloavezhioù pel-

loc'h. C'hwitet am eus. Atav am bez c'hwitet gant pezh a ran. Boas e veze va mamm da lavarout n'am bije morse chañs: ur groaz du he doa gwelet an amiegez war va c'havell pa oa o vont da lakaat ac'hanon e-barzh, ha me nevez-c'hanet. Ne fazie ket va mamm baour. Morse ne fazier war ar seurt traoù. Rak, e gwirionez, Aotrou Barner, den ne c'hello lavarout, den ebet avat, e ouzon petra eo kaout chañs."

Translation

Folk-Tale

"If I tell you all this in detail, Your Honour, it isn't that I am afraid of your sentence. I don't care what will be done. I don't mind being condemned to death. It's the opposite. I want to die. And it's easier to be sent to the scaffold by others than go yourself to the end of the jetty or tie a rope around your own neck. No. I don't care what your sentence will be. I'd just like to make you understand. That's all. Just make you understand.

Yet, however much I try, you don't understand. Indeed, you can't understand. You're not from this neck of the woods, that's all! You're not one of our people. Even though you've been living among us for a long time, but you're not one of us. You've never heard the Cart of Death pass by your house, have you? What's more, what's worse, you've never heard your mother explain that the Cart of Death passed in front of the door of her house, and that her husband was lost at sea the following day. I have heard that, Your Honour, more than once. And every time someone retold the story, I used to see, in the light of the fire, the thin shape of the Ankou appearing in the mirror at the other end of the room, and I started screaming. The others screamed too, when they knew what I'd seen, and the neighbours hurried out of the house, making the sign of the cross.

You smile, Your Honour. However, let me tell you once more: if I am guilty, then so are my mother, my grand-parents and my grand-parents' grand-parents. All my people are guilty. As for my mother, she had heard a cradle rocking in the attic. And listen! There was no cradle there to make that noise. And yet she heard it, and I heard it too. When we climbed the stairs to go and have a look, the noise stopped immediately. That happened three nights in a row. The third night, Matilig the newsagent came to sleep in our house, we were so frightened. And as the two of us were listening to the noise of the cradle rocking to and fro, gently and regularly, something or rather someone, came to knock on the window. Three times in a row. Just as I knock now on this table with my finger, Your Honour. We never knew who or what had come. When we came back to our senses, the noise of the cradle had stopped in the attic, and my little brother was lying dead in his bed. That's what happened.

We've always known when one of the family was about to die. You too, you'll say. But that was because the doctor had told you: 'Your old uncle won't last long,' and that way, the family knew to keep a day aside for the funeral. Death comes to you in a quiet, predictable way. You sometimes expect it. For you, it's an end to life.

For us, death has never been an end to life. It's a break in life. My father's mother fell ill when we was doing her washing at the lake and she didn't even have time to bring her washing home. Her three older children had to collect her body from the road. In those days, people still knew. They didn't know who was going to die, but they knew that someone in the family was going to pass away. The previous week a sheet had been spread out in the front yard of the house. Widow Chanig and the woman who tins the squids had seen it on their way home from the canning factory. The moon was full. No way could they be mistaken. And what's more, there was a little pile of stones on each corner to make it stay flat.

You're laughing at me, Your Honour. Well then, tell me why I did it? You know well that I wasn't bearing a grudge. You know well that I am not bearing a grudge. I loved him a lot, the poor little mite! Everyday he used to come and play with my son. Or else my son went to his house to play with him. They were like two brothers. Like two brothers. But then, they were not brothers, and a mother is always a mother. Blood, Your Honour, is thicker than water. Blood always wins.

Fate, you see, is fate, and everyone must bow to its cruelty. What happened was meant to happen from the very first day. From the day of the christening, to be precise. I don't know how people can do such stupid things. But as soon as I heard it, I knew something bad would happen. In the end it did happen. Since the very day of his birth, he had been sickly, the other little boy I mean, compared to my own child who was a chubby, big and strong baby; but when my son happened to be ill – you know, Your Honour, little children always have something going wrong with them – it looked as if the other was gaining in strength and colour. It was as if there was only one health between the two of them. That's it. As if there was only one health for both of them and one of them would have to do without when the other had it.

No, I don't understand how people can do such stupid things. Because it's his mother who's responsible for all this. She'd got it into her head that she wanted to be the godmother of one of my children and I was happy with that, of course, since she was the last one to join the family. But then she should have told me. I wouldn't have been offended. I'd have looked for another one. I'd have found another one. Whatever, it would have been better than to burden our two children with such a terrible fate. Oh, I could have beaten her when I heard the news. There was no excuse. She knew it well. She knew that one of the two children was bound to die if the godmother was pregnant.

It would be better if I stopped talking now. Because what I'll say, you'll understand even less. But I've started to tell my tale and I'll carry on. My son had not been able to breathe freely for two whole days. The doctors didn't know what was wrong with him. One said there was something wrong with his brain, another one with his lungs. The fools! I, his mother, knew very well what it was. And yet, I was strong. My little one was suffocating, his face was turning blue, and the whites of his eyes were awful to see. And yet I was strong. I knew very well what to do to save him. But I stayed strong. It was better to feel pain than to inflict pain on others. It was better to let my child die, yes, better to let him die, that's what I told myself over and over again as I tried to keep the awful thought away from my mind. You see how strong I was, Your Honour. Well, was it my fault if her son, the godmother's son, came to my house, just as my little one was about to pass away? I hadn't gone to get him. I knew very well I'd lose my courage if I happened to see him. And I lost my courage when I saw him, him and his rosy cheeks that used to be so pale, and what's more, he was biting into a juicy apple, although he never used to want to eat anything. Tell me, Your Honour, would you have stayed strong if your son had been suffocating for the past two days? Could you truly say that you would have stayed strong? I knew exactly what I would do if I happened to see him. And that's just what I did. I killed him, Your Honour.

Yes, I know what you'll say: 'But your son is dead'. It's true, my son is dead. But that's something else. When we were on our way back from the christening, we met Luiz Marot's funeral party going to church. That's how I knew that my son was destined to die very young. I was only trying to keep him for a few more years. I failed. Whatever I try I fail. My mother used to say that I would never be lucky, because the midwife had seen a black cross on my cradle when she was about to put me down in it, just after my birth. My dear mother never made mistakes with this sort of things. And to tell the truth, Your Honour, nobody, yes, nobody, can say that I know what it is like to be lucky."-

---

Per-Jakez Helias

Marh al lorh, *1986* (Lodenn)

N'eo ket gantañ e c'hoarvezas an taol, gant eur henderv dezañ a zo bet lazet er brezel pevarzeg ne lavaran ket. Bugel oa c'hoaz ar henderv-ze pa welas o tond d'e di an noz a-raog gouel an Anaon, eul labourer-douar anavezet gantañ, Tiñ ar Halvez, koumananter eun tammig feurm tostig aleze. Dislivet an den ha skeulfet, diouest da ranna ger da gentan. Hasta reas tud an ti da ginnig dezañ eur banne hini kreñv. Hag eñ o naha gant e zorn. Greet oe dezañ azeza war ar bank. Pa gavas e deod adarre e oe da lavared e-noa gwelet an Ankou e-pad ma oa war e vern kolo, da vad o kelhia anezañ gand neud-orjal war-bouez mein da viroud ouz an avel d'e gas ganti. Hag an Ankou e-noa sellet outañ beteg strad e zaoulagad gand e voullo goullo. Ne ouie ket penaoz e-noa greet evid tehoud kuit, med asur oa dezañ e oa dalhmad an Ankou o klask anezañ. Dibaouez e lavare kaoud yen. Tro all ebed dezañ d'en em denna digand pourvezer ar maro, hervezañ, nemed derhel peg e dorn eun bennag beobuhezeg. E gwir, paket e-noa dioustu dorn mestr an ti ha ne zispege ket ken dioutañ. Tremen a reas eur boutadig amzer. Ar re all a ree o zeiz gwella evid dizoania ar paour-kêz den, med ne oa netra d'ober hag int o-unan en em zante gounezet gant eun enkrez disklêr. War eun taol trumm, Tiñ ar Halvez a stagas da grial: "Eñ an hini eo! Emañ o tond! Ha kleved a rit ar harr o wigourad? Ha kleved a rit ar moueziou diniver endro dezañ o kana kantik an Ivern? Perak an Ivern? Ar Purgator ne lavaran ket, med an Ivern! Ne fell ket din mond ennañ. Dalhit ahanon stard!"

Diêz-tre oa d'ar re all derhel anezañ dre ma tispahe gant nerz daou pe dri, int o-unan a daole c'hwezenn an doan ha padal ne glevent netra, nag eun disterra trouz mouez pe garr. Ken pell e padas an taol ma oa brevet o divreh ganto. Ha goude-ze an den en em lezas da vond gant eun huanadenn hir: "Eet int kuit, emezañ". Neuze eh asantas lonka eur mell banne lambig ha kuit d'ar gêr goude trugarez d'ar gompagnunez.

Hogen, setu amañ ar haerra tra. Antronoz e teuas ar helou e oa kouezet Tiñ ar Halvez a-ziwar e vern kolo, an derhent, eun tammig a-raok serr-noz. Douget e oa bet beteg e wele. A-boan ma tenne e alan, ne fiñve ket eun disterra. E-doug an noz e oa chomet er stad-ze, beillet gand e dud. Da houlou-deiz e oa deut endro d'e benn ha bremañ e oa war e labour evel kustum. Med penaoz e oa bet posubl d'eur familh a-bez gweled anezañ, pell a-walh euz e di, e-pad an arvest a zo bet kontet? Penaoz e oa bet gouest da waska ken stard dorn ar mestr ma oa eet e ivinou tre er palv? Disklêriadur ebed. © Plon, 1986

Translation

The Horse of Pride, *1986* (Extract)

The misadventure did not happen to him but to one of his cousins who was killed in the first world war. This cousin was still a child when, on the evening preceding All Souls' Day, he saw Tiñ ar C'halvez, a farmer of his acquaintance who leased a small neighbouring farm, come into his house. The man's face was white and drawn, and at first he could not utter a single word. The people of the house rushed to offer him a glass of brandy, but he waved the suggestion aside. He was told to sit on the bench. When he recovered his speech, he said that he had seen the Ankou when he was tying his rick of straw with a wire weighed down by stones to prevent it from being blown away by the wind. The Ankou had looked deep into his eyes through his empty sockets. He did not know how he managed to escape, but he was sure the Ankou was still searching for him. He kept on saying that he was feeling cold. The only way to escape from the death messenger, he said, was to keep hold of the hand of some living person. In fact, he had immediately taken the hand of the master of the house and was not letting go of it. This lasted quite a while. The others were doing their very best to comfort the poor man, but it was to no avail and they themselves were beginning to feel a kind of vague apprehension. Suddenly, Tiñ ar C'halvez screamed: "There he is! He is coming! Do you hear the cart squeaking? Do you hear all these voices around him singing the Hymn of Hell? Why Hell? Purgatory maybe, but Hell! I don't want to go there. Keep hold of me!"

This was very hard for the others to do so as he had the strength of two or three men in him and was struggling hard. They themselves were sweating with fear and yet they could hear nothing that might resemble a voice or the noise of a cart. The tussle lasted so long that their arms were aching all over. Finally the man relaxed and breathed a sigh of relief: "They have gone," he said. He then agreed to drink a large glass of brandy, thanked the company and went home.

But the story does not end there. The following morning, the news came that Tiñ ar C'halvez had fallen off his rick of straw the previous day, shortly before sunset and was carried to his bed. He could hardly breathe and was unable to move. During the night, there was no change in his condition as his family kept watch over him. By early morning he had recovered consciousness and he was now working as usual. But how is it that a whole family had seen him, quite a way from his home, during the incident I have just described? How was it that he had been able to squeeze his master's hand so hard that his nails had left marks on his palms? No explanation can be offered.

Meavenn

An Ankou, *1933*

> Perak o deus lakaet eur stumm spontus warnout?
> N'out ket divalo,
> N'out ket doanius,
> Dianav hepken.
>
> Eun nor out
> A zigor,
> Ar vro gevrinus a vo hon hini.
>
> Ma rankfen mervel a-benn eur bloaz
> Ar bloaz-se 'vefe va bloaz kaera,
>
> Betek an devez
> Diweza,
> Goustad, goustadik,
> Me a vevfe
> 'N eur sellout ouz pep tra,
> 'N eur garout pep den.
>
> Mervel,
> Petra eo se?
> N'ouzon ket,
> Ha dare oun da vont kuit.

Translation

L'Ankou, *1933*

> Why are you made out to be fearsome
> You are not ugly;

You are not distressing,
Just unknown.

You are a door
Which opens up
The secret land which will be our land.

If I were to die in a year's time
That year would be my very best year.

Until the very last day,
Slowly, so slowly,
I would live
Looking at everything,
Loving all men.

To die.
What is it like?
I don't know
But I am ready to go.

Fañch Peru

Ar Vuoc'h Zu, *1985*

– "D'an ospital?"

– "Ya, d'an ospital eo red deoc'h mont, Lom. Gwashaad a ra ho kleñved, hag amañ ho-hunan epad ar gouañv! Nann, n'eo ket mad deoc'h chom er gêr. En ospital e vo tommder, boued d'ar c'houlz, tud oc'h ober war ho tro..."

– "D'an ospital!" a lavaras Lom ur wech c'hoazh, a vouezh isel.

– "Ya," eme ar medissin en ur vont er maes.

Pa oa aet ar medissin kuit e chomas Lom ur pennad amzer hanter vatorellet en e goasez douzh taol. Dewezhier e oa er Genkis, ur menaj bras e parres Kerwern. Mont a rae bemdez d'e labour kerkent hag an deiz ha diouzh an nos e teue en-dro araog koan d'ar Genkis vihan, ur penn-ti a oa bet prestet dehañ gant perc'henn ar Genkis Vras. Paotr yaouank kozh e oa chomet, daoust dehañ da vezañ bet war zimeziñ diw pe deir gwech, ha setu e vewe e-hunanig-penn en e damm ti bihan.

Mont d'ar bourk gwech ha gwech all da evañ ur chopinad ha da brenañ un tamm butun pe da c'hoari boulloù d'ar sul goude merenn, sell ase e oll blijadurioù war an tamm douar-mañ. Hirie, justamant, en doa ezomm da vont da gerc'had butun. Hag eñv da sevel diouzh taol ha da gerzhed war hent Kerwern.

Pa oa erru e ostaleri vihan ar bourk e oa gwersed douzh ar c'hontouer, beb a vannac'h gwin gante.

– "Ale, Lom, mad an traoù ganit?" eme ar wersed.

– "Derc'hel da vont," a respontas hemañ a vouezh isel.

– "Petra zo newez ganit?" a c'houlennas Anna, an ostises.

– "Nebeud a dra, Anna, nemed traoù kozh! Ro din, mar plij, ur pakad butun hag ur bannac'h gwin ruz, hag iwe ur vuoc'h du da gass ganin d'ar gêr."

Goût awalc'h a ouie Anna petra a oa ur vuoc'h du ha setu e lakas ur voutailhad 'Grappillru' war ar c'hontouer.

Lom a lonkas e vannac'h, a zastumas ar pakad butun en e c'hodell gleiz hag ar voutailhad 'Grappillru' en e c'hodell zehoù, hag eñ er maes. Klouar e oa an abardaez-nos. E dibenn mis Gwengolo e oamp, achu e oa an eost abaoe pell dija, ha tostaad a rae koulz an eost all, eost ar mais. Neuse avad e vo press ha mesk adarre er Genkis pa zeuio ar c'houlz da serriñ ar mais drailhet a vunudoù, gant ar mekanik. Nos ha deiz e vo klewet war ar maes safar an trakteurien o tont hag o vont gant o c'hirri leun-chouk eus ar geot glas-se malet d'ober boued gouañv d'al loened.

Lom a gerzhe war vord an hent bihan don dindan sklàerder al loar gwall gàer en nos-se. A beb tu d'an hent an targossioù divarret a seblante bezañ soudarded distumm un arme ramzed. Ne oa ket bet adlodennet c'hoazh an douaroù er barres, ha setu e chome ar gwez hag ar c'hleuzioù en o sav sonn.

O vont gant e hent etreseg ar gêr, e klewe Lom mouezh ar medissin o lâred dehañ bepred: "Red e vo deoc'h mont d'an ospital, Lom!"

Arru er gêr, digoret gantañ dor e di bihan, e roas Lom ur bannac'h laezh d'ar c'hazh loued a oa asezet war an oaled. Goude e tennas deus e c'hodell ar pakad butun newez prenet er bourk hag ur c'harned paper O.C.B. Neuse, war e boues ha gant ampartis ur butuner kozh e stummas e sigaretenn etre bis meud ha bis yod. Ur wech achu ha tanet ar sigaretenn e tiskargas Lom ur volennad 'Grappillru' hag e lonkas anehi en un taol, hag un all c'hoazh hag un all.

A greis oll en em lakae da ganañ komzoù kentañ kantik Sant Erwan:

"Na n'eus ket en Breizh,
Na n'eus ket unan,
Na n'eus ket ur sant,
Evel sant Erwan"

Ha goude e lonke ur volennad win adarre.

Pa voe dizolo ar roc'hell e foñs ar voutailh, e tapas dewezhier ar Genkis Vras ur pennad kordenn e traoñ an ti hag henn stagas douzh plankenn ar bara e-kichen ar prenest goude bezañ gwraet ur skoulm-red er gordenn.

Distreiñ a reas da benn an daol ewid peurriñsañ ar voutailhad win. Goude-se e sachas ur wech c'hoazh war e bennad sigaretenn ha neuse, goustadig, e tosteas douzh ar prenest hag e lakeas e benn er groug....

"Klewet hon oa anehañ o kanañ wardro deg eur da nos," eme an ameseien en deiz warlerc'h.

Translation

A Bottle of the Usual, *1985*

"To hospital?"

"Yes, Lom, you need to go to hospital. Your disease is getting worse. Here you are, on your own, and what with winter coming! Staying at home won't do you any good. In hospital, you will have heat, meals at the proper times, people to look after you…"

"To hospital," murmured Lom once again.

"Yes," said the doctor as he left.

The doctor gone, Lom sat for a while longer at the table, in shock. He was a day labourer at Kenkiz, a large farm in the village of Kerwern. Everyday he went to work at day-break and returned before dinner-time to Little Kenkiz, a cottage which he rented from the owner of Great Kenkiz. Although he had been on the verge of getting married two or three times, he had stayed single and now lived by himself in his tiny house.

His only earthly pleasures were to go to the village once in a while, to have a drink and buy tobacco or to play bowls after Sunday lunch. Today, as it happened, he needed to go and get some tobacco. He got up from the table and set on his way towards Kerwern.

When he arrived at the small village inn, a few men were standing at the bar, drinking wine.

"Hello, Lom, is everything alright?" they greeted him.

"I'm fine," he replied in a low voice.

"So, what have you got to say for yourself?" asked Anna, the bar-owner.

"Nothing much, Anna, nothing new! Please give me packet of tobacco, a glass of red wine, and a bottle of the usual to take home.

Anna knew very well what his usual was, and she put a bottle of 'Grappille rouge' on the counter.

Lom drank his glass, put the tobacco packet in his left pocket, the bottle of red wine in his right one and went on his way. The evening was warm. It was the end of September. The main harvest had been gathered a few weeks ago but the corn would soon be ready to be harvested. There would be plenty of comings and goings at Kenkiz as it prepared for the corn-mincing machine. Night and day he would hear the noise of the tractors crisscrossing the countryside with their trailers overflowing with the chopped green corn leaves used as winter cattle fodder.

Lom was walking on the edge of the sunken narrow road by the light of the brightly shining moon. On each side of the road, the branchless pollards looked like the misshapen soldiers of an army of giants. The trees and embankments were still in place as the village fields had not yet been regrouped.

On the way back, Lom could hear the doctor's voice saying to him again and again: "You'll need to go to hospital, Lom!"

On getting home, he opened the door of his cottage and gave a saucer of milk to

the grey cat sitting on the hearth. He then took out of his pocket the tobacco packet he had just bought in the village and a packet of O.C.B cigarette paper. Taking his time, but with the expertise of a confirmed smoker, he shaped a cigarette between his thumb and index finger. He then lit it and poured himself a bowlful of 'Grappille rouge' which he drank in one go. This was followed by another, and yet another.

Suddenly he started singing the opening verses of the hymn to Saint Yves:

'No, there isn't in Brittany,
There isn't another
There isn't a saint
Like Saint Yves.'

After which he drank another bowlful of wine.

When the dimple in the bottle appeared, the day worker of Great Kenkiz fetched a piece of rope from the other end of the house, made a slipknot in it and attached it to the bread plank above the window.

He walked back to the other end of the table and drank the dregs of the bottle. He then took another puff at his cigarette, walked slowly up to the window and put his head in the slipknot.

"We heard him singing at about 10 pm last night," said the neighbours on the following day.

Jakez Riou

Ur Barr-avel, *1934* (Lodenn)

Evit an trede gwech ar marc'hadour a c'hoarias en dro d'al loen.
– N'eus ket distaol?
– N'eus ket.
– Distaol kant lur.
– Daouzek kant em eus lavaret.
Ar marc'hadour a hejas e benn, hag a reas an asvan da bellaat.
– Unnek kant, emezañ en ur zistreiñ.
– Kant ouzhpenn.
– Disteurel a ri.... Unnek kant hanter?
– Boued a zo dezhañ er gêr.
Ar marc'hadour a dremenas e zorn war gein al loen, a-c'hin d'ar blev.
– Gra dezhañ redek un tregont kammed, emezañ.
An ebeul a rede skouer.
– Derc'hel a rez da briz?
– Ya.
– Kerik mat eo. Prez a zo warnon. Dao.
Palv o dorn dehou a stlakas an eil ouzh egile, div wech.

Graet e oa marc'had.

– Stag al loen, aze, ouzh tal an ti, ha deomp da evañ ur banne ha da renkañ ar gont.

Yann a selle ouzh ar bilhedoù o tarzhañ dirak e zaoulagad, displeget unan hag unan. Pa gontas: daouzek, e santas e galon skañvaet.

Evit mil lur en dije roet e loen.

Yann ar C'herneis a ziskenne eus marc'had ar c'hezeg. E galon a lamme taeroc'h eget kustum, ha, da heul lammoù e galon, priz ar marc'had tonket.

Lakaat a reas e zorn en e c'hodell evit meudañ ar bilhedoù ha klevout kan ar paper kras:

.... Ar skouarn.... ar rod ... An ahel... ...

– Echu ar foar, Yann?
– Echu, Herve. Ha ganit?
– Ne rin ket foar hiziv. Edon e soñj prenañ ur vuoc'h... Keraouez a zo war ar saout. Eus ur vuoc'hig e c'houlenner eizh kant lur. Ken din bezañ deut d'ar foar diwezhañ!... Evit ar priz-se em bije bet an dibab...
– N'em eus ket d'en em glemm. Koulskoude, gant ur miz all er c'hraou...
– ...

Ar c'harr a vezo rodet hag ahelet, hag an alar en devo ur skouarn nevez.

An abardaez oa klouar. Frond an nevez-amzer dastumet gant an avel en ur dremen dre ar parkoù, a nije a-dreuz kêr, a gaouadoù skañv. Ne bare mui an heol er straedoù. Harpet edo e sklerijenn gant turumell serz ar C'hastell. Bannoù en em sile e gwez al lein; an delioù, heoliet, a denne da laboused aour.

Tuf an tornaod gozh a voukae. Tren peder eur a c'hwitellas war bont Kerlobred. Gweturioù ar marc'had a rede etre ar plataned dizeil war-du Sant-Kouli ha war-du Meilhvern. Skeud an abardaez a c'houneze koad menez Bann-Nin, hag an heol o tiskenn, a enaoue war an diribin enep, aour al lann ha tan ar brug.

Pe soñj a zeuas da Yann ar C'herneis? Peseurt menoz diboell a reas dezhañ arseviñ war bont Kastellin? Peseurt planedenn yud a grogas en e zorn hag a reas dezhañ kemer e vilhedoù bank, hag o dispakañ war an aspled?... A-boan ma edont dispaket, ur barr-avel a c'hwezhas hag o skubas er stêr.

Izeloc'hik e trouze ar skluz...

Dizaon ouzh treid ar c'hezeg, ouzh kerniel ar saout, ouzh rodoù ar c'hirri, Yann a dreuz ar pont en ur redadenn, hag a vount kement den a ziwar e hent. Ur gwaz a grog en e chupenn hag a glask e harpañ. Yann e wint ouzh ur maen bennerezh.

Emañ dreist!...

M'emañ ket. Yann a c'hourvez ouzh moger ar stêr, evel taget gant ur pistig. E arc'hant a zo aet dreist ar skluz, hag e spered da heul.

E-harz ar skluz an dour a verv hag a eonenn ouzh ar c'herreg; pelloc'h e tiskenn lizidour gant paper distrempet, roget, divalvoud, war-du ar mor tost.

Yann ar C'herneis a chome da alvaoniñ ouzh an dour. O welout an dud oc'h en

em vodañ a-dreñv e gein, e teuas mezh dezhañ. Brallañ 'reas war e dreid; e gorf a gostezas war-du ar gêr.

Heuliañ 'reas hent ar stêr vras gant kas ouzh an hentoù darempredet. An dour a oa glas ha don. Aezenn ebet n'he c'hrize d'ar mare. Skeud an elo hag ar pupli gant o bodoù uhelvarr a oa difiñv. Koumoulennoù gwenn a dremene e don an dour. A-boan ma fiche war ar gorre ur bod elestr ha klogorennoù spoum.

En tu dehou, war an hent bras, un diaoul a stleje ur wezenn en istribilh ouzh an ahel. Ar rodoù a storloke hag a zraske war ar vein.

Ahel ha rodoù an diaoul ne dorrint ket.

Gweturioù ar foar a ya d'ar gêr d'an drot. Ur wetur a dremen skañv ha dillo. Un ebeul a zo staget ouzh al lost. Ne glever war an hent bras nemet hern marc'h al loc'hennoù. Saprennoù menez Bann-Nin a zo dilusk ha du.

En tu kleiz, 'harz e dreid, ar stêr a zo skedus ha moredet. An dour a zo touellus hag a sach. Ar c'hoabrennoù a dremen goustadikoc'h er strad ec'honaet.

Dre ma kerzh gant e hent, boud ur skluz all a dosta...

An dour a gan e bouilh an eonenn.

Hegas eo kann ar skluz.

Dre hentoù kozh ha meinek, Yann a dec'h e-giz ul laer.

Tennañ 'ra e dog en ur vont e-biou d'ar groaz.

Tavet eo kan ar skluz.

Ur barr-avel a dremen er gwez kistin.

Pa zegouezhas Yann ar C'herneis er gêr, edo ar wreg er stivell. Yann a ziwiskas e zilhad foar evit bouetañ al loened. Da c'hortoz ur rod nevez, e oa ret choukata bec'hioù geot eus al liorzh a-dreñv.

Yann a gemeras ur gordenn hag e falc'h.

Ar gwez avaloù a oa en o bleuñv. Ar frond tanav skignet el liorzh a oa heskinus en abardaez-noz.

Ar falc'h a skrijas er geot.

– Graet hoc'h eus foar, Yann? eme ur vouezh a-bell.

Yann a reas ul lamm.

– Ya, emezañ.

Ha Mari, o tiskuizhañ e toull ar gloued, a sammas adarre he boutegad dilhad kannet.

C'hwiled a safrone er serr-noz. Un askell-groc'hen a dremenas didrouz war an oabl. Ar girzhier a oa moredet. Ar bokedoù-laezh e tislive o delioù melen er gwrimennoù sin. Ur vogedenn a save eus ar siminal iliavek.

Frond ar geot, frond ar bleunioù, frond ar sev, frond an douar frouezhus a vouskane el liorzh...

Yann ar C'herneis a demmas un alanad hir, a leunias e skevent gant c'hwezoù an nevez-amzer, hag en em stagas ouzh ar groug.

Translation

A Gust of Wind, *1934* (Extract)

For the third time the man scrutinised the foal.
– Won't you give me a better price?
– No.
– A hundred francs less.
– I said twelve hundred francs.
The man shook his head and pretended to walk away.
– Eleven hundred, he said, turning round.
– Add another hundred!
– Surely you'll give me a reduction. How about fifty francs?
– I've got fodder for it at home.

The man stroke the back of the animal, from tail to head.
– Make it run thirty paces, he said.
There was nothing wrong with the foal's trot.
– Are you really keeping to your price?
– Yes.
– It's quite high, but I'm in a hurry. I'll have him.
Their two right hands met noisily, twice. The deal was done.
– Tie the horse over there, in front of the house, and let's go to have a drink and settle the matter.
Yann's eyes were on the banknotes, unfolded one by one, in front of his eyes. When the count of twelve was reached he felt light-headed. He would have sold his horse for a thousand francs!

Yann ar C'herneis was on his way home from the horse fair. His heart was beating faster than usual and each throb reminded him of the banknotes slammed down one by one on the inn's table. He put his hand in his pocket to feel the notes and hear the rustle made by the stiff paper. There was enough there to mend the plough, the wheel and the axle!

– Are you on your way back from the fair, Yann?
– Yes. Did you go to it?
– I did, but didn't get anything. I wanted to buy a cow, but Keraouez was selling and asking eight hundred francs for a small one. If only I had come to the previous fair! For that price I could have taken my pick.
– Well! I have nothing to complain about. However, I wish I could have kept the foal for another month at the farm!

Never mind, he thought. The cart will get a new wheel and a new axle, and the plough will be mended.

In the warmth of the late afternoon, the scents of spring, gathered by the wind in the fields, were blowing in light bursts over the village. The streets were no longer bathed in sunshine as the steep Castle hill blocked its rays. But on high, the sun was playing among the trees, turning their leaves into golden birds.

The shale of the old cliff was turning purple. The four o' clock train whistled on Kerlobred bridge. The market carts, seen between the bare plane trees, were dashing towards Saint-Coulitz and Meilhvern. The evening shadows were reaching the high woods of Bann-Nin and the setting sun was igniting the golden gorse and the blazing heather on the opposite side of the valley.

What went through Yann ar C'herneis's mind? What stupid thought made him stop on Châteaulin bridge? What hand of fate made him take out his banknotes and display them on the parapet? Hardly had they been lined up that a gust of wind lifted them up and tossed them into the river.

Downstream, the sluice gates were humming away.

Taking no notice of the horses' hooves, of the cattle's horns or of the wheels of the carts, Yann ran across the bridge, pushing aside those who were in his way. A man got hold of his jacket and tried to stop him. Yann threw him against a stone pillar.

He's going to jump!

No, he didn't. Yann was lying at the foot of the stone bridge, as if in agony. His money had gone over the lock and he was dismayed.

At the foot of the lock, the water was swirling and foaming against the rocks. A little further on, it was gently carrying towards the sea the soaked, torn, useless strips of paper.

Yann ar C'herneis stared for a while at the water, in shock. He finally noticed the group of people who had gathered behind him and came back to his senses. He steadied himself up and let his feet find the way back towards home.

He followed the river path, avoiding the busy roads. The water was deep and blue. There was no breeze to ruffle its surface now. The reflected image of the poplar-trees crowned with clumps of mistletoe were not moving. Deep in the water, small white clouds were passing by. On the surface the clump of irises and the foam bubbles hardly moved.

On the right, on the main road, a sturdy man was dragging a tree balanced on an axle. Its squeaking wheels made the road crackle.

This axle and those wheels won't break!

The fair carts were returning home. One of them passed by, light and fast. A foal was tied to the back of it. The only noise on the main road was ringing of the older horse's hooves. The pine-trees at the top of Bann-Nin were still and black.

On the left, at his very feet, the shimmering river was sluggish, its water both deceitful and alluring. The clouds were crossing the wider river-bed at a more leisurely pace. . . Further on, the murmur of another lock reached him. The water was singing and the foam dancing. The lock song irritated him.

Yann scampered away like a thief and took to the old stony paths. He took off his cap as he walked by the cross standing at the roadside. The song of the lock stopped. A gust of wind blew through the chestnut trees.

When Yann ar C'herneis reached home, his wife had gone to the spring. Yann took off his Sunday best to feed the cattle. Until he could get a new cart wheel, he had to carry on his back the bundles of the grass cut from the back garden.

Yann went to get a rope and his scythe.

The apple-trees were in blossom. In the late afternoon, their light scent permeated the garden and was annoying.

The scythe screeched through the grass.

– You've done business at the fair, Yann? said a voice far away.

Yann jumped.

– Yes, he said

Mari, who had been taking a rest by the gate, picked up again her washing basket full of clean clothes.

The early evening insects were buzzing. A bat flew silently in the sky. The hedges were sleeping. At the far end of the garden, the yellow primroses were losing their colour.

Smoke was rising from the ivy-clad chimney.

The combined smells of the grass, flowers, sap and fertile earth were whispering in the garden.

Yann ar C'herneis took a deep breath, filled his lungs with the smells of Spring and hanged himself.

Goulc'han Kervella

Ar Gambr Ruz, *1989*

Ar Pommerol eo ar gwin a blij din ar muiañ. Anaoudegezh am eus graet gantañ p'e-don oc'h ober va amzer-soudard e Libourne, damdost da Vourdel. Di eo e vez kaset ar vedisined yaouank e-pad ur miz hanter a-raok bezañ kaset, taol da vor, taol da zouar. An hañv oa anezhi pa'z is da ober va amzer da Libourne. N'on ket mat da chom da louediñ er c'hazarnioù nag e-ser medisined pe soudarded. A-vec'h echu an devezh-labour e tec'hen diouzh ar c'hazarn evit mont da gantren dre ar vro. E kêr Sant-Emilion e vezen alies, ur gêr kozh, mogerioù kreñv war he zro, tiez, ilizoù kaer enni. Ha neuze gor ha buhez e kêr, noz ha deiz, ar pezh na vez ket kavet e Breizh el lec'h ma yena an amzer kerkent ha ma kuzh an heol. Ken alies all e vezen o pourmen war ar maez, e-kreiz ar gwiniegi hag ar c'hestell. Chom a raen gant va c'hoan en un ostaleri bennak – evañ gwin ha debriñ fourmaj. N'oan ket pinvidik, va banne a gaven mat. Tremen a rae hep traoù all gant ma'm bije va banne eus gwin ar vro. Echu va amzer eno e oa deut ar poent da guitaat. Prenañ a ris pemp pe c'h-wec'h boutailhad eus gwin Pommerol a zo lec'hiet en hanternoz da Libourne, gant ar soñj d'o leuskel da gozhañ en ur skiber bennak. N'o deus ket bet amzer da goshaat siwazh. D'al lamm ez on aet dezho!

Bep tro ma'z evan gwin Pommerol e teu da soñj din eus ar Gambr Ruz. Laouenidigezh hag euzh war an hevelep tro. Ar Gambr Ruz a veze graet eus ar gambr seitek en ospital ar Vouster. Kambr ar re a varve diwar ar gwin. Ar ruz n'oa ket liv ar gwin, liv ar gwad e oa. Ar gwad taolet, strinket, rechetet, dislonket dre c'henou ar vezverien war o zremenvan. Kaer e veze gwalc'hiñ al leur, ar mogerioù, sel ar gambr, liv ar gwad ne dae ket kuit. Chom a rae anat. Setu ma voe divizet ober eus ar gambr-se kambr ar marv. Di e veze degaset ar vezverien a oa war o zalaroù. Rak fiziañs ne veze ket kalz diwar ar c'hleñved-se.

Sebezusat tra d'an danvez-medisin gwelet un den o tislonkañ gwad. Sevel a ra ar c'hlañvour en e goazez, gwenn-kann e liv, spont en e zaoulagad. Breugeudiñ a ra ha setu ur genaouad gwad ruz ha du o tiverañ diouzh e c'henou. Hag un all war-lerc'h hag un all c'hoazh, dirak daoulagad spontet an den klañv hag ar medisin yaouank. Ruziañ a ra liñselioù ar gwele tra ma wenna kroc'hen ar c'hlañvour. A-wechoù e strink poulladoù gwad ouzh ar mogerioù, an armelioù, ouzh ar glañvdiourien zoken. Al liz ruz ne vefe ket kalz a dra c'hoazh ma ne vefe ket a c'hwez da heul. Ur c'hwez pounner hag a chom stag ouzh an den, pell-pell war-lerc'h, pa vez o tebriñ pe oc'h evañ zoken pell diouzh an ospital. Ral eo e teufe ur vad bennak da heul seurt rechetadenn. Sin ar marv tost eo.

En ospital ma oan en em gavet war-lerc'h va amzer-soudard e varve kalz a dud diwar ar gwin. Ar braz diouto a rae o zremen en ur daoler gwad. Dre benn pe benn. Paotred yaouank kozh, merc'hed... Kalz a verc'hed a yae d'ar bed all dre an hent-se. Dre ar Gambr Ruz. Merc'hed yaouank ha merc'hed kozh ivez.

Pa oa deut Eujeni d'an ospital koeñvet he c'hof, melen-beuz he c'hroc'hen, e oa bet diaes deomp krediñ ec'h eve. Doare vat he doa, gwisket kempenn, pemzek vloaz ha tri-ugent bennak dezhi. An dielfennadurioù gwad ne lâront ket gaou. Kalet e voe ar wirionez da glevet: gwall glañv e oa Eujeni gant kaletadur an avu. Ha kement-se diwar goust ar boeson. Dre gomz aketus ganti e teujomp a-benn da c'houzout he doa bet evet kalz a win en he c'hozni. Perak? Diaes oa gouzout. Intañvez oa pell a oa, o chom he-unan en he zi, aet he bugale pell diouzh ar vro war-lerc'h o bara. A-walc'h d'ober un eil kanaouenn *Planedenn*. Ne oa ket anat diouzh he c'hlevet e vije gwasket he spered gant tra pe dra. Marteze e kave mat he banne hag ez ae ganti ouzhpenn ar gont ha netra ken. Perak mont atav da glask spazhañ laou?

Endra ma oa en ospital ne zeuas ket he bugale war he zro. Alies avat e pell-gomzent dezhi. Ur mab he doa o chom e-kichen Bourdel, rener ur stal-sevel-tiez diouzh e vicher. Ur pezh mell stal o oa gantañ diouzh doare. Bep an amzer e c'houlenne keloù diganin diwar-benn e vamm. Iskis e kave e vije bet kleñvet diwar ar gwin. Pell oa ne oa ket deuet d'ar vro, dalc'het ma oa gant e labour, setu ne c'helle ket gouzout petra oa deut e vamm da vezañ da fin he buhez. Mignoniezh oa savet etrezomp dre ar pellgomz. Kontañ a ris dezhañ an amzer em boa tremenet en e vro ahont hag eñ a gontas din amzer eürus e vugaleaj er Vouster. Un tammig brezhoneg zoken a zeue ganeomp bep an amzer.

En ospitalioù a-vremañ e vez sellet a-dost ouzh ar re glañv. Goude ma ouezfemp mat anv ar c'hleñved hag ar stad ma vez ar re glañv en em gavet gantañ e plij deomp, medisined, lakaat ober enklaskoù diouzh an druilh war gorf ar c'hlañvour. Gant Eujeni, forzh pegen kozh e ve, e voe graet heñvel. Ouzh he c'halon, he stomok, he avu, he empenn, e voe sellet pizh. Anat e teuas da vezañ e oa gwall dapet ha diaes d'ar c'hleñved dont war e giz. Ar pezh a rae ar muiañ a aon deomp oa gwelet gwazhied koeñvet en he stomok. Pa vez kaledet an avu diwar an alkol ne c'hell ket ar gwad tremen drezañ ken evit distreiñ d'ar galon. Ret dezhañ kemer hentoù-treuz, hent gwazhied ar stomok o vezañ unan anezho. Gwazhied bihan ha tanav int, kustum diouzh ul labour ha n'eo ket re bounner dezho. Pa vez lakaet re vec'h gwad enno avat ne badont ket hag e teuont da devaat, da doullañ ha da darzhañ. Hag ar gwad a-bouilhadoù er-maez dre ar genou.

Ma voe ranket lakaat Eujeni er Gambr Ruz. Daou zevezh war-lerc'h e taole he gwad. Kaer e voe reiñ skorn dezhi da sunañ, lakaat ur sac'had dour skornet war he stomok, lakaat louzoù da devaat ar gwad, gwad nevez en he gwazhied ha zoken ur gorzenn da waskañ war ar gwazhied tarzhet ne wellaas ket dezhi he yec'hed. Mont a rae ar vuhez diouti da heul ar gwad. Anken vras a welemp en he daoulagad, kropet e veze he bizied war hor bizied-ni. En he c'hichen, stag outi, edon pa daolas he genaouad diwezhañ ha ma varvas tamm-ha-tamm, he liv deut da vezañ gwennoc'h eget an erc'h. Ret e vefe gwalc'hiñ ar Gambr Ruz adarre. Unan klañv all a oa o c'hortoz e dro d'ober e dalaroù!

Un nebeud devezhioù war-lerc'h an interamant en em gavas ur c'hased koad en ospital. "D'ar medisin yaouank en deus bet soursiet ouzh va mamm," a oa skrivet warnañ. Ha me e zigeriñ. Pommerol, daouzek boutailhad gwin Pommerol eus ar re wellañ a oa er c'hased e-touez ar c'holo.

Pell hag hir on bet a-raok stagañ ganto. N'eo ket ar c'hoant a vanke din. Nemet bep tro ma krogen en ur voutailh e teue da soñj din eus ar Gambr Ruz. Bouilhadoù gwad ruz-tan o tont er-maez eus genou Eujeni. Daou pe dri bloaz eo chomet ar gwin ganin. Da gozhañ, emit-hu. N'oa ken 'met gwelloc'h a se evit doare. A-barzh ar fin n'em eus ket gellet padout ken. Ha bec'h dezho. Ur drugar oa evañ ar Pommerol hag un displijadur war ar memes tro: c'hwek ha c'hwerv. Evel ar gwin mat.

Translation

The Red Bedroom, *1989*

My favourite wine is Pommerol. I tasted it for the first time when I was doing my national service in Libourne, near Bordeaux. That is where young doctors spend six weeks before being posted either on a boat or on dry land. It was summer when I was sent to Libourne. I am not one to spend my time in the barracks or in the company of doctors or soldiers. As soon as the day's work was over, I fled from the barracks and went to visit the region. I often went to Saint-Emilion. It is an old town, surrounded with ramparts, with many beautiful houses and churches. I was also attracted by the constant heat and by city life. These are unusual in Brittany where the weather cools as soon as the sun sets. I also often went to take a stroll in the countryside, amidst the vineyards and castles. I used to stop for dinner in some restaurant or other, drinking wine and eating cheese. I was not wealthy, but I liked to have a drink. I did without other things in order to be able to afford a glass of the local wine. When my time there was over, I prepared to leave the region. I bought five or six bottles of Pommerol wine – Pommerol being a village to the north of Libourne – thinking I would let them mature in some shed or other. They did not have time to mature however. I drank them in no time!

Every time I drink Pommerol I remember the Red Bedroom, with pleasure but also with disgust. The Red Bedroom was the name given to room 17 in Mouster hospital. It was the room kept aside for dying alcoholics. Red does not represent the colour of wine, but that of blood. Blood thrown up, brought up, vomited, spewed through the mouth. No matter how well the floor, the walls, the ceiling of the room were cleaned, the colour of blood did not go away. It was enduring. So the decision was taken to make this room the room of death. Alcoholics on the verge of dying were transferred to it when there was little hope of them recovering from their disease.

The strangest thing a house doctor can see is someone vomiting blood. The patient sits up, his face white as a sheet, his eyes wide open with fear. He belches and a mouthful of red blood comes out of his mouth. And another one, and yet another one, as panic takes hold of the patient and of the young doctor. The sheets get redder as the patient's skin gets whiter. Sometimes pools of blood get sprayed onto the walls, the cupboards, and even on the nurses. The red colour would be tolerable if it was not for the attendant pungent smell which sticks to the doctor's clothes for a very long time afterwards, when he is eating – or even having a drink – far from the hospital. It is unusual for any recovery to follow such a vomiting session. It is a sign that death is near.

In the hospital where I was working after doing my national service, many people were dying from drink. Bachelors, women etc, died losing blood, from one end or the other. Many women, young and old, went to the other world in this way, through the Red Room.

When Eujeni arrived at the hospital, her belly blown up, her skin sallow, we found it hard to believe that she was an alcoholic. Her appearance was neat, her clothes tidy. She was about seventy-five years old. But blood tests do not lie. The truth was hard to hear. Eujeni's condition was critical: hardening of the liver caused by too much drinking. We questioned her and learnt that she had drunk a lot of wine in her old age. Why? It was difficult to know. She had lost her husband a long time ago and was living on her own in her house as her children had left the region to find work. Her story could make another song entitled *Planedenn* [Destiny]. From listening to her, it was hard to believe that she might have had any personal problems. Maybe she just liked to drink and drunk more than her fair share, and that was all. Why should we always look for complicated explanations?

When she was in hospital, her children did not come to visit her. However, they often telephoned her. She had a son who lived near Bordeaux. He was the managing director of a firm of architects, a very big one, from what I heard. He called me from time to time to know how his mother was doing. He found it strange that alcohol abuse was the cause of her illness. He had not returned home for a long time, as his job kept him away, and therefore did not know how his mother had coped towards the end of her life. We became friends over the telephone. I told him about the time I had spent in the region where he now lived and he told me about his happy childhood in Mouster. From time to time we even exchanged a few words in Breton.

In today's hospitals, many tests are carried out on patients. After putting a name on the disease and making a full diagnosis, doctors like to carry out a battery of tests on the patient's body. That is what happened with Eujeni, in spite of her advanced age. Tests were carried out on her heart, on her stomach, on her liver and on her brain. It became obvious that her disease was at an advanced stage and that it would be difficult to make it recede. What gave us the most worry were the swollen veins of her stomach. When the liver hardens under the effect of too much alcohol, blood can no longer run through it to return to the heart. It finds alternative routes, one of these being the stomach veins. But these are narrow and thin-walled, used to carry out a work which is not too heavy for them. When the pressure of blood in them becomes too great, they deteriorate. They thicken, perforate and burst, and blood gushes out of the mouth.

The time came when we had to put Eujeni in the Red Room. Two days later she was vomiting blood. Even though she was given ice-cubes to suck, a freezing-cold water bottle to put on her stomach, medicine to thicken her blood, a blood transfusion and an operation to ligature the burst arteries, her state of health did not improve. She was losing her life as fast as her blood. We could see the fear in her eyes as she sunk her fingers deep into our palms. I was by her side, holding her hand, when she threw up her last mouthful of blood and finally died, her face whiter than snow. The Red Room would have to be cleaned again. Another patient was waiting his turn to die in it!

A few days after the funeral, a wooden case arrived at the hospital. It was addressed "To the young doctor who looked after my mother." I opened it. Pommerol, twelve bottles of the best Pommerol were lying in the crate amongst the straw.

It took me a long time to start drinking them. It is not that I did not want to. But each time I picked up a bottle I remembered the Red Room and the spurts of bright red blood coming out of Eujeni's mouth. The wine stayed unopened for two or three years. To mature, you might say. It surely improved with age. In the end, I could no longer wait and I opened them. I both liked and disliked that Pommerol. It was sweet and sour, just as any good wine should be.

Fañch al Lay

Bugaleaj Bilzig; E hinivelez, *1924* (Lodenn)

Evel-se 'ta, e ti Bilzig emaoh. E-barz ar gwele-mañ e oe ganet, war an oaled-mañ eun amiegez hen mailluras, hag eun amezegez a roas dezañ da zena.

E dad? N'eus ket bet anavezet anezañ: beuzet e oa bet, a-raog ginivelez ar paotr. Ar hoaperien, an teodou fall a lavare "e stank ar vilin-avel"; e gwirionez, o tond d'ar gêr euz a Vro-Zaoz, evid dimezi da Janedig.

E vamm? Ar paour-kêz plah, mervel a eure en eur wilioudi. En deiz-se, trubuilh ha glahar en tiig: eur plah, ar vamm, war ar varv-skaoñ; eur bugelig en e gavell, emzivad an deiz kenta euz e vuhez.

Hini pe hini euz an amezeien a deue, eur wech an amzer, da deuler dour benniget war ar vamm, da lavared eur bedennig eviti. Pebezh kalonad!

Eur plah a drebase dre an ti: an amiegez. Unan all kosoh, azezet e penn ar havell, sioul, sioul a ouele, eur chapeled en he dorn, soublet he fenn ganti.

– Pebez kalonad!... Ho-pet truez oute, o va Doue!

– Red eo evelkent mond da gaoud an aotrou person, eme an amiegez.

– Ya, ya, eom, a lavaras ar plah koz, – Marharid a oa he ano, mamm-goz ar bugel, mamm e dad – red eo mond... Ar paotr a ranko beza badezet, hag ar vamm sebeliet... Ne zebro ket ahonom!...

Eet int o-diou d'ar presbital.

Tok! tok! war an nor, hag ar garabasenn da zigeri.

– Petra a hoarvez ganeoh, Marharid?... Petra a fell deoc'h?...

– Er gêr emañ an aotrou person, Frañseza?

– Ya. Antreit en ti, eme ar garabasenn, eul Leonardez talfazeg, eur dorgosenn a blah, teo ha ledan. Antreit, antreit.

Dirag an aotrou person, abaf an diou blah, ken abaf ha na gredent digeri o genou. Rust e oa an aotrou person, den a zoare, mad d'ar paour, med striz war al lezenn. Leonard e oa, hag o paouez erruoud er vro: ne anaveze ket c'hoaz oll dud e barrez. Ha c'hwi a oar: al Leonard paotr rog ma'z eo, gwall goapaer eo an Tregeriad, hag an eil atao e disfi ouz egile.

– Eur maleür braz, aotrou person, eme Marharid... Janedig a zo marvet en nozmañ... Janedig, Janedig Tangi...

– A!

– E-tro diou ha teir eur...

– A! eme adarre an aotrou person.

– Ha war e lerh e tilez eur mabig... Pegoulz e vo greet ar vadeziant, pegoulz an interamant?...

– Ar vadeziant, goude ar huz-heol, evelato, Marharid, c'hwi oar, badeziant ar re vastard. An interamant, n'ouzon ket, evelato... Maro heb anzav he fehed, maro heb sakramant!... Skwer fall d'an oll verhed yaouank... skwer fall d'an oll dud er barrez.

– Petra vo greet, aotrou person?

– Digasit ar paotr d'ar vadeziant d'an abardaez, evelato, ar vamm e korn ar vered. Marharid, c'hwi a dle gouzout petra da ober diouzh ar paotrig; hervez m'am-eus bet klevet, mab ho mab ez eo.

Ha Marharid, soublet ganti e fenn, kuzet en he jobilinenn, a ouele goustadig.

– Ya, aotrou person.

– Evelato savit anezhañ e doujañs an Aotrou Doue.

– Ya, ya, aotrou person.

– Ha gras dezañ ne heulio ket roudou e berhenn! Grit dioutañ, dre ho kelennadurez, ar pez n'eo bet nag e dad nag e vamm.

– Kaled ar blanedenn, aotrou !

– Petra a fell deoh!... Pep hini ahanom a steu e hini, dindan dorn ha skoazell an Aotrou Doue.

Ar paour-kêr Marharid, pleget dindan ar glahar, a zistroas war he hiz.

Bilzig en e wele a oa kousket mad, juntret gantañ ha stard e zaouarnigou. En e gichenn, war ar varv-skaoñ, e vamm lienet, dirazi eur houlaouenn goar benniget, eur chapeled hag eur groazig kouevr etre he daouarn; ha paneved sklas ar maro en he herhenn hag an disliou war he zal, ho-pije lavaret e vousc'hoarzhe d'he mabig bihan.

Ha Marharid, stouet d'an douar, a lavare dre he daerou:

– Va mabig eo, Janedig, va mabig eo!

Seblantoud a eure dezi pa zavas he daoulagad, penaoz ar vamm he-devoa eun tammig troet he fenn evit selled outi, evit trugarekaad mamm an hini he-devoa kement karet, mamm-goz he bugelig, euz he harantez hag euz he madelez.

– Janedig, va merh! va merh!... It gant an aotrou Doue!... Doue d'ho tigemer en e Varadoz!... It e peoh, Janedig, ho mab a vo va mabig!...

Ar plahig koz, savet en he sav, an daerou o ruilla var he diouchod, a roas eur pok d'ar vamm, serri a eure dezhi he daoulagad:

– Kousk, va merh, kousk! An dud ne absolvont ket... Doue a zo madelezuz!...

A-barz an abardaez, archedet Janedig, Marharid a wiskas he mantell, ha, dindan, paket ar bugelig. Gand ar paeron hag ar vaeronez setu-hi er porched. N'eo ket ar person a deuas da ober ar vadeziant: ar hure hag ar zakrist, ar hure, den a zouster hag a vadelez, eur hamarad da dad ar paotr.

– Petore ano, Marharid?

– Ivon, Ivonig, aotrou kure.

– Perag e son hizio ar hloh evel derhent eur gouel-berz? a lavare ar person, souezet meurbed, d'e garabasenn, hag e fredone da heul ar hloh:

Eun arhêl, a-berz an Aotrou,
A ziskennas euz an Neñvou
D'annoñs da Vari oa choazet
Evid mamm da Zalver ar bed.

Ar zakrist an-nevoa sonet an Anjeluz goude diwez ar vadeziant, greet an-neus

d'ar hleier kana ginivelez ar bugel dinamm evel hini ar gristenien all.

Goude ar vadeziant, raktal, eo bet sebeliet Janedig. Nebeud a dud o pedi evid ar paour-kêz plah, nebeud: an amezeien hag ar gerent. Eun toullig e korn ar vered, eun tamm douar war an arched.... Na kan na diskan; ar glazou, goude an Anjeluz, da vihanna, a gouezas truezuz, evel daerou an anken, war beziou ar vered lijennet dindan deñvalijenn an noz. Evel-se ar zakrist a ree gouela war bez ar vamm ar hleier 'devoa kanet bremaig badeziant he mab.

Marharid, mantret he halon, he-unanig, ar paotr dindan he mantell, a zistroas d'ar gêr. Lakaad a eure ar bugel en e gavell, hag hi, stouet d'an douar, war he daoulin noaz, a lavare en he fedenn:

– Doue da bardono d'an anaon benniget! Doue d'o fardono! Doue d'o digemer en e drugarez!

Translation

Bilzig's Youth; His Birth, *1924* (Extract)

So here you are now, in Bilzig's house. He was born in this very bed. A midwife wrapped him in swaddling clothes by this hearth and a neighbour suckled him.

His father? There was none about; he had drowned, before the birth of the baby. Malicious people said mockingly that he had drowned "in the pond of the windmill". To tell the truth, it happened when he was coming back home from England in order to marry Janedig.

His mother? The poor girl died in childbirth. On that day, there were tears and sorrow in the tiny house: a girl, a young mother, on the trestle-table for the dead; a baby in his cradle, orphaned on the first day of his life.

A few of the neighbours came in, one after the other, to sprinkle holy water on the mother and to say a quick prayer for her repose. What a heartbreak!

A woman was going to and fro in the house: she was the midwife. An older one, sitting at the head of the cradle, was crying softly, o, so softly, a rosary between her fingers, her head bowed down.

"What a heartbreak! Take pity on them, O Lord!"

"Yet we need to go and tell the priest," said the midwife.

"Yes, let's go," said the old woman. Her name was Marharid and she was the child's grand-mother, his father's mother. "We have to go. The boy needs to be baptised, and the mother buried. He is not going to eat us!"

The two of them set off for the presbytery.

Knock! Knock! on the door. The housekeeper came to open it.

"What's the matter, Marharid? What do you want?"

"Is the priest at home, Frañseza?"

"Yes. Come in," said the housekeeper, a sullen woman from Léon, a midget of a woman but fat and stout. "Come in! Come in!"

The two women were intimidated by the priest, so intimidated that they did not dare open their mouths. The priest was a harsh man, honest and good to the poor, but strict on religious matters. He came from the Léon region, had just arrived in the village and did not yet know all his parishioners. And, as you know, the people from Léon are haughty, the ones from Trégor sarcastic, and they distrust one another.

"It's a great misfortune, Father," said Marharid. "Janedig died during the night. Janedig, Janedig Tangi."

"Did she?"

"Between two and three."

"Did she?" repeated the priest.

"And she leaves a small son behind. When will the christening, when will the funeral take place?"

"The christening must be done after sunset. You know, Marharid, christening the illegitimates... As for the funeral, well, I don't know. She died without confessing her sin, she died without receiving the last rites. A bad example to all girls... A bad example to all the people in the parish.

"What will be done, Father?"

"Bring the boy to be baptised tonight. However the mother must be buried at the back of the churchyard. As for you, Marharid, you must know what your duty is towards the boy. According to what I heard, he is your son's son."

Marharid, her head bowed and hidden in the hood of her cloak, was crying softly.

"Yes, I do, Father."

"And bring him up to respect the Lord."

"Yes, Father."

"Let's pray that he will not follow in his parents' footsteps! Bring him up to be what his father and mother have not been.

"Man's destiny is a hard one, Father!"

"That is the way it is. Everyone of us weaves his own destiny with the support and help of our Lord."

Poor Marharid returned home, her grief weighing heavily upon her.

Bilzig was fast asleep in his bed, his little hands clasped together firmly. Next to him, on the trestle-table was his mother, dressed in a shroud, a holy candle at the foot of the bed, rosary beads and a small copper crucifix in her hands. If it had not been for the cold shadow of death on her face and for the paleness of her forehead, you could have said that she was smiling at her tiny son.

Marharid, her head bowed down, said between her tears:

"He is mine, Janedig, he is my little boy!"

When she raised her eyes, it seemed to her that the mother had turned her head slightly to look at her and thank the mother of the one she had loved so much, the baby's grandmother, for her affection and kindness.

"Janedig, my daughter! my daughter! Go and join the Lord! May the Lord take you into his paradise! Go in peace, Janedig. Your son will be my son!"

When the old woman stood up, tears were rolling down her cheeks. She kissed

the mother and closed her eyes:

"Sleep, daughter, sleep! People will not pardon you, but God is good."

By the evening, Janedig had been put into her coffin. Marharid put on her cloak, and held the wrapped-up baby underneath it. There she is now, in the porch of the church, with the godfather and the godmother. The priest had not come to do the christening, but had sent the vicar and the sexton. The vicar was a kind and gentle man, a friend of the baby's father:

"What name, Marharid?"

"Ivon, Ivonig, Vicar."

"Why does the bell ring as it does on the eve a holy day?" said the amazed priest to his housekeeper who was humming a hymn to the sound of the bell:

An Archangel sent by the Lord
Descended from Heaven
To tell Mary that she had been chosen
To be the mother of the Saviour of the world.

The sexton had rung the Angelus at the end of the christening. He had made the bells sing the birth of this innocent child as he did for any other Christian.

Janedig was buried immediately after the christening. Few people came to pray for the poor girl's soul, very few: only neighbours and family. A hole in a corner of the churchyard, some earth on the coffin... No singing. After the Angelus, the pitiful tolling of the bells felt like tears of grief falling on the graves of the churchyard bathed in night shadows. This is how the sexton made the bells, which had just sung the christening of the baby, cry on the grave of his mother .

Marharid returned home on her own, broken-hearted, holding the baby under her cloak. She laid him in his cradle, and then, on her knees, her head bowed towards the ground, she said her prayer:

"May the Lord forgive the blessed dead! May the Lord forgive them! May the Lord have mercy on them!"

Charlez Gwennou

Setu ar c'hloc'h o tinsan glaz! *1900*

> Setu ar c'hloc'h o tiñsañ glaz!
> Merc'hig, d'ar bez ez i warc'hoazh!
>
> Perak n'omp ket marvet ive,
> D'an Anjeluz eveldout-te,
> E-lec'h chom c'hoazh war an douar
> Da strivañ gant poan ha glac'har?
>
> Peseurt eurvad, diwar vremañ,

E kavfemp-ni war ar bed-mañ?
Hon holl dudi, merc'hig karet,
Ganit, er bez, a vo klozet.

N'eo ket a-walc'h! Ret eo deomp c'hoazh
Sebeliañ da gorf paour, siwazh,
Da gorfig ker koant, ken mibin,
A luskellemp war hon daoulin.

Ret eo deomp (pebezh kalonad!)
Serriñ, klozañ da zaoulagad,
Serriñ, klozañ da vuzelloù
Ur wech all c'hoazh gant hor pokoù.

Paouez, va gwreg, da skuilh daeroù
Hag e-touez he gwiskamantoù
Ra vo ar c'haerañ dibabet
Ha ra vint d'hor merc'hig lakaet!

Paour ha dister int, ni her goar,
Evel holl dilhad an douar,
Da wiskañ d'un aelig Doue,
Ken kaer, ken glan eveldout-te!

N'eus forzh! En Neñv, Ivonaig,
E kavi dilhad pinvidik!
Kaeroc'h evit aour hag arc'hant
En Neñv e vo da wiskamant.

D'az c'hoarezed, an Aeligoù
Doue, krouer bras an Neñvoù,
A ro dilhad, hon eus klevet,
Broudet gant loar, heol ha stered!

Ha bremañ Aelig, kenavo,
Da c'hortoz ma teuy an maro
Da zastum tad, mamm ha bugel
E memes bez, e Breizh-Izel.

Kenavo, va c'hrouadurig!
Sell ouzh da gerent reuzeudik!
Ped alies Mestr an Neñvoù
D'o c'hennerzhañ en o foanioù!

Setu ar c'hloc'h o tiñsañ glaz.
Aelig, diskenn er bez, siwazh!
Hep dale pell, gant gras Doue,
En Neñv en em gavimp adarre.

Translation

The Bell Is Now Tolling, *1900*

The bell is now tolling!
My little girl, tomorrow you will go to your grave!

Why did we not also die,
As the Angelus rang, just as you did,
Rather than stay on earth
To struggle on in sorrow and grief?

What happiness, from now on,
Would we find in this world?
All that we liked, dear little girl,
Will disappear with you in the grave.

And that's not all! We still have
To bury your poor body, alas,
The little body, so pretty, so supple,
We used to rock on our knees.

We have – what a heartbreak –
To shut and close your eyes,
To shut and close your lips
Once more with our kisses.

Stop, dear wife, to shed tears.
Amongst her clothes
Let us choose the loveliest
And put them on our little girl!

They are too humble and lowly, we know it well,
Like all earthly clothes,
To dress a little angel of God
Who is as beautiful, as innocent as you are!

Never mind! In Heaven, Ivonaig,
You will find splendid clothes,

Finer than gold and silver.
Your garments will be in Heaven.

We heard that God,
Sole creator of Heaven,
Gives your sisters, the little angels,
Garments embroidered with moon, sun and stars!

Now, little angel, goodbye,
Until death finally comes
To reunite father, mother and child
In the same grave in Lower Brittany.

Goodbye, my little child!
Look at your distressed parents!
Pray often to the Master of Heaven
To give them strength in their sorrow.

The bell is now tolling.
Little angel, go down into the grave, alas!
Soon, if God wills it,
We shall be with you in Heaven.

Roparz Hemon

Tartez an ognon, *1970* (Lodenn)

Edo ar beleg o vont er-maez eus an ti. Edo ar gerent o tistreiñ e-barzh ar gambr. Jozefin, ar vaouez toc'hor, hervez kustum ar re nevez nouet, en em gave gwelloc'h hag a selle a bep tu dezhi, hogos krak he daoulagad. Pep unan a oa en e lec'h, rak e kambroù ar re war o zremenvan eo kont evel en ilizoù: e blas da bep hini. He c'hoar Ambroazin a oa braket war ar gador-vrec'h, e-kichen ar siminal, he breur-kaer Tomaz war ar gador e-kichen ar prenestr, he niz Yann war ar skabellig ouzh troad ar gwele, he c'heniterv Felisite en he sav-sonn e-kichen ar gomodenn, – hag un eil Felisite, evel pa ne vije ket bet a-walc'h gant unan, spurmantet e melezour bras an armel, – he nizez Melani en he c'hluch war ar pouf, he niz Mark hag e wreg Tina e-giz patromoù koad war ar bank, harp ouzh ar voger.

– Va zud kaezh, – eme Jozefin.

An holl a selaoue. Ne oa trouz ebet er gambr. Nemet e traoñ al liorzh e kleved ur yar o sklokal dizamant en heol kaer Mezheven.

– Va zud kaezh...

War wanaat ez ae he mouezh. Hogen souden, kreñvoc'h, e lavaras:

– Me a fell din kaozeal gant Melani, Melani hepken.

Ambroazin, o krizañ he zal, a zastumas he brozh ledan, skignet ar plegoù anezhi en tu-hont d'he c'hador-vrec'h, a savas gorrek hag a gerzhas ken gorrek all etrezek an nor. Ar re all a heulias. Feuket e oant holl. Ne oa ket tu, avat, da zisentiñ.

Melani a oa chomet diflach. Pa voe serret an nor gant Tina, an hini diwezhañ da vont kuit, ar glañvourez a reas sin d'he nizez da dostaat. Melani a gasas ur gador betek kichen ar gwele.

– Va flac'h kaezh, – eme Jozefin, – emaon o vont da vervel!

– O nann, Tintin Fin!

Jozefin a hejas he dorn, evel o tibasiantiñ.

– Un dra a zo, va bugel, a rankan lavarout dit. Un dra n'am eus lavaret biskoazh da zen ebet. Ur sekred eo. Lavaret eo bet din gant va mamm-gozh, hag hi war he gwele a varv, eveldon hiziv, da virout kuzh a-hed va buhez. Ur sekred eo a zo manet en hon tiegezh abaoe amzer... amzer... ne ouzon ket pegeit amzer. Promet din Melani, e vo miret kuzh ganez ivez betek ar fin.

– Prometiñ a ran, Tintin Fin.

– Kemer paper hag ur bluenn, aze, war va "eurvad-an-deiz".

Ne oa ket ezhomm mont betek hec'h "eurvad-an-deiz", da lavarout eo, an daol-skrivañ a c'hiz kozh, gwerniset-du hag alaouret a oa o lufrañ er c'horn e-tal ar pren-estr. Melani, a oa sekretourez en ul labouradeg, he doa tennet, prim evel ul luc'hedenn, he boullbluenn hag he c'harned-berrskrivañ diouzh he sac'h ler. Lakaet he doa ivez he lunedoù stern platik skantbaotheñvel war he fri.

– Prest on, – eme ar plac'h yaouank, he c'harned en he dorn kleiz, he boull-bluenn a-bann en he dorn dehou.

– Soñj ac'h eus, Melani, – eme Jozefin, – eus va zartez?

He zartez? Melani ne gomprenas ket da gentañ. Neuze e veizas en un taol: an tartez! tartez an ognon, a veze graet ha servijet gant Tintin Fin, keginerez dispar, pa bede kerent ha mignoned d'ober lip-e-bav en he zi. Sellout a reas alvaoned ouzh he moereb. Daoust hag e oa he skiant vat o vont diouzh ar vaouez kozh? Ur berrad terzhienn emichañs?

Hogen dremm Jozefin a oa sioul ha parfet.

– Setu amañ ar sekred: penaos ober an tartez. Skriv Melani!

Melani a skrivas. Jozefin a yae goustad, souezhet o welout pegen buan e c'haloupe ar bluenn, un tamm anoazet marteze. Berrskrivañ a oa un arz n'he doa ket desket en amzer-hont ma rae pajennadoù skritur, saoz ha ront ha bastard, gant un doug-pluenn ha liv-du, dindañ evezh ar c'hoar Adela e skol ar seurezed.

– Mir an tamm paper-se, Melani. Bremañ e c'hallan mervel eürus.

Melani a yeas da c'hervel ar re all, a oa bodet er sal-debriñ. Selloù du a voe buket outi. Den avat ne rannas grik.

Translation

The Onion Tart, *1970* (Extract)

The priest was leaving the house. The family returned to the bedroom. Jozefin, the dying woman, like all those who have received the last rites, felt better and was looking around her, a definite glint in her eyes. Everyone was in place. In the room of a dying person, the same rule applies as in a church. Everyone has their rightful place. Her sister, Ambroazin, was slouching in the armchair, by the fireplace; her brother-in-law, Tomaz, was sitting on the chair by the window; her nephew Yann on a stool at the foot of the bed; her cousin Felisite was standing up straight next to the chest of drawers, and another Felisite – as if one of them was not enough – could be seen in the large mirror of the wardrobe; her niece, Melani was hunched on the pouffe; her nephew, Mark and his wife Tina, sitting on the bench by the wall, looked like wooden statues.

"My dear ones," said Jozefin.

Everyone was listening. There was no noise in the room, except for the constant clucking of a hen in the June sunshine.

"My dear ones..."

Her voice was failing her, but it suddenly gathered strength when she said:

"I want to talk to Melani. By herself."

Ambroazin, knitting her eyebrows, gathered around her wide skirt which was sprawled over the armchair, stood up slowly, and walked, just as slowly, towards the door. The others followed her. They all felt offended, but no way could they refuse to comply.

Melani had not moved. When Tina, who was the last one to leave the room, closed the door behind her, the dying woman waved her niece closer. Melani brought a chair to the bedside.

"My dear girl," said Josefin, "I am about to die."

"Of course, you are not, Auntie Fin!"

Jozefin, annoyed, waved the remark aside.

"There's something, dear girl, that I must tell you, something I have never told anyone. It is a secret. I got it from my grandmother when she was on her deathbed, just as I am today, and I promised to keep it my all life long. It's a secret which has been in our family for a long, long time, I can't remember for how long exactly. Melani, promise me that you will also keep it until the end of your life.

"I promise, Auntie."

"Go and get a piece of paper and a pen over there, from my secretaire.

Melani did not need to go to the secretaire, that is to say, to the old-fashioned writing desk, varnished in black with gold trimmings, which sparkled in the corner, by the window. Melani, who was a secretary in a factory, had taken her pen and notebook out of her handbag, quick as lightning. She had also put on a pair of plastic horn-rimmed spectacles.

"I am ready," said the young girl, holding her notebook in her left hand, her pen poised in her right hand.

"Melani," said Josefin, "do you remember my tarts?"

Her tarts? First of all, Melani did not understand. But suddenly she realised: the tarts! The onion tarts which Auntie Fin, a cordon bleu cook, baked and served when she invited family and friends to a meal in her home. She stared at her aunt in astonishment. Was the old dear losing her mind? Was it a fit of fever? But Jozefin's face was serene and serious.

"Here is my secret: the recipe for tarts. Write it down, Melani!"

Melani wrote it down. Jozefin spoke slowly. She was surprised to see how quickly Melani's pen was flying across the page, and might well have felt a little offended. Shorthand was not an art that she had learnt in her school days at the convent school where she used to do pages of handwriting, modern English handwriting, round-hand or slanting round-hand, with a penholder and black ink, under the watchful eye of Sister Adela.

"Take good care of this piece of paper, Melani. I can now die in peace."

Melani went out to the dining-room to call the others back in. They gave her a black look, but no one said anything.

Jakez Konan

Lannevern e kañv, *1949* (Lodenn)

N'ouzon ket kennebeut ha bet oc'h ur wech bennak en obidoù ur jeneral born? Mar doc'h, ne viot ket souezhet gant ar pezh a zisplegin deoc'h amañ. Setu: skeiñ a rae an heol ken kreñv war ar c'hlopennoù hag e c'hore kement an empennoù ma rankas ar baotred a-benn ur pennad goleiñ o fennoù. Goude-se, pan erruas ar c'harr-kañv e korn hent bihan ar vered e chomas kazeg Nikolaz a-sav ur munudig. N'eo ket dre ma'z oa skuizh koulskoude, nemet, en dro-gorn-se, e oa un ti bihan gwennet an talbenn anezhañ gant raz ha skrivet warnañ e lizherennoù du: *Café du Cimetière* hag un tamm izeloc'h *Allée de boules*. E c'hellit soñjal, hep drougiezh eus ho perzh, ez ae Nikolaz di alies a-walc'h da c'hlebiañ e c'hourlañchenn ha da c'hoari'r boulloù o tistreiñ eus ar vered. Perak avat e fazias an aneval en deiz-se, o chom a-sav pa oa o vonet? An dra-se n'ouzon ket ivez.

Bepred, Nikolaz ne voe ket pell o sachañ war ar rañjenn hag o krozal d'e gazeg. Ar sakrist hag a oa o kanañ dres d'an ampoent, a verzas an dra hag a fazias en e gan o cheñch ton div wech!

Gwelout al loen o nac'hañ kas an Aotrou Jeneral Kerangwenn war-du e ziskuizhlec'h diwezhañ ha klevout mouezh ar sakrist o fallaat, setu a voe kavet iskis adarre gant ar re a daolas evezh ouzh kement-se.

"Seblant fall," a anzavas an Aotrou Maer d'an Eilvaer en em gave en e gichen ha na c'hallas ket respont dre ma'z oa o cheñch jod d'e vutun-chaok.

Dres a-raok erruout e toull-dor ar vered, un ofiser hag a gleve, ur pennad oa, ur wigouradenn direizh er c'harr, a redas penn-follet a-raok d'ar gazeg.

"Chomit a-sav, chomit a-sav enta!" a grias-eñ da Nikolaz.

"Petra?" eme hemañ ken dichek ha dra diwar e azezenn, "Sodet oc'h?... Tec'hit alese!"

"Ne glevit ket?" a wic'he an ofiser. "N'eo ket marv ar jeneral".

"N'eo ket marv ar jeneral? 'M eus aon ez eo re domm dindan ho kalabousenn! Oust, tec'hit alese!"

"C'hwi an hini a zo bouzar! Emañ an Aotrou Kerangwenn aze o klemm en e arched! N'emaoc'h ket o vonet evelkent da gas un den bev d'ar vered, eo?"

E gwirionez e kleved trouz ha klemmadennoù o tonet eus an arched. Ken gwenn hag ul liñsel ez eas Nikolaz Briant.

"Noñdetout!" n'hallas ken balbouzat.

Kerc'het e voe buan an touller-bezioù, a oa kalvez ivez, da zigeriñ an arched, hag a yeas, en afer, da zigorer-archedoù. E-keit-se, tud ar c'hañvambroug, manet darn amgredik, darn aonik pe spontet, a chome difiñv, ar pezh a ziskouez sklaer hag anat pebezh galloud en devez ur jeneral, ha pa vefe o vonet d'e vez.

A-benn an diwezh, pa voe didachet an arched, e voe savet trumm ar golo anezhañ gant Olier Kerangwenn e-unan, hanter-baket gant e liñsel wenn, ruz e benn ha bev-mat. En e goazez ez eas hag e chomas ur vunutenn badaouinet ha mezevennet gant sklaerder an deiz. Goude-se, a-sav-taol, e lammas sonn en e sav. Stlepel a reas e liñsel pell dioutañ hag e frotas e elgez.

Marteze hoc'h eus-hu bet gwelet un dro bennak ur jeneral o sevel eus a varv da vev eus e arched. E gwir, un arvest divoutin eo, ur weladenn o tennañ war un dro d'ar burzhud ha da emgann Ballon. Evel-hen e c'hoarvezas gant Kerangwenn: da gentañ enta (ha gant kement jeneral o tasoc'hiñ e vez heñvel) e savas eus e arched. Kaer e oa, gantañ e splannañ gwiskamant-ofiser. Brasoc'h, duoc'h ha reutoc'h eget biskoazh e oa e vourroù, disbourbellet e lagad hag e selloù o parañ war ar vanden-nad tud en em gave dirazañ. Ar baotred a oa sabatuet, spontet e oa ar merc'hed, lod o lakaat sin ar Groaz en o c'herc'henn, lod o kouezhañ war bennoù o daoulin, lod all, merc'hed diwar ar maez, stardet ganto o disglavieroù war boull o c'halon, o pediñ Sant Paeron Lannevern. Holl e kave dezho e welent dirazo un tasmant pe un diaoul difluket eus an ifern.

Panevet e vourroù bras en dije gallet Kerangwenn krediñ e tegouezhe e-kreiz ar gristenien-se evel un ael a-berzh an Aotrou.

E wreg a stagas da huchal warnañ: "Olier" Olier!" D'ar c'houlz-se eo e tremenas traoù spontus. Ur gounnar ruz a grogas en Olier. N'ouzon doare pe eo mouezh e wreg o krial a vroudas anezhañ, pe eo ar c'hoant a savas ennañ da ober evel Nevenoe gwechall gozh oc'h argas ar Franked. Marteze e kredas e oa an holl dud-se oc'h ober goap anezhañ? Kavout a ra din kentoc'h ez eo pa welas an togoù-meloñs war bennoù ar maer hag e guzulierien eo ez eas trelatet.

Leuskel a reas ur youc'hadenn, bepred, unan spouronus evel ma tle bezañ yudadenn al leon er gouelec'h. Daoublegañ a reas da dapout e gepi ha neuze o tic'houinañ e gleze bras dorn-alaouret a oa bet lezet ouzh e gostez, e lammas diwar ar c'harr-kañv gant herr ur wabrigolenn o treuziñ an oabl en un nozvezh vac'hus a hañv, en ur youc'hal a-bouez-penn gerioù na gomprenas den. Ar gristenien gaezh, pa weljont ar c'hleze o luc'hañ en aer, a dec'has d'an daoulamm ruz dre straed strizh ar vered.

Mar demañ ar c'hustum evit ur jeneral da redek war-lerc'h e enebourien o tec'hel, em eus bet kavet a-viskoazh souezhus ha dizereat a-walc'h, evit un den marv, ar boaz da redek gant ur c'hleze war-lerc'h ar re a vez o ouelañ dezhañ.

Evit bezañ diduet da vat gant un hevelep arvest ez eo ret hen gwelout eus eil estaj un ti. Diwar ur pondalez-prenestr, dreist-holl, evel ma c'hoarvezas ganin sellout outañ, ho pije merzet ez-resis penaos e tremenas an traoù.

Kerkent ha ma krogas ar jeneral da redek, ho pije gwelet ur burzhud bras: digammet ar re gamm, sodet ar re fur, dispac'het ar re sioul, skañvaet ar re bounner, adyaouank ar re gozh! Er penn kentañ eus an diskampadeg-se, ar merc'hed a oa e penn diwezhañ ar c'hañvambroug o latennat, a sache o skasoù ganto mar gouient, en ur stardañ atav o disglaverioù ouzh o bruched hag en ur skuermal: "Biskoazh kemend-all, biskoazh kemend-all! An diaoul eo!" War o lerc'h e rede ar baotred a oa bremaik o kemerout nerzh dre "gleuziañ gwer" en ostaleri. Ret eo anzav ne voent ket pell (en abeg d'an nerzh-se) o tremen merc'hed o disglavierioù.

O klask tremen e-biou dezho holl, ho pije merzet ivez kuzulierien ar barrez, o dorn war o fenn, d'o zogoù-melons da chom, ha lonket e chaok-butun gant an eil-vaer (anat e oa rak ruz e oa e gokenn). War-lerc'h ar re-mañ e trote kichen-ha-kichen kamaradoù kozh Kerangwenn, unan anezho o sachañ gwreg ar jeneral d'e heul.

An Aotrou Maer, eñ, goude bezañ chomet ur pennadig da estlammañ ouzh ar jeneral advev, a skarzhas ivez, savet c'hwen pelloc'h dezhañ en e loeroù. A-rez an douflez ez ae ha hep dale, goude diskar Janed an Arc'her war he revr, e voe e-mesk ar re gentañ. Ken prim ez ae ma tegouezhas e-unan-penn war leurgêr ar vourc'h (Diwezhatoc'h, un den hag a c'haller fiziout ennañ, a c'hourlavaras din penaos en devoa maer Lannevern, sur a-walc'h, hag en desped d'e seiz vloaz ha daou-ugent, taolet d'an traoñ rekord-ar-bed an 800-metr-e-gwiskamant-d'ar-sul).

Kement-se holl a leunie ar straed hag a zaoulamme e-giz ur vandennad saout pennfollet. War o lerc'h e teue o maesaer, e-giz gwialenn en e zorn, e gleze o treiñ a-us d'e benn, hag o stirlinkat en aer an devezh flour-se a viz mezheven, e vruchedad medalinier. Hopal a rae, e vouezh o vezañ trec'h da holl safar an dec'hadeg: "Me a zesko deoc'h... ya, me a zesko deoc'h..."

E-keit-se e oa aet Nikolaz, Lom ar C'hezeg Bras ha Samson ar Fibleg da guzhat d'ar vered e logell an touller-bezioù, hag an Aotrou Person, pignet war ar c'harr-kañv a daole dour binniget a-dro-jouez.

N'echuas ar redadeg-parrez-se nemet e-kichen an iliz pa verzas unan bennak ne oa ket an Aotrou Jeneral Olier Kerangwenn ouzh o heul ken. Pep hini a c'hallas neuze ober war-dro e vloñsadennoù ha kempenn e zilhad.

Olier, avat, a oa sac'het e Tavarn ar Gazeg Wenn, berr warnañ ha torret dezhañ. Antronoz e kuitae ar barrez, brudet ha mezhek. Nikolaz Briant a skoas d'an douar e dog daougorniek. Dilezel a reas e garg a baotr Karr an Ankou peogwir n'houle ket kas tud vev d'ar vered ken.

Translation

Lannevern in Mourning, *1949* (Extract)

I don't know either if you have ever been to the funeral of a one-eyed general. If you have, what I am going to tell you now is not going to surprise you. Here we go: The sun was beating so strongly on the many heads and their brains were heating up so much that, after a while, the men had to put their hats on. Then, when the hearse reached the bend in the narrow road leading to the churchyard, Nikolaz's mare stopped for a few seconds. Not that it was tired, but in fact, in that very bend, there was a small house which bore in black letters on its white-washed front, the following words: *Café du Cimetière*, and a little further down: *Allée de boules*. You may well think – and no one will think the worst of you for it – that Nikolaz went there often enough, to wet his throat and play bowls on his way back from the churchyard. But why did the mare make a mistake on that particular day? Why did it stop on her way there? That is another thing I don't know.

Whatever, Nikolaz quickly pulled on the reins and muttered some angry words to the mare. The sexton, who was singing a hymn at the time, noticed the incident and changed key twice!

Again, those who noticed the incident thought it strange that the animal should refuse to bring the honoured General Kerangwenn to his last place of rest and that they should hear the sexton's voice falter.

"Bad signs," said the Mayor to the Assistant Mayor next to him. However the Assistant Mayor was not able to reply as he was in the process of moving his quid of tobacco from one cheek to the other.

Just before arriving at the entrance to the churchyard, an officer, who had been hearing for a while unusual squeals coming from the hearse, ran madly up to the very front of the procession.

"Stop! Stop! I tell you," he yelled to Nikolaz.

"What?" replied Nikolaz sharply from his seat, "Are you mad? Get away from here!"

"Can't you hear?" boomed the officer. "The general is not dead."

"The General is not dead? I am afraid that the sun is getting too much for you! Shoo! Get away from here!"

"And you must be deaf! Can't you hear General Kerangwenn protesting in his coffin! You are surely not going to bring a live man to his graveside, are you?"

It was true. There were noises and grumblings coming from the coffin. Nikolaz Briant turned as white as a sheet.

"Confound it!" was all he could say.

He quickly sent for the grave-digger, who was also a carpenter, in order to open the coffin; on that day he also became a professional coffin-opener. In the meantime, the mourners, who were either sceptical, frightened or frankly terrified, were standing perfectly still. This shows clearly and plainly the enormous power a general has, albeit one on the way to his grave.

In the end, as soon as the nails had been removed from the coffin, its cover was brutally pushed back by Olier Kerangwenn himself. He was half-wrapped in his white shroud, his head was red and he was well and truly alive. He sat up, at first stunned and dazed by daylight, but he suddenly stood up, drawing himself up to his full height. He threw his shroud down and rubbed his elbows.

Maybe you have, at some time or other, seen a general stepping out of his coffin after coming back to life. In fact, it is an uncommon happening, a vision which reminds one both of a miracle and of the battle of Ballon. This is what happened: first of all – but let me add that the same is true of any general who rises from the dead – Kerangwenn stepped out of his coffin. He cut a very handsome figure in his best army uniform. His moustache was bigger, blacker and stiffer than ever, as he stared wide-eyed at the group of people in front of him. The men were rooted to the spot. The women were frightened. Some of them made the sign of the cross on their chests, others fell to their knees, while the country women, clasping their umbrellas to their bosoms, were praying to the Patron Saint of Lannevern. They all thought that they were seeing a ghost or a demon sprung up from hell. If it were not for his big moustache, Kerangwenn could have thought that he was an angel sent by the Lord to appear in front of this assembly of Christians.

His wife then suddenly shouted at him: "Olier! Olier." That is when frightful things started happening. Olier flew into a terrible rage. I don't know if it was the shrill voice of his wife which spurred him on, or if he wanted to imitate Nominoé driving away the Franks centuries ago. Maybe he just thought that all these people were making fun of him. As for myself, I rather think that it was the sight of the bowler hats worn by the mayor and his councillors which made him furious.

Whatever it was, he let out a roar, a fearsome one, which I think was similar to the roar of the lion in the desert. He bent down to pick up his kepi and then, draw-ing the ceremonial sword with a golden handle which was resting on his hip, he jumped from the hearse with the speed of a meteor crossing the sky on an oppres-sive summer night, and screamed at the top of his head words that no one under-stood. The poor Christians, when they saw the sword glinting in the air, fled at full speed through the narrow path of the churchyard.

If it is the custom for a general to run after his fleeing enemies, I have always found it surprising and rather improper for a dead man to uphold the tradition of running with a sword after his weeping mourners.

In order to be thoroughly entertained by such a sight, one needs to see it from the second floor of a house. Had you been on a balcony, as I happened to be, you would have witnessed precisely what happened:

As soon as the general began to run, you would have seen a great miracle: lame people lost their limps, the wise turned mad, the quiet ones turned into rioters, the fat ones became light and the old folks regained their youth! The women who had been chattering at the end of the procession were leading the exodus. They were scattering away as fast as they could, still clasping their umbrellas to their bosoms, while bawling at the same time: "My goodness! My goodness! It is the devil!"

330 of the Ermine

Behind them ran the men who, a few minutes ago, had been gathering strength by having a drink in the inn. I must say that it did not take them long, thanks to their newly gathered strength, to overtake the umbrella-carrying women.

Trying to overtake them all, you would also have noticed the village councillors, their hands on their heads to prevent their bowlers from falling off. It was obvious that the assistant mayor had swallowed his quid as his face was bright red. Behind all these, Kerangwenn's old companions were trotting away, one of them dragging the general's wife by the hand.

As for the mayor, who had stayed for a little while to express his surprise at the resurrection of the general, his fear took the better of him and he scampered off too. He was running close to the roadside ditch, and, after knocking down Janed an Arc'her flat on her behind, he was amongst the leading ones. He was sprinting so fast that he arrived all by himself on the village square. Later, a perfectly reliable man stated to me that the mayor of Lannevern had, without a doubt and in spite of his forty-seven years, smashed the world record for the 800 metre race in Sunday clothes.

All these people filled the street, scuttling away like a herd of mad cows. Running after them was their cowherd. Instead of holding the usual stick, he was twirling his sword above his head and the medals on his chest were glinting in the sunshine of this balmy June day. He was yelling, and his voice could easily be heard above the pandemonium of the exodus: "I'll teach you! Yes, I'll teach you!"

During that time, Nikolaz, Lom ar C'hezeg Bras and Samson ar Fibleg had gone to hide in the gravedigger's hut while the priest, now perched on the hearse, was throwing holy water all around.

This village race only ended by the church, when someone noticed that General Olier Kerangwenn was no longer following them. Everyone started counting their bruises and straightening up their clothes. As for Olier, out of breath, all his strength drained away, he had stopped at the Inn of the White Mare. The next day he left the village, humiliated by his notoriety. Nikolaz Briant threw his cocked hat to the ground and gave his resignation as hearse driver because he no longer wanted to bring living people to their graves.

Snapshots of Brittany

Julius Caesar
The Veneti

From The Conquest of Gaul *by Julius Caesar, written about 52 BC and describing a battle that took place about four years earlier. The Veneti were a powerful seafaring and trading people and had been a thorn in the flesh of the Romans for some time. In the end Caesar gathered together an army and a large fleet of ships to do battle with the Veneti. As described in the following extract it took some time and a generous slice of luck for the Romans to defeat them. Caesar, afterwards, cut the throats of the council of the Veneti and sold the people as slaves.*

Such was the position of most of the enemy strongholds, situated at the ends of spits of land and on the headlands, that they could not be approached on foot at high tide (which happened regularly, twice a day, every twelve hours) and ships found themselves aground at low tide. For one or other of these reasons, it was very difficult to lay siege on such places. Sometimes, it was necessary by a huge amount of work, to build terraces or breakwaters, which kept the sea at bay and enabled the attackers to get on a level with the ramparts. But the besieged as soon as they saw that their position was impossible would bring up a number of ships, of which they had a large number, took all their possessions, and set off for neighbouring, equally well situated for defence, strongholds. For the best part of the summer they were able to pursue these tactics because they had little to fear when escaping from our ships which were weather-bound and sailing was difficult with the changing winds and made all the more difficult to navigate in that vast, open sea, subject to high tides and bereft of harbours.

The ships of the enemy were built and rigged in the following way: the bottoms were much flatter than ours, and that made it easier for them to ride shallow waters and low tides. Their bows were exceptionally high and their sterns were such as to be suitable for high seas and storms; their hulls made entirely of oak, so they were able to withstand any amount of shocks and rough usage; their cross-timbers, made of beams a foot wide, were joined together with iron bolts thick as a thumb; their anchors were secured with iron chain, instead of ropes; their sails were made of raw hides or thin leather, either because they had no flax, or did not know how to use it, or because they thought (and this is the most likely) that sails such as ours could not withstand the violent storms and squalls of the Atlantic and were not suitable for such heavy vessels as theirs. In meeting these ships the only advantage our ships had was their speed and that they could be propelled with oars; but in other respects the ships of the enemy were much more suitable in stormy weather. We could not damage them by ramming because they were so solidly built; their height made it difficult to reach them with missiles or board them with grappling irons; and when the wind blew and they were running before it, they weathered the storm more easily, they could enter shallow water with greater safety, and when they were left aground by the tide they feared nothing of the reefs and the sharp rocks; all these problems caused great risks to our ships [...]

One device prepared by our men, however, proved very useful – pointed hooks fixed on the ends of long poles, like grappling-irons used in sieges. With these the halyards were grasped and pulled taut, and then snapped by rowing hard away. This brought the yards down, and since the Gallic ships relied completely on their sails and rigging, when stripped of these they were immediately immobilised. After that it was a soldier's battle, in which the Romans proved by far the superior [...]

When the yards of an enemy ship were torn down as described, two or three of ours would get alongside and the soldiers would make vigorous efforts to board it. When the natives saw what was happening, and after the loss of several ships [...] they tried to escape. They had already put their ships before the wind when suddenly such a dead calm fell that they could not stir. Nothing could have been more fortunate for us. We were able to complete the victory by pursuing and capturing the vessels one after another, and only a few managed to make land when night came after a battle that lasted from ten o'clock in the morning until sunset.

Tangi Malmanche

Ar Baganiz, *1931* (Lodenn)

This three act play is about the lives of the ship wreckers of the north-western coast of Brittany, known as Bro Bagan. The play was first published in special editions of the literary magazine Gwalarn *in 1931 and performed in Plouescat on August 25, 1931. The Breton language publishing house, Al Liamm, published it as a separate book for the first time in 1976, rough-ly coinciding with the centenary of Malmanche's birth. Malmanche is one of finest playwrights in the Breton language and* Ar Baganiz *one of his most interesting works. The play, which deals with the lives and traditions of the people who lit fires and lanterns on the cliffs to attract ships on to the rocks, is set in August, 1681. The coastline of Brittany around Kerlouan is lit-tered with erratics – large stones carried in the ice age and shaped so that they often look like ani-mals – hence the references to* The Mare *in the first extract, and* The Dog *in the second.*

[From Act 1]

Sezni, *e-unan, en ur vousc'hoarzin*
Gant lezenn ar roue ne sav 'met disput;
gant Lezenn ar Mor 'vez unvan an dud.
Tangou a dremen
A 'ta Tangou

Tangou
A 'ta Sezni!

Sezni
Dec'h vintin,
m'em eus soñj ac'h eus kontet din
daou wenneg re 'vit ur c'harrad bezhin.
Setu int amañ. Dal.

Tangou
Den onest oc'h, Sezni.
A-enep an dud ne garit pec'hiñ,
'vel ar person 'n deus prezeget.
Klevet 'c'h eus ar sarmon?

Sezni
Da gomz gwir n'em eus ket.
Rak seul ma teuan koshoc'h-kozh
etretant e tapan repoz.
Un dra vat eo sertenamant
d'ar merc'hed ha d'an dud yaouank.
Peseurt 'oa ar sujed?

Tangou
Arabat ober gaou
ouzh an nesañ, dre gomzoù na dre oberioù.

Sezni
En-tailh setu ur sujed mat.
Ouzh an nesañ eo ret bezañ onest.
N'eo ket a-walc'h eo reiñ d'ar gest ...
Me 'oar meur a hini o deus laosket er plad ...
Hag e c'hoarzh gant un aer fin.

Tangou, *izeloc'h e vouezh.*
Sezni, un dra 'zo hag am rent nec'het:
aon am eus n'em befe pec'hed.
       Azezañ a ra e-kichen Sezni.
Te 'c'h eus soñj, da ouel Nedeleg,
al lestr 'zo deuet war ar c'herreg …
Un den eus ar mor 'm eus sachet.

Sezni
Pelec'h?

Tangou
War an traezh e-tal ar Gazeg.

Sezni
An den 'oa dit.

Tangou
Din 'oa an den,
n'eo ket gwir?

Sezni
Se 'zo al Lezenn.

Tangou
Outañ em eus, evel rezon,
goulennet paeañ e ranson.

Sezni
Arc'hant en doa?

Tangou
Ya. Da larout eo, ur gwennegig bennak …
Ha refuzet en deus.

Sezni
Pe 'vit tra?

Tangou
N'ou'n ket perak.
Neuze, gantan 'm eus darc'haouet …
Me 'oa droug ennon, me 'm eus skoet …
N'em eus ket skoet start 'elato,

ma 'z eo bet 'n em gavet maro.

Sezni
Kalz en em gav en doare-se
antronoz goude ur peñse …

Tangou
Ar gwir 'oa ganin sur … Nemet
ouzh va nesañ, gaou am eus graet!

Sezni
Da nesañ ne deo ket, 'n hini deuet a bell vro!

Tangou
'Gav dit? Me n'on ket dinec'h 'elato.
Sellet em eus ouzh an Daolenn:
spontusañ poan 'zo evel-henn:
ur rod vras warni kontelloù
da zisparfoeltrañ 'r bouzelloù …
Kement-se Sezni, a ra din tourmant.
Da vont da gofez 'm eus ur bras a c'hoant.

Sezni
Chom 'ta. 'Vit ar pezh a lerez,
nep hini ne da da gofez.

Tangou
Koulskoude, Sezni, me 'm eus keuz …
Ya, teruplamant, aon am eus
na vervo an nouenn em fenn
m 'z in diremed d'an Ifern.
Rak pa soñjan, 'n aotrou person
'zo desket mat e pep feson.

Sezni
Ar person? Re yaouank eo c'hoazh,
pa n'eo memes hanter-kant vloaz!
N'eo ket eus barrez ouzhpenn …
Ne oar banne eus al Lezenn …
'N aotrou person a-raok; nebaon,
n'en dije graet ar seurt sarmon.

Tangou
Te 'gred en dije laret er gador
e ve brav sentiñ ouzh Lezenn ar Mor?

Sezni
'Ket avat! Mes eus an traoù-se
Hennezh d'ihanañ nep tro ne gomze!

Tangou
Ar person nevez 'oar tout a zoare …
Lenn a rae war an Aviel
ma 'z eo merket ennañ an traoù selestiel …
Hon oberioù, 'mezañ, 'vo pouezet gant Doue,
ar re vat da gentañ, ar re fall da c'houde;
n'eo ket gant ur c'hrog-pouez, kompren,
gant ur valañs avat, ur valañs div bladenn
'vel 'z eus gant ar varc'hadourien.

Sezni
Un ober mat bennak ac'h eus graet ez puhez?

Tangou
Heu … me 'lar va fedenn bemdez …
ha bep sul ez an d'ar barrez …

Sezni
D'ur c'hristen se 'zo e zever anat.
Ober vad n'eo ket holl; ret eo ober ar mad.

Tangou
Me 'ro da gest ar veleien;
me 'laosk bara d'ar beorien …

Sezni
Abalamour ma 'z eo ar c'hiz
da vevañ an dud a iliz;
ha pa laoskez ur c'hozh gwenneg,
e kav dit ec'h eus laosket dek!
Panevet al lorc'h hag ar boaz,
peorien ha kloer 'yafe sur en noazh!

Tangou, *en ur c'hoarzhin*
Gwir eo … Ma ne vemp endalc'het …

Mantret
Ha n'em eus kempouez d'am pec'hed!

Sezni, *goude bezañ soñjet pizh ha pell*
An den a lerez … Te 'poa roet sikour
dezhañ da vont 'maez eus an dour?

Tangou
Ya sur. Don eo ar mor aze.
Panevedon en em veuze.

Sezni
Brav. Ar seurt ober hep douetañs
a gempouezo just er valañs.
Droug ha mad e pep a bladenn
hag e chomo sonn ar walenn.

Tangou, *laouen*
Droug en tu-mañ, mad en tu-se,
hag ar walenn a chomo sonn …
Sezni Falc'han, m'en tou Doue,
finoc'h out eget ar person!

Sezni, *o prezeg distag*
Pec'hed ne c'hall bezañ, na dizenor
gant a re a sent ouzh Lezenn ar Mor.
Rak ar lezenn-se 'zo ul lezenn vat,
diktet da Voiz gant Doue an Tad.
N'eus ket a berson ha n'eus ket a roue
a c'hallfe herzel ouzh al lezenn-se.
Tangou en em denn
Arabat meskañ e nep giz
traoù ar mor ha traoù an iliz.

★ ★ ★

[*From the Third Act of* Ar Baganiz. *Sezni, the old squire defends the shipwreckers' rights and methods in this conversation with The Officer. Ar C'hi (The Dog) is a rock on the section of coast considered to be the property of Sezni.*]

Sezni
Setu.
Erru eo bet an den da vare an noz du.

Degemer en deus bet. Riv ha naon 'oa dezhañ.
Bet en deus eus va zan, ivez eus va bara.
Eus va gwin, a zoare, – sellit, – en deus evet.
A-benn ar fin, e walc'h a bep tra pa 'n deus bet,
ha pa voe poent mont kuit, me, hervez al lezenn,
'm eus goulennet outañ paean 'vit e zaspren.

An Ofiser, *gant ur gourlamm*

E zaspren?

Sezni

E zaspren … Peogwir ur martolod,
taolet gant an dampest un tu bennak en aod,
a zo mestr warnezañ perc'henn an douar-se.
'N hini 've deuet e lestr ar C'hi e peñse
'dle paeañ e zaspren. Se 'zo Lezenn ar Mor.

An Ofiser

N'eo ket hini ar Roue. Mes n'eus forzh. Ha goude?

Sezni

Skoet am eus.

An Ofiser

Ha neuze?

Sezni

N'en deus ket fiñvet pelloc'h.

An Ofiser

Bo. – Me 'gav din ec'h eus klevet an ordrenañs,
embannet dec'h vintin. Formal eo an defañs
Da c'houlenn nag arc'hant na tra digant nep den,
Hag eñ eus ar vro-mañ, pe eus a vro estren.

Sezni

Marteze 'm eus klevet; ar soñj n'em eus ket ken.
Gant hoc'h ordrenañsoù, na koant ur saladenn!
Ar pezh laosket d'ur sul, d'ar sul all 'zo tennet;
un dra vrav er mintin, en noz 'zo difennet.
Ni avat etretant a rank da gaout hor boued,
pa'z a, goude 'vel kent, daouzek real er skoed!

A, e-lec'h disfoeltrañ 'n amzer, noz evel deiz,
ken pell du-hont, en e vaner bras e Pariz,
'kreiz e femelennoù o c'hoari ar brelan,
e deurenn ouzh an daol hag e gein ouzh an tan,
ra zeuio ar roue bras, e tro ar goañv digor,
pa yud ar barr-avel ha pa c'hlaour ar mor,
ra zeuio d'hor gwelout o firbouchal en traezh,
e-pad ma ouel er gêr bugale ha gwragez …
Ra dañvo-eñ hor boued, hor c'hozh bara ludu,
poazhet gant ar mannoù dastumet a bep tu …
Ra welo-eñ ar re 'vez plantet er vered,
pa ne vez kavet koad 'vit ober un arched …
Dezhañ dont da c'houzañv gant ar riv hag an naon,
ya, dezhañ dont, d'ho roue, da larout e gwirion
penaos al lestr, taolet gant an dampest en aod,
penaos an estrañjour, penaos ar martolod,
ha pa 'n defe hennezh trinket ganimp ouzh taol,
dezhañ larout penaos tud ha traoù aet da goll
n'int ket en hor galloud hag en hor perc'henniaj;
dezhañ dont, ha mar kred ober, dezhañ en nac'h!

Doue, d'an eizhvet deiz, pa grouas ar Pagan,
d'an abostol Moiz a ziktas al Lagan.
Hi 'zo Lezenn ar Mor, al lezenn veur a ra
d'ar Pagan e pep poent kavout e beadra.
Er parrezioù tro-dro, er memes rouantelezh,
ar re all o deus prad hag atil e-lec'h traezh;
aberioù mat o deus 'vit lakat e goudor
bageier ha rouedoù pa vez diroll ar mor.
'N ur larout o Fater int o deus en o soued
keuneud 'vit ober tan, gwinizh 'vit ober boued …
Ni avat, n'eus ganimp 'met kerreg ha tevenn.
Bep abardaez e reomp, ni ivez, hor pedenn
'vit kaout digant Doue an aluzen gaerañ,
pezhioù koad d'ober tan, ed mor d'ober bara,
ha skoedoù arc'hant sklaer a gaser d'ar veliaj
evit paeañ tailhoù, gabeloù ha fouaj …
Pe 'vern d'ar Roue, ket 'ta, mar deo ker ar panez!
Me n'em eus 'vit va rann 'met ur garreg en traezh.
Hounnezh a zo ar C'hi, va c'hi mat ha feal,
diwaller va ziegezh, prest atav da harzal
ouzh kement kantreer a red a-dreuz an dour,
ouzh an trubard daonet, ouzh al laer estrañjour.

Ar C'hi-se n'eo ket fall; ne ra nep hegerezh;
mes pa vez hegaset, ouzh den n'en deus truez;
ha pa'z eo desket-brav, bep taol ma pak ur c'had,
dezhañ ez a 'n eskern, ha dimp-ni ar c'hig mat.
A, grit ordrenañsoù, kreskit ar gobeloù,
diannezit an ti, skarzhit hor godelloù,
da gas va C'hi ganeoc'h biken ne viot gouest;
me 'ray va bolontez, ha me 'chomo ar mestr!

An Ofiser

Brav-tre eo da ziskours, 'met ar groug a dalvez.
Lazhet ec'h eus a-youl ur martolod, ur c'haezh,
n'en doa 'met e groc'hen evit e holl deñzor …

Translation

The Wreckers, *1931* (Extract)

Sezni, *alone, smiling*
The laws of the king do nothing but cause disputes;
The Law of the Sea brings people together.
Enter Tangou
Hello, Tangou

Tangou
Hello, Sezni

Sezni
Yesterday morning,
I think you gave me two pennies too many for a load of seaweed.
Here they are for you now. Take them.

Tangou
You're an honest man, Sezni.
No man should sin against his neighbour,
As the priest said in his sermon.
Did you hear his sermon?

Sezni
To tell you the truth, no.
As I get older
I need more sleep.
No doubt they are very good for women and children.
What was his subject?

Tangou
> That no one should do harm
To his neighbour, in word or in deed.

Sezni
It sounds like a good subject.
One should deal honestly with one's neighbour.
It is not enough to give to the collection …
I know of many who put money on the plate …
> *With a cynical laugh*

Tangou, *lowering his voice*
Sezni, one thing worries me;
I am afraid that I have sinned.
> *He sits next to Sezni*
You remember, at Christmas time,
a ship going on the rocks …
I pulled a man from the water.

Sezni
Where?

Tangou
In the cove opposite The Mare.

Sezni
He was yours.

Tangou
> That man was mine,
That's right, isn't it?

Sezni
That's the Law.

Tangou
From him, as it is reasonable,
I demanded a ransom.

Sezni
He had money?

Tangou

Yes. That is to say, he had a penny or two.
And he would not give them to me.

Sezni

Why not?

Tangou

I don't know.
So I hit him …
I was angry and I punched him …
it was not a hard blow …
but he died.

Sezni

Many are found like that
the day after a shipwreck …

Tangou

I was certainly within my rights… But to my neighbour
I did much harm!

Sezni

He who comes from a foreign land is not your neighbour!

Tangou

Is that so? But I worry nevertheless.
I have looked at the picture showing Hell:
the worse torture is that
of a large wheel with knives
to tear out the bowels …
I am tormented by it, Sezni.
I much want to go to the priest to confess.

Sezni

Don't. Of what you have just spoken,
no one goes to confess.

Tangou

Nevertheless, Sezni, I am truly sorry …
Yes, terribly; I am afraid
that the anointing oil will boil in my head
if I go to Hell for ever.

After all the priest
is well versed in all things.

Sezni

The priest? He is still far too young,
he is not yet fifty years old!
What's more, he is not from this parish ...
He knows nothing of the Law ...
The old priest, now,
he would never have preached such a sermon.

Tangou

You believe that he would from the pulpit
Preach that it is right to obey the Law of the Sea?

Sezni

I didn't say that! But at least
he never discussed such matters!

Tangou

The new priest knows everything ...
He reads from the Gospels,
and they talk about Heaven ...
Our actions, he said, will be weighed by God,
the good ones first and then the bad ones;
not with a spring scale, you understand,
but with proper scales, with two pans
like those which merchants own.

Sezni

Have you done a good deed in your life?

Tangou

Hum, I say my prayers everyday ...
and every Sunday I go to Mass ...

Sezni

But that's only your duty as a Christian.
To appear to do good is not enough; it is necessary to do good.

Tangou

I give to the priest's collection;
I give bread to the poor ...

Sezni

Because it is normal
to give to the people of the church;
and when you give a penny or two
you think that you have done well!
Were it not for pride and custom,
the poor and the clerics would have to go naked!

Tangou, *laughing*

Quite right ... if we didn't have to ...
With heavy heart
I have nothing to place opposite my sin!

Sezni, *after thinking long and hard*

The man you were talking about ... You helped him
To come out of the water?

Tangou

Of course! The sea there is deep.
He would have drowned were it not for me.

Sezni

Good. Such a deed without doubt
will be weighed in the scales.
Bad and good in each of the pans
and the needle will point straight up.

Tangou, *delighted*

Bad on this side, good on that one,
and the needle will point straight up...
Sezni Falc'han, on my word,
You are cleverer than the priest!

Sezni, *speaking seriously*

No sin nor disgrace will come
to those who obey the Law of the Sea.
Because that law is a good law,
given to Moses by God the Father.
It is not for a priest nor a king
to go against such a law as that.
Exit Tangou
Never should they be mixed,
the matters of the sea and those of the church.

★ ★ ★ ★ ★

The Wreckers, *1931*

From Act Three

Sezni
It was like this.
A stranger came here in the middle of the night.
He was welcomed. He was cold and hungry.
He was invited to the fire, and to eat my bread.
He drank well of my wine, as you can guess.
Finally he had his fill of everything,
and it was time for him to take his leave. I, as the law permits,
asked him to pay his ransom.

The Officer, *startled*
His ransom?

Sezni
His ransom … Because when a sailor,
is cast by the storm on the beach,
he becomes the property of the owner of that piece of land.
He whose ship is wrecked on the Dog must pay
a ransom to me. That's the Law of the Sea.

The Officer
But not that of the King. But that's beside the point. What then?

Sezni
I struck him.

The Officer
And then?

Sezni
He never moved after that.

The Officer
So! I take it that you heard the instructions
read yesterday morning. It is forbidden
to demand money or anything from any shipwrecked man,
whether he is from this country, or a foreigner.

Sezni

Perhaps I heard it but I can't remember.
As for your instructions, they are a fine mess!
What is permitted one Sunday, is forbidden the next;
it is fine to do something in the morning, in the evening it is unaccept-
able.
In the meantime we have to eat,
because, now as before, it takes twelve pence to make a shilling!

Instead of whiling away his time, night and day,
far away in his large palace in Paris,
amongst his women playing cards,
his belly to the table and back to the fire,
if only your great king would come here in the middle of winter,
when the storm howls and the sea foams,
that he would come to see us scouring the beaches,
while the children and women weep at home …
Let him come to taste our food, our stale brown bread,
baked on firewood gathered from wherever …
Let him see the dead placed in the earth,
when there is no wood to make a coffin …
Let him come to suffer the cold and the famine;
yes, let him come, your king, to tell us face to face
why we have no rights
on the ship, cast by the tempest on the shore,
on the unknown sailor
who may well have raised his glass at our table,
on all the drowning people and on all the wreckage:
Let him come, and should he dare, let him deny our claim!

God, on the eighth day, created the Pagans,
to Moses he spoke the Lagan.
It is the Law of the Sea, the great law
of the Pagans which provides them with sustenance.
In neighbouring parishes, in the same kingdom,
others have meadows and good fields instead of beaches;
sheltered estuaries to anchor their boats
and keep their nets safely when the sea is rough.
When they say their prayers in the morning they have
wood to light their fires, wheat to provide food…
As for us, we have nothing but rocks and dunes.
Every evening, we, too, say a prayer
that we shall receive from God his generous bounty,

pieces of wood to light a fire, algae to make bread,
and shining silver shillings to take to the bailiff
to pay our taxes, fire tax and salt tax ...
What difference is it to the King if the parsnips are dear!
My share is small, a rock on the beach.
It is called the Dog, my good and faithful dog,
It guards my family, is always ready to bark
at the thieves who come across the sea,
at the cursed traitor, and the foreign thief.
That Dog is not bad; he provokes no one;
but when he is provoked, he has no mercy for anyone;
As he is well trained, every time he catches a hare,
he keeps for himself the bones, and gives us the good meat.
Ha! Make your laws, raise your taxes,
rob our homes, empty our pockets,
you can never take away my Dog;
I shall have my way, and I shall remain the master!

The Officer
You speak well, but these words will send you to the gallows.
You have deliberately killed a sailor, a poor man,
who had nothing in this world but his skin.

Jakez Riou

Ar Run-heol, *1934* (Lodenn)

Brumenn wenn ar beure a deuze e goueled an draonienn gant heol mezeven o hori.

Rivanon, o pignad gand diribin an dorgenn, goustad, evel gwall zammet, a jomas harped e hanter hent. Teurel a reas eur sell a-dreñv e gein, hag e welas e oa kaer an draonienn gant ar gliz war ar hlazenn hag an heol o para enni penn-da-benn. Alanad a reas, evel huanadi, hag, e-kreiz-oll, en em gavas skuiz. Hogen, ne oa ket skuiz e gorv. E galon avad, ne lavaran ket.

Didrouz e oa an draonienn ha ne fiñve enni nemed lufr an heol war ar hlazenn hleb.

Rivanon a zellas en-dro dezañ ha ne welas hent-karr e neb leh. Hogen, ne glaskas ket gouzoud ha dond a ree kouerien da zastum eno ar geot hir. Ne zoñjas nemed eun dra: an draonienn a oa gwerh ha dizarempred.

Arvesti an draonienn didrouz ha dizarempred a oa dudi da galon Rivanon. Merzoud a reas e oa ar hlazenn, e-kreiz an draonienn, drusoh eget er gwrimennou. Eno, e brizheol ar geot hir hag an elestr, e piltrote moarvad eur wazig, hag he dour, en eur ziskenn, a hoarze en he lammouigou d'ar gleskeri o tihun e freskadurez ar prad.

C'hoant a zeuas da Rivanon diskenn beteg goueled an draonienn evit selaou mouskan ar wazig en he lammouigou ha selled ouz ar balafanned hag an nadoziou-êr o c'hoari er bleuniou o tigeri.

Trei a reas kein d'an draonienn hag e kendalhas da dostaad, goustad, ouz laez uhella an dorgenn. Evid arvesti an draonienn gwelloh, gand ar gliz war ar hlazenn ha mousc'hoarz an heol o para enni penn-da-benn.

Tost d'al lein eh azezas. C'hoant a zavas dezañ ranna eur gomz gant unan ben-nag. En-dro dezañ ne welas den ebet. Ar golveni, ar boh-ruziged hag ar zidaned a razailhe e strouez ar hleuziou hag er brouskoad. E-harz e dreid, ar raden tener, nevez savet diouz an douar skañv, a reutae da wrez an deiz o danteleziou kildroet, hag ar gwenan aketuz a dremene hebiou dezañ gant eur zardon skiltr.

Rivanon a zelle... Ne wele ha ne gleve. Chom a reas lent e spered en e brederiou, morzet ma oa ennañ e-unan e oll hoantou gourel.

Liver e oa dre vicher, ha brudet e ano e meur a vro. Steuet e-noa poltredou priñsezed ha rouanezed, hag euz ar broiou estren e teue dezañ ar vrasa meuleudi. E boltredou a oa dreist, a bell, da re an arzourien vrudeta, kement a wirionez ha kement a vuhez virvidig a lakae enno. Hogen, na brud na meuleudi ne gavas degemer e kalon an arzour. Livet e-noa, e gwirionez, poltredou priñsezed en o hened ha rouanezed en o gloar... O sellet outo, avad, goude ma oant peurechu, Rivanon en em gave doaniet, rag e daoulagad ar priñsezed e luhe atao pe ar vrasoni pe an hudurniez pe an techou all. Ne gavas morse poltred disi e-touez e oberou. Hag eñ e-noa klasket atao liva ar wirionez kaer, ar gened keneduz hag ar hlanded hlan...

Neuze, digalonekaet, e kuitaas ar gêrbenn. Dond a reas da gornog e yaouankiz, da gesta ha da gavout marteze, war ar mêz, er glaster hag en heol, eun distera euz ar vuhez hlan e-noa klasket beteg-henn, e leh all, en aner.

Rivanon a arveste an draonienn heoliet. Gant gwrez an deiz e save diouti fron-dou ar geot hag ar bleuniou, hag e peb tu e vouskane ar zeo nevez a-uz d'an douar o struja. Saouzanet e chomas, hag al levenez a waskas e galon a oa burzud hag estren-van.

An heol a oa uhel ha kreisteiz tremenet. Rivanon a oa azezet bepred en heveleb leh.

Boulhet-mad e oa an abardaez ha skeud ar gwez, en tu all d'an draonienn, a voukae en amhoulou. Sevel a reas hag e kendalhas da vond war-raog, en arvar, e c'hwez vad ar mêziou didrouz.

En em gavoud a reas gand eur houer o tond euz ar brouskoad gant eur gazeliad aozilh.

– Emaoh o pourmen, aotrou?

Ar ger aotrou ne blijas ket da Rivanon. N'e-noa mui, e feson, dremm eun den euz e vro?

– O pourmen emaon.

– Ar haerra mare euz ar bloaz hag euz an deiz evid an hini e-neus amzer d'ober

baleadennou war ar mêz. Me a zo bet o troha aozilh er brouskoad, aze, rag ar panerou nevez a zeu da veza, goude eur bloavez labour, panerou koz ha didalvez.

– Klevit, va eontr, daoust hag ez eus eun hent da vond beteg an draonienn?

– Feiz, n'eus hini ebed, va den. Ar foenneg dourenneg-se ne ziwan enni nemed
broenn hag elestr, hag he geot ne dalvez nag an troh nag an droug. A viskoaz eo bet
dizarempred.

Ar respont-se a reas plijadur da Rivanon. Selled a reas outi eur wech c'hoaz a-
raog ober hent gand an den.

Goude eur pennadig bale a-dreuz ar parkeier, e welas Rivanon war laez an dorgenn eun ti gwaskedet el liorzou. Diouz ar ziminal, kuzet a-dreñv ar gwez avalou, e
save eur vogedenn, o pignad evel eur zeisenn hlaz war aour ar huz-heol.

– Da bell ez it? a houlennas ar houer.

– D'an Ilvern ez an, ha,'m eus aon, en em gavan dihentet.

– Hent hir ho-peus d'ober c'hoaz. Ma karit, me 'gaso ar mevel bihan d'hoh
ambrouga. Setu emaon degouezet. Deuit beteg an ti hag e tañvoh sistr ar vro.

Rivanon a heulias an den. A-dreuz ar bodennou kelvez, an heol a zile e sklêrijenn velen e skoasellou an hent ha war man ar riblenn. El liorz, ar hegined a ragache
en avalenned, hag ar mouîlhi, kludet e kelenn ar hleuziou, a hwitelle diehan, en
abardaez blod.

E oant tost ouz an ti pa zilammas eur plah yaouank euz al liorz. He fennad-bleo
kazugel a oa paket e diou vailhadenn war he diouskoaz, hag eul lien gwenn a gelhie
he zal, evel eur gurunenn. Treuzi a reas an hent en eur redadenn, evel en eur
dehoud en he spont. Hervez eur gweled, e oa dremmet-kaer, hag he horv, stardet
en he houheledenn, a oa ivez direbech.

Ne gredas ket Rivanon goulenn eun disterra diwar he fouez.

– Deuit tre, eme an den.

Rivanon a yeas an ti. Ar plah yaouank, he fennad-bleo kazugel paket e diou
vailhadenn hag eul lien gwenn en-dro d'he zal, a oa azezet e-tal an oaled hag a
domme he zreid ouz an tan.

– Mari, ha deut eo ar mevel bihan eus ar hovel?

– Ne gredan ket, a respontas ar wreg stouet he fenn a-uz d'he filligou.

– Ne zaleo ket, emichañs. Pa vo en-dro, c'hwi a gaso anezañ da ziskouez hent an
Ilvern d'an aotrou-mañ.

Mari a zavas he fenn hag a zaludas an den.

– Azezit, aotrou, emezi, hag en eur hortoz, e tebroh marteze eur grampoezenn,
gand ma kavit mad ar hrampoez aozet war ar mêz?

– Ar hrampoez aozet war ar mêz a zo ar re wella, moereb.

– N'eus nemed sistr, eme an ozah, ha kaled eo moarvad da staon an hini n'eo ket
boazet outañ. Gand ma tiskenno...

Ma tiskenne?... Ne grede ket an arzour anzav e oa heb tamm abaoe ar beure,
chomet ma oa da henaouegi war an dorgenn.... Debri a reas a youl vad ar grampoezenn amanennet servijet dezañ war eur plad, hag ar sistr a floure en eur ziskenn.

– Gweled a ran, emezañ, n'eo ket kollet oll hiziou mad ar vro, hag e kaver c'hoaz maouezed dispar da veza an toaz.

An ozah a azezas ivez ouz taol dirazañ evit debri eur grampouezenn a-raog mond da voueta e loened.

– O! emezañ en eur respont, ne vez ket greet mui, en amzer hirio, kalz krampoez war ar mêz, hag amañ, evel e leh all, ez eo kollet ar hiz. Nemed evit ar verh an hini eo...

Evid ar verh azezet e-tal an tan...

Translation

Sun Hill, *1934* (Extract)

The white morning fog was melting away in the base of the valley as the June sun was gathering strength.

Rivanon was slowly walking up the side of the hill, as if carrying a burden, and stopped half-way up. Casting a look behind him, he took in the beauty of the valley, the dew on the grass and the sun shining down on it. He breathed in, sighed and suddenly felt weary. It was not his body which was tired but his mind.

The valley was silent and nothing moved in it except for the sparkle of the sun on the wet grass.

Rivanon looked around him, but did not see any path leading down. He did not ask himself whether farmers ever went right down to gather the long grass, but merely thought that the valley was virgin and isolated.

Gazing at the silent and isolated valley comforted him. He noticed that the grass at the bottom was growing more thickly than on the flanks. Down there, hidden by the long shining blades of grass and the wild irises, he knew that there was a stream bubbling along, and that its waters, skipping joyfully downwards, were laughing at the frogs waking up in the freshness of the meadow.

Rivanon wanted to go down to the bottom of the valley to listen to the babble of the bouncing river and look at the butterflies and dragonflies frolicking above the opening flowers. But he turned his back and continued to climb slowly towards the top of the hill. In this way, he could get a better view of the valley covered with dewy grass and basking in the cheerful sunshine.

He sat down near the summit. He would have liked to talk to someone, but there was no one around. Cantankerous sparrows, robins and pipits were twittering angrily in the undergrowth of the hedges and in the thickets. At his feet, the tender bracken, freshly sprung from the light soil, were uncurling their delicate lace in the heat of the day, as industrious bees buzzed by him shrilly.

Rivanon was looking but he was seeing nothing and hearing nothing. His mind was still sluggish and all his desires were muted.

He was an artist by trade and his name was famous in several countries. He had put on canvas portraits of princesses and queens, and his skill was much praised in foreign countries. His portraits, so truthful and life-like, were better than those of the most famous artists. However, neither fame nor praise gave him comfort. In truth, he had painted portraits of princesses in their beauty and those of queens in their glory, and yet, when he studied the finished work, he felt disappointed, because, in the glint of the princesses' eyes, there was always a gleam of either smugness or lust or some other defect. He never found a single of his portraits without some fault or other. Yet he had always aimed to paint the full truth, the perfect beauty, and the uncorrupted purity

Discouraged, he had left the capital and headed west, to the land of his youth, to search and hopefully to find, in the countryside, in the green landscape bathed in sunshine, a trace of the pure life he had always searched for in vain in other places.

Rivanon gazed on the sunbathed valley. As the heat of the day increased, he smelt the grass and flowers, and heard, from all sides, the new sap rising from the soil and turning it green. He was bemused, for the joy brimming in his heart felt like a miracle and amazed him.

The sun was high in the sky; it was now past midday. Rivanon was still sitting in the same place. At dusk, the shadow of the trees on the other side of the valley took on a purple tinge in the falling light. He got up and walked on, unsure where to go next, breathing in the pleasant smell of the silent fields.

He met a farmer coming out of a thicket, a bunch of willow branches under his arm.

"You are out for a walk, Sir?"

The title 'Sir' displeased Rivanon. Did he not look like a local man?

"Yes, I am out for a walk."

"This is the best time of year, and of day, for those who have time to go for walks in the countryside. I have been cutting willow branches in the thicket over there, because new baskets become old and useless after a year of use.

"Tell me! Is there a path leading down to the valley?"

"No, there isn't. Only reeds and irises grow down there, in the wet meadow. The grass has never been cut. It is not worth the trouble. The valley has always been left to its own devices."

Rivanon was pleased with the answer. He looked down at the valley once more and walked on with the man.

After cutting across a few fields, Rivanon saw a house and garden, sheltered by trees, on the hilltop. Smoke, climbing like a blue ribbon against the golden sunset, was coming out of a chimney hidden by apple-trees..

"Are you going far?" asked the farmer.

"I'm going to Ilvern, and I'm afraid I have lost my way."

"You still have a long way to go. If you wish, I shall ask the farmhand to show you the way. I am home now. Come to the house and I'll make you taste our local cider."

Rivanon followed the man. The sunrays, filtering through the clumps of hazel-trees, were leaving yellow specks on the uneven path and on the moss covering the verges. In the orchard, jays were twittering in the apple-trees, and blackbirds, perched in the holly bushes of the embankments, were whistling incessantly in the mellow evening.

They were near the house when a young girl dashed out of the orchard. Two plaits of dark hair reached down to her shoulders. A white headband circled her forehead like a crown. She ran across the path, at full speed, as though frightened. But a glimpse of her was enough to realise that she had beautiful features and that her body, squeezed in a corselet, was just as faultless.

Rivanon did not dare ask who she was.

"Come in," said the man.

Rivanon entered the house. The dark-haired girl with two plaits and a white hair-band around her forehead was sitting by the fireplace, warming her feet at the fire.

"Mari, is the farmhand back from the smithy?"

"I don't think so," replied his wife, her head bowed over her frying pans.

"I don't suppose he will be long. When he is back, send him to show this gentleman the road to Ilvern."

Mari lifted her head and greeted the man.

"Sit down, Sir. And since you have to wait, maybe you'd like to eat a pancake, if you like home-made pancakes, I mean."

"Home-made pancakes are excellent."

"There is only cider," said the host, "I know it feels rough to the palate if you are not used to it. But as long as you can drink it..."

As long as he could drink it? The artist did not wish to admit that he had not eaten the slightest morsel since breakfast, as he had stayed to gape at the hill. He hungrily ate the buttered pancake served to him on a plate, while the cider felt like velvet to his throat.

"I see," he said, "that all the old local customs have not been lost, and that some women still know how to mix a perfect batter."

The host sat in front of him at the table to eat a pancake before going to feed the cattle.

"Oh!" he replied; "Not a lot of pancakes are made in the countryside these days. Here, as in other places, the tradition has been lost. These were made specially for our daughter..."

For the daughter sitting by the fireplace...

Chrétien de Troyes

Yvain le Chevalier au lyon, Romans de la Table Ronde, *c.1177* (Extract)

This extract describes the Fountain of Barenton in Paimpont forest. Tradition says that if water from the fountain is sprinkled on the stone nearby – sometimes called Merlin's Stone – it will begin to rain.

I left the man after he had shown me the way. It must have been three hours later, noon even, when I saw the tree and the chapel. I can truly say that this was the finest pine that ever grew on earth. I do not believe that it could ever rain so hard that a drop of water could penetrate it, but would drip off the outer branches. From the tree I saw the basin hanging, of the finest gold that was ever for sale in any fair. As for the spring, you may take my word that it was boiling like hot water. The stone was of emerald, with holes in it like a cask, and there were four rubies underneath, more radiant and red than is the morning sun when it rises in the east. Not one word will I say which is false. I wished to see the marvellous appearance of the tempest and the storm; but in that I was not wise, for I would gladly have repented, if I could, after I had sprinkled the perforated stone with the water from the basin. But I fear I poured too much, for immediately I saw the heavens so break loose that from more than fourteen directions the lightning blinded my eyes, and all at once the clouds let fall snow and rain and hail. The storm was so fierce and terrible that a hundred times I thought I should be killed by the bolts which fell about me and by the trees which were rent apart. I was in great distress until the uproar was appeased. But God gave me such comfort that the storm did not continue long, and all the winds died down again. The winds dared not blow against God's will. And when I saw the air clear and serene I was filled with joy again. For I have observed that joy quickly causes trouble to be forgotten. As soon as the storm was completely past, I saw so many birds gathered in the pine tree (if any one will believe my words) that not a branch or twig was to be seen which was not entirely covered with birds. The tree was all the more lovely then, for all the birds sang in harmony, yet the note of each was different, so that I never heard one singing another one's note.

Yann-Vari Yann

Burzudo Breiz, *c.1860* (Lodenn)

Ma Breiz-Izel, te eo ar vro
Zo goloet ar vurzudo;
Ia, Breiz, ma vez anavezet
Dre ar bed holl e vez brudet.

Enn da greiz zo koajo teval,
Koajo dero, ledan ho zal;
Enn dro d'it e krozmol ar mor,
Te a zo koant, ma bro Arvor.

Da venezio, frost hag huel,
Zo brao da welet euz a bell;
Hag ar c'herrek, war ho c'hlipen,
Er c'houmoul aour a guz ho fenn.

Ez traouienno zo brouskoajo
Ha ieod med ebarz da brajo;
Till ha pin war grab an dosen
Hag er parko eosto melen.

Da sterio kamm gand ho dour skler
War zu ar mor a red zeder;
War da hencho, tort ha meinek,
Da gezek skanv a oar redek.

Redek buan er c'hlazenno
Da c'honid maout ha rubano,
Chasa goude war ann ara
Da hada ed d'ober bara.

Da botred vad, da verc'hed koant
A weler enn hent, kant ha kant,
O vont da bardon Gwir-Zikour,
Da Zant-Matelin Monkontour.

D'ar Releg, da Zantez-Anna,
War ho zroad hag enn eur gana;
Da Remengol, Zand-Iann-ar-Biz,
Ar fe a zo gant-he diskuiz.

Setu aze, e berr gomzio,
Skeuden Breiz enn he douaro;
Hogen e kichen ar mor glaz
Me gav anezhi bravoc'h c'hoaz.

Translation

Breton Miracles, *c.1860* (Extract)

Brittany, you are a land
Full of miracles.
Yes, Brittany, by those who know her,
Is celebrated throughout the world.

Inland grow the dark woods,
Oak woods, large and leafy;
On the edges, the sea growls,
You are pretty, land of Arvor.

Your mounts, proud and high
Are lovely to see from afar;
The rocks on their crests
Hide their heads in the golden clouds.

The thickets grow in your valleys,
The luscious grass in your meadows;
Elm and pine trees on the flanks of dunes
And yellow harvests in the fields.

Your meandering rivers of clear water
Flow gently towards the sea;
On your winding and stony roads,
Your sprightly horses effortlessly trot along.

Gallop away on the grassy banks
To win the race and get ribbons,
And then drag the plough
To sow the wheat, our bread to be.

Your good men, your pretty girls,
By the hundreds, are making their way
To the pardon of Our Lady of Good Aid,
To Saint-Matelin Moncontour.

As they walk to Le Relecq, to Sainte Anne,
To Rumengol, to Saint-Jean du Doigt,
They sing.
The faith is strong and brings relief.

This is, in a few words,
The picture of inland Brittany.
But close to the blue sea,
I find her more beautiful still.

Kuilhandr

Labour ar mor, *1903*

Klevit! dirollet eo war aochou Breiz
Ar barr-amzer, spouron an dud a vor,
A rann kaloun an intanvezed geiz
Hag a laz tad bugaligou Arvor.

E korn an tan ha prennet mad ho tor,
O tud eürus a gomz, a gan dinec'h,
Sonjit, tud vad, sonjit en dud a vor
HaG er gragez o pedi er gwelec'h.

Ar mor a darz en dro da Vreiz-Izel,
Trouzal a ra noz ha deiz heb ehan;
En he c'hounar e flastr, war ar rec'hel
Goloet a eon, eur paourkez bag vihan.

War gein kommou, e kreiz iouc'h an avel,
Strakl ar gurun o krozal uz d'e benn,
An den a neunv, a stourm, a glask gervel
Kerent, du-hont war an aot, en anken.

Teurel a ra eur griaden doaniuz,
Galvaden skiltr ar re zo vont da goll...
Med den na glev e kreiz an trouz spontuz
Mouez braz kurun, avel, mor o tiroll.

Stourm, o stourm c'hoaz, bremaik teuio sikour!
Nan, dinerz eo ar c'heaz, n'hall mui herzel...
Sikour a deu... Siouaz ne'z euz mui gour:
E strad ar mor e ma o peur-vervel!

Gant ar mor braz setu great e labour,
E labour kriz, e labour a varo...
Wel, intanvez, ha wel, emzivad paour!
M'euz mui netra nemet pense tro-dro.

O mor gouez, bremaik vezi tener;
Great da labour, paouez a ri tarza,
Ha da vouskan zavo klemmuz en er
Epad ma vo an noz sioul o koueza.

Translation

The Work of the Sea, *1903*

Listen! On the coast of Brittany
Howls the storm, the sailors' scourge,
Which breaks the heart of poor widows
And kills the fathers of the children of Arvor.

By the fire, your door tightly shut,
You chatter and sing merrily,
But think, good people, think about the fishermen
And about their wives praying in solitude.

The sea rages around Brittany,
It is heard day and night, relentlessly;
In its fury it hurtles onto the rocks
Covered with foam, a tiny boat.

In the wild sea, in the wailing wind,
As thunder growls above,
A man is swimming, fighting, trying to call
His distressed family, over there on the shore.

He lets out a plaintive cry,
The shrill call of those losing their life,
But no one hears him in the dreadful noise
Of thunder, wind and raging sea.

Fight! Fight on! Help will come soon!
But his strength is failing him; the struggle is too hard.
Help arrives.... But there is no one there:
On the sea floor, the drowning man is dying.

The ocean has done its work,
Its cruel work, its deathly work.
Look, young widow! Look, dear orphan!
There is nothing but driftwood around.

Wild sea! You will soon be calm;
Your work done, you will no longer seethe.
Your soft plaintive voice will soon rise in the air
As the quiet night descends upon you.

Ar Rumeur

Enez Eussa, *1913*

E kreiz mor brumennus an hanter-noz, kollet,
Enez Eussa, enez an heuzusded, evel
En eur c'havel a hun... hep arzao luskellet
Gant krozmol ar c'hommou ha iud gouez an avel.

Mesk ar reier, a nij 'uz d'ezo morvrini,
A vev paotred hardiz, hep aoun rag an arne,
Ha merc'hed koant ha fur mez leun a velkoni
Ha gant broud a anken strafillet o ene.

Rag tro war dro d'ezhi ar vorgragez daonet
A vouskan hag a chalm dre zellou entanet
O c'halonou da galz euz he merdaïdi.

Pere, eun deiz pe zeiz, en em daol gant dudi
'N ho divrec'h 'vit gellout (hervez an danevel)
Tanvât eur pennadik d'ho c'harante marvel!

Translation

Ushant, *1913*

Lost in the middle of the foggy North Sea,
Ushant, island of many evils,
Sleeps as in a cradle... forever rocked
By the roaring billows and the wild wailing wind.

Among the rocks, circled by cormorants in flight,
Live bold men, fearless of storms,
And pretty girls, wise but full of melancholy
As their minds are burdened by the sting of worry.

For, around the island, dwell malicious mermaids
Whose soft songs and fiery looks charm
The heart of many local sailors

Who, one day or other, throw themselves eagerly
In their arms, in order – so tells the story –
To taste, for a short while, their deathly love.

Maodez Glanndour
Beg ar Raz, *1953*

Yud ar Raz, froud a lazh,
Toulloù trouz ifern,
Ha spouron traezh an Anaon!
Evelato e vleugn al lann melen war an tevenn
Lec'h e nij lamperezed askellet glas.
O leñvadeg ar peñseoù!
Evelato, en pleg an ant e vored al lennig
Lec'h e neuñv, skañv ha flour, bagadoù an douryer,
'Tre inizi frondus bleunioù gwenn al lugustr.

Translation
The Pointe du Raz, *1953*

Roar of the ocean at Raz, lethal undercurrents,
Hellish noise of the abysses,
And terror of the Bay of the Dead!
And yet, the yellow broom blooms on the cliffs
Where blue-winged grasshoppers fly.
O the sorrow of ship-wrecks!
And yet, in the fold of the furrow dozes a pond
Where flocks of water-hens lightly glide
Between fragrant islands of white water lilies.

Kenan Kongar
Dichal, *1982*

Gwelout a rit ar vagig wenn
A vorede e korn al lenn,
A-dreñv ar c'horz, e-mesk ar broen,
Nerzhus ha flamm evel ul loen;

Ar paotrig koant en deus kavet ar vag,
Stignet ar gouelioù ha brevet ar stag,
Sellit outañ o vleinañ 'tal ar stur,
O tridal gant al lorc'h, seder ha fur.

– Emañ o vont dre 'n avel hag al lano
Evel un den kollet gantañ e ano.
Perak 'ta bezañ dilezet ar porzh,
Ar goudor sioul, an elestr hag ar c'horz?

War gern an donn e vag a vrall,
En amzer vat, en amzer fall;
'Mañ-eñ o vont da redek bro
A-dreuz ar bed, ha tro-ha-tro?

– Emañ o vont da Veg ar Raz
Da glask e deun he falez glas
Morgan a gan gant trouz ar mor
Pa roc'h an avel 'tal ho tor,

Morgan a zeu d'an aodoù pell
P'eo diskennet an nozioù gell,
Evit klevout trouzioù ar maez
D'astenn he c'horf a-dreuz an traezh.

Pa ziskenno an heol, da serr an noz,
Klevit a-hed an aod ar c'hlemmvan kozh;
Oc'h astenn war ar bili hag an traezh,
Ar mor a groz e skleur an abardaez.

– Un deiz marteze vo doaniet hor spered,
Pa 'z aimp hor-pevar da zougen d'ar vered
Ar paotr a gare Morgan ar mor-bras
Hag aet d'he c'hlask da gichen Beg ar Raz.

Translation

Carefree, *1982*

Before your eyes is the little white boat
Which was dozing at the edge of the lake,
Behind the reeds, amongst the rushes,
Robust and bright like an animal.

A nice young boy discovered the boat,
Hoisted the sails and cut the rope.
Look at him, his hand on the tiller,
Full of pride, serene and wise.

He is cutting through the wind and the waves
Like a man who no longer knows his name.
Why did he leave the harbour,
The sheltered spot, the irises and the reeds?

At the top of the wave his boat dips,
Weather fair or foul;
Is he going to journey on,
Across the world and around it?

He is going to the Pointe du Raz
To look, in the depths of her blue palace,
For Morgan who sings to the sound of the sea
When the wind howls at your door.

Morgan comes to the distant shores
When the dark night has fallen,
To listen to the country sounds
And recline her body on the sand.

When the sun sets, at twilight,
Listen to the old lament along the shore;
Lapping the pebbles and the sand,
The sea foams in the faint light.

Maybe one day we shall grieve
When the four of us carry to the churchyard
The boy who loved Morgan of the Ocean
And went to find her around the Pointe du Raz.

Tudual Huon

Beaj diwezhañ Gwilhou, ar chalboter huñvreoù, *1979*

Kaer en deus Gwilhou astenn e zivaskell gwenn ha bresk, heuliañ pizh lamm ha
pleg ar gwag ne c'hell mui talout ouzh ar barrad amzer. Ken stank eo ar vorenn
ma ne wel takenn. Ar mor, kollet gantañ pep kuñvelezh, a greñch hag a skop kunujennoù sall war e dal skuizh. Ne gavo ket repu, evel a-ziagent, war ar mor,
    mestr eo al lanv du, trubard ha treitour, ur wech c'hoazh war gein kromm an

houl. Pistigañ a ra ar fru-mor e zaoulagad hag al lard gwechall ken stank war e gorf a zo aet tanav. Nijal a ra marblu Gwilhou gant an avel-vor evel delioù sec'h an diskar-amzer.

Torret eo kelc'hiad ar beder amzer ha morzet ar boan en e galon moan ha treut gant an anken. Dont a ra ur wennili he bruched gwenn d'e flourat gant hec'h askell gizidik. Gwilhou, avat, a zo dall ha ne gren ket e gorf ouzh he flouradenn zous. Gwriziennet don eo en e askre frond c'hwek ar bezhin o tañsal war ar spoum ha tousmac'h ar fru-mor o stekiñ ouzh ar chaoser.

Gant poan e lonk boued ar gounnar sac'het en e gorzailhenn.

N'eus kasoni ouzh den; n'eo morse bet e lod.

"Klev, Gwilhou, grozmol an avel e fulor e korf koeñvet an noz prest da wilioudiñ un diaoul

Klev gliziennoù he c'horf toc'hor, brazez gant bugale dinatur,

bugale liammet gant begeloù neud-orjal dreinek, sparloù an huñvreoù digabestr. Klev lammoù da galon bronduet, bloñset ha tragaset war-nes sankañ en donvor..."

"Diwall, Gwilhou, eme an eil mouezh, diwall ouzh an erv traezh hir ha lemm evel un aotenn. Un ehan a ranki ober avat dindan boan da veuziñ. N'eo ket echu ar veaj." "Klev fistilherezh an touseged-mor o c'hoari gant an houl er beure luzennek,

bugale lez-ober ha dinec'h.

Flemmet ha ruziet en deus al linad-mor e zivjod gwenn ha blevek. Diheñchet eo bet ar paour-kaezh loen gant ar c'hantolorioù melen o lugerniñ d'al lazh-goulou. Mouget da vat eo tour-tan enez Gwerc'h gant ar c'hoummoù o sevel dibreder.

"Klev hirvoudoù an dud."

Ar mor en deus gwisket e vantel-gañv...

Bez en deus spoum ar c'hoummoù blaz ar marv war e vuzelloù.

"Taol pled, Gwilhou, lampreiz 'zo gant ar mor ha keler-noz a zaskren war ar maezioù."

"Klev c'hwez ar rost o sevel eus genou ar stêr, klev ograoù ar gorventenn o fraoñval en iliz-veur ar vezh

laosk an daouar da gemer e gozh ha da yudal

ledet eo bet an teil mil bell 'zo."

Ne vo burzhud ebet.

Emañ ar stêr o rechetiñ bouzelloù al lazhdi.

"Hast buan, Gwilhou, rak ne zevero mui ar mesper: aet eo ar plouz da ludu hag an amzer a zo faziet diwar he hent."

Emañ ar "bez-hinerien" o lifreoù liv kaoc'h o skuilhañ tremp bec'hius ha lazhus war ar Garreg Hir ha war an Daouioù.

Enezennoù dir ha betoñs 'lec'h ma c'hoari ur c'hrank houarn gant un durkez divent... da valañ ar beorien.

Setu an douar bras, kribennoù rostet menezioù Are, aret, poazhet ha du-hont rele- gennoù bruzhunet o horjellañ, un ankou krignet o koroll en o daoulagad disliv.

"Truez, eme Gwilhou, truez ouzh ar merien-tud, gozed dall ha bouzar skoachet en

o zoulloù teñval, preñved o sunañ o c'hoantoù diroll war lenn skornet o buhez."
Tud o tislonkañ bep a sac'h-bestl leun a hudurniachioù, lastez, astuz ha preñved o
fourgasiñ... marnaoniet.

"E pelec'h emañ da dammig eñvor ganez, Gwilhou, 'peus ket soñj bezañ beajet
betek aodoù Kembre! Moged louet Port Talbot hag Abertawe kemmesket gant
c'hwezh ar "fish and chips" d'ar sadorn da noz!

ha Jon y glo o tistreiñ eus ar vengleuz un tamm duad-glaou ouzh e jod ha pemp pe
c'hwec'h "ceiniog" en e chakod toull da vagañ e seizh a vugale.

ha Loeiz ar mesaer, baleer digenvez, o kas e dropellad deñved en draoñienn evit ar
wech diwezhañ. Ar chas, a-ruz-kof, a souch d'e c'hwitelladenn.

Sell, du-hont, tud trist o vont da interamant o mignon, dilhad da sul ganto ha bep a
vleunienn ruz ivez.

Du-se, Mari Losog oc'h hastañ davet an atant en noz teñval
ur bouch a zo ganet marv
trist e vo an traoù e Rangranog fenoz...
Aet out kuit, te ivez, Gwilhou paour
paotr ar poulloù, kiger eus e vicher, masikod ha ribouler war an dibenn sizhun, en
deus da zouared e bered da barrez (hag ur barrez 'poa?)
Ar gurun a strak, a voud, a sourr war bered bras Kergoullo
Preizherien o lifreoù vil a goag goap war dismantroù an ti kozh
Ne vo dasorc'hidigezh ebet
n'eo nemet skraperezh la laeroñsi
gaou ha koumoul
Ur bouilh moged, kellider ar marv, par d'ur c'habell-touseg ramzel a sav bramm
diwezhañ ur c'hantved distaget gant mil boan
Aet out kuit, Gwilhou,
ha va lezet, me ha va mignoned, gant hon esperañsoù taer hag hon daouarn noazh
ha gwadek
evel da re dit-te, Gwilhou
evel da re dit-te..."

Translation

The Last Journey of Gwilhou, the Dream Carrier, *1979*

Try as he may extend his white and fragile wings, follow carefully the blade and the
swell of the wave, Guilhou is no longer able to fight the bad weather. The fog is so
thick that he cannot see anything. The sea, having lost its gentleness, spits and
spews its salty abuse on his weary forehead. He will not find refuge, as he had done
previously, on the sea,
        the black tide rules once more, perfidious and treacherous, on the round
back of the waves. The sea-spray stings his eyes and the fat layer, which used to be
so thick on his body, has now grown thin. Gwilhou's downy feathers fly in the sea
wind like the dried leaves of autumn.

The ring of the four seasons is broken and his frightened and alarmed heart is gripped with the sting of distress. A white-fronted tern comes to stroke him with her delicate wing, but Guilhou is blind. His body does not shiver under the soft caress. Ingrained in him is the pleasant smell of the seaweeds dancing on the foam and the uproar of the waves crashing down on the sea-wall.

He painfully swallows the morsels of rage stuck in his throat.

He does not feel hatred; this never was his way.

"Listen, Gwilhou, to the roar of the furious wind in the swollen body of the night on the verge of giving birth to an evil spirit

Listen to the convulsions of her dying body, pregnant with deformed children,

children joined with umbilical cords made of barbed wire, chaining up all dreams of freedom.

Listen to the beats of your swollen, bruised, aching heart about to plunge into the open sea..."

"Be careful, Gwilhou," said the second voice, "be careful about the narrow sand strip as long and sharp as a barber's razor. But you will need to stop or else you will drown. The journey is not over."

Listen to the chitchat of the small crabs playing with the waves in the misty morning,

unflustered and carefree.

The sea anemones have stung and reddened his white and downy face. The poor little bird has been led astray by the yellow candlesticks shining in the twilight. The Ile Vierge lighthouse is totally concealed from view by the heedless surge of the waves.

"Listen to the people groaning."

The sea has put on her mourning coat...

The foaming sea brings the taste of death on his lips.

"Be careful, Gwilhou, there are tiny creatures glowing in the sea and will-o'-the-wisp above the fields."

"Smell the burning smell coming from the mouth of the river, listen to the drone of the great storm organ in the cathedral of shame.

Let the land lie fallow and scream. The manure was spread ages ago."

There will be no miracle.

The river is vomiting guts from the abattoir.

"Hurry up, Gwilhou, for there is little time left. Dust has gone back to dust and time has lost its track."

The "grave" wrack-gatherers in their turd-coloured clothes are tipping out heavy lethal manure on Karreg-Hir and on Daouioù.

Steel and concrete islands on which an iron crab moves its huge pincers to crush the poor.

Here is the land, the baked ridges of Monts d'Arrée, ploughed, burned down and, over there, broken tottering remnants, the shadow of death dancing in their colourless eyes.

"Take pity," said Guilhou, "take pity on the ant-like people, blind and deaf moles hidden in their dark holes, worms sucking at their unleashed desires on the frozen lake of their lives."

People who vomit – each and everyone of them – their sack of bile full of obscenities, of rubbish, of vermin, while famished maggots and worms bustle about... .

"Where is your memory gone, Gwilhou, don't you remember travelling to the coasts of Wales! The grey smoke of Port Talbot and Swansea mixed with the smell of fish and chips on Saturday nights!

and Jon y glo [Johnny the Coalminer] returning from the pit, his cheeks blackened by coal and five or six "ceiniog" [pennies] in his pierced pocket to feed his seven children.

and Loeiz ar mesaer [Lewis Shepherd], solitary rambler, bringing his flock to the valley for the very last time. His dogs, creeping stealthily around the sheep, crouch down at his whistling.

Look, over there, at those sad people going to their friend's funeral. They are dressed in their Sunday best and they all hold a red rose.

On that side, Mari Losog hurrying towards the farm in the dark night.

The foal was still-born

there will be sadness in Rangranog tonight...

You too went away, dear Gwilhou

the grave-digger, a butcher who, at week-ends, serves mass and chases women, has buried you in the churchyard of your parish (Did you have a parish?)

The thunder growls, roars, snarls over the large Kergoullo [Emptytown] church-yard

Looters in their ugly uniforms croak their sarcasm on the ruins of the old house

There will be no resurrection

It is no more than theft and robbery

lies and clouds

A column of smoke, the seed of death, rises up like a huge mushroom

like the last painful fart of a constipated century

You went away, Gwilhou,

and left me, me and my friends, with our brutal hopes and our naked and bloody hands

like your own, Gwilhou

like your own..."

Añjela Duval

Karantez-vro, *1963*

> E korn va c'halon 'zo ur gleizhenn
> 'Baoe va yaouankiz he dougan
> Rak siwazh, an hini a garen
> Ne gare ket pezh a garan

Eñ na gare nemet ar c'hêrioù
Ar morioù don, ar broioù pell
Ha ne garen 'met ar maezioù
Maezioù ken kaer va Breizh-Izel

Ret 'voe dibab 'tre div garantez
Karantez-Vro, karantez den
D'am bro am eus gouestlet va buhez
Ha leset da vont 'n hini 'garen
Biskoazh abaoe ne'm eus e welet
Biskoazh klevet keloù outañ
Ar gleizhenn em c'halon 'zo chomet
Pa gare ket pezh a garan.

Pep den a dle heuilh e Donkadur
Honnezh eo lezenn ar Bed-mañ
Gwasket 'voe va c'halon a dra sur
Met 'gare ket pezh a garan
Dezhañ pinvidigezh, enorioù
Din-me paourentez ha dispriz
Met 'drokfen ket evit teñzorioù
Va Bro, va Yezh ha va Frankiz.

Translation

For the Love of My Country, *1963*

Hidden in my heart there is a scar
Which has been there since my youth
Because, alas, the one I loved
Did not love what I love.
He loved only the towns,
The deep seas, the distant lands,
Whereas I only loved the fields,
The lovely fields of Brittany

I had to choose between two loves
Love of the country, love of a man
I devoted my life to my country
And let go of the one I love
I never saw him again
I never heard from him again
The scar in my heart is still there
As he did not love what I love

To every man his destiny
Such is the law of this World
It certainly was a heart ache
But he did not love what I loved.
To him wealth and respect
To me poverty and contempt
But I would not trade for all earthly treasures
My Country, my Language and my Freedom.

Erwan Bertoù

Pa zeu, d'abardaez-noz, *1904*

Pa zeu, d'abardaez-noz, ar c'huzh-heol da ruziañ,
Pa weler ar balan hag ar brug o krenañ,
Pa zeu an hentoù kleuz da vezañ teñvaloc'h,
Pa ya d'ar gêr ar saout, en o fenn an ejen,
'N ur leuskel a-wechoù, spontus, ur vlejadenn,
Neuze 'kreder klevout raktal trouz dizoare:
Kezeg o c'haloupat, ha trompilhoù-arme.
Lez-Breizh a zo er vro gant e varc'heien vat:
Setu int en oabl ruz o tremen 'us d'ar c'hoad;
Set' ar Roue Arthur, setu Sent an Arvor:
War an oabl e weler displeget hon istor.

Translation

When in the Early Evening, *1904*

When, in the early evening, the setting sun reddens,
When the gorse and heather are seen to shiver,
When the sunken lanes start becoming darker,
When the cows go home, the ox leading the way
And sometimes letting out a frightful bellow,
It then seems that one hears unusual noises:
Horses galloping by and military bugles.
Lez-Breizh is around with his good knights:
Here they are in the red sky passing above the wood;
Here is King Arthur, and here the Saints of Brittany:
In the sky, our history is plain for all to see.

Yann ar C'hamm

An Neizh dilezet, *c.1930*

Bugel, pa c'haloupen er parkoù 'tal ma c'hêr
Me 'gave alies e-kreiz ur vodenn spern
Un dornad brankoù kras, disac'het en ur bern,
An dra-se oa un neizh drailhet gant an amzer.

Pa welen goude-se ur vandenn evned kaer
O nijal ken laouen 'us d'ar c'hleun ha d'ar wern
Me c'houlenne perak n'en eus ket un ifern
'Vit neb ankoue e neizh pa ve savet en aer.

Allas! An dud ivez a zo ken ankoueus...
Neizh ar vugaleaj, ar c'havell burzhudus,
N'int netra d'ar galon pa vez hir an askell.

Paour pe binvidik-mor, aet int lec'h all da chom.
Diforzh, pe leun a lorc'h, n'o devo ken ur sell
'Vit an ti bihan yen a oa gwechall ken tomm.

Translation

The Empty Nest, *c.1930*

When a child I ran in the fields close to home
I often found in the middle of a thorn bush
A handful of dried twigs, crumpled up in a heap,
Which was in fact a nest mangled by the weather.

When, a little later, I saw a flock of handsome birds
Flying so happily above the peat bog and the marsh
I wondered why there was no hell
For those who forget their nest when they have taken to flight.

Alas! Men too are forgetful...
The nest of youth, the miraculous cradle
No longer speak to the heart, when wings have grown.

Whether poor or wealthy, they have moved somewhere else.
Unconcerned or full of pride, they will no longer glance
At the cold little home which used to be so warm.

Yann-Bêr Kalloc'h

Tristedigeh er Helt, *c.1910*

Yaouank on. N'em es ket hoah gwélet uigent hañù,
En héol tro-ha-dro dein e skuill é vanneu-tan,
Er bleu ar en aùél e zégas dein o hwéh,
Ha neoah me zo lan a velkoni dalbéh...
Perag 'ta? Doué e oér. Pe grouéas er Breton,
Eañ lakas en dristé de chom én é galon;

Dégouéhet on én oed é vourrér é véùein,
E rédeg ér parkeu, é hoari, é kanein,
Én oed ha ne chonja nag é bé nag é mén,
Nag é stér er vuhé ken fonnuz é tremén...
E kreiz me 'flijadur, neoah, ankinet on;
Doué 'lakas en dristé é kalon er Breton.

En dud tro-ha-dro dein e hoarh d'en neùé-hañù,
Én estig ar er barr e lar é son vraùañ,
Rah en éned e strèu o 'fozieu gwiù én ér.
Med mé, pe geméran me zelennig distér,
Hirvoudein 'hra bepred, ne oéran med un ton:
Doué 'lakas en dristé é kalon er Breton.

Peb tra e rehkehé gobér dein leùiné:
Youankiz ha frankiz, bleu ér prad, héol én né,
Petra zo red muioh eid em anùein eurus?
Ha neoah, er bed-man ne gavan ket bourruz,
Un dra bennak ataù 'm es diovér dehoñ:
Doué 'lakas en dristé é kalon er Breton.

O men Doué, en dra-sé e vank d'em hoanteu-dén,
Hwi é! Rag, ar en Douar ne hram nameid tremén,
Rag, n'é ket aveitoñ 'ma groeit or haloneu...
Med pa wélim é tond karrig gwenn en Ankeu,
Eid on dougein du-hont, genoh, 'barh en néañù don:
Neuzé vo leùiné é kalon er Breton!

Translation

The Sadness of the Celts, *c.1910*

I am young. I am not yet twenty;
The sun around me darts its fiery rays,
The flowers bring me their fragrance on the wind,
Yet I am constantly full of melancholy.
Why is it? Only God knows. When He created the Bretons,
He sowed lasting sadness in their hearts.

I am at an age when one enjoys living,
Running through the fields, having fun, singing;
At an age when one does not think of the grave or the tombstone,
Of the meaning of life which passes so fast;
Yet I feel restless among my life's delights.
God sowed sadness in Breton hearts.

People around me smile at the new Spring;
On a branch, the nightingale sings her sweetest song;
All the birds fill the air with their melodious notes.
Yet when I pick up my own little harp
It always sighs. I only know one tune:
God sowed sadness in Breton hearts.

Everything should make me happy:
Youth and freedom, the flowers in the fields, the sun in the sky,
What more do I need to call myself happy?
Yet I do not find this world enjoyable;
Something is constantly missing:
God sowed sadness in Breton hearts.

My Lord. This thing which, as a man, I miss so much
Is You! For we are only visitors on this earth,
Our hearts were not designed for it.
But when we see the blessed cart of the Ankou approach,
To bring us over there, next to you, in the deep heaven:
Then there will be joy in Breton hearts!

Yann-Vari ar Joubiouz

Karanté er Vretonned doh ou bro, *1844*

Diskan:
> Me halon zo
> Ghet mem Bro;
> Oh! Ya, prepet e vo!

I
Hag é vehen é pèn er bed,
Doh Breih me halon vo staghet.

II
En heol, m'er gouér, a huél broïeu,
El léh m'en dès mui a vadeu.

III
E Paris é huélan treu bràu,
Treu kaer d'em deulagad attàu.

IV
Me zo bet é mesk er Sauzen:
Etal d'hai é omp paorien.

V
Rom hag er Pab e mès gùélet,
Ha Breih ne mès ket ankoéhet.

VI
Er broïeu-zé, deusto ker kaer,
Prepet me halon oé ér ghér;

VII
Mem diskoarn a hoanté komzeu
A lar d'emb é Breih hur mameu;

VIII
Mem deulagad a glaské lann,
Kelen glas ha bleun er belann;

IX
Ne huélen ket mui er bragheu

En dès miret d'emb hun tadeu;

X
Ne gleuen mui er binieu
Nag er Barz ghet é gùerzenneu.

XI
Bet me dremeinei mem buhé
E Breih é chomein, mar vèn Doué.

XII
Me vèn bihuein é ty me zad:
Ino hemb kin é on erhat;

XIII
Me vèn choukein idan er gùé
En dès ean bet skedet ehué;

XIV
Me vèn trezein er morik douz
En dès trezet e vaghik kouz;

XV
Dreist peb-tra me vèn pedein Doué
Ghet-n-oh, broïsèd, lan a fé;

XVI
Me vèn èl oh, ar mèn deulin,
Er vinèd eit me zud pedein;

XVII
Ghet-n-oh me larei pedenneu
En un ilis dû dré vlaïeu.

XVIII
Me vèn é Breih bout béïet
Hag étal me mam beur laket.

Translation

Love of the Bretons for their Country, *1844*

Chorus:
>   My heart is
>   With my country;
>   Oh, yes. It always will be.

I
Should I be at the end of the world,
My heart would be in Brittany.

II
The sun, I know, sees many countries
Which hold many more treasures.

III
In Paris, I see lovely things,
Which are always beautiful to my eyes.

IV
I have been among the English:
Compared to them, we are poor people.

V
I have seen Rome and the Pope,
But they did not make me forget Brittany.

VI
In these countries, lovely as they were,
My heart was always back home;

VII
My ears wanted to hear the words
Which our mothers speak in Brittany;

VIII
My eyes were looking for moors,
For green holly, for flowering bloom;

IX
I could no longer see the breeches
Which our fathers bequeathed us;

X
I could no longer hear the bagpipes
Nor the Bard singing his ballads;

XI
When my working life is over,
I shall settle in Brittany, if God wishes it so.
XII
I want to live in my father's house:
The only place where I feel at ease;

XIII
I want to lie under the trees
Which also gave him shade;

XIV
I want to cross the calm stretch of sea
Which his old boat used to cross.

XV
Above all, I want to pray to God
With you, my compatriots full of faith;

XVI
I want, like you, to pray on my knees,
For my parents in the churchyard;

XVII
With you, I shall say prayers
In a church darkened by the years.

XVIII
I want to be buried in Brittany
And lie next to my dear mother.

Prosper Proux

Mouez ar c'hleier, *1866* (Lodenn)

Bim! baon! me zo strobineller;
Me oar petra gan ar c'hleier,
Selaouid holl ho mouez zantel,
Ha sentit mad ouc'h ho c'hentel.

Bim! baon! baon! kloc'h an ofern bred,
Lared a ra: "Hasted! Hasted!
Kalz ne zigwezond enn Iliz,
Nemet enn hanter ann ofiz;

Darn na reont nemed roc'hal,
Ha darn all (resped d'hoc'h) strakal,
Trompillad gand ho diou froen,
Pe riboullad ho c'horzaillen.

Ar botret lemm, dindan ho zao,
A lugern ouc'h ar plac'hed vrao,
Gand eur zell flemmuz, ar merc'het,
A lavar d'ezho: Kendalc'het.

Iann Bitoch a glask, n'he spered,
Penaoz ienna he vignouned,
Lakaad enn he ialc'h eur bern kresk,
Dre ar burzud ouz ar pemp Pesk.

Ar Persoun moal zo baroduz,
He brezegen zo moreduz,
Ar zouben, hep mar, vo ienet,
Hag ar patatez kaledet.

[...]

Bim! baon! baon! eur vadiziant!
Ar bugelik, ma feiz, zo koant!
Hag ouc'h he dad eo hanvel tre,
Fri he baeroun n'euz kouskoude!

Gant ann holen kriz, ma elig,
Ec'h eo ruzied da vuzellig:
Er vuez, enkrez ha daero,
A gavi c'hoaz muioc'h c'houero!

Mar bevez koz, war hor bern pri,
Da ene c'hlan a vaztari,
Da galoun, liez, vo roged
Gant drez ha spern, dre hend ar bed!

Bim! baon! brinbalomp a nerz brec'h!
Miket eo *Pao-krog*, ar c'hruk-sec'h;
Ognoun! Kignoun! a zruilladou,
Ken a strinko eur mor daelou!

Tad eunn tiad braz bugale
A zo galved dirag Doue:
Ann holl a wel gant wir c'hlac'har,
Ar c'hi a iud warlec'h ar c'harr!"

– Bim! baon! Petra ne leront ket
E kement iez zo dre ar bed?
Koulz ec'h eo d'in ta troc'ha berr,
Zard oun... vel eunn teuzer kleier!

Translation

The Voice of the Bells, *1866* (Extract)

Ding dong! I am a wizard;
I can tell what the bells sing,
Listen, people, to their angelic voices,
And make sure you do what they tell you.

Ding, dong, dong! This is the bell for mass
Which says: "Hurry! Hurry!
A good many people enter the church
When mass is half-over;

Some do nothing there but take a nap,
While others, if I may say so, snore,
Trumpeting through their nostrils,
Or making gargling noises with their throats.

Some lewd boys secretly
Ogle the pretty girls;
With a piercing look, the girls
Reply: "Do carry on!"

John Rogue is pondering on the best way
To deceive his friends
And multiply his gains
As shown by the miracle of the five Fish.

The bald priest is boring,
His sermon is sleep-inducing;
The soup will no doubt be cold,
And the potatoes hard as rocks.

[...]

Ding, dong, dong! A christening!
The baby, I must say, is pretty!
He looks just like his father,
He has, however, his godfather's nose!

The harsh salt, little angel,
Has reddened your little lips:
In life, you will find that
Worries and tears are a lot more bitter still.

If you live till old age on our grimy earth,
You will soil your untainted soul.
Often, your heart will be torn
By the brambles and thorns of the paths of the world!

Ding, dong! Let's us ring a peal of bells!
Scrooge, the skinflint, has snuffed it;
Onions galore, please, and garlic too!
Until an ocean of tears is shed!

The father of a large family
Is called in front of the Lord:
Everyone weeps, from genuine grief,
The dog whines too as it follows the hearse."

– Ding dong! What can't the bells say
In all the world's languages?
It is time for me to finish,
I feel as happy as a bell-maker.

Travelling Through Brittany

W. Ambrose Bebb

Pererindodau (Extract)

Bebb was a lecturer and historian who visited the Pardon of Sainte-Anne-de-la-Palud in 1924, 1927, 1928, 1929, 1931 and 1937, but this description is the result of his visit in 1927 – "the occasion I went most like a true pilgrim". Pererindodau – a series of essays and articles written over many years, was published by the Welsh Book Club in 1941.

The Grand Mass at Sainte-Anne was scheduled for eleven in the morning. It was in that direction that I set off, in good time to see the pilgrims gather from the dunes and the beaches, from the fields and from their carriages. It was an open-air service, from an altar built up on both sides of the church. On the nearby stage there are thirty or more priests, and in front of them, sitting on the grass on the slope opposite, is one of the most beautiful crowds of people that the eyes of any man can feast upon. The variety in age and dress, posture and colour, is remarkable. There are beautiful women – beautiful in a virginity of body and thought, born of health and the skills of the land – from all the neighbouring areas. And those from Pont l'Abbé are more prominent than any, not because they are more beautiful nor more numerous, but because the pointed tops of their *coiffes* are easier to see. Look at the *coiffes* of all of them, and you read, as if in an open book, the parishes and the towns they come from – Plounevez-Porzay, Plomodiern and Locronan; Ploaré and Douarnenez; Saint-Guénolé and Audierne; Quimper, Concarneau, Pont-Aven and Quimperlé; Scaër, Pontivy and Vannes; Huelgoat, Landerneau and Morlaix. Who are these in their black – dressed in black from head to toe? Undoubtedly, they are the children of the great tribulations! They all come from Ile de Sein, and their dress is always black as is appropriate to the inhabitants of the storm, where everyone, so it is said, is daily in mourning. As their tears drown in the sea that

sings its lyre around their island, so their mourning clothes melt into the many colours of the crowd.

Amongst these noble women – and I make no apology for using the word noble to describe them – are the men in their velvet hats, decked with ribbons and buckles, in their blue waistcoats with black and yellow velvet, and rows of colourful buttons. They, in turn, appear like chieftains and princes, and almost as dignified as their queenly sisters.

The audience join in to sing the *Gloria in Excelsis* and the *Ave Maria* in all its magnificence. Then parts of the Gospels and the Epistles are read, and the prayers are sung. All this, and much more, is followed by a sermon in Breton. The priest who delivers the sermon is a master of the Breton language in all its elegance. He possesses a sonorous voice that can be heard from the first syllable to the last. He gives high praise to *Santez Anna*, and talks of the Bretons' indebtedness to her. But the main thrust of his short but interesting sermon is to stress that there is but one God, that He above all else should be served, that we seek His Kingdom, that we should serve mankind with love. The rich should make proper use of the wealth with which they have been entrusted, and behave justly and lovingly towards them who are below them. *Doue a zo just*, said the preacher; God is just, repaying good with good *en e bed* (in the world) and in the land of *Paradoz*. But his wrath shall descend heavily on those who are governed by injustice, hate, envy and enmity.

It is the duty of all Bretons to read *Buhez ar Zent*, to meditate much on the lives of the Saints, and in particular that of *Santez Anna*, who is so ready to listen to the pleadings of her children. She was the mother of the Virgin Mary, and taught her to *lenn lezen Doue*, that is to read the law of God. *N'eus ked den parfait er bed mân, ma breudeur ker* [there is no perfect man in this world, my dear brothers], he said in words dewy with brotherly gentleness. But Anna, *Mamgoz Jesus, Patronez ar Vreiziz* [Grandmother of Jesus, patron of the Bretons] will give to every Breton *nerz, sicour a bennoz* [strength, succour and blessing].

On this comforting note the preacher ended his open-air sermon, so short, so pleasant. The service did not end there. The sermon ended by singing the *Credo* and the *Ave Mari Stella*, a kind of greeting to the Star of the Sea, so fitting, so pleasant, in this place.

H.G.Wells

Apropos of Dolores (Extract)

Brittany was fashionable with the English in the period 1880 and 1920, a fact reflected in the number of English travel books published about the country in that period. H. G. Wells came a little later and his "novel" Apropos of Dolores was published in 1938. A spat between Wells and a mistress who, in a literary effort of her own, was seen as having slighted him inspired this work. The revenge he sought was less than complete as the portrayal of the lady – as Dolores – pleased her greatly.

(Torquéstol, August 31st, 1934)

We went to Roscoff to see the great fig tree and the Marine Laboratory. Dolores dressed as though she was going to tea in the Place Vendôme – what do they call the place? […] We met Foxfield at Roscoff as I had appointed.

At first Dolores was disposed to treat Foxfield … since she knew that occasionally I paid him money … with considerable condescension. He did not appear to observe that. She also addressed several almost audible asides to me. "Why do you let him come so untidy? It is a slight on both of us. Does he *never* cut his hair?" These also, if they were heard, went unheeded. After one glance at her, he paid her no more attention, until we were among the salt-water tanks, to which he led us with a sort of round-shouldered determination. Then suddenly addressing himself to her, he began a lucid and detailed account of the love life of the octopus.

"I find it the most hideous of created things," she had said.

"But consider its sensitiveness," he remonstrated, becoming extraordinarily like an octopus himself as he said it, and then, with a touch of wonder, "See! It is *looking* at you."

Dolores became interested. "Mind you – they don't often take notice of things outside the glass," Foxfield said very gravely, and regarded her with a speculative eye, as though he sought some reason for it.

Dolores made an elegant gesture at the uncoiling creature in the corner. "C'est un monstre," she said relenting, noted a sort of invitation in an extending arm, and was reluctant to turn away.

"But in those unfolding undulating movements – a certain grace?"

"A certain grace," she admitted. "Yes."

"Sophisticated perhaps. But could a man do that? See. *There*!"

"M'm'm," she considered.

"Few people realize the capacity for passion among marine animals," Foxfield went on in that ample piggish voice of his, and it dawned upon me that in his own peculiar way he meant to get even with her for that preliminary phase of patronage. "Mind you – floating in the sea as they do – un-distracted by gravitation …"

This was a new idea to Dolores.

"Like painted Gods upon a ceiling," said Foxfield.

"Naturally," she agreed, reflected, and then pursued knowledge. "But in water – do they make love? Can they?"

"Incessantly. For example …"

It was a new view of an aquarium to Dolores that it could be an arena of passion.

"For example?" she echoed.

Foxfield hesitated for a moment and sought my eye. His large loose mouth was interrogative. But he found nothing in my eye to restrain him, and with a sort of modest reluctance, speaking very gently, he proceeded to instruct Dolores on the hidden ways of nature. I had never realized before how much livelier an imagination he has than Creation, and what a brighter world we should have had if affairs had been in the hands of this trained biologist.

"Of course," he said with an apologetic sigh, "the sea here gets a lot of *warm* water from the Gulf Stream – a lot of warm water. Even the vegetables in this part of Brittany are – " he sank his voice – "*precocious*."

"Yes?" said Dolores.

"Even the early flowers. When English bulbs are still in the nursery. And there is a great fig tree – but you will see that for yourself … But consider these dogfish. Now *they* …"

I see no reason for recording the coarse selachian scandals he retailed to her.

Dolores was so artlessly interested that she forgot to be the ultra-fashionable lady altogether. She became the last and brightest and indeed slightly gaminesque pupil of a great savant, who told her things, wonderful things, that he had never been able to unfold before to so quick and intelligent a mind.

He talked and talked, gravely but unedifyingly, and grew more and more solemnly happy as he talked.

She was much excited by the idea of sea water as something into which an infinitude of spawn and gonads were perpetually liberated, as Foxfield explained, "without the slightest precautions," and the more he pursued the subject the more disordered his hair became, the more wicked his great spectacle-magnified eyes, and the more gravely preposterous his slowly enunciated biological exaggerations. The life of the ocean became an orgy tempered by massacre. "But they hardly notice they are eaten," he said.

I had never seen Dolores in such eager pursuit of knowledge, and when Foxfield appealed to me to confirm his statement that Tritons and Mermaids were "conceivable – in actual practice I mean – conceivable" – I did so, like one who betrays the arcana.

"Of course they hush it up," said Foxfield very confidentially.

"And now, Steenie," she said, "You see how sound my instinct was!"

"?!" said Foxfield by means of a suitable noise.

"Against bathing in the sea."

"There was a young lady of Sark," began Foxfield, and then turned away and blew his nose violently. His feelings were suddenly too much for him. Over his handkerchief he watched his effect on me. Was he going to far? I looked judicious. My eye counselled moderation. For a time he desisted from the topic of the salt salacious sea. I doubt if anything further is known about the young lady from Sark. It becomes just one more Mystery of the Sea.

That trip to Roscoff was indeed an unexpected success. Dolores explained to Foxfield how superior the marine laboratories there were to the marine biological station at Plymouth – which she heard of for the first time – and how inferior the British scientific mind was to the clear logic of the Latins. "You dream," she said, "you dream. Your women do not wake you up and inspire you. Look at Steenie? What would he be if he never came to France?"

"*Ah!*" said Foxfield and looked at me accusingly with magnified eyes.

And when we contemplated the great fig tree in the Enclos des Capucins, she made us both jump and look round guiltily for nuns, for their flavour still lingers, by her remark, coming clear and abrupt out of pensive stillness, "Regard it, Steenie. A chic costumier could not have invented a better leaf. It almost makes one believe in what you call Papa Bible, all over again."

It was one of her brilliant days. She came near to being happy – and I liked her.

She approved vociferously of the restaurant upon the *plage*, its cleanliness, its unaffected simplicity and the fishiness of its fish; she toyed with the idea of installing Breton servants in the flat; she told the proprietor that she was an Egyptian princess in her own right, and that Foxfield and I were producing a book about Brittany in which he would certainly figure very honourably; and later in the town she went some way towards the purchase of a large salt-water tank which could be installed in the flat for the closer supervision of marine morality. But the price and cost of transport, she decided, were prohibitive.

And so home, leaving Foxfield chuckling heavily as we receded – he had begun a sort of chuckle soliloquy to himself after lunch – and obviously puzzled that I should ever have betrayed discontent with my married lot.

In the car Dolores relapsed towards fatigue and intimations of her pain, but revived abruptly to express her amazement at the fullness of a sea anemone's life as Foxfield had expounded it. "I thought they were mere pretty dolls," she said.

Also she remarked: "You publishers underpay men like Foxfield. What are his opportunities? None! He is like the great Curie. Who worked all his life in a shed … Afterwards they were sorry."

"Did you talk to him about that?"

"He wouldn't talk. He is too loyal to you. But I could see through him."

Then in an apt voice: "The things he knows! The things he might still discover! He makes Nature *live*. He goes to the core of things. How dull your talk is in comparison, Steenie; how banal! How English! Never have you told me anything of all this. If I were a rich woman I would endow him. Like Rousseau. Like Catherine the Great and Voltaire."

"Damn!" I said suddenly.

"What?"

"Nothing. Only that I went to Roscoff just to get Foxfield to hurry up with his copy – and from first to last I never said a word about it."

Arthur Young

Travels in France (Extract)

Young, an English squire from Suffolk, travelled extensively in France in 1787, 1788 and 1789 – witnessing the beginning of the Revolution and the years immediately prior to it. Alone, unarmed and ignorant of the many languages and dialects of France he visited one remote region after another.

September 1, 1788 – To Combourg [Ile et Vilaine], the country has a savage aspect; husbandry not much further advanced, at least in skill, than amongst the Hurons, which appears incredible amidst enclosures; the people almost as wild as their country, and their town of Combourg one of the most brutal filthy places that can be seen; mud houses, no windows, and a pavement so broken, as to impede all passengers, but ease none – yet here is a château, and inhabited; who is this Monsieur de Chateaubriant, the owner, that has nerves strung for a residence amidst such filth and poverty? [*It was, in fact, Monsieur de Chateaubriand – father of the great writer, who also spent his youth there.*] Below this hideous heap of wretchedness is a fine lake, surrounded by well wooded enclosures. Coming out of Hédé, there is a beautiful lake belonging to Monsieur de Blassac [*Count de Blossac, actually*], inten-dant of Poictiers [*the promenade of Poitiers was named after him*], with a fine accompa-niment of wood. A very little cleaning would make here a delicious scenery. There is a chateau, with four rows of trees, and nothing else to be seen from the windows in the true French style. Forbid it, taste, that this should be the owner of that beau-tiful water; and yet this Monsieur de Blassac has made at Poictiers the finest prom-enade in France. [...] The lake abounds with fish, pike to 36lb, carp to 24lb, perch 4lb and tench 5lb. To Rennes – the same strange wild mixture of desert and culti-vation, half savage, half human – 31 miles.

September 2, 1788 – Rennes is well built, and it has two good squares; that par-ticularly of Louis XV where is his statue. The parliament being in exile, the house is not to be seen. The Benedictines garden, called the Tabour [*Le Thabor, in fact*], is worth viewing. But the object at Rennes most remarkable at present is a camp, with a marshal of France [de Stainville], and four regiments of infantry, and two of dra-goons, close to the gates. The discontents of the people have been double, first on account of the high price of bread, and secondly for the banishment of the parlia-ment. The former cause is natural enough, but why the people should love their parliament was what I could not understand, since the distinction between the *noblesse* and *roturiers* is nowhere stronger, more offensive, or more abominable than in *Bretagne*. They assured me, however, that the populace have been blown up to violence by every art of deception, and even by money distributed for that purpose. The commotion rose to such a height before the camp was established, that the troops there were unable to keep the peace.

W. Ambrose Bebb

Llydaw (Extract)

From Llydaw (Brittany) *by Ambrose Bebb (1894–1955), published in 1929. The book is based on the time the author spent in Tremel in June 1923. Bebb, one of the most interesting Welsh language writers of the twentieth century, was a lecturer at the Sorbonne from 1920 to 1925.*

There was no separation of the people of the village from the inhabitants of the country cottages. They were dependant one on the other, living content as two pears on a branch. The carpenter and the blacksmith got their work from the country, and it was in the village that the farmers baked their bread. Dozens of farms were within a little distance of the village. In whatever direction you set off, you would arrive in no time at all at a farm, and ten more steps, you would be at another. Turning up a narrow lane, and you would be at another, and across the yard from it, the next. Thus it was every time, in every direction. They were very small, about ten acres, or five *devez arez* (a day's ploughing) each. There were two or three bordering on twenty acres, even forty acres, and those were considered to be very large indeed. For such small farms, it was necessary for the fields to be even smaller. They were fields of one acre, an acre and a half, two acres, and occasionally three. Fine crops of wheat, hay, oats or barley, potatoes and turnips grew in them. There were many crops of clover to be cut early in the spring to feed the cattle and the working horses. Many of the farms grew buckwheat, which was used to feed the animals. It was also used to make a kind of pancake, *krampouez*. There was no farm that did not have a good orchard with an excellent crop of apples, pears and, less often, plums and cherries. Fertile gardens were full of cabbage, potatoes, carrots, peas and beans. Hemp could be seen in the corner of a field and from it cord and ropes, halters and lines would be made. There was no farm without its rick, or ricks, of wood. *Bern coat* (wood rick) or *bern keuneut* (firewood rick) as they were called, and as necessary as the rick of peat to a cottage in the heart of Ceredigion.

There would often be as many as two or three of these ricks in a farmyard, and they were invariably neat and tidy. This firewood was cut from the branches of trees that had fallen to the ground. They are then left there to dry then tied like sheaves and placed together. Later, after a time they would be garnered to the vicinity of the house. Should there be many loads of them, the neighbours would come to help with the work. The loads would be brought alongside the rick, and four men would go on top of the rick and one on to the cart to unload. He would unload, a sheaf – or a *fagodenn* – at a time, while the other four would build the rick, each with his own section to look after, making sure that the thicker bases were on the outside and the twigs towards the centre. It was, as I experienced, hard work, as each sheaf was very heavy; and many gallons would be drunk that day. Six cartloads would make a considerable rick, but some of them would be twice that size. They were very useful, summer and winter, always convenient, and would burn like withered sticks. These were the only fuel for the fireplace in the district. There was no coal and no peat, summer or winter.

The other thing that caught my attention while walking past the farmhouses was the abundance of furniture. The door faced out to the road, and you could see the furniture exactly opposite. A grandfather clock from floor to the ceiling, of gleaming yellow oak, with a shining pendulum, was one of the most beautiful of the all the furniture. Nearly all were both solid and artistic, of pure oak, carefully looked after and respected even more so. They were old, often the family's oldest inheritance. Tradition was tied to it, and with it, the history of their predecessors, the wisdom of the fathers and the preservation instinct of the mothers.

When there was a knock on the door, there would be, after a moment or two's pause, an invitation to enter. Sometimes someone would get up to see who was there, but the usual practice was not to get up, just call out to invite the caller to come inside. You then had the opportunity to see the Breton's kitchen, and experience its hospitality. A palisade stretched forward two yards from the door. The other side of the palisade there was a table, nearly always of a good size, with two benches, one on each side. Whenever you entered, the huge round loaf was sure to be there, and a plate of yellow butter. Sitting on the bench next to the palisade you faced the fire, a fire on the hearth under the wide mantle, under which the entire family could sit. In the evening, you would see *tad koz*, the grandfather, sucking his clay pipe, listening with enjoyment to the rest of the family chattering around the table as they ate their *soubenn avalou douar*, potato soup, from the cauldron over the fire, and drink coffee and cider.

Turning to your right, you would see a row of oak furniture, full of plates and cups, then the *gwele clos*, the cupboard bed revealing a little of the clean clothes. The house had an earthen floor, which was the poorest part of the house. It was never flat, or dry, or clean. Clean? How could it be as it was always damp with a houseful of children walking on it all day? It was no small task to keep such a house tidy. Especially when considering how the kitchen was always in constant use. Not only was it the place where the food was prepared, this was where it was eaten, and where the people lived throughout the day. If that was not enough, this was also the bedroom. This was the room of the *gwele clos*, even two or three of them. It was here that a good number of the family slept every night. And Breton families were numerous. As yet, unlike France, its population is not in decline. Wherever we went, the children were numerous and this to a certain extent was responsible for the untidiness of the houses. There was much work to be done to nurse and feed so many, knit socks for them and clothe them, on top of the other daily tasks of a mother. There were cows to milk, twice a day; the cowshed had to be cleaned out and pigs fed. She had to help her husband to load manure into the cart, lead the horses when ploughing and sowing, help with the haymaking, to load the carts in the field and unload them in the rickyard. The Breton women work hard on their small farms. There is hardly anything that they cannot do, and do for that matter. They are as strong as the men and just as dexterous with the farm implements. Loading manure or hay, cutting and tying the corn, weeding the potatoes or thinning the turnips, is as often done by the women as by the men.

They are greatly respected by the men. No Breton would ever consider that his wife is nothing but his equal. After all she can do all the tasks that he can, and able to do some that he would only make a mess of! After all, is not Brittany a feminine nation? So believed [Ernest] Renan who was himself one of them. There is much truth in that. The Parisians have a saying, "obstinate as a Breton." It is right to accept that he can be determined, that he sticks to his beliefs and opinions. The obstinacy of a woman, at the same time. He is all heart.

Mrs Lewis Chase

A Vagabond Voyage Through Brittany (Extract)

From A Vagabond Voyage through Brittany *by Mrs Lewis Chase, published in 1915. This is a travel book rather in the style of today, where the writer goes on an eccentric journey. The kind of book where the reader learns more about the writer than the country through which the journey is made. In this book Mrs Chase, an American, and her husband, always referred to as "Himself," travel around Brittany along the canals. "Himself" walks along the towpath pulling the boat in which she sits, writing about the journey and taking the occasional photograph. The journey was made just before the outbreak of war.*

Before there were often three or four locks in the charge of two men who lived at either extremity and accompanied boats through those where there were no keepers. From now on we were to be perpetually escorted. Each keeper would go with us till we reached the next, whether we had more than one lock to attend or not, and in every instance offered to tow us.

If Himself was not in a talking mood (which was seldom), he would get into the boat and on one of these occasions we were towed by a bicycle. Usually he walked along with the keeper who helped pull the boat, and it was a droll picture to look upon two men dragging a boat which one of them often towed for miles with one finger. But as they both declined to ride in order to chat (the keeper usually had a bicycle), it added to the sociability to be occupied in the same task.

From time to time Himself would call back the salient points of the conversation:

"This man killed a wild boar near this spot last year, weighing two hundred and thirteen pounds."

The man, not content with this meagre translation of his prowess, would shout back more details, such as: it had been in the papers, that it was very good meat, but that he had had very little of it, being obliged to turn it over to his superior.

Another keeper explained how difficult it was for children to learn French in school when the home language was Breton. For that reason he and his wife always spoke French, but being the only people round them who did, their desires were more or less frustrated, as their children learned Breton from the others at school.

Another recounted his experiences when he was in China with his regiment at the time of the Boxer uprising. A German went over to the enemies' side, and "when his desertion was discovered and he was shot it gave me more pleasure than anything that ever happened," said our Teuton-hating companion.

Others would be interested in hearing of the world outside their towpath, and so the happy days would be walked and talked away.

There was one matter which became more and more complicated – that of the "tip". Our boating adviser at Dinan had said that two sous were expected for pleasure craft, and the habit of getting within convenient reach of the dispenser thereof,

as we left the lock, made it an easy thing to do.

As we could find no one with a pleasure-boat who had been the other side of Redon we were forced to make our own rules. At the first house where we spent the night on this unknown portion of the trip we met with the first "*Comme vous voulez*" when we asked what we owed them for sleeping in the attic. All the others refused to be paid for a lodging which did not include a bed, and frequently when it did.

The mode of refusal differed according to the temperament of the host or hostess. Occasionally, it was a wounded "*Monsieur*", and nothing more. Again, what might be called a dignified and well-adjusted refusal; and some of them would greet the offer with such rollicking guffaws and good-natured banter that we went away feeling positively comfortable.

The most difficult moments were those when, instead of giving us a price or refusing to be paid, they would only add one apology to another that their accommodation for the entertainment of strangers was so poor. That required a niceness of French of which our joint stock was lamentably deficient.

Naturally, when we met this expectation of remuneration for two nights on the hay we began wondering whether the keepers on this "other side of Redon" were going to expect more than two sous for filling the locks. We were increasingly astonished as the days wore on to find that they expected nothing whatsoever. In nearly every case Himself was told, "It is not necessary," as he handed it out. Then on the next section, "the other side of Pontivy," their surprise at being offered anything was not feigned. Even the keeper who was on holiday and had taken too much cider said "*Pas la peine*" and two men absolutely refused it.

It was not the smallness of the amount to which they objected, for Himself kept it concealed, and when he extended it many of them thought he wished to shake hands. Particularly was this true of those with whom he had walked for any distance, and whose constantly offered snuff he had gone through the motions of accepting.

Unquestionably the scenery reaches its superb climax between Guerlédan and Malvran. The hills and crags are higher and wilder as the river serpentines deeper and deeper into the heart of the forest of Quénécan, and each day the colouring became more gorgeous; but in contrast to the bright leaves we came upon the most dismal sight of the voyage. It was nothing but a group of three or four houses leaning against the foot of a drab slate hill. They were built of slabs of slate; the decaying thatched roofs were the colour of slate; an aged woman and child came out to watch us, and they too looked as though they might have been quarried from the gloomy background. Their flesh was drab, their clothes were drab, and it was altogether the dreariest spot I think I ever saw.

The keeper accompanied us to a house and woodshed and asked whether there was something else he might do, then left us to the most remote, most solitary lodging we had found. The nearest neighbour in either direction was close to a kilometre distant, and because the Blavet forms a U, high hills encircled us. The house was at the foot of one, in the curve of the U, and somewhere across the river and up the hill before us, somewhere through the forest on the slope, behind the row of sentinel pines on the skyline, were the few farmhouses known collectively as the village of Malvran.

The house was like the one at Guerlédan, except there was no hall; so we entered into the stone-floored kitchen. Into this Himself rolled a stump from the wood shed, to serve as a chair, and the stove box answered for another. Then on the hearth he built a fire that would have roasted an ox, but our being without one only diverted its usefulness by getting the room above ready to be slept in after having been deserted for five years.

We ate our supper by the glow of the fire and in unaccustomed silence, for each of us was so busy with one persistent thought that neither remarked the other's preoccupation. Not until the dying embers reminded us of the hour did we come from our reveries and surprise the look in each other's eyes, which said as plainly as words:

"Let us live here."

John Dyfnallt Owen

From the Breton Headland (Extract)

The Welsh journalist and minister of religion, John Dyfnallt Owen, knew Brittany well and in 1934 published O Bentir Llydaw *(From the Breton headland). The following extract translated from the Welsh describes a visit to Concarneau.*

The country on both sides of the main road from Pontaven to Concarneau is flat, fertile and wooded, and we passed through no village of consequence apart from Trégunc. But we saw many a standing stone, manor and church, each one of which would take hours and days to pursue and explain their histories; but we were intent on getting to Concarneau [...]

The moment we arrived at the corner of the quay, every hint of the placid, restful, dreamy and magical atmosphere of Quimperlé and Pontaven vanished. We progressed slowly along the quay through the crowds of fishermen and women. The harbour was alive with fishing boats – boats unlike any to be seen anywhere in the world. There was movement, bargaining, buying and selling everywhere, and the stench of fish filled our nostrils. The streets were filthy.

We ventured to point a camera at a group of fishwives who were knitting and sewing on the quay. Their costumes, in the middle of the noise and chatter and dust, were a delight. But no sooner had they spotted the camera than all twelve of them got up, turned their faces to the wall and their backs to the camera. We went to them, begging them to turn, but they were hard as flint, until we explained that we were *Bretons d'outre-mer* (Bretons from beyond the sea, i.e. Welsh). In an instant their attitude changed and we were honoured with a pose for a splendid photograph.

Near them was another group, and they demanded payment for a photograph. The reason, they said, was that they objected to the French from Paris making fun of them. We had no time to argue and explain – and the women of Concarneau quay are unsurpassed at bargaining.

Opposite us stood the old walled town – the *Ville close*. This side of the river is the new town, the old on the other side, and a narrow bridge linking the two. The old town is home to the remnants of the Middle Ages. It is there that the ancient porches, the sturdy defences and the old houses are found.

Life in Concarneau revolves around ships, fish and fishermen. One of its most stunning views is of the scores of sailing ships setting out to sea or returning. With the blue of the sea and the fiery reflection of the sun on the water and the miraculous tricks of the wind in the folds of the sails there is nothing as elegant as the Concarneau fishing fleet. The circle of fishing ports around Brittany are like a crown on the forehead of a fair maiden, and one of the hidden pearls, the finest of them all, is Concarneau.

Who can forget the excitement when the fleet returns, the dexterity with which the fish are cleaned and their heads removed, the weighing and the washing, the dozens of errand boys with full baskets stepping barefoot from boat to boat and on to the quay, and off to the sellers. For hours after the return of the fleet the quay is like a beehive. Sails are lowered, nets are cleaned, the fish handled and arranged – there never was a busier place.

In the streets behind the quay are the large factories employing hundreds of women and girls. The sardines are washed in large tanks, their heads chopped off, and then immersed in hot oil, their aroma and taste perfected in the *bain de soleil*, before they are placed safely in the tins.

Sails are spread to dry on the masts. The craft of repairing and drying the nets after the trip is like that of the coracle fishermen on the rivers Towy and Teifi.

Finally the weariness of frantically running around the town caught up with us and it was a luxury to rest on the rocks at the entrance to the harbour. Our eyes were drawn to the ever-changing colours on the westerly horizon, the ships moving as if in a dream on the edge of the sea in the heavy hues of the restless scenery. This constant change of colour and ships on a horizon is the enchantment that attracts the world's artists to the area.

Perhaps Concarneau is now one of the seaside towns of Brittany weaned by politics away from the traditions of its past. Communism prospers amongst the seamen. Sun and breeze vying in the folds of a sail were the last view we had as evening descended on Concarneau.

M. Betham-Edwards

Literary Rambles in France

From the chapter 'Brittany of Emile Souvestre' out of Literary Rambles in France *by M. Betham-Edwards, Constable 1907.*

At Roscoff I had a friend's friend, a learned Breton doctor.

"You should cross over to the Ile de Batz tomorrow in time for vespers and see the Druidesses," he said to me one Saturday afternoon. "These people are quite unlike any other in Brittany; they go to mass and are called Catholics, but their real religion is still the purest Druidism."

... In the little mail-boat were about a dozen passengers, all talking Breton as fast as they could. Among them was one of the so-called 'Druidesses', or women of the Ile de Batz, a very young woman – though she wore a wedding ring – who now very modestly put on the shoes and stockings she had wisely taken off to get down to the boat. She was a pretty brunette, and her look of physical strength and animal spirits was delightful to see. Her dress was severely simple and dignified: skirt of the softest, finest black French merino, scrupulously white linen habit-shirt with embroidered collar and sleeves, and a hood of creamy white cashmere, so spotless, soft, and graceful that a duchess might have put it on to go to the opera... Inside [the church], the congregation presented so strange an appearance that it was difficult to believe we were not assisting at some solemn ceremony instead of an ordinary Sunday service. There was not a bit of colour in the church except a gay baby's hood, the assemblage of black-robed, white-hooded women looking more like a concourse of nuns than like ordinary country folks...

Anonymous

From the *Carmarthen Journal*

The following article, together with an introduction and postscript presumably by the editor, appeared in the Carmarthen Journal *of February 25, 1825, translated into English from the French. We do not know who wrote the article quoted at such length. The introduction and postscript are not untypical of Welsh attitudes towards their Celtic cousins in the nineteenth century, that a good injection of Protestant religion and the Bible in the Breton language would inspire an improvement in morality, cleanliness and standards of living. The Cymreigyddion of Abergavenny, in which the Reverend Thomas Price – better known by his bardic name Carnhuanawc – and Lady Augusta Hall, Llanover, were among those who tried to persuade the British and Foreign Bible Society to pay for the translation and publication of the Bible into Breton. Carnhuanawc did, in fact, help the Breton grammarian Le Gonidec with the translation, but it was Hersart de la Villemarqué who paid for the publication many years later.*

Inasmuch as a laudable sympathy has of late been excited in the natives of Cambria for the Bretons in France on account of their superstition and want of civilization and their anxious wishes for their welfare has been manifested on several occasions, the following account of some of their manners and customs written originally in the French language, will, it is presumed, be perused with no small interest by our readers.

The manners of the natives of Bretagne, of those, at least, who have religiously preserved the traditions of their ancestors, are well worthy [of] the attention of travellers. In the midst of an immense population, whose natural physiognomy is so much altered, as not to present the remains of its peculiar type, how great must be the surprise of an observer at meeting with a peasantry ten times renewed in the course of five centuries, without having adopted any new habits, any alteration in their costume, any change in their language, any modification from their original character which they derive from the Gothic ages. The peasant of Bretagne, and especially the Bas-Breton, keeps up the habits which he has inherited from his fore-fathers, rather out of respect for an old-established practice, than from national motives.

The spirit of superstition governs almost every action of his life; traces of his coarse ignorance are to be discovered on almost every occasion. A child is no sooner born than he must be instantly protected from the devil. Will baptism at least be resorted to against the power of the evil spirit? No, this comes afterwards. They first apply to the head, and heart of the child, a piece of scarlet cloth cut in the form of a lozenge, which is supposed to possess the miraculous property of repelling the attempts of the devil. The parents of the newborn child are assembled to celebrate its birth round an oak table, upon which are placed the sweet milk and curds, the crisp buckwheat, the brown loaf, and the hotchpotch – a real porridge, which is a hundred times more insipid than the most detestable ragout. One of the parents no sooner gives an affectionate kiss to the hero of the feast, than he is immediately handed from one to another, beginning with the guest whose age, or whose quality of stranger has entitled him to sit on the mother's right hand; the child at last comes to the guest who asked for it, and returning by the left hand to the starting point, is given back to the nurse, whose anxious eye has followed it on the journey, which might have proved fatal to it, if one of the guests had chanced to forget for a moment the consequences of sending it back to the mother by the shortest route in a direct line, across the table, for the devil stood there waiting for it, and nothing, not even the *scarlet lozenge*, could have saved it from such a danger.

It may be easily conceived that a country almost unknown to the rest of France – a country, the soil of which is naturally poor, and still more impoverished through the ignorance and incapacity of its cultivators, would show for a considerable time the traces of hereditary barbarism. The revolution, which has changed the state of the empire, and in so doing has expanded to almost every province, the benefit of the new ideas, whether as connected with agriculture or with industry, has effected little more with respect to Bretagne, than its mere discovery. It has created with difficulty a communication between the centre of knowledge, and these dwellings, wherein customs had been preserved unchanged for centuries, which were totally at variance with others rendered by the force of instruction so generally popular in the rest of Europe. Villages and hamlets, though without any anxiety on the subject, are prepared to receive an administration that may at least bring the manners of their inhabitants into a character of harmony with those of Frenchmen; so that a stranger who may visit our country in all its extent, will no longer be struck with these strange inconsistencies; the prevalence of which, amongst a people governed by uniform laws, is so difficult to be accounted for.

The people of Bretagne appear to take a delight in slovenliness; their dress always covered with dust and filth, is composed of coarse stuff, and in shape resembles that of the Dutch peasantry. In some districts of Bretagne, the men add to a large waistcoat with sleeves thrown over a shorter one, a goat's skin, which exhales a smell more offensive than the hair and bodies of these savages.

Long and bushy hair is not an object of mere ornament for the natives of Bretagne; it is suffered to grow without any care, in order that it may be offered under certain circumstances of life, to some saint or virgin who may be held in some repute among them. We have seen in the church of the small town of Dinan, a chapel where the image of a saint (an ill-shapen piece of wood bedaubed with glaring colours) had several consecrated heads of hair about it, forming together, as may be imagined, a very whimsical figure. These grotesque saints ranged about the chapel presented the appearance of casks placed in a row in a vinegar manufactory; and when adorned with these repugnant offerings conveyed the idea of a temple of cannibals decorated by the devotion of a warlike tribe, with the only remains of the vanquished which they could not devour.

The women are generally of short stature; their costume is not becoming their small figure; they are not cleaner than the men. Those who carry on the fishing trade, and have frequent intercourse with the towns, are habitually in a state of drunkenness. The greater number of these women, since we must call them by that name though they have little resemblance to a sex in which they appear to be ranked as it were by mistake, retain all the habits of men of a corresponding class. It is common to see them chewing tobacco, and getting intoxicated at the same time with the fumes of the tobacco leaf, which they are in the habit of smoking.

The women of the interior of the country do not exhibit such extraordinary customs and inclinations as those who live among the rocks, and on the seashore; they are however as little careful of their persons. We have found cottages, into which we could not have entered without running the risk of sinking into a pool of stagnant water that infested the atmosphere of an unpaved habitation; which proceeded from the abundant rain of Bretagne, and from the drainings of the ox-stalls, and pigsties. We have seen many a young girl whose freshness and beauty could hardly be distinguished through the filth that disguised the features of her charming face, and who wanted nothing more than an elegant dress and the habit of daily ablutions, in order to bear the palm in a circle of handsome women. In the greater part of the dwellings of the peasantry of Lower Bretagne, the beds are found to be of a totally different construction from those in use in other parts of France. A simple piece of furniture not unlike the large elevated wardrobes, which contain the dresses and household linen of the most affluent of our country, serve the purposes of bed: for the parents in the first shelf, the girls the next, higher up for the young men, and in the last for children under ten years of age.

As we were travelling though the country, in which everything bears so extraordinary an aspect, we were benighted at the entrance into a small village, and forced to apply for hospitality to a worthy peasant, who in the most obliging manner gave us shelter in his hut. This man was marrying his daughter, a full grown, handsome lass, for two years betrothed to a young husbandman, who had served in the ranks of the brave legions of the west, and made with them that campaign so glorious to the Bretons, by their having decided the success of the battles of Lutzen and Bantzen, to which the division of marine artillery had so powerfully contributed. We were presently invited by the head of the family to partake of the repast, which our arrival had interrupted; and when it was the hour of rest – when the national *sons* [i.e. the Breton 'sonoù' or folk songs] had ceased – when the nasal instrument, which resembles a bagpipe, and produces a harsh and shrill sound, had given the signal to the company, who joined in chorus with a mournful noise: the worthy peasant kindly accosted us, and said in a language of which we could only collect a few words, "that the only shelf of his bed-press that could afford us any accommodation, was that of his son, a lad 16 years old. We thanked our landlord and accepted his offer. A man of tall stature and open countenance next accosted us in these words: "Should you feel incommoded by what is going forward, and wish for a quiet sleep, you will oblige me by coming with me and taking share of my bed." "We would eagerly accept your kind offer," was our reply to this open-hearted obliging Breton, on whose breast shone a large gold cross hanging by a red ribbon, and who, we soon discovered, had served as captain in the old guard. "We would eagerly accept it, were we not afraid of offending the person who has given us such a hearty welcome." "You are quite right then," said the officer, smiling at our military dress. We, accordingly ascended to the third storey, the second was occupied by the new couple. When the night was far advanced we heard a noise like the grunting of a pig. We enquired the next morning from whence had proceeded the noise: it was in fact from a hog who was an old inmate of the press, and lodged in the lower part of it.

The inhabitants of Bretagne being, according to the above account, in so low and abject a state of civilisation, what Cambrian breast is there which does not become warm, even at the probability of this ancient people, which are descended from the same stock as the Welsh themselves, and speak nearly the same language, having their minds cultivated, and habits of civilization promoted through means of literature, and the Holy Scriptures in their own language being introduced among them. The Cymreigyddion of Brecon and of other places, have, much to their credit, exerted themselves on their behalf, whose efforts deserve to be seconded by the ample donations of affluent individuals; and as it is understood that the Committee of the British and Foreign Bible Society propose to undertake the business shortly, the performance of much may be expected and the Bretons receive incalculable benefits through the powerful means, which the extensive patronage bestowed on the Society, enables them to confer.

H. A. Vachell

The Face of Clay (Extract)

The novel, published in 1906, is set among the artistic community in Pontaven. It is dedicated to Mademoiselle Julia Guillou (1848 – 1927), who owned the Hôtel des Voyageurs, and was popular with the richer, mostly amateur artists, in Pontaven. Paul Gauguin, and the more talented artists lodged in the less expensive Pension Glouanec. Mademoiselle Yvonne in the novel is probably based on Mademoiselle Julia and the hotel on the Hôtel des Voyageurs.

Not many changes had been wrought in Pont-Aven. The houses, built of grey granite, built to endure forever, seemed to greet Téphany with a sober smile; the familiar watermills, with their huge wheels, looked not a day older. They had, so Téphany reflected, the sane, mellow appearance of faithful servants who had worked hard and were now enjoying a well-earned rest. The doors of the houses stood open as of yore. Peering into the dark interiors, Téphany caught a glimpse of furniture black with age and smoke, polished by the use of a hundred years. The villagers were busy in the prosecution of the small daily tasks so important to their welfare. The old women knitted, chattering together in pairs; the wives and daughters were washing down by the river, or preparing the simple noon meal, or at work in the fields; most of the children were at school. In a window Téphany recognised the face of a friend, Mère le Beuz, who glanced up as Téphany passed. The dear soul smiled pleasantly, thinking, perhaps, of the fat five-franc pieces which strangers brought to the village, but in the keen, kindly eyes Téphany perceived interest only, not recognition. Time had been generous to Mère le Beuz. Perhaps her shoulders and hips were a trifle broader; a few more lines lay upon the brown, clear-skinned face which glowed between the snowy collar and coif; but she still looked strong, the mother, the wife, the sister of strong men.

The sight of this plain honest face gave Téphany a thrill of delight. Then, in the reaction, she compared her own life during the past decade with that of the peasant. The hurry and scurry from town to town, from country to country, from continent to continent, the never ending competition, the jealousy of rivals, the glare of the footlights, the hot, tainted atmosphere of the theatre, the adulation of the mob. And at the end, a physical breakdown, a tiny rift within the lute. Had it been worthwhile?

The marketplace was empty save for a couple of carts standing opposite a tavern. The carts, very long in the body, deftly balanced between high wheels, gave Téphany another thrill. How often she had lain snugly curled up in masses of sweet-scented clover and hay, half dreaming, hearing the tinkle of the bells upon the horses' necks, as these same carts carried her back from the fields to the small house where she and her father lived!

At the east end of the marketplace she saw the ancient inn, and at its side a large annexe built since Téphany had left Pont-Aven. Téphany smiled at the old tavern,

and frowned at the new. A moment later she was walking up the stone steps, walking, so she felt, into the past, as one strolls into a place where time has recorded its sunniest hours.

To the right, through an open door, she could see the dining room, panelled from floor to ceiling with pictures and sketches painted by her dear artists for Mademoiselle Yvonne. And Mademoiselle Yvonne was still Mademoiselle Yvonne (Téphany had learned this at Quimperlé), and, as ever, the loyal friend of all painters.

Téphany walked into the small office to the left, where a young girl, in the dainty coif and collar of the commune, sat writing behind a broad counter. In answer to Téphany's questions, the girl informed Mademoiselle that as the season had not begun she could have any accommodation, any room almost, she might require. Mademoiselle Yvonne was in the kitchen. Certainly, if one wished to see her, she could be summoned. Téphany asked for a room in the old house, and, without giving her name, wandered into the dining room and up to a panel at the farther end of it. The panel held a portrait of herself. Gazing at it, she wondered if it were possible that she ever presented so wild, so disordered an appearance. For the first time she experienced an honest sympathy for the uncle and aunt who had welcomed their unknown niece so coldly, who had stared with such horror at unkempt locks, untied strings, badly laced boots: all, in fact, that Michael Ossory had faithfully reproduced upon the panel.

In a minute, however, Téphany recognised herself, the essential spirit which still dominated her. The eyes, burning out of the panel with such fiery interrogation, were her eyes; the smile was her smile. Such as she had been she still was; only the envelope had changed.

A step, not a light one, upon the well-scrubbed floor, warned her that Yvonne was approaching. Ah, thank heaven! Her kind friend had altered hardly at all. Her hair was now iron-grey; her fine figure had grown massive; but the shrewd, twinkling eyes, the square chin, the mobile, humorous lips, were the same. She greeted Téphany courteously, but indifferently. Téphany smiled as she returned the formal salutation.

"Who is that?" she asked, indicating the portrait of herself.

"It is one of my best panels," said Yvonne.

"But how ugly!"

"Ugly?" Yvonne frowned, then she added sharply: "Evidently Mademoiselle is not an artist. The sketch is very fine. I have been offered a thousand francs for that panel."

"You ought to have taken it," Téphany murmured, still scrutinising her elfin locks. Vanity hinted that such a terrible witness ought not to be at large.

"Never!" Yvonne's voice was flatteringly emphatic. "And to me, Mademoiselle, that child is beautiful."

"Sinfully ugly," said Téphany. Then as Yvonne's kind eyes began to blaze, she burst out laughing, holding out her hands. "Why, Yvonne," she said – and although she was laughing, tears shone in her eyes – "you have told me a thousand times that I was ugly, and naughty, and an imp of Satan, and that you never wished to set eyes on me again."

"Ma Doué!" exclaimed Yvonne, relapsing into Breton under the stress of violent emotion. "It is thou, my blessed one. The Saints be praised!"

Téphany flung herself into those sturdy arms, gasping with delight.

★ ★ ★ ★ ★

The road to Nizon is on the other side of Pont-Aven, but Téphany wished to take the short cut through the woods and fields; the path she had trod so often with her father, which passes the chapel of Trémalo. She knew every tree, every stone and stile. Presently she came to a delightful avenue of oaks; upon each side of the way are wheat-fields and apple-orchards. Téphany looked at the trees, stunted, misshapen, many of them, but sturdy and vigorous, deeply rooted in the soil, twisted by a thousand storms, yet surviving them as they would survive others, almost imperishable, honoured in legend and song – the oaks of Finistère. The avenue leads into a wider, more beautiful avenue of beech trees – an approach to the château [*this would be the Manoir du Plessis, where Hersart de la Villemarqué spent much of his childhood*]. But Téphany, turning sharp to the left, came suddenly upon the small chapel of Trémalo, a miniature church built of granite, extremely old, but in a state of remarkable preservation, and surmounted by a delicately carved spire, an ornament added probably in the sixteenth century. [*Inside this chapel, today, can be seen the wooden statue of Christ on the Cross, which inspired Paul Gauguin's famous Le Christ Jaune – the Yellow Christ.*]

Téphany paused on the threshold […] a strong desire assailed her to dip her fingers into the *bénitier*, to cross herself with holy water. She was distressed when she discovered that the *bénitier* was dry.

Téphany entered the chapel. Inside it is paved with rough granite flagstones. Wide arches, surmounting big, round, whitewashed pillars, support a wooden roof, painted sky blue. Between the roof and the walls is a frieze with extraordinary heads of men and animals carved upon it, all grimacing violently to keep at bay evil spirits. Some ostrich eggs hung in front of a painted figure of the Virgin. The stained glass in a window, very old and very good, deflected oddly the light, throwing splotches of vivid colour upon the stone floor.

Téphany noted these details before she perceived at the further and darker end of the chapel a man sitting upon a rude bench, with his face hidden by his hands. The man sat so silent and motionless that he seemed to have no more life than the figure of the Virgin. Téphany's presence, seemingly, did not excite his interest. This, however, aroused no surprise in her. Some fisherman, doubtless, who had wandered into the chapel to pray and meditate. She felt sorry that she had disturbed him. Possibly he had covered his eyes on purpose. Her imagination flared, seeing a fellow creature suffering in spirit, yearning to be alone with his Maker,

resenting bitterly, perhaps, the advent of a strange woman. His attitude was one of profound dejection. With a shy, backward glance, Téphany left the chapel.

[She went] to the Calvary upon whose pedestal she had spent so many hours. The Calvary at Nizon is triple, richly ornamented, carved out of granite, the hardness of which has been softened by centuries of rain. It is probable that it was set up after one of those fearful visitations of sickness which ravaged the country of Cornouailles about the middle of the sixteenth century. During the Reign of Terror the crosses had been pulled down and broken up. All over France madness wreaked its fury upon such sacred emblems. And yet, the madness passed away, the emblems remain, replaced by pious hands, venerated, as before, by pious souls. Téphany, gazed at the stones worn by the feet and knees of countless pilgrims, reflected that another thunder-cloud of madness and violence hung over the province, and she believed that, as before, it would pass, having spent itself, but that the faith, enduring as the granite of these monuments, would not perish, but would rise again, purged, maybe, by fiery ordeal, refined, tempered, glorified.

Ambrose Bebb

Pererindodau

To this day men – and a few women – from Roscoff, St-Pol-de-Léon and the neighbouring countryside and villages come to Britain to sell strings of onions carried around on the handlebars of their bicycles. The trade of the 'Johnnies,' as they are known, goes back to 1828. They spend six months from August to February in Britain and the rest of the year home in Brittany. The following extract is translated from Pererindodau *(Pilgrimages) by Ambrose Bebb, published by the Welsh Books Club in 1941.*

Of the towns and villages within reach of St-Pol-de-Léon, the largest is Roscoff. It was a place I had to visit. It is a journey of around four miles and it would not take me more than an hour at a brisk pace. I started out early on a Thursday morning. With a fair wind to urge me on, I had walked from the station to the Kreisker and the cathedral, indeed I had left the town, almost without realising it. I saw little of interest in the flat, fertile countryside with its valuable crops – an uninspiring land lacking in splendours. As I strived a little harder, and lengthened my stride on the dusty, stony road, I saw a man with a horse and cart on the bend ahead of me. I was alongside him in no time, and addressed him in my best St-Pol Breton, which was very important, as the language varies much in colour, tone and accent, from place to place. It is the rule – or the fashion – for the people of neighbouring parishes to claim not to understand each other's Breton!

Evidently, I succeeded quite well. I was invited to ride with him in the cart. Although not in the least tired, I jumped up without hesitation. Without any prompting the man told me his life's story. He lived nearby, and had travelled abroad many times. He had been to Wales, and knew Swansea, Carmarthen and Llanelli at least as well as I did. We had to speak Welsh, and his Welsh was fluent, although his vocabulary was rather limited. He spoke the dialect of South Wales, the dialect of Llanelli, with its glory and its faults. He held Llanelli in great affection, despite admitting that he and his compatriots led a hard, wooden life, while they were in Wales.

"It's not home, you see, no comforts. Walking in the wind and rain and all weather. Soaking wet, and having to be in those wet clothes from morning to night. Eating a cold onion from the hand and an occasional crust of bread. Then there was Sunday, the saddest day of all for us in Wales. No cathedral like the one in St-Pol. No praying and singing in Latin and Breton. No presence of brothers and sisters around us, to warm us. And no dressing up in our Sunday best. Have you ever seen us Bretons in our best clothes?"

"Yes, many times."

"In St-Pol?"

"Yes, and in Guingamp, Morlaix, Trémel and ..."

"O, well, I don't have to tell you anything about our clothes – especially those of the women. But many people in Wales think that we are tramps because they only see us in our working clothes."

So true! And so sad!

The man with the cart turned off the road, for his home, which was within sight. By now we were the best of friends, and causing some bemusement as we chatted away in Welsh. In fact, it should not have caused people any surprise, as there were many others in the neighbourhood who spoke Welsh exceptionally well. I met a few as I wandered from place to place, and I recall one who spoke Welsh with even great fluency than my friend with the cart. When I commented on the suppleness with which he spoke Welsh, he replied:

"O, you see, I have been going to Wales every year for a long time. I also have a brother-in-law who lives nearby, and he speaks Welsh as well as I do."

"Do you converse in Welsh sometimes?"

"Don't we just! Every time we meet – and especially if we don't want people to know what we're talking about. It pays to be able to speak Welsh!"

Childhood memories

Anne Douglas Sedgwick

A Childhood in Brittany (Extract)

These memories of a Breton lady were recorded by Anne Douglas Sedgwick and published in 1919. It is an interesting portrait of life among the nobility in the mid-nineteenthth century.

I was born at Quimper on the First of August, 1833, at four o'clock in the morning, and I have been told that I looked about me resolutely and fixed a steady gaze on the people in the room, so that the doctor said, "She is not blind, at all events."

The first thing I remember is a hideous doll to which I was passionately attached. It belonged to the child of one of the servants, and my mother, since I would not be parted with it, gave this child, to replace it, a handsome doll. It had legs stuffed with sawdust and a clumsily painted cardboard head, and on this head it wore a *bourrelet*. The *bourrelet* was a balloon-shaped cap made of plaited wicker, and was worn by young children to protect their heads when they fell. We, too, wore them in our infancy, and I remember that I was very proud when wearing mine and I thought it a very pretty headdress.

I could not have been more than three years old when I was brought down to the *grand salon* to be shown to a friend of my father's, an Englishman, on his way to England from India, and a pink silk dress I then wore, and my intense satisfaction in it, is my next memory. It had a stiff little bodice and skirt, and there were pink rosettes over my ears. But I could not have been a pretty child, for my golden hair, which grew abundantly in later years, was very scanty, and my mouth was large. I was stood upon a mahogany table of which I still see the vast and polished spaces beneath me, and Mr John Dobray, when I was introduced to him by my proud father, said, "So this is Sophie."

Mr Dobray wore knee breeches, silk stockings, and a high stock. I see my father, too, very tall, robust, and fair, with the pleasantest face. My father's figure fills all my childhood. I was his pet and darling. When I cried and was naughty, my mother would say: "Take your daughter. She tires me and is insufferable." Then my father would take me in his arms and walk up and down with me while he sang me to sleep with old Breton songs. One of these ran:

> *Jésus péguen brasvé,*
> *Plégar douras néné;*
> *Jésus péguen brasvé,*
> *Ad ondar garan té!*

This, as far as I remember, means: "May Jesus be happy, and may His grace make us all happy."

[*This song from* Barzaz Breiz *should read as follows: Jezuz! Peger bras eo/Plijadur an eneoù, Pa'z int dirak Doue/Hag en e garante! – Jesus! How great is/The pleasure of the souls/When they are before God/and in His love!*]

At other times my father played strange, melancholy old Breton tunes to me on a violin, which he held upright on his knee, using the bow across it as though it were a cello. He was, though untaught, exceedingly musical, and played by ear on the clavecin anything he had heard. It must have been from him that I inherited my love of music, and I do not remember the time that I was not singing.

I see myself, also, at the earliest age, held before my father on his saddle as we rode through the woods. He wore an easy Byronic collar and always went bareheaded. He spent most of his time on horseback, visiting his farms or hunting.

My father was of a wealthy bourgeois family of Landerneau, and it must have been his happy character and love of sport rather than his wealth – he was Master of hounds and always kept the pack – that made him popular in Quimper, for the gulf between the *bourgeoisie* and the *noblesse* was almost impassable. Yet not only was he popular, but he had married my mother, who was of an ancient Breton family, the Rosvals. One of the Rosvals fought in *La Bataille des Trente* [in 1350] against the English, and the dying and thirsty Beaumanoir to whom it was said on that historic day, "Bois ton sang, Beaumanoir," was a cousin of theirs.

My mother was a beautiful woman with black hair and eyes of an intense dark blue. She was unaware of her own loveliness, and was much amused one day when her little boy, after gazing intently at her, said, "*Maman,* you are very beautiful." She repeated this remark, laughing, to my father, on which he said, "Yes, my dear, you are."

My mother was extremely proud, and not all flattered that she should be plain Mme Kerouguet, although she was devoted to my father and it was the happiest *ménage.* I remember one day seeing her bring to my father, looking, for all her feigned brightness, a little conscious, some new visiting-cards she had had printed, with the name of Kerouguet reduced to a simple initial, and followed by several of the noble ancestral names of her family.

"What's this?" said my father, laughing.

"We needed some new cards," said my mother, "and I dislike so much the name of Kerouguet."

But my father, laughing more than ever, said:

"Kerouget you married and Kerouguet you must remain," and the new cards had to be relinquished.

My mother, with her black hair and blue eyes, had a charming nose of the sort called "*un nez Roxalane*." It began very straight and fine, but had a flattened little plateau on the tip which we called "*la promenade de maman*". My memory of her then is of a very active, gay, authoritative young woman, going to balls, paying and receiving visits, and riding out with my father, wearing the sweeping habit of those days and an immense beaver hat and plume.

Quimper is an old town, and the *hotels* of the *noblesse*, all situated in the same quarter and on a steep street, were of blackened, crumbling stone. From *portes-cochères* one entered the courtyards, and the gardens behind stretched far into the country.

In the courtyard of our *hotel* was a stone staircase, with elaborate carvings, like those of the Breton churches, leading to the upper stories, but for use there were inner staircases. My mother's *boudoir*, the *petit salon*, the *salle-à-manger*, and the billiard-room were on the ground floor and gave out upon the garden.

The high walls that ran along the street and surrounded the garden were concealed by plantations of trees, so that one seemed to look out into the country. There were flowerbeds under the salon-windows, and there were long borders of wild strawberries that had been transplanted from the woods, as my mother was very fond of them. Fruit-trees grew against the walls, and beyond the groves and flowerbeds and winding gravel paths was an orchard, with apricot, pear and apple trees, and the clear little river Odet, with its washing-stones, where the laundry-maids beat the household linen in the cold, running water.

It was pleasant to hear the *clap-clap-clap* on a hot summer day. Is it known that the pretty pied water-wagtail is called *la lavandière* from its love of water and its manner of beating up and down its tail as our washerwomen wield their wooden beaters?

Beyond the river were the woods where I often rode with my father, and beyond the woods distant ranges of mountains. I looked out at all this from my nursery-windows. Near my window was a great lime-tree of the variety known as American. The vanilla-like scent of its flowers was almost overpowering, and all this fragrance gave my mother a headache, and she had to have her room moved away from the garden to another part of the house. How clearly I see this room of my mother's, with its high, canopied four-poster bed and the pale-grey paper on the walls covered with yellow *fleur-de-lis*!

The wallpaper in my father's room was one of the prettiest I have ever seen, black, all bespangled with bright butterflies. Of the *grand salon* I remember most clearly the high marble mantelpiece, upheld by hounds sitting on their haunches. On this mantelpiece was a huge *boule* clock, two tall candelabra of Venetian glass, and two figures in *vieux Saxe* of a marquis and a marquise that filled us with delight. On each side of the fireplace were two Louis XV court chairs – chairs, that is, with only one arm, to admit of the display of the great hoop-skirts of the period. I remember, too, our special delight in the foot-stools, which were of mahogany, shaped rather like gondolas and cushioned in velvet; for we could sit inside them and make them rock up and down.

The houses of the *noblesse* swarmed with servants; many of them were married, and their children, and even their grandchildren, lived on with our family in patri-archal fashion. Men and maids all wore the costumes of their respective Breton cantons, exceedingly beautiful some of them, stiff with heavy embroideries, the strange caps of the women fluted and ruffled, adorned with lace, rising high above their heads and falling in long lappets upon their shoulders, or perched on their heads like butterflies. These caps were decorated with large gold pins and dangling golden pendants, and these and the materials for the costumes were handed down in the peasants' families from generation to generation. My young nurse Jeannie – there was an old nurse called Gertrude – wore a skirt of bright-blue woollen stuff and black-cloth bodice opening in a square over a net fichu thickly embroidered with *paillettes* of every colour. Hers was the small flat cap of Quimper, with the odd foolscap excrescence, rather like the horn of a rhinoceros, curving forward over the forehead. Needless to say, the servants did not do their daily work in this fine array; while that went on they were enveloped from head to foot in large aprons.

The servants and the peasants in the Brittany of those days had a pretty custom of always using the *thou* when addressing their masters or the Diety, thus inverting the usual association of this mode of address; for to each other they said *you*, and on their lips this was the familiar word, and the *thou* implied respect. Our servants were of the peasant class, but service altered and civilised them very much, and while no peasant spoke anything but Breton, they talked in an oddly accented French. I remember a pretty example of this in a dear old man who served my little cousin Guénolé du Jacquelot du Bois-Laurel. Guénolé and I, because of some naughtiness, were deprived of strawberries one day at our supper, and the old man, grieving over the discomfiture of his little master, said, or, rather chanted, half in condolence, and half in playful consolation: "Oh, le pauvre Guénolé, que tu es désolé!" accenting the *o* in a very droll fashion.

The servants were all under the orders of a very stately autocratic person, the steward or major-domo. It was he who directed the service from behind his mas-ter's chair at the head of the table and he who proscribed the correct costume for the servants. His wife had charge of Jeannie and of me; it was she who, when two little sisters and a brother had been added to the family, took us down to our break-fast and supervised the meal. We had it in a little tower-room on the ground floor, milk soup or gruel and the delicious bread and butter of Brittany.

We lunched and dined at ten and five – such were the hours of those days – with our parents in the dining room, and it was here that one of the most magnificent figures of my childhood appears; for my devoted father bought me back from Paris one day a splendid mechanical pony, life-sized and with a real pony skin, the apparatus by which he was moved simulating an exhilarating canter. Upon this steed, after dessert, we children mounted one by one, and we resorted to many ruses in order to get the first ride of the day. This dear pony accompanied all my childhood. He lost his hair as the result of an unhappy experiment we tried upon him, scrubbing him with hot water and soap, one day when we were unobserved. He had a melancholy look after that, but was none the less active and none the less loved. When I saw his dismembered body lying in the garret of a grand niece not many years ago I felt a contraction of the heart. How he brought back my youth, and since then how many generations had ridden him!

We played at being horses, too, driving each other in the garden, where we spent most of our days when at Quimper. Strange to say, even while we were thus occupied, we always wore veils tightly tied over our bonnets and faces to preserve our skins from the sun. We all wore, even in earliest childhood, stiff little dresses with closely fitted boned bodices. My sister Eliane was delicate and wore flannel next to her skin; but my only underclothing consisted of cambric chemise, petticoats, and drawers, these last reaching to my ankles and terminating in frills that fell over the foot in its sandaled shoe. When I came back from a wonderful stay, later on, of four or five years in England, a visit that revolutionized my ideas of life, I wore the easy dress of English children, with bare arms, much to my mother's dismay. Another change that England wrought in me was that I was filled with discomfort when I saw the peasants kneeling before us at Loch-ar-Brugg, our country home; for in those days, although the Revolution had passed over France, it was still the custom for peasants to kneel before their masters, and my mother felt it right and proper that they should do so. I begged her not to allow it, but she insisted upon the ceremony to her dying day, and only when I came as mistress to Loch-ar-Brugg with my children and grandchildren was it discontinued.

Another early memory is the long row of family portraits in the *salle-à-manger*. I think I must have looked up at these from my father's shoulder as he walked up and down with me, singing to me while my mother went on with her interrupted dessert, for the awe that some of them inspired in me seems to stretch back to babyhood. Some were so dark and severe that it was natural they should frighten a baby; but it was a pastel, in flat, pale tones, of an old lady with high powdered hair, whose steady, forbidding gaze followed me up and down the room that frightened me most. This was an elder sister of my grandmother's, a March'-Inder, who, dressed as a man, had fought with her husband and daughter in the war of the Chouans against the republic. Her husband was killed, and her daughter, taken prisoner by a French officer, had hanged herself, so the family story ran, to escape insult. Another portrait of a great-grandmother enchanted me then, as it has done ever since, a charming young woman seated, with her hands folded before her, her golden hair un-powdered, her dress of citron-coloured satin brocaded with bunches of pale, bright flowers. And there was a portrait of my grandmother in youth, with black hair and eyes as black as jet. I thought her very ugly, and could never associate her with my dearly loved *bonne maman*.

I must delay no longer in introducing this most important member of the family, my mother's mother, with whom we lived, for the old Quimper *hôtel* was her dower-house.

Poor *bonne maman*! I still see her, in her deep arm-chair, always dressed in a long gown of puce-coloured satin, a white lace mantilla, caught up with a small bunch of artificial buttercups, on her white hair. She wore white-thread lace mittens that reached to her elbows, and her thin, white hands were covered with old-fashioned rings. My mother was her favourite daughter, and I, as the eldest child of this favourite, was specially cherished. Both of *bonne maman*'s parents had been guillotined in the Revolution. I do not think her husband was of much comfort to her. He came to Quimper only for short stays. He was *directeur des Ponts et Chaussées* for the district, but also a deputy in Paris, and these political duties, according to him, gave him no leisure for family life. He was at least ten years younger than *bonne maman*, very gay and witty, *l'homme du monde* in all acceptations of the term, full of deference to *bonne maman*, which he treated like a queen, with respectful salutes and gallant kissing of the hand. He seemed very fond of his home at Quimper when he was in it, but he seldom graced it with his presence.

When I went up to see *bonne maman* in the morning, she would give me her thumb to kiss, an odd formality, since she was full of demonstrations of affection toward me. I did not find the salute altogether agreeable, since *bonne maman* took snuff constantly, and her delicate thumb and forefinger were strongly impregnated with the smell of tobacco. Taking me on her knees, she would then very gravely ask to see my little finger, and when I held it up, she would scrutinise it carefully, and from its appearance tell me whether I had been good or naughty. Beside her chair *bonne maman* had always a little table, the round polished top surrounded by a low brass railing. On this were ranged a number of toilet implements, her glasses, scent-bottle, workbag and various knickknacks. A very unique implement, I imagine, was a little stick of polished wood, with a tuft of cotton wool tied by a ribbon at one end. This she used, when her maid had powdered her hair or her face, to dust off the superfluous powder, and I can see her now, her little mirror in one hand, the ribboned stick in the other, turning her head from side to side and softly brushing the tuft over her brow and chin. The table was always carried down with her to the *petit salon*, where, her morning toilet over, she was borne in her chair by means of the handles that projected before and behind it.

Bonne maman had an old carriage, an old horse, and an old coachman. None of these was ever used, since she never went out except on Easter day, when she was carried in a sedan chair to hear mass at the cathedral near by. The sedan chair was grey-green with bunches of flowers painted on it, and upholstered with copper-coloured satin. It was carried by four bearers in full Breton costume. They wore jackets of a bright light blue, beautifully embroidered along the edges with disks of red, gold and black; red sashes, tied round their waists, hung to the knees; their full knee-breeches were white, their shoes black, and their stockings of white wool.

Like all the peasants of that time, they wore their hair long, hanging over their shoulders, and their large, round Breton hats were of black felt tied with a thick chenille cord of red, blue and black which was held to the brim at one side by a golden fleur-de-lis, and that had a scapular dangling from the end. Within the chair sat my grandmother, dressed, as always, in puce colour; but this gala costume was of brocade, flowers of a paler shade woven upon a dark ground, and the lace mantilla of every-day wear was replaced by a sort of white tulle head-dress, gathered high upon her head and falling over her breast and shoulders. I remember her demeanour in church on these great occasions, her gentle authority and *recueillement*, and the glance of grave reproach for my mother, who was occupied in looking about her and in making humorous comments on the odd clothes and attitude of her fellow-worshippers. On all other days the *curé* brought the communion to my grandmother in her room. I remember the first of these communions that I witnessed. I was sitting on *bonne maman*'s bed when the *curé* entered, accompanied by his acolytes in red and white, and I was highly interested when I recognised in one of these important personages the cook's little boy. The *curé* was going to lift me from the bed, but *bonne maman* said: "No; let her stay. When you are gone I will explain to her the meaning of what she sees". This she attempted to do, but not, I imagine, with much success. Old Gertrude, Jeannie's chief in the nursery, had of course already told me of *le petit Jésus*, and I had learned to repeat, "*Seigneur, je vous donne mon coeur.*" But *bonne maman* was grieved to find that I did not yet know "Our Father".

"Sophie does not know her *Pater*," she said to my mother. "She must learn it."

"Oh, she is too young to learn it," said my mother. But *bonne maman* was not at all satisfied with this evasion and saw that the prayer was taught to me. She was very devout, and confessed twice a week; but more than this, she was the best of women. I never heard her speak ill of any one or saw her angry at any time, nor did I ever see her give way to mirth, though I remember a species of laughter that at times shook her thin body.

Bonne maman was devoted to my father, even more devoted than to her own sons, of whom she had eight. They had been so severely brought up by her, but especially, I feel sure, by my grandfather, that through exaggerated respect and absurd ceremony they almost trembled during the short audiences granted to them by their parents. My father trembled before nobody. He was always cheerful, good-tempered, and kind. During our life in Quimper he was not much at home, as he had a horror of receptions and visits – all the bother, as he said, of social life – and the time not spent in hunting was fully occupied seeing after his farms, his crops, and his peasants. Therefore, when he came back for a three-or-four days' stay with us, it was a delight to young and old. I see him now, sitting in a low chair beside *bonne maman's bergère*, his head close to hers, his pipe between his teeth – yes, his pipe – for *bonne maman* not only permitted, but even commanded, him to smoke in her presence, so much did she value every moment of the time he could be with her. So they smiled at each other while they talked – the snowy, powdered old head and the fair young one enveloped in the midst of smoke – understanding each other perfectly; and although their opinions were diametrically opposed, politics was their favourite theme. They must have taught me their respective battle cries, for I well remember that, riding my father's knee, while he varied the gait from trot to gallop, I knew just when to cry out, "*Vive le Roi!*" in order to please *bonne maman*, and "*Vive la République!*" to make papa laugh. When disputes occurred in *bonne maman*'s room, they were between my father and mother, if that can be called a dispute where one is so gay and so imperturbable. It was *maman* who brought all the heat and vehemence to these differences and, strange to say, *bonne maman* always took my father's side against her beloved daughter. My mother's quick temper, I may add, displayed itself toward me pretty frequently in slaps and whippings, no doubt well deserved, for I was a naughty, wilful child; whereas in all my life I never received a punishment from my father. I remember his distress on one of these occasions and how he said, "It is unworthy to beat someone who cannot retaliate." To which my mother, flushed and indignant, replied, "It would indeed need only that." She was a charming and loveable woman, but I loved my father best.

Bonne maman was very musical, and in the *petit salon*, when he was installed there for the day, I heard music constantly, performed by two young protégés of the house. One of these was Mademoiselle Ghislaine du Guesclin, the youngest descendent of our great Breton hero. It was a very poor, very haughty family, and extremely proud of its origin. Ghislaine's father, the Marquis du Guesclin (for with a foolish conceit he had separated the particle from the name) had died, leaving his daughter penniless and recommending her to my grandfather, who placed her as *dame de compagnie* beside my mother and *bonne maman*. Ghislaine was an excellent musician, and their relation was of the happiest. The other protégé was called Yves le Grand, and was the son of *bonne maman*'s coiffeur. His story was curious. As a boy of fourteen or fifteen he had come three times a week to wash the windows and doors, and while he worked he sang all sorts of Breton songs and strange airs that, as was learned later, were his own improvisations. *Bonne maman*, noticing his talent, had him taken to Paris by her husband, and he was educated in the conservatory, where, after ten years of admirable study, he took the second prize. He returned to Quimper, and earned a handsome livelihood by giving pianoforte lessons while remaining in a sense our private musician, for he was much attached to us and accompanied us on all our travels. Ghislaine sang in a ravishing fashion, and Yves accompanied her on the clavecin that stood in the *petit salon*, mingling the grave accents of his baritone with her clear soprano. When I first heard them I was almost stupefied by the experience, cuddling down into *bonne maman*'s arms, my head sunk between her cheek and shoulder, but listening with such absorption and with such evident appreciation that *bonne maman* loved me more than ever for the community of taste thus revealed between us.

I must often have tired her. I was a noisy, active child, and sometimes when I sat on her knee and prattled incessantly in my shrill, childish voice, she would pass her hand over her forehead and say: "Not so loud, darling; not so loud. You pierce my ear-drums; and you know that *le bon Dieu* has said that one must never speak without first turning one's tongue seven times round in one's mouth." At this I would gaze wide-eyed at *bonne maman* and try involuntarily to turn my tongue seven times, an exercise at which I have never been successful. I may add that I have often regretted it. Another amusing adage I heard at the same time from Gertrude. If a child made a face, it was told to take care lest the wind should turn, and the face remains like that forever. I was much troubled by this idea on one occasion when *maman* and Ghislaine had been to a fancy dress ball. Ghislaine told me next day about the dances and dresses. *Maman* had danced a minuet dressed in a Pompadour costume, and she herself had gone as a deviless, with a scarlet-and-black dress and little golden horns in her black hair. I felt this to have been a very dangerous proceeding, for if *le bon Dieu* had noticed Ghislaine's travesty, He might have made the wind turn, and she would then have remained a deviless and been forced to live in hell for all eternity.

A pretty custom at that time and in that place was that the young matrons who went to such balls and dinner-parties were expected to bring little silk bags in which they carried home to their children the left-over sweetmeats of the dessert; so that we children enjoyed these entertainments as much as Ghislaine and *maman*.

Ghislaine taught me my letters from a coloured alphabet in the *petit salon*, showing an angelic patience despite my yawns and whimperings. My memories of the alphabet are drolly intermingled with various objects in the *petit salon* that from the earliest age charmed my attention. One of these was an immense tortoise-shell mounted on a tripod, and another a vast Chinese umbrella of pale yellow satin, with silk and crystal fringes, that, suspended from the ceiling in front of the long windows that gave on the garden, was filled with flowers. This had been an ingenious contrivance of my father's, and *bonne maman* found it as bewitching as I did, never failing to say to visitors, after the first greeting had passed: "Do you see my Chinese umbrella?" When I had learned seven letters *bonne maman* gave me four red *dragées de baptême*, the sugar-almonds that are scattered at Christenings – and promised me as many more for each attainment. Thus sustained, I was able to master the alphabet and to pass by slow degrees to Aesop's Fables, with pictures and a yellow cover. It was later on that Ghislaine began to coach me in all the *départements* of France and their capitals. *Maman* lent a hand in this and instituted a method that was singularly successful. I still laugh in remembering how at any time of the day, before guests, at meals, or while we were at play, she might suddenly call out to us, "Gers!" for instance, to which one must instantly reply "Auch". Or else it was "Gironde!" and the reply, "Bordeaux!" must follow without hesitation. If I replied correctly, I was given fifty centimes; if incorrectly, I received a slap. I used to dream of the *départements* and their capitals at night. One rainy day I was playing in the petit salon, lying at full length on the floor and making a castle of blocks, when maman, coming suddenly out of the library, a great tray of books in her arms, cried out to me as she came, walking very quickly, "Gare!" [*"Take care!"*] Without moving and without looking up, I replied obediently, "Nîmes" [the capital of Gard], and an avalanche of books descended upon me, poor *maman* and her tray coming down with a dreadful clatter. *Maman* was not hurt, but very much afraid that I was. When she found us both, except for a few bruises, safe and sound, she went off into a peal of laughter, and I followed suit, much relieved; for I had imagined that I had made a mistake in my answer, and I found the punishment too severe.

"You are sure I have not hurt you, darling?" said *maman*, kissing me; and I replied with truth:

"No, *maman*; but I should have preferred the *gifle* [slap.]" On that day, instead of fifty centimes, I received a franc for consolation.

It was not until my bother's tutor came to us, when I was eight or nine years old, that I ever had any teacher but Ghislaine.

Poor Ghislaine! Hers was a rather sad story. She had great beauty, thick, black hair, white skin, her small prominent nose full of distinction, but one strange peculiarity; there were no nails on her long pointed, fingers. This, while not ugly, startled one in noticing her hands. As I have said, she had been left penniless, and it was difficult in France, then as now, to find a husband for a *jeune fille sans dot*. Ghislaine only begged that he should be a gentleman. But after *bonne maman*'s death, when we had gone to live in Paris, Ghislaine was left behind with my aunt's family, and they finally arranged a marriage for her with a notary. My mother was much distressed by this prosaic match. She had for a time cherished the romantic project of a marriage between Ghislaine and Yves, who, besides being an artist, was the best of men, sincere, devoted and delicate.

For a descendant of Du Guesclin the *coiffeur*'s son would, however, have been as inappropriate as the notary. The latter, too, was an excellent man, and Ghislaine was not unhappy with him.

Lan Tangi

Devezhioù peurbadelezh, *1997*

Sevel a rae abred
Evid mont d'ar red
E-touez aelez ar balan

Sebezadur ar c'haol el liorzh
Ur salud d'al lapined ha d'ar melchon
Ar yer c'hoazh er c'hlud

Strakal a rae e votoù-koad
En oabl sklaer
War hent Kroaz-en-Bod

Oc'h ober tro e rouantelezh e oa
E devezhioù diwezhañ miz Ebrel

Er bloavezh mil nav c'hant hag hanter-kant

Hennezh a anaveze mat
Pep lodenn eus an douar-se
Anvioù ar parkoù hag al laboused
Nij ar vran, kan ar bistrak
Etre delienn ha gwezenn
Uhel war 'r brank betek izel er fank
Kantvedoù sioul o doa treset bedoù divent
E pep brochenn goad

Hennezh a anaveze mat
Vioù glas ar rouzegan en e neizh,
Emsavadeg ar c'hleuzioù
Kan ha diskan mil amprevan
O lufrañ o iskilli
O ruzañ o divorzhedigoù evit ar fest
Evit friko ar c'hlazenn

Pell e oa Park-Tost bremañ
Hag an elfenn e geneil
Gwezenn marsoñj e amzer paotr-saout
E penn an hent e troas war-du ar reter
    "hei do marc'h Hamo'"
Tre an derv hag ar fav
A-dreuz ar c'hoadoù ha faltazi ar moc'h-gouez
        "marc'h Hamo' a ya da Vrest"
Betek ar stêr en avalenneg e eontr
Buanoc'h e-kichen toull al louarn
Eñvorennoù marvailh ar bleiz
"dishouarn ha digabestr"
A-hed ar wazh kontilli an hesk

Koroll ar fubu en e vlev
"tre an drez, tre an drein
ar paotr bihan war e gein"
Redek a rae, fistoulig
Etre taboulinoù an oabl hag an dour
Blaz an triñchin war e ziweuz
En ur goumoulenn spern-gwenn
Bomm-nij ar c'hwervizon en aer
Un ehan evit reiñ kalon

Da basianted ar broen beuzet
Da lenn diougan ar raden
E ganedigezh o zroellennoù yaouank
O tostaat ouzh an ti

Trouz karnoù ar c'hezeg e kraou an amezeg
Ar golveni war 'r bern teil
C'hwezh e naon war an daol
Bara krazet ha boued kafe

E lagad ar vroñsenn
E-kreiz kalon ar vleunienn
E c'hellez lenn ma sellez mat
Huñvre an irin hag hini an aval
Ar c'hraoñ-kelvez
Ar sistr hag ar glav

Hennezh n'anaveze ket c'hoazh
Avel-dro ar pevar amzer o vuanaat

Bugaleaj
Devezhioù peurbadelezh

Translation

Days Held Eternal, *1997*

A Breton nursery rhyme, similar to 'Ride a cock horse...', becomes entwined in these happy childhood memories translated by Bev Newman.

He rose early
To run
Among the broom-angels

Astonishment of the cabbages in the kitchen garden
A greeting to the rabbits and the clover
The hens still roosting

His clogs clattered
Under the clear sky
On the Kroaz-en-Bod road

He was walking the frontiers of his kingdom
In the last days of April

In the year nineteen hundred and fifty

He did know well
Every little corner of the land
The names of the fields and birds
The crow's flight and the thrush's song
Between the leaf and the tree.
High on the branch down to the mud
Silent centuries had drawn immense worlds
In every twig

He did know well
The blue eggs of the warbler's nest
The rebellion in the hedges
The buzzing of a thousand insects
Polishing their wings
Rubbing their thighs for the feast
For the banquet in the meadow

Park-Tost was far now
As was his friend the poplar
The tree of his daydreams when he watched over the cows.
At the road's end he turned eastward
    "Giddy up, giddy up"
Through oak and ash
Across the woods, past imaginary wild boars
    "My little horse is off to Brest"
Until the river in his uncle's orchard
Faster past the fox's earth
Remembrances of the wolves folktale
    "Unshod and unshackled"
Alongside the stream the blades of sedge

Midges' dance in his hair
    "Through the bramble, through the thorn
    The little boy on its back"
He was running and wriggling
Between the snare drums of the sky and the water
The taste of sorrel on his lips
In a cloud of hawthorn
Dandelion time blown in the air
A short break to encourage
The patience of the drowned rushes

To read the predictions of the ferns
In the birth of their budding spirals
He was nearly home
Clip-clop of the horseshoes in the neighbour's stable
The sparrows on the dunghill
The smell of his hunger on the table
Toasted bread and milky coffee.

In the eye of the buds
At the heart of the bloom
You may read, if you watch closely
The dream of the sloe and that of the apple
Of the hazelnuts
Of the cider and of the rain

He did not yet know
The whirlwind of seasons gathering speed

Childhood
Days held eternal

Youenn Drezen

Skol-louarn Veig Trebern, *1972* (Lodenn)

Sellout a rejont an eil ouzh egile ur vourenn. Ne ouient ket pet eur oa. Sklaer oa un dra evelkent: dale du-mañ, dale du-se, diwezhat e oant adarre evit ar skol.

Sell amañ, vat!... M Karadeg!... Peseurt digarez rentañ da M Karadeg?... Lakaomp n'en dije ket skandalet re evit un devezh mank. Mes degouezhout diwezhat er c'hlas, kerkent hag an devezh goude? Aze oa pinijenn da gaout, ha mezh 'ta, dirak ar baotred!... Gast! gast! gast!...

"O, met!..." a daole Veig, trumm, tra ma treuzent ar blasennig, hep hastañ nemeur. "Hiziv emaomp ar sadorn.

– Ya

– Hama! N'eo ket dav mont d'ar skol.

– N'eo ket dav mont d'ar skol?...

– Memes goude kreisteiz.

– Memes goude kreisteiz?...

– Nann! Kompren ac'hanon, 'frai choj!" Ma'z eomp bremañ d'ar skol, e klevimp pater, hag e vimp lakaet e pinijenn. Ma ne'z eomp d'ar skol nemet goude kreisteiz, e vo goulet ganeomp, memes tra, perak n'omp ket bet er skol, dec'h hag ar mintin-mañ, ha pinijenn kaletoc'h deomp. Ma ne'z eomp ket tost, ne vo goulet netra diga-neomp; n'eo ket gwir?... Ha, 'benn arc'hoazh, *frai* bihan, emañ ar sul. Ha, 'benn dilun, M Karadeg n'en do ket mui soñj. Hennezh zo kozh.

– Koulskoude, me garfe gwelloc'h mont d'ar skol."

... Pezh ne viras ket ouzh Paotr-Teo – ha stad ennañ a vezañ kavet ar riboul, e-unan, – da grapat ar c'hentañ dreist kleuz park ar C'hoseg Ruz, ha da sankañ e sac'h en e skoachig, e toull ar strouezh.

Ha dao, o daou, d'ar c'hoad en-dro, da lenn *Intrépide* hag *Epatant*, e-harz traoñ ar wezenn faou, en ur c'hortoz kloc'h unnek eur.

Peadra o doa da lenn evit ur sihunvezh, d'an nebeutañ.

A-benn nemeur, ne voe mui, dindan bolz deliaouek ar gwez glas, na Veig na Trebern-Doue ebet. Hogen Texas-Jack e-unan hag eeun-hag-eeun. Sombrero ledan war e benn, kentroù lemm ouzh e heuzoù, ur rifle war gein e chupenn ler, hag ur c'holt war bep a groazell, loc'het oa, ouzh daou-lamm ruz e varc'h prim-tan, e Foenneg Vras ar Far-West, war roudoù an *outlaws*.

Skrapet e oa bet, gant an difallidi-se, merc'h ar c'horonal Callaghan, ur plac'h yaouank he blev hir, brav e-giz an deiz, ha karet gant ar Gomanched valc'h zoken. Ret groñs e oa tapout an outlaws da brizonidi, kent na vije tizhet ganto kevioù ar Menezioù Roc'hellek, a weled, du-se, e penn pellañ an dremmwell, heñvel ouzh ur goumoulenn c'hlas.

Amañ ez echue ar bajenn, gant ar meneg: "Da genderc'hel, er sizhun a zeu". Skrijañ a rae hol lenner diwar e from. Ruflañ a reas.

"Dav vo din kavout daou wenneg da brenañ niverenn ar sizhun a zeu", emezañ, en ur dreiñ ar bajenn.

Ifig Korku, gouzout a reomp, e oa ur paotrig sioul anezhañ. Harp e gein ouzh ar wezenn faou, ne fiñve ket eus kichen e geneil. N'em eus ket lavaret, avat, e kave berr e amzer evel egile. Ne gare ket lenn. Ne gare ket lenn evit meur a abeg. Da gentañ, ne ouie ket c'hoazh en em zibab mat-mat en e lizherennoù. Ha, d'an eil, ne gomprene seurt er pep brasañ eus ar gerioù a lenne. Marteze, ma vijent bet e brezhoneg!...

A-benn ur reuziad eta, ha, goude bezañ troet ha distroet pajennoù e gelaouenn da sellout ouzh an 'imachoù', e santas c'hwen en e benn a-dreñv. Bazailhat a reas:

"Veig, me 'zo vont da vale."

En-dro dezhañ, an douar sec'h, rak ar gwez faou ne c'houzañvont ket ar geot dindan o deil, a oa goloet a giviz. Dibluskañ a reas gant e zent tri pe bevar eus ar frouezhigoù-se, a vez graet ivez finij anezho, ha, du-mañ, kraoñ-pichon. Mes re zifonn e oant da zebriñ. Ober a reas e venoz diskenn, e traoñ ar c'hoad, betek c'hae, da sellout ouzh al lestr *Inga Harner*.

Klevout a rae ar wazed da vat o tiskargañ ar vag. Skoachet e oa outañ tud ha bag gant ar plenk berniet uhel, en tu-mañ d'an hent, dindan ar gwez evlec'h, da c'hor-toz bezañ sammet kuit gant kirri an ti-heskennerezh.

C'hwitellat a rae Ifig e-giz ur pintig disoursi. Edo o vont da dreuzañ an hent, pa voe stouvet naet e c'hwitell.

E-mesk ar wazed e oa, gant o douarn en o chakodoù, o sellout ouzh ar fiñv, un den eus ar Waremm-Mên, harpet war e vazh! Ha piv e oa, nemet Izidor Kefeleg, ar c'hemener kamm?

Ur c'hemener penn-da-benn, gant un teod a bike evel e nadozioù, hag a droc'he evel e weltre. Ha katell abalamour d'e vicher, prest atav da dopinat – evit farsal, sañset! – kement a gleve hag a wele. Ul lesanv en doa evel an holl: Pik-Chupenn. Mont a rae dezhañ e lesanv e-giz e veskenn d'e viz. Hag, evit echuiñ tout, o chom e oa dor ouzh dor gant tad ha mamm Veig.

Hopala! Jañ-Mari. Amañ zo dañjer! Arabat bezañ gwelet gant hennezh!

Ha Paotr-Teo d'ar c'haloup da laez an durumell, en ur droc'han berr, dre douez ar gwez.

"Veve! Veve! N'ouzez ket piv zo war ar c'hae? Pik-Chupenn kamm!...

– Oi!... N'out ket bet gwelet gantañ?"

Eus al lec'h e oant, ne verzed na porzh, na lestr, na den. Nemet garennoù ar gwez hag an delioù glas. Mes n'eo ket mui daou louarn eo a oa kas anezhi e Koad Karmez; daou wiñver spontik ha war-c'hed, ne lavaran ket, prest da skampañ, aon leun o c'hof na zeuje Pik-Chupenn, kement ha koll e benndevezh, da gas e dreid tre betek laez ar c'hoad.

Ne fiñjont ken diouzh o repu, ken na sonas kloc'h ar Frered.

Me lavar ivez; petra en doa ar c'hemener-laou-se da zont da straniñ war ar c'hae, e-lec'h bezañ gant e labour en e di?

Translation

Veig Trebern Playing Truant, *1972* (Extract)

[*Veig (Herve, Veve) Trebern and his best friend, Ifig (Fatty) Korku are playing truant.*]

They looked at each other and pulled faces. They did not know what time it was. One thing was clear however: they had lost time here and lost time there, and they were late again for school.

Fair enough; but what about Mr Karadeg! What excuse could they dream up for Mr Karadeg? Let's suppose he would not have rebuked them too much for missing one day at school. But being late again on the very next day? They would be punished and humiliated in front of the other boys! Damn it! Damn it!"

"Yes, but!" uttered Veig suddenly as they were taking their time crossing the square, "today is Saturday."

"So it is."

"Well then! We don't need to go to school."

"We don't need to go to school?"

"No. Not even after lunch."

"Not even after lunch?"

"No. Let me explain, mate. If we go to school now, we'll get hell and we'll be punished. If we go to school after lunch, we'll still be asked why we were not at school yesterday or this morning, and we'll be punished even more. But if we don't go at all, nothing will be asked. Don't you agree? Tomorrow is Sunday. By Monday, Mr Karadeg will have forgotten. He is an old man.

"I still think it would be better for us to go to school."

But this did not prevent Fatty, who was very proud to have discovered the new path, from being the first one to climb the embankment surrounding the field named Kozeg Ruz and from throwing his school-bag in its hiding-place among the bushes.

So, the two of them went back to the woods, to read their comics, *Intrépide* and *Epatant*, at the foot of the beech tree, waiting for the eleven o'clock bell.

They had enough reading material to last them for at least a week.

Very soon afterwards, it was no longer Veig Trebern who was sitting under the leafy vault of the green tree, but Texas-Jack himself, as large as life. He had a wide sombrero on his head, spurs on his boots, a rifle on the back of his leather jacket and a Colt on each of his hips and he was galloping away, on his fast horse, to the Great Plain of the Far-West, on the trail of outlaws.

The baddies had abducted Colonel Callaghan's daughter, a girl with long hair, pretty as a picture, and much loved by all, even by the proud Red Indians. He had to catch the outlaws before they reached the caves of the Rocky Mountains which loomed, like a blue cloud, on the distant horizon.

The story stopped there, with the words: "To be continued next week". What a spine-chilling tale! The young reader heaved a big sigh. "I'll need to find a few pennies to buy next week's issue," he said, turning the page over.

We have already established that Ifig Korku was a quiet child. His back leaning against the beech tree, he did not wander off from his friend's side. I did not say, however, that time was flying for him as quickly as for the other boy. He did not like to read. For several reasons. First, he did not know his letters all that well. Secondly, he could not make any sense of the majority of the words he read. It might have been a different story if they had been written in Breton!

Some time later, when he had finished turning the pages of his comic again and again to look at the pictures, he started fidgeting and yawned:

"Veig, I'm going for a walk."

Around him, the dry earth – grass does not grow under beech trees – was covered with beechnuts. He peeled with his teeth three or four of these tiny fruits which are also called beechmast. But they were too small to eat. He decided to go down to the edge of the wood, by the quayside, to look at the ship *Inga Harner*.

He heard the men unloading the ship. He could neither see them nor the boat because of the wooden planks stacked up high under the elm trees, on his side of the road, waiting to be carted away to the sawmill.

Ifig was whistling like a carefree bird. He was on the verge of crossing the road when the whistling suddenly dried up in his throat.

Among the bystanders who stood, their hands deep in their pockets, looking at the flurry of activity, was a man from Waremm-Mên leaning on his walking stick! And would you believe it? It was Izidor Kefeleg, the lame tailor.

He was a tailor through and through: his tongue was as sharp as his needles and as cutting as his scissors. His job gave him ample opportunity to gossip, to grass on other people – although he pretended he was only joking – and to pass on everything he heard and saw. Like anyone else he had a nickname, Pik-Chupenn [Prick Jacket], which fitted him like the thimble on his finger. To top it all, he lived right next door to Veig's parents.

"Wow! What a narrow escape! I mustn't let him see me."

Fatty ran as far as he could to the top of the hillock, taking a short cut through the wood.

"Veve! Veve! You'll never guess who is on the quayside? Limping Pik-Chupenn!"

"What! He didn't see you, did he?"

From where they were, they could see neither the harbour, the ship nor anyone. Only the tree-trunks and the green leaves. They no longer felt like two crafty foxes playing truant and having fun in Karmez Wood, but like two frightened watchful squirrels, ready to scamper off, fear gnawing at their heart, in case Pik-Chupenn turned up, right here, in the middle of the wood, in an attempt to thoroughly waste his afternoon.

They did not move from their hiding-place until they heard the school bell ring.

Let me ask you: what was that stupid tailor doing on the quayside when he should have been hard at work at home?

Erwan Kervella

Yud, *1973*

Skrivañ 'raen va anv
gant lizherennoù ar soubenn
war vord feilhañs un asied dantet

Mirout 'raen gwerzennoù diheson
en ur c'haier-skol glas
breset ha prizius

Pegañ 'raen war mogerioù va c'hambr
skeudennoù divlaz ha koll-o-liv
broioù kevrinus

Tresañ 'raen en traezh
d'ar skreved da c'hoarzhin
enkrezioù disouezhet

Engravañ 'raen er c'hoad tener
gant ur gontell laeret
karantezioù dispi

Livañ 'raen war dremmwelioù louet
ar baradoz arnevez
trelat va dic'hoanag

> Me eo ar bleiz digenvez
> hag aet on skuiz
> Me eo ar bleiz digenvez
> hag aet on da greviñ

Translation

Scream, *1973*

I used to write my name
with the soup alphabet
on the edge of a chipped earthenware plate.

I used to keep second-rate poetry
in a blue-covered exercise book
dog-eared and treasured.

I used to stick on the walls of my room
tasteless fading posters
of secret countries.

I used to draw in the sand
to give the gulls something to laugh at
my disillusioned anxieties

I used to engrave in the soft wood
with a stolen knife
my hopeless loves

I used to paint on grey horizons
a modern heaven
in the delirium of my despair

> I am the lonely wolf
> grown tired
> I am the lonely wolf
> gone to die

Meven Mordiern

Al Lez a ris da Jorjeta, *c.1935* (Lodenn)

Biskoaz ne welis Mari Brindeau nemet eus a bell. Ledander neo an iliz a oa etre-zomp. Biskoaz gant-se n'am eus bet tro da gomz d'ezi. Jorjeta a welis a-dost meur a wech. Mare a oa bet – etro ar bloaz 1884 pe 1885 – m'he gweled hogos bemdez o vale war an hentou en-dro d'hon liorz, eun danvadezig wenn ganti, a-ere eur seizenn. Nemet re vihan e oa d'ar c'houlz-se evit tenna va sellou. Pa voe brasoc'h ha kenedusoc'h d'am daoulagad, e kejis outi a-wechou p'edon o vont gant va zad d'ar c'hoadou war an uhelgompezenn. An hent-pign o kas d'an uhelgompezenn a dremene dirak dor-borz ti Roussineau. Gwechou-all, diwar korn mervent an eil leurenn-liorz – aet e oa ar c'horn-se da welva ganen – am eus gwelet Jorjeta o tiskenn gant an hent-pign. Biskoaz ne liviris ger d'ezi, nemet eun iskis a les a ris d'ezi, eur wech, diwar ar gwelva-se.

Deuet e oan sioulig d'ar gwelva, va fuzul em daouarn (pa valeen hon liorz, e veze bepred ganen eun arm bennak: fuzul dre emors pe dre gapsulenn, gwareg, kraozwareg, goaf, kleze pe sabrenn; er-maez eus hon liorz, ne dae ganen nemet pis-tolennou a guzen em godell). Ha me sellout er-maez, ouz traon, war an hent, ha gwelout dindanoun Jorjeta en he c'hluch, o kutuilh bleunv a-douez ar geot, e troad hor moger. Laket didrouz ganen va fuzul ouz an douar, e lakis plastrennouigou diwar lein ar voger da goueza war Jorjeta. Sevel a reas evel eun tenn ha sellout ouzh krec'h. Ouz va gwelout, e reas pez a hanvalas d'in beza eur mousc'hoarz goapaüs. Brouezet krenn gant-se ha dre ma welen ne ziskoueze ket beza na spontet nag abafet zoken, e stlapis outi meinigou diwar ar pengenn em c'hichen pe diwar an alez a-drenv d'in. Tec'hout a reas war an hent, pouez-traon gantan, a gase da garrdi an tad Fulup. Seul belloc'h ma tec'he diouzin, seul bounneroc'h e tibaben ar mein a strinken war he lerc'h. Eun arsavig a reas e-harz ar c'harrdi, sounn en he sav, ouz va daea gant sell skedus ha faeus he daoulagad glas-mor ha minc'hoarz goapaüs-kenan he diweuz koant. Kaer evel eun ael pe evel eur brinsezig wall-gaset en harlu e oa da welout evel-se, nemet seul vrouezekoc'h, seul gounnaretoc'h a-se e vezen outi, ha seul stankoc'h e koueze ar mein war he zro. Ma tec'has a-ziwar-wel d'in neuze, war ar frankizenn etre karrdi an tad Fulup (diouz tu ar c'hreisteiz) hag e di-annez (diouz tu an hanternoz). Prad briellek ar Graonenn Vras hag ar c'harz spern-gwenn war vevenn gornok ar prad-se a harze ouzin da welout kement a oa war ar frankizenn. Kenderc'hel a ris kouskoude da deurel mein dreist d'ar c'harz, ken ma savas mouez voud ha garo an tad Fulup: "Piou a zo o vanna mein evel-se?"

Gorren e ris va fuzul dioustu, ha skampa kuit ac'hano, ha mont d'an trede leurenn-liorzh d'en em sila e dounderiou kuzeta al lireueg vras. Eno, goude trei an emorsiou hag ar c'hapsulennou war va fuzuliou, e c'houezis eun tantadig-brechin, e kanis va c'hanaouenn a varo o tansal en-dro d'ar brechin, hag e livis va dremm e ruz, e du, e gwer hag e melen, en doare spontusa, d'am lakaat henvel ouz eur preiziataer indian war hent ar brezel. Liva va dremm er c'hiz-se a oa bet difennet

grons ouzin gant va mamm, hag ivez c'hoari gant an tan. Nemet n'oa ket bepred ac'hanoun eur bugel sentus.

En aner e kemeris an holl ziarbennou-se. Roussineau na zeuas ket da gavout va zad abenn ober klemm ouzin dre m'am boa labezet (meinataet) e verc'h koant.

Translation

How I Courted Jorgeta, *c.1935* (Extract)

I only ever saw Mari Brindeau from afar. The width of the nave separated us and I thus never got the opportunity to talk to her. But I did see Jorjeta several times from close by. There was even a time – around 1884 or 1885 – when she could be seen, practically everyday, taking a walk on the paths surrounding our garden, leading a small white sheep by a ribbon. But she was too young at that time to attract my attention. When she was older and prettier – or so I thought – I sometimes met her as I walked with my father up the steep path which passed by the carriage entrance to the Roussineau's home and led to the upland woods. From the southwest corner of the second garden terrace which I used as an observation point I have, on other occasions, seen Jorjeta go down the hill path. I never said a word to her, yet I once courted her in a strange fashion, from this vantage point.

Holding my gun – I always used to carry some kind of weapon when I played in our garden: a toy gun, a bow, a crossbow, a spear, a sword or a sabre, whereas outside our garden, I only carried pistols which I hid in my pocket – I had quietly gone up to my observation post. As I looked over the side of the wall, and down towards the road, I saw Jorjeta squatting, picking flowers among the grass at the foot of our wall. I laid down my gun quietly and threw little bits of plaster on Jorjeta. She jumped to her feet and looked up. On seeing me she smiled in what I thought was a mocking way. Annoyed at her reaction, all the more so because she seemed to be neither frightened nor even intimidated, I started throwing gravel from the border next to me or from the path behind me. She fled down the steep road which led to Father Fulup's garage. The further away she fled from me, the heavier the stones I chose to throw at her. She stopped for a short while on reaching the garage, raised herself to her full height and challenged me with her bright and mocking sea-blue eyes, a most sarcastic smile on her pretty lips. She thus looked as pretty as an angel or as a kidnapped princess, except that, the more irate and infuriated I felt towards her, the heavier the shower of stones which fell around her. She finally fled out of my sight to the patch of ground which lies between Father Fulup's garage, on the south side, and his residence, on the north side. The Kraonenn Vras clay field and the hawthorn hedge on the west side of this field prevented me from seeing what was on that patch of ground. However, I continued to throw stones over the hedge, until the deep and severe voice of Father Fulup rose: "Who is throwing stones like this?"

I immediately picked up my gun and ran off to the third garden terrace to worm my way into the most hidden depths of the big lilac trees. There, after playing with the reel of my cap guns, I lit a small straw fire, I danced around it singing my death song and I painted my face red, black, green and yellow, in a most frightening way, to make me look like a Red Indian raider on the war path. My mother strictly forbade me to paint my face like this and to play with fire, but I was not always an obedient child.

I took all these precautions in vain. Roussineau never came to see my father to complain that I had thrown stones at his pretty daughter.

Charlez Rolant

Paotr Breiz, *c.1885*

En eul lann vraz, war lein ar mene
En gwarez an ivin, ar fo,
Dirag an avel hag an arne,
En kornik eul lochen kolo,
Ia eno, tud keaz, 'n eur gwele kaled
E tritaz ma c'halon o tond war ar bed,
    Ia eno 'on bet ganet
    Luskellet ha maget.

Eno 'meuz sonj mad, pa oan bugel,
Meuz bet aliez tom ha ien,
Gwisket fall, divotou, diskabel,
Renken mond en dro vel peb den,
Ma, eno tud keaz, en kreiz ma zruillou
Ma c'halon lampe o redek ar parkou,
    Ia eno me 'n em gare
    En kreiz ma faourente.

Eno na zav netra en erven
Med kanab, segal hag ed-du,
Eno na ve bleun med er spern-gwenn,
El lann, er balan, er bruk ru,
Ma, n'eus forz, tud keaz, gant bleun ar mene
Me vije seder, lawen eveltê
    Sard ha iê korf hag ene
    Gant bleun koant ar mene.

Eno, lec'h an holl drouz a glever
Eo kloc'h braz ar barrouz en brall,
Garm ar c'horn-boud, mouez voan ar mesaër,
Ar biniou o son da zansal:

Ma, eno tud keaz, demeuz eur sort son
Me chome da zilaou a greiz ma c'halon,
   N'oa ket evidon er bed
   Musik muioc'h karet.

Eno, ekreiz ar goanv aliez
Me 'meuz bet poaniou diniver,
Nec'hamant, riou, naon, ha dienez,
Glac'har hag hirvoud leiz ma ler!
Ma, n'euz forz tud keaz, e kreiz ar goanv kri
Me zante ma c'halon meur wech o virvi,
   O virvi gant karante
   Despet d'am faourente!

Eno c'hoaz en dro d'an tantajou,
En nozvejou ar souben-laez,
Meuz bet kanet rimoustadennou
Laket c'hoarz ha gouel aliez!
Ha neblec'h tud keaz, n'on bet 'n em dommet
Vel deuz al lannou lec'h on bet savet!
   Eno, kreiz ma faourente,
   Em bro ar garante!

Me c'houlen achui ma deiou
Pa na vin ken mad da netra,
Eno, pell pell deuz trouz ar c'heriou
Ha brazoni ar bed paour-ma,
Eno c'hoaz tud keaz, lec'h ma ren bepred
Gant giziou hon zadou, an evurusted,
   Ar peoc'h hag ar garante
   Em bro ar baourente!

Brema, tud keaz, ô pa vin galvet
Da vont lec'h eo eat hon zud koz,
Grit, 'n han Doue, ma vin douaret
En bered vihan ar barroz!
Eno c'hoaz e lec'h drito ma c'halon
O klevet biniou ar mesaër o son,
   Hag an holl moueziou karet
   Deuz ma Bro binniget!

Translation

Breton Boy, *c.1885*

On an open moor, on top of the mount,
Sheltered by yew and beech trees,
Facing both wind and storms,
In a small thatched cottage;
This is where, dear friends, in a hard bed,
My heart started beating when I came into the world.
    This is where I was born,
      Rocked to sleep and brought up.

There, I remember, as a child,
Often suffering from heat and cold;
Dressed in rags, bare-footed, bare-headed,
I had to survive like everyone else.
There, dear friends, in my shabby clothes,
My heart would throb as I ran through the fields,
    This is where I loved being
      Although I was poverty-stricken.

There, nothing grows in the furrows
But hemp, rye and buckwheat;
There, the only flowers are those of the hawthorn,
Broom, gorse and heather.
But no matter, dear friends, the mountain flowers
Made me feel calm and happy;
I was cheerful, sound of body and mind
    Among the pretty flowers of the mount.

There, the only sounds I heard
Was the ringing of the big parish bell,
The call of the fog-horn, the faint voice of the shepherd
The bagpipes calling for a dance.
Well, dear friends, I listened to them
With all my heart,
    There was not in the world
    Any music I loved more.

There, often in winter,
I was beset by numerous pains,
Disappointments, cold, hunger, deprivation,
Distress and sadness, much more than I can tell.

But, no matter, dear friends, in the middle of the harsh winter
I frequently felt my heart ready to burst,
    To burst with love
    In spite of my poverty!

There again, at the fireside,
In the evenings when milk soup was served,
I have sung rhymes,
Made others laugh or even cry.
Nowhere, dear friends, have I felt so happy
As on the moor where I was brought up.
    There, in spite of my poverty
    In my land of love.

I ask that I may end my days,
When I will no longer be able to work,
There, far away from city noises
And the arrogance of the world;
There, dear friends, where the old customs
Are still alive and foster happiness,
    Peace and love
    In my land of poverty.

Now, dear friends, when I am called
To the land where our ancestors went,
Let me, I beg you, be buried
In the small parish churchyard.
There again my heart will rejoice
At the sound of the shepherd's bagpipes
    At the sound of all the loved voices
    Of my hallowed Land.

Youenn Drezen

Foenneg an Dourig Kozh, *1958* (Lodenn)

Stlapet oa bet ar botoù-koad du-mañ du-hont, war ar c'hlazenn, deomp da redek buanoc'h, oc'h ober an hu war skrilhed lammennek ar prad ha kemenerien ar ganol, pe o c'hoari alc'houeder ha toutig-penn. Unan pe zaou eus ar re oadetañ a ziskennas war an aodig hag a soubas o zreid en dour. Sin e oa an dour. Pebezh skrijadenn gant ar blijadur! Pebezh cholori daoust d'hor mouezhioù munut! N'oa chomet na paotrig na plac'hig war ar sec'h. Holl en dour! Troñset betek o begel. Ha stlapig, ha saflig, ha bountadegoù, ha gwic'hadegoù gant hon tudigoù. Ken oa tec'het, diwar o strafuilh rak kement a zispac'h, raned ha penndologed, e-barzh goudor an elestreg.

Mamm-gozh, d'an ampoent, a oa o tont eus ar c'hraou, gant ur sailhad laezh, a oa bet o c'horo.

– Pelec'h emañ ar vugale? emezi da voereb Katell, tra ma fenne al laezh eonennek en ur varaz velen gwerniset. Pelloc'h eo poent merenn-vihan.

Moereb Katell, ur vigoudenn yaouank ha yac'h, a oa o veskañ an dienn, e-kichen maen an oaled. Teurel a reas ur sell ouzh an horoloj en hec'h armel hir.

– El leur, aze, oant bremaik, emezi. Feiz! n'o c'hlevan ken.

Lezel a reas ar vazh er ribod evit mont da welout. Bugel ebet war al leur.

– Feiz! Da belec'h int aet adarre?

Hopal a reas diwar an treuzoù:

– Voñvoñ!... Nana! ... Mar-Louizig!...

Ne respontas nemet geiz al laboused, e gwezenn bêr al liorzh, dirak an ti.

– Feiz! eme voereb Katell. 'Maint kuit adarre. Me 'bari int aet adarre war dro an dour. Gisti bihan fall!

Moereb Katell, daoust ha rust en he c'homzoù hag en he doareoù, ha prim da skandalat – tra eus an efedusañ da lakaat forzh piv da sentiñ diouzhtu, evel ma rae tad-kozh – a gare kalz bugale he div c'hoar.

– Mont a ran da welout, emezi, betek foenneg an traoñ.

Hag hi kuit, difrae warni, dre ar parkad avaloù-douar.

Goude bezañ en em ziwisket e-unan en noazh-pilh, Voñvoñ en doa tennet spilhoù tavañjer ha sae e geniterv Mar-Louizig vihan, d'he sikour en em ziwiskañ ivez. Hiviz hag all.

A-benn neuze o doa an "houidi" all tapet meur a lamm en dour, en ur ober soubig d'o feskennoùigoù, hag e oa gleb-teil o dilhad. Voñvoñ, hardiz evel ur bleiz, a ruze e gofig tev war c'horre an traezh, oc'h ober van da neuiñ evel un den bras. Ur pezh kofig tev a oa da Voñvoñ, ur sac'h-yod, a lavare e dad, ha morzhadoù gwenn-roz, kuilh ha tener, ur revr bonner, en ur ger. Mistroc'h oa Mar-Louizig, ha gwennoc'h kroc'hen dezhi.

Neuze eo e tarzhas, evel un talm-kurun, ur garm, diwar laez an dorgenn, a-us d'ar prad.

– I che! Gisti bihan fall! Gortozit, ma vo pradet deoc'h ho revr!

Moereb Katell!...

N'oa ket ar "gisti bihan fall" diestlammet, ma oa erru warno.

– Petra 'lavaro ho mammoù? a fuc'he... Ha ma vijec'h bet beuzet!... En dour e oant, va Jezuz!... En dour, mar deo permetet!... Hag en noazh!... Pa ouezo ho mammoù!...

Me 'lavar e oa difretadeg gant ar vugale. Ne gavent mui na sae, na botez, na spilhenn. Kollet oa ar spilhoù e-touez ar geot. Lakaet ar botoù kleiz da zehou. Ha prest an holl da zifronkañ.

– Hag ho merenn-vihan?... Disoñjet ganto o merenn vihan gant ar mall c'hoari!...

Gwir oa. Ha souezhus. Disoñjet oa bet ganeomp hor c'hofoù, gant ar blijadur c'hoari.

Houpet he doa moereb Katell Nana vihan war he brec'h, ha kroget gant he dorn all e dorn Mar-Louizig, ha kuit da Venez-Piked, a gammedoù bras, hon tropellad d'he heul, d'ar piltrotig.

Ha mamm-gozh, ouzh hor gwelout o tont:

– Hag ho merenn vihan, bugale droch! Ha kerkent: Sed e pe stad emaint!

Ne voe ket seizhdaletoc'h dorn prim moereb Katell o tennañ diganeomp hon dilhadoù d'o lakaat da sec'hañ, keit ha ma frape Voñvoñ war davañjer mamm-gozh.

– Mamm-gozh, me 'm eus naon.

– Ma n'eo ket un druez en em lakaat e seurt stal, a lavare mamm-gozh, en ur vont da laez an daol, e-tal ar prenestr, da gerc'hat an dorzh a-zindan an daol. Hag e roe deomp da zebriñ.

Troc'hañ 'rae deomp melloù felpennoù bara hag amann. Bodet oamp en-dro dezhi evel un torad poñsined en-dro d'ar yar-gloch. Moereb Katell a ribote a-zevri-kaer. Ha mamm-gozh a lavare:

– Ar grouadurien kaezh!... Ma n'eo ket un druez!... Rostañ o c'hein en heol berv, ha riellañ o zreid en dour sklas.

Translation

Dourig Kozh Meadow, *1958* (Extract)

We had tossed our clogs anywhere on the grass so that we could run faster, chase the grasshoppers in the fields and the harvestmen on the stream, frolic in the field and play roly-poly. A couple of the older children went down to the stream and put their feet in the water. It was cool. They screamed with pleasure! What a noise we made in spite of our tiny voices! Not a single boy or girl stayed dry. All the children were in the water, their clothes hitched up to their waists, as they splashed, sprayed, pushed and shrieked so much that the frogs and tadpoles, confused by all this upheaval, fled to the shelter of the iris-covered bank.

At that very time, Grandma, who had been milking the cows, came out of the cowshed with a bucketful of milk.

"Where are the children?" she asked Auntie Katell as the milk was now frothing in a yellow-varnished churn. "It is well past tea-time."

Auntie Katell, a young and strong girl from the Bigouden region was churning butter by the fireplace. She threw a glance at the grandfather clock.

"They were on the threshing area a little while ago. But you're right! I can't hear them anymore."

She left the pole in the churn and went to have a look. There were no children on the threshing floor.

"Where have they disappeared to again?"

From the threshold she started shouting: "Voñvoñ! Nana! Mar-Louizig!" The twittering of the birds in the pear tree in the front garden was the only reply.

"Well!" Said Auntie Katell. "They have disappeared again. I bet the scallywags went to the river's edge, once again!"

Although she spoke harshly, acted brusquely and was quick to reprimand – a very effective way of making everyone, including Granddad, obey immediately – Auntie Katell loved her two sisters' children a lot.

"I'll go down to the lower meadow," she said as she hurried away across the potato field.

Voñvoñ had first undressed himself completely and then had taken out the pins from his young cousin's apron and dress to help little Mar-Louizig out of her clothes, out of all her clothes.

In the meantime, the other 'ducklings', trying to dip their bottoms into the water, had fallen in several times and their clothes were wet through. Voñvoñ was boldly dragging his plump body on the surface of the sandbank, pretending to swim like an adult. Voñvoñ had quite a fat belly – his father called him fatso – chubby and tender pink thighs. He was quite a big child. Mar-Louizig was thinner and her skin was whiter.

A shout suddenly exploded like a clap of thunder from the top of the cliff which overlooks the field.

"There you are! Scallywags! Just wait there and I'll come and smack your bottoms".

Auntie Katell!...

Before the 'scallywags' could recover from their surprise, she was among them.

"What will your mothers say?" she raged loudly. "What if you had drowned! Playing in the water, dear God! In the water. Can you believe it! And stark naked too!.. Just wait till I tell your mothers!"

I can assure you that the children were thoroughly bewildered. They could no longer find their dresses, clogs or pins which had been lost among the grass. Left shoes were put on right feet. All the children were on the verge of tears.

"And what about your tea?" They had forgotten about their tea, so engrossed had they been in their games.

This was true, as well as surprising, but in the excitement of play we had forgotten about our tummies.

Auntie Katell picked up little Nana, grabbed Mar-Louizig's hand with her free hand, and we all returned to Menez-Piked at such a pace that the other children had to trot along behind them.

As she spotted us, Grandma said:

"What about your tea, you naughty children!" and immediately afterwards she added: "Look at the state they are in!"

Auntie Katell's hastily removed our clothes so that they could be dried, but Voñvoñ was already pulling at Grandma's apron.

"Grandma, I am hungry."

"Fancy getting into such a state," said Grandma as she went to the window, to the head of the table, to fetch the loaf from the table drawer. She cut and handed us large slices of buttered bread. We were gathered around her as a brood of chicks around the mother hen. Auntie Katell was busy churning butter when Grandma said:

"Poor children! Can you believe it! Roasting their backs in the scorching sun and freezing their feet in the icy water."

Fañch Elies-Abeozen

Un Danvez-den, *1958* (Lodenn)

Pa zeue an hañv hag ar vakañsoù ez ae Frañsa da di e vamm-gozh, da dremen ur pennad. En e vleud e veze e Krec'h-ar-Bleiz. Den ebet da zifenn outañ mont a-gleiz pe a-zehou, netra kaeroc'h d'ur bugel. Hag ez ae Frañsa d'ar vengleuz da welout tennañ taolioù-min, da graoñ-kelvesa, da vouara, pe da vesa ar saout gant moused all er gêriadenn. Un dro en doa kavet plijus redek en ur wazh-dour n'ouzon pegeit amzer ha da c'houde e tapas war e gofoù-divhar daou daol heol a-zoare. N'ouie ket, avat, petra a c'hoarie gantañ nemet e ouele en e wele-kloz an noz war-lerc'h hag ar vamm-gozh a ouele gantañ. Kalonoù tener 'oant o daou.

Pegen plijus da Wener pa stage mamm-gozh d'ober krampouezh. Un dudi 'oa evit Frañsa sikour c'hwezhañ an tan dindan ar billig vras ha gwelout goude mamm-gozh o ledañ bravig an toaz gant he rozell hag o plegañ ar c'hrampouez diwar ar bern pa vezent distanet un tamm. Ne c'hortoze ket Frañsa poent koan evit kaout un tañva anezho. Ha da echuiñ an abadenn, mamm-gozh gant an dilerc'h eus an toaz a aoze un doare kouign tevoc'h eget ur grampouezhenn. Hag ar gouign-se, un tamm amann o teuziñ warni, a veze un dra lipous da zebriñ, me 'lar deoc'h!

Ar vakañsoù, avat, ne badont ket bepred hag un deiz e veze red adkemer hent Landi. Ur wech da nebeutañ ez eas Frañsa d'ar gêr war e droad gant e vamm-gozh. An dud a zegouezhe ganto war an hent a c'hellas gwelout un arvest teneraüs: an hini bihan hag an hini gozh o vont gant an hent en ur ouelañ dourek. Kañv a zougent d'unan bennak, moarvat. Nann, tudoù keizh, o kas ar mab bihan da di e vamm, netra ken. Pebezh glac'har!

Translation

A Man in the Making, *1958* (Extract)

In the Summer, Frañsa used to go to his grandmother's house to spend part of the school holidays. He liked to be in Krec'h-ar-Bleiz where no one prevented him from exploring the surrounding area. What more could a child ask for? Frañsa thus used to go to the quarry to see mines being blown, to pick hazelnuts or blackberries, or to herd the cows with the village boys. He once had fun running in a stream for such a long time that the calves of his legs got badly sunburned. He did not know for sure what was wrong with him but, on the following night, he cried in his box bed and his grandmother cried with him. They were both soft-hearted.

What a pleasure on Fridays when Grandma started making pancakes. Frañsa enjoyed helping to light the fire under the large frying pan. He then watched Grandma spread the dough with her wooden spatula and fold the stacked pancakes when they had cooled a little. Frañsa did not have to wait till dinner time to taste them. At the end of the cooking session, Grandma used the remainder of the mixture to prepare a kind of cake, thicker than a pancake, and that cake, covered with melting butter was a delicious treat, believe me!

However, holidays do not last for ever and the day would come when it was time to return to Landivisiau. Once at least, Frañsa walked back home with his grandmother. The passers-by who met them saw a very tender scene as the young boy and the old woman walked along the road crying their eyes out. They were mourning someone, you might think. Not at all. The child was returning to his mother's home, nothing more. How distressing that was!

Yann Ezel

Va Fesk kentañ, *1943*

Aet e oan, un dervezh evel unan all, e kreiz an hañv kaer, ur votez-koad e pep dorn hag ar galabousenn pillig krampouezh war ar penn, da gantren ar c'herreg hed an oad. Bliv oan d'ar mare-se da redek war ar c'herreg ha rouez ar gwechoù ma c'hoarveze ganin risklañ war ar bezhin gleb, ha kouezhañ en ur poull. Ha kavout dres war ar garregenn blat ur c'hanfard un tamm mat koshoc'h o klask sevel ar c'hastreged gant ul linenn-sont. Goulenn a ris digantañ ha n'en doa ket ul linenn da zioueriñ e-touez ar strobad linennoù a welen gantañ en e baner malastrañ.

Dresañ a reas din eta ul linenn gant ur maen e penn evit ober pouez, lakaat a reas ur garvenenn ruz ha reut e penn an higenn hag e reas din mont pelloc'h da deurel va jeu er-maez gant aon da droc'hañ dezhañ e hini. Rak n'eo ket ur soubenn dirouestlañ linennoù pa vez rouestlerezh. Ha me, avat, da zibunañ war ar garregenn pemp pe c'hwec'h gourhed sifell ha teurel an traoù er-maez, en ur ziwall mat da luziañ an higenn em biz ha da vezañ, me va-unan, brasañ pesk eus va feskerezh. Ne lavaran ket e voe ar bann kentañ eus ar bravañ ha marteze zoken e voe ret din en em gemer meur a wech a-raok teurel mat va linenn er poull. Met selaou a raen ar c'hentelioù a veze roet din gant va c'heneil kozh. Hag erfin, e santis e penn va biz un taolig, un taol brasoc'h c'hoazh. "Emañ e penn," emezon. "Bec'h d'al lasenn!" Frapañ a ris buan-buan gant va holl nerzh. En em zifretañ a rae ar pesk en dour, met kaer en doa ober, ret e voe dezhañ dont er-maez hag e welis petra? Ur c'hastreg bihan divalav na oa ket hiroc'h eget ur penndolog. N'eus forzh, joa a oa ennon, ken e ris un hej-skoaz hag un taol-sav-otoù gant al lorc'h.

Met penaos disklaviañ al loen? Kaer am boa sachañ, ne zeuen ket a-benn da zistagañ va higenn. Rak ar seurt pesked, par d'ar wrac'h, o deus muzelloù troñset ha gwareget start, diaes da ziframmañ. Atav gant kuzulioù va c'heneil e voen gouest erfin da zieubiñ va labousig-gwrac'h. Ha me d'e flac'hotañ flourik gant palv va dorn, dres evel ul labousig gwirion. Kenderc'hel a ris gant va feskerezh, peogwir e pege ker brav ar pesk d'ar vouedenn. N'ouzon ket mui hag e pakis kalz a besked all: tri pe bevar marteze. Dresañ a ris anezho, pare da vont war ar baelon: diskantet, divouzellet hag istribilhet dre ur penn-fard a-dreuz d'o genou. Setu na fogas gant ar paotr o vont d'ar gêr da ziskouez e beskerezh! Met ne blijas ket kalz ar seurt bugale pesked d'am mamm.

"Va faotrig bihan, emezi, petra a rin gant ar struj-se? N'int mat nemet da lipat amanenn?"

Hag e voe taolet va feskerezh d'ar c'hazh. Ken am boa c'hoant grial.

Translation

My First Fish, *1943*

On a beautiful midsummer day which was in no way special I went to the rocks by the shore, a wooden clog in each hand and a wide beret on my head. At that time I was agile and could run from rock to rock without constantly slipping on the wet seaweed and falling into a pool of water. On a flat rock, I met a youth a few years older than myself who was trying to catch wrasse with a sounding line. I asked him if he could spare one of the lines from the bundle I could see in his fishing basket.

He got me one, tied a stone to the end of it to weight it, put a stiff red bait at the end of the hook and told me to try my luck further afield, so as not to be in his way, as it is not easy to unravel lines which have become tangled. I unwound ten or twelve yards of line and threw them into the water, taking care not to catch the hook on my finger, thereby becoming the biggest fish of my own catch. I would not say that my first attempt was particularly stunning. In fact I had to try several times before throwing my line properly into the water. But I listened to the advice given by my older comrade. Finally, I felt a little pull at the end of my finger, followed by a stronger one. "I've got one!" I said "Get the net, quickly!" I pulled on the line with all my strength. The fish was struggling in the water, but to no avail. It had to come out, and then, what did I see? An ugly little fish, no longer than a tadpole. It did not matter. I was exhilarated and felt so proud that I threw my shoulders back and pulled my trousers up.

But how was I to unhook the beast? I tugged and pulled but did not manage to free the fishing hook. This kind of fish, which belongs to the wrasse family, have strongly arched and turned-up mouths which are not easily freed. Still following my friend's advice I finally managed to unfasten my tiny fish. I stroked it gently with the palm of my hand, as if it had been a baby bird, then carried on fishing, as the fish seemed so keen to go for the bait. I cannot remember if I caught many fish, maybe three or four more. I got them ready for the frying pan: I scaled them, cleaned them and hung them on a piece of string strung through their mouths. Such was the boy's conceit going on his way home to show off his catch! But this kind of tiny fish did not impress my mother:

"My dear son," she said, "whatever can I do with this small fry? They only soak up butter."

My catch was thrown to the cat. I felt like crying.

Tadevab

Ar Gartenn-oferenn, *2003* (Lodenn)

Ha neoazh, bugale ar labourizion "ruz," èl ar re 'rall, a veze kaset d'ar c'hatechim d'ar yaou vintin. Adal seizh vlez c'hoazh! D'ober ar gomunion vihan. Pemp blez àr-lerc'h: ur Pask arall, hag ar goñfirmasion evit echu. Ha katechim hag oferennoù a-hed an amzer-se. Ur wezh disklabet tennadoù pennañ hor bugaleaj kristen, ne dostae ket kalz ac'hanomp doc'h an iliz. Ne oa hani ac'hanomp a yae e dud d'an oferenn d'ar Sul. Kaset e veze ar vugale neoazh ha ne veze ket roet deomp da zibab. Gwisket e vezemp brav get, alies-mat, ur chupenn re vras pe re vihan. Re vras pa oa nevez-prenet (pa vize bet dres a-vod n'he dize ket padet), re vihan ar blez àr-lerc'h (ret e veze padiñ, ker a-walc'h e oa bet prenet). Botoù-lêr koaret-mat, ur gravatenn "beg-yod" oc'hpenn kement-se d'an deizioù bras. Blev rannet ha distennet. Nag aes en em gavemp èl-se! Ne oa ket tu ebet d'ober netra: ret e oa donet d'ar gêr ken distenn ha digousi èl ma oamp bet kaset d'an oferenn. Ar gwashañ a oa ar gravatenn "beg-yod". E-lec'h ur gravatenn èl ar re vras e prene alies ar mammoù brizhkravatennoù bugale dalc'het gęt ur lastik a veze kuzhet edan gougenn ar roched. Ya, met gozik bep taol en em gave ur lapous brasoc'h evidoc'h (hag en doa-eñ ur gravatenn "den") evit sach àr veg ho tamm danvez betek lakaat ar lastik d'ar stegnañ. Pa zileze e grog e tae an neudenn stirennek, a-drumm, da stardiñ àr ho koug en-dro. N'eo ket an dra-se a rae ar muiañ a zroug, kentoc'h e oa ar frazenn distaget hep mank ebet, dirak an holl: "A! A! Ur gravatenn beg-yod zo getañ!" Gozik e vezec'h laouen, a-benn eno, da frammiñ buan en iliz evit un euriadig.

Ar baotred a-gleiz, ar merc'hed a-zehoù, er groazenn. Ur paotr kozh, a gave deomp atav, met marse ne oa ket hant-kant, ar "Saeg tev" a veze graet anezhañ, a oa aze d'hon diwall. Eñ eo a lakae ar siell àr ho kartenn. Graet e oa ar gartenn-se evit tri miz, tri bann a oa enta àrnezi, unan evit pep miz, peder pe pemp linenn e pep bann evit an oferennoù hag unan en diaz evit kofesaat. Ret e veze monet da "zisklêriiñ ho chistr", pe o chistroù, bep miz. Tu 'veze marse mankiñ un oferenn ur wezh en trimiziad met da ziwall a veze! Ensellet e vezent ingal! Un nebeudad c'hwiled o doa, ur wezh, kavet an tu da chom hep mont d'an oferenn. Roet e oa bet dezhe, a-guzh, get ur c'hensort hag a oa masikod, ar siell benniget. Amzer pemp munutenn e oa bet karget o zrimiziad d'ar pevar pe bemp istrelog a oa e-barzh an taol, ar gwalldaol! Unan a oa bet re hir e deod? Unan arall a oa bet é toupiniñ marse? Savet e oa da benn ar person, a-drumm, gwiriekaat ar c'hartennoù re goulz? Dastumet e oant bet atav ha diandellet ar floderion sielloù, a daolioù Pater ha Ave Maria. Ha trouz er gêr da heul! An tadoù, neoazh, evit ar muiañ, ne ziskouezent ket skouer. Lod ac'hanomp o doa soñj bout gwelet o hani monet d'an oferenn, get o mamm ive. Ne bade ket. Buan e yae ar boaz da goll. Hoalusoc'h e oa ar chapel evit an davarn! Evit dek eur hanter e oa aet lod-kaer ag ar wazed er-maez, didrouz, a-guzh, dre-laer. Lezenn pe get, atav e oa ur "chapel" pemp metr a-zoc'h an iliz. Amezeg tostañ ar person e oa an tavarnour. Tremen d'ur c'harr a oa etre an daou savadur. "Ne vin ket pell," a veze lâret d'ar maouezed, "n'eus banne aer amañ, eh an d'ober un dro er-maez, ne badan mui!" "Eh an da gerc'hat ar bara atav, àr-lerc'h an oferenn e vo re a dud!" Muioc'h a blijadur a veze er chapel. Ne oa ket stummet ar wazed gant ar c'hantikoù ha diaes da vat e kavent gwelet ar person ec'h evet gwin (ha "kani mat" a lârent), goude bout savet e galirenn er vann, diskouezet d'an holl hep kinnig ul lomm da zen! Ne gredent ket re d'ar person pa lâre e oa gwad hor Salver ha neoazh, ne oa aze netra souezhus ebet: meur a unan, en o mesk, a oa e wad tost-tre doc'h ar gwin, ma ne oa ket gwin penn-dre-benn: mesket-mat e oa atav! Danvez salverion e oant holl, hep gouiet dezhe. Salverion hag a gave hir an oferenn. Ha ni ivez, an hanter re hir, met ne oa ket tu deomp monet d'an davarn.

Translation

The Mass Card, *2003* (Extract)

However, children of communists were sent, just like the other ones, to catechism on Thursday mornings. And that from as young as seven! In order to do their first communion. Five years later, another communion and confirmation to finish with. We had to go to catechism and mass during all that time. Once the main achievements of our Christian youth had been attained, few of us went anywhere near the church. None of our parents attended Sunday mass, but the children were sent to it, whether they wanted it or not. We were dressed up for the occasion, and, most of the time wore a jacket which was either too big or too small. Too big when it had just been bought (if it had been the right size it would not have lasted), too small the following year (it had to last, it had been expensive enough to buy). To top it all, polished shoes and a ready-made tie for special occasions. Hair parted and plastered down. How at ease we felt like this! We could do nothing: we had to return home, as neat and tidy as we had been sent to church. The worst was the ready-made tie. Instead of the tie worn by adults, our mothers often bought children's imitation tie with a knot sewn on an elastic which was hidden under the shirt collar. Fine, but practically every single time, a boy bigger than you – one who had a proper man's tie – would pull on the strip of fabric in order to stretch the elastic. When he let go of it, the taut knot would spring back suddenly around your neck. This is not what did the most harm, but the words which never failed to be spoken for everyone to hear: "Ah-ha! He's wearing a ready-made tie." All things considered, we were almost pleased to rush into church for an hour or so.

Boys on the left, girls on the right, in the chancel. An old man – we found him old but he could well not have been fifty – nicknamed "Fat Saeg", was there to keep an eye on us. He was the one who stamped our cards. The card was valid for three months. It was arranged in three columns, one for each month, four or five lines in each column for mass attendance and an extra line at the bottom for confession. We had to declare our catalogue – or our catalogues – of sins every month. You could arrange to miss mass once a month, but had to be careful. The cards were inspected regularly! Once, a few scallywags found a way not attend mass. They had been handed the blessed stamp, on the sly, by one of the choirboys. In less than five minutes, the cards of the four or five free spirits who were in on the deed – on the misdeed, rather – was filled in for the whole three months! Was one of them unable to hold his tongue? Did someone tell on them? Or did it suddenly enter the priest's head, out of the blue, to check the cards early? Whatever it was, the cards were collected and the trick pulled by the receivers of stolen stamps came to a sudden halt, with a whack and a wallop, in the name of the Father, the Son and the Holy Spirit. And ditto at home! However, the majority of fathers did not set a good example. Some of us could remember our fathers going to mass, together with our mothers. It did not last. The habit did not stick. The "chapel" was more attractive than the church. By half past ten, a good number of fathers had gone out, silently, secretly, furtively. Whether it was a lawful requirement or not, there was always a "chapel" within five yards of the church. The priest's next door neighbour was the publican. There was the width of a car between the two buildings. The women were told: "I won't be a sec! It's too stuffy in here; I'm going out. I can't stand it any more!" "I'll go and get the bread; after church there will be too much of a queue!" There was more fun to be had in chapel. The men were not keen to sing hymns and also found it hard to see the priest drink wine – and "good wine too" they said – after lifting the chalice in the air and showing it for all to see, without offering anyone a drop! They did not believe the priest when he said it was our Saviour's blood, and yet there was nothing strange there: many of them had blood very similar to wine: if it was not entirely made of wine, it was a well blended mixture. They were all potential Saviours without knowing it. Saviours who found mass too long. We did too, much too long, but there was no way we could go to the pub.

The Bretons and their Language

From the French Revolution to the present day the Parisian administration made many attempts in the name of national unity to eradicate the mosaic of regional languages and dialects spoken on French Republican soil. The attacks on 'patois' of all sorts used to be led primarily by school teachers who, from the middle of the nineteenth to that of the twentieth century, punished children heard speaking their mother tongue on school premises. For a couple of years at the very beginning of the twentieth century, the French Government also banned the use of Breton in the church. In Lower Brittany many priests disregarded the order and refused to speak French to their monoglot Breton speakers, consequently losing their salary. The separation of Church and State put an end to this language war in religious affairs. However Catholic schools turned out to be no defenders of the Breton language. They were competing with State schools to attract pupils and often enforced the sole use of French, partly in response to the wishes of the majority of parents who had learnt to consider Breton as a backward language and wanted to secure their children's future by having them educated in French.

In the western part of Brittany Breton remained the language of social and family interactions until the end of the first world war. The numerous magazines and books published in Breton had a consistent readership and many children learnt to read Breton from them. Changes in the way of living, such as compulsory national service, emigration of Bretons to French cities, the development of the railways, the opportunities offered for social promotion by the French civil service and the first world war which forced men out of their villages, probably did as much as laws and decrees to bring the Breton language to its present precarious state.

Contemporary writers who, having been schooled in French, choose to write in Breton, point repeatedly to the harmful influence of the education system on the language, to the psychological impact of the enforced use of French and to the constant impoverishment of their mother tongue as French encroaches ever deeper into the Breton-speaking heartland.

Pêr Bronost

E Skol va farrez, *1902*

A-boan me ioa ken huel ha botez eunn archer,
Ma'z oann kaset d'ar skol evit deski gallek,
Rag euz ar iez-se c'hoaz ne gouienn ket eur seurt ger,
Ne gouienn, evel va mamm, nemed ar brezounek.

M'ho pije va gwelet, diskabel ha diarc'henn,
Oc'h en em gaout er-skol, holl ho pije c'hoarzet;
Va ginou, digor-braz, e pep leac'h e sellenn,
Gant em fenn daoulagad eur bugelik dianket.

Renket oc'h eur voger, evel ar zoudarded,
Tro-war-dro d'ann ti-skol, me wele taolennou
Warn-ho livet e du pep seurt anevaled
Gant ann Aotrou skolaer hanvet lizerennou.

Med ne jomiz ket pell eur c'hrouadurik gouez;
Sonjezonou nevez a deuaz buan em spered;
Ann anevaled du, kentoc'h hag eiz dervez,
A ioa deuet da veza va braza mignouned.

Ma vijen bet ken fur ha m'oann mad da zeski,
N'em bije ket skubet ann ti-skol d'ar pardaez,
Med, evel m'oann dibenn ha ma karenn c'hoari,
Em euz skubet, siouaz! leur an ti-skol aliez.

Biskoaz n'em euz klemmet o chom e pinijenn
Da c'houde beza great eur farserez-bennag,
Lenvet em euz avad o kaout ar 'zimbolenn'
Evit komz brezounek!... goulenn a rit perag!

Ra zigoro Sant Per d'in dor ar baradoz:
M'em euz hen gounezet dre gement a zaelou!...
Med penaoz pardouni d'ann Aotrou skolaer-koz
D'am beza kastizet 'vit komz iez hon Tadou!

Translation

In My Parish School, *1902*

The poet recalls his very first school-days and the sanctions taken against the pupils heard speaking Breton at school. The 'symbol', an object which recalls the 'Welsh not', was given to the child caught speaking Breton on school premises, and then passed on from offending child to offending child. The last child denounced by his comrades for speaking Breton was punished at the end of the school-day.

> I was hardly as high as a policeman's boot
> When I was sent to school to learn French;
> I did not yet know a single word of that language.
> Like my mother, I only knew Breton.
>
> If you had seen me, bare-headed, bare-footed,
> On my first day at school, you would all have laughed;
> Mouth wide-open, I looked all around
> With the eyes of a lost child.
>
> Lined up like soldiers on the walls
> Of the classrooms, were posters
> On which were painted all kinds of strange black animals
> Which the teacher called letters.
>
> But I did not stay ignorant for long;
> New thoughts soon entered my mind;
> The black animals, in less than a week,
> Had become my greatest friends.
>
> Had I been as well-behaved as I was quick to learn,
> I would not have swept the classroom floor at the end of the day,
> But, as I was absent-minded and liked playing tricks,
> I regrettably often had to clean them.
>
> I never complained when I was punished
> For playing some trick or other,
> But I cried when I was given the 'symbol'
> For speaking Breton! And you are asking why?
>
> May Saint Peter open the doors of paradise to me:
> I deserve it for having cried so much!
> But how can I ever forgive the old teacher
> Who punished me for speaking the language of our Fathers?

Frañsez Vallée

Eñvorennou eur Brezonegour, *1941*

E Treger em eus gwelet dreist-holl an aod adalek Sant-Brieg betek Plistin. Va mamm a yae pep bloaz war ribl ar mor. Da genta ez ae da Sant-Ke, a oa aet diwar-se d'eul lec'h a herberc'herez evit ar Barizianed. Gwelet em eus eno, p'edon yaouank-flamm (war-dro 1867 pe 1868) an Ao. Littré hag an Ao. De Hérédia. Er bloaz 1872 pe war-dro, e feurmas va mamm eun ti-kenkiz e Sant-Eflam, a oa d'ar c'houlz-se, er c'hontrol, dieub-tre a estrenien ha brezonek penn-da-benn. Ne gomzed nemet brezoneg er vro tro-dro, ken e-touez al labourerien-douar, ken e-touez ar besketaerien. Abaoe ez eus deuet kemm bras, savet eun ostaleri giz-nevez e-harz eur roc'h uhel a zo graet anezhi er vro Roc'h al Laz. Evel ma oa ar ger-se re c'harv da gorzailhenn ar Barizianed, divadezet ar roc'h ha kemeret gant an ostaleri an ano a *Hôtel du Grand-Rocher*! N'ouzon ket pegement e koust ar bevañs en ostaleri-se, nemet gwechall em eus bevet tri pe bevar devez e tavarn Pont ar Yar evit c'houezek real en holl. Ha c'hoaz em boa eur vag hag eur martolod koz anvet Hippolit d'ober baleadennou evit netra war ar mor.

Bro-Leon em eus gwelet dreist-holl gant va breur Juluan, a oa neuze war e studi-beleg. Eus Sant Yann ar Biz, e-lec'h hor boa tremenet eun nebeut sizhun-vezhiou, ez ejomp war droad, a-hed an aod, betek Landerne, en eur dremen dre Montroulez, Karantek, Kastell-Paol, Lesneven, ar Follgoad. En em gavout a rejomp er Follgoad evit ar pardon.

Meur a wech all ez oun aet da Blougastell-Daoulas a oa neuze distag-krenn diouz pep hent. N'oa ket bet savet ar pont ramzel, hag e ranked mont dre eur vagig-dre-lien. Da enez Vaz ha da enez Vriad oun aet ivez evel-se, dre vagou-dre-lien. Nebeut-tre a zarempredou a oa neuze etre an enezennou-se hag an Douar-bras. Bro-Gerne em eus darempredet gwechall-goz, p'edon bihan. Eno e chome c'hoaz kerent a-berz va zad-koz a oa eus ar Gemene. Gant eur voereb d'in, c'hoar d'am mamm, ez is eur wech da welout eun eontr koz, an Ao. Samzun, hag a oa person en eur vourc'hig vihan eus Gwened. Eno e vezen lojet er presbital, hag e rejomp anaoudegezh gant kerdirvi, kenitervezed, holl labourerien-douar evel va zad-you, o tougen ar gwiskamant breizat hag o komz brezoneg. Koun em eus dalc'het dreist-holl eus eur genitervez a oad ganen pe eun tammig kosoc'h, hec'h ano Visanta, hag a servije ouz taol.

Moerebezed koz, lez-c'hoarezed d'am zad-koz, a oa d'ar c'houlz-se e Korle hag em eus bevet pell-amzer en o zi. Korle n'oa ket c'hoaz peurzivrezonekaet evel bremañ. Skoliou a zo bet abaoe, ken kristen, ken lik, hag a zo bet heligenta etrezo da zivrezonekaat ar vro. Va moerebezed, unan anezho dreist-holl, anvet Matilda, a gare hag a gomze mat-tre ar brezoneg.

Pa ergerzan ar vro bremañ, souez eo ar c'hemm a welan en-dro d'in. Ar gwiska-mant dreist-holl, a oa ken dereat gant ar merc'hed gwechall, a zo distreset euzus pa n'eo ket bet peurzilezet. Ar merc'hedigou gwechall a veze holl gwisket e gwiskamant ar vro gant eur boned bihan ruz pe c'hlas e-lec'h koef ar re goz. Bremañ e tougont holl togou. Evit ar yez kement-all. Em yaouankiz ne gleved war ar maez ger gallek ebet, hag er c'hêriou, e veze komzet hag enoret ar brezoneg keit-ha-keit gant ar galleg. Bremañ, e kêriou bihan evel Gwengamp, a-vec'h ma teurvez zoken tud ar bobl komz brezoneg. Ouspenn ma veze komzet stankoc'h, e veze ivez komzet kalz gwelloc'h eget bremañ. Nebeut-tre a c'heriou gallek o tont da saotra ar yez, dreist-holl evit an traou-bemdez hag evit ar vuhez war ar maez. Ar skoliou dreist-holl a zo bet penn-abeg da se.

Pa oan bihan, e veze graet eun nebeut skol d'ar vugale. E Benac'h e veze dalc'het skol ar merc'hedigou en eun ti-soul hag e weled eun nebeudig anezo bemdez o vont d'ar skol en eur gomz brezoneg etrezo, gwisket holl e gwiskamant ar vro, bonedou ruz war o fenn. Degemeret e vezent gant ar vestrez-skol, nizez d'ar per-son, gwisket kerkoulz-all, e gwiskamant ar vro, hag o komz brezoneg evelto. Desket e veze lenn ar pedennou dreist-holl e brezoneg hag e latin. Evit ar baotred, diwar neuze e veze e penn ar skoliou pabored da vistri hag a oa ganto en o genou eur galleg bras: *Nous partîmes dès l'aurore et nous rentrâmes au crépuscule*. Ha koulskoude brezoneg mat a zesked er skol, rak an euriou rôet da zeski ar galleg a veze daztrouc'het gant eur bern labouriou a dïegez hag al labouriou-se, graet a-unvan gant ar vugale, a veze d'ezo eur c'hoari na gomzed ennañ nemet brezoneg. Va breur Olier en deus heuliet ar skol-se ha desket enni gant ar vugale all komz brezoneg ervat. N'oa meneg ebet neuze eus ar *certificat* (testeni-studi) hag eus an arnodadou all divrezonekaus.

Translation

Memories of a Breton Speaker, *1941* (Extract)

In Tregor I chiefly saw the coast from Saint-Brieuc to Plestin-les-Grèves, as my mother used to go every year to the seaside. She went first to Saint-Quay which had become a resort for Parisians. When I was very young (in 1867 or 1868) I saw Monsieur Littré and Monsieur de Hérédia there. In or around 1872 my mother hired a villa in Saint-Efflam which was at that time, on the contrary, free from out-siders and totally Breton-speaking. Only Breton was heard in the area, amongst farmers as well as fishermen. The state of affairs has changed since then. A modern hotel has been built at the foot of a high rock called Roc'h al Laz by the locals. As this was too rough for Parisian throats, the rock lost its name and the hotel was renamed *Hôtel du Grand-Rocher*! I do not know how much it costs to stay there, but, in the old days, I managed to stay for three or four days in the inn at Pont ar Yar for £3, including meals. What is more, I used the services of Hippolit, an old seaman, to go for free trips on the sea.

I mostly know the region of Léon from the holiday I spent there with my broth-er Juluan who, at that time, was studying to be a priest. We spent a few weeks in Saint-Jean-du-Doigt and then walked along the coast to Landerneau, having passed through Morlaix, Carantec, Saint-Paul-de-Léon, Lesneven and Le Folgoat.

We arrived at Le Folgoat on the day of the "pardon".

I had many other occasions to go to Plougastel-Daoulas which, at that time, was not linked to any major roads. The huge bridge had not yet been built and one had to take a small sailing boat to get there. This is also how I also went to the Isle of Batz and to that of Bréhat, on sailing boats. At that time there were very few links between these islands and the continent.

I went to Cornouaille many years ago, when I was little. Some relatives of my grandfather, who was born in Guéméné, still lived there. I once accompanied one of my aunts – one of my mother's sisters – to see an old uncle, Father Samzun, who was in charge of a small parish in the diocese of Vannes. I stayed in the presbytery where we met, for the first time, male and female cousins. They were all farmers, as my great-grandfather had been, dressed in the traditional Breton costume and they spoke Breton. I particularly remember a female cousin of mine, my age or slightly older, named Visanta, who served us at meal-times.

At that time, there lived in Corlay old aunts who were my grandfather's half-sisters. I stayed with them for a long time. Corlay had not yet lost the use of Breton as it has now. Since those days, the schools, whether church schools or not, have competed amongst themselves to make the area lose the Breton language. My aunts, particularly the one called Mathilda, loved Breton and used to speak it very well.

When I travel up and down the country nowadays, I am surprised by the many changes around me, like the one brought to the costume which suited women so well in the past and which has been dreadfully distorted if not been totally abandoned. In the old days, all young girls used to be dressed in the local costume, but they wore a small red or blue bonnet instead of the headdress of the older women. Now they all wear hats. The same happened to the language. In my youth, one did not hear a single word of French in the countryside. Breton was well regarded, even in towns, and spoken as often as French. Nowadays, in small towns like Guingamp, ordinary people hardly condescend to speak Breton. Not only was Breton spoken more widely, it was also spoken better than it is now. There were very few French words to pollute the language, particularly as regards everyday things and those referring to life in the countryside. The schools bear the main responsibility for this loss.

When I was young, the children spent a year or two at school. In Belle-Isle-en-Terre, the girls' school was held in a thatched house. Some of them could be seen everyday on their way to school, chatting in Breton among themselves, all dressed in the local costume, a red bonnet on their heads. They were met by the schoolmistress, one of the priest's nieces, who also wore the local costume and also spoke Breton. They were mostly taught to read the prayers in Breton and in Latin. As for the boys, pretentious schoolmasters who spoke very pompous French were already in charge at that time: *Nous partîmes dès l'aurore et nous rentrâmes au crépuscule.* And yet good Breton was learnt in school, because the hours dedicated to learning French were interrupted by a great number of farming tasks, and these, done with the help of the children, were like a holiday during which nothing but Breton was spoken. My brother Olier went to that 'school' where he learnt to speak good Breton from the other children. At that time, no one yet cared about the *certificat* (end of primary school diploma) or about the other examinations which have led to the loss of Breton.

Rojer Brison

Ar Chapeled, *c.1950* (Lodenn)

Echu ar gousperoù, ar beleg nevez a bignas gant ar gador-brezeg, juntañ e zaouarn ha kregiñ evelhen: "Mes bien chers frères..."

Chann Gozh a savas he fenn sebezet. Biskoazh n'en doa ar person kozh komzet galleg en iliz, nemet e vefe da vare an douristed, pa veze e penn all an nev ur paotr bennak en e vragoù berr pe un doare gast eus Pariz, livet he muzelloù hag he ivinoù ma selle an holl outo gant fae, ha c'hoazh ne zeue gantañ nemet ur frazenn c'hallek, pe ziv en deizioù ma veze imoret mat. Chann a droas he fenn hag a sellas pizh a-dreñv, a-gleiz hag a-zehou. Den estren ebet ne welas en iliz, ne oa nemet tud ar barrez. Den ebet n'en dije bet ar soñj iskis da gomz galleg oute. Stouiñ a reas buan he fenn, evel m'he dije graet ur fazi bennak, o treiñ he sebez en he spered.

Ar beleg yaouank a zistagas c'hoazh ur geriennoù bennak e galleg, ne glaskas ket Chann kompren anezhe. Tostaat a reas he fenn ouzh penn ur vaouez all en he c'hichen hag a oa paouez tennañ, goude ul lajadig termal, ur chapeled diouzh godell he zavañjer, ha goulenn diganti: "Petra 'zo o tremen?" – "Me gred din e fell dezhañ e lavarfemp ur chapeled evit ar person kozh."

Ar beleg a reas sin ar groaz ha kregiñ: "Notre Père qui êtes aux cieux..." Chann Gozh a savas he fenn adarre, mezh ha spont a sante en he c'halon. Ar wazed, a-dreñv dezhi a respontas a vouez uhel, o teukañ avat dre m'o doa poan oc'h adkavout ar gerioù estren.

Teukañ a rejont, ha diaes e oa dezhe ivez. Evit pediñ e oant deut amañ ha sklaer e oa dezhe ne oa ket ar bedenn a zeue gant ar beleg yaouank an hini wirion, a darzh eeun ha splann evel ur voaz hir, al lavar ma oant stummet outañ a-vihanik hag a c'hoantae ezhommoù reizh o c'halonoù hep m'o dije o muzelloù da glask ar gerioù. Ar bedenn, o fedenn-i a oa garanet e don-donañ o c'halon e troioù-lavar deut dezho eus penn-pellañ ar ouenn. O fedenn a oa ar gerioù kavet hep bezañ klasket hag o adlavarout a oa al lusk a dostae anezhe ouzh Doue.

Hogen ar bedenn-mañ ne oa ket o fedenn, ar bedenn bet laret gant o zadoù ha tadoù o zadoù.

Ar beleg yaouank a gendalc'he: "Je vous salue Marie..."

Den ebet ken avat en iliz ne soñje mui e Doue, Jezuz pe Vari. Pep hini a glaske en e benn ar gerioù dianket gant strivoù seul vrasoc'h ma strebote o zeodoù, da bep frazenn c'hallek, war al lavar brezhonek kozh a felle dezhañ dont er-maez en desped dezhe.

"Notre Père qui êtes aux cieux..."

Chann a oa chomet hep pediñ e-pad ar merkad kentañ. Leun e oa he c'halon gant ur c'hwervoni disoñjet ganti abaoe pell, abaoe an amzer ma oa skoliadez vihan e skol ar seurezed, an amzer ma veze dornet bewech ma zifloupe diganti ur ger brezhonek.

Gwelout a reas a daol-trumm, gant lagad hec'h ene, sal ar c'hlas gwennrazhet, ar groaz e krec'h an daolenn du, delwenn plastr an Itron Varia en tu dehou, brizh livet, ur vandenn lien en-dro dezhi ma lenned warni: "Gloire à Marie".

Daoust hag e oa hanter kant pe tri ugent vloaz a-raok? N'oa mui evit kaout soñj. Soñj mat he doa avat eus ar verc'hig vihan ma oa, daoulinet, ha mezhek o lavarout: "Pardon, ma Mère, je ne parlerai plus breton," hag o kinnig en ur zaskrenañ he bizied evit ma vefe skoet outo taolioù reolenn, ar verc'hig ruziet he divjod gant ar palvadoù, hec'h unan penn e sal ar c'hlas dilezet hag a skrive gant poan: *Je fais de la peine au Bon Dieu chaque fois que je parle breton*, kant gwech war ur follenn kaier a veze roget da c'houde gant ar seurez faeüs.

Chann a voustras war he soñjoù. Edo an eil merkad o paouez echuiñ. A-greiz-holl e teuas soñj dezhi eus: *Sainte Marie, mère de Dieu…* met diouzhtu e chomas berr ha ne gavas en-dro *Pauvres pêcheurs* nemet d'an ampoent ma tistage ar beleg e *ainsi soit-il*!

Chom a reas dilavar e-pad an Ave diwezhañ, o damselaou ouzh ar pezh a veze hiboudet en-dro dezhi. Sourrad boaz ar rozera ne oa ket. Sellout a reas e kuzh en he c'hichen, gwelout a reas ar muzelloù o fiñval, oc'h ober un harp, an talioù o krizañ gant ar preder. A-dreñv dezhi, mouezioù boud ar wazed a veske brezhoneg ha galleg en ur fuilhadeg truezhus.

Neuze e troas en he soñj lavarout ar bedenn e brezhoneg. Kregiñ a reas e dibenn ar merkad kentañ, o klask heuliañ mouez ar beleg ha mougañ en diabarzh "Hon Tad a zo en neñv…" Hogen ne oa ket echu ar Pater ganti ma oa dija echu gant ar beleg. Klask a reas kenderc'hel gant he merkad buan-buan o soñjal e c'hellfe gortoz en dibenn.

Hogen klaskit 'ta da skouer, kontañ ar c'hammedoù emaoc'h oc'h ober, tra m'e-mañ unan all o toumpiñ war an douar gant e votoù koat. Unan, daou; ho taou gammed kentañ hoc'h eus kontet. Mat. Tri, pevar; kammedoù an hini all hoc'h eus kontet, pemp, c'hwec'h; kammedoù an hini all a gendalc'hit da gontañ. Ha Chann gaezh a luzie, a veske galleg ha brezhoneg, a echue un Ave, bet kroget e brezhoneg, gant un hanter Bater galleg a droe a-greiz-holl da gaout soñj anezhañ.

Neuze e reas he menoz tevel. Sevel a reas he fenn, dijuntañ he daouarn ha sellout difiñv dirazi. Blaz ar c'hwervoni a oa aet kuit. Bremañ edo emsavadeg he ouenn o tichalañ enni. He ouenn! Dianaoudek krenn e oa anezhi ha n'eo ket seurez ar skol he dije desket tra dezhi war he divout. Krediñ a rae, evel an holl Vretoned, e oa bet he zadoù tud baour a-viskoazh, o krakvevañ diwar an douar krin hag o klask dalc'hmat ur mestr evit e servijañ. Bez ez eus avat, en tu-hont da goun mab-den, koun enskuilhet ar meuriad, hag a-dreñv da dal ar wrac'h gozh-mañ en em strolle mil vloaz emgann hag emsavadeg.

Sellout a reas ouzh ar beleg yaouank. E anavezout a rae mat-tre koulskoude hag a-vihanik; n'eo ket abaoe dec'h diwezhañ, avat, e oa deut da vezañ un estren evit tud ar vro. E welet he doa o kreskiñ, o vont davet kêr, o tont en-dro da vare ar vakañsoù, lorc'h ennañ gant e zaouarn gwenn, leun a fae evit tud ar vourc'hig, o klabousañ ur gallegach ne oa den ebet er vro evit e gompren, ar C'hallaoued ne-beutoc'h c'hoazh abalamour d'e vomm-lavar spontus. Aon en dije bet rak louzañ e c'henou en ur gomz brezhoneg.

Chann a savas e-touez ar maouezed daoulinet. Un ehan e rouzmouzerezh ar bedenn a ziskouezas sebez ar re all. Sellout a reas ur wech diwezhañ gant kasoni en he daoulagad ouzh ar beleg yaouank er gador-brezeg, ha mont er-maez an iliz, sonn he c'horf.

Treuziñ a reas ar vourc'h evel pa vije bet oc'h huñvreal ha kemer penn he hent davet he mereuri.

Ar re a geje ganti a c'henaoue ouzh ar wrac'h gozh-mañ, fero he sell, erv arc'hant an daeroù o lugerniñ war c'hwrac'helloù he dremm. "Sur, e soñjont-i, kañv bras a dle bezañ en he zi."

Sur, kañv bras a oa er vro, petra bennak ma ne oa ket bet brallet kleier an anaon, petra bennak ma ne oa ket bet stignet ar pallennoù du ouzh pileroù an iliz. Ur sell a daolent war o c'hiz, ha ne welent nemet ur vaouez gozh, stroñset he c'herzhed.

Pezh na welent ket avat eo amheuliadeg an tasmantoù ouzh hec'h ambroug: Nevenoe, houarnwisket, gwadek c'hoazh diwar emgann Ballon, Yann Pevar, ban-nieloù skedus an trec'h en-dro dezhañ, Pontkallek, war e chafod, Kadoudal, ar galon sakr war e vruched hag an Aotrou Perrot o tougen ar Sakramant dre lanneier Skrignag, hag ar re all, tout ar re all, ar re vihan, ar re zister, ar re n'en deus ket an istor miret o anvioù, ar re a zo bet avat ar Seizh Sant ouzh o c'hortoz e toull dor ar Baradoz evit o bleniañ davet Breizh all.

Translation

The Rosary, c.1950 (Extract)

The old parish priest has died and been replaced by a young Breton priest.

Evensong now over, the new priest climbed in the pulpit, joined his hands in prayer and started thus: "Mes bien chers frères..."

Chann Kozh raised her head in surprise. The former priest had never spoken French in church, except during the tourist season, when a man wearing shorts or a racy-looking Parisian woman with red lips and nails – and everyone stared at them with disapproval – sat at the back of the nave. Even then, he only said a single sentence in French, maybe two if he happened to be in a good mood. Chann looked carefully behind her, then to the right and to the left. There were no strangers in the church, only parishioners. Surely no one could have the strange idea of speaking French to them. She quickly bowed her head, as if she had made a mistake, and pondered her surprise.

The young priest uttered a few more French words which Chann made no attempt to understand. She leant towards the woman sitting next to her who had, after a small hesitation, taken out a rosary out of her apron pocket, and asked her: "What's happening now?" – "I think he wants us to say a rosary for the old priest."

The young priest made the sign of the cross and started: "Notre Père qui êtes aux cieux..." Old Chann raised her head again, her heart brimming with shame and fear. Behind her, the men answered in a loud voice, although they kept faltering as they found it hard to recall the foreign words.

They kept faltering; so, it was hard for them too. They had come here to pray, and it was obvious to them that the young priest's prayer was not the real one, one which unfolds easily and clearly after a lifelong habit formed in early childhood and which their hearts rightly called for and their lips could utter without having to search for words. The prayer, their prayer, was embedded in the depths of their hearts in terms uttered by their people from times immemorial. Their prayer was those words recalled effortlessly and their repetition formed a pattern which got them closer to God.

But this prayer was not their prayer. It was not the prayer recited by their parents and their parents' parents.

The young priest went on: "Je vous salue, Marie..."

Everyone in church had stopped thinking of God, Jesus or Mary. They were all searching their mind for the missing words but, despite their ever-increasing efforts, their tongues stumbled over every French verse as, in spite of themselves, the Breton words wanted to come out.

"Notre Père qui êtes aux cieux..."

Chann had not taken part in the first prayer. Her heart was full of a bitterness which had not been there for a long time, since the days when she was a little girl in the convent school and was slapped every time a Breton word escaped from her mouth.

She suddenly saw, in her mind's eye, the whitewashed classroom, the crucifix above the blackboard, and on the right, the plaster cast of the Virgin Mary with its faded paintwork and the sash bearing the words : "Gloire à Marie."

Was it really fifty or sixty years ago? She could not remember for sure. But she did recall the little girl she used to be, kneeling down, humiliated, saying: "Pardon, ma Mère, je ne parlerai plus Breton," as she presented her trembling fingers to the ruler, the little girl whose cheeks were red from being slapped, on her own, in the deserted classroom, who struggled to write a hundred times: *Je fais de la peine au Bon Dieu chaque fois que je parle breton*, on a page of her exercise book which was then torn up by the sneering nun.

Chann made an effort to stop reminiscing. The second prayer had just finished. Suddenly she remembered: *Sainte Marie, mère de Dieu*... but could go no further and only remembered *Pauvres pêcheurs* when the priest was saying *Ainsi soit-il!*

She kept silent during the last Ave, half-listening to the mutterings around her. It definitely did not sound like the usual humdrum recitation of the rosary. She surreptitiously looked sideways. She saw lips moving, stopping, foreheads wrinkling under the strain. Behind her, the deep voices of the men were uttering a pitiful muddle of Breton and French.

She then thought she might say the prayer in Breton. She started at the beginning of the next one, trying to follow the priest's voice and saying to herself in Breton "Our Father who art in heaven..." But she was still going through the Lord's prayer when the priest had finished his. She tried to rush up through the remaining prayers, thinking that she could wait at the end.

But try counting, for instance, the number of steps you are doing when someone else is pounding the soil with his wooden clogs. One, two. You have counted your first two steps. Fine. Three, four. You have now counted the steps of the other person. Five, six. You still keep counting the other one's steps. Poor Chann made mistakes, mixed up French and Breton, ended an Ave started in Breton with the second half of the Lord's prayer which she had suddenly remembered in French.

So she decided to keep silent. She raised her head, put her hands on her lap and looked straight in front of her. The feeling of bitterness had gone. Her fiery temper, common in her people, was now cooling off. Her people! She did not know anything about them, as the nun would not have taught her anything about them at school. She believed, as do all the Bretons, that her ancestors had always been poor, earning a difficult living from a barren soil and always looking for a master they could serve. But beyond man's memory lies the collective memory of the tribe, and behind this old woman's forehead stood a thousand years of battles and insurrections.

She looked at the young priest. She knew him well, from the day he was born in fact, but he had started becoming a stranger to the villagers a good many years ago. She had seen him grow up, leave to be educated in town and return during the holidays, proud of his soft hands and full of contempt for the villagers, in spite of the fact that he spoke such bad French that no one could understand him, least of all the French because of his very strong accent. But he would have been afraid to foul his mouth by speaking Breton.

Chann stood up among the kneeling women. An interruption in the drone of the prayer showed the others' surprise. She cast a last look full of hate at the young priest in the pulpit, and walked out of church, her head held high. She crossed the village as if in a dream and took the road leading to her farm.

Passers-by were amazed to see this old woman looking so fierce despite the silvery rivulets of tears which glimmered in the deep wrinkles of her face. "One of her close relatives must have just passed away," they thought.

To tell the truth, the whole village was mourning, even though the bells had not tolled, even though the black shrouds had not been draped round the pillars in the church. They looked back but could only see an old woman walking stiffly.

What they were not seeing however was the procession of ghosts which walked with her: Nominoe in his suit of armour, still bleeding from the battle of Ballon; Yann IV surrounded by the glowing flags of victory; Pontcallec on the scaffold; Cadoudal wearing the insignia of the Sacred Heart on his chest; Jean-Marie Perrot carrying the host through the moors of Scrignac, and the others, all the others, the insignificant ones, the unimportant ones, those whose names have been forgotten by history but who have been greeted at the gate of Paradise by the Seven Saints and shown the way to the other Brittany.

Roparz Hemon
Breizh hag ar bed, 1972 (Lodenn)

Mar gweler ervat e tleer labourat evit spered Breizh, — skrivañ, prezeg, sevel kelaouennoù, skolioù, kelc'hioù-studi; en ur ger, ober un dra bennak, n'eus forzh petra, da zihuniñ spered ar vro, — ne weler ket peurliesañ e vefe tamm ezhomm ebet enebiñ ouzh spered Bro-C'hall.

Un torfed e vefe evit darn: an daou spered, war o meno, a zo bet enebourien gwechall, a dle mont diwar bremañ, evel keneiled, dorn-ouzh-dorn, evit brasañ gounid an div vro. Penaos e teufe se da vezañ, avat, ne lavaront ket. Rak da gentañ, war veur a boent, ez eo an eil spered kontrol bev d'egile. D'an eil, n'o deus ar C'hallaoued c'hoant ebet da welout spered Breizh o tihuniñ, — pe a-du ganto, pe en o enep, — diskouezet o deus an dra-se splann a-walc'h. D'an trede, e vefe ur seurt unvaniezh, unvaniezh an dañvad hag ar bleiz.

Evit darn all, labourat evit Breizh a zo labourat a-enep Bro-C'hall. Hag ar wirionez eo a-wechoù marteze. Hogen amañ e ranker digemmeskañ.

Da ober labour mat evit Breizh, ret eo da gentañ kaout spered ur Breizhad. Daoust hag o deus ar Vrezhoned ar spered-se? Savet int, an darn vuiañ anezho, e skolioù gall, gant Gallaoued alies, hervez doareoù gall. E galleg int bet kelennet war gement tra a ouzont. Hag ar pezh a ouzont ar gwellañ a sell ouzh Bro-C'hall: lennegezh Bro-C'hall, istor Bro-C'hall, douaroniezh Bro-C'hall. An holl amzer, ur c'hoant hepken, ur mennad hepken o deus bet o mistri: o sevel e-giz Gallaoued. Hag ur wech deuet er-maez a skol, petra lennont, nemet levrioù gall, nemet kelaouennoù gall? Petra glevont, nemet prezegennoù gall, nemet pezhioù-c'hoari gall? Traoù gall, ha netra ken. En doare ma teuont, pep hini anezho, hag i a-wechoù Brezhoned vat, daoust dezho o-unan alies, hep gouzout dezho aliesoc'h, da vezañ Gallaoued penn-kil-ha-troad, peogwir ez eo gall o spered.

Ha setu bremañ ar fazi bras a reer: krediñ ez eo a-walc'h treiñ kein ouzh Bro-C'hall, a-walc'h lavarout "Me a zo Breizhad" da vezañ digabestr. Aes e vefe diskouez pegen kreñv eo chomet dalc'h an estren betek war ar re ac'hanomp o deus stourmet da enaouiñ ar spered breizhat. Sellit ouzh hol lennegezh, ha kement he deus amprestet digant lennegezh Bro-C'hall, ouzh stumm hor barzhoniezh heñvelekaet diouzh hini Vro-C'hall, ouzh hor pezhioù-c'hoari, savet diouzh skouer re Bro-C'hall. E pep lec'h hag e pep giz, betek en hon doare-skrivañ, e kaver merk Bro-C'hall.

Ar wirionez eo hon eus e Breizh, — evit bremañ da vihanañ, — da zizober kalz muioc'h eget d'ober, da ziskar kalz muioc'h eget da sevel. Hag en ur skignañ ur gelennadurezh nevez, e rankomp stourm war un dro ouzh ar gelennadurezh kozh.

Pe e vo evel hadañ war ur bod-spern ha gortoz un eost fonnus.
Diarbenn spered Bro-C'hall, eno emañ an dalc'h evidomp.

Translation

Brittany and the World, *1972* (Extract)

If we are well aware of the need to work for Brittany's spirit, through writing, giving talks at conferences, setting up magazines, schools, study centres, in short, through doing something, anything, to revive the country's spirit, we do not usually see any need to fight against France's own spirit.

Some would consider this a crime: according to them, the two spirits – which used to be enemies in the old days – must now go, like friends, hand in hand, for the greater benefit of the two countries. Yet they do not say how this could happen. In the first place, on several points, the two spirits are diametrically opposed. In the second place, the French do not have the slightest desire to see an awakening of the spirit of Brittany, whether it be for or against them. They have made this plain. In the third place, it would be a kind of union, the union of the sheep with the wolf.

For others, working for Brittany means working against France, and they may not always be wrong. But this requires clarification.

In order to work efficiently for Brittany, one must have the mind of a Breton. Do the Bretons have such a mind? Most of them are educated in French schools, often by French people, according to French ways. Everything they know was taught them through the medium of French, and what they know best relates to France: French literature, French history, French geography. During the whole time, their teachers had a single wish, a single thought: educate them as French people. When they leave school, what do they read but French books and French magazines. What do they hear but French speeches and French theatre plays? French things and nothing else. In this way, all of them – although they may sometimes be good Bretons, and this often in spite of themselves, and even more often without realizing it – become Frenchmen through and through, because their mind is French.

And now for the grave mistake one makes: to believe that it is enough to turn one's back on France, enough to say "I am Breton" to be liberated. It would be easy to show the present strength of the foreigner's grasp, even on those of us who have fought to arouse the Breton spirit. Look at our literature and at what it borrowed from French literature, at the versification of poetry which replicates that of France, at our theatre plays, composed on the French pattern. Everywhere, in every mode, even in our style of writing, one finds the stamp of France.

The truth is that we have in Brittany – at least for the time being – to undo a lot more than we have to do, to destroy a lot more than we have to build. And in spreading a new teaching we must also fight the old teaching. Or else it will be like sowing seeds on a thorn-bush and expect a fine harvest.

Overcoming the spirit of France. Such is our main objective.

Sten Kidna

Me a garfe bout, *1977*

Me 'garfe bout
 Ur Gall.
Ur Gall, a rafed anezhañ
Martin pe Durand.
Ur Gall goapaus,
Fin pe darsod
– Met lorc'hus –
A gav dezhañ
E vez e vro kreizenn ar bed.

E lec'h bout
Unan eus ar varmouzed-se
O chom er c'hornog – er pell pellañ –
Prest bepred da bismigañ ha da dagañ
Labour o c'henvroiz.
Unan eus ar varmouzed-se,
A fell dezhe en em ren o-unan,
Gante tri doare da skrivañ o yezh,
Hep mervel gant ar vezh.

Translation

I Would Like to Be, *1977*

I'd like to be
 A Frenchman.
A Frenchman who would be called
Martin or Durand.
A sarcastic Frenchman,
Brainy or thoroughly stupid,
But definitely proud,
Who thinks that is country
Is at the centre of the world.

Instead of being
One of these bungling idiots
Who live in the West, right at the fringe,
Always ready to criticise and condemn
The work of their fellow countrymen.
One of these bungling idiots,

Who want to govern themselves
But have three different ways of writing their own language
And don't even die from embarrassment.

Jarl Priel

Va Zammig buhez, *1954* (Lodenn)

Brezhonegerien eus an dibab a oa an daou gozhiad ez on bet savet ganto, met ne ouie lenn nag an eil nag egile. Dont a rae a-wechoù, hag ur ral e veze, pennadoù galleg saout gant an hini-gozh, evel skouer "il a frigassé son pied", (friket eo bet e droad) pe "un pitit morçon du pain", hogen biskoazh em buhez n'am eus klevet digant he fried nemet ur ger galleg, hag eñ distaget fall: ar mor *Atélantik*, emezañ. A drugarez d'an azenerezh-se, evel ma lavarfe darn 'zo, ha d'o diouiziegezh venniget, hervez ma kredan-me, rak daou benn he deus pep bazh, desket ha desket mat am eus va yezh a-vihanik, ha mil bennozh Doue dezho evit se! Gwir eo, er mare-se ne veze ket klevet ar vugaligoù o trailhañ gallegach dre an heñchoù; holl a raent, krennarded koulz ha merc'hed, gant ar brezhoneg dalc'hmat, er gêr, er c'hatekiz, er parkeier pa vezent o vaesa pe o neizhata, e pep lec'h nemet er skol, rak eno e veze krozet dezho, ha kastizet e vezent zoken gant ar "Symbol", ar "Vuoc'h goad", kerkent ha ma tifloupe diganto ur ger en o yezh vroadel. Allas Doue! Bremañ 'vat n'emañ ken kont evelse gant Yann grenn, da vihanañ em bro Dreger.

Translation

My Modest Life, *1954* (Extract)

The two elderly people who brought me up were excellent Breton speakers but neither of them could read. Sometimes, though it was unusual, my grand-mother would utter a few words in bad French, for instance "il a frigassé son pied," [his foot has been crushed], or "un pitit morçon du pain," but I only ever heard a single French word from her husband, and that was pronounced badly: he would say the *Atélantik* Ocean. Thanks to their stupidity, as some would call it, or thanks to their blessed ignorance, as I would put it myself, as there are two sets of opinion on the matter, I have learnt and learnt well the language in my tender youth, and I thank them for this! It is true however that, at that time, one did not hear little children speak pidgin French in the open. All of them, whether boys or girls, always spoke Breton, at home, at Sunday school, in the fields when they looked after the cattle or went searching for birds' eggs, in fact everywhere, except at school, because there they were told off or even punished by being made to wear the 'symbol' or the 'wooden cow' as soon as a word of their mother tongue passed their lips. Unfortunately, this situation is no longer the case with youngsters, at least in my area, in Tregor.

Thierry Chatel

An Tokarn, *1987*

E-tro ar bloaz 2004, ar galleg a oa en e zalc'h Bro-Dreger, Bro-Wened ha Bro-Gernev hogos holl.

"Emañ ar marv ouzh hor gedal," a lare gerioù Brezhoneg Bro-Leon."

– Aret em eus, aret e-leizh. Ha c'hwi bemdez netra ne raec'h!" a responte gerioù ar Galleg galloudus.

Goude un amzer a freuz hag a reuz e savas un tammig peoc'h. "Daoust pegen izel eo kouezhet ar Brezhoneg en amzer hiziv, n'on ket gouest da zisfiziout anezhañ a-grenn," a lare Kelenner diwezhañ Kevrenn geltiek Skol-Veur Brest.

Bro-Leon a voe liñvet d'he zro... e 2077. Trec'h e oa ar Galleg. Den ne reas dezhañ divarchiñ ur paz eus an hent en doa kemeret.

Pevar bloaz warn-ugent a oa aet e-biou abaoe m'edo ar Galleg e Bro-Leon a-bezh. Ne oa ket troet ken al Leoniz gant al labour. A-barzh pell e voe flutet ganto danvez ar vro. E-lec'h ur bobl nerzhus, ne gaved nemet ur bobl doc'hor. Pe walenn 'ta a oa kouezhet war douaroù Bro-Leon? Gwall-gemeret e oa bet gant un aer-ouant?

Ar brud en devoa va zad da vezañ un den didalvez ha ne rae ket kalz a dra eus ar mintin betek an noz. Hogen eñ a dride en e galon ar youl d'ober un draig bennak evit e Vro. Un deiz e oa deut en ti gant un tokarn elektronek kalfichet gantañ e-pad an noz. Pebezh fromadenn pa glevis digantañ e venoz! Lakaat a reas an tokarn war e benn...

E deod a oa distagellet mat. Komz brezhoneg 'rae koulz ha tud a veve e 1900!... Ha kompren a raen...

Ul labouradeg a voe savet gant va zad. Gwerzhet e voe gantañ tokarnoù a-vili-adoù. Adsevel a reas va zad ar Brezhoneg ha nerzh ar Vro. Bremañ e kaver e pep lec'h e Breizh tud a laka un tokarn elektronek war o fenn evit komz Yezh ar Vro. Gant an tokarn-se e voe gwarezet Breizh ouzh alouberezh ar Saozneg pa voe beuzet Bro-C'hall a-bezh gant ar Yezh-se.... e tro ar bloaz 2222.

Translation

The Helmet, *1987*

Around the year 2004, French held sway over the greatest part of the districts of Tréguier, Vannes, and in Cornouaille.

"Death is on our heels," said the words of the district of Léon.

"We have toiled hard, toiled away constantly while you were doing nothing at all!" replied the words of powerful French.

After arguing and quarrelling for a while, some kind of peace was restored. "Although Breton is now at an all time low, I haven't lost all hopes for it," said the only remaining lecturer in the Celtic Department of the University of Brest.

The district of Léon was overwhelmed in its turn.... in 2077. French was victorious. No one had been able to make it deviate a single step from the path it had taken.

Twenty-four years had passed since French prevailed in the whole district of Léon. Its people were no longer keen to work. The local resources were squandered in no time. This formerly dynamic community was now moribund. Which calamity had befallen the land of Léon? Had a dragon laid it to waste?

My father had the reputation of being an idle man who did very little from morning to night. He had however this deep-seated longing to do something or other for his Country. One day he came into the house holding the electronic helmet he had fabricated during the night. What a thrill when he mentioned his idea to me! He put the helmet on his head...

He spoke with ease. He spoke Breton as well as the people who lived in 1900! And, what is more, I understood...

My father opened a factory. He sold millions of helmets, breathed new life into Breton and revitalised the Country. Nowadays one finds that, everywhere in Brittany, people put an electronic helmet on their heads in order to speak the country's language. Thanks to this helmet, Brittany was protected from the invasion of English, whereas France was totally taken over by that Language... around the year 2222.

Yann-Loeiz Emili

Prizoniad er Ruhr, *1992* (Lodenn)

Rouez oa, en ur c'hamp boch, ar re a rae o stalig o-unan: un ingrouin bennak, marteze, ha ne zesko biken petra eo bevañ, pa n'en deus ket desket eno. E nep lec'h all muioc'h eget eno, e gwirionez, ne'z eus tro da welout pegement e c'hell an eil kaout ezhomm eus egile pa soñjer an nebeutañ.

Peurvuiañ ec'h en em gleved daou, tri, pevar asambles, pe ouzhpenn, evit lakaat e boutin kement tra a deue eus Frañs; hag etre tud eus ar memes bro ec'h en em gleved an aliesañ: aesoc'h eo en em glevout, e gwirionez, pa vez demdost ar memes boazamañchoù. Evidomp-ni dreist-holl, Bretoned, n'en em santemp en hon aez nemet kenetrezomp; ha pa gavemp tro da ragachat en hor yezh, ar galleg a veze lezet a-gostez. En ur c'hamp evel hon hini – hag a oa ennañ tud eus a bep seurt bro, Saozon, Gallaoued, Beljed, Rused, Serbed hag all, hep kontañ ar Voched hon diwalle, – ne raed van ebet o klevout un den o tremen e-biou deoc'h o komz ur yezh ha ne gomp0rened ket. Evelato, o klevout paotred an Nort o komz en o galleg ken farsus, em eus bet lavaret ouzhin va-unan naouspet a wech: pegement n'eo ket kaeroc'h hor yezh vrezhonek eget ar c'hozh galleg-saout a deu gant ar re-se! Pa deuent da lavarout deomp: "*Mi j'te compreno nein,*" e c'hellemp respont dezho: "N'eus netra 'zrol e kement-se, pa'z eo gwir hor yezh n'eo ket hoc'h hini. Mes ar pezh a zo farsus eo ne c'hellfemp-ni ket, daoust deomp gouzout galleg, dont a-benn da c'houzout peseurt a c'hoantait lavarout deomp." Ha ne'm beus ket gellet en em virout da drueziñ war un darn eus Breizhiz yaouank a-vremañ, a ra fae war yezh o mammoù, hag a gav gwelloc'h drailhañ, en un doare iskis a-wechoù, ur galleg ha ne gomprenont ket – ur galleg ha ne gomprenint gwelloc'h nemet en dervezh ma vezo desket dezho, er skolioù, lakaat anezhañ e kemm gant ar yezh o deus desket war barlenn o mamm.

Translation

Prisoner in the Ruhr, *1992* (Extract)

In a German prisoner of war camp, those who kept themselves to themselves were a rarity. There may have been one or two weirdoes who will never learn what life is about as they did not manage to learn it in the camp, but, if you think about it, there is no better place to realise how much an individual needs other people.

By and large, groups of two, three, four or more, got together and pooled whatever they received from France. These groups were usually made up of fellow countrymen as it is easier to get on with people who have more or less the same habits in common. This was especially true for us Bretons, who only felt at ease amongst ourselves. Every time we found a way to chatter away in our language, French was left aside. In a prisoner camp like ours, which drew together all sorts of nationalities, English, French, Belgian, Russian, Serbs and others, without mentioning the Germans who guarded us, no one found it strange to come upon people who spoke a language they did not understand. However, when I met men from the north of France speaking their very odd French, I often thought how much more beautiful our Breton language was compared to the pidgin French they spoke. When they came towards us and said: "*Mi j'te compreno nein*" [Me can't understand you nein"] we were able to say to them "That is no surprise, as we speak a different language from yours. What we find strange is that we cannot, even though we know French, manage to make out what you are trying to tell us." Furthermore, I could not prevent myself from taking pity on a lot of young Bretons who, these days, look down on their mother tongue and prefer to make do, often in a very peculiar way, with a French language that they do not master and that they will only learn to master properly when it will be taught in school side by side with the language they have learnt on their mother's knees.

Roparz Hemon

Kilañ ha mont war-raok, *1953*

Kiladenn

Ur sell ouzh Breizh a zo a-walc'h da ziskouez ar giladenn a zo bet graet abaoe 1944.

Berr-ha-berr, adkouezhet eo er stad ma edo war-dro 1900. Ar renerien wellañ eus an amzer etre 1919 ha 1944 a zo bet lazhet pe o deus ranket kuitaat ar vro. Ar gouelioù n'int mui nemet maskaradennoù. Ar C'helc'hioù hag ar Bodadoù, an

touller-bez a zo roue enno.

Ur skouer hepken: e roll-labour kevredigezhioù nevez e welomp: 1) an dañs, 2) ar sonerezh, 3) ar gwiskamant, 4) an istor, 5) ar yezh.

Ya, ar yezh a vez lakaet e renk an traoù da studiañ... ma'z eus amzer...

Da lavarout eo, al labour a vez graet e galleg, hep an disterañ mezh. Hag ar brezhoneg ne vez graet anv anezhañ nemet evel un danvez-studi e-giz ar re all, mat evit an nebeut tud iskis na ouzont na kanañ, na dañsal, na seniñ ar biniou, na gwiskañ ur jiletenn vrodet hag un tog voulouz, pe un davañjer seiz hag ur c'hoef dantelezh d'en em ziskouez dirak an douristed.

Ur ger kaer a zo bet kavet: Foklor. Komzomp galleg ha skrivomp galleg kement ha ma karomp. Gant ar Foklor e vimp saveteet!

Reiñ lamm d'ar galleg

An holl koulskoude a lavar ez int "a-du gant ar brezhoneg". Ha gwir, mar deo a-walc'h evit bezañ "a-du gant ar brezhoneg" reiñ dezhañ un tammig lec'h, dek linenn amañ ahont war ur gazetenn, pe skrivañ pennadoù e galleg diwar e benn, ez int "a-du".

Evit neb en deus soñj mat, bezañ a-du gant ar brezhoneg a zo un dra disheñvel. Bez' ez eo ober eus ar brezhoneg ar yezh n'eus nemeti e Breizh, ha, sklaer eo, reiñ lamm d'ar galleg.

An holl yezhoù keltiek hag an holl vroioù keltiek a zo tost o vont da goll, hag an abeg pennañ eo: n'o deus ket an darn vuiañ eus ar Gelted komprenet e rankont ober gant o yezh keltiek ha diskar ar yezh estren, diskar ar saozneg e Breizh-Veur hag en Iwerzhon; war an Douar-Bras, diskar ar galleg.

(Ar galleg a rank bezañ diskaret ha distrujet e Breizh.) Kentañ a zo d'ober eo e ziskar en Emsav. Etrezek ar pal-se hon eus labouret start etre 1919 ha 1944.

Hag e 1950, petra welomp? Emsaverien o c'hallegañ etrezo adarre, koulz ha gwashoc'h eget emsaverien an naontekvet kantved.

Petra ober?

Lezel ar folkloristed da foklorachañ e galleg kement ha ma karont, ha bodañ en un Emsav nevez tud ar Brezhoneg.

Menozioù-stur an Emsav Nevez

1. Chom hep ober gant ar galleg.
2. Bodañ kement emsaver ha kement kevredigezh a ra gant ar brezhoneg hepken.
3. Mont eeun d'ar vrezhonegerien, ur milion anezho.

Ober disheñvel a zo koll amzer, ha koll Breizh.

Translation

Decline and Progress, *1953*

Decline

A look at Brittany shows easily enough the decline which has happened since 1944.

To put it briefly, Brittany is back to where she was around the year 1900. The ones who worked most between 1919 and 1944 have been killed or have had to leave the country. The festivals have become masquerades. The grave-digger now rules over Breton Societies and Clubs.

Let me give a single example: in the list of activities of the new associations, one finds: 1) dancing; 2) music; 3) traditional costumes; 4) history; 5) language...

The language is indeed listed under things worth studying ... if one can find the time.

In other words, the work is done, openly and without second thought, through the medium of French. Breton is only mentioned as one of many subjects worth studying, good enough for the few peculiar people who cannot sing, dance, play the bagpipes, put on an embroidered jacket and a velvet hat, or a silk apron and a lace headdress, to exhibit themselves in front of tourists.

A nice word has been invented: Folklore. Let us speak French and write French to our heart's content. We shall be saved by Folklore.

Getting rid of French

However everyone says that they "agree with Breton". As long as "agreeing with Breton" means giving it a bit of space, ten lines here and there in a newspaper, or writing articles in French on the subject of Breton, they indeed "agree".

For anyone whose memory is not too short, agreeing with Breton means something different. It means making Breton the only language in Brittany and, in consequence, getting rid of French.

All the Celtic languages and all the Celtic countries are on the verge of disappearance for the following main reason: the majority of Celts have not understood that they need to use their Celtic language and wipe out the foreign one, wipe out English in Great Britain and in Ireland; on the continent, this means wiping out French. French needs to be wiped out and obliterated in Brittany.

The first thing one needs to do is to wipe it out within the Breton Movement. This was the aim at which we worked hard between 1919 and 1944. But in 1950, what do we see? Breton militants are again speaking French among themselves, as much or even more than their nineteenth-century counterparts did.

What should we do? Let the folklorists folklorise in French to their hearts' content and regroup the defenders of Breton in a new network.

Guidelines for the New Emsav:

1. Do not use French.
2. Bring together every single activist and every single association that only use Breton.
3. Go and meet the million Breton native speakers.

Doing anything else is a waste of time and will lead to the disappearance of Brittany.

Arzhig

Klemm ar Brezhoneg ouzh ur Brezhoneger, *2004*

'Al laou a beg start o genoù
Ouzh divrec'h treut va c'hemmadurioù.'

'Ouzh al laou on deut da voaziañ;
Kaer em befe klask o spazhañ.'

'Ar c'hwen a lamm, a-viliadoù,
Dreist divrec'h izil va zroiennoù.'

'Na dister 'kavan laou ha c'hwen;
Problemoù all en deus mab-den.'

'Ar gorioù 'sav, bras ha kornek,
War dremm eskernek va geriaoueg.'

'Ne gav ket din e vent ken stank;
Din out mibin, yac'h ha yaouank.'

'Al lenkern blot, ouzh va diskar,
A sun e kof va zroioù-lavar.'

'Ha koulskoude n'int ket marvel;
Bezomp fur, ha c'hoazh naturel!'

'Gant an tagn ez on mac'hagnet,
Va holl yezhadur digroc'hennet.'

'Goût a rez n'on 'met rambreer;
Ker e koustfe kaout louzeier.'

'Ar c'hontron 'lonk, rok ha divezh,
Takennoù gwad ha talm va zaol-mouezh.'

'Na sellomp ket ouzh an tu koll,
Rak te zo priziet, goude holl.'

'Gant katar, lin, glaour ha goulioù
E tremper korf va holl frazennoù.'

'Selaou 'ta – me 'gar ac'hanout,
Met n'eus ket amzer d'ober tout.'

Translation

Complaints from the Breton Language to a Breton Speaker, 2004

'Lice grab, teeth in motion,
At the thin arm of every mutation.'

'I have got used to lice;
Anyway, they are too small for me to slice.'

'Fleas jump in their millions
Over the spindly limbs of my expressions.'

'Lice and fleas hardly count;
Man has others problems to worry about.'

'Abscesses grow, big and scabby,
On the emaciated face of my vocabulary.'

'I don't think they are that many;
To me you are agile, young and healthy.'

'Squashy tapeworms in me do hide,
Sucking at my idioms from the inside.'

'Yet they survive. Be practical!
This in fact is quite "normal!"'

'With ringworms I am totally crippled;
My grammar is all but dismembered.'

'You know, I am only a day-dreamer;
But it would cost a lot to call in the doctor.'

'Maggots, brazen and arrogant,
Gobble up the blood and pulse of my accent.'

*'Let's not look on the bad side of things
After all you are still part of our belongings.'*

'Mucus, pus, spittle and wounds – it is no pretence –
Cover the whole body of their every sentence.'

*'Listen to me: – I do love you,
But have other things to do.'*

Women Writing About Women

As in most languages the voice of women is not as strong as that of men. Lack of education, social expectations, daily duties, the fact that the literary scene has always been dominated by men have been evoked to explain the relative dearth of works by women. Until fairly recently most Breton women tended to use their skills in the shadow of male writers, as story tellers or reviewers of other people's works. Those who did offer their own work to a wider public did not often publish more than a few pages. Nevertheless a few women did achieved some measure of fame, amongst them Filomena Kadored, Añjela Duval, Ivona Laorañs, Loeiza ar Meliner in the field of poetry, also Anna Vezmeur who wrote a history of Brittany. By and large however women's writing up to the present day tends to be very personal, concentrating on recollections and childhood memories rather than on works of fiction.

Benead who published the first of what was meant to be a two-part article on 'Women in Breton Literature' (cf *Al Liamm* No 7, March-April 1948) gives a very positive – if controversial – picture of the way in which women are described by men in their works. The controversial aspect of her analysis must have been made plain to her as the promised follow-up article never appeared. In 1968 in the 126th issue of the same magazine she offers a study on birds, "a problem – not as risky as that of .... women – which I have not yet been able to solve properly."

The literary scene is now more open to women than it ever was. Poetry and childhood memories still form the majority of the works published yet the range is widening. In 1995 Annaig Renault made her entry into a new field with the publication of *Dec'h zo re bell dija*, the first novel ever written by a woman in Breton. Others such as Annaig Rozmor are making an impact on Breton theatre. Although it would be difficult to find a loud feminist voice amongst women writers, they sometimes deal with issues of particular interest to women such as birth, lesbianism, the place of women in society... as will be seen from some of the extracts below.

Naig Rozmor

Eur Mister joaiuz, *1977*

Euz peleh 'ta teu ar c'hoant iskiz
A darz em hreiz
Pa harpez war va zellou da zellou?

Euz peleh e teu a skrij
A red dindan va hrohenn
Da heul da vizied ouz va floura?
Hag ar gliz, dre guz, ouz va ferlezenna?

Petra 'm laka klañv ha terziennet souden?
Petra 'ra da hinkinou va divorzed tridal?
Petra 'ra din alteri etre da zaouarn?
Ha skei war va 'fenn
Hag en em rei, o pegement!
Hag en em renta d'az faltazi?

Med, perak klask kompren?
Evel ma tiskenn an heol er mor digor
Da hada eun deiz nevez,
Deus da honid ganin eun eost a joa.

Translation

A Mystery of Love, *1977*

Where does the strange desire
Which bursts in me come from
When your eyes rest on my eyes?

Where does the quivering
Which runs under my skin come from
As your fingers caress me?
And from where those secret beads of dew?

What makes me suddenly ill and feverish?
What makes my slender thighs quiver?
What makes me so elated under your touch?
Makes me thump my head,
And give myself so completely
And surrender to your fantasy?

But why try to understand?
Like the sun coming down on the open seas
To sow the seeds of a new day,
Come and reap with me a harvest of love.

Annaig Renault

Divroet, *1993* (Lodenn)

Boas e oamp da vale tro-dro d'an Iskonk. Met n'eo ket alies e oamp-hi hon-daou. Bepred gant tud all. Da zaou-ugent vloaz pe dost e oamp lent evel bugale. Fresk 'oa an aer d'an eur-se. Un avelig a save evel ma c'hwezh anal ur babig o kousket, habask. Ar seurt enkrez a santen abaoe ma oa erruet Mikael du-mañ a oa nijet kuit. Dastum a reas Mikael ur vleunienn penn-glas. He lakaat a reas en e c'henou.

– Ha plijet out bet gant ar bloavezh labour aet e-biou? Em eus goulennet digantañ.

– Eürus-tre. Nemet ez eo skuizhus labourat e-unan. Ne c'hell ket ma zad skoazellañ ac'hanon kement-se bremañ.

– Poent bras dit kavout unan bennak, neuze?

O lâret an dra-se, e seblante din bezañ kasi noazh dirazañ. Ruziet em eus sur a-walc'h. Er wenodenn e veze klevet bremañ trouz ar mor o ruilhañ war ar bili. Ken dous e oa din an trouz-se, galvet ken alies e-pad ar goañv gant ma c'halon... Erruet oamp war an draezhenn, 'benn ar fin. Gleb oa an traezh. Roudoù hor pazioù a dec'he kuit en a-dreñv, pell-tre, kichen-ha-kichen. Mut e chome Mikael.

N'em boa ket bet tro d'e welet alies e-pad an hañv. Beuzet e oa bet gant al labour. E skoazellet am boa evit labourioù 'zo. Ken plijus oa bet an devezhioù-se. E welet em boa en e vleud gant ar mor a dud o skoazellañ anezhañ.

A-daol-trumm, e teuas da soñj din ma buhez e Pariz; ar monedonea etre ma randdi ha ma burevioù. Ha ma oa plijus al labour e oa ret gouzañv gouli buhez un divroadez. En harlu diouzhin, diouzh donder ma ene ha ma bro.

– Ma ouefes pegen alies e soñjan em c'horn-bro, ma faour-kaezh Mikael!

– N'eo ket ken displijus-se buhez Pariz, memes tra? Tud 'vez gwelet eno?

– Arabat dit ijinañ an dra-se! N'hon eus ket amzer da gejañ gant tud all en un doare gwirion. Ar re a labouran ganto a red buan-tre d'ar gêr goude o labour. Me ivez am eus ezhomm adkavout ul lec'h evit diskuizhañ. Hag e tistroan buan bemnoz. Evidon ez eo buhez ar c'hêrioù bras ur mallozh ruz. Digas a ra ar c'hleñved d'an ene. Hag un deiz e tihunez diene. Disoñjet t'eus petra oa keneilded etre an dud.

– Me 'soñje din e oa anavezet Bretoned all ganit? Ur bern a zo du-hont, memes tra.

– Ya, un niver bras a Vretoned a zo du-hont. Met tapet o deus ar c'hleñved-se, re alies. Anavezet em eus ur plac'h yaouank hag a oa mignonez din. Kroget eo, un deiz bennak he mousc'hoarzh da deuziñ. Ken dislivet e oa he c'hroc'hen ma veze gwelet he nerzh-kalon o vont diouti. Douaret eo bet; marvet gant an naonegezh a ganoù

laboused, a livioù frank bleuñv 'zo. Flouradenn an avel en he blev a rae diouer
dezhi. Pa ne vez ket maget ken an ene, e varv an dud…
— Netra ne vank dit, memes tra…
Paouezet e oa da gomz. Ne oa ket tu din respont. Ken bras oa ma sec'hed a
vuhez. Ne oa ket ur ger pe ur frazenn evit e zisplegañ. Ur jestr en dije diskouezet e
vent divuzul met n'em boa ket desket seurt jestroù em bugaleaj. Ha traoù 'zo na
c'heller ket deskiñ pe krediñ ober pa'z eo aet kuit da vat oad an dieubidigezh, oad ar
vugaleaj.

Mut e chomemp. N'eo ket aes bezañ e toullbac'h an dud deuet. Gouelani a
huche a-us deomp. Teñval e teue an oabl da vezañ hag em eus bet ur gridienn.
— Riv 'teus? Distroomp eta!

Ne oa ket Mikael en e vleud. Ken aes e oa da welet an trefu a oa ennon ma'n em
sante sammet gantañ eñ ivez. Tapet hon eus hent an distro. Keuz am eus bet da
vezañ lavaret gerioù em bije bet c'hoant diverkañ. Met kiriek oc'h, er vuhez, eus ar
pezh hoc'h eus lavaret. Betek ar ger diwezhañ. Nebeut a amzer a chome din da
vezañ gantañ ha moc'het em boa pep tra. Fuloret e oan.
— Skrivañ a ri din ar pezh t'eus divizet evit da labour?
— Ya. Evel-just.

Perak? A soñjen. Netra ne cheñcho. N'out ket gouest paour-kaezh Mikael, da
zisplegañ ar pezh a zo pouezus evidout. Neuze. Erruet e oamp dirak ma liorzhig.
Koantik e oa ha sioul. Aet 'oa ar gwesped da gousket. Pelloc'h, el liorzh e-kichen
marteze, e kane ur skrilh. Kan, kan, bihanig! Ra vo klevet da vouezh gant ar bed a-
bezh!

Harpet e oa Mikael ouzh moger an ti. Sellet en deus pell, pell war-du
dremmwelioù kuzh ha leuniet eo bet e zaoulagad a-daol-drumm gant ur
ganaouenn ne oa ket anavezet ganin.
— Un dra a-bouez am eus da lâret dit hag a gavi iskis…
Ur spi divent a darzhas ennon.
— Pa 'm eus anzavet dit e oa re ziaes din labourat ma-unan. Ne chomin ket ma-
unan.

Mousc'hoazhin a raen dezhañ. Gant piv 'teus c'hoant chom, Mikael? Gant piv e
chomi, a gane ma soñjoù.
— Eurediñ a rin ar bloaz-mañ.

Paouez a reas ar bed da dreiñ, amzer d'en em silañ e kendentadurioù ar vuhez e-
pad un eilenn.
— Dimeziñ a rin gant Mariannig Kemenner e miz Kerzu. Da greisteiz Bro-C'hall
eo aet d'ober ur staj labour-douar e-pad miz Gouere. Abaoe deiz he ganedigezh
ec'h anavezan anezhi.

Translation

Exiled, *1993* (Extract)

We usually went for a walk to Iskonk, but the two of us were not often alone. Always with other people. At the age of nearly forty we were as shy as children. At that hour the air was cool. A breeze was blowing, as light as the breathing of a sleeping baby. The mild anxiety that filled me since Mikael has arrived home had now gone. Mikael picked a blue flower and put it in his mouth.

– Are you pleased with the past year's work? I asked him

– Yes, very happy, except for the fact that I find it tiring to work alone. My father can't help me as much now.

– Well! Now is the time for you to find someone else.

As I said this, I felt as if I was half-naked in front of him. I am certain that I blushed. On the path, we could hear the sea rolling over the pebbles. How pleasant was this noise to my ears! How often I had tried to recall it in my heart during the winter months! We finally arrived on the beach. The sand was wet. Our footsteps, side by side, were imprinted in it, right into the distance, far behind us. Mikael was silent.

I did not often get the opportunity to see him during that summer. He had too much to do. I had helped him on occasions, and those days had been very pleasant. I had seen him in his element amongst the crowd of people who had come to give him a hand.

Suddenly, I remembered my life in Paris. The toing and froing between my flat and my offices. Although I enjoyed my job, I had to endure the life of an expatriate, exiled from myself, from my soul, from my country.

– If only you knew how often I think of this place, dear Mikael!

– Surely, life in Paris is not as bad as that. There are plenty of people to meet.

– That's not the case! There is no time to get to know other people. Those I work with rush back home after their day's work. I also feel the need for a place where I can rest and get back home quickly. I think that city life is a plague. It attacks your very being and one day you wake up soulless, having forgotten what companionship was.

– I thought that you knew Breton people. Many of them live there, don't they?

– Yes. Many Bretons live there, but the majority of them have been contaminated. I used to have a young woman as a friend. One day, her smile started to disappear. Her skin was so white that you could see the will to live leaving her. She was buried. She died from lack of bird songs, of brightly coloured flowers. She missed the caress of the wind in her hair. When there is nothing to feed one's inner self, one dies...

– You have everything there, however.

He stopped talking. I could not answer him. My thirst for life was so strong. There were no words to describe it. A gesture would have been enough to show how deep it was, but I had not learnt to show my feelings when I was young. There are things that one cannot learn or do when the age of youth, that of freedom, is well and truly behind you.

We stayed silent. It is not easy to be in the prison of adulthood. Seagulls were screaming above our heads. The sky was darkening and I shuddered.

– You're feeling the cold. Let's go back.

Mikael did not feel at ease. My agitation was so obvious that it had reached him too. We turned back. I regretted having said these words and wished I could take them back. But in life one is responsible for what has been said, right to the very last word. I had little time left in his company and I had made a mess of everything. I felt irritated.

– Will you write and tell me what decision you make concerning your work?

– Yes, of course.

Why? I thought. Nothing will change. You are incapable, dear Mikael, of explaining what is important to you. So?

We had reached my front garden. It was well-kept and silent. The bees had gone to sleep. Further on, and it could have been in next door's garden, a grasshopper was singing. Sing! Sing, little one! May the whole world hear your voice.

Mikael was leaning against the wall of the house. He looked in the distance, towards unknown horizons, and suddenly his eyes filled with a song that was unknown to me.

– I have something important to tell you. You'll find it strange, though...

I was filled with immense hope.

– I did tell you that I find it hard to work on my own. Well! I shan't stay on my own.

I smiled at him. My thoughts were singing a song of joy: "Who do you wish to share your life with, Mikael? With whom will you live?"

– I am getting married next year.

The earth stopped turning for a second to give it time to tweak back into the cogwheel of life.

– I shall marry Mariannig Kemener in December. She is spending the month of July on a farming course in the south of France. I have known her since she was born.

Maguy Kerisit

Bali ar gouleier, *1999*

O tremen em c'hichen edout
Ha koulskoude n'em eus ket galvet
Marteze e ouien ar respont
Aesoc'h 'oa din sellout ouzh ar gouleier
Gouleier kreiz-kêr
Liv al levenez warno
Gouleier o teverañ em daoulagad

Ha te o tremen em c'hichen
Stardet 'm eus ma mantell en-dro din
Yen eo dre-amañ
Neketa?
Gwelloc'h eo mont d'ar gêr
Met pelec'h 'mañ ar gêr?
Amañ ez eus gouleier...
Hag en aer lemm 'vel un aotenn
E kavan dirak ma daoulagad
Eñvor da skeudenn
O tremen.

Translation

Street of the Lights, *1999*

You passed by my side
And yet I did not call you
Maybe I knew the response
It was easier for me to look at the lights
The lights of the town centre
Which looked so cheerful
Lights which streamed down my eyes
And you passing by my side
I wrapped my coat around me
It is cold here
Isn't it?
It is better for me to go home
But where is home?
Here there are lights...
In the air, sharp as a razor,
I find in front of my eyes
The memory of your shadow
Passing by.

Pierrette Kermoal

Karantez, *2000* (Lodenn)

Bep beure ez aen tre e sal ar gelennerion, liv an trec'h war va dremm. En tu-hont da vorad ar c'heinoù du e spurmanten da sell glas, hag e oa tarzh-an-deiz; mousc'hoarzhin a raen, hag e teues war-du ennon. Dihejet gant kas ar c'heinoù teñval, e tostaes c'hoazh. Va dremm stouet war-du da hini, ha te o kontañ din da skolidi, ez even da sinadurezh aouraval. Mont a raemp er-maez a-gevret, ha treuziñ ar porzh, hag emzivizout. Met da hesk ez eas buan danvez ar C'hwec'hved: goude div sizhunvezh e oa nijet kuit da chal a zeskardez. N'hor boa netra ken da eskemmañ.

Neuze e komzen: va soñjoù, va albac'hennoù, va lennadennoù. Ne oa ket evit o rannañ ganit. Nemet lusk ar gaozeadenn a c'horrekae hon c'herzhed, ha ne veze ket echu va frazenn e koulz, ret-mat dit chom a-sav un hanter vunutenn dirak da sal neuze, ha sevel eeunik davedon da zaoulagad ken glas, evit ur c'himiad un eurvezh. Ne c'houzañven e nep doare ouzh da guitaat evit un eurvezh. Nag evit un devezh, pe veur a hini. Nemet war-lerc'h un eurvezh, un devezh, un sizhunvezh, da adkavout a walc'he pep c'hoant ennon. Dour hag heol e oas; te a oa aze, dous ha diogel, bev, fetis, douarel, ha padal o skediñ, aourheñvel, mezvus.

... Hag e konten dit ar bed, ha va sell war ar bed; hag e tisplegen, hag ez ouzhpennen, hag ez arguzen... Hag e oa Baldwin pe Kundera, ar re zu er Stadoù Unanet, ha me 'oar... Ken buan e'm eus dibunet dit va rambreoù war saviad ar merc'hed. Ne oa ket evit komz dit diwar da benn. Respont a raes? N'ouzon ket. A c'hell bezañ. 'M eus aon ne selaouen ket. Sellout a raen ouzh da vuzelloù o stummañ ar gerioù; chom a raen va sell o kantren en egor lufr da dal. Pezh a dremene a-dreñv d'an talse? Ne oan ket deuriet. Va dislavaret 'c'h eus ur wech bennak? Sur a-walc'h. C'hoarzhin a raen. Ennon e save ar c'harm hud: "Mir da vennozhioù, Dominique a galon; soñj pezh a garez, evel-just; marteze emañ ar gwir ganit, piv 'oar. Soñj, ar gwir 'c'h eus da soñjal. Prof din da zremm rous-mel, aour roz da zivjod, dameuc'h da c'houloù-deiz, va c'hoantenn ken dous, ken brav, ken flour, ha voulouzennek."

Trellet da vat... tañva da sked...

O lavarout e oa sac'het va c'harr, e oan deuet a-benn ur wech pe ziv da ober hent ganit e-barzh da hini. Gouzout a raen pelec'h edos o chom, ha da ijinañ a raen e'z ranndi karrezek er c'harter nevez. Gwaz ha bugel 'z poa – ur bugel a oad gant va hini, pe war-dro: un nebeud goulennoù 'm boa graet. Karet a-walc'h 'm bije gwelout penaos e veves ganto. O anavezout? Nann. Nemet e vijent bet parzh ac'hanout evit gwir. Met ne greden ket. Petra o dije gallet deskiñ din diwar da benn? Petra a ouient muioc'h egedon? Pa edo amañ pep tra, e roz mel da groc'hen, e boulder glas da zaoulagad, galv dieil, douar va fromesa. O! tremen, ya tremen en tu all d'ar melezour-se!

Hag un deiz e chomas teñval sal ar gelennerion. E goueled ar pezh edos, evel boaz. Mousc'hoarzhin a rejout din, evel boaz. Hogen ne voe mui na tarzh na trec'h. Tamm luc'h ebet gant ar c'hroc'hen-se. Demer an daoulagad-se. Netra ken ne skede. Hag aze e vanen saouzanet ha yen, evel unan he dije kollet a-greiz-holl ar bed strink a oa bet profet dezhi. Diskredik, e klaskis e-pad daou, tri devezh adkavout entan ar mizvezhioù kent, an eienenn voemus a'm lakae mezvez. Aner. Fulenn ebet. Steuziet ar voem. Dipitet, ginet, e sellen ouzh an dremm c'hoular-se dindan rizenn ar blev plat. Eus ar muzelloù-se e teue lec'hiennoù boutin, a'm enoee. War ar marc'had e'z poa mourroù. Neuze e trois kein, rak gant da bersonelezh ne raen ket an disterañ forzh.

Ha setu ma tarzhas ar wirionez: sed aze doare ar baotred d'hon c'harout!
Ar moc'h!

Translation

Love, *2000* (Extract)

Every morning I walked into the teachers' staff room, looking triumphant. Over
the tide of black backs I would catch sight of your blue eyes and it was dawn. I
would smile and you came towards me picking your way through the flow of dark
backs. My face tilted towards yours as you talked about your pupils, I drunk your
juicy freshness. We would leave together and cross the playground, talking. But the
subject of the first form soon dried up: after two weeks, the apprehension you had
felt as a new teacher had disappeared. We had nothing more to share.

So I started talking, about what I thought, what obsessed me, what I read. It was
not to share them with you. But the heat of conversation slowed our steps down.
My last words were never finished on time and you had to stop for half a minute at
your classroom door and then openly raise your pure blue eyes to me to take your
leave for an hour. I had no problem leaving you for an hour, for a day, for several.
Yet after an hour, a day or a week, being once again with you washed away all my
longings. You were water and sunshine to me. You were there, gentle and self-
assured, alive, tangible, earthly, and yet you shone, gold-like, intoxicating.

... So I told you about the world and my views on the world. I explained,
enlarged, argued my points about Baldwin and Kundera, about the blacks in the
United States or whatever. I was also swift to tell you my thoughts on the position
of women. But I was not trying to talk to you about yourself. Did you reply? I don't
know. Maybe you did. I'm afraid I was not listening. I was looking at your lips shaping words; my eyes were wandering over the bright space of your forehead. What
was going on behind this forehead? It did not matter to me. Did you ever contra-
dict me? Probably. I laughed. A mysterious cry was rising in me: "Keep on thinking, darling Dominique; think whatever you like, of course; you may be right, who
knows? Think. You've got the right to think. Just give me your honey-coloured
face, the golden pink of your cheeks, mirror-image of dawn, my lovely, so gentle,
so beautiful, so soft, so velvety."

Dazzled for good... I taste your brightness...

Once or twice, alleging that my car had broken down, I had managed to get a lift
from you. I knew where you lived and imagined you in your four-sided flat in the
new quarter of town. You had a husband and a child, a child of roughly the same
age as mine. I had asked a few questions. I would have liked to see for myself how
you lived with them, but get to know them? No, unless they were really part of you
and I did not think so. What could I have learned from them about you? What
more did they know that I did not? Everything was there, in the pink honey of your
skin, in the blue transparency of your eyes, matchless beacons and promised land.
If only, yes, if only I could get to the other side of the mirror!

But one day, the staff room stayed dark. You were in the back of the room, as usual. You smiled at me, as usual. But the brightness and feeling of elation had gone. No more luminescence in that skin. Those eyes were opaque. Nothing was shining any more. I stayed there, stunned and cold, like a girl suddenly losing the sparkling globe given to her as a present. Filled with disbelief, I tried for two or three days to rekindle the fire of the past months, to revive the magic spring which made my head spin. In vain. No more sparks. The magic has gone. Disappointed, I looked dourly at the bland face framed by flat hair. Trite remarks which bored me fell from those lips. What is more, you had a moustache. So, I turned my back on you, because I was not in the least interested in your personality.

Then the truth exploded: this is how men love us!

The pigs!

Meavenn

Merc'hed Brest, *1942*

Eürus ar merc'hed savet e Brest dindan ar glav war gafe tomm ha bara kras, rak n'eus tu ebet ken da lavarout muioc'h a zroug diwar o fenn. Divalav int, difeson, divergont, fougeüs, hegasus, heugus, komerezed, teodoù fall; kement ha kement a zo bet lavaret ma chomont bremañ diseblant, ha tost da grediñ n'eus ket par dezho er bed a-bezh. Ha n'eus ket evel-just. N'eo ket vijent marteze, skouerioù a basiant-ed. Ne vint ket lakaet da santezed evel Anna-Vari baour eus an Itali a selle dousik ouzh he gwaz o oa o teurel ar chaodourenn hag ar skudelloù dre ar prenestr, un noz. Ur Jani a anavezan he dije taolet he gwaz dezhi war-lerc'h ar chaodourenn aes a-walc'h, met n'he doa ket ezhomm d'hen ober o vezañ ma chome da bep taol mestrez war an dachenn, keit ha ma tiskenne an den skuizh ha sioul evit mont da gaout e vamm en he zi war an tu all d'an hent. "Ha peur ez aio da vamm da vouzhañ e ti da vamm-gozh?" a c'houlenne Jani. Nann, n'int ket skouerioù.

Soñj am eus eus honnezh vras a oa deuet en he gloar da gontañ deomp er skol e Brest penaos e ranker da vevañ, ivez, hag e welan c'hoazh he fri hir ha dismegañsus. Eviti kennebeut ne oa ket hor mammoù skouerioù a basianted, na skouerioù a netra, loudourenned e oant, setu. "Em bro-me," emezi. Nec'het e oa ganeomp-holl, hag ez eas kuit gant he fri war-zu he bro, hag a oa, dre chañs, bro an dud ha na walc'hont morse o skalerioù – evit ar peurrest, n'em eus ket gwelet. Loudourenned, ya 'ta – ha diouzhtu pa'z eus un tammig heol dindan ar c'houmoul, setu ar gweleoù er-maez, red-avel an ti, sailhadoù dour e pep lec'h, ha dav d'ar poull, gant ur samm ponner, betek gortoz unan eus ar barradoù "a-raok ar glav" a raio pri eus pep hentig kamm tro-dro d'ar gêr, ha botoù lous war al leur nevez-gwalc'het; – kalon a vije ret da gaout evit chom laouen.

★ ★ ★ ★

Merc'hed Brest, evel o gwazed, evel Brest, n'eo ket bet krouet evito ar vuhez sioul a renont – a renent kentoc'h. Merc'hed Brest a zo bet krouet evit kaout dousen-nadoù bugale war ur gompezenn ec'hon ha digenvez, hag ober burzhudoù. Kezeg-labour int, hag a zo bet lakaet da vevañ war o leve kalz a-raok o amzer; piv en o lec'h ne vije ket beuzet er c'hwervoni? Merc'hed Brest, dizaon dindan an oabl o kouezhañ – evel ma'z eo kouezhet re alies war o c'hein – a zo gouenn ar merc'hed brokus ha pinvidik, a oar reiñ buan ha prim kement tra o deus d'ar re a garont, gant ma ne vo ket lavaret Bennozh Doue dezho, gant ma ne vo ket klasket teneraat anezho, gant ma c'hellint krediñ e chomont stag dre gaer ha n'eo ket dre heg.

Translation

The Women of Brest, *1942*

Blessed are the women brought up in rainy Brest on hot coffee and dry bread as they cannot be denigrated anymore than they have already been: they are ugly, uncouth, insolent, hot-headed, irritating, loathsome, gossipy, spiteful. So much has been said that they are now totally unruffled and ready to think that they stand head and shoulders above the rest of humanity. And this is true, of course. Not that they are, for instance, models of patience. They will not find their place amongst saints, as poor Anna-Mari from Italy who, one evening, was looking mildly at her hus-band throwing the cooking pot and the plates out of the window. Jani, one of my acquaintances, would have thrown her husband out after the cauldron without any qualms, but she never felt the need to do so as she was always in charge in her own home, so much so that the tired and gentle man would go out to see his mother who lived on the other side of the street. "When will your mother go and sulk in your grand-mother's home?" used to ask Jani. No, they are not models.

I remember this lady who came in school, cloaked in her self-importance, to tell us how one should live, and I can still see her long and scornful nose. She too thought that our mothers were not models of patience nor models of anything. They were slatterns, full stop. "Where I come from," she used to say. We made her feel distraught. She left us, her nose pointing back to wherever she had come from, which was – who knows? – a place where staircases are never scrubbed clean. As for the rest, I have not been there to take a look. Why call them "slatterns" when, as soon as the sun appears from behind the clouds, the bed linen is put out, doors and windows are opened wide, bucketfuls of water are everywhere to be seen? And then off they go to the washing-place, with their heavy loads, before one of these "showers before the rain" which turn into quagmires all the winding paths leading home, not to mention the footprints soiling the recently washed floor. It would require a lot of willpower not to complain.

★ ★ ★ ★

The women of Brest, their husbands, even the town of Brest itself, have had to fight to gain the quiet life that they live, or rather that they used to live. The women

of Brest were born to give birth to dozens of children on a vast and deserted plain and to do miracles. They are beasts of burden who need to live on their widows' pensions much before their time. Who in their place would not sink into bitterness? The women of Brest, unruffled in the face of fate which hits them more often than anyone else, come from this generous and powerful race who can give, without a second thought, everything they own to the ones they love, as long as no one thanks them for it, as long as no one tries to soften their hearts, as long as they can believe that they do so willingly and not by force.

Benead

Disparti, *1979*

Pelec'h emaout-te, Soazig?
Ne'm eus ket poket d'az plev
Pell 'zo.

Ne glevan ken da vouezhig
O sevel drant ha sklintin
Er mintin.

Etrezomp ez eus douaroù ec'hon, morioù divent,
Koroll euzhus ha ramzel
Ar brezel.

    Etrezomp-ni, kasoni an dud.

Kreñvoc'h eget o fallentez eo va c'harantez.
Petra 'vern bagadoù diniver ar gadourion?
Va soñjoù a nij a-us d'an harzoù:
Goullo eo va divrec'h, nemet leun va c'halon.

Klevout a ran frond bev da vlev,
Ennon e viran douster da sell glan,
Da ene, Soazig, a vev em ene.

Translation

Separation, *1979*

Where are you, Soazig?
I have not kissed your hair for a long time.
I no longer hear your cheerful and silvery voice in the morning.
Between us lay vast lands, deep seas, and the horrendous giant dance of war.

Between us is man's hatred of man.

My love is stronger than their insanity
What matter the countless armies of fighters?
My thoughts fly above the borders
My arms are empty, but my heart is full.

I can smell the living fragrance of your hair,
I keep in me the sweetness of your innocent eyes
Your soul, Soazig, lives in my soul.

Meavenn

Ar Follez yaouank, *1936* (Lodenn)

D'an interamant e teuas hon eontr eus Galiv. Degaset en doa dimp sukantin, a zebras e-unan pa ne gavas ket ac'hanomp seven a-walc'h. Ne ouzin ket piv a lavaras dezhañ e oa ret dezhañ hor c'has da C'haliv gantañ, pa ne c'hellemp ket chom hon-unan-penn en un ti kollet e-kreiz ar paludoù. Lavarout a reas ya, hag e c'houlennas ouzh kement den a oa deut d'hor sikour ha chom a rae arc'hant gant va zad. Eñ a oa breur va mamm. Ispiser e oa e Galiv.

Kaset e voemp gantañ d'e di. Bevañ a rae e-unan-penn. Avaloù-douar gant laezh a zebre bemdez, hag e skoe gant an dud a vanke arc'hant dezhañ. D'an noz e lakae ur vantell souezhus. Lavaret ho pije ur gaouenn. Ne oa ket drouk e gwirionez. Ar stal e oa, a oa re vihan, ha blaz al loued ganti. An dud a c'houlenne traoù ouzhin. Hag an eontr a c'harme:

"Respont, respont, morwaz!"

En iwerzhoneg eo e kare sakreal ouzhin. Lavarout a rae e oa bravoc'h. Ha gwir eo e tirolle ar c'hunujennoù eus e gorzailhenn evel mein stlapet en un islonk. Ne ouien ket respont outañ. Faziañ a raen em c'hontoù, ha merc'hed Galiv, gant o zeodoù lemm evel kontilli, a youc'he a-bouez-penn hag a golle o chalioù du gant ar gounnar.

Kevin a yae d'ar skol. Daouzek vloaz e oa, ha me pevarzek. Treut-ki e oamp, hon daou.

Div wech e tec'his kuit diouzh ar stal, gant Kevin. Hag e teuis en-dro. An eontr en doa lakaet ar polis war hol lerc'h.

N'ouzon ket penaos e tremene an devezhioù. Hir e oant. D'an noz e teue Kevin. Ha bemnoz e teske din kement en doa desket e-pad an devezh. Hag eñ, biskoazh ne folle pa deue an eontr da lazhañ ar goulou.

Devezhioù hir daou vloaz hir. Ha Kevin a yeas da Zulenn. Ur yalc'had-studi en doa gounezet. Petra a c'haller lavarout diwar-benn ur vuhez c'houllo? Ne skrive ket alies, n'en doa ket peadra da brenañ timbroù.

Pa deuas en-dro, e oa seitek vloaz. Gouere 1921. Ha setu ma voe digoret evidon ur bed nevez.

E stal va eontr e oa bet komz eus Iwerzhon evel just, eus ar sodien emsavet da Lun Fask, eus an trubuilhoù. Ha laouen e oa ar mammoù o doa kaset o mibien da Amerika. Va eontr a drouze muioc'h eget ne vern piv, hag e felle dezhañ deviñ ur Republikan pe zaou war blasenn ar Frankiz, gant dour-tan, evit ma'z afe brav an tan daoust d'ar glebor daonet. Ha sur on e oa fouge ennañ o soñjal en dije gellet kinnig ur saihlad dour-tan da saveteiñ Impalaeriezh Bro-Saoz. Ur Judaz e oa, ha bet en doa e dregont pezh-moneiz, pa oa lezet gant ar polis da ober e botin evel ma kare. Ha bremañ e rank bezañ evit frankiz peurglok Iwerzhon, evel an holl dud, hag e oar en em zifretañ gant ar polis nevez...

Kemm a oa deuet war Gevin. Penn ur paotr ne gousk ket en doa, daoulagad brasaet. Hag e fri-Nolan a yae war hiraat c'hoazh. Hag e c'henou, Doue! Evel pa ne vije ket bet evit e zigeriñ, evel m'en dije ranket mirout ennañ ar c'hevrinoù en doa aon da goll. Ne zigore ket alies e c'henou, nann. Ha nebeutoc'h c'hoazh, pa gomze an eontr dezhañ. Ne forane ket e varradoù kounnar eveldon, ha pa deue ez echuen kerkent.

Da c'hwec'h eur beure ez ae kuit. Sportoù, marteze. Ur seurt doujañs en doa an eontr evitañ, dre ma teue eus Dulenn. Mestr e oa war e amzer. Er-maez eus ar stal e kase e zevezhioù hag e soñjen em boa kollet va breur. Ne raen nemet faziañ muioc'h-mui em c'hontoù hag e soñjen: "Mont a ri da Amerika hag e labouri ha berzh a ri, ha gant ur c'harr-tan e teui en-dro da C'haliv, hag e stlapi fank ouzh an holl."

Nag a gasoni am boa outo, ouzh kement den!

Ha setu Kevin o tont er gegin, ha me kousket em gwele.

"Sav, Enda. Ezhomm am eus ac'hanout."

An noz-se, eñ ha me, ha daou baotr all n'am boa morse gwelet, hon eus harzet ur c'harr-tan leun a armoù, war hent Galiv-Dulenn. Ne ouzon ket mat penaos. Sentet em eus. Tennoù a zo bet evel-just. Me eo am eus kempennet ur seurt chaos-er skourroù gwez a-dreuz-hent. Da beder eur mintin omp deuet en-dro. Pep tra a zo bet nevez goude.

Soudarded a-nevez e oa Kevin. Yaouankoc'h egetañ ne oa ket. Kement-se a lavaras ha netra ken. Ne gare ket displegañ traoù. Ne c'houlennas ket ha c'hoant am boa da gerderc'hel. Gouzout a rae.

E-pad an noz eo e vevjomp, a-hed an ehan-skol. Kement-mañ, kement-se. Kement tra a c'hoarvez pa stourmer dre guzh a-enep d'ur mell mekanik evel Bro-Saoz. N'eo ket dudius da gontañ goude. O bevañ! deskiñ d'ar galon da chom sioul pa dostaer ouzh traonienn skeud ar Marv. N'ouzon ket perak e lavarer: traonienn... na skeud ar Marv. Un dra sklerijennus eo ar Marv, evit an hini a varv. Ar re all, gwazh a se evito... n'o deus nemet gortoz d'ober.

Ne gomzemp ket. Ha koulskoude, tostoc'h biskoazh ne oamp bet an eil ouzh egile, daoust d'an holl draoù c'hoarvezet e ti an taouarc'hegi.

"Gwelout a rez, Kevin..."

Met ne wel mui. Me kennebeut.

Eñ, me 'gav din, en doa soñjet e Dulenn:

"Me a vo eus ar re a savetaio Iwerzhon."

En e wad e oa kasoni ouzh ar Saozon – moarvat abaoe an deiz m'en deus taget Lord Rydell, gant e vizied aotrou, ur wreg da Nolan, war-dro 1807. Ha va vamm a gomze alies eus ar gernez e 1848. Me, kavet em boa peadra da leuniañ va buhez, ha gwell e oa eget mont da Amerika ha dont en-dro da sabatuiñ tud C'haliv. Gwerzhañ soavon bouk ha te louedet, hag a-greiz-holl lakaat ar polis da redek ar vro, o c'haout war ho lerc'h evel ur vandenn vleizi marnaoniet, ha gouzout he deus ar vro ezhomm ac'hanoc'h.

Hogen ar polis ne oa ket ken diot-se. Pakañ a reas Kevin, ha me ivez. Me, avat, a voe kaset d'ar gêr buan a-walc'h – ha kaset ker buan all d'ur genitervez d'am eontr, a oa o chom en ur gouent e Tibrad-Arann. Aze pe e "lec'h all". Gouzout a raen e vije bet dieubet Kevin.

Er gouent-se, ne lavarin ket e vezis gwalleürus. Un doare kakouzez e oan. Ur gambr a voe roet din, e traoñ al liorzh, a veze prennet warnon bemnoz. Ar Seurezed a gerzhe pell diouzhin pa gejen outo war an alezioù, met brav e oa, mezv e oan gant gwin ar vuhez digenvez. Dismegañset ma oan ganto, ne c'hellen ket koll va nerzh en ur vont da c'houlenn outo truez o furnez santel, o furnez daonet goudoret, hag e chomen va-unan-penn en o zouez, klok ennon, c'hwerv ha kalet.

C'hwez al lab-yer hag ar glebor o doa an devezhioù er gouent, neuze. Hag ez erruas Kevin, gant feur-skrid miz kerzu 1921, da welout ac'hanon, d'ar red. Ha me, taer evel boaz, me a felle din mont kuit gantañ, da geginañ evitañ, da labourat.

"Me a raio dit te du, evel ma karez."

Leñvet em bije, o soñjal en te du. Hag an arc'hant, hag al labour da c'hounit arc'hant, astud ma oamp. Ha ne oa ket echuet ar stourm, emezañ. A-enep da Vro-Saoz, hag a-enep d'an holl Judazed.

"Neuze ez eus ezhomm ac'hanon," emeve.

"Nann, re a blac'hed a zo bet dija."

★ ★ ★

24 a viz Kerzu 1922. C'hoant am boa da laerezh un dra bennak. Ne oa ket e oa bet Nedeleg evidon ur gwir c'houel gant loereier ouzh an oaled hag ur wezenn-bin gant goulou-koar. Va zad a soñje e traoù all, ha va mamm – aon he divije bet ouzh e welout o kemer ar wezenn-bin da skourjez. E ti va eontr e oa aes-meurbet. En em vezviñ a rae, d'an deiz-se. Neuze ne oa ket ezhomm da c'hortoz tra ebet, ne oa ket ezhomm da vezañ fromet gant mouezhioù dizanvevel dibersonel ar seurezed, mouezhioù a sav d'en em goll en ur meurvor a beoc'h – a vije kredet. Peoc'h ar gouent – peoc'h ar vuhez sparlet, moanaet, a-wechoù kollet da c'hounit ar bed amezek, a-wechoù kollet da c'hounit netra.

Ha neuze c'hwez ar gegin. Un tamm "pudding" am bo, un tamm "soda-bread", koaven evit an te, hag ur vi fresk. Ouf! Kevin eo a felle din. Ur vi fresk evitañ, koaven en e dasad te, ha Kevin. Amañ, va-unan-penn, gant ar seurezed. N'int ket drouk. N'int ket mat kennebeut. Ne rae forzh, Kevin eo a felle din.

Ha gellet em bije leñvañ, terriñ va fenn, leñvañ, gouelañ, hopal, ober pezh a ra ur plac'h n'he deus ket he c'hoant, ha ne raen tra. Didalvoud, an daeroù. Ar brezel. Kelou ebet eus Kevin. Pe ne gase tra, pe neuze kelou ebet ne c'helle treizhañ stêr ar gouent betek ennon. Hag e felle din laerezh un dra bennak evit Nedeleg. Da noz ar Pellgent, e oa moustret va spered gant ar c'hoant mont da vurev ar Vamm-Abadez da laerezh he c'helaouennoù. An alc'houez a vez bepred e-harz treid ar Galon-Sakr.

Betek nav eur e c'hortozis. Edont er chapel. Lufrañ a rae an diri – dre garantez Doue eo e laboure seurez vihan ar skubelloù, ar paour-kaezh merc'h diskiant. Ha ne oa bet biskoazh lavaret dezhi piv a oa karet neuze gant Doue.

C'hwez ar burev, c'hwez ar galloud sioul kempenn. Ar Vamm-Abadez n'anavez ket an aon. Nag an naon. Ar C'hrist du. Ar c'hloc'hig kouevr skiltrus. Ar gador-bediñ. An daol. Ar c'helaouennoù.

Ar pakad ganin dindan va c'hazel, e redis gant an diri ha war alez vras al liorzh. Un tamm goulou-koar a oa ganin em c'hambr hag em gwele eo e krogis da lenn. Ket ar c'heleier, nann, ket ar c'heleier da gentañ – kement tra all da gentañ, ha goude: Krog-evit-krog e menezioù Dulenn. Lenn a ris. Lakaet e oa e oa bet kavet korf marv ur studier, Kevin Nolan, eus Galiv, e-giz-se, korf marv ur studier, lazhet, tennet warnañ, marv. Lenn a ris. Adlenn. Hag e sellen tro-war-dro ouzh ar mogeri-où gwenn. Kevin Nolan! Kevin Nolan, eus Galiv, studier naontek vloaz, pe ugent vloaz. Un taol war ar penn, ha goude ez en em c'houlenner: E pelec'h emaon? Ne gomprener ket. Va breur e oa. Va breur e oa. Va breur – a oa me, ha muioc'h. Ya, just a-walc'h, ne c'helle ket bezañ marv.

Ne c'helle ket bezañ marv. Sevel a ris, ha kemer an arc'hant am boa gounezet er gouent, ha revolver za zad – ne chome nemet ar paour-kaezh revolver-se eus ti an taouarc'hegi. Malizenn ebet.

"Sell, a soñjis. Malizenn ebet. Pegen fentus eo."

Er-maez edon bremañ. Sellout a ris ouzh ar chapel e-pad ur pennad. Ne ouien ket da belec'h mont. An oferenn, a! ya. Ne soñjen ket e Kevin. Ne soñjen e tra ebet. Dre ar parkeier eo e tapis hent an ti-hent-houarn evit an treñ-noz. Me a gave din e oa un treñ-noz. Treñ ebet. Penn an ti-hent-houarn a oa oc'h evañ te. Paotred ar polis gantañ. D'ar mare-se e oa gwarezet an tiez-hent-houarn evel pa vijent bet aouregi pe eskern sent Doue.

"Dulenn? O! O!"

An "O! O!" a lakaas penn an ti-hent-houarn da soñjal en un dra bennak hag e kanas:

"The Cambells are coming, oh! oh! oh!"

Ne oa ket te hepken a oa kouezhet dindan e groc'hen. Hag ez adlavaren, diotoc'h-diotañ:

"An treñ evit Dulenn..."

"Ret eo mont war droad da Zurlas. Er bloaz a zeu e viot erru. Kemerit te gan-imp."

Ar re-se, spered gouel Nedeleg a oa ganto. Hag e oan losket gant an te daonet o tiskenn ennon, hag e kleven hennezh o lavarout:

"Arabat sellout ouzh Séan hepken. Ha n'on ket kaer me ivez?"

Kaer ha mezv, a drugarez Doue.

"Ha c'hwi 'oar pelec'h emañ ti ministr ar Gwir e Dulenn? a c'houlennis.

Aon am boe a-greiz-holl. Ar re-se a oa o klask tapout ac'hanon, mirout ac'hanon, stagañ ac'hanomp. Hag e tec'his, ur wech muioc'h.

Translation

The Young Mad Woman, *1936* (Extract)

[*Enda and her brother, Kevin, get involved in the activities of the IRA.*]

Our uncle from Galway came to the burial. He had brought sugar candy for us, but ate it all himself as he did not find us polite enough. I do not know who told him that he had to bring us back with him to Galway, as we could not stay on our own in an isolated house in the middle of the marshes. He agreed, then asked all the people who had helped us if my father had left any money. He was my mother's brother. He was a greengrocer in Galway.

We went back with him. He lived alone. Every day, he used to eat potatoes with milk, and beat up the people who owed him money. At night he would put on a strange coat that made him look like an owl. He was not really a nasty man. It was the shop. It was too small and smelt musty. Customers asked me for things, and my uncle would scream:

"Answer, you stupid girl, answer!"

He liked to swear at me in Irish. He said it sounded better. The insults rolled off his tongue like stones thrown into the ocean. I did not know how to react to him. I made mistakes in the shopping bills, and the Galway women, their tongues sharp as scissors, shouted as loudly as they could, losing their black shawls in their fits of anger.

Kevin went to school. He was twelve. I was fourteen. Both of us were thin as rakes.

Twice I fled from the shop with Kevin but we came back as our uncle had put the police after us.

I do not know how the days went by. They were long. Kevin returned home in the evening, and every night he used to teach me what he had learnt during the day. He never lost his head when the uncle came to turn off the lights.

Two long years made up of long days. Then Kevin went to Dublin. He had won a scholarship. What can be said about an empty life? He did not write often, as he did not have enough money to buy stamps.

When he returned, he was seventeen. It was in July 1921. That is when a new world opened in front of me.

In my uncle's shop, I had, of course, heard about Ireland, about the fools who had risen on Easter Monday, about the troubles. The mothers who had sent their sons to America were happy. My uncle argued louder than anybody else. He wanted to douse one or two Republicans with petrol on Freedom Square, so that the fire would burn brightly in spite of the stupid rain. I am sure he felt proud to think he could have offered a bucketful of petrol to save the British Empire. He was a Judas who had pocketed his thirty pieces of silver, for the police always turned a blind eye to his illegal home distilling. Nowadays, he must be for the total freedom of Ireland, like all the others, and have made arrangements with the new police force…

Kevin had changed. His face looked like that of a man who never slept. His eyes were enlarged and the nose he had inherited from the Nolan side of the family kept getting longer. And his mouth! Dear God! It was as if he could not open it, as if he needed to keep in it secrets he feared to lose. No, he did not often open his mouth. And less so still when the uncle was talking to him. He did not have fits of anger as I did, but every time he came in, I calmed down immediately.

He used to leave at 6 am. Possibly to play sport. The uncle had a kind of respect for him, as he had been in Dublin. He could do what he liked with his time. He spent his days away from the shop and I thought I had lost my brother. I kept making more and more mistakes in the bills but kept saying to myself: "You will go to America, find work and be successful, and you will come back to Galway in a car and you will show off in front of everybody."

I hated them, hated every one of them.!

One day Kevin came into the kitchen where I was asleep in bed.

"Get up, Enda. I need your help."

On that night, Kevin and I, and two other boys I had never seen before, stopped a car full of weapons on the road between Galway and Dublin. I do not quite know how. I obeyed orders. There were shots, of course. I built a kind of barricade made of branches across the road. We came back at 4 am. Afterwards, it was like a new beginning.

Kevin was a new recruit. He was the youngest of them all. He did not give me any more details. He did not like to explain things. He did not ask me if I wanted to carry on. He knew.

During the school holidays, we lived at night, doing one thing or another. What happens during covert fights against a huge and wealthy machine like England is not interesting to recount later. But did I live! I taught my heart to stay calm as I approached the valley of the shadow of Death. I do not know why one says 'valley' or 'shadow of death'. Death is something that gives out light, for the one who dies. The others – too bad for them – just have to wait.

We did not speak. And yet we were closer to each other than we had ever been, in spite of all that had happened in the house on the marsh.

"You see, Kevin…"

But he does not see. Neither do I.

I think that, when he was in Dublin, he had thought: "I shall be one of those who will save Ireland."

Hatred for the English ran in his blood, probably since around 1807, when Lord

Rydell strangled one of Nolan's wives with his noble fingers. My mother often used to speak of the famine of 1848. I had found something to fill my life that was better than the idea of going to America and coming back to dumbfound the people of Galway, for there I was, selling musty soap and mouldy tea, and suddenly making the police search the whole countryside, having them hot on my heels, like a pack of hungry wolves, and knowing that my country needed me.

But the police are not that stupid. They caught Kevin, and me too. I was sent back home quickly enough, and sent just as quickly to one of my uncle's cousins who lived in a convent in Tipperary. There or somewhere else! I knew Kevin would be set free.

I cannot say that I was unhappy in that convent. I was seen as a kind of leper. I was given a room, at the bottom of the garden, and I was locked in every night. The Sisters walked away from me when I met them on the garden paths, but I liked it. I felt drunk on the wine of my solitary life. They despised me, but I was not prepared to lose my nerve and ask for the pitiful consolation of their holy wisdom, of their blinkered wisdom. I stayed solitary amongst them, complete in myself, bitter and hard.

These convent days smelt like a hen-house in wet weather. Then Kevin made a lightning visit and showed me the December 1921 treaty. As impulsive as ever, I wanted to go with him, to cook for him, to work.

"I'll make black tea for you, the way you like it."

I could have cried at the thought of black tea, of money, of a job which would bring in a salary, we were so deprived. He replied that the fight was not over yet, the fight against England, against all the traitors.

"Good, then I am needed," I said.

"No, there are already too many women."

★ ★ ★

24 December 1922. I wanted to steal something. Not that Christmas had ever been a proper day of celebration for me, with stockings by the hearth and a Christmas tree decorated with candles. My father had other things on his mind, and my mother, well! she would have been frightened in case he used the Christmas tree to beat us up with. In my uncle's house, things were very simple. He just got drunk on Christmas day. Therefore I was expecting nothing. Nor was I moved by the ethereal, impersonal voices of the nuns, voices rising to lose themselves in an ocean of peace, or so they would have us believe. The convent's peace was that of a gagged, restricted life which was lost either to gain access to the other world, or worse, to gain nothing at all.

But there were those kitchen smells. I'll have a bit of pudding, a piece of soda-bread, cream in my tea and, a fresh egg, I thought. In truth, it was Kevin I wanted. The fresh egg was for him, the cream for his tea. Kevin! But there I was, alone among the nuns. They were not bad. They were not good either. But that did not matter. It was Kevin I wanted.

I could have whimpered, groaned, moaned, cried, screamed, done whatever a girl does when she does not get her own way, but I did nothing. Tears are worthless.

The war? I had no news from Kevin. Either he had not kept in touch, or his letters had not crossed the convent's walls to reach me. It was Christmas and I wanted to steal something. On Christmas Eve I was haunted by the desire to go to the Mother Superior's office and steal her newspapers. I knew the key was kept at the feet of the Sacred Heart.

I waited till nine. They were all at chapel. The stairs were shining, a labour of love performed by the cleaning Sister, an endearing mentally-disabled girl who had never been told of God's special love for her.

The smell of the office was the smell of calm, orderly power. The Mother Superior does not know what fear is, nor what hunger is. The black Christ. The shrill small copper bell. The low prayer chair. The table. The newspapers.

The bundle under my arm, I ran downstairs and along the wide garden path. I had a candle in my room. I jumped into bed and started to read. Not the news, no, not to start with. Everything else first, and then: "Fight in the mountains outside Dublin." I read on. They said that the body of a student named Kevin Nolan, from Galway had been found. Just like that: the body of a student, killed, shot, dead. I read. I read again. And I looked around me at the white walls. Kevin Nolan! Kevin Nolan, from Galway, a nineteen or twenty-year-old student. Get a knock on the head, and afterwards you ask yourself: "Where am I?" You do not understand. He was my brother. My brother was me and more than me. That is why he could not be dead.

He could not be dead. I got up, took the money I had earned in the convent, and my father's revolver. That was the only thing left from the house on the marsh. I had no suitcase.

"Ha! Ha!" I thought, "no suitcase. Isn't that funny?"

I was now out. I looked at the chapel for a while. I didn't know where to go. Was that the sound of mass? Yes. I was not thinking of Kevin. I was not thinking of anything. I cut across the fields towards the station to catch the night train. There was no train. The station manager was drinking tea. There were policemen with him. In those days, train stations were guarded as if they were gold mines or relics of Christian saints.

"Dublin? Ho! ho!"

The "ho, ho!" reminded the station manager of something, and he started to sing:

"The Campbells are coming, oh! oh! oh!"

He had been drinking more than tea. And I repeated, in the stupidest way:

"The train for Dublin …"

"You need to walk to Durlas. You'll get there by next year. Have a cuppa with us."

They were full of the Christmas spirit. I burnt my throat on the blasted tea, and heard one of them say:

"Don't keep looking at Sean. Don't you think I am handsome too?"

Handsome and drunk, thank God.

"Do you know where the Minister for Justice lives in Dublin?" I asked.

Suddenly I got frightened. These men were trying to catch me, to keep me, to bind me. And I fled, once again.

Soaz an Awen

Suo Gân, *1996*

Bremañ e c'hallan diskuizhañ, dre m'az omp hon-unan-penn. N'eus ket ezhomm ken bezañ mestr war ar santadoù pe klask tec'hout diouzh selloù truezus an dud. Serr eo an nor, ha laouen e vin e-pad un nebeut munutennoù. N'em eus ket ezhomm displegañ kement-se da zen ebet. Dezho, dezhañ na da Zoue. C'hoant am eus luskellat ar c'henavo dit.

Sioulder 'zo er gambrig-mañ. Pell emañ diouzh ar rann wilioudiñ gant he garmoù ganedigezh ha buhez. Amañ ez eo un enezenn a c'hlac'har. N'out ket ponner em div vrec'h, dre ma'z out ken difiñv. N'am eus ket aon d'ober poan dit bremañ, tennet o deus ar binviji a oa o terc'hel ac'hanout bev hag o lakaat da galon da dalmiñ. Stag ouzhin emaout bremañ, ket ouzh ur benveg.

Gwelout a ran sklaer da benn. E-pad tost nav miz em boa klasket ijinañ doare da zremm. Sañset e vez heñvel ar babig ouzh unan bennak en e familh gant e griadenn gentañ zoken, hag en da sioulder e welan tal da dad hag e vlev du. Gleb eo da vlev bepred. Sur a-walc'h n'o deus ket bet amzer d'az sec'hiñ na d'az kwareziñ rak yen e oas dija. Bremañ ez eo va daeroù 'zo o c'hlebiañ ac'hanout.

Tadig 'zo aet d'ar gêr. Goulennet 'm eus digantañ lakaat da zilhad e-barzh seier plastek ha kas anezho war an tantad. 'M eus ket c'hoant e vefent gwisket gant unan all. Ne vo ket unan all, unan all eveldout, heñvel ouzhit. Heñvel ouzh ma huñvre, ma buhez, ma foan. Da gambr 'vo goullo, hag a zeuio da vezañ burev en-dro. Ret eo douarañ an huñvre ganit. Livet 'vo gris ha trist ar mogerioù, hag ar c'havell 'vo lakaet e korn pellañ ar c'hrignol. Met, da gambr 'vo evidon bepred. N'on ket en egar, n'on ket e kounnar. Ne gomprenan ket perak, setu tout. Ne gomprenan ket perak eo c'hoarvezet din. Ne gomprenan ket perak out bet kemeret diganin. Aes eo bet ar c'hanedigezh a-benn ar fin. N'ac'h eus ket graet re a boan din, ma babig. Bez' e oa un nebeut segondennoù a levenez na c'hell nemet ur vaouez kompren. Un nebeut segondennoù a levenez, ha goude ar gortoz diziwezh da glevout da griadenn gentañ. Gortoz a rin ar griadenn-se ma buhez-pad.

Kemeret out bet diganin diouzhtu. Troc'het o deus kordenn ar begel etrezomp, ha kemeret out bet. N'am eus ket bet ar gwir derc'hel ac'hanout em divrec'h. Ne ouien ket hag-eñ e oas paotr pe blac'h. Laosket on bet er gambr-se da c'hortoz. Emichañs n'o deus ket graet poan dit, ma babig. Ret 'oa dezho klask, kompren a rez. Diaes 'oa dezho ivez. Met, benveg ebet n'en deus gellet dihuniñ ac'hanout. Da lagad 'zo chomet serr war ar bed-mañ. Ne felle ket dit anavezout muioc'h marteze.

N'anavezi ket poan ha dipit ar bezañ. Met ret eo din bevañ gant ar boan hag an dipit da c'houzout n'anavezin morse ac'hanout. Ne welin ket ac'hanout o kreskiñ, ne welin ket da gammedoù kentañ, ne glevin ket da gomzoù kentañ. Ne welin ket ken, ne glevin ket ken, ne santin ket ken.

N'on ket fachet gant Doue. Ne soñjan ket ennañ tamm ebet er mareoù-mañ. Soñjal a ran ennout. Hiziv, bremañ, amañ ez eo te an hini nemetañ a gont. Ma vefe tu din chom amañ, hep soñjal ha gwelout tra ebet ken, e rafen. C'hoant 'm eus luskellat ur c'henavo dit da viken ha setu ar pezh a rin. Gouzout a ran e vo ret din reiñ ac'hanout en-dro. Met, te 'oar, bemdez e soñjin ennout. Luskellat a rin va doan dirak an tan e krizder ar goañv, ha pa vez bannoù heol kentañ an hañv o tommañ ac'hanon. Luskellat a rin va doan o welout, marteze, bugale all din o kreskiñ. Luskellat a rin va doan dre ma n'eus den ebet na soñj ebet da c'hellout kemer da blas.

Bremañ n'eus netra da zihuniñ ac'hanout. Pegen diaes eo evidon lakaat ac'hanout en-dro e-barzh ar c'havell. Ar c'havell a zeu 'vo un arched bihan. Gouzout a ran n'out ket amañ e gwirionez, luskellat a ran da gorfig divuhez. Da ene 'zo aet da lec'h all.

Translation

Lullaby, *1996*

Now I can relax since we are alone together. I no longer need to control my feelings or try to flee from the compassionate looks of others. The door is shut and I shall be content for a few minutes. I do not need to explain this to anyone, to them, to him nor to God. I want to rock you as I say goodbye to you.

This small room is quiet. It is far from the delivery rooms with their cries of birth and life. This is an island of grief. You are not heavy in my arms as you are so still. I am not afraid to hurt you now. They have removed the machines which kept you alive and made your heart beat. You are now linked to me, not to some apparatus.

I can see your face clearly. For nearly nine months I tried to imagine your features. One says that a baby takes after a member of the family, even in their very first cry. As you lay still, I can see that you have your father's forehead and his black hair. Your hair is still wet. They obviously did not have time to dry you or cover you as you are already cold. Now it is my tears which make you wet.

Daddy has gone home. I asked him to put your clothes in plastic bags and make a bonfire. I don't want others to wear them. There won't be another one, another one like you, like my dreams, my life, my sorrow. Your bedroom will be empty and will again become an office. The dream must be buried with you. The walls will be painted grey and gloomy and the cradle will be put in a far corner of the attic. But your room will always be there for me. I am not enraged, I am not angry. I don't understand why, that's all. I don't understand why it happened to me. I don't understand why you were taken away from me. In fact it was an easy birth. You did not hurt me much, my baby. There were even a few seconds of joy that only a woman can appreciate. A few seconds of joy, and then, the endless wait for your first cry. I shall wait for this cry my all life long.

You were taken away from me immediately. They cut the umbilical cord which linked us and took you away. I was not allowed to hold you in my arms. I did not know if you were a boy or a girl. I was left in that room to wait. I hope they did not hurt you, my baby. They needed to try, do you understand? It was hard for them too. But no machine was able to waken you. Your eyes stayed closed to this world. Maybe you did not want to know anymore. You will not know the pain and bitterness of being. But I need to live with the pain and bitterness of realising that I shall never know you. I shall not see you grow up, I shall not see your first steps, I shall not hear your first words. I shall no longer see, no longer hear, no longer feel.

I am not angry with God. I don't think of him at all at the moment. I think of you. Today, now, you are the only one that counts. If I could stay here, without thinking or seeing anything at all, I would do so. I want to rock you as I say an endless goodbye to you, and that is what I will do. I know I shall need to give you back. But, I assure you, I shall think of you every day. I shall rock my grief by the fireside in the depth of winter, even when the first sunrays of summer come to warm me. Maybe I shall rock my grief when I see my other children growing up. I shall rock my grief as there is no one or no thought able to take your place.

Nothing can wake you up now. How hard it is for me to put you back in your cradle. Your next cradle with be a small coffin. I know you are not really here, that I am only rocking your lifeless body. Your soul has gone to another place.

Anna Mouradova

Ret eo plegañ, *1994*

> Perak e plegez
> Gwezenn gaezh
> Perak out stouet?
> Da skourroù louet
> A glemm hep abeg:
> "Na rust an avel!"
>
> He mamm a lâre:
> "Perak e klemmez,
> Va merc'hig kaezh?
> Ma tuf hennezh
> E-kreiz da zremm
> Arabat leñvañ,
> Arabat klemm.
> Ret eo plegañ
> Dirak an den.

Arabat sevel
Da sell..."

Hogen
Ar plac'h a leñve
Hep teurel pled.
Ma, bezañ kreñvoc'h
A oa ret...

Translation

You Must Accept, *1994*

Why do you bow
Dear little tree
Why are you bent?
Your grey branches
Complain senselessly:
"How strong is the wind!"

Her mother said:
"Why do you complain
My dear little daughter?
If he spits
In your face
Don't cry
Don't complain.
You must give in
In front of a man.
Don't raise
Your eyes..."

But
The girl cried
Taking no notice.
Well, she had to become
Stronger.

Madalen an Amour

Leoni, *1992* (Lodenn)

Leoni, ur vaouezig dister a-walc'h, a oa o chom e-kichen atant hon tud. Un atantig he devoa dalc'het gant he familh nepell ac'hane, er bloavezhioù a-raok. Eno n'he devoa nemet peder buoc'h hag ur gazeg.

Dre ma oa tost d'ar gêr, e oa deut Leoni da sikour hor mamm pa oamp bihan ha niverus en tiegezh. Soñj 'm eus he gwelout bepred en-dro dimp!...

Ur boned ganti war he fenn d'ar pemdez pe un tog plouz e-kerz an hañv, e lakae ur c'hoef evel-just d'ar Sul evit mont d'an oferenn-veure e chapel Kerofern... Ur saro du a c'holoe he brozh hag ouzhpenn-se, un davañjer vras a rae c'hoazh an dro dezhi!... Kenkoulz e-pad an hañv evel e-kerz ar goañv, e veze ganti en he zreid loeroù gloan du ha botoù-koad gant choukennoù lêr.

Bez' e oa Leoni ur gwall labourerez, ur skoazellerez talvoudus evit hor mamm. Ober a rae war-dro al lienaj: lakaat an dilhad hag al liñselioù da sec'hañ war an orjalenn staget ouzh ar gwez-avaloù e-lec'h ma stlakent en avel fresk; dastum ha plegañ al lienaj: kalz a labour a oa er gêr d'ar c'houlz-se gant lienennoù ar vugale peogwir e veze daou vihan hep kerzhout e-pad un toullad bloavezhioù!... Sikour a rae aozañ ar predoù: peliat ar patatez pe al legumaj evit ar soubenn; pe c'hoazh goro ar saout, treiñ an digoavenerez pe ar ribot...

A-hend-all e rae ivez war-dro al loened: karzhañ kraou ar saout ha degas boued dezho – daoubleget dindan forc'hadoù plouz pe foenn ne veze gwelet nemet he zreid!... – dougen kelorniadoù boued d'ar moc'h en ur vrañskellat un tammig gant o fouez eus an eil tu d'egile...

Bep ma kreskemp, ha pa veze koulz ar vakañsoù, e teskemp ganti ober meur a dra eus an holl labourioù-se: peliat ar patatez hep lakaat an hanter anezho e plusk, reiñ da zebriñ d'ar yer ha d'al lapined, skubañ an ti, torchañ al listri, hag all.

Poan he devoa da zebriñ rak pell oa ne oa dant ebet ken en he genoù!... Moarvat e oa tener he divskouarn: un tammig kotoñs a veze bepred enno!...

Butun a lakae en he fri hag a-wechoù e roe dimp ur veudadenn da 'dañva' un tammig. C'hoarzhin a rae neuze o welout ac'hanomp o tistreviañ!...

Translation

Leoni, *1992* (Extract)

Leoni, a rather ordinary little woman lived near our parents' farm. In previous years, she and her parents had kept, in the neighbourhood, a little farm in which there were only four cows and a mare.

Since she lived close to our house, Leoni came to help our mother when we were young as there were several children in our family. I remember that she was always around, looking after us.

On normal days she used to wear a bonnet on her head or a straw hat in summer, but of course on Sundays she wore a lace headdress to go to early mass in the chapel of Kerofern. She wore a black smock over her dress and, on top of that, a wide apron. In winter as in summer she wore black woollen stockings and wooden clogs with a leather border.

Leoni worked very hard and was a precious help to our mother. She looked after the washing, put the clothes and sheets to dry on the washing line attached to the apple trees, where they flapped in the wind. She took them in and folded them. At that time, there was plenty to do at home, what with the nappies and all as, for a number of years, there were two little ones too young to walk in our home. She helped prepare the meals, peeled the potatoes and vegetables for our soup. She also milked the cows, turned the cream and the milk churns.

On top of that she looked after the farm animals: she cleaned the cowshed and gave them fodder. When she went to feed the cattle, only her feet were to be seen, as she was bent under the weight of the pitchforks laden with straw or hay. She also brought bucketfuls of food to the pigs, swaying from one side to the other under the weight.

During the summer holidays, when we were a little older, she taught us to do some of these tasks: how to peel potatoes without discarding half of them as peel, how to feed the hens and rabbits, sweep the floor, dry the dishes, etc.

She found it difficult to eat as she had lost all her teeth many years ago. Her ears must have been sensitive too as she always stuffed them with bits of cotton-wool.

She used to take snuff and, every so often, she would give us a pinch of tobacco to "try", and then would laugh when we sneezed.

Soaz Maria

En-dro d'an inizi, *1996*

Hag amañ pell doc'h ar ragach
ha doc'h trubuilh ar vuhez-se
ec'h an paz ha paz adarre.

Kerzhout war an douar-se 'zo din
hag a zo ac'hanon
ur wezh 'darre
hag ur wezh c'hoazh
ur wezh diwezhañ marteze.

A-raok an deiz
ma vo cheñchet ma zremened
ma vo cheñchet liv an dazont
ma yel ma eñvorioù da get...
A-raok an deiz.

Kerzhout adarre em fazioù
hag e pazioù ma hendadoù
pa anavezan tro-ha-dro
kement riboul, kement korn-tro
kement toull war an hent hedro.

'Pad ma buhez war ar roc'h-se
'tal ar chapel, 'tal an avel
n'eus nemet-se, n'eus nemet-se
betek ar fin, chal ha dichal, lanv ha tre
kalon ar mor em c'halon-me.

Hag an amzer o vont e-biou
ha me zo chomet koulskoude
evel releg o relegoù
evel test eus an amzer-se
evel pennhêrez marteze.

N'am eus bet na ti na douar
na madoù, nag argant ebet
ha koulskoude ma hêrez-me
'zo dalc'het e kleuz ma spered
evel un teñzor kaer-meurbet.

E roudoù un amzer bennak
o vuzuliañ ma amzer-me
mem douar, mem bro
hag andon ma buhez
avel an inizi o talmiñ em askre.

Translation

Around the Islands, *1996*

Here far from the rumours
and worries of this life
I walk again one step at a time.

Walking on this land is my pleasure
and is me
another time
one more time
for the last time maybe.

Before the day
when my past will be changed
when the potential future will be changed
when my memories fade...
Before the day.

Walking again in my own footsteps
and in the footsteps of my ancestors
as I know through and through
every path, every turn
every hole of the winding road.

During my life on this rock
close to the chapel, close to the wind
there is nothing else, nothing else
until the end, ebb and flow, high tide, low tide
the heart of the sea in my own heart.

Time passed by
and yet I stayed
like the relic of their relics
like a witness of past times
like sole heiress maybe.

I have had neither house nor plot of land
neither property nor money
and yet my legacy
is there, in the dykes of my mind
like a wonderful treasure.

In the tracks of some time or other
measuring my own time
my land, my country
and the source of my life
the wind of the islands beating inside me.

Biographical notes on Breton language writers

Abeozen: (Fañch Elies) 1896–1963. A graduate in Celtic studies, he was an active participant in the Gwalarn movement which aimed at creating a literature in Breton comparable with that of other European countries. He was a fiction writer and poet but is also known for his articles and books on the history of Breton literature, *Istor Lennegezh vrezhonek an amzer-vremañ* and *Damskeud hol lennegezh kozh*, essays on middle Breton, his study of *Barzhaz Breizh* and for his translation of the Welsh *Mabinogion* into Breton. He earned his living as a teacher but wrote for various magazines, including *Breiz Atao*. He was also a broadcaster on the Breton radio during the second world war. In 1945 he was sent to prison, lost his teaching job and was banned from Brittany. In his short story, *Kell 5*, he recalls the fate of Breton activists at the end of the war. The other texts chosen are taken from *Dremm an Ankou*, a collection of short stories on the first world war and from *Hervelina Geraouell*, a love story set in Northern Brittany. He also wrote books on the Welsh language, a collection of short stories, *Pirc'hirin Kala-goañv*, and other works such as *Argantael* and *Bisousig, Kazh an Tevenn*.

Marianna Abgrall: 1846–1926. Lived all her life in Brittany. A poet, she also wrote songs and stories which were published in *Feiz ha Breiz*, *Kroaz ar Vretoned* and in *Dihunamp*. Her collected poems, *Gwinizh hepken*, were published by Al Liamm in 1962.

Madalen an Amour: Born ca. 1933. Her childhood memories were published in two books, *Kostez ar Pemp Kroaz* and *Bugale Kerugan*.

Arzhig: (Rhisiart Hincks) Born in 1954. A Senior Lecturer in Breton and Welsh at the University of Wales in Aberystwyth, he is editor of *Keleier Breizh/Newyddion Llydaw*, now *Breizh/Llydaw*, translating Breton ballads and proverbs into Welsh. He is a regular contributor to *Al Lanv* writing about contemporary Wales.

Soaz an Awen: (Ffran May-Prijent) Born c.1970 in Wales, she learnt Breton at university in Wales and in Brittany where she now lives and works. She has published a number of poems and short stories in *Al Liamm*.

Benead: (Madeleine Saint-Gal de Pons) 1907–1994. Born in France to a Breton father and a French mother, she learnt Breton as an adult and was one of Maodez Glanndour's closest friends and assistants. Creator and editor of *Ar Bedenn evit ar vro*, she published articles, essays, translations and poems in several magazines. Her poems were published in a book entitled *Gwiadenn ar vuhez*.

G.B. Bertou-Kerverziou: (Guillaume Berthou) 1908–1951. A graduate in chemistry, he published articles in many Breton magazines, including *Gwalarn, Arvor, L'Heure Bretonne, Kad, Ogam*. He is best remembered for his poems in which he occasionally makes use of the traditional method of Celtic versification. A collection of his poems, *Barzhaz Kerverzhioù*, was published by Al Liamm after his death.

Erwan Bertou: (Yves Berthou; Kaledvoulc'h; Alc'houeder Treger...) 1861–1933. Worked as an engineer in the French Navy before returning to Brittany to look after his parents' farm. He was initiated into the Welsh Bardic Circle at the 1898 Eisteddfod in Cardiff and was a founder member of the Breton bardic circle. He wrote for several magazines but is best known for his compilation of poems, *Dre an delen hag ar C'horn-Boud*.

Herve Bihan: Born in 1956. Works as a senior lecturer in the Celtic Studies Department of the University of Rennes. He is the editor of the magazine *Hor Yezh*. His short story *Remi* won a prize in 2001.

Alan Botrel: Born in 1954. Works as a lecturer in the Celtic Department of the University of Rennes. He is known for his translations from Greek into Breton, but also writes poems and short stories, including 'Ar pok/The Kiss' included in this anthology, from *Orea ha danevelloù all*, published in 1999. He also reviews books for *Al Lanv* and for *Ar Men*.

Yann-Vari Branneleg: 1759–1794. During the French Revolution this Breton priest refused to take an oath of allegiance to the French Republic and went into hiding in a private house where he was eventually arrested. He was condemned to death by a revolutionary court and beheaded. It is said that he wrote his Testamant while awaiting execution, although doubt has been cast on his authorship.

Charlez ar Braz: 1811–1877. Worked as a currier in Morlaix. He wrote the majority of his poems in French but also published a few in Breton.

Rojer Brison: (Arz; Arz-mor; Roger Brisson) Born in 1921. His short stories were published in *Al Liamm*.

Aogust Brizeug: (Auguste Brizeux) 1803–1858. Born in Lorient, he learnt Breton from his uncle, Abbé Lenir. He travelled to Flanders, Marseilles, Montpellier – where he came into contact with the newly emerging Occitan cultural movement and Frederic Mistral – and to Italy. He settled in Paris where he became a major figure in Breton circles. He is famous for the poems he wrote in French which were inspired by his love of Brittany.

Pêr Bronost: (Pierre Pronost, Barz Treflez) 1861–1909. A journalist who took an oath in youth to help the Breton language. He wrote several short stories, folktales and articles which were published in *L'Espérance Bretonne*, *Spered ar Vro*, *Ar Vro* and *Kroaz ar Vretoned* but is best remembered for his love poems published under the title *Annaïk, Lili ha Roz-Gouez*.

Reun ar C'halan: (René Galand) Born in Western Brittany in 1923, he has spent most of his life in the United States where he still lives. He has written several books of poetry and still contributes learned papers, poems and short stories to *Al Liamm*. The first part of his autobiography, *War hentoù an tremened*, was published in 2002 in *Al Liamm*. He also writes in *Bro Nevez*, a magazine on Brittany published in the USA.

Yann ar C'hamm: (Jean Le Cam) 1898 –1940. A doctor by profession, he was of the leading campaigners for *Ar Brezoneg er skol*, an organisation which fought for the teaching of Breton in schools.

Thierry Chatel: Born in 1958. A primary school teacher who studied Breton at university, he has written authoritatively about the poet Erwan Bertou. As well as writing short stories, he has published a multilingual dictionary on plants names.

Per Denez: Born in 1921. A retired Senior Lecturer in Breton at the University of Rennes, Per Denez has led the fight for the Breton Language since the end of the second world war. His role as President of *Skol-Uhel ar Vro* and of many other Breton organizations did not prevent him from writing numerous novels (*Diougan Gwenc'hlan, Glas evel daoulagad c'hlas*...,), collections of short stories (*Hiroc'h eo an amzer eget ar vuhez, Evit an eil gwech*), poems, manuals for learning Breton, essays and a dictionary on the dialect of Douarnenez. He is one of the best, most prolific and most influential of Breton contemporary writers.

Youenn Drezen: 1899–1972. He was selected by a religious order as a promising schoolboy and sent to the Basque country to be educated at a time when religious orders had to leave France. There he was encouraged to learn more about his native language. He decided not to go into the Church (cf his partly autobiographical novel *Sizhun ar breur Arturo*) and returned to Brittany, where he became, together with his fellow seminarians Jakez Riou and Jakez Kerrien, one of the main figures of the *Gwalarn* movement, to which he gave many translations and original works. He worked successively for a wine merchant, then as a journalist for *Le Courrier du Finistère* and *Ouest-Journal*. He published several books in Breton such as *Itron Varia Garmez*, which was illustrated by René-Yves Creston and subsequently translated into French under the title *Notre-Dame Bigoudenne*. He also worked for the Breton radio and for the magazines *Heure Bretonne* and *Arvor*. At the end of the second world war he was imprisoned in Rennes together with many other Breton nationalists. Later he wrote a lively autobiographical work, *Skol-louarn Veig Trebern*, which was published a few months after his death.

Añjela Duval: 1905–1981. This well known Breton poet never left her native village in Northern Brittany. She worked on her parents' farm, running it by herself after their death. She started writing in Breton when she was in her fifties, often in the evening after working all day. She published her first poems in *Ar Bed keltiek*. Others were brought together in a book which bears the name of her farm, *Traoñ an Dour*. Her complete works, *Oberenn glok Añjela Duval*, were published in 2000.

Yann Loeiz Emili: 1884–1923. During the first world war, Emili spent time in a prison camp in Germany, the inspiration for his book, *Prizoner er Ruhr*. He is also known for his translations of Shakespeare into Breton.

Yann Ezel: (Herle Blomarc'h) 1908–1957. A doctor by profession who spent most of his adult life in Douarnenez, the setting for most of his stories, published in *Gwalarn* and in *Arvor* and played on Breton radio during the second world war. He supported the nationalists during the German occupation.

Farnachanavan: (Louis-Fernard Andouard; Erel Keralban; Farnachavan) 1904–1985. Began his adult life as a sea-going captain, then became a journalist before working for the Fisheries Council in Paris. He translated American and Irish literature into Breton but the sea remained his favourite subject in his own work. He was one of the members of the *Gwalarn* movement, along with his wife Fant Rozeg (Meavenn) who introduced him to Irish Gaelic. While living in Paris he nevertheless worked to develop the Breton theatre. During his retirement in Brittany he worked for the magazine *Barr-Heol* and, amongst other works, published a dictionary of maritime terms.

Yann Gerven: (Yvon Gourmelon) Born in 1946 in Plougastel, he works as a teacher of mathematics and Breton. He has published an amusing thriller, *Brestiz o vreskenn*, many humorous short stories for adults and adolescents, novels such as *Bouklet ha minellet*, and *War un ton laou*, and essays on the Breton language.

Maodez Glanndour: (Louis Augustin Le Floc'h) 1909–1986. Brought up to speak French by his parents he began learning Breton as a child from his school-mates and other members of his family and subsequently deepened his knowledge of the language in the seminary in Saint-Brieuc where he met Frañsez Vallée. After a couple of years in Rome he returned to Brittany, first as a teacher then as a priest. He met Roparz Hemon who published his first poems in *Gwalarn*. He created and ran several Breton magazines including *Studi hag Ober*, *Kaieroù Kristen*, *Ar Bedenn evit ar vro* and published other works in *Sterenn*, *Al Liamm*, *Barr-Heol* and *Skol*. He is well known for his translation of part of the Bible into Breton, for his poem *Imran* and his collections of poems *Milc'hwid ar serr-noz* and *Komzoù bev*.

Yeun ar Gow: 1897–1966. Spent all his life in Brittany where he worked as a solicitor. He was a fervent defender of the Breton language, took an active part in *Breuriez ar brezoneg er skoliou* which aimed to get Breton taught in catholic schools and wrote articles in many Breton magazines. He was also known as a Breton nationalist, was arrested at the end of the second world war but managed to keep his job. His most famous work is *E Skeud tour bras Sant Jermen* in which he recalls his youth in Pleiben.

Charlez Gwennou: 1851–1915. He began studying to become a priest but left the seminary at the age of 20. He then moved to Paris to work for the railways. He became a member of the Paris Breton circle where he met Yann-Vari ar Yann, Kelien and Renan. He taught Breton in Paris and worked for several Breton maga-zines including *L'Hermine*, *Kroaz ar Vretoned* and *Ar Vro*.

Youenn Gwernig: Born in 1925. After working as a sculptor in Huelgoat, he emigrated to the United States where he made friends with Jack Kerouac. He came back to live in Brittany in 1969 and was one of the main actors in the fight for the renewal of Breton culture in the 1970s. He published an autobiographical novel and several collections of poems, including *Toull an Nor* and *An Diri dir*. He is also a well known Breton singer.

Per-Jakez Helias: 1914–1995. Born to Breton-speaking parents, his most famous work, *Le Cheval d'orgueil*, recalls the events of daily life in his native village, Pouldreuzig, and was translated into 18 languages (*Marh al Lorh*, *The Horse of Pride*…) and became the subject of a French film. He worked as a teacher of French in a teacher-training college in Brittany. He wrote several plays in Breton, includ-ing *Mevel ar Gosker* and *An Isild a heul*, sketches and books of poetry which he trans-lated himself into French and published in bilingual editions, such as *Manoir secret/Maner Kuz* and *An Tremen Buhez/Le Passe-vie*. He was also a respected story-teller on the radio.

Roparz Hemon: (Gawain) 1900–1978. The founder of modern Breton literature was trained as a linguist and earned his living for many years as a teacher of English. A controversial figure he devoted his life to the Breton language. His own work includes novels, short stories, poems, plays, radio broadcasts, as well as dictionaries, grammar books and course books for learning Breton. He published translations, essays, songs and hymns and also wrote for children. He founded several magazines, the most important of which being *Gwalarn* – a literary magazine whose influence can be felt right up to the present time – which aimed to create a literature of international standing in Breton and offered translations into Breton of works from other Celtic countries as well as those of famous writers such as Shakespeare, Cervantes and Pushkin. His insistence on using a unified way of writing Breton modernised the language and enabled it to be taught in schools during the second world war. However these reforms, approved during the Occupation of Brittany by the Germans, were shunned by some Breton activists after the end of the war and thus divided the Breton literary movement. Roparz Hemon was very adept at spotting new literary talents. He gathered around him many of the most famous contemporary Breton writers such as Fañch Elies Abeozen, Jakez Riou, Youenn Drezen, Meavenn, Frañsez Kervella, Langleiz and many others. At the end of the second world war the publication of *Gwalarn* and that of many other Breton magazines was banned. Roparz Hemon was condemned to 10 years of national indignity. He moved to Dublin where he continued to work for the Breton Language in the Institute for Advanced Studies. Though he never returned to Brittany, he continued to contribute to various Breton magazines and even created a new one, *Ar Bed Keltiek*, which eventually merged with *Al Liamm*, the successor to *Gwalarn* after the war. His works of fiction for adults include the novels *Nenn Jani*, *Mari Vorgan*, *Tangi Kerviler*, collections of short stories including *Ho kervel a rin en noz*, *Kleier eured*, *War ribl an hent*, and a futuristic novel, *An aotrou Bimbochet e Breizh*.

Loeiz Herrieu: 1879–1953. Worked as a farmer, hence one of his pseudonyms, 'Er Barh Labourer'. He used the dialect of Vannes to write his poems, plays and comedies but also published a history of Breton literature in French. He set up and ran the magazine *Dihunamp*, and created a Sunday school for children to learn Breton. He collected ballads and songs in both French and Breton. His war diary, *Kamdro en ankeu*, was rewritten in standardised Breton by F. Louis.

Ronan Huon: 1922–2003. A graduate from the University of Rennes he worked as a teacher of English. At the end of the second world war when the majority of Breton language magazines were banned he created *Tir na n-Óg*, which three years later merged with *Al Liamm*, already strengthened by a merger with Per Denez's magazine, *Kened*. *Al Liamm* thus became the true successor of Roparz Hemon's *Gwalarn* and Ronan Huon remained its editor until his recent death. As well as writing editorials and reviews, he published a collection of poems, *Evidon va-unan* and two books of short stories, *An Irin Glas* and *Ur Vouezh er vorenn*.

Tudual Huon: Born in 1953, he is a teacher of English, book illustrator and author of several short stories, some published in a book entitled *Ar Chalboter hunvreoù*. He became the editor of *Al Liamm* after his father's death in 2003.

Lan Inizan: 1826–1891. Lan Inizan was a priest and teacher who published many articles in the magazine *Feiz ha Breiz*. He wrote three books: two novels and a *Life of Saint Francis of Assisi*, all of which were reprinted several times after his death. The historical novel *Emgann Kergidu* is his most famous work.

Yann-Vari ar Joubiouz: 1806–1888. After taking his religious vows he worked for a while as a teacher before falling ill and going to live for some years in Italy, where he wrote some of his best poems. On his return he was appointed canon of Vannes cathedral and prelate to the Pope. He wrote in the Vannes dialect of Breton and published prose work and translations in *Brediah er Fé*. He is best remembered for his collection of early poems, *Doué ha mem bro*, published in 1844.

Yann-Bêr Kalloc'h: (Bleimor) 1888–1917. Had to leave the seminary for health reasons but remained a fervent Catholic. He worked as an assistant teacher in Paris, Reims and Mesnières (Normandy). He met Loeiz Herrieu and published poems in the dialect of Vannes in several magazines including *Dihunamp* and *Ar Vro*. He died in the war in 1917. He is one of Brittany's greatest poets and draws his inspiration from his love of God and of his country. His collection of poems, *Ar en deulin*, was translated into French as *A Genoux*.

Narsis Kelien: (Narcisse Quellien) 1848–1902. He is known for his stormy friendship with Ernest Renan and his participation in the Paris 'Celtic Diners'. Educated in Northern Brittany, he went to live in Paris and was given the task of collecting the folk-songs and slang-words of Western Brittany by the Ministry of Education. He wrote novels and poems in Breton and in French. He was run over by a car and buried in Paris.

Maguy Kerisit: Born in 1975. Learnt Breton at school and at the University of Brest where she completed a Master's Degree. She has published a number of short stories and poems in *Al Liamm* and also collaborates with TES, a publisher who specialises in books for young people.

Ronan de Kermene: (Joseph Duchauchix) 1882–1957. Born in Eastern Brittany, he learnt Breton in his youth. He was a Breton nationalist and held the post of secretary and managing editor of *Breiz Dishual*. After the first world war he entered a seminary, became a monk and left Brittany to work first as an archivist in an abbey, then as a priest during the second world war. He published several articles and poems in *Dihunamp*, *Kroaz ar Vretoned* and *Al Liamm*.

Pierrette Kermoal: A writer of short stories and essays on Breton literature, she learnt Breton as a young adult and worked as a teacher. She is particularly interested in the works of Roparz Hemon, the subject of her recent prize-winning book, *Un Ene tan*. She has published in *Al Liamm*, *Preder*, and *Emsav* and is the editor of *Aber*, a new literary magazine. She has translated *Le Petit Prince* by Saint-Exupéry into Breton.

Kervarker: (Hersart de la Villemarqué) 1815–1895. Trained as an archivist, this key figure in nineteenth-century Breton literature gained fame throughout France with the publication of *Barzaz Breiz*, a compilation of songs and ballads collected and embellished by himself which were translated into several other languages. He was made a bard at the 1838 Eisteddfod in Abergavenny (Wales). He devoted his life to the Breton language, edited Middle Breton texts and had the works of the grammarian and lexicographer Ar Gonideg published. He wrote many articles on Breton and Celtic literatures.

Erwan Kervella: 1949–1984. Brought up in a family of Breton militants (his father is the famous grammarian and writer Frañsez Kervella/Kenan Kongar) he started writing light-hearted short stories and poems at a young age. Left unfinished at his death was a comic book he wrote and illustrated himself. He took an active part in Celtic circles and held various jobs connected with Breton, such as teaching in a Diwan school or being a broadcaster for a private Breton radio. Most of his writings were published a year after his sudden death in a book entitled *Yud*.

Goulc'han Kervella: Born in 1951. Graduated as a doctor and practised for a short time before deciding to devote his life to the theatre. He runs one of the most famous Breton theatre troupes, Strollad ar Vro Bagan. He has written a novel, *Ar Chase*, and a study of Laenneg, the inventor of the stethoscope. He also wrote a medical thesis in Breton and several short stories published in *Al Liamm* and *Brud Nevez*. Some of these were published in a book entitled *Lara*.

Sten Kidna: 1916–1982. Learnt Breton during his youth and tried to instil the love of the language in his state-school pupils. He wrote articles and poems in the dialect of Vannes as well as in standard Breton. A collection of his poems entitled *Kanenn d'ar vuhez* was published in 1974.

Jakez Konan: 1910–2003. A keen musician who played the violin and the bagpipe he earned his living as a salesman and spent his leisure time organising the activities of the Celtic Circle in Perros Guirrec. He then worked as a journalist and as a German interpreter during the war and emigrated to Canada in 1952 where he ran the Celtic Circle in Montreal. He came back to live in Brittany on his retirement. He wrote in many magazines such as *Feiz ha Breiz*, *Arvor*, *Gwalarn*, *Barr-Heol* and *Al*

Liamm, translated books into Breton and published three books, *Ur marc'hadour a Vontroulez*, *Lannevern kañv* and *Kenavo Amerika*.

Kenan Kongar: (Frañsez Mari Kervella) 1913–1992. One of the most prolific and famous figures of the Breton literary scene. He studied sciences at the University of Rennes and worked as a geologist in France and abroad. He published in *Feiz ha Breiz* for over 20 years and for two years in *Breiz Atao*. He never stopped writing in his native language and published in many magazines such as *Gwalarn*, *Barr-Heol*, *Al Liamm*, *Skol* and *Hor Yezh*. He was a novelist, short story writer, poet, translator and linguist. His masterpiece is his Breton grammar, *Yezhadur bras ar brezhoneg*.

Kuilhandr: 1880–1955. While studying French at the University of Rennes, Kuilhandr attended the lectures given by the celticist Joseph Loth. He was particularly interested in Breton and Cornish which he taught for a short time in Brest. He wrote in Breton and French in several newspapers and magazines. He is particularly known for his collection of Breton poems, *Mouez an Aochou*.

Yann-Vari al Lae: 1749–1802. Worked as a priest in Brittany until c. 1789, but had to take refuge first in Jersey and then in England where he composed a long poem on the misfortunes brought to France by the Revolution. During this period he also wrote a history of the French Revolution. Both works were published after his death. He returned to live in Brittany in 1800.

Langleiz: (Xavier de Langlais) 1906–1975. A renowned writer and graphic artist. He studied art in Nantes and Paris and became an eminent member of Seiz Breur, a group of artists led by René-Yves Creston who took their inspiration from traditional Celtic and Breton themes and projected them into the modern world. While in Paris he met Roparz Hemon and became a member of the early twentieth-century literary movement, *Gwalarn*. His works are often illustrated with his own wood engravings. He was also a prolific writer in Breton and in French. His Breton publications include a long poem and a theatre play but he is mostly known by Breton speakers for his powerful retelling of the Arthurian legend and of the Tristan and Iseult love story. He was very conscious of the need to keep the Breton language alive and, in 1948, he became a founder member of KEAV, an association which still gives Breton speakers an opportunity to meet and live together for a few weeks every summer.

Fañch al Lay (François-Marie Le Lay): 1859–1937. Son of a poor Breton fisherman, he started working as a ship's boy on his father's boat until the local doctor decided to pay for his education. He graduated in 1881 and worked as a history teacher while carrying on with his doctoral studies. He started his literary career writing French and Breton poems which were published in *L'Hermine*. On his retirement he returned to Locquirec, his native village, became its republican mayor and increased his literary production. His masterpiece, *Bilzig*, was serialised before being published as a book. It contains many autobiographical features and is considered one of the best novels ever written in Breton.

Tangi Malmanche: 1875–1953. The work of this most eminent of Breton dramatists was not recognised during his own life-time. Born in northern France, his parents returned to Brest when he was 14 years old. The young Malmanche was fascinated by the tales he heard from the workers on the family estate in Plabennec and he subsequently integrated many of them into his own plays. Although well educated he worked as a blacksmith for most of his life. He published a number of poems and his very first play, *Marvailh an ene naonek*, in *L'Hermine*. In 1903 he founded a short-lived literary magazine, *Spered ar Vro*. He taught Breton for a couple of years in Paris and produced his lessons in book form. His plays, most of which he printed himself in his garden shed, include *Gurvan ar marc'hek estranjour*, *Ar Baganiz* and *Buhez Salaun lesanvet ar Foll*. He also contributed to a range of magazines such as *Gwalarn*, *Sav* and *Al Liamm*.

Soaz Maria: Born in 1962. Has published a study on the magazine *Ar Falz*, several articles in *Bremañ* and many poems in *Al Liamm*.

Roperzh ar Mason: 1900–1952. After graduating from Polytechnique he worked as a naval officer and a sea captain. He first published in French but, influenced by his friend Loeiz Herrieu and by the writings of Y-B Kalloc'h, he wrote in Breton for the last 20 years of his life. A collection of his poems in the dialect of Vannes, *Chal ha dichal*, illustrated by Langleiz, were published in 1942. Other poems were published in *Kened* and in *Al Liamm*. He also wrote plays and a well known novel, *Evit ket ha netra*, which takes place in southern Brittany at the time of the second world war.

Meavenn: (Fant Rozeg) 1911–2001. Born in Brest, Meavenn learned Breton as an teenager. She lived for a few years in Ireland where she learnt Irish Gaelic. She was the only woman writer of the Gwalarn literary movement and published several short stories inspired by Brittany (*Pa c'houez Avel Walarn*), articles on Ireland (*Iwerzhon dishual*, *Skol Sant-Enda*) and poems (*Kanou en deiz*) in *Gwalarn*. Her most famous work, *Ar Follez yaouank*, which takes place in Ireland, was made into a film in French in 1952. During the second world war she wrote short plays for the Breton radio where she worked and also published translations and articles in *Galv*, *Arvor* and *Al Liamm*. She stopped writing in 1945.

Reun Menez-Keldreg: (Alain-René Autret) 1914–1984. Born in Brittany he worked as a school bursar before retiring to Eastern Brittany. He wrote twenty-six short stories, most of which appeared in *Al Liamm*. Two of these *Lili* and *Elena* were published in a book entitled *Merc'hed* in 1969.

Paol ar Meur: Born in 1960 in Brest. He has published articles and short stories in *Al Lanv*, *Al Liamm*, and *Cholori*. He is a regular contributor to *Bremañ* and has written a book of short stories published by *Skrid*.

Anna Mezmeur: (Anne Le Bastard de Mesmeur, Anna Vezmeur) 1823–1909. After passing her *baccalauréat*, unusual for a girl at that time, Anna Vezmeur studied law, then classic and modern languages, before deciding to become a nun. She founded and ran a catholic school in Crozon. She contributed several articles to *Feiz ha Breiz* and wrote two books, including a history of Brittany entitled *Istor Breiz e 36 nozvez*.

Erwan ar Moal: (Dir-na-Dor and many other pseudonyms) 1874–1957. Worked for a few years as an assistant teacher in Saint-Brieuc where he met Frañsez Vallée who encouraged him to write articles for *Kroaz ar Vretoned*, a magazine he ran for seven years up to 1914. He also created *Arvorig*, *Breiz* and *Breizadig*, a periodical for children. He published folk tales (*Pipi Gonto*) and worked for the preservation of Breton by setting up *Breuriez ar Brezoneg*. He was Secretary, then President of the Catholic association *Bleuñ-Brug* and a founder member of *Emgleo Sant Iltud*, a publishing company which specialised in works of a religious nature. He published many articles, poems, songs and theatre plays.

Pêr Mokaer: (Pierre Mocaër) 1887–1961. Born in Paris, he was educated in Quimper then at a Paris business school. A keen traveller, he learnt several languages, working as an interpreter in Brest before moving to Lorient where he met Yann-Ber Kalloc'h and Loeiz Herrieu and learnt the dialect of Vannes. He became a member of the bardic circle in 1912. He became involved in left-wing politics, continuing to work as a Breton militant, creating a journal and publishing company, *Buhez Breiz*, and joining the campaign for Breton to be taught in schools. In the last ten years of his life he was president of *Kendalc'h*, an organisation federating Breton cultural associations. He published articles in Breton and French and also a book in Welsh.

Meven Mordiern: (René Le Roux) 1878–1949. Although his family had no connections with Brittany he learnt Breton for his own pleasure. He was a great friend of Frañsez Vallée and of Emil Ernod (Emile Ernault). With their help he wrote some very influential books, such as *Sketla Segobrani*, *Notennoù diwar-benn ar Gelted koz* and *Istor ar Bed*. His Breton was of a very high standard and inspired other writers to express a wide range of ideas and subjects. A collection of his fiction work, *E fealded va c'houn hag e padelezh va c'harantez*, was published in 2001.

Anna Mouradova: Born in 1972 in Moscow, she studied Breton at the University of Rennes and published several short stories in *Al Liamm*. She is known for her translations of short stories from Russian into Breton, for a book on translation techniques, and for a collection of her own short stories entitled *Un dornad kraoñ-kelvez*. She teaches Breton at Moscow University.

Filip Oillo: Born in 1956 he was brought up in Brittany, Algeria and Senegal before studying engineering in Paris and Toulouse. He started publishing short stories in *Al Liamm* in 1988. His first novel, *Blaz an holen*, won a literary prize in 1995.

Youenn Olier: 1923–2004. One of the most prolific of contemporary writers, he was been the editor of several Breton periodicals including *An Avel, Avel an trec'h, An Trec'h, Imbourc'h* and *Kannadig Imbourc'h*. He wrote numerous books of poetry, short stories, novels (*Poanioù an Tad Gwazdoue, E penn an hent, Porzh an Ifern*), dramas, translations, diaries, books on Breton literature (*Skol Walarn, Un tonkad hag un oberenn*) and political pamphlets published by Preder.

Urvan Perennes: 1881–1947. This parish priest was asked to work as a teacher during the first world war. He published a single collection of poems entitled *Pe Is pe Ahes* in 1944.

Fañch Peru: Born in 1940. This teacher of Breton and French also pursued a career in local politics. He wrote many short stories for *Ar Falz, Brud, Skol Vreizh, Tregor* and *Pobl-Vreizh*. Many of these were subsequently published in book form: *Ur c'huzhiad avaloù douss-trenk, Glizarc'hant, Teñzor run ar Gov, Kernigelled ar goañv*.

Jarl Priel: (Charles Trémel) 1885–1965. A writer and dramatist, Priel worked during and after the first world war as a Russian interpreter. He resigned this position to become secretary to Charles Dullin, a well known French theatre manager and actor. Priel went on to write for the theatre, first in French then in Breton. He is also known for the three volumes of his autobiography which was written in Breton and for his novel *An Teirgwern Pembroke*.

Prosper Proux: 1811–1873. This spirited man, who liked playing pranks and telling jokes, spent most of his life in Brittany. He held several jobs before becoming a law graduate and marrying a rich heiress. Although he worked as a tax-inspector for about 30 years, he never took his work seriously and was, in due course, made to resign. From the age of twenty he composed many humorous, ironic and irreverent songs which brought him immediate fame amongst the ordinary people and a fair share of disrepute among the gentry and the Church. These songs were brought together to form two books, *Canaouennou grêt gant ur C'hernewod* (1838) and *Bombard Kerne* (1866).

Annaig Renault: Born in 1946, she studied Breton at the University of Rennes and is currently General Secretary of the Cultural Institute of Britanny. Her poems and short stories were published by *Skrid* and in *Al Liamm*. She is the first woman who to publish a novel in Breton: *Dec'h zo re bell dija*. In 2004 she published a bilingual book on her travels, *Carnet de voyages/Karnedig beaj*.

Jakez Riou: 1899–1937. One of the best writers of the Gwalarn literary movement, Jakez Riou is famous for his short stories, poems and theatre plays. Like his childhood friends, Youenn Drezen and Jakez Kerrien, he was educated in the Basque country with a view to becoming a priest. He left the seminary before the end of his studies and returned to Brittany, briefly living in Paris. He got his first stable job as a journalist in *Le Courrier du Finistère* on Youenn Drezen's recommendation. He met Roparz Hemon around 1930 and published his best known short story, *Geotenn ar Werc'hez*, in *Gwalarn*. This is also the title of his collection of short stories which were first published in 1934. In 1931 he left *Le Courrier* to work for *Ouest-Journal* in Vannes, along with his friend Youenn Drezen. The lung disease he contracted during the first world war was never cured and he died at the age of 38. His legacy includes humorous plays, *Gorsedd digor*, *Nomenoe-oe* and a light-hearted tale, *An ti satanazet*, published posthumously.

Charlez Rolant: 1862–1940. Politically on the extreme left Rolant joined the navy before becoming a watchmaker and a town councillor in Guerlesquin. He is best remembered for the poems and songs he wrote in Breton.

Anna-Vari Roparzh: 1839–1913. A member of the druidic circles, her poems were published during her life time and collected in book form after her death by her son, Taldir Jaffrennou, the poet.

Naig Rozmor: (Anna ar Bian) Born in 1923. She began writing stories and rhymes for children in 1975 but also published translations, poems and theatre plays for adults. Her collection of love poems, *Karantez ha Karantez*, were published by Brud Nevez in 1977. The contemporary Breton theatre scene owes a lot to this dramatist and actress whose plays include works about the Breton onion sellers from Roscoff – the Johnnies – such as *Ar Mestr* and *Johniged an Hilda*.

Ar Rumeur: (Mathaliz) 1882–1942. Learnt Breton from his grandparents in Lannion and deepened his knowledge of the language in Rennes where he joined a Breton students association and formed his enduring nationalist ideas. He published poems in magazines such as *Kroaz ar Vretoned* and *Ar Vro* and was made a bard in 1907. He worked as a watchmaker in Azay-le-Rideau and was one of the first members of the PNB (*parti nationaliste breton*). His collection of poems, *Breiz divarvel*, was published in 1913.

Olier Souetr: (Olivier Souvestre) 1831–1896. Abandoned his studies at the seminary after doing his national service, then worked for a wine merchant and as a

clerk with the French Railways in Paris. He took an active part in the 1871 Paris Commune and, losing his post as a result, went on to work for a publisher. He wrote mostly in French. His fame as a Breton writer is based on his ballad, *Gwerz ar roue Gralon ha Kear Is*.

Tadevab: (Daniel Doujet) Born in 1956. Formerly a teacher in a Diwan school, he is now lecturer in Breton at the University of Rennes. He has written stories for children and is a regular contributor to *Al Lanv*. His trademark is a humorous style.

Lan Tangi: Born in 1951 to Breton-speaking parents, he travelled the world before creating Roudour, a Breton language school for adults based in Huelgoat. *Mousafir*, a collections of poems published in 1997 and *Da Goulz an avaloù*, a compilation of short stories published in 2001, take their inspiration from his travels.

Fañch an Uhel: (François-Marie Luzel) 1820–1862. Remembered for the part he played in the renaissance of Breton folk literature. He was educated in Rennes and Brest and trained as a doctor in Paris. He abandoned his studies to pursure his literary intetrests and spent a few years earning his living as a teacher. After the publication of a mystery play, *Santez Tryphina hag ar roue Arzur* in 1863, the Ministry of Education sent him on a mission to Brittany to collect Breton traditional songs and folk-tales from the Trégor region. He published many of the ballads in a book entitled *Gwerziou Breizh-Izel*. His friendship with Kervarker (Hersart de La Villemarqué) came to an end over a dispute regarding *Santez Tryphina hag ar roue Arzur* which both wanted to publish. An Uhel also cast doubt on the authenticity of the ballads of *Barzaz Breiz* which Kervarker published in 1839. In 1874 an Uhel resigned as a teacher to become a journalist and later an archivist. He published several books in French and in Breton, amongst them *Soniou Breiz-Izel*. His collected folk tales, *Kontadennou ar Bobl e Breiz-Izel*, were first published in 1939. His own poems were published in two books, *Ma c'horn-bro* (1943) and *Yezh ar vuhez* (2002).

Frañsez Vallée: (Abherve) 1860–1949. Lexicographer and linguist. His interest in Celtic languages came from meeting Joseph Loth, a professor in Celtic studies at the University of Rennes, where he was reading philosophy. His poor health prevented him from working as a teacher of Breton but gave him time to deepen his knowledge of Celtic languages, particularly Breton. He was the founder of the influential magazine, *Kroaz ar Vretoned* which lasted for 22 years until 1920. He also worked for several Breton associations and was made a bard in the 1899 Eisteddfod in Cardiff. With his friend Emil Ernod (Emile Ernaud) he devised a way of unifying the writing of Breton dialects (with the exception of the Vannes dialect). He created and ran Emgleo ar Skrivagnerien which succeeded in getting the newly devised rules adopted by the vast majority of Breton writers. He published books for learning Breton, articles in many magazines, co-authored *Notennou diwar-benn* *ar Gelted koz* (with Meven Mordiern) and *Sketla Segobrani* (with Meven Mordiern and Emil Ernod). With the help of these two close friends he also published an influential dictionary in 1931, *Grand dictionnaire français-breton*, which earned him the nickname of Tad ar Yezh, 'father of the language'.

Yann-Vari Yann: (Eostik Koat an Noz) 1831–1877. Worked for most of his life as a primary school teacher in Brittany. He composed hymns, ballads and poems and took an active part in the nineteenth-century Breton Revival Movement.

Bibliography

FE-Abeozen, 'Kell 5', *Al Liamm-Tìr na n-Óg*, No. 6

–, 'Un danvez den', *Kontadennoù an amzer-vremañ*, Mouladurioù Al Liamm, Brest, 1960

–, *Dremm an Ankou*, Skridou Breizh, 1942

–, *Hervelina Geraouell*, Mouladurioù Hor Yezh, Lesneven, 1988 [1943]

Marianna Abgrall, 'Ar Roue Grallon hag an Dr Laenneg', *Gwinizh hepken*, Mouladurioù Al Liamm, Brest, 1962

Madalen an Amour, *Kostez ar pemp kroaz*, Mouladurioù Al Lanv, Kemper, 1992

Arzhig, 'Klemm ar brezhoneg ouzh ur brezhoneger', *Keleier Breizh*, No 37, 2004

Soaz an Awen, 'Suo gân', *Al Liamm-Tìr na n-Óg* No 296–297

Sabine Baring-Gould and John Fisher, *Lives of British Saints*, facsimile reprint by Llanerch, Felinfach

Ambrose Bebb, *Llydaw*, Foyle, London, 1929

Ambrose Bebb, *Pererindodau*, Clwb Llyfrau Cymreig, 1941

Benead, 'Disparti', *Gwiadenn ar vuhez*, Mouladurioù Al Liamm, Brest, 1979

Erwan Bertou, 'Pa zeu, d'abardaez-noz..'., *Barzhaz Al Liamm* No 41

M Betham-Edwards, *Literary Rambles in France*, Constable, London, 1907

Herve Bihan, 'Remi', *Al Liamm-Tìr na n-Óg* No 320

Alan Botrel, 'Ar pok', *Orea ha danevelloù all*, Mouladurioù Hor Yezh, Skrid, Lesneven, 1999

Yann-Vari Branelleg, 'Testamant an Aotrou Branellec', *Santimanchou diveza an Autrou Branellec*, c.1794

Charlez ar Bras, 'Son nevez war un danvez kozh', *Barzhaz Al Liamm* No 41

Rojer Brisson, 'Ar chapeled', *Kontadennoù an amzer-vremañ*, Mouladurioù Al Liamm, Brest, 1960

Brizeug, 'Mari', in Taldir-Jaffrennou, *Breiziz* (1810–1910), Carhaix, 1911

Rachel Bromwich, *Trioedd Ynys Prydein or The Welsh Triads*, University of Wales Press, Aberystwyth, 1961

Julius Caesar, *The Conquest of Gaul*,

translated by S.A. Handford, Penguin Classics, 1951

Thierry Chatel, 'An tokarn', *Al Liamm-Tìr na n-Óg* No 242–243

Reun ar C'halan, 'Emsav', *Klemmgan Breizh*, Mouladurioù Al Liamm, Brest, 1985

Yann ar C'hamm, 'An neizh dilezet', *Barzhaz Al Liamm* No 41

Edward Davies, *Celtic Research on the Origin, Traditions & Language of the Ancient Britons*, London, 1804

Per Denez, 'Aelig va buhez', *An amzer a ra e dro*, Mouladurioù Hor Yezh, Lesneven, 1995

–, 'Milliget ra vezin…', *Hiroc'h eo an amzer eget ar vuhez*, Mouladurioù Hor Yezh, Lesneven, 1981

–, 'Kontadenn bobl', *Evit an eil gwech*, Mouladurioù Hor Yezh, Lesneven, 1982

Valère Depauw, *Breizh Atao*, Uitgevenj Westland, Merksem, Belgium, 1968

Youenn Drezen, *Skol-louarn Veig Treben*, Lodenn gentañ, Mouladurioù Al Liamm, Brest, 1972

–, 'Foenneg an Dourig Kozh', *Kontadennoù an amzer-vremañ*, Mouladurioù Al Liamm, Brest, 1960

–, *An Dour en-dro d'an inizi*, Mouladurioù Al Liamm, Brest, 1970

Añjela Duval, 'Karantez-Vro', *Traoñ an dour*, Mouladurioù Al Liamm, Brest, 1982

Yann-Loeiz Emili, *Prizoniad er Ruhr*, Mouladurioù Hor Yezh, Lesneven, 1992

Yann Ezel, 'Va fesk kentañ', in Per Denez, *Kentelioù brezhonek*, *Al Liamm*, Brest, 1971

Farnachanavan, 'Diavaez', *Barzhaz Al Liamm* No 41

Geoffrey of Monmouth, *The History of the Kings of Britain*, translated by Lewis Thorpe, Penguin Classics, 1966

Gerald of Wales, *The Description of Wales*, translated by Lewis Thorpe, Penguin Classics, 1978

Yann Gerven, 'Walpurgisnacht', *Ifern yen ha merc'hed klouar*, Mouladurioù Al Liamm, Brest, 1995

Maodez Glanndour, 'Beg ar Raz', *Komzou Bev*, Mouladurioù Al Liamm, Brest 1985

Yeun ar Gow, *E Skeud tour bras Sant Jermen*, Mouladurioù Al Liamm, Brest, 1978

Charlez Gwennou, 'Setu ar c'hloc'h o tiñsañ glaz', *Barzhaz Al Liamm* No 41

Youenn Gwernig, 'Ni hon-unan', Identity, (CD), 2003

Per-Jakez Helias, *Marh al lorh*, Plon, Paris, 1986

Roparz Hemon, 'Kilañ ha mont war-raok', *Al Liamm-Tìr na n-Óg* No 38

–, 'Tartez an Ognon', *Ho kervel a rin en noz*, Mouladurioù Al Liamm, Brest, 1979

–, 'Pirc'hirin ar mor', *Barzhonegoù*, Mouladurioù Al Liamm, Brest, 1967

–, 'Ar Marc'heg bale-bro', *Barzhonegoù*, Mouladurioù Al Liamm, Brest, 1967

–, 'Breizh hag ar bed', *Ur Breizhad oc'h adkavout Breizh*, Mouladurioù Al Liamm, Brest, 1972

–, *Santez Dahud*, Mouladurioù Hor Yezh, Lesneven, 1998

Algernon Herbert, *Britannia after the*

Romans, Bohn, London, 1836

Loeiz Herrieu, *Kammdro an Ankoù* , Mouladurioù Al Liamm, Brest, 1994

–, 'O huidérig euruz!' *Dasson ur galon*, Brud Nevez, Brest, 1984

Ronan Huon, 'Ar Gwennili-mor', *An Irin Glas*, Mouladurioù Al Liamm, Brest, 1966

Tudual Huon, 'Beaj diwezhañ Gwilhou', *Ar Chalboter huñvreoù*, Mouladurioù Al Liamm, brest, 1979

Lan Inizan, *Emgann Kergidu*, levrenn 1, Mouladurioù Al Liamm, Brest, 1977

Gwyn Jones and Thomas Jones, *The Dream of Macsen Wledig*, from *The Mabinogion*, Everyman, London, 1948

Yann-Vari ar Joubiouz, 'Karante er Vretonned doh ou bro', *Doué ha mem Bro*, Vannes, 1844

Yann-Bêr Kalloc'h, 'Er Vernikenn', *Ar en deulin*, Breizh hor Bro, Edition Kendalc'h, 1986

–, 'Tristedigeh er Helt', *Ar en deulin*, Breizh hor Bro, Edition Kendalc'h, 1986

Narsis Kelien, 'Gouspero an Anaon', *Breiz*, J.Maisonneuve, Paris, 1898

Maguy Kerisit, 'Bali ar gouleier', *Al Liamm-Tìr na n-Óg* No 312

Erwan Kervella, 'Yud', *Yud*, Mouladurioù Hor Yezh, Skrid, Lesneven, 1985

Goulc'han Kervella, 'Ar Gambr ruz', *Lara*, Mouladurioù Al Liamm, Brest, 1989

Ronan de Kermene, 'Pa vin maro', in Camille Le Mercier d'Erm, *Les Bardes et poètes nationaux de la*

Bretagne armoricaine, Rennes/Paris, 1918

G.B.Kerverziou, 'Matezh al loar', *Al Liamm-Tìr na n-Óg* No 48

Sten Kidna, 'Me a garfe bout', *Al Liamm-Tìr na n-Óg* No 181

Jakez Konan, 'Lannevern e kañv', *Lannevern e kañv*, Mouladurioù Al Liamm, Brest, 1980

Kenan Kongar, 'Dichal', *Barzhonegoù*, Mouladurioù Al Liamm, Brest, 1982

Kuilhandr, 'Labour ar mor', *Mouez an Aochou*, Rennes, 1903

Langleiz, 'Feunteun Varanton', *Romant ar Roue Arzhur*, Marzhin, Mouladurioù Al Liamm, Brest, 1975

Langleiz, *Tristan hag Izold*, Al Liamm, Brest, 1958

Yann-Vari al Lae, *Reflexionou christen war Revolution Franç*, 1836

Fañch-Mari al Lay, 'Bugaleaj Bilzig. E hinivelez', *Bilzig*, Emgleo Breiz, Brest, 1995

Liber Landavensis (The Book of Llandâv or The Llandaff Charters), 1841

Letters by Bretons, *Baner ac Amserau Cymru*, 1946

Tangi Malmanche, *Ar Baganiz*, Mouladurioù Al Liamm, Brest, 1976 [1931]

Soaz Maria, 'En-dro d'an inizi', *Al Liamm-Tìr na n-Óg* No 298

Marie de France, *The Lais of Marie de France*, Translated by Glyn S. Burgess and Keith Busby, Penguin Classics, 1986

Roperzh ar Mason, *Evit ket ha netra*, Mouladurioù Hor Yezh, Lesneven, 1986

Meavenn, *Ar Follez yaouank*, Mouladurioù Al Liamm, Brest, 1973

Meavenn, 'Merc'hed Brest', *Gwalarn*, Gwengolo-Here 1942

Reun Menez-Keldreg, 'Lili', *Merc'hed*, Mouladurioù Al Liamm, Brest, 1969

Paol ar Meur, *Kontadennoù an Emsav*, Mouladurioù Hor Yezh, Skrid, Lesneven, 1992

Erwan ar Moal, 'Kloareg Kersoazon', *Pipi Gonto*, Le Goaziou, Kemper, 1925

Pêr Mokaer, 'Er glau', in Camille Le Mercier d'Erm, *Les Bardes et poètes nationaux de la Bretagne armoricaine*, Kelen, Guipavas, 1918

Meven Mordiern, 'Al lez a ris da Jorjeta', *Envoriou Bugeliez*, Mouladurioù Hor Yezh, Lesneven, 1983

John Morris, *Translation of Excerpta or Selected Documents of Early British History by Nennius*, Phillimore, Chichester, 1980

Anna Mouradova, 'Ret eo plegañ', *Al Liamm-Tîr na n-Óg* No 287

Filip Oillo, *Blaz an holen*, Mouladurioù Al Liamm, Brest, 1996

Youenn Olier, 'Barnedigezh laouen', *Al Liamm-Tîr na n-Óg* No 24

J. Dyfnallt Owen, *O Ben Tir Llydaw*, Gwasg Aberystwyth, 1934

Urvan Perennes, 'Kan an drouiz', *Pe Is…Pe Ahes?*, E ti ar Chourrier, Brest, 1944

Fañch Peru, 'Ar Vuoc'h zu', *Eur c'huzhiad avaloù douss-trenk*, Skol Vreizh, Morlaix, 1985

David Powel, *History of Cambria*, London, 1584

Jarl Priel, 'Va zammig buhez', *Al Liamm-Tîr na n-Óg* No 44

Annaig Renault, 'Divroet', *Al Liamm-Tîr na n-Óg* No 278–279

Jakez Riou, 'Ur Barr-avel', *Geotenn ar Werc'hez*, Emgleo Breiz, Brest, 1957

–, 'Ar Run heol', *Geotenn Ar Werc'hez*, Emgleo Breiz, Brest, 1917

Charlez Rolant, 'Paotr Breizh', in Taldir-Jaffrennou, *Breiziz* (1810–1910), Carhaix, 1911

Anna-Vari Roparzh, 'Dihun Breiz', in Camille Le Mercier d'Erm, *Les Bardes et poètes nationaux de la Bretagne armoricaine*, Kelen, Guipavas, 1918

Naig Rozmor, 'Eur Mister Joaiuz', *Karantez ha Karantez*, Brud Nevez, Brest, 1977

Ar Rumeur, 'Enez Eussa', in Taldir-Jaffrennou, *Breiziz* (1810–1910), Carhaix, 1911

Anne Douglas Sedgwick, *A Childhood in Brittany Eighty Years Ago*, Century, London, 1918

Olier Souetr, 'Ar Roue Gralon ha Kaer-Is', in Taldir-Jaffrennou, *Breiziz* (1810–1910), Carhaix, 1911

Edward Stillingfleet, *Origines Britanniacae or The Antiquities of the British Church*, 1685

Tadevab, 'Ar Gartenn-oferenn', *Al Lanv*, Niv 100

Lan Tangi, 'Devezhioù peurbadelezh', *Mousafir*, Mouladurioù Hor Yezh, Lesneven, 1997

Fañch an Uhel, 'Ar plac'h hag an naer….', *Kontadennoù ar Bobl*, levrenn 1, Mouladurioù Al Liamm, Brest, 1984

H.A. Vachell, *The Face of Clay*, John Murray, London, 1905

Frañsez Vallée, *Envorennoù eur brezonegour*, Sterenn, Lambezellec, 1941

Hersart de la Villemarqué, *Barzaz Breiz*, Perrin, Paris, 1867

Anna Vezmeur, 'Amzeriou kenta hon bro', *Histor ar Vreiz*, 1869 [1855]

H.G. Wells, *Apropos of Dolores*, Cape, London, 1938

William of Malmesbury, *The Kings Before the Norman Conquest*, Facsimile reprint of translation by J Stephenson, Llanerch, Felinfach

Hugh Williams, *Two Lives of Gildas by a Monk of Ruys and Caradoc of Llancarfan*, Facsimile reprint of 1899 original by Llanerch, Felinfach, 1990

Yann-Vari Yann, 'Burzudo Breizh', in Taldir-Jaffrennou, *Breiziz* (1810–1910), Carhaix, 1911

Further reading

English

An Naihl, B. (1997) 'Barzhaz Breizh: A Breton Kalevala' in *The Celtic Pen* 12.

Aubert, O. L. (ed.) (1993) *Celtic Legends of Brittany*, Kerangwenn: Coop Breizh.

Boussell du Bourg, Y. (1994) 'Early Breton Literature' in *The Celtic Pen* 2:1.

–, (1996) 'Breton Theatre' in *The Celtic Pen* 10.

Ellis, P.B. (1993) *The Celtic Dawn: A History of Pan-Celticism*, London: Constable.

–, (1999) *Chronicles of the Celts: New Tellings of their Myths and Legends*, London: Robinson.

Denez, P. 'Modern Breton Literature' in Williams, J.E.C. (ed.) (1971) *Literature in Celtic Countries*, Cardiff: University of Wales Press.

Fleuriot, L. (1995) 'The Origins of Brittany' in *The Celtic History Review* 2:1.

German, G. 'The French of Western Brittany in Light of the Celtic Englishes' in Tristram, H.L.C. (ed.) (2003) *The Celtic Englishes* III, Heidelberg: Winter.

Giot, P.R., Guigon, P., Merdrignac, B. (2003) *The British Settlement of Brittany: The First Bretons in Amorica*, Stroud: Tempus.

Guehennec, Y. (1996) 'Elements of a Breton Dialect' in *The Celtic History Review* 2: 2.

Harvey, D.C., Jones, R., McInroy, N., Milligan, C. (eds.) (2002) *Celtic Geographies: old culture, new times*, London and New York: Routledge.

Heusaff, A. (1995) 'Yann Ber Kalloc'h: A Breton War Poet' in *The Celtic Pen* 3:1.

–, (1997) 'Brittany during the French Revolution' in *The Celtic History Review* 2: 4.

Kent, A.M. (2000) *The Literature of Cornwall: Continuity, Identity, Difference 1000–2000*, Bristol: Redcliffe.

–, and Saunders, T. (eds.) (2000) *Looking at the Mermaid: A Reader in Cornish Literature 900–1900*, London: Francis Boutle.

Knefsey, M. 'Rural Tourism and Identity: Stories of Change andResistance from the West of Ireland and Brittany' in Hale, A. and Payton, P. (eds.) (2000) *New Directions in Celtic Studies*, Exeter: University of Exeter Press.

Le Duc, G. (1994) 'An Aspect of Medieval Breton Poetry' in *The Celtic Pen* 2: 2.

Le Mat, J. P. (1995) 'Literature and the Breton Cultural Revival' in *The Celtic Pen* 2: 4.

–, (1995) 'The French Revolution in Brittany' in *The Celtic History Review* 1: 2.

–, (1996) *The Sons of Ermine: A History of Brittany*, Belfast: An Clochán.

Le Menn, G. (1993) 'Breton Popular Theatre' in *The Celtic Pen* I: I.

Le Stum, P. (1994) 'The Union Regionaliste Bretonne' in *The Celtic History Review* 1: 1.

Madeg, M. 'A Learner's Selection from Breton Literature and Press' in Ó Luain, C. (ed.) (1983) *For a Celtic Future: A tribute to Alan Heusaff*, Dublin: The Celtic League.

–, (1994) 'Writing in Breton Today' in *The Celtic Pen*, 1: 4.

Minard, A. 'Pre-Packed Breton Folk Narrative' in Hale, A. and Payton, P. (eds.) 2000.

Ó Breasláin, D. (1994) 'A Brief Guide to Breton Literature' in *The Celtic Pen* 1: 3.

–, (1996) 'Brittany, WW II and Bezen Perrot' in *The Celtic Pen* 2: 3.

Renault, A. (1993) 'Women Writers in Breton' in *The Celtic Pen* 1: 2.

Russell, P. (1995) *An Introduction to the Celtic Languages*, Harlow: Longman.

Tanner, M. (2004) *The Last of the Celts*, New Haven and London: Yale.

Wilhelm, J.J. (ed.) (1994) *The Romance of Arthur*, New York and London: Garland.

Williams, J.E.C. (ed.) (1971) *Literature in Celtic Countries*, Cardiff: University of Wales Press.

Breton

Abeozen (F Elies), *Istor lennegezh vrezhonek an amzer-vremañ*, 1957

Abeozen (F Elies), *Hol lennegezh kozh*, 1962

Andouard L, *Ar c'hoariva brezhonek*, Skrid (Hor Yezh), p 28-57, 1978

Carré D, *Dihunamp*, Hor Yezh, 1987

Favereau F, *Lennegezh ar brezhoneg abaoe 1945*, Skol Vreizh, Montroulez, 1991

Kerdraon M, 'Tangi Malmanche', *Al Liamm*, no 114, p 33-41, 1966

Olier Y, *Istor an Emsav*, Imbourc'h, Roazhon, 1972

Raoul L, *Geriadur ar skrivagnerien ha yezhourien*, Al Liamm, Brest, 1992

French

Balcou J, Le Gallo Y (Dir.), *Histoire littéraire et culturelle de la Bretagne*, Champion-Slatkine, Paris-Genève, 1987

Croix A (& Veillard JY) *Dictionnaire du patrimoine breton*, Rennes : Apogée, 2000

Dujardin L, *Hor skrivagnerien, Hor Yezh*, Lesneven, 1992 & 1995

Favereau F, *Bretagne contemporaine – langue, culture, identité*, Skol Vreizh, Morlaix, 1993

Giraudon D, *Chansons populaires de Basse-Bretagne sur feuilles volantes*, Skol Vreizh, 1985

Gourvil F, *Langue et littératures bretonnes*, PUF : Que sais-je, 1962

Hélias PJ, 'L'œuvre de Tanguy Malmanche', *Ar Falz*, no 9 & 12, 1953

Herrieu L, *La Littérature bretonne des origines au XXè siècle*, PUF: Que sais-je, 1943

Jaffrennou F, Breiziz, *Ar Bobl*, Carhaix, 1911

Kerdraon M, *T. Malmanche témoin du fantastique breton*, Bayeux, 1975